PRINCES AND PRINCELY CULTURE 1450–1650

VOLUME ONE

BRILL'S STUDIES IN INTELLECTUAL HISTORY

VOLUME 118/1

PRINCES AND PRINCELY CULTURE 1450–1650

VOLUME ONE

EDITED BY

MARTIN GOSMAN
ALASDAIR MACDONALD
ARJO VANDERJAGT

TUTA SUB AEGIDE PALLAS · 1683 ·

BRILL
LEIDEN · BOSTON
2003

Illustration on the cover: Porte Saint Denis, with Francion and Pharamond, from Simon Bouquet's *Bref et sommaire recueil de ce qui a esté faict, et de l'ordre tenüe à la joyeuse et triumphante Entrée de tres-puissant, tres-magnanime et tres-chrestien Prince Charles IX de ce nom Roy de France, en sa bonne ville et cité de Paris, capitale de son Royaume, le Mardy sixiesme jour de Mars … M.D.LXXI* (Paris, printed by Denis du Pré for Olivier Codoré, 1572, K13[R]).

This book is printed on acid-free paper.

Library of Congress Cataloging-in-Publication Data

Princes and princely culture, 1450-1650 / edited by Martin Gosman, Alasdair MacDonald, Arjo Vanderjagt.
p. cm. – (Brill's studies in intellectual history, 0920-8607 ; v. 118)
Includes bibliographical references and index.
ISBN 90-04-13572-3 (v. 1)
1. Europe—History—15th century. 2. Europe—History—1492-1648. 3. Princes—Europe—History. 4. Europe—Court and courtiers. 5. Europe—Kings and rulers. 6. Art patronage—Europe—History. 7. Politics and culture—Europe—History.
I. Gosman, Martin. II. MacDonald, A. James (Alasdair James), 1954- . III. Vanderjagt, Arie Johan. IV. Series.

D203 .P75 2003
305.5'22'09409031-dc22

2003061017

ISSN 0920-8607
ISBN 90 04 13572 3

PRINTED IN THE NETHERLANDS

CONTENTS

PREFACE

The princes, princely courts and court cultures of the late Middle Ages and the early Modern Era held as great a fascination for contemporaries such as Machiavelli and Guicciardini as for modern scholars such as Norbert Elias and Richard Vaughan. This interest has involved the desire to penetrate the dynamics of princely power and the reasons of princes to be patrons of culture as well as the wish to understand the development of European social patterns and political institutions. It is not surprising that literary scholars, historians of culture and institutions, politics and society, and even historians of ideas are ardent students of princely culture. Many products of medieval and renaissance culture – literature, music, political ideology, social and governmental structures, the fine arts, and even forms of devotional practice – found their best expression in the context of the courts of greater and lesser princes. Malcolm Vale has recently pointed out in his *The Princely Court. Medieval Courts and Culture in North-West Europe* 1270-1380 (Oxford, 2002) that medieval court culture was particularly open to external forces: 'it was essentially permeable and absorptive of a wide range of influences'. Thus the study of courtly culture not only elucidates the working of the princely court itself, but it can tell us something as well about the world at large. It might be said that the significance of many aspects of society outside the court gains in focus as they are viewed within the perspective of a princely court.

The present book is the first of two volumes devoted to princes and princely culture in Europe between 1450 and 1650. This first one contains essays on selected European courts north of the Alps and the Pyrenees; the second will discuss the courts of England and of southern Europe. When the editors first conceived the plan for this project in the mid 1990s, they were, of course, aware of the many learned studies both of medieval princely cultures and of the magnificent courts of the seventeenth century. It seemed, however, that the transitional period between the late Middle Ages and the early Modern Era had not received the attention it deserved. It was then decided to solicit the help of friends and colleagues who are involved in speciality research within this period. Their findings about the princely cultures of this era appear in these two books. The focus of this work is especially on two aspects of princely culture: the problem and range of princely friendship and patronage, and the ideology and symbolism of rulership and statehood. The two introductory essays by Martin Gosman and Olaf Mörke set the stage; they are devoted systematically to these two important themes.

The discussions and analyses presented in the ensuing chapters are variously surveys of culture and the arts at princely courts (Hoogvliet on Catherine de Médicis, MacDonald on James III and James IV of Scotland, Eichberger on Margaret of Austria in Mechelen, Swanson on the princely courts of Scandinavia), studies centred on the political and cultural functioning of these courts (Vanderjagt on the Burgundian court, Finley-Croswhite on Henry IV of France, Lynch on Mary, Queen of Scots, and James VI, Müller on Maximilian I, Schlusemann on the court at Heidelberg under Frederick the Victorious and Philip the Upright), and case-studies of princely attitudes to the arts (Brunelle on cartography under Francis I, Hadley Williams on the literary patronage of James V of Scotland). Each article is essentially multidisciplinary in focus, and they all include material from other areas and disciplines to enhance their specific considerations.

The editors are grateful to the contributors to this volume for their polite and enduring patience. Due to the everchanging pressures of academic politics, the editorial process took far longer than was first anticipated. It is hoped that this volume meets their expectations and those of our readers. Thanks go also to Nella Gosman-Scholtens who did much of the word-processing necessary in these modern times of camera-ready copy. We are pleased that Brill Academic Publishers (Leiden, Boston) is publishing this book in Brill's Studies in Intellectual History.

CONTRIBUTORS

Gayle K. Brunelle is Professor of History, California State University, Fullerton.

Annette Finley-Croswhite is Associate Professor of History and Graduate Program Director in History, Old Dominion University, Norfolk, Va.

Dagmar Eichberger is Privat Dozentin, Department of the History of Art, University of Heidelberg.

Martin Gosman is Professor of Older Romance Languages and Cultures, University of Groningen.

Janet Hadley Williams is Visiting Fellow in English, School of Humanities, Faculty of Arts, The Australian National University.

Margriet Hoogvliet is researcher at the Faculty of Arts, University of Groningen.

Michael Lynch is Professor of Scottish History, University of Edinburgh.

Alasdair A. MacDonald is Professor of Medieval English Literature and Language, University of Groningen.

Olaf Mörke is Professor of History, University of Kiel.

Jan-Dirk Müller is Professor of German Philology, University of Munich.

Rita Schlusemann is Assistant Professor for Dutch Literature and Culture at the University of Leipzig.

Alan Swanson is Professor of Scandinavian Literatures, Languages and Cultures, University of Groningen.

Arjo Vanderjagt is Professor of the History of Ideas and Medieval Studies, University of Groningen.

LIST OF PLATES

FIGURES 1–2*

FIGURES 3–9**

* Figures 1–2 belong to *James V of Scots as Literary Patron* by Janet Hadley Williams.
** Figures 3–9 belong to *A Cultural Centre in the Southern Netherlands: the Court of Archduchess Margaret of Austria (1480-1530) in Mechelen* by Dagmar Eichberger.

P· ROSSETI POETÆ
Laureati De insignibus Scotorum Regum
Carmen.

TErra viris belloq; potens clarissima rebus
Scotia, quam toto oceanus disiungit ab orbe
Vnam hominũ extremam, sed primam viribus vnam.

Fig.1. Hector Boece, *Scotorum Historiae a Prima Gentis Origine* (Oxford, MS Ashmole. G.1, Sig a ii recto).

Fig. 2. John Bellenden, *Heir beginneis the Hystory and Cronikles of Scotland, 1536-40* (The Royal Arms of Scotland).

Fig. 3. Anonymous, Netherlandish, *Margaret of Austria as a young princess* (private collection; photo: Jochen Bayer).

Fig. 4. Auguste van den Eynde, *View of Margaret's Residence in Mechelen, seen from Voochtstraat, circa 1840* (Mechelen, Stadtarchiv, no. 345; photo Markus Hörsch).

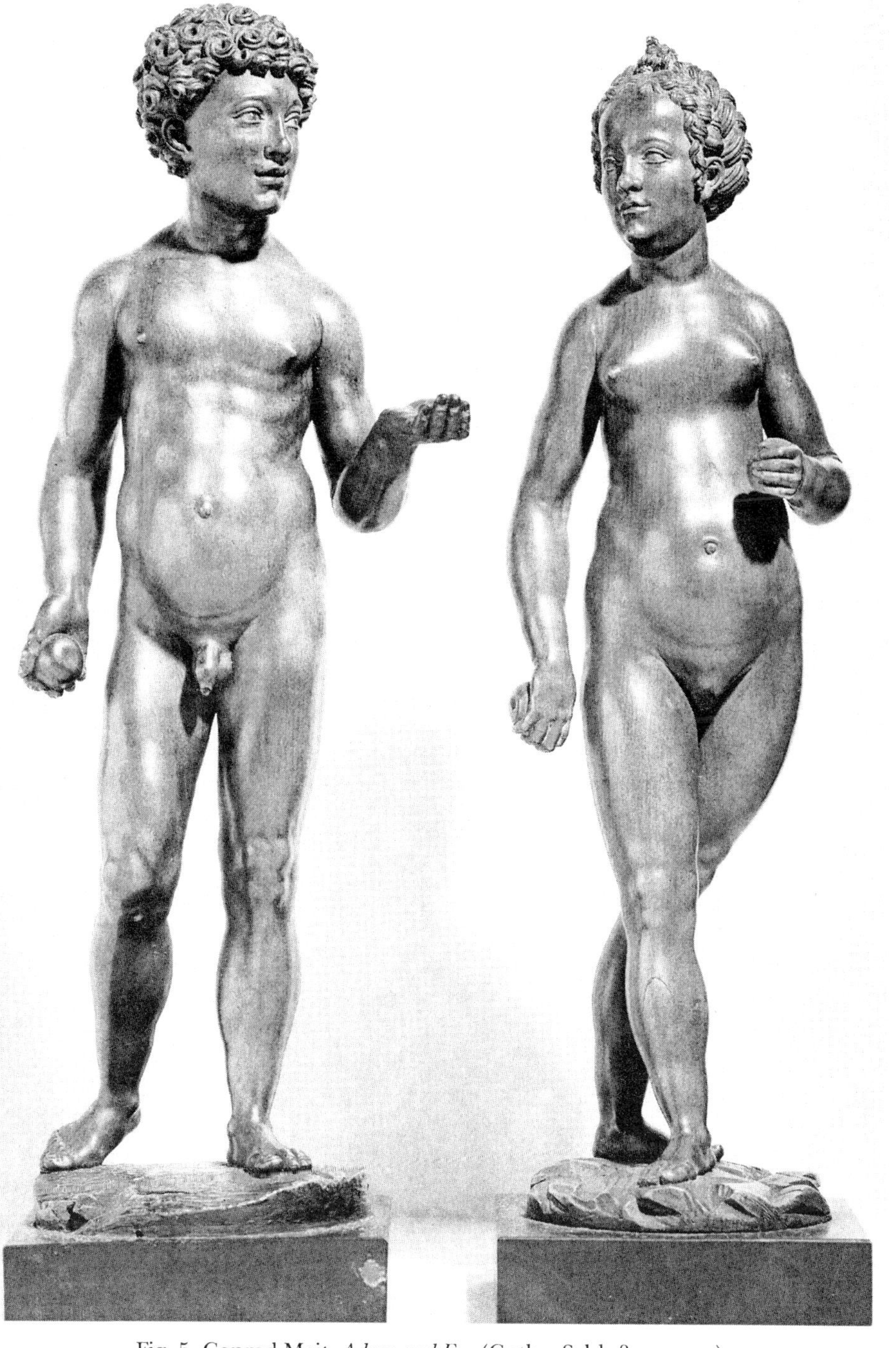

Fig. 5. Conrad Meit, *Adam and Eve* (Gotha, Schloßmuseum).

Fig. 6. Jan van Eyck, *Arnolfiniwedding* (London, National Gallery).

Fig. 7. Jan Gossaert, *Hermaphroditus and Salmacis* (Rotterdam, Museum Boijmans van Beuningen).

Fig. 8. Jan Mostaert, *Ecce Homo* (Hamburg, Kunsthalle).

Fig. 9. Henri van Lacke, *Genealogical tapestry for Margaret of Austria* (Budapest, Museum for Applied Arts).

PRINCELY CULTURE
FRIENDSHIP OR PATRONAGE?

Martin Gosman

Although sixteenth-century cultural production confronts us with the first steps towards what nowadays we should call an 'open market-situation', where the artist hopes to sell his creations, there is no question yet of the artist's being really independent: patronage remains the dominant factor.[1] The relationship between patron and artist, however, is a complex one and is not easily described: reality shows a myriad of possibilities, exhibiting in one way or another the tension between, on the one hand, the patron who likes to see his wishes respected and his exclusive status confirmed and celebrated, and, on the other, the individual creative artist who seems to accept the inevitability of his dependence but who nevertheless resents being treated as a subordinate and who tries to cast off the yoke.[2] Even if in earlier centuries artists – I take this qualifi-

[1] In the following I ignore the patronage of ecclesiastical authorities exercised within the scope of their official status. I shall also disregard the widespread tradition of the commissioning of religious artefacts by lay people. The ideas of the medieval Church with regard to the visual arts are widely known and need no comment. The religious controversies of the sixteenth century, however, reanimate the discussions concerning the relation between the visual arts and the faith. A striking example of this problem is the decree concerning the images of saints promulgated in 1563 by the Council of Trent. One example: the Church was quite willing to promote the cult of Mary Magdalen, but it did not appreciate at all the sensual way in which painters tended to represent that repenting sinner. The attitude that Protestant theologians adopted towards the arts in connection with Holy Writ bears witness to the same tensions: Luther, for instance, accepted the use of non-allegorical art, but Calvin's vision of God's inscrutability remained purely scriptural. According to the latter, pictorial products only concealed God's intentions. Cf. Delenda, 'Sainte Marie Madeleine'; Michalski, *The Reformation and the Visual Arts*, pp. 39, 65; Trevor-Roper, *Renaissance Essays*, p. 228.

[2] I use here the designation 'artist', although in the period discussed there is no real distiction between 'artist' and 'artisan'. The same applies to the confusion between terms such as 'author', 'translator' and 'editor'. See Welch, *Art and Society*, p. 39; Hauser, *The Social History of Art*, vol. I, pp. 31-340; Burkolter, *The Patronage System*. Remarks pertinent to this issue can be found in Burke, *The Italian Renaissance*, pp. 105-110 as well as in Salet, 'Mécénat royal et princier au Moyen Age'. For the relation between sciences and princely power, see Eamon, 'Court, Academy, and Printing House', pp. 27-31. For the role played by cultural production in propaganda,

cation in a broad sense: painters, sculptors and authors are all inhabitants of the realm of creativity – existed practically in a state of total dependence (art was merely the *ancilla theologiae*), they seem to have been able to live with the restraints imposed by those in power. In the pages that follow I start with some general remarks. After that, I concentrate on the situation in late fifteenth and sixteenth-century France. From time to time I shall adduce occasional examples related to the situation in Italy and Spain; after all, cultural production in this period functions as it were as an international affair.

Towards the end of the Middle Ages the relation between patrons and artists changes: some artists show signs of unhappiness and even of unwillingness when confronted with patrons who try to condition their creativity or impose unfavourable working conditions. Artists, as a rule, want to have their merits recognised. This consciousness may bring some of them to decline invitations to establish themselves at a specific court, to change patron, and even to refuse to finish objects which had been commissioned. In 1469 Mantegna, desiring to have his professional excellence duly recognised, goes to the Emperor to receive the title of Palatine Count. The historiographer Philippe de Commynes exchanges the patronage of Charles the Bold for that of Louis IX. The sculptor Pietro Tacca, well aware of the fact that his capacities are in great demand, declines James I's offer to come to London, where the king wishes to have an equestrian statue celebrating his own personal glory. Instead, Tacca heads for Madrid, where he creates the statue of Philip III in the Plaza Mayor (where it still stands).[3] At the request of Francis I, Giovanni Battista Rosso and Primaticcio come to France and transform Fontainebleau into a real royal palace. Sometimes the extant documentation confronts us with protests against the constraints of authority (Michelangelo's reluctance to obey the very authoritarian Julius II is a perfect example), or else with messages reiterating the patron's prescriptions or reformulating his explicit wishes. From time to time the artist wants his patron to recognise his genius and to pay him better.[4] Infor-

see, among others, Von Beyme, *Die Kunst der Macht*, pp. 11-34.

[3] Elam, 'Mantegna at Mantua', p. 16; Howart, *Images of Rule*, p. 138; Blanchard, *Commynes l'Européen*, pp. 29ff. Rivalry between princes makes artists understand that they can attempt to make the best terms they can. See Scaillierez, *François Ier*, pp. 18, 27; Cassagnes, *D'arrt et d'argent*, p. 161.

[4] For Michelangelo's bitter fights with the pope, see Noufflard, transl., *Vi de Michelange*, pp. 29-30; Salvini, *Michel-Ange*, pp. 59-93. Francesco del Cossa's problems are of a different nature: in 1470 he writes a letter to the duke of Ferrara in which he complains about the non-recognition of his exceptional genius, and he demands more money. The duke, however, plays deaf. Cf. Barker, Webb and Woods, eds, 'Historical introduction' in their *The Changing Status of the Artist*, p. 12. See also Campbell, *Cosmè Tura of Ferrara*, p. 1; Baxandall, *Painting and Experience in Fifteenth-Century Italy*.

mation of this kind concerns the 'contractual aspects' of the relationship between the parties. It is true that other parts of the extant documentation may suggest a peaceful cohabitation of both patron and artist; but arguments from silence do not prove much.

In this same period, furthermore, we see self-confident members of the *République des lettres* claim that their creativity is on a par with that exclusive divine *sapientia* with which rulers are gifted (or are said to be). Some poets see themselves as seers, who should really live in close proximity to their respective (princely) patrons in order to allow the latter to profit from those seers' exclusive capacities. This classical topos is also exploited by humanists, who consider themselves as being on a level with Plato's philosophers and for that reason perfectly able to advise those in power about the way the *res publica* ought to be directed. Typically, this is the attitude adopted by many humanists in the Italian city-states, where *artes* and governmental or other administrative activities often went together (Dante, Salutati, Porcari, Machiavelli, and so many others were simultaneously authors and civil servants). A man like Ariosto was regularly sent on diplomatic missions on behalf of his very demanding patrons, activities which left him little time for writing.[5] In the opinion of such poets, they are better placed to serve the prince than are his courtiers, who only think about themselves and despise the wisdom provided by literature, art and knowledge. To the courtiers who only want to be in his immediate *proximidad* the wise prince will refuse the opportunity to defend their own interests.[6] The poets pretend to be of more use to their master than the ambitious legists whom he employs.[7] The attitude adopted by Ronsard and his colleagues is a perfect illustration of all this, and many other examples could be adduced.

Whether the information provided by the texts is correct or not, is irrelevant. What counts is, first, the way the relationship between patron and artist is perceived, and, second, the efforts of the latter to implicate the patron in the exclusive interpretation-process, to which only the initiated are supposed to have access. It is here that we see the artist present himself as the mediator par excellence. is not he the only one who can 'explain' the secrets of his creations? It goes without saying that the Renaissance philosopher-

[5] Bonino, ed, *Ludovico Ariosto*, pp. 18-25.

[6] The notion *proximidad* is of the utmost importance in Baltasar Gracián's *El Héroe* (1637). See Del Hoyo, ed, *Baltasar Gracián*. There are, of course, the Urbino soirées where, under the aegis of the marchioness Elisabetta, nobles together with artists harmoniously idealise courtly life. But Castiglione's world belongs to fiction. For the (political) role of the *Accademie* in sixteenth-century Italy, see my 'Les académies du Cinquecento: aventure scientifique ou politique?'; Barzman, *The Florentine Academy*.

[7] In his *Art Poétique françait*, Thomas Sébillet states that virtue and the arts are of di-vine origin; in Sébillet's eyes, however, *art* means poetry. See Goyet, ed, *Traités de poétique et de rhétorique*, p. 51.

king is considered as the most important among those who are able to understand, and that is up to the artist to create a worthy environment.[8] The illusion is complete: instead of presenting the relationship between patron and artist as sociologically asymmetrical (as harsh reality shows), the artist prefers to evoke the impression of a *sodalitas*, all members of which strive for aesthetical and intellectual fulfilment. This, of course, belongs to the world of exaggerated wishes, since the prince and his court want only to be amused, and it does not really matter how. This impressive attitude on the part of the prince in what could be called a throw-away culture, is seriously at odds with the claims of the artists and humanists to produce things which should last for ever.[9] The suggestion, however, of an intellectual and cultural in-group is perceptible, and it goes without saying that the prince is its most outstanding and most learned member. As I hope to show in the following pages, it is on this particular level that the artist tries to neutralise the competition of the much hated courtier, and that he refers to what could be called a 'princely culture'.

Certain artists enjoying great prestige are put on a pedestal, and it comes to seem as if they can do whatever they want. Of course, a pedestal is only for the most popular and most excellent of those artists, who lay down new standards and who reveal themselves to be extraordinarily gifted or so prove themselves exceptionally useful to the prince whom they serve. The great majority of artists, however, are in a position of utter dependence. For the practioners of the so-called *arts mécaniques* things are even worse, because those who belong to the *République des lettres* consider themselves superior to those who work with their hands. This attitude of disdain, which humanists, like noblemen,[10] adopt in order to keep painters, sculptors, engravers and others at a distance, derives essentially from the classical tradition, according to which only those who had mastered rhetoric were able to advise the ruler: with the help of rhetoric one could explain, and therefore facilitate, dis-

[8] According to Jean d'Auton, Louis XII's official historiographer, the king's château at Blois was not only 'new and sumptuous' but also 'worthy of a king'. See Baumgartner, *Louis XII*, p. 162.

[9] Anglo, 'Humanism and the Court Arts', p. 86.

[10] In this view the fatigue resulting from the exercise of physical labour makes the body weak and effeminate, and reduces the vigour as well as the virtues of the heart. The conclusion of this thesis, already defended by Xenophon and adopted by sixteenth-century authors, is that those who practise the 'arts mécaniques' can never be virtuous. The next step is, of course, a sociological differentation between 'those who work with their hands' and the virtuous noblemen who never make their hands dirty. The humanists, eager to distance themselves from the artisans, quickly adopt the same attitude. Hence their attempts to present themselves as noble and as good as the *bene nati*. Cf. Jouanna, *Ordre social*, pp. 41-43.

cipline, peace, justice and power.[11] The case of printers is somewhat different. The cultural prestige of Aldus Manutius, for instance, is undisputed: the man had received a solid humanist training, and he was a master of Greek as well as of Latin. Other printers, too, know the classical languages. And this is precisely the reason why they consider their activities as being totally different from the ones linked to the *arts mécaniques*. Sometimes printers have an important status in university life, but – and here reality shows its grim face – this privileged position does not necessarily lead to an improvement of their social position.[12]

Of course, not every artist accepts the lowliness of his status. Leonardo violently protests that the power of expression of a work of visual art yields in nothing to that produced by discourse (whatever the nature of the latter may be); in his eyes both the concrete object and the abstract reasoning are integral parts of the analysis of moral and/or aesthetic ideas (such as those formulated, for instance, in many contemporary philosophical treatises) which, therefore, have to be treated equally. Painters often refer to a passage in Pliny the Elder's *Naturalis Historia* mentioning the esteem enjoyed by artists like Apelles in ancient Greece.[13] Others follow in Leonardo's footsteps. Although Giorgio Vasari's *Vite de' più eccellenti pittori, scultori e architetti* (1550) over-emphasises Florentine supremacy – he has to please his Medici masters – his work confirms the change in the position of the creative artist. It is similar with Benvenuto Cellini's *Vita* (started in 1558 and never really finished). Notwithstanding the artist's egocentricity and conceit, his 'autobiography' betrays a remarkable tendency towards artistic and intellectual independence. But protests like these do not really help. In the eyes of a Ronsard real images are always purely verbal constructs, and the creations of painters and sculptors cannot be considered as the results of intellectual operations. Opinions, however, change: in 1578 Blaise de Vigénère, who knows Vasari's *Vite*, publishes his *Images de Philostrate*, in which he defends the thesis that any separation between mental image and material image is a misinterpretation of the arts as well as a denial of the potential of the visual arts; three years later, Balthazar de Beaujoyeulx sees the combination of all the arts as the only possible way to glorify the political system.[14] The ideas of De Vigénère and Beaujoyeulx, however, are not accepted easily.

[11] Enders, 'Rhetoric, coercion, and the memory of violence', p. 28.

[12] The Moretus family are very proud of their professional skill: however, after having been ennobled, and having thus had their merits recognised, they go on printing. See Lefèvre and Martin, *L'apparition du livre*, pp. 207-215.

[13] Jex-Blake and Sellers, eds, *The Elder Pliny's Chapters*, pp. 121-127.

[14] Rèpaci-Courtois, 'Blaise de Vigénère', pp. 103-110.

Since the period under discussion here confronts us with passionate debates on the way society ought to be organised, as well as with numerous discussions on the position of the ruler, it is not surprising that we should see the artistic need for freedom of creativity clash with the then current ideas about the perfect society. Though earlier centuries had produced numerous treatises offering princes the necessary legal and moral excuses with which they might liberate themselves from feudal constraints, the sixteenth century begins to see power not only as an abstraction answering only to its own rules but also as a matter which is in urgent need of codification and illustration. Works like Machiavelli's *Il Principe* (written around 1513, but published in 1532), More's *Utopia* (1516), Seyssel's *Grant Monarchie de France* (1519), Bodin's *Les Six livres de la République* (1576), and so many others, are to be considered as attempts to reconsider man's position within a *christianitas* which is not the unified and happy *ecclesia* which Augustine desiderated. Rather, it is a mere collection of particularistic and strictly self-interested nation-states. Within this perspective it is not surprising to see artists trying to reformulate their position vis-à-vis their patron(s) and the nation in which they live and work.

It is not only the position of the artists that exhibits many variations from place to place; the same can be said of their patrons. The situation in Italy, where the political landscape is dominated by several small city-states together with a powerful *patrimonium Petri*, is not the same as that which we encounter in England, Spain and France, where centralisation conditions life. The variations, however, are remarkable: in England the crown has to deal with a Parliament which is not always cooperative; in the Iberian Peninsula the authority of the king is undermined by strong local particularism. Reality shows that the king has effective control only over Castile and hardly any over Catalonia and Aragon, whose *cortés* passionately try to preserve local autonomy; in France royal authority is regularly confronted with political, legal and financial opposition, even in times when the country is not either at war with foreign powers or disunited by religious antagonisms. Theories – and the sixteenth century loves theorising – can be perfect and promising, but reality shows that the exercise of authority is always confined to a political *hic et nunc*, a fact that 'official' propaganda happily ignores. Hence it is not surprising to see propaganda and panegyrics present princely authority as if it were total, complete and non-contested: whatever the prince wants to do, he is allowed to do. The exploitation of statements such as St. Paul's *non est potestas nisi a Deo* (Rom. 13,1) together with the Roman formula *Quod principi placuit, legis habet vigorem* proves highly functional in propaganda. Dozens of other apposite Biblical or classical references might also be given. The question of whether this kind of propagandistic assertiveness is motivated by political reality or by abstract theory is irrelevant: rulers want their virtual realities to be confirmed, and they are not interested at all in having true realities discussed.[15] It goes without saying that the occasional attempt to give a politically correct perception of reality cannot but put a strain on the relationship between patron and artist, especially in cases where the artist has to respect standard ideological concepts (see below).

The situation with which we are dealing always implicates several actors. On the one hand there is the prince, who is both the incarnation of the *persona* who represents ontologically as well as theatrically the *institutio,* and who is also just another human being; however, in the period concerned individualisation processes are schematic, and there is no real 'individualism' yet as such. Royal propaganda likes to present people as mere 'subjects' of the realm, a thesis which, of course, does not always correspond to reality, since princely authority is not always, and not automatically, acknowledged.[16] On the other hand, there is the artist who is both servant and subject of the prince as well as being an actor who has personal traits and/or specific artistic ideas. Since sixteenth-century power structures are in urgent need of motivation, illustration and even (re)definition, some princes are more interested in legalistic and political argumentations than in literary and artistic products that only the initiated can appreciate. Hence the opposition, mentioned above, between artists and legists at the prince's court. Other princes, on the contrary, are quite aware of the importance of the instrumental power of persuasion and they try to combine the political and the artistic. Had not Cicero already suggested a direct relation between the use of rhetoric and the exercise of power?[17] Isabella d'Este of Mantua, Francis I, Cosimo I de' Medici, Henry VIII, Charles V and his son Philip II are well-known for the intelligent and conscious use of patronage. But other princes are less easily convinced of the utility and effectiveness of cultural propaganda: Ronsard finds out how difficult it is to open Henry II's eyes to the political interest of the *Franciade*,[18] a text meant to highlight the glory of the nation as well as of the ruler and his poet. Of course, patron-client relationships are incurred voluntarily, and no artist (not even in the sixteenth century) is really compelled to seek and to accept the protection of a patron (generally with the help of some court broker).[19] But if the artist does wish to make a living out from his skills, he has to accept patronage. Unfortunately, even if he

[15] For the role of suggestion in French royal entry ceremonial, see my 'The Best Present Ever'.

[16] For *persona* and *institutio*, see Kantorowicz, *The King's Two Bodies*, pp. 364-400.

[17] Coleman, 'The science of politics', pp. 181-214.

[18] Chambers, 'The Earlier 'Academies' in Italy'.

[19] An excellent example of such a court broker, who makes the artist's life difficult, is the cardinal of Ferrara, whom Francis I uses many times as an intermediary. See Camesasca, ed, *Benvenuto Cellini. Vita*, pp. 431-433; also Knecht, *Renaissance Warrior and Patron*, pp. 425-477.

does so, his material worries are not over – far from it. Mantegna's position at the Gonzaga court is a relevant example here. Theoretically he is rather well off, since he has a contract guaranteeing him a house and a steady income; the reality, however, is different, since his patroness, Isabella d'Este, is always short of money, and he does not always receive his due. The situation confronting the lesser artists whom the Gonzaga may have lured into their service is even more precarious.

A striking example of the attitude that Renaissance patrons adopt towards artistic creativity can be found in the well-known correspondence between Isabella d'Este and Perugino concerning the *Battle between Love and Chastity*, which the master was commissioned to paint. Isabella gives detailed literary and technical prescriptions which the painter is to follow to the letter. Although Perugino may, eventually, omit some minor details from these instructions, he is not allowed to add anything of his own invention: any change in the scenes planned by the marchioness would have consequences for the meaning of the painting as well as for the iconographical design of the first *Studiolo* where it was to be displayed.[20] In order to achieve maximum narrative, iconographic and aesthetic coherence, Isabella decrees that not only should the canvases be of the same format, but even the main figures on the paintings should be of the same size. When, in 1505, the *Battle* is delivered, the marchioness is not happy at all: Perugino, she now decides, would have done a better job if he had used oil paint. Isabella has forgotten that the man has loyally obeyed her order to execute the painting in tempera.[21] Such details reveal the close and strictly hierarchical relationship between patron and artist, implicating not only the desired work of art but also the artist himself, and even his modus operandi. In other cases, the exercise of authority implies risks of physical punishment: Isabella threatens to throw Liombeni, another artist in her employ, into the dungeon if he does not deliver in time.[22]

From time to time, however, the artist's professional excellence as well as his self-confidence protect him. In his autobiography Cellini mentions a silver *acquereccia* [a water jug], commissioned by the bishop of Salamanca, a patron described by Cellini as *molto mirabile uomo, ricchissimo, ma difficile a contentare* ... [a very admirable man, but difficult to please]. The qualifications

[20] Sometimes instructions were given in carefully drawn up contracts which could even be accompanied by sketches specifying the patron's wishes. For this, see Welch, *Art and Society*, pp. 104-114; DaCosta Kaufmann, *Court, Cloister and City*, chapters 7 and 8.

[21] Fletcher, 'Isabella d'Este, p. 52; Canuti, *Il Perugino*; Martindal, 'The Patronage of Isabella d'Este', pp. 183-191.

[22] For other examples see Hollingsworth, *Patronage in Sixteenth-Century Italy*, pp. 248-249, 274-275; Kempers, *Painting, Power, and Patronage*; Hacke, 'Isabella d'Este'; Huse, *Studien zu Giovanni Bellini*.

used are revealing: every day the bishop sends someone to verify the progress made. Whenever the artist is found not working on the *acquereccia*, the bishop threatens to give the commission to someone else. After three months the bishop gets his jug, but he refuses to pay for it immediately: now it is Cellini's turn to wait. One day, however, the handle of the jug breaks and the bishop wants it to be repaired. Here Cellini seizes the opportunity to outsmart the bishop and to prove his own indispensability. Despite various threats made against the artist, the affair has a happy end: Benvenuto not only gets his money, but also obtains important commissions from Pope Clement VII, who, if we are to believe Cellini's account, is quite amused by Cellini's firmness.[23] This episode confronts us with quite different circumstances: though Cellini wants the commission from the Spanish prelate, he stages himself as the self-confident artist who has a workshop of his own and who is not afraid of a powerful and difficult patron. Moreover, faced with the bishop's unfair behaviour, he does not hesitate to defy him openly. The conflict does not concern the quality of the object (as a matter of fact the bishop is quite happy with Cellini's work), it only refers to the contractual aspects of the relationship of patron to artist. Benvenuto gives his readers the impression that he is independent. Even if the exact details of the adventure will never be known (Cellini's account is certainly not to be taken at face value), it is clear that the artist here is in a position different from that of Perugino. What Isabella does to the latter is diametrically opposed to what the Spanish bishop can do to Cellini.

Although the exact nature of the relationship between Isabella and her artists is something which could lead to interesting discussion, the reasons why princes buy cultural products are more pertinent to the present topic. These reasons can be political or aesthetic. In 1453 Philip the Good ordered Jean Wauquelin to rewrite the Old French epic *Girart de Roussillon*, a poem which was to provide the ducal dynasty with the necessary typological motives with the help of which it could substantiate Burgundian claims to independence and even to a royal crown. In order to ensure that he would obtain what he wanted, the duke supplied Wauquelin with the necessary sources, and he even checked the latter's handiwork very carefully.[24] However, Isabella d'Este's attitude towards art is strictly eclectic. She loves things for beauty's sake and, since she is chronically insolvent, she sometimes goes to great lengths in order to get the objects she has set her mind on: flattery, emotional blackmail and even threats are quite admissible in the achieving of her aim.[25] In the foregoing Cellini's

[23] Camesasca, ed, *Benvenuto Cellini*, pp. 130-4.

[24] See Thomas, Zink, Guerrand, eds, *Girart de Roussillon*, pp. 21-23; Gosman, 'Le nationalisme naissant et le sentiment de la *natio*'.

[25] Her appetite for works of art is said to have been insatiable. That is why Baldassare Castiglione, when he came to Mantua, hid his collection of paintings from the *appe-*

Vita has been mentioned as a valuable source of information about the status of an artist who owns a workshop producing either objects for the open market or others to commission. The conflict with the bishop of Salamanca is the result of a purely *ad hoc* relationship between an artist and a patron who wants the artist to manufacture a beautiful object. Cellini was able to show down the anger of the Spaniard but a less gifted (or a less popular) artist would not have dared to stand up to a prince of the Church. The behaviour displayed by the marchioness and the bishop is altogether illustrative for the way the magnates of sixteenth-century society expected their wishes to be obeyed. Perugino's painting and Cellini's jug also illustrate the need felt by high-placed persons to decorate their dwellings with works of art. The examples noted suggest that the commissions by the bishop and the marchioness were only inspired by aesthetic motivations, and that there were no political implications. This, of course, is not the general rule, since power and prestige go together as one can see in the case of Wauquelin's *Girart de Roussillon.*

Things become even more complicated in the case of iconographical programmes such as those encountered in the following list: in the Gonzaga *Camera degli Sposi*; Lorenzo de' Medici's villa at Poggio a Caiano; Henry VII's palace at Richmond; Francis I's Fontainebleau; the Sala dei Cinquecento in the Palazzo Vecchio; the famous Valois tapestries commissioned by Catherine de' Medici, etc. In such cases the works produced by the artist have to function within the framework of what nowadays we should call a political ideology. This cannot but have put a strain on the creative process. Of course, ideological connotations are not limited to programmatic ensembles; in itself the ruler's image is ideological – the word is to be taken in a broad sense, ranging from the effigies to the heraldic symbol. One has only to think of the way the statue of Francis I functioned within the French royal entry ceremonial, of the family tradition maintained or (re)created in Medici portraits, or of the desire for conformity manifested by the Spanish kings who were fully aware of the evocative power of the isolated detail in state portraits.[26] However, as soon as an artistic creation is to be fitted into a narrative or iconographical framework determined by ideological notions, the situation with which its maker is confronted becomes subject to very particular constraints: the creation has to respect the norms of the programme echoing the patron's way of thinking, and this, as we know, is the way of thinking of the *institutio* which the patron's *persona* is supposed to represent. Programmes like the one in the Sala dei Cinquecento function as a coherent entity: every part of it has to harmonise with

titosa [voracious] marchioness; see Fletcher, 'Isabella d'Este', p. 53.

[26] MacFarlane, ed, *The Entry of Henri II*, pp. 27-28; Hollingsworth, *Patronage in Sixteenth-Century Italy*, pp. 252-254; Van Veen, *Cosimo de' Medici*, pp. 82-90; Brown and Elliott, *A Palace for a King*.

the ensemble. Should it fail to do so, the propagandistic effect of the whole is inevitably reduced. Ideological programmes need not always be materialised; they can also be virtual, and the above-mentioned effigies refer to a virtual catalogue which has infinite propagandistic possibilities. It goes without saying that the inhabitants of the *République des lettres* have to respect these demands in their turn.

Normative pressure in contexts dominated by pure authoritarian behaviour, by centralism and/or by absolutism can easily degenerate into pure tyranny, and that is what sometimes happens in the period under discussion. Only exceptional artists, whose capacities are universally recognised, can maintain their freedom (as long as they do not antagonise the authorities). El Greco is a much appreciated artist but after his criticism of Pius V's prudery towards the nakedness of Michelangelo's *Last Judgment*, he has to flee the papal state. Titian's position, by way of contrast, is exceptional: Charles V, who considers him *huius seculi Apelles*, not only promotes him to the post of official court-painter, but also makes him a Palatine Count and even knight of the Order of the Golden Spur.[27] The emperor also employs Jan Vermeyen, who paints his victories at Pavia (1525) and Rome (1526) and who makes the designs for the tapestries which are to commemorate Charles's victory at Tunis, an event that induces some panegyrists to depict the emperor as another Scipio Africanus.[28] Vermeyen's prestige is uncontested, but he is never allowed the privileges enjoyed by Titian. Philip II orders from the same Italian two major allegorical paintings: *The Allegory of Lepanto* and *Spain coming to the Aid of Religion*. Titian is honoured by the commission, but he jealously guards his independence, stays in Italy, and has the paintings shipped to Madrid. On the other hand, his colleagues El Greco and Federigo Zuccaro (the latter is *pintor regio* from 1586-89) live at Philip's court, where they discover that the king is not only a difficult man to please, but also wants to regulate everything.[29]

I have referred, above, to the main reason why intellectuals tend to distance themselves from those who practise the *arts mécaniques* and who,

[27] Trevor-Roper, *Princes and Artists*, pp. 29, 66. Rubens was likewise considered the Apelles of his century. The remarkable thing is that both painters are compared with an abstract icon of perfection, since none of the Greek artist's creations has survived. Although the only work of art left by Alexander the Great's painter is his fame, Apelles' reputation was everywhere conceded. In his influential *Della pittura* (1435-6) Alberti refers to the description of Calumny which Lucian claimed was made by Apelles; cf. Spencer, transl., *Leon Battista Alberti*, p. 90). A non-existing norm, therefore, and one based on an entirely lost production, becomes the standard which Renaissance artists have to respect; Levy, *High Renaissance*; Rubinstein, 'Lorenzo de' Medici: his statecraft'.

[28] Trevor-Roper, *Princes and Artists*, p. 30; Zeitz, *Tizian. Teurer Freund*, pp. 1-20.

[29] Kamen, *Philip of Spain*, pp. 211-241.

mostly, are illiterate men united in guilds or other professional associations. I have also mentioned Leonardo's protests and Blaise de Vigénère's statement about the dysfunctional separation of mental and visual arts. It remains, however, a fact that the university-trained are very reluctant to give up territory, and that they go on pretending to belong to the 'international' elite whose advice is appreciated by secular as well as by ecclesiastical princes. This point of view seems to refer to another kind of superiority, a sociological one. Nothing, however, is less true, and in reality the position of the humanists is not essentially better. As a matter of fact, their position may even be less favourable than that occupied by some of the despised artists. It cannot be denied that many rulers are able to appreciate the beauty of philosophy, literature and poetry and that they can recognise the usefulness of the written word in propaganda and panegyrics. Both Lorenzo il Magnifico and Francis I wrote love poetry.[30] Texts singing the love of a lady are rather harmless, but philosophical, theological or political treatises are not. Like all sixteenth-century rulers the Medici and the Valois princes fear the impact of unorthodox ideas circulating on a large scale and that is why they seek to control the stream of ideas disseminated by the printing press and to divert it towards goals politically more correct. In general this is not too difficult a task since the great majority of authors – I limit myself here to the producers of narrative, philosophical and/or moralistic documents and not to poets wooing their ladies – have a subordinate status. With the exception of outstanding figures such as Cellini, Da Vinci and Titian, the mass of artists have to respect the normative system of their society which, as is well known, is set by the prince's court.[31]

It is important to stress the fact that those in power are mainly interested in strengthening and consolidating their position. There are, of course, many ways in which to achieve such a goal. Though Renaissance princes exploit everything, their main instruments are legal treatises and artistic creations. It goes without saying that the exact formulas of the treatises produced by the lawyers whom they employ can reveal themselves as politically highly convenient, and that they push the rich multivalences of artistic creations into the background. Propagandists, on the contrary, prefer to produce a discourse as vague as possible. It does not really matter whether the inhabitants of the *République des lettres* claim to have the same excellence and genius as the legists; the prince considers himself better served by the latter, who can produce

[30] For Lorenzo, see Rinaldi, *Storia della civiltà letteraria italiana*, vol. II: 2, pp. 903-906 and Orvieto, ed, *Tutte le Opere di Lorenzo de' Medici*. For the French king, see Jacquart, *François I*, p. 16, as well as Champollion, ed, *Les Poésies du Roi François Ier*.

[31] The remarkable thing is that even authors belonging to the upper classes of society have to conform to the norms fixed and upheld in the prince's court. This particular aspect of literary and socio-politically correctness will not be discussed here. See Firth Green, *Poets and Princepleasers*.

the required unambiguous statements.[32] The artists and the humanists cannot do this, and this is their Achilles' heel. Herein lies the vital difference between the legists on the one hand and the scholars from the faculties of arts and theology on the other. This disparity explains the desperate efforts made by the latter to be counted among the *intimi* of the prince, with whom they claim to share the same intellectual, artistic, and political, interests. Hence the emphasis on the correct interpretation of artistic creations: only the elite, of whom the prince is the most outstanding representative, are capable of the intellectual *tours de force* which bring about a correct interpretation of the artist's or the humanist's work. It is for this very reason that all artists – and in this they are merely following the example of the competitive courtiers – like to stress the importance of (Ciceronian) *amicitia*, based on mutual openness, frankness and loyalty so perfectly well evoked in Castiglione's *Cortegiano*.[33] Of course, all this theorising has only one goal: to mask the structural dependence of many of these theorists upon the patrons who, ultimately, sustain them. Only recognised geniuses like Leonardo and Titian can afford to stay away from the patron's court and still obtain commissions. Less fortunate artists and authors have to make a real effort if they want to earn some money, and, if their creations do not please, they have no income.

The relationships between patrons and authors are as diverse as the ones linking patrons and those who practise the *arts mécaniques*, as can be shown by several examples. The Spanish playwright Juan del Encina, who is in the service of the Alva family, seems to benefit from a rather stable position, and this also seems to be case of George Chastelain and Jean Molinet, who are both in the service of the Burgundian dukes. A career like that of Jean Lemaire de Belges, however, is far more representative for the vulnerability with which authors are confronted. *Clerc de finances* in the service of Pierre de Bourbon, Jean finds himself without a patron in 1503; his new protector, Louis de Luxembourg dies immediately; from 1504 to 1511 Jean is *indiciaire* of Marguerite of Austria; in 1511 he exchanges the Habsburg for the Valois and until 1514, the year of her death, he is *historiographe* of Queen Anne de Bretagne; after 1514, finally, we lose track of him.[34] Some thirty years later Rémy

[32] There is, of course, quite a distance between the politically adequate statement and its implementation in reality: in practice, however, this does not seem to matter very much

[33] Carnazzi and Battaglia, eds, *Baldassar Castiglione*; Rudd, *Themes in Roman Satire*, pp. 132ff. For Cicero's opinion, see the text as well as the translation by Falconer, ed, *Cicero*, pp. 108-211.

[34] Frappier, ed, *Jean Lemaire de Belges*, pp. vii-xxii; Rothstein, 'Jean Lemaire des Belges', pp. 594-595; Thibaut, *Marguerite d'Autriche*, pp. 134-158. Part of Jean's mobility can be explained by the fact that, long before 1511, he was already considering the possibility of a post at the prestigious Valois court; for this see Abelard, *Les Illus-*

Belleau finds himself totally dependent on the goodwill of the very catholic De Guise family, and even the famous Ronsard, who is the official court poet, has to contend with the fickleness of life. Juan del Encina writes *églogas* which sometimes give off the odour of church candles, but at least do not contain politically or religiously incorrect statements; his *Égloga de Cristino y Febea*, for instance, is as innocent and conformist as can be.[35] Lemaire de Belges's works betray the influence of his successive patrons, since Jean knows very well on which side his bread is buttered. In the first book of the *Illustrations de Gaule et Singularitez de Troye* he highlights the Burgundian ideals of unity and holy war against the Turks and he happily exploits the flexible and neutral concept of 'Gaule', which he sees as covering all the Habsburg territories, whether French- or German-speaking. However, once the poet has entered into the service of the Valois, the politically distinctive notion of 'France' takes over (the different 'titles' which the *Illustrations* have in the course of time been given demonstrate this clearly), and this explains why the contents of the second and third books are French, that is to say Valois.[36] In his *Bergeries*, Rémy Belleau transforms the intensely religious De Guise household into a fictitious and pastoral landscape allowing him to present his patrons as 'shepherds' belonging to a restored Age of Gold (in his days a politically very useful notion). The euphoria displayed in the text keeps the artist in business.[37]

The case of Pierre de Ronsard is even more interesting: although passionately hoping to write his *Franciade*, heralded to become the French *Aeneid*, he fails to convince Henry II to subsidise the long-term project. Henry's successor, Charles IX, does accept the proposal but, as we shall see, not without imposing ideas of his own. In the meantime, Ronsard has to produce a stream of occasional poetry confirming the ideology of the French royal *institutio*. Reality is harsh: as a court poet he can benefit from some *ad hoc* advantages but he has no real privileges. Moreover, he even has to sing the glory of two of Henry III's deceased minions, men whom the poet loathed.[38]

Like their competitors from the *arts mécaniques*, authors have to respect the norms of society. Conformity is the key-word, though it is actually very difficult to determine what is allowed and/or correct, and what is not. In authoritarian societies the subject's behaviour is judged on the basis of a rather vague conglomerate of political, religious and moral concepts that are thought of as coherently organised, perfectly understandable and politically (or even

trations de Gaule et Singularitez de Troye, pp. 23-25.

[35] Gimeno, ed, *Juan del Encina*, pp. 3-92.

[36] Rothstein, 'Jean Lemaire de Belges', p. 596.

[37] Delacourcelle, ed, *Rémy Belleau, La Bergerie*.

[38] Py, ed, *Ronsard. Hymnes*, p. 253; see also Smith, *The Anti-Courtier Trend in Sixteenth-Century French Literature*, pp. 197-198.

theologically) adequate and correct. Such a collection of *idées reçues* is that exploited by rulers in order to confirm or to strengthen their position, and by contrast, non-conformity or contestation – whatever form the latter may assume – leads to exclusion or persecution.

The question of whether such collections of ideas are to be seen as what nowadays is called an 'ideology' is a rather tricky one. Although no sociopolitical system, however primitive, has ever existed without an 'ideological' motivation, the fact is that before the second half of the sixteenth century political science is no more than a collection of notions taken from *ethica*, *philosophia* and *theologia*. As for the term 'ideology' itself, it did not even exist before the late eighteenth century.[39] The paradox, however, is that every system had an 'ideology' of its own with the help of which it it was able (or was thought to be able) to set itself off from other sociopolitical systems: medieval and early modern France loved to stress its difference from other nations, with the help of, among other things, its so-called 'lois fondamentales'.[40] This explains why the (re)construction of a 'system' which is not – in our terms – a real one, is quite an endeavour. But the paradox is that there always *is* a system. Alternatively – and more precisely – there is a congeries of *idées reçues* which provides people with a referential framework permitting adequate interpretations of every act of life, as well as with norms of socio-political correctness. These *idées reçues* can be found in literature, art, philosophy, theology, law (written or customary), etc.

It goes without saying that the cultural production in authoritarian systems cannot fail to echo (parts of) the ideological programme. The question, however, of the extent to which the individual artistic creations respond to the demands of such 'ideological' programmes as the monarchical rulers try to implement, is difficult to answer. However, it remains true that secular rulers try to play down the traditionally universalist perception of the sublunary world, which was highly soteriological, and attempt to replace it with some kind of functional 'nationalism' steered by a specific 'ideology'. Since there is simply no adequate definition of 'ideology', I opt here essentially for a purely pragmatic approach, whereby ideology is taken to be a steering-programme implicating the following:

1. a collection of sociological and ethical ideas supposed to be known, actively or passively, by the people concerned;
2. the premise that this collection has a certain coherence,

[39] Coleman, 'The science of politics', pp. 183-184; Kelley, *The Beginning of Ideology*, p. 1; Boudou, *L'idéologie ou l'origine des idées reçues*.
[40] See Richet, *La France moderne*, pp. 37-54; Barbiche, *Les institutions de la monarchie française*, pp. 28-33.

3. the effective functionality of this group of ideas within the socio-political collectivity which it conditions;
4. the acceptance (voluntary or not) of the necessity of this group of ideas by the subjects living in the context which it is supposed to characterise;
5. a tangible impact on the behaviour of these subjects;
6. the effective control, by those in power, of the way in which the subjects respect the 'ideologically adequate';
7. the certainty that the ideological system in which the subjects live is superior to all others; this superiority manifests itself in time and in space: life in the subject's *hic et nunc* is not only better than the one in former times, but is also better than life in other, contemporary, societies.

It is not unimportant to stress the point that not only in medieval but also in early modern society both the production and the correct interpretation of the 'ideological' connotations of complex cultural phenomena is the privilege of an intellectual and artistic elite (as has been said above, this is the trump card played by the humanists of the sixteenth century). Even if the traditional four-layered interpretation system, widely applied in the Middle Ages in Biblical exegesis, loses its effectiveness in the period discussed here, it may still remain functional where the one interpreting possesses the necessary keys. The presence of Roland's statue among those of saints on the façade of the cathedral of Modena not only presupposes specific knowledge of Charlemagne's legendary Iberian adventure, but the juxtaposition of Christian and legendary elements can also trigger theological interpretations, whereby the emperor's nephew comes to be seen as a *miles Christi*, a martyr of the Faith, an incarnation of the succesful collaboration between secular and spiritual powers, a perfect knight willing to sacrifice himself for the good of the nation (in the manner of a good *subjectus*).

The problem is greater, however, when we have to deal with learned, mostly pagan 'icons'.[41] Here access to the 'truth' is limited to the intellectuals in society. The mention of Alexander the Great in Chaucer's *Monk's Tale* illustrates this perfectly well:

> The storie of Alisandre is so comune
> That every wight that hath discrecioun
> Hath herd somwhat or al of his fortune.[42]

[41] For the *idées reçues* as well as for the use of 'icons' here, see my *La légende d'Alexandre le Grand,* chapters 3 and 8.
[42] Blake, ed, *The Canterbury Tales*, vol. II., pp. 253-257.

This is a traditional exploitation of the mechanism evoked above: the implied reader/listener has to actualise some of the ideals that the icon 'Alexander' is supposed to stand for in order to obtain a correct interpretation of the passage in question. In the present case, the icon referring to the Macedonian has no factual content whatsoever, but that is no hindrance: the reader/listener will take from the virtual catalogue of *idées reçues* those elements that he judges appropriate for his personal interpretation. In addition, it goes without saying that education, initiation and judgment (*discrecioun*) also play a role. The same goes for the reference to Apelles mentioned above: only the cultivated reader/listener who has heard *somwhat* (to use Chaucer's term) of the painter's reputation will grasp the importance of the comparison.

An identical phenomenon, though much more complex because of the telescoping of materials taken from Christian, pagan, legendary, mythological and even pseudo-Egyptian sources, can be detected in the way that learned and esoteric material is used in princely entries. Access to the semantic charges of the signs displayed on those occasions depends on the intellectual and cultural baggage of those who belong to the target group. The interpretation of all secrets, however, becomes a matter for the initiated only: that is to say, for the intellectuals, who try to turn their specific knowledge to their own advantage.

It is this aspect which reveals itself as of vital importance to the artists who desire the loosening of the straitjacket of cultural policy, and who, for this reason, seek to convince their patron of the fact that not only is he the initiated *par excellence* but that he can have access to the full meaning of artistic and intellectual creations only if he first accept the artist's or the scholar's help. The psychological implications of this attitude are very interesting indeed, as one may see with reference to several examples. During his entry into Vienne (1490) Charles VIII is Hercules, who will restore order in the *hortus Franciae*, an idea which even the common people are able to grasp.[43] On other occasions things are more difficult: the learned inscriptions in French, Latin and Greek, as well as the complex iconographical programmes on the triumphal arches made for the entry of Henry III into Paris (1573), can only have been understood by the intellectual elite. Although the king and his nobles were not complete *illitterati*, they would undoubtedly have required explanations of the Latin and Greek texts as well as of the allegories used.[44] Sometimes the poets, who were anxious to furnish proof of their scholarly knowledge, made the programmes as complicated as possible. Jean Dorat, *excellent poete es langues grecque, latine et françoyse*, creates for the entries of Charles IX (1571) and Henry III a programme telescoping Greek, Latin and French 'national' material in a manner so complex that the spectators need help. The pseudo-hiero-

[43] Jung, *Hercule dans la littérature française du XVIe siècle*, pp. 38-39.
[44] Houston, *Literacy in Early Modern Europe*.

glyphs on the imitation obelisks planned for the entry of Alessandro Farnese into Ghent (1584), are another illustration of this elitist approach.[45] The same occurs in 1616 during a *naumachia* on the Arno where the mythological references are so learned that the Florentine upperclass, though by no means unfamiliar with mythological references, has to be given the libretto of the nautical festival: in such displays cultural elitism embraces esotericism.[46]

As said earlier, it is the desire of humanists to leave unworthy competitors behind, especially those who belong to the much contemned 'working classes' whose members desire to climb the social ladder. One of the most effective ways to make life difficult for these unworthy persons is to 'hide the truth of things', since the truth is part of the *arcana Imperii* to which only the ruler and the initiated (the worthy) have access.[47] This consideration allows Ronsard to claim that *bien déguiser la verité des choses / D'un fabuleux manteau dont elles sont encloses* is an activity most honorable.[48] More than merely typical humanist snobbery and self-assurance is involved here; it is also a conscious effort to telescope sacred power (here also poetic power, since the Pléiade-poet considers himself as a *vates* whose duty it is to guide and inspire the worthy) and esoteric cultural production in order to widen the gap between the lower layers of society and the upper ones: only the educated and the virtuous have access to the real significance of elitist poetry. This classical idea, which had already been discussed by Petrarch and exploited by his imitators, does not cease to be effective in humanist writing.[49] Those who can read with discrimination are fully able to grasp the meaning hidden behind the liturgy of French entry ceremonial. The image is a strictly verbal construct. The illiterate, however, only see the external part of things, which the propaganda-machine announces as being in the interest of the people: for example, the king, *père du peuple* (this is how Louis XII was qualified by the representatives of the Estates, in 1506),[50] is good and just: he loves his subjects, and they love him. The meticulous protocol transforms these ceremonies into live illustrations of socio-political harmony: everything seems to be, as Voltaire was to put it, 'pour le mieux dans le meilleur des mondes possibles'. The real ideological connotations are only accessible to those who can 'read the signs'. This is the result of

[45] Waterschoot, 'Hieroglyphica te Gent', pp. 48-85.
[46] Blumenthal, *Theater Art of the Medici*, p. 11.
[47] Yates, *The French Academies*, p. 15.
[48] Laumonier, ed, *Pierre de Ronsard*, vol. IV, p. 313; De Nolhac, *Ronsard et l'Humanisme*, p. 93. A man such as Jodelle bluntly states that the ignorant plebs will never grasp the meaning of symbols. Cf. Demerson, *La Mythologie dans l'œuvre de la 'Pléiade'*, p. 518. See also my 'La matière "classique" dans la littérature française'.
[49] Baccou, transl., *Platon*, pp. 277-278 (= 519bcd). See also Gadoffre, *Du Bellay et le sacré*, pp. 111-112.
[50] For this, see Quilliet, *Louis XII*, pp. 314-334; Baumgartner, *Louis XII*, pp. 209-227.

a deliberate action on the part of the artist who wishes to refer to the above-mentioned *arcana Imperii*, to strengthen the intellectual *amicitia* between his princely patron and himself, and to mark his own indispensability.

Though it cannot be denied that even illiterate people understand direct statements of superiority on the part of their betters, the question remains, whether erudite comparisons referring to instances of long gone socio-political and cultural perfection are really functional outside the university, the court and the immediate spheres of influence. What is the use of a comparison between sixteenth-century France and the former Roman Empire if only the learned can see the implications of, for instance, the Roman *res publica* and *bonum commune* concepts, which are used in political treatises in order to jusify the position of the kings in society vis-à-vis the Church and the magnates in society? The concepts are common enough in official French propaganda (cf. *chose publicque* and *chose commune*) but it is not always clear whether they refer to Roman republican virtues or to imperial ones. In some other cases propagandistic effects are held in check on account of sheer material impediments: the message of the fresco painted, in 1516-7, by Raphael's assistants in the Vatican, where Leo III (pope from 795 to 816 but depicted here with the features of Leo X, pope from 1513 to 1521) crowns Charlemagne, who in turn has the looks of king Francis I of France, can only have limited significance, since only a few members of the elite have access to the papal palace.[51]

Things, however, are not always as complex as this. As soon as the illiterate or the uneducated accept the basic principle that their country is superior to others, and that the dynasty in power is the best thing that could happen to them, propaganda has achieved its aim. Such is the ultimate effect of the lavish imagery displayed on the triumphal arches in French royal entry ceremony: classical and 'national' elements are exploited, in order to illustrate both the king's and the nation's supremacy. The subjects easily recognise standard symbols like the 'fleur de lys', the Parisian 'nef', the allegorised damsel representing 'France' etc. Though the exact significance of the Latin and Greek inscriptions escapes the greater part of the onlookers – to them this scholarly activity is just a *pesant faix* (Ronsard) – they will undoubtedly take the esoteric signs and symbols for effective expressions of the supremacy of *their* king and *his* (and *their*) country. Propaganda succeeds here in underlining the exclusive relationship between the nation and its ruler, who is presented as its guardian,

[51] Lecoq, *François Ier*, p. 207. It is not impossible, however, that the French king would have liked the direct link between his Valois dynasty and the canonised Carolingian to be made more explicit: the French never abandoned the imperial dreams which they shared with their rulers. On the other hand, there can be no doubt at all about the feelings of the Habsburg candidate for the Empire, who can scarcely have been disappointed at the reduced accessibility of such a politically sensitive message.

as its *paterfamilias*. In his *Hymne de Pan* Jean Antoine du Baïf assimilates Pan and the king. With his 'divine' music the king *A qui fort triple & vn Dieu fauorise* guarantees *Le vray bon heur ou toute France aspire.*[52] Like Du Baïf's text, most others contain easily accessible statements: Jean Lemaire de Belges speaks of *nostre France* and so does Etienne Pasquier in his *Recherches de la France.*[53] If the king is a man like Saint Louis life will be good. This approach can take different shapes, by preference complex mythological ones stressing the esoteric aspect of power. The 1549 entry of Henry II into Paris illustrates this very well. Typhis, the helmsman of the Argo, says:

> Par l'antique Typhis Argo fut gouuernée,
> Pour aller conquerir d'or la riche toison:
> Et par vous Roy prudent à semblable raison,
> Sera nostre grand nef heureusement menée.[54]

The link between the royal helmsman and the 'ship of state' must have been clear to everybody, even though the non-learned will not have understood the implications of the mythological details.

The quintessence of propaganda is distortion (negative or positive): here factual truth is ignored, and replaced by a vision acceptable or desirable in a socio-political sense, and one preferably presented in a lapidary way. Though it may sound rather cynical, political truth is merely the result of a wholly *ad hoc* sociological relationship between the ruled and the ruler, with the latter claiming unlimited, supreme authority. In reality, however, princely power is never unlimited, total, absolute or uncontested (even Louis XIV, the 'model' of absolutism, cannot do everything he wants). Rather, official propaganda voluntarily papers over any suggestion of imperfection or incompleteness. In the period discussed here propaganda is not vertical, as in dictatorial states, but mostly horizontal, as in most modern states. This implies that everybody is supposed to respond to the same set of denotative and connotative elements (the above-mentioned *idées reçues* which inform both perception and interpretation. The result is what may be called an 'integration-propaganda', where the persuader asserts that he shares the same code as the people whom he wishes to persuade. In essence the system is confirmative as well as conservative.[55]

[52] MacFarlane, ed, *The Entry of Henri II*, pp. 5, 9.
[53] Gillot, *La Querelle des Anciens et des Modernes*, p. 101; Dubois, *Celtes et Gaulois*, p. 117.
[54] MacFarlane, ed, *The Entry of Henri II*, p. 15 (text).
[55] Dowell and Donnell, *Propaganda and Persusasion*, pp. 14-16; Foulkes, *Literature and Propaganda*, p. 42. For Louis XIV, see Lavisse, *Louis XIV*, pp. 161-187, 1161-1165; Goubert, *Louis XIV*, pp. 233-314. A perfect example of 'integration-propaganda' is to be found in Corneille's *Le Cid* (1637), where one of the *personae* states, rather

This is a codification-process based on the premise that all things and all ideas judged essential by the system are part of the *ordo naturalis*, that is to say of the system in which the parties concerned live. This *ordo* is protected by the prince who is ruler by the grace of God. Good Christians respect God's commands and they understand the necessity of obedience. Small wonder that the *raison d'être* of patronage and/or of censorship is conformity.

A few examples, taken from the theatrical tradition so severely supervised by authorities on account of possible breaches of peace, illustrate the phenomenon. The first example confirms the changing of values: Tasso's *Aminta* (1573) presents love as a natural affair (*ama, se piace*), while Guarini's *Pastor Fido*, though acknowledging the laws of nature, shows the real effectiveness of post-Tridentine discipline, whereby society's law only accepts regulated love (*ama, se lice*). Towards the end of the century a statement like that of Tasso's would have been politically incorrect (that is to say, in the eyes of the Church). This is an indirect way of confirming the existence of new norms. Direct political propaganda may be illustrated from two other examples: in Lope de Vega's *La Estrella de Sevilla*, where one of the *personae* states *que aunque injusto el rey es obedecerle ley* [however injust the king may be, one always has to obey him] and in Molière's *Tartuffe*, where the impasse is overcome by the king's officials, since the king is the guardian of *justitia* (as well as of other virtues, such as *caritas*, *fides* etc.) royal justice punishes the wicked.[56] The plays mentioned here confirm the excellency of the status quo and refer to the standard virtues, which the prince is supposed to incarnate.

The *livret* of the entry of Charles IX into Paris on the occasion of his marriage to Elisabeth of Austria (1571) provides references to the adventures of Francion, who after the fall of Ilion came to the Germanic regions, where Pharamond built the empire of Gaule. The text gives: *quas gentes Carolus ambas / Ut primus iunxit, sic tu nunc Carole iungis*.[57] ['O Charles, you are now joining the two peoples whom Charles (the Great) was the first to join']. The inscriptions address the king, who is presented as equal to Charlemagne. Among the images displayed on the arches is the Habsburg imperial emblem with the columns supporting the arches (evidently in honour of Elisabeth), with the columns appearing here in convoluted shape suggesting both an architectural

casually: *Mais on doit ... respect au pouvoir absolu / De n'examiner rien quand un roi l'a voulu* (I, 3); see Couton, ed, *Corneille*, vol. II, pp. 163-164.

[56] Ariani, ed, *Il teatro italiano*, vol. II, pp. 671 (= *Aminta*), 870 (= *Il Pastor Fido*); Maravall, *Teatro y literatura*, p. 125). Louis XIV, *ennemi de la fraude*, is the object of a discourse singing his perfection; cf. Jouanny, ed, *Molière*, vol. I, pp. 704-5. I do not imply, of course, that the fiction of a play mirrors the reality of a society. But, since conformity is a *conditio sine qua non*, Molière's play works towards a solution that the official ideology is bound to welcome.

[57] Graham and Johnson, eds, *The Paris Entries*, pp. 110-111.

analogy and a political one: the French king, who is the successor of Charlemagne, does not neglect the French imperial pretensions. André de la Vigne, who wrote an account of Charles VIII's expedition into Italy, had already mentioned France's imperial dream and so had Jean Lemaire de Belges.[58] For Ronsard, the court poet responsable for many of the inscriptions, the union of a Habsburg princess with a French king will restore the Age of Gold, because *Roy en terre n'est si grand qu'un Roy de France*.[59] Indeed, there is no need to stress the fact that the Age of Gold has a 'Roman' ring. The princess's veins are filled with imperial blood. Compulsory flattery and propaganda here meet, with the happy consequence that the king and his subjects get what they need. The special faculty of poets is to be able to combine Mars and Minerva.[60]

Like Lemaire de Belges, whom he admires very much, Ronsard exploits the Trojan connection distinguishing the French régime. In his *Hymne de France* (1549), his *Ode de la paix* (1550) and his *Cinquiesme livre des Odes* (1552) as well as in many other texts, he announces his intention of singing the deeds of France's Trojan ancestor as well as of the country's national heroes in a truly French *Aeneid*. This, he suggests, is something France needs. However, if the king wants such a national epic, he will have to give his official poet a good benefice (a bishopric or, at the least, a rich abbey).[61] In the dedication to the third edition of his *Odes* Ronsard claims his due:

> Les vertus & le bien que je veux recevoir,
> ...
> ... il te faut paier les frais de ton arroy.[62]

Even when totally subject to the whims of the mighty, the Pléiade-poets refuse to let themselves be overcome by modesty. They consider themselves divine seers, classical *vates* who can recreate and restore order with their sublime poetry. Here Ronsard exploits the myth of the artist-genius.[63] This attitude, based on the presumption that patron and artist belong to a circle of kindred spirits united in what resembles a Ciceronian *amicitia*, suggests that the parties involved can speak to each other in total freedom; hence the rather haughty style of the dedication (see above: *que je veux* and *il te faut*), which is a trifle surprising, since patronage upholds the illusion of freedom. The client offers his

[58] See Slerca, ed, *André de la Vigne*, vol. II, pp. 4365-70; Britnell, ed, *Jean Lemaire de Belges*.
[59] Graham and Johnson, eds, *The Paris Entries*, p. 144.
[60] Leiner, 'Mars et Minerve', pp. 161-163.
[61] Laumonier, ed, *Pierre de Ronsard,* vol. XVI, *La Franciade (1572)*, pp. vi-vii.
[62] Laumonier, ed, *Pierre de Ronsard*, vol. VII, p. 9.
[63] De Nolhac, *Ronsard et l'Humanisme*, p. 74; Ménager, *Introduction à la vie littéraire*, p. 7; Barker, Webb and Woods, eds, *The Changing Status of the Artist*, p. 9.

services to his patron who is not obliged to offer something in return. Such an obligation is impossible in an essentially asymmetrical relationship. However, that other *grecque Iliade*, which Ronsard is going to create, will be immortal, and it is a political and poetical must that Henry II simply cannot refuse.[64] However, as we know, statements of this kind do not always correspond with reality.[65]

Unfortunately for Ronsard, Henry dies; however, an endless stream of petitions addressed to the latter's widow, Catherine de' Medicis, is finally crowned with success. Ronsard is granted an abbey, which he exchanges as soon as possible for the priory of Saint-Cosme-lez-Tours, in his beloved Loire country.[66] When Henry's successor, Charles IX, finally gives the green light for the *Franciade*, Ronsard's triumph might seem to be complete, but nothing is less true. Though Charles IX accepts Ronsard's proposal, he imposes the *décasyllabe* of the French *chanson de geste*, which in earlier centuries had been used to sing the great deeds of the Franks and their kings. Ronsard, on the contrary, prefers the *alexandrin*, the *vers heroique*, to the *décasyllabe*, which he considers nothing more than a *vers commun*. 'National' tradition, however, tilts the balance.[67] In his preface to the first edition of Books I-IV Ronsard shows himself a truly servile creator: it would have been easy, so he says, to write the *Franciade* in *alexandrins*, but he prefers the *décasyllabe*, which is more difficult, more poetic. Obedience and creativity are forced to meet.[68] We do not know what happened in the years that followed, but in one way or another Ronsard seems to have lost his enthusiasm for the *monumentum aere perennius* which he was supposed to write. In September 1571 Amadis Jamyn reads Book IV of the *Franciade* to the king, who is the supervisor of the activities of his creative servant. It is impossible to ignore political control. In the next year, one month after the St Bartholomew massacre, the first four books of the poem are published. Thereafter there are some new editions, but Ronsard never writes the other twenty books, and in 1578, four years after the death of Charles IX, he abandons the project.[69]

Ronsard's position is highly illustrative. As the most outstanding Pléiade-poet he enjoys an enormous prestige, but as official court poet he is constrained to hover somewhere between his personal ambitions and the reality of

[64] Laumonier, ed, *Pierre de Ronsard*, vol. XII, p. 84; vol. VII, pp. 24-34.
[65] See Peck, *Court Patronage and Corruption*, pp. 18-19.
[66] Laumonier, ed, *Pierre de Ronsard*, vol. XVI, p. xiii.
[67] Py, ed, *Ronsard. Hymnes*, pp. 243, 265.
[68] Laumonier, ed, *Pierre de Ronsard*, vol. XVI, p. 9.
[69] Again, the poet gives the truth a little twist by blaming circumstances beyond his control: *Si le roy Charles eust vescu, / J'eusse achevé ce long ouvrage: / Si toost que la mort l'eut veincu, / Sa mort me veinquist le courage* (= Laumonier, ed, *Pierre de Ronsard*, vol. XVI, p. 330).

social relations. Although he frequently manifests his dislike of court life, he cannot ignore the source of his fortune, and like all other courtiers he bows to the inevitable. This applies not only in secular matters but also in religious ones: that is, in the religious wars he sides with the Catholic Church. Whether he does so out of conviction or merely for opportunistic reasons cannot be determined. One thing, at any rate, is clear: as an artist he remains vulnerable. In his rather cynical *Hymne de l'Or* (1555), written, significantly, this time in *vers heroiques*, and dedicated to his friend Jean Dorat, he admits:

> ... mon amy, puis qu'il nous faut joüer
> La farce des humains, vaut-il pas mieux loüer
> Qui peut, l'habit d'un Roy, d'un grand Prince, ou d'un Conte,
> Que l'habit d'un coquin, duquel on ne faict conte ...[70]

In order to earn a living, Ronsard has to send his poems not only to the king but also to key figures in society, people such as Odet and Gaspard de Coligny, Charles de Lorraine, brother of François de Guise, and many others. They are the *Prince* and *Conte* whose glory the court poet has to sing, but whom he would gladly exchange for a really qualified audience, such as the one that Joachim du Bellay had identified in the preface to the first edition of his *Olive* (1549). There Du Bellay states, in terms which betray Horatian influence: *Je ne cherche point les applaudissements populaires. Il me suffit pour tous lecteurs avoir un S. Gelays, un Heroât, un de Ronsart, un Carles, un Sceve ....*[71] The classical concept of social *amicitia* is here married to a humanist *idéologie de la fraternisation* which only the initiated are privileged to understand.[72] However, the courtiers – not to mention such other competitors as the king's legists – do not belong to this fraternity, and neither do those who practise the *arts mécaniques*.

It is not surprising that in his official court poetry Ronsard ignores as much as possible life's negative aspects. In his *Hymne de la France* he sings as an authentic *Françoys* of his *France aux belles villes: / Et son sainct nom*, of that country of *equité* and *justice*, where Astrea and her sister have restored the Age of Gold, and where Jupiter himself sends the *Françoys* (the French nation), *qu'il estime / Enfant d'Hector, sa race legitime* a king who will protect and guarantee happiness.[73] That king is Henry II, who is not only prince by the

[70] Py, ed, *Ronsard. Hymnes*, pp. 241-262.

[71] Simonin, ed, *Du Perron*, p. 13; Chamard and Bellinger, eds, *Joachim du Bellay*, p. 9. It is, of course, a reworking of Horace's statement in his *Satires* (vol. I ,10, 73-5): ... *neque te ut miretur turba labore,/ contentus paucis lectoribus. an tua demens / vilibus in ludis dicari carmina malis?* (in Färber, ed, *Horaz*, pp. 66-67).

[72] Dubois, *L'Imaginaire de la Renaissance*, pp. 74-75.

[73] Py, ed, *Ronsard. Hymnes*, vol. II, pp. 20-30.

grace of the Christian God but also a hero who rules also with the approval of the pagan Jupiter, which is why he favours justice, promotes equity, punishes evil and rewards virtue. In the *Hymne du Treschrestien Roy de France Henri II de ce nom* (1555) our poet, once again, displays the whole range of traditional 'patriotic' topics. Seen in this perspective, his poetry demands to be considered political. Ronsard's conception of 'France' ignores, however, any legalistic connotation. It is emotional. His 'France' is not a *natio* with a bureaucratic machinery but rather a territory full of people living in happiness and abundance, thanks to its king who is *presqu'un Dieu.*[74] Only a few texts – one thinks in this context of the *Hercule Chrestien* – refer to the religious controversies which are destroying the country's original happiness. Ronsard's later texts, however, pass over in silence the conflict between the different religious factions which is tearing the country apart, or the anarchy with which Henry III is confronted. Everything must be seen to be perfect.

It is precisely here that we encounter the poet, when Ronsard admits his disinterest in historical truth: aux *Historiographes d'esplucher toutes ces considerations, & non aux Poetes, qui ne cherchent que le possible.*[75] Little wonder that in the preface to the *Franciade* he boldly states that things have been altered in order to illustrate the superiority of France. In the eyes of Ronsard and of other such poets, what counts is not precision, but functionality. Although this claim allows the artist to avoid some of the constraints of necessity and ignore (parts of) harsh reality, the final result of the poet's licence is the defence of the political *ordo* as well as the conservation of the truth of the prince. This, of course, is exactly what the prince wants the artist in his service to do.

Conclusions

In the period discussed here, creative artists cannot permit themselves the luxury of ignoring the wishes of their patrons, who have very definite ideas about their own position in society. Even if Cellini's *Vita* is not to be taken at face value, the high-handed Spanish bishop mentioned by him is a patron who knows what is his due. When patrons are also rulers, their personal ideas implicate the interests of the sociopolitical system as well. There is, however, no standard system which can be invoked to explain every situation, since the relationships between artists and patrons are always fluctuating and uncertain. Isabella d'Este has no political power as of herself, but her husband's authority is hovering in the background. For this reason Liombeni must take her threats

[74] *Hymne du Treschrestien* (Py, ed, *Ronsard. Hymnes*, p. 117); Yates, *Astrée,* pp. 227-251.

[75] Laumonier, ed, *Pierre de Ronsard*, vol. XVI, p. 340 (= preface to the 1587 edition).

seriously. The exceptional and volatile Leonardo, however, is more fortunate: he may be allowed to count as Isabella's 'friend'. Though the distinction seems to echo the traditional Roman difference between *cliens* (Liombeni) and *amicus* (Leonardo), it would be unwise to pretend that Isabella knew the formal difference between the two terms. Even if she did – she was, after all, a very educated woman – rhetoric, as well as basic psychology, might also have played a role. But there can be no doubt that Leonardo's position appears better.[76] The emperor Charles V, in his attitude towards artists, shows an identical differentiation: while practically all the painters whom he employs have to respect his wishes, the brillant Titian may follow his own fantasy. The situation, however, with which El Greco and his colleagues are confronted is a more typical one: Philip II, master of centralisation, seeks to control everything. Like his counterparts in other countries, the Habsburg ruler understands very well that patronage and political control go together. The artist's world cannot escape from being conditioned by sheer opportunism.[77]

Once more, however, an exception proves the rule: the very traditional Philip buys the non-conformist paintings of the strikingly unorthodox Hieronymus Bosch (d. 1516) and keeps them in his private collection.[78] The apparent discrepancy here has no significance in reality, since palace walls may be hung with paintings which present concepts diverging from traditional standards or deviating from the norm.[79] According to the legists present in his court, Philippe is allowed to do so. Is not he above the law?[80] In any event, the exuberance of Bosch's paintings allows – even elicits – interpretations, which only the initiated can interpret. A ruler like Philip II must actually have appreciated the very inaccessibility of the works of the Flemish painter, and it is not inconceivable that he even relished the possibility of strictly personal explanations. After all, a good king possesses the divine *sapientia*.

The situation in the *République des lettres*, however, seems different. Since the printing press allows vast audiences to become acquainted with ideas which in themselves might seem to be politically questionable, the authorities inevitably seek to control the dissemination of information. The consequences are well-known, and need no repetition here. Within the scope of this essay it is more interesting to note the potential of panegyrics and propaganda to stress

[76] Rudd, *Themes in Roman Satire*, pp. 132ff.; Fletcher, 'Isabella d'Este', p.51; Luzio and Renier, 'La cultura e le relazioni letterarie di Isabella d'Este Gonzaga', p. 151.

[77] Peck, *Court Patronage and Corruption*, p. 17

[78] Trevor-Roper, *Princes and Artists*, pp. 75-78.

[79] The same remark can be made with regard to the images and inscriptions in the Medici theatre, which evoked Cosimo I's princely pretensions in a politically harmless environment. Cf. Van Veen, *Cosimo de'Medici*, pp. 66-68.

[80] It may be noted that the king is only *legibus solutus* with regard to his own laws; he cannot ignore natural or divine law.

both the superiority of the ruler and the happiness of the subjects, who profit from the ruler's *vis perfectiva.* In Tasso's *Aminta*, where the fictitious pastoral life (a mere stone's throw from the all too real Ferrara) is supposed to furnish the key to happiness, the duke's palace reveals itself as a *felice albergo* where people become *pien di nova virtù, piena di nova deitade.*[81] Tasso's dependence is evident, and he can do nothing but sing his master's glory. At the same time he can also praise the happiness of his shepherds. One might wonder, what his real intentions are.

The *Aminta* is an intelligent exploitation of learned references to classical authors, the identification of which can only be realised by the initiated. Though most princes had been been exposed in their youth to some elements of classical learning, only a handful could ever hope to qualify as real scholars. In such a situation the artist is offered an opportunity to stake out for himself some measure of independence, and to claim, perhaps, some respect: by providing the patron and his courtiers with learned references or with symbols of which the interpretation has to be mediated by the artist himself, the servant establishes for himself an aura of (temporal) indispensability.[82] As a qualified mediator, he communicates real knowledge to his master who – and this is the quintessence of the manoeuvre – sees his natural (and divine) superiority confirmed. After all, the artist is only telling the prince what the latter already knows. To the patron the artist is no more than an 'instrument' with the help of which the prince is enabled to demonstrate his own perfection. Since the excellent prince can tolerate the presence of nothing but what is outstanding (is it not his *vis perfectiva* which makes the artistic commission perfect?), it is against the background of this nexus that artists like Ronsard and his learned friends claim to be the only ones who can properly serve their prince.

All obligatory references to Antiquity, to the virtues of the Bible, to the innocence of the Age of Gold or to the exemplary heroes of the past whose status evokes a proverbial perfection can therefore be entirely replaced by the euphoric circumstances of the patron's natural *ordo* (not to be confused with that of the Church Fathers). After all, the prince's present is the best there ever has been. Since the ontologically reassuring message of panegyrics and propaganda implies a comparison between two perfections, one belonging to a past (not necessarily remote) and the other to the prince's present, which is also better than the present in which his competitors and enemies live, we are dealing with a kind of game, albeit a serious one. On the one hand there is the virtually unknown past, which is said to have harboured standard models of conduct supposedly applicable to all circumstances; on the other there is the actual

[81] Fubini and Maier, eds, *Torquato Tasso*, p. 87.

[82] See Gombrich, *Symbolic Images*, vol. II, pp. 158-60. For Ariosto's role at the Ferrara court see my 'Ariosto's *Orlando Furioso* and the restoration of the Este image'.

prince's present, which is not described in its particulars, but which seems to have its own set of rules with the help of which the prince governs his society.[83] This is the explanation of the ephemerality of court culture, where cultural production is serviceable and essentially based on the catalogue of *idées reçues* which, in the relevant context, function as a kind of ideological framework.

It is this catalogue of *idées reçues* that the creative artist has to take into account. Although he has to deliver a clear message identifying his patron and the society which the latter rules, he has to be careful with his examples taken from the past. If he leans too heavily on the perfection suggested by those examples, he will merely produce a conventional portrait, making his princely patron look like every other ruler with similar virtues. Such a thing would be unacceptable: could Francis I have lived with the idea that his enemy and rival Charles V was as perfect as he was himself?

On the other hand, if the artist should insist too much on the perfection of the *hic et nunc*, and should not provide the required quantity of adequate learned – and thus normative – references, he will not really have honoured his patron, who – and herein lies the real task of the artist – has to be given the opportunity to deduce and to extract from the icons of perfection proposed by the artistic creation, the politically appropriate interpretation. This operation can succeed only if it receives the necessary help from the contents of the approved canon of ideas. The initiated artist, who sees his capacities grow as soon as and for as long as he is within close proximity of his master. This exclusive *proximidad*, so much desired by the artist's eternal competitors, the courtiers and the legists, whose position is otherwise essentially similar, comes to be realised in a palace like Tasso's *felice albergo*. There man becomes a better creature altogether, in a better world, created and controlled, by his prince. This then is the quintessence of cultural production in the courtly contexts of the Early Modern Period. Creativity is a gift only the privileged artist pretends to possess, but it is the prince who makes that creativity work.

How, then, should the artist, who claims to belong to the same intellectual and cultural fraternity as his princely patron, deal with the information provided by the tradition – a tradition which the artist is able to exploit as well as to explain? The answer seems to be simple: as a servile creator he will pretend to do exactly what he has been told to do and he will perform the ritual dance. However, as a creative servant he will allow his patron to think that it is he, the patron, who is making the correct interpretation, and that the patron is only able to do so if he uses the exclusive knowledge furnished by the artist. In this way the latter becomes the real *amicus*, and the person uniquely qualified to tell the world that his master is a real prince. In his turn, the master becomes minded to

[83] Von Beyme, *Die Kunst der Macht*, pp. 17, 34, 44-45.

acknowledge the merits of his loyal 'friend', and he will give the latter, whom he no longer considers as a servant, access to princely bounty. In this way, each and everyone plays his role in the new theatrical *ordo* which is the princely court.

THE SYMBOLISM OF RULERSHIP

Olaf Mörke

In every age, power and rulership involve the problem of communication. Though that might be a truism, it nonetheless contains the essence of the subject we have to deal with. Success in rulership depended and depends on the ability to legitimate the relationship between ruling individuals or groups and those being ruled. The reliability and stability of rule also depended and depends on the predictability of the procedures in which the ways of political decision making are specified. The ranking of those taking part in processes of decision making was a crucial aspect of pre-modern political techniques. Order of rank had to be recognised as legitimate and permanent by both those involved in the process of decision-making and those affected by it, in order to facilitate a measure of rule itself as well as its future validity. Politico-social hierarchies are first of all noticeable through symbols, and the latter serve the aim of 'directed conspicuousness'.[1]

In his *Catalogus gloriae mundi* of 1546 the jurist Barthélemy de Chasseneux, president of the *parlement* of Provence, stressed the necessity to visualise social ranks as a fundamental element through which to understand the cosmic order: *honor consistit in signis extereoribus*.[2] By this, he not only summarised the experience of his time but also expressed the significance which the symbolism of hierarchy retained up to the end of the *ancien régime*. Since hierarchy is a precondition of rule, symbolic visualisation of that hierarchy is an integral part of the technique of rulership. It cannot be denied that physical force and material resources such as, for example, the administrational and military apparatus, are effective instruments with which to impose rule. However, the potential of such forces to secure rule can last only for a short time unless they are backed up by a consensus between rulers and ruled concerning the normative basis of the socio-political system in which both live. This consensus has to be proved in everyday communication, as well as in particular demonstrations confirming their mutual relationship.

[1] Stollberg-Rilinger, 'Zeremoniell als politisches Verfahren', p. 95.

[2] Bartholomaeus Cassanaeus, *Catalogus gloriae mundi* (Lyon 1546), quotation: 2nd edition (Frankfurt 1579), vol. I, p. 1. Quoted after Stollberg-Rilinger (see note 1).

In his book *The Fabrication of Louis XIV*, Peter Burke deals with the ways of constructing this mutual relationship under conditions of absolute monarchy. Among others, he stresses the techniques of 'persuasion', the channels and codes through which the image of the *roi soleil* was embedded in the political consciousness of the country, of those who had to recognise the king's claim to be the decisive bearer of power.[3] Emphasising in this way the element of persuasion as the crucial element of the communication process between king and country may give a somewhat distorted impression, since it lays the main stress on a one-sided relationship in which the ruler and his propagandists are seen to be the only, or at least the most active, and creative element. Nobody denies that this was the case under the conditions of a 'centralised state', which *ipso facto* 'needs a symbol of centrality'. Burke clearly stresses that 'the ruler and his court, often seen as an image of the cosmos, function as a sacred or an 'exemplary' centre for the rest of the state',[4] and he convincingly demonstrates the development of a wide spectrum of political symbolism serving that task. However, the mutual character of rule – on the one hand, the claim to power, on the other hand, the recognition of power – and the diversity of participants acting as individuals or groups representing interests *sui generis* may disappear from sight. Both in theory and practice, this mutuality was characteristic of the late medieval and early modern political systems in the pre-absolutistic era. All over Western and Central Europe these systems were centred around the idea of the *monarchia mixta*, the mixed constitution of a complementary interaction between monarch and Estates.[5] Recent works on the era of absolutism emphasise that even theoretically absolute monarchic systems depended in practice on success in negotiating the interests of different groups and individuals.[6] One might conclude that the stability and durability of a political system depended on its ability to shape a reliable set of communication patterns which were flexible enough to react to new demands which did not touch the political order in general, and which were stable enough to secure that order in principle. In that context the symbolism of rulership played a decisive role.

The development from more open, scarcely institutionalised forms of communication, both in cooperation and conflict, between the monarch and politically influential individuals and groups – the nobility, the high clergy, and the rising urban elites – to an institutionalisation of that relationship

[3] Burke, *The Fabrication of Louis XIV*, pp. 15-37.
[4] Burke, *The Fabrication of Louis XIV*, p. 11.
[5] Koenigsberger, 'Dominium Regale or Dominium Politicum et Regale'.
[6] Asch and Durchhardt, eds, *Der Absolutismus – ein Mythos?*; Henshall, *The Myth of Absolutism*; Hinrichs, *Fürsten und Mächte*.

marks the state formation process in the period from the high Middle Ages up to the sixteenth or even early seventeenth century. In his book on the Empire between 1250 and 1490, the German medievalist Peter Moraw has expressed that development with the formula 'from open constitution to structured intensification'.[7] By that he means the constitutional and institutional formation of the Empire as well as the emergence of the social and political estates which both organised the socio-political order up to the end of the *ancien régime*, not only in Germany but all over Europe. The increasing codification of that order, resulting in a growing number of ordinances concerning the relationship of political and social status groups, indicated the new demands for the ways of organising and visualising political and social hierarchies. The mutual face-to-face relationships of the high medieval feudal order did not completely lose their meaning for the representation of that hierarchy. But they were integrated into a more complex system of social and political lines of communication and interdependences, concerning the organisation not only of the state-internal structures of rule but also of interstate relationships. The increasing importance of written statutes concerning both the political and the social order since the late medieval period is indicative of the process whereby those relationships were rationalised. That this process fundamentally affected the symbolism of rulership and policy making is, for example, expressed by the emergence of a new scientific discipline in the late seventeenth century; this was especially true of the Holy Roman Empire, with its highly complex political system. The so-called 'Zeremonialwissenschaft' tried to fix the political and social order around the prince and his court in a rational and predictable shape.[8] It stood at the end of the development of the symbolism of rulership with which we have here to deal.

Those elements mentioned as crucial by Burke – the king or prince, and his court – undoubtedly played a decisive role in the symbolism of rule not only in France during the reign of Louis XIV but also in monarchic Europe during the entire period considered in this volume. That the German *Zeremonialwissenschaft* was centred around the relationship of those components proves the validity of that statement for a political culture differing plainly from that of absolutist France. But it has to be stressed again that for the era between around 1450 and 1650 the prince and court were enmeshed in the mutual tension of competing pretensions to power. In the following, I present a depiction of the role which political symbolism played in that process. First of all, the concept of symbolism both in the general context of rulership and also that of late medieval and early modern relations of power

7 Moraw, *Von offener Verfassung zu gestalteter Verdichtung*.
8 Vec, *Zeremonialwissenschaft im Fürstenstaat*; Bauer, *Hofökonomie*.

will be outlined briefly. After that, I present a series of examples, in order to show the effects of the symbolism of rulership on the way of political decision making and the shaping of state constructions. Finally, I discuss whether the process of state institutionalisation had an effect upon the way of symbolising the distribution of political power and rule. The depiction cannot be strictly limited to the period from 1450 to 1650, because some of the basic socio-political structures of 'Old Europe' started to develop earlier and persisted longer.[9]

In the humanities, various disciplines, such as art history, anthropology, sociology, and recently political history, deal with the concepts 'symbol' and 'symbolism'. It is not the place here to present the highly differentiated and controversial attempts to apply these concepts to the multitude of specific questions raised by each of those disciplines. Our question is a precisely historical one. It concerns the function and the status that princes had in late medieval and early modern political culture, and the activities which princes developed to mark their function and status in order to secure and to extend their power in competition with other groups and individuals. Political culture in that context means, on the one hand, the institutional and constitutional framework of the state constructions within which the princes act, and on the other, it means the not necessarily institutionalised and codified practice of constructing coherence within a state as a system of rule. This coherence is realised by interaction, in which the participants come to an understanding about the basis of the value of the constitutional framework and about the forms of practising power within that framework.

The more a political order lacks clearly defined institutionalised and codified competence for rulership, the more it depends on techniques of permanent negotiation about the distribution of power and the binding nature of norms and values which make the working order of the political construction possible in daily practice. Otherwise said, the relationships of rule were logically hierarchic ones. The hierarchy had to be fixed to generate stability. That was especially necessary at the end of conflicts in which those relationships were discussed. The result of those conflicts could sometimes be a return to the *status quo ante*; however, concerning the distribution of power among the competing participants and the organisation of rule during and after such conflicts, a development could take place. Accordingly, more often than by a mere return to the *status quo ante* restabilisation could be founded on a new, mostly slightly different level. New persons or groups could be integrated into the inner circles of power, and, as a countermove, old ones could be invalided out. However, especially after

[9] This is the key thesis of the concept of 'Old Europe' developed among others by Gerhard, *Old Europe*.

those dynamic periods of crisis, the fixation of the societal hierarchy in everyday policy was even more a *conditio sine qua non* for ensuring the reliability of political decision making. In this context of policy making under the auspices of preserving or generating stability – not least also in the face of political and social crises – the symbolism of rule is of particular importance.

'Symbol' and 'symbolism' are relatively open and general concepts, which have to be filled with concrete contents. 'Symbol' only means a sign which enables somebody to visualise an abstract object, an idea or context of action – as for example 'rule'. It reflects an imagined order.[10] 'Symbolism' orientates towards a specific abstract object, and implies the variety of a set of symbols in which that object can be crystallised – not least in order to make it communicable. That in particular the imagination of transcendental orders – 'religion' in the broadest sense – works with a developed symbolism, is something that implies the necessity of reducing the complexity of abstract normative systems to a set of symbols, in order to make the communication about them, and consequently their general recognition, possible.

The same goes for systems of rule which are closely connected to the general recognition of abstract norms and values. The success of any rule depends not only on that recognition but also on the standardisation of techniques of behaviour within the hierarchic order of rulers and ruled. That behaviour expresses the degree of recognition of that relationship. The success of rule also depends on the reliabilty of procedures by which the practice of rule is organised.[11] Those procedures can integrate symbolic elements in order to mark, for example, their beginning and end or the distinction of the locality where they take place.[12] They can thus be seen as performed symbols.

The participants in the political communication process made sure of the socio-political order they were acting in by using non-verbal, perhaps more than verbal, communication.[13] If the latter played a role, it was therefore in combination with and subordinated to non-verbal forms. In order to

[10] Bak, 'Symbolik und Kommunikation im Mittelalter'.

[11] The importance of the reliability of procedures for the stabilty of rule in the Middle Ages and the Early Modern Period is recently shown by the contributions in: Stollberg-Rilinger, ed., *Vormoderne politische Verfahren*

[12] Stollberg Rilinger, *Vormoderne politische Verfahren*, pp. 15-16.

[13] The problem of power stabilisation by submitting political communication to a routine of fixed forms and symbols is coherently discussed by Reinhard, *Geschichte der Staatsgewalt*, pp. 80-100. The importance of non-verbal regulations in the medieval political culture is among others stressed by Althoff, 'Ungeschriebene Gesetze'.

stabilise a political system consisting of individuals and groups with at least partly different interests, the basic values and the specific localisation of each individual or group within that system could not permanently be up for discussion; rather, they had to be unquestionable common property. One had, therefore to visualise them in acts of communication which were likewise unquestionable. That was managed by operating with a set of symbols, signs and acts, signalising that particular common value basis and localisation of those participating in a socio-political hierachy. The non-verbal manifestation of power relations – the symbolism of rule – is among other things expressed by gestures, by the constellation of individuals and groups in both informal and formal direct contacts in social situations, such as a conversation, a dinner, or a reception.[14] In all of those cases power relations are realised by constructing a relationship which reflects the construction of a social space, and within this space the acting individuals or groups are defined by their position to each other.[15]

Social space constructions play a crucial role in the symbolism of rule. They may be depicted by those constellations that individuals and groups enter into, when they meet on the occasion of real events. They may also be expressed in a less volatile manner by works of art, paintings, and architecture, in order to demonstrate and represent the relations of power and rule in a stable material way beyond the momentary social contact. The architecture of castles and palaces, moreover, gives shape to the material space in which the direct social contact demonstrating the individual position in the distribution system of power competence by action takes place.[16] In this way, architecture becomes part of a symbolic system which organises the relationships between the acting subjects of the political system, just as it represents the pretension of rule and its legitimacy. Scholars interpret this 'representation' through objects, gestures and actions as the crucial socio-political function of the princely court, and it is both architectural manifestation and social configuration.[17]

In dealing with the symbolism of rule in the form of concrete social configurations, one has to introduce a conceptual specification. When

[14] For a systematic overview, see Paravicini, 'Zeremoniell und Raum'.

[15] For the concept of social space, see Bourdieu, 'Espace social et genèse de "classe"'.

[16] The architectural structuring of princely dwellings as an expression of societal structures and esp. power relations was for the first time discussed in detail by Elias, *Die höfische Gesellschaft*, esp. chapter III, elsewhere. Also Chroscicki, 'Ceremonial Space', pp. 199-207.

[17] The discussion of different approaches to the definition of 'representation' in the context of late medieval and early modern rule is informativly lined out by Ragotzky and Wenzel, eds, *Höfische Repräsentation*, pp. 1-15.

writing about 'symbolism', scholars use two other key concepts: 'ritual' and 'ceremonial'. The latter refer to the social techniques in which the configuration around the prince receives expression in a formalised and organised way of social acting.[18] As concepts, neither 'ceremonial' nor 'ritual' can be separated sharply from the other. Indeed, they are often used in combination. A precise definition, summing up the results of recent research and useful in the discussion of the problem of the symbolism of rule is offered by Wolfgang Reinhard: 'Ritual gives behaviour security by stereotyped repetition, it is primarily action and not representation. Ceremonial makes the action a drama, it is an aestheticised and visually accentuated ritual. [...] But before all, ceremonial is a sytem of rituals, which at least in the seventeenth and eighteenth centuries even became a science in itself'.[19] From that, one may conclude that the development of the symbolism of rule from the late Middle Ages up to the end of the *ancien régime* is characterised by a rationalisation of rituals into the form of ceremonial, in order to subject the communication about rule to a coherent system of regulations.[20]

Despite a certain vagueness of definitions the close systematic connection of symbol, ritual, and ceremonial is obvious. The latter are components of a symbolic system which shows the various levels within a hierarchy of opportunities of participating in a highly complicated order of social and political relationships and dependencies between individuals and/or groups. This system should define, and, first of all, confine, the possibilities of concrete individual or collective action, in order to safeguard the structural permanence and security of that order. It is quite clear that the successful achievement of those functions depends on the recognition of rituals and ceremonial by those involved. Although authority may sometimes impose its will by sheer, brute force, this is actually the less preferable strategy, since it lacks the essential element of legitimacy. A much more effective way for authority to gain recognition is via the free agreement among the participants on – as mentioned above – the basis of commonly shared norms and values.

To illustrate the latter case I give an example which at first glance does not have much in common with monarchic rule. The free agreement would arise where the ideal of late medieval and early modern urban republicanism, with its notion of the city as a community of legally equal burghers all

[18] A wide range of attempts to define 'ritual' has recently been presented by Muir, *Ritual in Early Modern Europe*, pp. 1-9. For 'ritual' and 'ceremonial' see: Paravicini, 'Zeremoniell und Raum'; Stollberg-Rilinger, 'Zeremoniell, Ritual, Symbol'.

[19] Reinhard, *Geschichte der Staatsgewalt*, p. 91 (translation OM.) – The concept of ceremonial is widely discussed by Duindam, *Myths of Power*, pp. 102-107, 133-136.

[20] In that sense argues Bojcov, 'Qualitäten des Raumes', esp. pp. 130-131, elsewhere.

of them obliged to serve the city's common weal and liberty, were to be transformed into political practice.[21] We know that this ideal was an argument used to justify the setting-off of cities against their larger political environments, and in justifying the establishment of city regiments during this period, with its multitude of inner urban conflicts.[22] But even such a thing could not prevent the urban political structures from developing oligarchic forms of rulership. Nonetheless, elements of the ideal of citizenship centred around common weal and liberty were shared by all groups participating in urban politics.[23] As crucial elements of the common basis of values they played a decisive role in solving internal conflicts. Although different groups could have fundamentally different understandings of what the common weal meant in substance, discussion existed as to the basis of those at least generally shared values. Differences of interest could be overcome by a discourse which was led by morphologically identical concepts of common weal and liberty. The identity in the morphology of political language among the parties in the conflict made it achievable to conceal those differences, at least at times. This technique made possible the restabilisation of the political and social urban order after a conflict, if an agreement about the meaning of common weal could be found regarding the concrete problem which had produced the conflict. Furthermore, the highly standardised, or rather 'ritualised', course of events during urban uprisings made the latter into events whereof the participating groups could rationally assess, and thus predict, the consequences. The ritual of oath, which constituted the coherence of the community by confirmation of the mutual obligations of burghers and council, often played a part at the end of a conflict, in order to restore the communal peace and the consensus about the common weal among the conflicting groups. Those values were activated in concrete action, when townsmen came together to swear the burgher's oath. Political practice was not only closely connected with the political basis of values in the sense that the latter formed the ideological foundation for action; this basis of values rather became part of the action itself and through this could be redefined for the future.

This pattern applies to more than merely late medieval and early modern urban society with its non-hierarchic ideal of equal citizenship expressed by the oath ritual. In the same way, the symbolism of hierarchic systems of rule – especially those elements which not only represent preten-

[21] Isenmann, *Die deutsche Stadt im Spätmittelalter*, pp. 74-97, elsewhere; concerning the urban value system: Rublack, 'Political and Social Norms'.

[22] With numerous hints for further reading: Blickle, *Unruhen in der ständischen Gesellschaft*, pp. 52-58.

[23] Rublack, 'Political and Social Norms'.

sions for rule but organise the relationship of those involved in the system of rule – could work as an active element of political culture. At the beginning of the period, which is of interest here, the case of fifteenth-century Burgundy shows how ritual and ceremonial worked as instruments wherewith the socio-political coherence between the prince, the nobility, and the cities as participants of the communication system could be constructed into a composite state which developed exemplary forms of a *monarchia mixta*.[24] In the particular case of the complex of territories comprising the Burgundian Netherlands, which significantly differed from each other in their internal social structure – ranging from the highly urbanised Flanders and Brabant to the rural Luxemburg – the ruling princes had always to take the autonomy and the privileges of the territorial Estates into consideration.[25] The princes' relationship to the rich and influential cities of Flanders and Brabant was now and then especially precarious. Princely power and the unification process of the whole state formation depended on the degree of consensus between the prince, on the one hand, and, on the other, noble and civic territorial and local Estate elites. In that context the *Blijde Inkomsten* or *Joyeuses entrées* of the Burgundian dukes, the splendid state entries into the most important Burgundian cities, played a crucial role as both ceremonial and constitutional acts. As a ritual, the entry of the prince into 'his' city or territory was an act of taking possession. As with constitutional charters, the *Blijde Inkomsten* – for example, of Brabant – fixed the privileges of the territory and the Estates. The obedience of the subjects was bound to conditions and was rendered invalid if the prince did not keep the treaty.[26]

State entries, considered as rituals legitimising the princely rule over a territory and fixing the mutual obligations between princes and subjects, were not exclusive to Burgundy; among other examples, we find them in late medieval and early modern Scandinavia. The *eriksgata* of the Swedish monarchs, their traditional tour of the realm, where the *ting*, the law-giving body of the various provinces, hailed the new elected king, was an integral part of the ceremonial which made kingship legitimate by letting it be recognised by the Estates in the various provinces.[27] Like the Burgundian *Blijde Inkomsten*, the *eriksgata* was a ritual and a constitutional act as well. It was inalienable, because the king both as person and institution, embodied the unity of the composite state by accepting the mutual obligations of

[24] Elliott, 'A Europe of Composite Monarchies'.

[25] For the Burgundian Netherlands, see also the contribution of Arjo Vanderjagt in this volume.

[26] Prevenier and Blockmans, *Die burgundischen Niederlande*, pp. 202, 263.

[27] Schück, 'Sweden's Early Parliamentary Institutions', pp. 13, 15,16, 56; Sawyer, *Medieval Scandinavia*, p. 90.

monarch and country. The *eriksgata* of king Charles IX in 1609 took place in a strained political period. Charles had to struggle with his proble-matic kingship, because the catholic Sigismund III Vasa, since 1587 the elected king of Poland and since 1592 Sigismund I, king of Sweden, had not accepted his own deposition by the *riksdag* of 1599. It was therefore all the more necessary for the new king to prove the legitimacy of his rule and so to solve a fundamentally crisis-prone situation. Charles's *eriksgata* was the last link in a chain of constitutional acts, beginning with the coronation of 1607, which were designed to rid his reign of the suspicion of usurpation. Besides its character as an act symbolising that the king was taking possession of the country, the *eriksgata* also had a both practical and symbolic task. During his royal progress, the king administered justice as supreme judge of the realm. Charles himself and those who recognised him in that particular function, could thereby demonstrate that he alone could guarantee the country's peace under the law – one of the main tasks that a ruler had to perform.

The order in which the king's procession set off from Stockholm in 1609 clearly symbolised his claim to legitimate rule and dynastic continuity. Twelve horses covered with blue and yellow caparisons, the colours of Sweden, not of the Vasa familiy, formed the beginning. The coat of arms of the realm followed. In this first part of the procession there came also the nobles of the respective court district to be visited by the king. These nobles changed, when the border between two districts was crossed. The centre of the procession was formed by the sons of the king, Gustavus Adolphus and his younger brother Charles Philip, together with his nephew. Charles then followed on horseback, accompanied by members of the royal household. His wife came after him in a state coach, surrounded by her entourage. Office bearers of the court and the royal bodyguard concluded the parade. On different occasions during Charles's *eriksgata*, magnates such as duke John of Östergötland, who was considered as being a not completely reliable follower of Charles and also the noble and non-noble Estates of the regions swore an oath to the king.[28] The character of the *eriksgata*, as a triumphal procession representing both the magnificence of the king by the splendour of his court and his dynastic continuity, as a demonstration of royal justice through which the king served the country's peace, and as an opportunity for the country to pay homage to the king, was one of considerable programmatic complexity. The fact that the monarch was coming to the provinces of his country could be interpreted in a double sense: on the one hand, it was an act wherby the king took possession of the country; on

[28] Barudio, *Gustav Adolf – der Große*, pp. 82-99.

the other, it was one whereby the country took possession of the king. *Obligatio mutua* and *recognitio mutua* went hand in hand.

Thus was fulfilled a typical task of the ceremonial visualisation of a *monarchia mixta*, in which was demonstrated the functional complementarity of king and Estates for the construction of authority.[29] Complementarity, however, did not mean equality in rank for king and Estates. Of crucial importance was the distribution of power between those elements. That distribution was not fixed, and it would change over time, to the benefit of either party. The symbolic programme of the 1609 *eriksgata* documented impressively that in this particular situation the king should be profiled as the dominant factor concerning the competence of rule. Nonetheless, that had to be managed without hurting the traditions of the Swedish *monarchia mixta*, otherwise the legitimacy of Charles's reign might be called into question. In the precarious dynastic constellation of the Vasas, and as long as there was another serious pretender to throne in the person of Sigismund of Poland, that was something particularly to be avoided. The *eriksgata*, had, on the one hand, to stress the tradition of the *obligatio mutua* between king and Estates, while on the other, the order of the procession also emphasised strongly that the king and the dynasty stood in the centre of public interest and at the top of the socio-political hierarchy. The medieval custom of the *eriksgata* therefore played an important role in 1609 in stabilising the Swedish monarchy in the period which was to be decisive for the future development of the country as a European great power. Nonetheless, the *eriksgata* was an extraordinary event, and it could fall into oblivion, when the conditions of the distribution of power in the Swedish *monarchia mixta* changed. It was confined to a specific stage of the reign, and it was not integrated into the daily routine of rule. Because of that it was more a ritual than a ceremonial in the sense of a coherent and continous system of rituals.

A continous presence of the king as the centre of the political system was deliberately constructed by the propagandists of Gustavus Adolphus, the son and successor of Charles IX. In a masterly way, these men developed an image of the young king which located him in the unassailable context of historical mythology. The origin of the Swedes from the Goths, a people with a glorified past and said to have been the most powerful people

[29] Recently the concept 'komplementärer Reichs-Staat' (the Empire as complementary state) was introduced by Schmidt to characterise the early modern Holy Roman Empire: *Geschichte des alten Reiches*, pp. 40-44. As such, it mainly refers to the systematic connection between the competence of the Imperial Estates on both the territorial and imperial level, and the Emperor, in order to form a coherent political construction which preserved the Empire as a peace keeping association. Despite some differences, elements of the same intention can be found in the symbolic representation of the Swedish state in the *eriksgata* too.

of the world, gave Sweden under the rule of Gustavus Adolphus the necessary framework with which to legitimise its ambition to be the dominant power in Northern Europe.[30] Since the young king is profiled as standing in the tradition of the mythical leaders of the Goths and as being the one who brings the Gothic heritage to fulfilment, he has been placed in the position of a heroic leader whom the country has to follow without reservation. On the occasion of Gustavus's coronation in 1617, a tournament was held in Uppsala, where the king performed as Berik, the king of the Goths who is said to have led his warriors over the Baltic sea against the people of the South, in order to avenge the injustices which he and his own people had suffered from that direction.[31]

It was the task of the princely leader to restitute the honour of his people, and Gustavus Adolphus seized the opportunity to portray an image of himself as the champion of that honour. That *honor consistit in signis exterioribus*[32] is obvious in the successful attempt of Gustavus Adolphus and his advisers – among them his teacher Johannes Bureus, who is regarded as one of the most prominent propagandists of gothicism during the early sixteenth century[33] – to bind the political intentions of the new king into a dramaturgical context, in which the latter appears as the only guarantor of collective honour.

Gustavus Adolphus, as Berik, thus justified in a fictitious letter his intentions as being suitable to disseminate his own glory and that of his subjects all over the world through his virtues and deeds.[34] His performance as Berik, in the context of a theatrical ritual tournament which assembled the most prominent members of the country's nobility around the king, clearly testifies to the fact that he had recognised the importance of the symbolism of rule to the task of introducing a new accent to the programme of policy making. The aim of the specific symbolism of that event was the common recognition of the new role of leadership that he intended to fill in the future. To that end, a historic context, which suggested tradition but meant change, was constructed and performed symbolically. In a symbolic action, the history of the people and its leaders passed to Gustavus Adolphus, the

[30] Concerning the development of gothicism in the sixteenth and seventeenth centuries, see Johannesson, *The Renaissance of the Goths*; Svennung, *Zur Geschichte des Goticismus*, esp. pp. 84-87; Schmidt, *'De clara antiquitate et antiqua claritate Gothorum'*.
[31] Almquist, 'Tornérspelet vid kröningen 1617'; Barudio, *Gustav Adolf der Große*, pp. 24-30.
[32] See above, note 2.
[33] Concerning Bureus see Roberts, *Gustavus Adolphus*, vol. 1, pp. 519-520; Barudio, *Gustav Adolf – der Große*, pp. 73-76.
[34] Almquist, 'Tornérspelet vid kröningen 1617', p. 5.

one who would define the standards of the country's future.[35] Sweden had to be prepared for its role as a great power and it had to accept the king as the centre of political decision-making. This fact marks the difference between the reign of Gustavus Adolphus and that of his predecessors, including his father Charles IX. Charles's *eriksgata* was a manifestation of stability through its placing of the king in a constitutional tradition which lent his reign legitimacy. The tournament of Uppsala, however, created something different. It slightly but nonetheless effectively changed the socio-political hierarchy, since never before in Sweden had the king presented himself in such an obvious manner as the centre of the political cosmos. It was a symbolic milestone in a development characterised by the strengthening of royal power and the administrative centralisation, which would climax in the theocratic legitimation of princely sovereignty under Charles XI (1672-1697) and Charles XII (1697-1718).[36] It has to be stressed that the construction of the image of Gustavus Adolphus around the myth of the Goths did not lead to the direct annulment of the constitutional construction of the Swedish *monarchia mixta*. Nonetheless, the latter had been challenged by a concept of leadership lent itself to the fundamental transformation of the character of kingship in the direction of personal rule in consensus with the Estates.[37] The symbolism of the tournament drama at Uppsala initiated an obviously well calculated dynamic for the development of rule in Sweden, and as such the tournament demonstrates effectively how an event which was both ritual and ceremonial could be instrumentalised in the formulation of a programmatic intention of rule.

But ritual and ceremonial could also develop a dynamism of their own, especially when they were not only the intentionally used instruments of rule in a concrete and isolated event, as has been the case in the examples presented up to now. The scientification of ceremonial in the seventeenth and early eighteenth centuries indicates the rationalisation of ritual and ceremonial as routine in a complex and permanent communication process. In that context these factors not only served as instruments of rule brought into play by the ruler himself; they also had an impact on rule itself – *inter alia* by shaping the scope of action of those individuals and groups involved in relations of rule. As a result, such people could influence the pattern of rule, as has been demonstrated by the Swedish examples.

Within the same context, another aspect is of particular interest. Since the last decades the importance of princely courts as ceremonialised social

[35] Ringmar, *Identity, interest, and action*, pp. 160-164.

[36] For further reading see Mörke, 'Bataver, Eidgenossen und Goten', p. 115.

[37] Concerning the demand of Gustavus Adolphus to the Estates to follow the king without any reservation, see Runeby, *Monarchia mixta*.

systems for the relationship between the monarchic ruler, the nobility and other groups of functional state elites has been discussed intensively. Up to now, that discussion has been focused on the classical works on court culture of Norbert Elias and Jürgen von Kruedener, as this is seen mainly in early modern France and Germany.[38] According to Jeroen Duindam, these cultural historians overestimated 'the extent to which the ruler could use ceremonial – although they did recognise the restrictions ceremonial placed on the ruler'.[39] Here Duindam indicates the crucial problem mentioned above: princely rulers were integrated into a complex system of communication which was ceremonially regulated – that Duindam does not deny – but one which they obviously could not manage completely for their own purposes.

The intention to use elements of the court ceremonial – as for example the *levée* of the king and the architectural construction of the royal chambers[40] – as symbolic manifestations of rule and of the socio-political hierarchy culminating in and determined by the king alone, is not called into question. Nonetheless, the reality and effectiveness of the court ceremonial as an unambigious instrument of princely rule has to be discussed. Elias presented a model which might indicate the general direction in which the intention of monarchic rule, expressed by the patterns of court ceremonial, developed in seventeenth-century France. French court ceremonial deliberately intended as an intentionally used instrument to subdue the nobility to the rule of the king and to shape its behaviour to that end, did seem to work successfully to a certain extent. Ellery Schalk stresses that from the end of the sixteenth century the French nobility grew to accept the court as the measure of noble life style. Furthermore, the royal court became the aim of noble adaptability.[41] But even this perception does not allow a reliable statement about the working mechanism of court ceremonial. The relationship between, on the one hand, the court's function as a motivating force behind the change in noble behaviour and the definition of princely rule, and, on the other, the way in which the court reflected other developments of the political and social system, still cannot be explained satisfactorily.

Here another critical argument against Norbert Elias and his functionalistic model in explaining the role of ceremonial especially under the rule of Louis XIV has to be stressed. 'For Norbert Elias's purposes it is not relevant to know where the elements of etiquette came from nor how they are

[38] Elias, *Die höfische Gesellschaft*; Von Kruedener, *Die Rolle des Hofes*.

[39] Duindam, *Myths of Power*, p. 135. Duindam mainly refers to Elias, *Die höfische Gesellschaft*, chapt. V 'Etikette und Zeremoniell', pp. 120-177.

[40] Elias, *Die höfische Gesellschaft*, pp. 125-129.

[41] Schalk, 'The Court as "Civilizer" of the Nobility'.

pieced together. What counts for him is how they functioned as a structure of social relationship. [...] Certainly it has never been proved that the introduction of new forms of etiquette in Louis's court (not to mention their codification) was a product of deliberate planning'.[42] This objection is mainly directed against a methodological approach which neglects the historic genesis of ritual and ceremonial and which, in that account, stresses only the element of intentional control concentrated on the person of the ruler.

The integration of the historic evolution of rule clearly shows that the display of court ceremonial and its orientation towards the king underwent fundamental changes in early modern France. Those changes were influenced by *inter alia* the relative strength of the crown and the nobility. Under Henry III (1574-89) the court ceremonial functioned largely to cut the king off from his courtiers; under Henry IV (1589-10) and Louis XIII (1610-43) admittance to the king was temporarily made somewhat easier, however, under Louis XIV (1661-1715) ceremonial once more distanced the king from the courtiers.[43] This oscillation cannot be explained sufficiently by stressing a monocausal functionalism of ceremonial as an instrument in the hands of the king. A better interpretation is to see it as an element wherewith the court, as the country's central market for patronage relationships, might be organised.[44] Through their visualisation in ceremonial, those relationships acquired effective and calculable value for all individuals and groups involved. As much as court ceremonial was part of the symbolism of rule, it was also part of the symbolism of societal complexity, and this varied diachronically.

The functionalistic approach, which follows the paradigm of absolutism as including the entire socio-political reality, does not take into consideration that the royal intention of controlling and shaping the political and social elites could fail, even under the conditions of courtly absolutism. To an important degree, it depended on the will of the prince as individual. Louis XV (1715-74) and Louis XVI (1774-92) upheld their ceremonial role, but they did not fill it convincingly, since they both retreated into a parallel private life. More importantly, however, was the emergence of a political discourse on the financial situation of the state, with which the mechanism of courtly representation increasingly collided.[45] This excursion into a later

[42] Giesey, 'The "King Imagined"', p. 56.

[43] For this development see Solnon, *La cour de France*, pp. 140-141, 163-185, 237-243.

[44] Concerning patronage in a multipolar court society, see Mettam, *Power and Faction*, esp. pp. 20-22; Kettering, *Patrons, Brokers and Clients*, pp. 175-177, 232-237.

[45] With a concise overview over the development of the French court in the

period does not vitiate the general message, that ritual and ceremonial structure the perception of social relations in a system of political communication. But it does shift the emphasis away from concentration on the intentional shaping of ceremonial to a more open concept which integrates the study of ceremonial within an analysis that takes both the diachronic and synchronic dynamics of socio-political relationships and their influence on ceremonial into account. The result could be – as I have tried to indicate – that the function of ceremonial in the organisation of social relationships within a hierarchy of power should be interpreted more in the light of its offer of standards for behaviour which have to be accepted by the participants in a complex communication process, rather than of its being the outcome of a situation of order and obedience. Acceptance of ceremonial obviously depended on factors other than the rationality of ceremonial alone.

The interpretation of court ceremonial by Elias and others was centred too exclusively on the king's ability to manipulate it as an instrument of power and on the paradigm of absolutistic rule. Its genesis can be understood in the context of the older historical research, which took the idea of a rule *legibus solutus* as a given concerning the practice of rule. Recent research into absolutism in Europe has proved that this was not the case.[46] Diverse elements of the *monarchia mixta* model had survived – at least in political practice. The court nobility was by no means only a creation of the king's absolute power. New, however, were the ideas of absolute rule formulated by Bodin or Hobbes between the late sixteenth and the middle of the seventeenth century, although these ideas resulted in part also from developments that had taken place since the late Middle Ages. The process of state formation, which can be described by the concepts of territorialisation, institutionalisation and centralisation, indeed produced new challenges for rulership and changed the relation between, on the one hand, the ruling princes and kings and, on the other, the elites of nobility and clergy.

The process of state formation in Europe also affected the pattern of interstate relations. Step by step, beginning in the early sixteenth century, the European political system changed from the idea of an imperial universalism, as the expression of a christian order of salvation which placed the Roman emperor at the top of an ideal hierarchy of rulers within a feudal order, to a system of sovereign states with in principle equal political rights as was recognised in the peace negotiations at the end of the Thirty Years War.[47] All that brought new demands for the organisation of the complexity of state-internal and interstate political relations, in order to secure a

eighteenth century, see Bauer, *Hofökonomie*, pp. 254-259.

[46] See note 6.

[47] Burkhardt, 'Die entgipfelte Pyramide'.

minimum degree of reasonable regulation in these matters. In this context, new requirements were made of the symbolism of rule, and especially concerning those elements which were directly focused upon the organisation of po-litical action – in brief, ritual and ceremonial. The case of Gustavus Adolphus's performance as Berik has shown how both the relationship between king and country and between the country and the international sphere was symbolically performed under the conditions of the growing competition for power on the part of the European states and the imperative of concentrating the interior socio-politcal system on the royal ruler.

Finally, emphasis should be laid on one example which demonstrates, on the one hand, the cermonial shaping of an act which was crucial for the medieval constitutional system of the Empire and the idea of imperial universalism, and, on the other hand, the fate of that ceremonial under the conditions of changed political patterns in the early modern period. The Golden Bull of 1356 organised the election of the king in the Holy Roman Empire.[48] Its importance for the process of state formation has been summarised precisely in one sentence: 'The bull created an increase of state'.[49] Even during the most severe crises of the sixteenth and seventeenth centuries it maintained its role as the centrepiece of the constitution of the Empire up to the end of the latter, in 1806. The regulations of the Golden Bull show the connection between an important step in the institutionalisation of state formation and the symbolism of rulership. They solved one of the key problems of an electoral monarchy, the succession of the ruler and the integration of both the king and the electing Estates into a regulated system of symbolic communication suited to represent the political order of the Empire and the functionality of its feudal hierarchy.[50] First of all, it definitively codified the circle of the Electors and fixed their pre-eminent position against the other imperial Estates. But it was also a written ceremonial schedule, which was to prevent future conflicts of rank among the Electors and as concerns their relationship to the other Estates of the Empire. The seating plan of official acts such as imperial court days, banquets and especially the Imperial Diets, stressed the dominant position of the Electors, and gave visualisation to their internal functional differentiation and their position within the symbolic system representing the Empire as a whole.[51] By profiling a ceremonially expressed *theatrum praecedentiae*,[52] the Golden

[48] Moraw, *Von offener Verfassung*, pp. 149-169, 247-251.
[49] Moraw, *Von offener Verfassung*, pp. 248-249.
[50] Hofmann, 'Der spätmittelalterliche Rechtsbegriff der Repräsentation', pp. 24-28; Kunisch, 'Formen symbolischen Handelns'.
[51] Shown in detail by Kunisch, 'Formen symbolischen Handelns', pp. 264-270.
[52] Kunisch, 'Formen symbolischen Handelns', p. 274.

Bull served in principle to stabilise the Empire's constitutional and sociopolitical order for the following centuries.

To belong to the exclusive circle of the Electors was obviously attractive, until the end of the *ancien régime*. In the seventeenth-century, Bavaria and Hanover, and at the very end of the Empire Salzburg, Baden, Württemberg and Hesse-Kassel, also became electorates.[53] But it has to be questioned, whether this attraction resulted from the intention to maintain the order which was created by the Golden Bull. The fact that in 1764, on the occasion of a banquet after the election and coronation of king Joseph II, only the three ecclesiastical Electors, the archbishops of Trier, Mainz and Cologne, joined the meal, while the secular electorates allowed themselves to be represented by legates, who furthermore, dined in a side chamber, indicates the erosion of the meaning of the Golden Bull.[54] The symbolic content of this absenteeism is quite clear. It expressed the exact opposite of the traditional role of ceremonial in stabilising the order of the Empire. The role of the king and the Electors was fundamentally called into question by this symbolic act. The traditional ceremonial was maintained in form, because the secular electorates took part in the banquet, albeit, only represented by subordinate ranks. However, the ceremony was no more than an empty shell. At a crucial moment of the Empire's constitutional life, the celebration of royal succession, a new symbolism was set off against the symbolism of stability. The complementary dualism of king and Electors (or alternatively, the Estates) no longer appeared as an eternal *ordo*. The secular Electors knew of the effect of their symbolic action. It demonstrated that the relationship between them and the king had changed. Precisely that which the Golden Bull had tried to prevent – to make use of the ceremonial framework of the Empire as a forum within which to compete for influence and power – now occurred, as the Electors instrumentalised that ceremonial for their own actual purposes. In doing so, they undermined the feasibility of presenting the Empire as a sacred order, and on the symbolic level the Empire became merely a political construction dominated by the secular interests of the participants.

Here a development has come to an end, which had started in the early sixteenth century with the Reformation: the shattering of ceremonial.[55] Martin Luther's criticism of the pope and of the salvation dependent on good works already contained elements criticising ceremonial as superficial and

[53] Concerning the long term development, see Neuhaus, *Das Reich in der frühen Neuzeit*, pp. 21-27.

[54] Möller, *Fürstenstaat oder Bürgernation*, p. 247.

[55] With hints for further reading, see Stollberg-Rilinger, 'Zeremoniell als politisches Verfahren', pp. 128-131.

thereby irrelevant for salvation.[56] But only from the early eighteenth century onwards did this criticism fall on fertile ground. Johann Christian Lünig, one of the most effective compilators of European state ceremonial in that period, considered ceremonials as mere superficial signs of deference.[57] As such they could be disputed and instrumentalised in the service of the daily conflicts of political interests. That is what the Electors did in 1764. Nearly one hundred and fifty years earlier Gustavus Adolphus had also dynamised the political order by instrumentalising ceremonial. But the difference is notable, and Gustavus Adolphus succeeded in his attempt to give a visualisation through ceremonial of a new stability of princely rule. The symbolic content of his performance as Berik was more than a superficial sign of deference. It placed the ambition for rule within the unchallengeable context of historic myth, and it profiled the king as the executor of a mission which could be interpreted as the fulfilment of the *Heilsgeschichte* of the Swedish people. Thus, Gustavus Adolphus symbolically made use of the dialectic of dynamics and tradition. He created something new with reference to the traditional – and hopefully eternal – roots of his task as a ruler. In that respect his symbolism of rule is similar to the late medieval pattern of ceremonial enacted by the regulations of the Golden Bull. These regulations promoted the future process of the state formation of the Empire by codifying its socio-political shape as an expression of an eternal order. The chances of this remaining so vanished to the extent that the symbolism of rule eventually ruptured its connection with the transcendental legitimation of rule.

[56] Berns, 'Luthers Papstkritik als Zeremoniellkritik', pp. 160-161, 165.
[57] Lünig, *Theatrum Ceremoniale Historico-politicum*, vol. 1, preface.

THE PRINCELY CULTURE OF THE VALOIS DUKES OF BURGUNDY

Arjo Vanderjagt

By a curious paradox, the princely culture of the fifteenth-century Valois dukes and duchess of Burgundy – Philip the Bold (Pontoise, 1342-1404, Halle), John the Fearless (Rouvres, 1371-1419, Montereau), Philip the Good (Dijon, 1396-1467, Bruges), Charles the Bold (Dijon, 1433-1477, Nancy) and Mary of Burgundy (Brussels, 1457-1482, Bruges) – is hardly Burgundian at all if that adjective is taken to refer geographically to the duchy and the county of Burgundy.[1] Philip the Bold governed his duchy of Burgundy and the many lands he acquired in 1369 through his marriage to Margaret of Male, heiress of Flanders – Franche-Comté (the county of Burgundy), Nevers, Rethel, Flanders, Artois, Lille, Douai and Orchies –, mainly from Paris. His only important forays into Flanders and Brabant were to his border town of Tournai in 1385 in order to enter into a peace treaty with Ghent and to Halle in 1404, where he died in the Stag Inn. Yet, Philip was a Burgundian at heart and thus it was at Dijon that he founded the Charterhouse of Champmol as 'a gigantic sepulchral monument for himself and his heirs'.[2] Ironically, it was designed and executed not by a Burgundian but by Claus Sluter, from the city of Haarlem in the county of Holland.[3]

[1] The standard account of the dukes of Burgundy is Vaughan's tetralogy: *Philip the Bold. The Formation of the Burgundian State*; *John the Fearless. The Growth of Burgundian Power*; *Philip the Good. The Apogee of Burgundy* and *Charles the Bold. The Last Valois Duke of Burgundy*. Of many other books, special mention must be made of Calmette's *Les grands ducs de Bourgogne*. On Mary of Burgundy see the slightly outdated but highly entertaining work by Hommel, *Marie de Bourgogne* and for Mary's most important political activities the articles in Blockmans, ed, *Le privilège général*. For Charles see also Paravicini's *Karl der Kühne*. The latest important study of fifteenth-century Burgundy is Schnerb's *L'État bourguignon*.

[2] Vaughan, *Philip the Bold*, pp. 202-206; cf. Calmette, *Les grands ducs de Bourgogne*, pp. 288-298.

[3] Morand, *Claus Sluter*; cf. for stunning photographs the *Actes des journées internationales Claus Sluter*.

Philip's descendants, too, increasingly absented themselves from the two Burgundies to take up their affairs in *les pays de par dela* in the North which, of course, soon in their turn became *les pays de par deçà*. The dukes 'returned' from 'foreign' parts to Dijon only after their death.[4] Still, it is easy to overestimate the congruence of the culture of the ducal court with that of the dukes' northern territories, the Low Countries. There was little love lost between the dukes and the cities of Holland, Flanders, Brabant and their other possessions in the Low Countries. In describing these lands under Philip the Good as *terres de promission*, the fifteenth-century chronicler Philippe de Commynes selectively forgot divisive events such as the terrible Ghent Wars of 1449-1453.[5] Richard Vaughan, the modern historian of the dukes, is clear on the bloody antagonisms between ruler and ruled:

> The power of the Valois dukes of Burgundy had been established in Flanders in the 1380s over the dead bodies of thousands of Ghenters, slain on the field of Roosebeke, and Ghent remained a trouble-spot for every one of Philip the Bold's successors. In Bruges, too, revolt flared up from time to time, notably in 1437, when Philip the Good only just escaped with his life. In 1439 and 1445 it was the Dutch towns, Rotterdam, Amsterdam and Leiden in particular, which were convulsed by civic commotion and revolt, though here the situation was complicated by party struggles.[6]

Nor were these the only frictions between the dukes and their northern territories.

Nonetheless, the cultural tastes and perceptions of the dukes may seem at first sight to concur with those of their subjects. In the elaborate and solemn 'entrées joyeuses' or *blijde inkomsten* which the dukes made into

[4] Great pains were taken to inter the dukes at Champmol; see for example the fune-ral procession in the summer of 1420 of John the Fearless from the Notre Dame at Montereau – where he had been summarily buried after his murder in 1420 – to Champmol: Schnerb, 'Les funérailles de Jean sans Peur'; Vanderjagt, *Laurens Pignon*, pp. 5-8; as late as 1474, Charles the Bold, who visited the Charterhouse only rarely, had the remains of his parents re-interred there. The principal residences of Philip the Good were at Brussels, Bruges, Lille, Hesdin and Dijon, with Brussels taking pride of place: Vaughan, *Philip the Good*, pp. 135-136.

[5] Commynes's term was used for the title of their book by Blockmans and Prevenier, *The Promised Lands*, pp. 141-142. Commynes painted Philip the Good's lands as a terrestrial Paradise in order to maximise the contrast between Philip and his son Charles the Bold, the great adversary of Louis XI of France, to whom the chronicler had defected.

[6] Vaughan, *Philip the Good*, p. 303.

towns and cities, ducal and civic cultures appear to mirror each other. Gordon Kipling has devoted a large part of his mould-breaking *Enter the King* precisely to the theatre, liturgy and ritual in the medieval civic triumph of the Burgundian Low Countries.[7] He shows how meticulously the ducal and communal authorites each played their set parts in this kind of pageantry, for example, in the first civic triumph in Flanders, held at Bruges in 1440.[8] Following principles and enacting rituals that can be traced back to the *adventus* processions of the Roman emperors and Christ's entry into Jerusalem on Palm Sunday, these productions were directed emphatically by those citizens who hoped

> to achieve their rehabilitation as faithful subjects of their sovereign lord. In effect, by playing their roles in the civic triumph, the Duke and his subjects strove to reconstitute an ideal of Christian polity that had been destroyed in the rebellion. The civic triumph offered the citizens a symbolic and theatrical means of reuniting the head and body of the state in their proper, divinely ordained relationship. [...] However extravagant, such a ritual of repentance and pardon redeems the political bonds destroyed in the rebellion. Formerly a tyrant prince and rebellious citizens, they now adopt ideal roles characteristic of a Christian *corpus reipublicae*: a saviour prince receives the joyful homage of his repentant subjects.

The roles of the duke and his subjects are very different but they are part of the same cultural phenomenon, and their actors understand its structure in the same way. Thus, in a sense, what Robert Muchembled has sought to distinguish as popular culture and the culture of the elites is here at one to exorcise the demons of discord and injustice.[9]

In an astute study, Peter Arnade juxtaposes the urban public which constituted the central and political pillar of the Burgundian Netherlands with the 'brilliant court' of the dukes.[10] He investigates the civic realm:

> Behind the smooth, almost static surface of Burgundian ceremony was a turbulent urban landscape teeming with townspeople's opposition to Burgundian state centralisation. At the heart of the Burgundian public world, then, were town-state antagonisms, a bundle of shifting relationships that fundamentally shaped Burgundian life. A central dynamic behind Burgundian ritual was the fractious encounter between an ambitious ducal house-

[7] Kipling, *Enter the King*.
[8] Kipling, *Enter the King*, pp. 49-60.
[9] Muchembled, *Culture populaire et culture des élites*.
[10] Arnade, *Realms of Ritual*.

> hold and a world of townspeople. Behind ducal power in the fifteenth- and early-sixteenth-century Burgundian Netherlands was an urban core; towering over the powerful cities of the Low Countries was Burgundian sovereignty.[11]

Yet Arnade insists that this dialectic ensures that 'in fact, cities and the court were culturally contiguous insofar as Burgundian residences were urban based'.

Important as the recent studies by Arnade and Kipling are, they seem to this reader to exaggerate the cultural contiguity between the dukes and their subjects. In these and most other works the concept of 'Burgundian culture' is employed rather too generally and diffusely, lumping together all the different cultural activities of the Franco-Burgundo-Netherlandish realms, whether princely, civic, religious or devotional. The following pages are an exercise in distinction. The present paper will not discuss the kind of 'Burgundian' *civic* culture and ritual that is shared by what might loosely be called 'the ducal court', the local authorities and their populace. Neither will it treat the courtly religious devotion that is held in common with non-courtly society, although, of course, the former is more richly endowed. The focus instead will be on the culture that is typical for the *courts* of Philip the Good, Charles the Bold and Mary of Burgundy. This *princely* cultural activity may be divided broadly into two general areas that often overlap: the conglomerate of activities associated with the institution of the Order of the Golden Fleece and crusading ideals, possibly to be cast as a fascination with the Orient in general, and, second, the ideological and political justification of ducal rule as that of a sovereign prince. Thus this article will deal with the development of the *political culture* of the dukes.

Civic Ritual, Crusading Ideals, and the Golden Fleece

As Kipling and Arnade have shown, the two aforementioned specific phenomena of Burgundian princely culture played a role, too, albeit a relatively small one, in the strongly theologised Burgundian civic ritual and theatre. Thus entries of the dukes into their towns afforded them – at least symbolically – a princely, even regal aura which has religious and ritualistic overtones and foreshadows divine right theories of kingship.[12] Princely and

[11] Arnade, *Realms of Ritual*, p. 5.

[12] Kipling, *Enter the King*, discusses at length Philip's entries into Bruges in 1440 and Ghent in 1458: pp. 48-61, 264-280; emphasis is on the theological symbolism of which the upshot is: 'By selecting so many images based upon the iconography of the Nativity, the citizens of Bruges clearly attempt to shape the political occasion

civic desires and needs often clashed but as often they were again resolved, although elastic tensions always remained. Arnade gives an extensive analysis of Philip's entry into Ghent in 1458, in which he stresses that Ghent's aldermen knew that their political future rested on securing Philip's favour. In fact the aldermen begged Philip to make a joyful entry and they even decided to pay him handsomely to do so. Together with ducal officials the Ghenters 'prepared a spectacle unlike any other entry ceremony in the history of the Low Countries'.[13] To prove their fidelity to the duke, they remade their city into a terrain of symbols hospitable to Burgundian princely culture, even mixing ducal and civic symbols with common religious images and rituals in order to convey a sense of interdependence between the politics and goals of the city and those of duke Philip. Yet, the strong display of guild arms in this context also made a less conciliatory point: 'the guildsmen had some powerful symbols at their disposal and were thus to be reckoned with'.[14] It should, however, also be pointed out, that once these marvellous entries had been held, the street theatre concluded, the colourful banners taken down, the parades ended, and the final religious ceremonies held, the specific, 'non-Christian' ducal symbols, such as that of Jason and the Golden Fleece, were soon no longer in evidence in the city while the symbols of Christianity and of the civic community and the guilds remained.[15]

into a new beginning: Philip's reign begins anew and he approaches the city as if he were being inaugurated for the first time'. There is more than 'only' symbolism here. Philip the Good and Charles the Bold both sought a regal crown; in fact, at Trier in 1473, Charles hoped to be created king of the Romans and successor to the emperor or at least a territorial king, probably king of Burgundy; everything had been brought to readiness for the official ceremony, and, '[i]ndeed the duke was within a hair's breadth of wearing a crown'; the crown and the sceptre had already been made. At the very last moment, however, emperor Frederick absconded; see Vaughan, *Charles the Bold*, pp. 140-155; cf. Blockmans and Prevenier, *The Promised Lands*, pp. 188-189; Jongkees, 'Het koninkrijk Friesland'.

[13] Arnade, *Realms of Ritual*, p. 133.

[14] Arnade, *Realms of Ritual*, p. 139. Philip was well aware of how much the Ghenters hated him. In a personal, bantering letter (ca. 1452) to his nephew duke John I of Cleves he writes in his own hand: 'The Ghenters still have as much love for me as for the Devil, and are as amiable as they are wont to be'; cf. Vaughan, *Philip the Good*, p. 131.

[15] Kipling, *Enter the King*, pp. 274-276, gives as an example Van Eyck's altarpiece which had already by 1458 become a notable civic sight at Ghent. By contrast, very few of the princely, non-Christian elements of the entries became a part of civic cul-ture after their staging. Hence in works devoted to city culture, such as the magni-ficent volume edited by Vermeersch, ed, *Brügge und Europa*, only small mention is made of these Burgundian courtly symbols; this lack of interest is true even for Bruges, which was probably the favourite city of Philip, Charles and Mary.

A clear illustration of this cultural disjunction is furnished by the contents of the library of the Adorno family of Bruges. The family originally hailed from Genoa; they made good in Flanders as merchants and bankers, and they played an important political role in local administration as well. In the 1420s their wealth gave the Adorno brothers Jacob and Peter the opportunity to found the Jerusalem chapel in Bruges, which was completed by Peter's son Anselm later in the century. To this chapel, Peter in 1452 bequeathed his books, and his example was followed by Anselm's son Jan in the will the latter drew up in 1494.[16] In this library there is much mention of the Holy Land and the Orient generally, as might be expected from a wealthy family with a penchant and the money for pilgrimages to Jerusalem.[17] However, it lacks books that can be associated with the ducal focus on *princely* ideology, the trappings of the Golden Fleece and the noble art of arms, and this is understandable for such a *civic* family. In fact, Peter must have been rather devout: among the books he willed to the chapel are a *Vitae patrum*, an *Aurea legenda*, sermons by St Bernard and Petrarch's moralistic *De remediis utriusque fortunae*. From the fact that his son Anselm transcribed the *Somnium Scipionis*, knew his geography and mythology, and admired ancient Rome and quoted its authors, it cannot, however, be concluded – as Albert Derolez does – that Anselm is a humanist; not a few late-medieval, non-humanist intellectuals have similar interests. But things are different only half a generation later. The library that Anselm's son Jan (1444-1511) collected and in 1494 gave to the Jerusalem chapel is clearly early humanist. Jan studied at Paris and Pavia, where he became interested in humanist texts. Besides French and Dutch works like Christine de Pisan's *Othéa la déesse* and the Flemish work *Van Heer Erentrijk*, and devotional works like those of St Bonaventure and Suso, he owned books by Poggio, Bruni and Valla, and a gathering of classical Latin books by Valerius Maximus, Caesar, Cicero and Vergil.

International aristocrats like the Adornos with their base at Bruges exemplify civic culture with an intellectual bent. There is, for instance, a manifest difference between their bibliophile interests on the one hand and on the other those of their fellow citizen of Bruges and possibly friend: Louis of Bruges, lord of La Gruthuyse and earl of Winchester, who was governor of Holland and Zeeland for dukes Philip and Charles, and a knight

[16] Derolez, 'Vroeg humanisme en middeleeuwse bibliotheken'; cf. Macquarrie, 'Anselm Adornes'.

[17] They travelled to the Holy Land in the early decades of the fifteenth century and again in 1470-1471; of this last journey Anselm wrote an *Itinerary*, which he presented to James III of Scotland; cf. Macquarrie, 'Anselm Adornes'; MacDonald, 'The Chapel of Restalrig', pp. 40-41, who also gives an extended bibliography in his footnotes.

of the Order of the Golden Fleece; thus he was closely allied with the ducal court. Although they were closely related in local politics, trade and business, and perhaps also in 'international' relations on the behalf of Flanders and also of the dukes, the tastes in reading of the Adornos and of Louis were as different as can be. Louis's library is entirely modelled on the collection of the dukes, and in this sense it is clearly 'princely'; the Adorno library, on the other hand, can only somewhat prematurely for Bruges be described as humanist.[18] Malcolm Vale and Alasdair MacDonald have demonstrated how closely these wealthy citizens and knights were both connected with the aristocratic cultures of Guelders, Scotland and England, of which the rulers had a predilection for Burgundian courtly manners, styles, and literary productions.[19] How exactly these very different interests and fashions might be brought together intellectually – if indeed that is what happened – is a subject for further study. Perhaps Johan Huizinga is correct when he suggests eloquently in the first chapter of *Herfsttij der middeleeuwen* that the utter opposites of late-medieval Franco-Burgundian culture cannot be bridged.

Another interesting example of the juxtaposition and yet total separation of princely and, in this particular case, religious and philosophical literary culture in fifteenth century 'Burgundy' is the fascinating library of St Bavo's Abbey at Ghent.[20] The library in point is the private collection of Raphael de Marcatellis, abbot from 1478 until 1507, when he withdrew to his palace in Bruges, where he died in 1508. Marcatellis was one of Philip the Good's many bastards and thus a half-brother of both Anthony, the 'Grand Bâtard' of Burgundy, and Charles of Charolais, Philip's legitimate son and heir. Anthony was a well-known patron of the arts at the ducal court, a jouster, knight of the Order of the Golden Fleece, and the leader of the Burgundian crusading party in 1464; he was legitimated by pope Sixtus IV in 1475.[21] Marcatellis's library had some fifty-seven manuscripts, each often containing several distinct individual works. Obviously an abbot's interests are likely to be different from those of a courtier; the true distinction of Marcatellis, however, might be that he was 'among the first in the Netherlands to set up a collection of manuscripts of a markedly humanistic nature'.[22] Most of his books are in Latin; these are scholar's works like Martianus Capella's encyclopedia, works of the Church Fathers – especially

[18] For the library of Louis of Bruges: Martens, ed, *Lodewijk van Gruuthuse*, who gives a wealth of information.
[19] Vale, 'An Anglo-Burgundian Nobleman'; MacDonald, 'The Chapel of Restalrig', pp. 40-47.
[20] On this library see Derolez, *The Library of Raphael de Marcatellis*.
[21] See Cauchies, 'Antoine de Bourgogne', pp. 118-120.
[22] Derolez, *The Library of Raphael de Marcatellis*, p. 298.

those in fashion in Italy at the time like Chrysostomos,[23] treatises by Plato, Plotinus, Apuleius, Hermes Trismegistus, and Ficino, ethical and moralistic guidelines by Seneca, Alain Chartier, Francesco Barbaro, Poggio Bracciolini and Aeneas Silvius Piccolomini. There is much more, but from this short list it is clear that this collection shows almost no overlap with the ducal library – except for a few authors like Seneca, whose moralistic works had earlier been rendered into French for various princes of France and Burgundy. Neither has the collection anything in common with the fashion created by the knights of the Golden Fleece such as the Grand Bâtard; nothing at St Bavo's, therefore, can be connected to Burgundian *princely* culture. There is, though, a kind of scientific interest in the Orient. This is illustrated by a series of treatises authored by Piccolomini, the 'crusader pope' of the fifteenth century, letters from the Grand Turk, Marco Polo's account of his travels, and tables with trade-routes through Europe and the Levant. Derolez thinks that this part of the library 'evidently must be related to the plans for a crusade forged by Marcatellis's father Philip the Good and to the ideas set up by the humanist pope Pius II' (Piccolomini).[24] However, although these manuscripts are luxurious in execution, their language, style, and very form had little in common with those of the ducal library. Whether they can be connected directly to a crusade is debatable; it is more likely that they illustrate a general interest for the Orient in the light of the latest 'Turkish' news and, too, for travel guides useful to pilgrims. However this may be, there is little or no sign of 'trickle-down culture' from the princely, ducal court to either the civic or religious communities.

The civic culture of the Burgundian lands clearly stood at a distance from the extravagant semi-public, princely culture of book collecting, the design, manufacture and hanging of tapestries, and the elaborate culinary creations for their feasts which incorporated themes from both pagan and Christian antiquity, and the Orient. Similary, a great distinction can be detected between the specific princely culture of the dukes on the one hand and on the other their munificent funding of religious architecture and the devotional arts – the illumination of books of hours, for example, or the commissioning of music for their private chapel from Gilles Binchois or Anthoine Busnois. For instance, the wonderful Charterhouse at Champmol, so close to the heart of Philip the Bold and his heirs, suggests nothing that

[23] A high servant and ambassador of Philip the Good, Jean Jouffroy, who was bishop of Arras from 1453-1462 and defected from Burgundy to Louis XI in 1461, was particularly fond of Chrysostomos, and some of the latter's works were translated from the Greek into the Latin on the bishop's behalf; cf. Märtl, *Kardinal Jean Jouffroy*, pp. 286-287.

[24] Derolez, *The Library of Raphael de Marcatellis*, p. 302.

might be connected to the dukes' favorite stories of the Trojans, Jason and the Golden Fleece and Hercules, the histories of Alexander the Great, Hannibal, Publius Cornelius Scipio and Julius Caesar. There is no congruence with typically 'Burgundised' romances such as the fifteenth-century version of Gautier de Tournai's thirteenth-century poem devoted to Gilles de Chin and the 'history' of Gillion de Trazegnies. Both romances deal with the complicated travels and pilgrimages of their protagonists to the Holy Land and with their subsequent fights with infidel princes; besides, the Burgundian version of Gilles de Chin waxes eloquent with descriptions of Burgundo-French tournaments, gala-dinners, dances and parades ceremonial. Neither are there in the Charterhouse any references that harmonise with the rendition by Jean Miélot, one of Philip's secretaries, of the work of the Italian civic humanist Buonaccorso da Montemagno to say nothing of that of the much favoured ancient writer Lucian.[25] In their eternal repose, the dukes were concerned with other matters.[26]

It is true that the famous collar of the Order of the Golden Fleece – consisting of interlocking flints and a pendant golden fleece – was incorporated into the heraldic arms of the dukes and the knights of the Order. Thus it is also often displayed in public space. Symbols and badges of this kind were no doubt regarded as matters of princely prerogative and they could not, of course, be adopted by the citizens who fancied them. But more important is the fact that the relevant background stories are not adopted in non-courtly manifestations of civic culture. The same symbols, of course, are also quite common as emblems both on Burgundian coins and on medals, such as the famous one of Charles struck by Giovanni Filangieri di Candida around 1474. This, again, has but little to do with devised, ritual civic culture, since coinage and the mint were seen as the personal prerogative of the ruler. At the very least he governed the mint for the benefit of the common good if indeed he was not considered its 'owner'.[27] As far

[25] For Gilles de Chin and Gillion de Trazegnies see Doutrepont, *La littérature française*, p. 47, and the texts and literature mentioned there. I am unaware of more recent work on or editions of these romances except for a dissertation by Cormier, *An Edition of the Middle French Prose Romance*. For editions of the French translations of the *novella* by Buonaccorso and of the *controversia* by Lucian after the version made in Latin by the Italian humanist Giovanni Aurispa: Vanderjagt, *"Qui sa vertu anoblist"*; for the term 'Burgundised' see also his 'Expropriating the past'.

[26] Morand, *Claus Sluter*, pp. 19-21, claims that the significant devotion to the Virgin displayed by Sluter's monument shows a connection to the movement of the 'modern devotion'; this possible link, however, is not typical for Burgundian courtly culture.

[27] Cockshaw, 'La présence de l'ordre de la Toison d'or', pp. 163-165; Vanderjagt, 'Expropriating the Past', pp. 177-179. Cf. Spufford, *Monetary Problems and*

as medals are concerned, it is clear that these were made especially for courtiers and the high servants of the court; possibly they were also used as gifts to the other courts of Europe in order to further Burgundian ducal interests.

Admittedly, sometimes these areas of cultural activity seem to overlap. This was the case at the stupendous Feast of the Pheasant hosted by Philip at Lille on Sunday, February 17, 1454, which is described by both contemporaries and modern scholars as unsurpassed in the fifteenth century.[28] Here the duke and many of his noble knights individually pledged solemnly on a live pheasant adorned with priceless jewels to go on crusade to deliver the Church, eastern and western, from the demands and hands of the Grand Turk. How seriously this pledge was taken is shown by the fact that vows were also extracted from those knights who were unable to be present at the banquet, and that they were all put into writing and stored away for safekeeping. The chroniclers Olivier de La Marche and Matthieu d'Escouchy also report these individually. In the banqueting hall, the religious sphere was represented by the model of a church large enough to host a small choir with an organ and the worldly sphere was designated by a huge pastry or pie filled with musicians. After each of four theatrical productions of Jason's adventures, religious motets and organ music would sound out from the church and from the pie a worldly *chanson* and the airs of flutes or other instruments.[29] However closely associated, the ecclesiastical sphere and the sphere of Jason remain merely neighbours, and there is no joint chorus. There is nothing in the quite elaborate accounts of the productions of Jason's adventures that in any way even suggests the plight of the Church. Similarly, the Church, here represented as a grieving lady, with her long

Politics; Vanderjagt, *"Qui sa vertu anoblist"*, pp. 51-52.

[28] Vaughan, *Philip the Good*, pp. 143-145, describes it as by common accord the 'best known, most bizarre and extravagant of all fifteeenth-century banquets'; in a letter discovered by Vaughan someone who attended the feast writes 'I believe that nothing so sublime and splendid has ever been done before'. The most important works on this gala are: Caron and Clauzel, eds, *Le Banquet du Faisan*, and Lafortune-Martel, *Fête noble*; Caron, *Le Banquet du Voeu du Faisan*, prints the contemporary full accounts by Olivier de La Marche and Matthieu d'Escouchy; an analysis of the different accounts is given by Cockshaw, 'Les voeux du Faisan', pp. 115-117.

[29] The prose of contemporary authors is filled with wonder; for example, after one of the first entertainments, Escouchy reports: *commença l'en, en l'eglise à jouer des orgueues moult doucement; et quant l'eglise ot achevé, dedens le pasté fut joué d'un cornet d'Allemaigne, moult estrangement*; for his account: Caron, *Le Banquet du Voeu du Faisan*, pp. 40-45. There is a rendition of this music on CD 7243 5 61818 2 3 by the Ensemble Gilles Binchois under the direction of Dominique Vellard, and curiously entitled *Le Banquet du voeu* (EMI Virgin Veritas 1991).

plaint – which played a relatively short but very colourful part in the feast – alludes to Jason only obliquely in the penultimate stanza of her poem:[30]

Vous, chevalliers, qui portez la thoizon,
N'oubliez pas le très divin service,
Aussi les autres nés de bonne maison,
O gentilz hommes! vecy belle occoison,
Pour acquerir de los le benefice:
Mon secours est pour jones gens propices;
Les noms croistront en l'ame enrichira
Du service que chascun me fera.

Possibly it was all quite obvious to all those present how these spheres were or could be joined together, but the contemporaneous accounts leave this far from clear.[31] Even Lady Church is fearful that the fleeced knights and their less gilded fellows are forgetting their divine duties:[32] punning, she promises to increase (*croistre*) their names and to enrich their souls if they crusade on her behalf.

Isabella of Portugal, Philip's duchess, was present at the High Table of the feast.[33] It has not come down to us what she thought of all of this. She had once been deeply involved in Burgundian naval exploits in the Eastern Mediterranean and the Black Sea that were closely connected to possible

[30] For Escouchy's text, see Caron, *Le Banquet du Voeu du Faisan*, p. 49.
[31] Strangely, however, Vaughan, *Philip the Good*, p. 162, writes: 'As to the possible connection of the Golden Fleece with Philip's crusading projects, contemporary records bear little or no trace of this'. This Banquet, however, is the most magni-ficent and sumptuous piece of propaganda for a crusade in the Middle Ages, and it is clearly replete with Jason, Gideon and the Golden Fleece; the problem inheres not in the fact that these things are not represented in connection with the crusade, but rather in the manner in which this is communicated. Furthermore, bishop Fillastre, chancellor of the Order and the author of an enormous work on its origins and his-torical diversification, was also one of the chief Burgundian activists for a crusade. For the connection between the crusade and another of Philip's authors, Raoul Le-fèvre, who wrote an *Histoire de Jason*, see Nieuwstraten, 'Vervaardigers en be-zitters' and also Morse, *The Medieval Medea*, chapt. 4: 'The Romance of Jason'. It is remarkable that the latter does not mention the prolific Fillastre.
[32] The attending knights were apparently required to pay alms. Philip paid his in the following way: 'The second table side-piece was a totally nude small child sitting atop a rock and constantly pissing rose water; and it was placed well, so that a silver ship into which were put the duke's alms was on its right side; in a short time it was completely filled with the said rose water'; see Escouchy in Caron, *Le Banquet du Voeu du Faisan*, p. 35; Lafortune-Martel, *Fête noble*, pp. 112-113.
[33] On Isabella, see the study by Monique Sommé, *Isabelle de Portugal*.

crusading activities, commerce and also to ancient legend.[34] However, after 1445 she seems to have become increasingly sceptical about the grand plans of Philip the Good with regard to the Empire as well as to his desire to join or even initiate a Crusade.[35] Soon after the Feast of the Pheasant and Philip's first delegation of power to their son Charles, Isabella retreated from active politics to the castle of La Motte-au-Bois in the forest of Nieppe. Far from the madding crowd intent on defining the activities of the princely culture of the dukes and formulating its propaganda, she henceforth gave all her energies to religious devotions and to charity.[36]

The lavish literary production associated with the Burgundian court made virtually no inroads into the civic space of Flanders, Brabant or Hainault, Artois or the Burgundies. This is tellingly illustrated in Arras during the particularly cold winter of 1434-1435, not very long after the colourful nuptials in 1430 at Bruges of Philip the Good and Isabella of Portugal, during which the Order of the Golden Fleece had been ceremoniously instituted. A special memoir written on the express instruction of the local authorities gives a census of *plusieurs choses de neges*, snow-men, sculpted for the streets and squares of Arras.[37] Among these are figures of the Emperor, the King, Death, the Seven Sleepers, some local noblemen and high officials, Reynard the Fox, and *le Grande Pucelle* – interesting because her nemesis was Philip the Good, by whom she was delivered into the hands of the English. None of these figures in the town's central venues has much to do with specific courtly interests. Indeed, the figure of Joan of Arc might be interpreted as a representation of the distance the citizens of Arras at this time were putting between themselves and the house of Burgundy, even though Philip was very much at home in that city. Some twenty years later there was at the same place a possible closing of the gap between civic and princely culture. Richard Vaughan writes that the duke received a rapturous welcome when he entered the town by St Michael's gate on February 24,

[34] Paviot, *La politique navale*, pp. 106-111, 122-123, 151-155; Vanderjagt, '"En in de zomer doorkruisten zij de hele Zwarte Zee"', pp. 241-243.

[35] Remarkably, Isabella's 'retreating decade' coincides with Philip's greatest activity in collecting manuscripts that are directly related to the justification of his power, his crusading ambitions, and chivalric 'play' (to quote Stanesco, *Jeux d'errance*).

[36] Sommé, *Isabelle de Portugal*, esp. pp. 437-478, 482-483. Duke Philip was a very pious man: cf. his extreme religious scruples at the Congress of Arras. It seems that this kind of devotion is stronger at the Burgundian court than in the other princely establishments of Europe. It is hence one of the defining elements of Burgundian princely culture.

[37] The complete text is published in Muchembled, *Culture populaire et culture des élites*, pp. 161-165; cf. Besnier, 'Quelques notes sur Arras et Jeanne d'Arc'; Vaughan, *Philip the Good*, p. 67.

1455: the streets and the Petit Marché were fitted out with scenes from the life of Gideon.[38] There is little doubt that this is a direct allusion to the Order of the Golden Fleece whose second, Christian, patron after Jason the Argonaut was the Old Testament figure Gideon.[39] A month later, plans for a similar entry into Mons were drawn up. Here a *tableau vivant* was presented of the conquest and capture of Constantinople in 1204 by Baldwin, count of Flanders and Hainault. But these symbols, designed for the common understanding of both the citizens and the duke, must be interpreted less in the terms of a *rapprochement* of ducal and civic culture than as a general reaction to the shockwaves that everyone in Europe in 1454 felt in the wake of the fall of Constantinople to the Infidel.

[38] Vaughan, *Philip the Good*, pp. 334-336.

[39] In his *Espitre pour tenir et celebrer la noble feste du Thoison d'Or*, which Olivier de La Marche wrote for Maximilian in 1481, he describes Gideon even as a *replacement* of Jason on the initiative of bishop Jean Germain, first chancellor of the Order, in the course of the 1431 chapter meeting: *Et ainsi rompit messire Jehan la premiere opinion qui estoit de Jason et le changea sur Jedeon, dont l'histoire de la Bible fait mencion*; La Marche, *Mémoires*, vol. 4, p. 166. For the Order: Vale, *War and Chivalry*, chapt. 2: 'Orders of Chivalry in the Fifteenth Century'; Boulton, *The Knights of the Crown*, chapt. 13; Van den Bergen-Pantens, ed, *L'ordre de la Toison d'or*. In 1453, Philip ordered eight large and expensive pieces of tapestry depicting the history of Gideon and the Golden Fleece: the account specifies that 'the figures and emblems [are to be] decided on and explained to them [the artisans] by my lord [the duke]': Vaughan, *Philip the Good*, p. 154. In daily courtly practice, however, Jason remained at the very front of everyone's imagination; cf. Doutrepont, *La littérature française*, pp. 147-171. Still, in a closely argued article Barbara Haggh, 'The Virgin Mary', convincingly demonstrates that the Marian *officium* used at meetings of the Order after 1458 'elaborates the Biblical story of the fleece of Gideon to an extent not found in any other local or courtly liturgy'; of course, this illustrates also the distinction between princely culture on the one hand and civic and common devotional cultures on the other; the devotion to the Virgin evident in Sluter's monument at Champmol is of a completely different sort. It is perhaps to be doubted that all these intricacies of the Golden Fleece, Gideon, and the *officium* of Mary – to use a modest expression – were immediately understood by actors as well as by the onlookers. There is possibly some over-interpretation here. The theme of Philip's joyful entry into Ghent in 1458 is the 'Wedding of the Lamb' in which Jan van Eyck's famous altar-piece, *The Adoration of the Lamb* (1432), in St Bavo's Cathedral plays an important role; Van Eyck, of course, was Philip's *valet de chambre*; cf. Arnade, *Realms of Ritual*, pp. 131-142, and Kipling, *Enter the King*, pp. 264-280. In both entries there is some reference to elements from pagan, classical mythology but these are always immediately connected to Christian symbolism; Gideon's fleece is related directly to the Lamb of God but also to the Order of the Golden Fleece and thus to Jason. Anyone today who has carefully examined Van Eyck's altar-piece might well be excused from seeing it as the ultimate syncrisis of Christian and pagan symbols.

Ideals of nobility and success in matters of political authority, Jason and the Golden Fleece, ducal considerations of the Orient: understandably these are not analysed in *Realms of Ritual* or *Enter the King*, which treat Burgundian culture first and foremost as a civic culture that balances the antagonisms between ruler and subjects with a view to a kind of mutually coercive political and economical concord. They were, however, part and parcel of the dukes' propaganda effort and of their elaborate ceremonial.[40] In this connection it is important to point out that the court of Philip the Good certainly during the first half of the fifteenth century did not have a 'set' ceremonial. Increasingly, however, during the course of Philip's reign, there was a development of courtly ritual and 'representation' which clearly culminated in the activities of Olivier de La Marche under the tutelage of Charles the Bold. This ceremonial was copied by other European princes and their courts or at the very least it influenced the way the literature of ceremony was received by them. The Burgundian princely court thus became something of a model for rituals of the representation of political power and for cultural tastes – even ranging to fashions in clothing, modes of making music, demeanour at courtly events and receptions, and to the practice of the extravagant politeness for which the dukes were renowned. This exemplary function was further strengthened by the fact that many young nobles and princes of a variety of other courts were guests of the Burgundian dukes, not seldomly for long periods of time. Here they associated directly with the young Charolais and his friends such as La Marche, Jean le Chassa and Guy de Brimeu. The lion's share, too, of the non-devotional books of the grand library which the dukes and their courtiers such as Louis of Bruges and Guillaume Hugonet collected is devoted directly to these defining cultural activities of the courts of Philip the Good, Charles the Bold and Mary of Burgundy.[41]

[40] Paravicini, *Karl der Kühne*, pp. 44-46, who in a few well-chosen sentences also points out the 'Repräsentation und Selbstdarstellung' explicitly inherent in these activities. Kipling, in a recent, as yet unpublished paper entitled 'Were Royal Entries Propaganda?', insists wisely that 'if we are to get at the ways that the royal entry creates political meaning we have to understand first its liturgical and ritual principles'. To a large degree, the ducal ceremonial was derived from Mallorca and the Spanish court of Aragon; cf. Schwarz, *Aragonische Hofordnungen*; Paravicini, "Ordre et régle" and the literature cited there.

[41] The ducal library also contains much devotional literature, many books of hours and such. These are not generally 'defining' works for the princely culture of the Burgundian court. In other words, similar works can be found in many fifteenth-century libraries that are not Burgundian; thus they are not directly relevant for the present study. For the library: Doutrepont, *La littérature française*; see also especially the catalogues of the many exhibitions of Burgundian manuscripts mounted for anniversary years, for instance Dogaer and Debae, eds, *La librairie de Philippe*

Much as it differed from the mutually convenient ritual of civic behaviour, this princely culture in all its magnificence, pomp and circumstance obviously did not at all go unnoticed by the dukes' civic subjects. The townspeople of the prospering cities in the northern lands were much taken by the dazzle and the novelty of courtly feasts and ceremony, and they seemed not unwilling to pay for a close view without actually participating directly in the revels. Olivier de La Marche, *maître d'hôtel* of Philip the Good and Charles the Bold, explains the presence of members of the city elites at banquets of the Order of the Golden Fleece by pointing out that 'it must be kept in mind that those from the cities regularly give gifts and gratuities to support these feasts'.[42] Citing the fifteenth-century French and Burgundian authors Eustache Deschamps and Ghillebert de Lannoy, Arnade rightly distinguishes this courtly ceremonial from the civic ritual: 'familiarity [...] breeds disrespect; the purpose of the public interaction [at these courtly extravaganzas, AV] is more to emphasise the power and privilege of monarch or prince than to create bonds of affinity'.[43] Officers and servants of the court and especially the princes' subjects must stand in awe and fear of their noble masters, a point often made with a vengeance in particular by Charles the Bold. A harangue such as the following, made during a meeting with the Flemish estates in 1470, is not untypical:

> *et, entre vous, Flamengs, avecq vous dures testes, avez tousjours contempné ou hay vostre prince, car, quant ilz n'estoient point bien puissant, vous les comtempnastes, et, quant ilz estoient puissans et que vous ne leur povoyés riens faire, vous les haystes. J'ayme mieulx que vous me hayéz que contempnéz.*[44]

Not only was this princely culture not ignored by the dukes' subjects, on more than one occasion the latter for their part, felt seriously threatened by it. Thus, when Philip appeared to be making serious plans for putting into practice his crusading ideal, describing it as *nostre voyage que entendons faire au plaisir de Dieu, au secours et service de la foy catholique*, the

le Bon; Cockshaw, *et al.*, eds, *Karel de Stoute*; Lemaire and Henry, eds, *Isabelle de Portugal*; Martens, ed, *Lodewijk van Gruuthuse*; a new series on the library has recently been initiated: Bousmanne and Van Hoorebeeck, eds, *La librairie des ducs de Bourgogne*. A comprehensive recent study on the way the presentation miniatures of books in the Burgundian library represent ducal power is Cyriel Stroo's fascinating *De celebratie van de macht*.

[42] Arnade, *Realms of Ritual*, p. 27.

[43] Arnade, *Realms of Ritual*, p. 31.

[44] Gachard, ed, *Collection*, vol. 1, p. 223; cf. Vaughan, *Charles the Bold*, pp. 178-180; Vanderjagt, *"Qui sa vertu anoblist"*, pp. 62-64.

estates of the Low Countries which he had officially called together to discuss these matters – Brabant, Flanders, Lille, Douai and Orchies, Artois, Hainault and Valenciennes, Holland, Zeeland, Namur, Malines, and Boulogne – were truly alarmed. Their delegates to the general meetings at Bruges in January and early February 1464 and again at Lille in the first half of March 1464 insisted that Philip carefully make arrangement for the governance of his lands during his absence. Angrily the duke upbraided them for even thinking that he would be so stupid and ignorant as to abandon them without having provided for *nosdits pays*.[45] Apparently Wouter van der Meere and Philips van Heurne of Audenarde in Flanders allowed themselves to be convinced that he *en zoude zijne landen so voorsien dat elc daarvan te vreden zijn zoude* [he would provide for his lands in such a way that each of them would be satisfied]; similar phrasing is found in the reports which Jan van der Broucke, Gerard van Baussele and Bellen van Zuften wrote for the town of Leuven and Jacques-en-Croix and Julien Daudenfort for St Omer in Artois.[46] In early June of 1464, Guillaume Fillastre, chancellor of the Order of the Golden Fleece and its great propagandist, bishop of Tournai, one of the duke's councillors, and one of the most trusted for his advice, sent an enthusiastic letter to Jehan Jouard, president of Burgundy, that an army of 3000 had set out to the Holy Land. Sadly for him and like-minded proponents of religious adventure, the enterprise failed miserably at Marseilles.[47] There is no doubt, though, that this

[45] For this episode see Cuvelier, *et al.*, eds, *Actes*, vol. 1, pp. 54-104, especially for Philip's letter pp. 71-72; Vanderjagt, *"Qui sa vertu anoblist"*, pp. 49-50. All of this was taking place when Philip and Charles were still falling out mightily over policy and household matters; thus the estates were doubly alarmed. Chastelain in his *Chronique* of Philip's reign gives a vivid account of these altercations and how they were resolved: vol. 4, pp. 471-492; cf. La Marche, *Mémoires*, vol. 2, pp. 414-427, for a colourful and moving version of the family feud between 1454 until it was more or less resolved in 1464.

[46] Cuvelier, *et al.*, eds, *Actes*, vol. 1, pp. 76, 98, 100; there are similar reports from other delegates.

[47] Vaughan, *Philip the Good*, pp. 370-372. According to Blockmans and Prevenier, *The Promised Lands* (table on p. 152), the population of the northern lands stood around 2.5 million in 1470; if the figure in Fillastre's letter can be trusted, about 1.2 men per thousand inhabitants went on the ill-fated crusade of 1464; for the city of Ghent this works out just a little higher, at about 1.7 per thousand, which might be expected from a city quite close to the ducal propaganda machine with priests ready to hand out indulgences to those who took up the cross. By comparison, at the peak in 1968 of that modern crusade, the Vietnam War, 550,000 Americans served out of a U.S. population of about 200 million; this comes down to 2.75 per thousand (this does not include those Americans serving in the rest of Southeast Asia in positions of logistic support; that would double this figure). On Fillastre see Prietzel, *Guillaume Fillastre der Jüngere*.

failure was a matter of relief for Philip's subjects. All of this shows just how much princely culture was at odds with the civic sensibilities of the estates – no matter that arrangements were indeed in the end made by the duke to safeguard *le bien publicque* during his expected absence.

Arras to Malines and Ghent: Political Practice to Ideology of State

It has been pointed out succinctly by Blockmans and Prevenier that the Congress of Arras in 1435 laid down the very political foundations for a Burgundian state, as will be seen below.[48] It is only after the Congress that we can technically refer to ducal political practice and culture as princely in their own right, and for this reason attention must be given to it here. In the introduction to his full study *The Congress of Arras 1435*, Joycelyne Dickinson sums up the results of his analysis of the Congress for the future of Burgundy thus:[49] '[...] the 1435 treaty was an acknowledgement of Burgundy's eminence as a brilliant new-comer to the medieval concert of Europe. It marked the highest point of her influence and prestige, and by territorial and other concessions it consolidated the power of a state which might have become one of the greatest in Christendom'. The Hundred Years War had come to the point where Charles VII of France had been reduced to the regions of the Loire while Lancastrian Henry VI ruled England, Paris, Normandy and Gascony. The murder of his father John the Fearless by the dauphin of France on the bridge over the Yonne River at Montereau in 1419 had detached Philip from Valois France. The duke thereupon concluded an alliance with England through a treaty signed at Troyes on May 21, 1420. This treaty stipulated that king Henry V of England, husband of Catherine, the daughter of Charles VI, was to be the sole heir to the crown of France. The dauphin – the later Charles VII – was disinherited, and both Henry V and Philip the Good solemnly pledged not ever to enter into separate negotiations with him. On the deaths of Charles VI and of Henry V in 1422, Henry VI thus succeeded to the French throne.[50] No matter how great his economic, political and military powers, this made duke Philip, who until then was not a sovereign prince but a vassal of the French throne, subservient to Henry in the latter's function as king of France. For the time being this suited the duke well for '[b]y

[48] Blockmans and Prevenier, *The Promised Lands*, p. 81.
[49] Dickinson, *The Congress of Arras*, p. viii.
[50] Dickinson, *The Congress of Arras*, p. ix ff.; Vaughan, *Philip the Good*, pp. 3ff., 98ff.; Blockmans and Prevenier, *The Promised Lands*, pp. 62-64; 79-81.

balancing the English interests against those of the Dauphin, Philip found himself in an enviable bargaining position'.[51]

By the early 1430s, however, the political landscape of western Europe had changed. The duchy of Burgundy was under threat from Orleanist France; there was a pro-French party in Burgundy and some of Philip's noblemen, for example Louis de Chalons, prince of Orange, defected to Charles VII; further, a continuous war wreaked havoc throughout France, destroying towns and devastating the countryside.[52] In 1434 Sigismund, the Holy Roman Emperor, in an alliance with Charles, declared a *Reichskrieg* against Philip. Seeking then to undermine the Anglo-Burgundian treaty of Troyes, Charles offered Philip a truce that would break the Franco-imperial encirclement of the duke's lands.[53] Philip countered by convoking the magnificent Congress of Arras, the first token event of his princely reign.[54] Its goal was to broker a general peace between the main combatants England, France and Burgundy.

In the summer of 1435, representatives, deputations and delegations from almost every self-respecting power in Europe began converging on Arras in an attempt to make an end to the Hundred Years War, in what most historians of one accord call the first international peace conference. Duke Philip, a master of ceremonial meetings, made sure that the political negotiations took place with all the pomp and circumstance for which Burgundian princely culture is notable.[55] Vaughan has calculated that there must have been 5000 strangers in Arras who were in one way or another connected to the Congress; among these were heralds and poursuivants and kings of arms, knights and secretaries, clerks and churchmen, *maîtres d'hotel* and chroniclers; and, for their own safety, the main contenders brought large bodyguards: 'Everybody sent ambassadors or observers to attend the

[51] Vaughan, *Philip the Good*, p. 63.

[52] This last point, which has all the hallmarks of propaganda – but in spite thereof not necessarily less true – is the theme of the *Moralité d'Arras* written by Michault Taillevent, Philip's *joueur de farces*, for performance as an entertainment during the Congress; Deschaux, *Michault Taillevent*, p. 22, describes Taillevent as *ce poète qui fut avant tout un serviteur du Philippe le Bon*; for the *Moralité*, see. pp. 87-110; cf. Estaing's sermon cited in note 65.

[53] See for concise and clear accounts: Blockmans and Prevenier, *The Promised Lands*, pp. 79-81; Schnerb, *L'État bourguignon*, pp. 182-185.

[54] Blockmans and Prevenier, *The Promised Lands*, p. 81, term it one 'of the most solemn circumstances that northern Europe ever witnessed'.

[55] Charles the Bold took after his father in this respect, and he was a master of the propagandistic effects of ceremony; an impressive example is the duke's entourage that entered Trier in the autumn of 1473; cf. Vaughan, *Charles the Bold*, pp. 140-144: the list of more than 1000 participants and their fitting out at enormous expense is impressive; but as we know this propaganda was not to have the desired effect.

public sessions of the conference.'[56] Most important, of course, were the chief negotiators from England, France and Burgundy and the two cardinals who presided over the public sessions of the congress: Hugues de Lusignan, cardinal of Cyprus, representing the Council of Basel and Nicolò Albergati, cardinal priest of Santa Croce, delegate of pope Eugenius IV. Thus the Church in its entirety was represented as well. Frantz Funck-Brentano has pointed out how important religion was to the medieval politics and rituals of peace-making, and he uses the Congress of Arras as his primary example.[57]

The official negotiatiors were accompanied by large retinues, richly dressed for the occasion; in fact, clothes were tailored with designs specific for the congress. Antoine de La Taverne, who was the provost of the abbey of St Vaast, where the congress was held, kept a famous journal of the proceedings.[58] He was informed about many of its transactions by his personal guest Laurens Pignon, the Dominican confessor of duke Philip, who was also one of the main celebrants of the religious services that accompanied the disputations, discussions and finally the jubilant closing ceremonies of the congress.[59] No doubt Pignon was also closely involved in the moral decision Philip had to make with regard to undoing the commitment he had made to the English at Troyes in 1420.[60]

In fact, the issue of breaking his oath was taken extremely seriously by Philip, illustrating his extraordinary piety even in the face of what must have been the personally very gratifying terms of the treaty; very clearly, he did not want to endanger his soul. No less than five documents about this issue were circulated at Arras. Albergati instructed his lawyers carefully to study the terms of the treaty of Troyes, and he, together with Lusignan, decided in the name of the Church that Philip could be released from his oath. Philip, however, was not satisfied until Hugues d'Estaing, archdeacon of Metz, preached a long sermon outlining the entire matter on September 6,[61] and until he received sealed and witnessed letters of release from his oath from both cardinals; these were given to him on September 20, the day before the official promulgation of the treaty between Burgundy and

[56] Dickinson, *The Congress of Arras*, pp. 106-108, discusses the archers that accompanied the Burgundian, French and English delegations; Vaughan, *Philip the Good*, p. 98.
[57] Funck-Brentano, 'Le caractère religieux de la diplomatie du moyen âge'.
[58] La Taverne, *Journal de la Paix d'Arras*.
[59] Vanderjagt, *Laurens Pignon*, pp. 22-30.
[60] On all of this and the following paragraph: La Taverne, *Journal de la Paix d'Arras*, pp. 69-72; Toussaint, *Les relations diplomatiques*, pp. 99-101; Dickinson, *The Congress of Arras*, pp. 174-176.
[61] See note 65.

France. Although there was a sizeable pro-English party in the duke's council which vociferously and angrily defended the treaty of Troyes, it was soon clear to the English that Philip would renege on the treaty of Troyes, and the English embassy angrily departed from the congress on the day of Estaing's sermon, two weeks before the final session. Philip had thus been strategically too weak to conclude a general peace between Burgundy, France, and England. A particular Franco-Burgundian treaty was the fruit of the Congress. Richard Vaughan points out that Charles VII never intended to honour the terms of the peace but that 'Philip was duped in this way partly by the allure of the terms themselves. [...] Above all, full moral satisfaction promised for the crime of Montereau, including a formal apology from King Charles VII, and expiatory religious foundations'.[62]

Most important, however, the nullification of the Treaty of Troyes and the terms of the Peace of Arras released Philip personally from all the obligations of a vassal to the crown of France, whether Henry VI or Charles VII. As a sovereign prince he was now able to work towards the establishment, certainly in legal terms, of a Burgundian state. A process could now begin that allowed him to replace the appellate authority of the Parlement of Paris over his fiefs in Flanders and France by his own Great Council. This became a 'full-fledged central high court' and eventually evolved into the Parlement of Malines in 1473.[63]

It is not very clear to what extent Philip understood that he was dramatically changing the apparatus of the governing culture of the Burgundian lands. It may be that he was at first intent only on his personal, princely independence in a feudal sense. Until 1464 he gave little indication that he was fully aware how the rallying cry of the Burgundian dukes and their adherents from as far back as 1402 in the streets of Paris against the Armagnacs – *le bien publicque*! – might serve ideologically as the mainstay of a Burgundian state in the sense of a seventeenth-century *raison d'État*.[64] It is wonderfully appropriate that as early as 1435, Estaing's technical,

[62] Vaughan, *Philip the Good*, p. 99.

[63] Blockmans and Prevenier, *The Promised Lands*, p. 81; Vaughan, *Philip the Good*, chap. 6: 'The Government at Work', pp. 164-204; Schnerb, *L'État bourguignon*, chap. 16: 'Le gouvernement de l'état bourguignon', pp. 228-261; but see especially Van Rompaey, *De Grote Raad*. Jongkees, 'Vorming van de Bourgondische staat', pp. 232-234, does not consider Philip's release from vassalage as the beginning of this process; he dates it rather too late, from the Thionville ordinances of 1473, which established the Malines parlement.

[64] Vanderjagt, *"Qui sa vertu anoblist"*, pp. 45-63; Huizinga has pointed out the connection to seventeenth-century political thought: 'De Bourgondische macht en Frankrijk', p. 117. Armstrong gave a lecture at Louvain in 1958 in which he discussed especially this concept in the development of the political thought of the

juridical sermon at Arras, on the eve of Philip's public decision to enter into a treaty with Charles VII, uses precisely the term *le bien publicque* as a linchpin for the rationale of the peace.[65] It thus lies at the very heart of the political, princely culture of the dukes, even if Philip did not see the structural implications of the term at the time. Indeed, it would have been surprising if anyone at all in 1435 could have envisaged the potentiality of such a concept for the development of ideas about the state that were ultimately to issue into the political ideology of Charles the Bold and his chancellor Guillaume Hugonet.[66] At Arras, *le bien publicque* is still closely connected to ideas about the duties of the knightly second order of the time-honoured tripartite division of society, as these had been developed in the late fourteenth and early fifteenth centuries. The call to honour the commonweal is here a kind of moral injunction in the sense of the literature of mirrors for princes. This can be seen clearly from the words Estaing attaches to *le bien publicque* in his sermon: *bonnes meurs*. Only a few years before the Congress, Laurens Pignon, too, had made that association. At the end of his French translation for duke Philip of Durand of St Pourçain's (ca. 1275-1334) *Circa originem potestatum et iurisdictionum quibus populus regitur*, Pignon adds a discussion on the overthrow of tyrants – possibly implicitly referring to the murder by John the Fearless of Louis d'Orleans in 1407[67] – and in that context he also couples *matiere de foy et* [...] *bonnes*

dukes; it was finally published in 1995: 'Les ducs de Bourgogne, interprètes de la pensée politique du 15ᵉ siècle'. Just how strong the influence of the Burgundian party must have been in Paris is illustrated by the reports of chroniclers concerning the events of 1411; the *Chronique du Religieux de St Denis*, Juvenal des Ursins, and the *Journal d'un bourgeois de Paris* report that priests there made the sign of the cross not vertically and horizontally but at the angles of St Andrew's cross, the symbol of Burgundy.

[65] La Taverne, *Journal de la Paix d'Arras*, p. 72; Toussaint, *Les relations diplomatiques*, p. 100, summarises concisely why Philip was allowed to break his oath: *Une obligation ne peut aller à l'encontre* du bien commun*; un serment ne vaut pas s'il n'engendre que le mal* (emphasis, AV). In a barrage of eloquence, Estaing in his sermon paints a vivid picture of the state of France; La Taverne cites him: *Item, ce ainsi dit et proposé, ledit archediacre adrecha ses parolles a monseigneur le duc de Bourgogne, lui remonstra le desolation dudit royalme, les grans maulx qui s'en estoient ensieuyz et ensieuoyent chascuns jour, le perdition des amez, le destruction des eglises et de* la chose publicque, *les homicides, adulteres, enforcemens de femmes, deffloracions de pucelles aveuc aultres maulx innumerablez. Item lui remonstra les sermens faiz contre carité,* bonnes meurs et le bien publicque... (emphasis, AV): La Taverne, *Journal de la Paix d'Arras*, p. 72.

[66] Vanderjagt, 'Terechtgesteld', pp. 37-44, and 'Expropriating the past', pp. 191-193. The latest study on Hugonet is Paravicini, 'L'arsenal intellectuel d'un homme de pouvoir'.

[67] Jan Veenstra has pointed out the connections between the ideas of Laurens

meurs with *le bien publique* and *la chose publicque*.[68] All of this illustrates the importance of this idea at a time when the Burgundian state was in the process of being established.

By the time of the chapter meeting of the Order of the Golden Fleece at Ghent on November 30, 1445, the context of *le bien publicque* had begun to change. La Marche reports the core of a sermon delivered by bishop Guillaume Fillastre thus:[69]

> *L'offerande achevée et faicte, l'eveque de Verdun, qui deppuys fut chancellier de l'ordre, fit ung sermon où fut ramentue la cause de la fondacion d'icelluy noble ordre, et dont l'intention singuliere fut pour le remede et l'ayde de l'Église et de saincte foy chrestienne, et aussi ce que les chevaliers* debvoient et en quoy ils estoient obligés envers Dieu et la chose publique plus que ceulx de moindre estat, de l'amour et union qui debvoit estre en eulx, de la loyauté qu'ilz debvoient porter à leur chief et leur chief à eulx, et l'ung envers l'autre (emphasis, AV), *et moult d'aultres belles et notables choses, qui trop longues me seroient à escripre*.

Obviously the knights' duty towards God entails aiding the Church: in the context of the Order this means putting into practice crusading ideals. With regard to *la chose publique*, the knights have a special task when compared to those of the lesser estate; but more importantly, though they are to be loyal to each other, their first loyalty is to their *chief*. His knights do not serve the commonwealth as individual moral agents, but they are to unite as a single force under their leader, duke Philip, much in the same way as Jason was the leader of his Argonauts in the fifteenth-century perception. It is exactly this personal loyalty that Philip used politically to structure his dominions.[70] There is no mention in the report of this sermon of *bonnes*

Pignon in *Contre les devineurs* (1411) and Jean Petit's *Justification* (1408) of John the Fearless for his successful plot in 1407 to assassinate Louis of Orleans. The *Justification* rests on three important indictments of Louis: his usurpation of the throne and therefore of the *chose publique*, his unfair taxation proving him to be a tyrant, and, perhaps most gravely, his practice of sorcery which allied him with the Devil; hence John was duty bound to rise up against such an evil heir of France. Cf. Veenstra, *Magic and Divination*, chapt. 2: 'The Pact with the Enemy'; cf. Schnerb, *Les Armagnacs et les Bourguignons*, chapt. 4: 'Le Tyrannicide'.

[68] Vanderjagt, *Laurens Pignon*, p. 133, lines 1686-1723.

[69] La Marche, *Mémoires*, vol. 2, p. 92.

[70] Armstrong, 'A Policy for the Nobility', p. 235, points out 'that the Burgundian government preferred to deal with a nobility segregated in territorial units and having no other bond of union than the prince'. Paravicini has drawn attention to the fact that knights, particularly those of the Order of the Golden Fleece, had very special rights in connection with the ducal household. At other courts in Europe,

meurs, which inform the earlier moral sense of *le bien publicque*. Of course, the knights of the Order often addressed each other on their moral obligations, and small fines were levied for inebriety and sexual extravagance. But far more importantly, the duke could by his selective policy of membership use the Order to strengthen his grip on his territories, and hereby it became an instrument of state.[71] Mario Damen has acutely demonstrated the centralisation policy of duke Philip around 1445 with a view to Holland and Zeeland.[72] He shows how much the duke was concerned with the balance of power among his lands and how he used appointments to the Great Council of all his territories and to the Order of the Golden Fleece to that purpose. By holding such a balance, he was himself clearly the main-stay.

Thirty years after Arras, there is a further development in which this personal loyalty is evolving in the direction of a collective force representing all the Burgundian lands of the North. No longer assemblies of the estates of each of his lands individually, they now met as a collective Estates General, even if the duke was not happy that they had at first convened themselves. Philip seems to be acquiring a taste for consulting the Estates of his territories, from his first muster of them in January 1464 in the specific case of the crusade, no matter that there were some shouting matches on that occasion. He and his successor Charles consulted the Estates twelve times between 1464 and 1477, mostly over financial matters. From their first convocation onwards, these meetings of the Estates resound with the familiar words *le bien publique* and *bonum commune* especially on the part of the dukes, but these terms have now taken on a political meaning.[73] After Charles's demise at Nancy, the Estates themselves established the permanence of these meetings by extracting from Mary of Burgundy her Great Privileges at the Ghent meeting of February 1477 and a second one in March.[74] As Blockmans and Prevenier have shown, these Great Privileges are not a conservative and local-minded reaction to the idea of a modern state. Leaving the territorial councils, the Chambers of Account and even the Great Council of the Burgundian lands intact, '[w]hat the Estates General achieved was an agreement to keep ducal institutions like the Parlement of Malines from trampling all existing rights. [...] [T]he

such as those of Anjou or Milan, knights did not have this kind of position: Paravicini, 'The Court of the Dukes of Burgundy', pp. 87-88.

[71] See for a helpful summing up and bibliography: Cools, *Mannen met macht*, pp. 61-63.

[72] Damen, *De staat van dienst*; for an English summary see pp. 432-434.

[73] See note 65.

[74] Wellens, ed, *Les États généraux des Pays-Bas*, pp. 159-166; Blockmans, *Le privilège général*.

Burgundian state seems to have attracted and united its subjects more than it repelled them.'[75]

The development in Burgundian princely political culture of the meaning of *le bien publicque* and the role of knights with the duke as their leader in its maintenance can be nicely illustrated by examining three texts from the ducal library. The first two dukes, Philip the Bold and John the Fearless, acquired copies in French of the manual that Ramón Llull (ca. 1232-1316) wrote on the order of chivalry.[76] This widely circulated work, popular at courts but also in religious circles throughout Europe, is a rambling, moralistic interpretation of the duties of a knight in which the three Christian virtues of faith, hope and charity have a prime place; it continues to describe in a high voice and in technicolour the ceremonies of knighthood familiar from boy's stories, such as *Men of Iron.* Knights are seen here literally as benefactors to the poor and protectors of widows and orphans; they are intensely humane but there is little or no political angle to their good works. All their struggles are related directly to the divine grace they are to receive in the Heavenly Order after death. There is a glimpse– but no more than that – of this image of a knight in the socio-political term *bonnes meurs* discussed above.

The second treatise that must be mentioned was written by a knight of the Order of the Golden Fleece, Ghillebert de Lannoy.[77] Lannoy was one of Philip's counsellors who belonged to the pro-English party at the Congress of Arras. Between 1439 and 1442 he dedicated a copy of his *Instruction d'un jeune Prince* to Philip; much later a copy was also made for Charles the Bold, which was illuminated by Jean Hennekart.[78] Lannoy's *Instruction* reads like an amplification of Estaing's sermon at Arras. In contrast to that of Llull, his accent is not on the knight as an individual moral agent, but on the knightly prince who loves *la chose publique* and governs his people with reason and justice, while he leads a highly moral life which is founded in the fear of God.[79] This might indeed be expected of knights of the intensely political Order of the Golden Fleece more than of Llull's knights-errant. It is not unreasonable to assume that the interpretation of *le bien publicque* put forward by Estaing and earlier by Laurens Pignon and Jean

[75] Blockmans and Prevenier, *The Promised Lands*, pp. 196-197; but see also Israel, *The Dutch Republic*, pp. 28-29.

[76] For a clear introduction see Keen, *Chivalry*, pp. 8-17.

[77] Van Leeuwen, *Denkbeelden van een vliesridder*, gives a modern edition with introduction and analysis; on Lannoy also Paviot, 'Ghillebert de Lannoy', pp. 42-45.

[78] Doutrepont, *La littérature française*, pp. 314-315.

[79] Lannoy, *Instruction*, lines 5ff. in: Van Leeuwen, *Denkbeelden van een vliesridder*, p. 5ff. and p. 18ff.

Petit, and now by Lannoy, informed the political culture of the duke and his entourage in these years.

The final stage of the evolution of the political culture of knighthood and *la chose publicque* at the Burgundian court is represented by the French translation which Gonzalve de Vargas made around 1459 of Diego de Valera's *Espejo de verdadera nobleza* and by its incorporation in 1481 into a compilation called *Des drois d'armes de noblesse* at the request of Gilles, king of arms of Flanders under Maximilian.[80] Basing himself on *les anciens*, Diego puts the practice of religion at the bottom of his list, between the defence of widows and orphans and the preservation of good manners with regard to matrons and young ladies. But the first duty of a noble knight is to honour and serve his prince; the second is *qu'il garderoit le bien et prouffit de la chose publique*.[81] Thus political culture has here become almost entirely secularised, and the individualistic moral primacy of knighthood as it is found in Ramón Llull's work plays only a marginal role.

In this context there is a remarkable reversal of the role in Burgundian princely culture of two texts that were popular in the *civic* communities of the *communes* of early-Quattrocento Italy: Buonaccorso da Montemagno's *Dialogus de nobilitate* and Giovanni Aurispa's Latin translation of Lucian's *Twelfth Dialogue of the Dead* entitled *Opusculum de presidencia*.[82] In their Quattrocento form they are both concerned with the status of the nobility in the municipal sphere: is 'true' nobility derived through inheritance or by service to the common good? Buonaccorso treats this question by weaving a story of Lucretia, the beautiful and learned daughter of senator Fulgentius Felix and his wife Claudia. Two young men of the city of Rome vie for her hand in marriage. The first is Publius Cornelius who has inherited his nobility from a long line of outstanding ancestors but who is himself given to feasting and hunting. The second is Gayus Flaminius, a scholar who has put his not inconsiderable gifts of learning and practice to use in helping to build the *res publica*. Lucretia means to marry the more noble of the two, and because this is a case of 'eternal' and mundial significance she asks the highest court – the senate of ancient Rome – to hear what her suitors have to say for themselves. Each delivers a speech, Publius Cornelius defending inherited nobility and Gayus Flaminius the virtues of public service. Buonac-

[80] For editions of French translations of Valera's work and the prologue to the 1481 compilation: Vanderjagt, *"Qui sa vertu anoblist"*, part II, chapt. 4: 'Diego de Valera in Burgundy'.

[81] Diego de Valera, *Ung petit traictyé de noblesse*, lines 1069-1102 in: Vanderjagt, *"Qui sa vertu anoblist"*, pp. 262-263.

[82] For an English translation of Buonaccorso, see Rabil, ed, *Knowledge, Goodness, and Power*, pp. 24-52, who gives an extensive bibliography; for Aurispa's texts and its variations, see Cast, 'Aurispa, Petrarch, and Lucian'.

corso does not give a solution but leaves the resolution of the question to the readers of his dialogue, who are the wealthy merchants and non-noble aristocrats mainly of Florence. However, the implicit answer to this case is clear. In keeping with the tenets of what Hans Baron in his *The Crisis of the Early Italian Renaissance* has called 'civic humanism', Gayus Flaminius must be the suitor who gains Lucretia's hand in marriage.

Aurispa's version of Lucian stages three great generals of Antiquity – Hannibal of Carthage, Alexander the Great, and Scipio Africanus – who in the underworld debate before judge Minos the question which of them has precedence as a general. In Lucian's original Alexander is judged to be the greatest on the basis of his conquest of 'the world', and Scipio makes only a fleeting entry. Aurispa, however, changes the judgement of Minos. He allows Scipio a speech as long as those by Alexander and Hannibal. In it, Scipio describes himself in the terms of the ideals of civic humanism: he deserves precedence because he has fought not for his own honour but *pro patria* and because his love of the fatherland – *pietas patriae*– excels that of his two opponents who love only their own prowess. For Buonaccorso and Aurispa true nobility is a quality that is not delimited by genealogy; instead, it is acquired through the service to the *res publica* of the Quattrocento *commune*.

In the middle of the fifteenth century, Jean Miélot translated these two texts into French for Philip the Good: Buonaccorso's dialogue he called *La controversie de noblesse* and Aurispa's debate is entitled *Le debat de honneur*.[83] At least fourteen copies were made, and around 1475, Colard Mansion printed a presumably very small run of Miélot's version at Bruges. The manuscripts of the French translation are among the most expensive and lavishly illuminated books of the ducal library. The owners that can be traced belong to courtly circles. Thus these texts made a transition from a civic, humanist culture to the princely political culture of the court of Burgundy. In fact, there appears to have been no interest in Buonaccorso and Aurispa in the duke's cities such as Ghent, Bruges, Antwerp or Dijon, even among their Italianate citizens such as the Adornos or the Arnolfinis. Given the extreme popularity of these booklets in the cities of northern Italy, this is remarkable and it shows just how completely the cultural meaning of these texts was changed at the ducal court. It also demonstrates the chasm between the princely political culture of the ducal court and the municipal culture of the dukes' lands. In the introduction to his translation of the Buonaccorso, Miélot asks that duke Philip decide the merits of the case for the hand of Lucrece, presumably because he is noble by genealogy and also by his service to *le bien publicque*. Philip is, therefore, in the very best position

[83] See note 25 above.

to adjudicate the debate. The final judge of nobility, then, is himself a hereditary nobleman.

Near the end of the century, William Caxton, England's first printer, who had worked in close proximity to the Burgundian court of Margaret of York and repaired to England in 1476, translated Llull's aforementioned book into English and printed it for king Richard III in 1484.[84] He adds to it an Epilogue, bristling with moralisms completely in the vein of Llull himself. Quite immune to the many discussions at the Burgundian court ever since the 1450s on the relative merits of nobility through inheritance or through service to *la chose publique*, he writes about his translation:

> Which book is not requysyte to every comyn man to have, but to noble gentylmen that by their vertu entende to come and entre into the noble ordre of chyvalry, the whiche in these late dayes hath not ben used acordyng to this booke hertofore wreton, but forgeten and th'excersytees of chyvalry not used, honoured ne excercysed as hit hath ben in auncyent tyme.[85]

The virtues that Caxton recommends are 'manhode, curtosye and gentylesse', through which the knight will come 'to grete fame and renommee'. This is a kind of general civility or politeness. There is, however, no indication at all in this epilogue of anything that can be connected to the commonweal in a meaningful political sense.

Indeed, Caxton does not print or translate the widely circulated texts from the Burgundian court that put forward the idea that nobility and chivalry are political, even politico-princely qualities. Yet, he was undoubtedly aware of these works because he had collaborated closely with Colard Mansion, who had printed the texts by Buonaccorso and Aurispa.[86] Antoine Vérard, too, one of the first printers at Paris, published versions of the Franco-Burgundian Valera and Buonaccorso in 1497 for the benefit of king Charles VIII of France.[87] In his compilation, he reverses the chrono-

[84] Painter, *William Caxton*, pp. 141-143; Caxton's version of Llull's book was edited by Byles for the Early English Text Society in 1926.

[85] The discussion on nobility in ducal circles is clear from the popularity of the French translations of Buonaccorso da Montemagno and of Aurispa's version of Lucian's *Twelfth Dialogue of the Dead.* The basics of the debate are repeated theoretically in Valera's work. Caxton's epilogue is printed by Blake, *Selections from William Caxton*, pp. 111-113; cf. Byles, *The book of the ordre of chyvalry*.

[86] Vanderjagt, *"Qui sa vertu anoblist"*, pp. 43, 85, 124, 187.

[87] The latest, voluminous study on Vérard is by Winn, *Anthoine Vérard*. In 1496 or 1497 this interpretation of knighthood and chivalry also made inroads into the Tudor culture of 'new men' at Court: Henry Medwall published his version of Buonaccorso entitled *Fulgens and Lucrece*, which was probably based on the translation

logical order of Buonaccorso and Valera, thereby perhaps indicating that the latter is the key to the former. Vérard's epilogue, echoing Miélot's prologue, professes his expectation that the king will be able to come to a decision in the matter of Cornelius and Flaminius on the grounds that he has *travaillé a mettre bonne paix en vostre royaulme de France.*[88] In this wish, Vérard is clearly referring to the idea that work on behalf of the commonweal enables the king to make a judgement on the construction of nobility. Caxton, however, must be placed in the context of the very earliest Burgundian perceptions of nobility and chivalry, suggested by the literary purchases and commissionings of the first two dukes. Vérard's ideas on the workings of political culture, on the other hand, are akin to and probably derived from those of Philip the Good and courtiers such as Jean Miélot. Another version of the Valera text expresses the idea that nobility was first instituted as a coercive force to redress the effects of the first fall and disobedience of the first parents;[89] hence political nobility is based upon virtue, notably the virtue of justice in its minimal sense.

It is this idea of *justice* that is closely connected to the concept of *le bien publique* in the development of the princely, political culture of Burgundy between the Congress of Arras and the deaths of duke Charles and chancellor Hugonet in 1477 and duchess Mary in 1482.[90] *Justice* came to be seen as the personal, princely prerogative of duke Charles, independently acquired by him through the course of history – 'nature', as it is called by Hugonet – and by law. Moreover, the duke's magnificence and magnanimity in dispensing justice are beholden neither to imperial and regal nor to ecclesiastical rights and powers; he has been invested in his high place directly by God himself, according to the model of Cyrus the Great presented in the Old Testament.[91] It is important to note here that Charles was not

made by John Tiptoft, member of the circle of queen Elizabeth Woodville, more than twenty years earlier; cf. Kipling, *The Triumph of Honour*, pp. 12 -22.

[88] For Vérard's *explicit* of his edition of 1497: Vanderjagt, *"Qui sa vertu anoblist"*, p. 224; for the reception of Buonaccorso's work in different circles in northern Europe: Vanderjagt, 'Three solutions' and 'Il pubblico dei testi umanistici'.

[89] Cf. Valera's text: the first reason for the institution of politcal or civic nobility *fut par necessité car pour ce que les hommes de ce tempz comme dit est estoient promptz et enclins a tous maulx, il convint pour corrigier et reprimer les assaulx de mauvaiz a l'encontre des bons eslire un bon homme plus juste et vertueux des autres qui presidast par dessus la commaulté, eslevast et promeust les vertueulx, les moyens deffendist et les mauvaiz contraingnist et meist a raison*: Vanderjagt, *"Qui sa vertu anoblist"*, p. 274.

[90] Paravicini, *Karl der Kühne*, pp. 27-29, and Vanderjagt, *"Qui sa vertu anoblist"*, pp. 47-65; his 'Terechtgesteldt', pp. 40-43; and his 'Practicing nobility', *passim*.

[91] Chastelain, *Advertissement au duc Charles*, p. 294; Gallet-Guerne, *Vasque de Lu-cène*, pp. 183-186; Guillaume Hugonet, *Proposicion faicte à Brouxelles* in:

content only to reign, that is to say: to have intermediaries carry out his orders. He governed hands-on and carried out justice himself gladly and frequently in order to ensure that *le bien publique* was as well served as it could be. But he demanded that all of this be done according to his own princely insights and his interpretations of codified law,[92] and he mostly ignored local jurisdictions as he went about what he regarded as his high duties.

Charles himself died in the siege of Nancy and so the citizens of his cities could not call him to account for what they regarded as his usurpation of their rights, but Hugonet, the duke's faithful servant and ideologue, lost his head for this princely, political culture on the scaffold of Ghent in April 1477. Casting his historian's eye ahead, Werner Paravicini elegantly observes: 'Trois générations plus tard, son arrière petit-fils Charles Quint réussira à imposer aux Pays-Bas ce que Charles avait deviné et tenté en vain d'instaurer une première fois'.[93]

Cuvelier, ed, *Actes*, p. 182. Cf. Armstrong, 'Les ducs de Bourgogne'; Vanderjagt, 'Expropriating the Past', pp. 191-193 and the bibliography cited there; on this point in Chastelain: Van Hijum, *Grenzen aan macht*, pp. 51-54. Werner Paravicini is preparing a study on *magnificentia* in this context; until it appears see the remarks by Kipling, *The Triumph of Honour*, pp. 28-30; pp. 160-168 discuss the relations between this Burgundian concept and Edmund Spenser's, *The Faerie Queene*; on *magnificence* at Charles' court see also Franke, *Assuerus und Esther*, chapt. 4:1: 'Die Fürstentugend der Magnificenz'.

[92] Raynaud, 'Humanism and Good Government', gives an analysis of Jean Miélot's translation of the *Romuleon* by Roberto Della Porta; she connects the illumination programme of the manuscript (executed among others by Jean le Tavernier) directly to Burgundian political insights, and more specifically she draws a parallel between the illuminator's rendition of Marcus Aurelius in his judicial capacities and Charles the Bold; see especially pp. 165-166.

[93] Paravicini, "Ordre et régle", p. 351.

IMAGES OF EMPIRE

FRANCIS I AND HIS CARTOGRAPHERS

Gayle K. Brunelle

A significant but often neglected aspect of Renaissance courtly culture was cartography. The 'Age of Discovery' ushered in an era of European expansionism in which, in the competition for wealth and glory among rulers, it no longer sufficed merely to rule a single, integrated territory. Truly educated princes had to be well versed in the newest overseas discoveries; truly powerful ones needed to acquire overseas possessions of their own. Typically, historians seeking to assess the cultural impact of European overseas exploration, trade, and colonisation have focused on cross-cultural exchanges between Europeans and indigenous peoples, and the effects, mostly deleterious, of the conquest on native cultures. When evaluating the implications of expansion for European society, however, they tend to follow the lead of J.H. Elliott, and argue that whereas the 'Columbian exchange' brought Europe manifold benefits that forever altered the course of Europe's economic and political development, the voyages of discovery did little to change European culture, popular or elite.[1] By the same token,

[1] For an overview of the topic of European colonial expansion, see Brunelle, 'The World Economy and Colonial Expansion'; for a discussion of the 'Columbian Exchange', see Crosby, *Ecological Imperialism*; Elliot's seminal work, *The Old World and the New, 1492-1650*, was the first to point out how little the discovery of the New World altered the world view of the Old World in the early modern period; for a similar interpretation, see Schlesinger, *In the Wake of Columbus*. Geoffroy Atkinson notes 'les *mentions* des pays d'outre-mer' in the works of certain French humanists. He emphasises, however, that most writers had little or nothing to say about the new discoveries: Atkinson, *Les nouveaux horizons de la renaissance française*, pp. 301ff. Greenblatt, *Marvelous Possessions*, argues that not only did European culture fail to change very much as a result of its experience with the non-European 'other', but that rather Europeans 'took possession' of indigenous cultures as a necessary step in appropriating their lands as well. The literature on the encounters between Europeans and non-Europeans, and the impact of them on indigenous societies is rapidly expanding. See, for example, the two volumes of reprinted articles in Forster, ed, *European and Non-European Societies;* the essays in Schwartz, ed, *Implicit Understandings*, and those in Greenblatt, ed, *New World En-*

historians of cartography and geography have emphasised primarily a positivist narrative of the evolution of map making from a highly imaginative art to a 'valid' science where geographers excised culture from maps in the name of scientific 'objectivity'. They also examine the geopolitical power struggles that spurred rulers to seek the latest and most accurate maps to be had. Rulers competing for power and access to the wealth of the New World eagerly sought to obtain geographical data on the best routes to the Indies for themselves and to deny it to their rivals, because in the race to stake a claim to territory in the New World, or to trading entrepots in Asia, accurate information could spell the difference between success and failure.[2]

During the 1980s and 1990s, however, historical geographers began to garner new insights from the anthropologists, sociologists, and philosophers whose work was expanding the focus and methodology of historical scholarship. Brian Harley, an already eminent scholar of the history of cartography, was an especially important pioneer in this trend. After reading the work of Michel Foucault, and especially Foucault's remarks on geography, Harley found that he could never read a map in quite the same way again. Maps, he realised, were as much texts and cultural artifacts, deeply ambivalent in meaning, and replete with symbols, as the scores of written texts cultural historians were busy deconstructing. Of most significance, Harley and those who have built upon his insights concluded that maps, like other texts, were about power, and not merely because they reflected power relations that already existed, but also because they asserted special knowledge, power and possession.[3] As Harley put it in 1989: 'Cartogra-

counters. See also Cervantes, *The Devil in the New World*; Clendinnen, *Ambivalent Conquests*; Seed, *Ceremonies of Possession*.

[2] Mollat du Jourdin and De La Roncière, *Sea Charts of the Early Explorers*; Parry, *The Age of Reconnaissance*, pp. 53-113; Quinn, 'The Americas in the Rotz Atlas of 1542' and 'Maps in the Age of European Exploration'; Skelton, *Maps*; Thrower, *Maps and Civilization*; Tooley, 'Map Making in France'.

[3] Harley drew his inspiration for his cultural approach to maps especially from the writings of Michel Foucault, and in particular from Foucault's brief discussion of geography in an interview with the editors of the French journal *Hérodote*. Cf. Foucault, 'Questions on Geography'; Harley, 'Maps, Knowledge, and Power', 'Silences and Secrecy', 'Deconstructing the Map', 'Rereading the Maps', and 'Historical Geography'; Harley and Zandvliet, 'Art, Science, and Power'. For discussions of the impact of Harley's work on the historiography of cartography, see Belyea, 'Images of Power'; Pelletier, 'Les enjeux de la cartographie européenne'; Petto, 'Cartography and Power'; Wintle, 'Renaissance Maps and the Construction of the Idea of Europe'. For other cultural approaches to map history, see Brotton, *Trading Territories*; Conley, *The Self-Made Map*; Cosgrove, ed, *Mappings*; Lestringant, *Mapping the Renaissance World*; Mignolo, *The Darker Side of the*

phers manufacture power: they create a spatial panopticon. It is a power embedded in the map text'.[4]

Thus, it has also become apparent that European rulers, great and small, from the Doge of Venice to the king of France, who competed with each other over the talent of map makers like Jean Rotz, Diogo and Andreas Homem, and Abraham Ortelius, and sought to lure geographers to their courts by creating official posts for them, did so in the hope of enhancing their own power and prestige.[5] Moreover, maps did more than merely reflect those aspirations, or record triumphs already attained. Rather, maps possessed agency; they were, in and of themselves, a source of power that was not dependent on actual conquest and territorial control. Obviously it was ideal to possess both the map and the territory but, as I shall argue below, in the absence of an empire, a map asserting possession of one could be almost as empowering.

France has always been considered something of a laggard in the race to acquire overseas colonies, eager to follow in the footsteps of the Spanish and the Portuguese, but incapable of carving out a durable French empire before the eighteenth century.[6] Moreover, historians of French colonisation have criticised Francis I in particular for his weak response to Portuguese and Spanish attacks on French commerce in American and Asian waters which the Iberian powers claimed to have divided between themselves by virtue of the 1494 Treaty of Tordesillas.[7] Francis rejected the Spanish and

Renaissance, especially Part 3, 'The Colonization of Space'.

4 Harley, 'Deconstructing the Map', p. 13.

5 The manifold ways in which early modern rulers sought to use maps to enhance their power are discussed in Black, *Maps and History*; Buisseret, ed, *Monarchs, Ministers and Maps*; Broc, *La géographie de la Renaissance*, especially the discussion on the role of government in sponsoring geographic learning (pp. 187ff).

6 Broc, *La géographie de la Renaissance*, p. 66; Chaunu, *Conquête et exploitation des nouveaux mondes*, pp. 345-349; Julien, *Les voyages de découverte*, p. 4; Morison, *The European Discovery of America*, pp. 316, 454. Trudel, *Histoire de la Nouvelle-France*, actually entitles the volume covering the sixteenth and early seventeenth centuries, 'Les vaines tentatives'.

7 Francis has been criticised most severely for his failure to support Jean Ango, and for turning a blind eye to the machinations of his admiral, Philippe Chabot, with the Portuguese ambassador, which resulted in a temporary prohibition on French voyages to the New World (although French vessels continued to sail there in reduced numbers) and the revocation of the letters of mark which had permitted Ango's ships to prey on Portuguese vessels in Brazil. *Déclaration portant défense de faire le commerce au Brésil, en Guinée, et dans les autres possessions portugaises d'outre-mer', 30 mai, 1537*; *Lettres interdisant derechef toute navigation et tout commerce au Brésil, en Guinée et dans les autres possessions portugaises d'outre-mer'' 8/1537, Commission du Roi et mandement au Parlement de Rouen, contenant défense à tous marchands, mariniers et autres d'envoyer des navires á la*

Portuguese pretensions to monopoly, demanding to see the clause in Adam's will excluding him.[8] He argued strongly in favour of liberty of the seas (less out of principle than because he lacked an empire to protect), sanctioned the voyages of Jean Ango's pilots as long as it was diplomatically possible, and sponsored those of Verrazano and Cartier. Still, his failure consistently to support this principle in the teeth of determined Iberian opposition has permanently tarnished his reputation among historians of French colonisation.[9] Even his biographers tend to avoid the subject. While more sympathetic to his plight, especially after Pavia, scholars of his reign give very little space to its overseas dimensions, acquiescing in the general judgement that because his initiatives bore little practical fruit, especially in comparison to the conquests of Mexico, the Yucatan, and Peru, or the expansion of Portuguese power in the Indian Ocean, they had little relevance. More importantly, they rarely put them in the context of Francis' patronage of humanists at his court. To most historians, European oceanic voyages, long distance trade, and cartographic representations of Asia, Africa, and the Americas, were about the expansion of European economic and naval power, and not really connected to the cultural changes taking place in Europe during this same period.[10] This attitude reflects the still poor integration of the history of European expansion into 'mainstream' European history, as well as the persistent disconnection between cultural and economic history.

I dispute this interpretation of the role of the discoveries in Francis I's reign, not so much because I seek to vindicate Francis on this score as because I think it underestimates the purpose, and power, of cartography in early modern culture, and the significance of images and symbols in propagating power. A number of historians have begun to explore the central role of the symbols which abound in medieval and Renaissance paintings,

Guinée ni au Brésil, données á la requête du roi de Portugal, 24 ou 25 janvier 1538(9); this royal order was revoked in 1540; see *Catalogue des Actes de François Ier*, vol. 8, pp. 657, 661, 698. See also Barrault, *Le Sacre et la Pensée*, p. 247; Calderon, *Étude biographique sur Ango*, p. 187; Guénin, *Ango et ses pilotes*, pp. 103-104, 147, 167; Julien, *Les voyages de découverte*, pp. 71-76. For a more positive assessment, see Le Roy Ladurie, *The Royal French State*, p. 127.

[8] Bideaux, 'Le discours expansionniste', p. 179. See also the *Lettre de marque accordée en 1530 à Jean Ango, et achetée par l'ambassadeur portugais* in: Guénin, *Ango et ses pilotes*, pp. 249-255.

[9] Chaunu, *Conquête et exploitation*, p. 348, states, for example, that 'le roi de France, en 1534, n'en est pas au niveau d'Henri le Navigateur un siècle plus tôt'.

[10] Guerdan, *François Ier*, pp. 425-426; Jacquart, *François Ier*, pp. 408-409; Knecht, *Renaissance Warrior and Patron*, pp. 368-384; Pernoud, 'L'inventeur de la monarchie', p. 177.

sculpture, and texts in shaping how Europeans interpreted their world, and power relationships within it. Anne-Marie Lecoq, in *François Ier imaginaire* examines the creation of Francis as an imagined ideal Renaissance ruler, an erudite humanist, a lover of peace but a redoubtable crusader as well, the rightful head of Christendom in its struggles with the infidel.[11] Historians of cartography have come to recognise that maps were an integral part of this symbolism of power, and that rulers accordingly used them to express and assert authority. As yet, however, few scholars have attempted to produce case studies examining the role of cartography and geography in the reign of a specific ruler.

I propose in this essay to attempt such a case study for Francis I, and in doing so demonstrate that, immersed as he was in the visual and textual symbols the humanists around him marshalled in support of his reign, maps were at once an assertion of, and confirmation of, his rightful equality with, or even precedence over, his imperial rival, Charles V, and his imperial ally, the Turkish sultan. I shall also show that Francis I, like other early modern rulers, competed for the service of cartographers, and treated cartographic knowledge as a potent source of royal propaganda and as a means to assert effective possession over territories. Although rulers, and especially the Portuguese and Spanish, often attempted to suppress maps that might aid foreign interlopers in reaching their new overseas trade routes and colonies, at other times maps were proudly displayed as tangible indicators of the extent of the power of the possessor. Francis I used maps to assert his right to share in the bounty of the New World, and to deny the claims of the Portuguese and Spanish to exclusive control over the trade routes to the Americas and Asia. But in acquiring maps, Francis was asserting more than simply the right of French vessels to ply the seas freely. For in Renaissance art and imagery, 'not only the distinction between symbolisation and representation is removed but that which threatens even the distinction between the symbol and what it symbolised'.[12] Through his maps, Francis also insisted on the reality of his right to possess the New World.

Part of the 'imagined' Francis I which Anne-Marie Lecoq analyses lies in the realm of geography and cartography. To keep pace with Charles V, who had inherited an empire in Europe and had the good fortune to acquire another in the Americas, Francis too needed to obtain an empire. Fortunately for Francis, however, effective occupation was not the sole, or even necessarily the prime, criterion in early modern empire building. After all, it

[11] Lecoq, *François Ier imaginaire*. See also Beaune, *The Birth of an Ideology*; Bryant, *The King and the City*; Gombrich, *Symbolic Images*; Pelletier, 'La symbolique royale française'.

[12] Gombrich, *Symbolic Images*, p. 172.

was a German cartographer, Martin Waldseemüller, at the court of Claude de Guise, the first Duke of Lorraine, who erroneously but successfully named the New World after the Italian geographer Amerigo Vespucci in a 1507 map of the New World. Although Waldseemüller soon realised his error and attempted to credit Columbus in subsequent works, his 1507 *Cosmographia Introductio* and its famous map had by then been reprinted, and plagiarised, throughout Europe. His map had taken on a life of its own, and the name 'America' stuck.[13] Thus maps had a power to shape perception on their own, at least partially independently of the situation in the actual territories depicted in the map. What a ruler could not conquer materially, he could at least possess symbolically, and in a society where symbols were often conceived to be no less 'real' than matter, symbolic possession in the form of a map was enough at least to save face, even if it did little to enlarge the royal treasury. Maps in the early modern world constituted a form of possession. Recognising this, European rulers of the sixteenth century frequently used maps to assert power over territory in which they had at best a tenuous presence on the ground. Moreover, even those who lacked the means to conquer any colonies participated in the European appropriation of the Americas through maps, one reason why Flemish, Italian, and German map makers flourished during the Renaissance and found eager patrons at home as well as abroad.[14] '*Mappae-mundi* therefore operated as vast visual encyclopaedias, which offered their patrons a privileged and highly flattering perception of their place in an expanding world, as well as reflecting their particular acquisitive commercial and political agendas'.[15]

The decorative maps which adorned the libraries of princes everywhere in Europe were for the benefit neither of sailors, who had their own form of

[13] Broc, *La géographie de la Renaissance*, pp. 58ff.
[14] This eagerness of princes, merchants, and adventurers from regions lacking colonies of their own explains the ubiquitous presence of Italian merchants in the financing of voyages of discovery, and of Italian sailors like Columbus, Verrazano, and Cabot, in heading them. Cf. *Participation des financiers lyonnais à l'expédition de «jehan de Varrasenne», 523 - 23 et 26 mars*, in: Mauduech, ed, *Normandie et la Nouvelle France d'Amérique*, pp. 21-22, and on pp. 22-23 the *Constitution de procureurs par «Jehan de Varasenne» avant d'«aller au voiage des Indes», 1526, 11-12 mai*; Broc, *La géographie de la Renaissance*, pp. 26ff; Brotton, *Trading Territories*, p. 154, Pelletier, 'Les enjeux de la cartographie européenne', pp. 163-164. See also Heers, 'Le rôle des capitaux internationaux'; Knecht, *Renaissance Warrior and Patron*, pp. 371-374; Rau, 'Les marchands-banquiers au Portugal'; Verlinden, 'Italian Influences in Iberian Colonization'; Wroth, *The Voyages of Giovanni Verrazano*. For excellent illustrations of the international participation in early modern cartography, see Mollat du Jourdin et La Roncière, *Sea Charts of the Early Explorers*; Tooley and Bricker, *Landmarks of Mapmaking*; Wolff, *America*.
[15] Brotton, *Trading Territories*, p. 31.

maps, portulans, to help guide them in their journeys, nor of the indigenous peoples who were well aware of the nature and limits of European power in their lands. Thus it is a mistake to dismiss them for their imprecision and fantastic imagery. Rather, they should be read as texts that served as a form of propaganda which, like other precious objects princes collected, were designed to illustrate the extent of the ruler's power. They were produced by and for court culture. 'At the very time maps were being transformed by mathematical techniques, they were also being appropriated as an intellectual weapon of the state system. If their study had become, by the end of the sixteenth century, the 'science of princes', it was because maps were by then recognised as a visual language communicating proprietorial or territorial rights in both practical and symbolic senses'.[16]

Francis I, nourished on symbolism throughout his life, understood the power of maps, and accordingly patronised cartographers and humanists to affirm the imperial stature of his rule and his equality with Charles V. Among the most significant among his map making clients were Oronce Fine (or Finé) and Jean Rotz. Fine was the quintessential loyal courtier whose career was closely intertwined with that of Francis I, and whose maps were dedicated to his patron and meant to emphasise the true, if mystical, global reach of Francis' rightful authority. Fine's strongly mystical bent and reverence for Ptolemy situate him in the late medieval trend of cartographers who found their inspiration primarily in antiquity and the religious iconography of medieval Catholicism. Rotz, by contrast, was a more modern, if enigmatic figure, who transferred his loyalty, and his cartographic skills, from the French monarchy to the English, and back again. Trained in cartography and navigation by the seamen of Dieppe, Rotz was less interested in mysticism than Fine, but no less aware of the potency of maps to inspire empire building. Although these were by no means the only cartographers Francis patronised, their works illustrate both the evolution of map making in France during the first half of the sixteenth century and the influence of cartography on Francis I's reign.

Francis I: The king who would have been emperor

When Francis I ascended the French throne in 1515, he appeared to have all the qualities of a great king, and everyone expected his reign to be a golden one. More handsome and charming than Charles of Habsburg, heir to the Spanish throne and future Holy Roman Emperor, more urbane than Henry VIII, victor at Marignano in the first year of his reign, he seemed the perfect candidate finally to complete the Crusades, and unite the world under

[16] Harley, 'Silences and Secrecy', p. 59.

Christian rule.[17] Humanist scholars and artists employed a plethora of images drawn from pagan and Christian antiquity, and often mingled with striking anachronism, to express their image of the young king. Francis was 'God's elected king', a 'second Caesar', a 'new Constantine'. even 'God's image on Earth'.[18] Guillaume Budé, humanist scholar and founder under Francis' partronage of the *Collège de France*, firmly believed that Francis embodied all the qualities of the ideal prince, and was destined to revive the fortunes and glory of France.[19] Another poet avowed that Francis would soon fulfil an ancient prophecy and subjugate Africa and Asia.[20] One especially telling 1517 image illustrates the struggles for precedence among European leaders and the full expectation of the French that Francis would impose peace upon Christianity and with the blessing of the Pope lead the next, and final crusade. Oronce Fine, court mathematician, geographer, and astronomer, produced two illustrations for the *Grant voyage de Jhérusalem* (Paris, 1517), in which Francis is shown accepting thc standard of the crusade from the Pope in the presence of the other European rulers, while Charles V skulks off to the side.[21] Moreover, Francis benefited from the advice of sage counselors like Claude de Seyssel, who urged him to rule wisely and justly, and incidently, to build a strong navy in order to 'perpetually secure the kingdom of France in all quarters', so that France would 'attain to such greatness and reputation that it would give law to all others'. In addition to 'the glory that the king who did this would acquire thereby and the reputation he would confer on the whole French nation', control of the seas would open the way for France to conquer new territories.[22] Globes or orbs also symbolised world sovereignty, and in 1515 a medal was struck for Francis with two globes, one terrestrial and the other celestial, and the devise *Unus non sufficit orbis* [one world does not suffice].[23]

No one could have foreseen in 1515 that within a decade Francis would

[17] Knecht, *Renaissance Warrior and Patron*, pp. 86, 88-90; Lecoq, *François Ier imaginaire*, pp. 17ff.

[18] Anne-Marie Lecoq, *François Ier imaginaire*, p. 23, outlines twelve separate themes, each examined in a separate chapter, that characterised the idealised portrait of Francis I between 1504 and 1525. See also Le Roy Ladurie, *The Royal French State*, pp. 110-116.

[19] Guillaume Budé, *De l'institution du prince*; Lecoq, *François Ier imaginaire*, pp. 166-167; Pelletier, 'La symbolique royale française', p. 61.

[20] Lecoq, *François Ier imaginaire*, p. 273.

[21] Lecoq, *François Ier imaginaire*, pp. 260-262.

[22] Hexter, transl., *Claude de Seyssel*, p. 140; Pernot, 'De l'importance des territoires extérieurs et du contrôle des voies maritimes'.

[23] Harley, 'Maps, Knowledge, and Power', p. 295; Pelletier, 'La symbolique royale française', p. 61.

suffer defeat at Pavia and captivity in Spain at the hands of Charles V, and within two decades would defy Europe by entering into an alliance with the Turkish Sultan. Yet from the beginning of his reign, Francis had to contend with an aggressive and wily rival in the person of Charles V. The issue of imperial power and prestige was at the centre of their contest from its inception. Several years before the death of the Holy Roman Emperor Maximilian, Francis had already begun his campaign to win election to the imperial throne in the place of Maximilian's grandson and preferred successor, Charles. Francis had good reason to be concerned about Charles, as the latter already ruled Spain, and through it a new source of revenue from his territories in the New World, as well as the extremely wealthy Netherlands, the Franche-Comté, and Naples. All Europe knew that as Holy Roman Emperor, Charles would possess the means not only to threaten all of France's land frontiers, but also to displace Francis as pre-eminent protector of Christianity against the Turk. Francis was not alone in his concern about Charles' ambitions, therefore, and was able to find substantial support in Germany and in Italy for his own imperial aspirations, with which even the Pope sympathised. In the end, however, Charles's superior income won him the imperial crown by affording him the ability to offer richer bribes to the imperial electors than Francis could muster. Francis attempted to counter Charles's growing prestige by an Anglo-French *détente* sealed at the famous Field of the Cloth of Gold', a magnificent, if costly, orgy of chivalric symbolism designed to cement Francis's golden reputation. If he could not be Holy Roman Emperor, Francis was determined to remain Europe's quintessential knight. Pavia shattered that image too, however, and Henry VIII proved to be an untrustworthy ally. If Europe was unprepared to allow Francis to be dethroned and France to be dismantled, and England, the Pope, and Venice were willing to offer tepid support to Francis in order to counter the now omnipresent Charles, Francis' dreams, and those of his subjects, of France at the helm of Christendom were irretrievably lost in the sixteenth century.[24]

Francis did not give up the game, however. Determined to find a reliable ally against Charles, and unable to trust the English, he turned finally to Suleiman the Magnificent, Sultan of the Ottoman Empire. This tactic, which earned him much opprobrium throughout Europe, turned out to be an excellent solution for Francis, although not for the reasons most historians have offered. Although Francis likely hoped that the Turks would offer him needed military support against Charles by attacking Habsburg

[24] Knecht, *Renaissance Warrior and Patron*, pp. 165ff; Mignet, *Rivalité de François Ier et de Charles-Quint*; Russell, *The Field of the Cloth of Gold*; Seward, *Prince of the Renaissance*, pp. 45ff.

frontiers in Eastern Europe and the Mediterranean, he could not have expected that the Turks would turn the tide of European political power in his favour. Suleiman in fact proved to be Francis' most faithful ally; he kept his part of their deal and deployed his army and navy (and corsairs) to distract Charles V on more than one occasion, and despite the fact the Francis proved a far less loyal partner. The Turkish forces could not tie Charles V down for very long, however, and in 1544 the emperor was even able to invade France and oblige Francis to sign the Peace of Crépy in which Francis agreed to abrogate his entente with Suleiman. As usual, Francis proceeded to ignore the treaty before the ink was dry, and secretly renewed the Turkish alliance just before he died.[25] Still, like the voyages to the New World that Francis sponsored, the Turkish alliance has generally been viewed at best as a modest success useful primarily for sowing the seeds of future French commercial expansion. In the absence of significant tangible results, they have seemed secondary to the other achievements, and the enormous losses, of Francis' reign.[26] Yet after Pavia, Francis needed above all to restore his lost prestige and honour after his captivity in Spain. He had to find new symbols to shape his royal identity for his own subjects and the rest of Europe, allies of a stature equal or greater than his own, who would address him as a peer, and efface the humiliating memory of defeat and imprisonment. In that respect at least the Turkish alliance was a success.[27]

As in his struggle to dominate Europe, Francis had to face persistent Spanish and Portuguese opposition to his efforts to carve out French colonies in the New World. From the 1494 Treaty of Tordesillas, the Iberian

[25] *Catalogue des Actes de François Ier*, vol. 9, pp. 84-87: 'Ambassades et Missions'; Charrière, *Négociations de la France*, offers the most complete account of French-Turkish diplomacy during the reign of Francis I, including numerous copies of correspondence between the two rulers and their ambassadors; see also Ursu, *La po-litique orientale de François Ier* for an account of Francis' diplomatic relationship with the Turks that emphasises the mediation of John Zápolyai, Voivode of Transyl-vania.

[26] Knecht, *Renaissance Warrior and Patron*, pp. 295-296; Guerdan, *François Ier*, pp. 337-341, 351-352.

[27] Suleiman wrote Francis a comforting letter during the latter's imprisonment, and although he never accorded Francis quite the same number of titles as his own in subsequent letters, by 1539 he was addressing Francis as the *très excellent et honoré le prince des princes des chrestiens, grand, clément et vaillant en toutes vertu, le plus renommé ès actes et gestes de toute la génération du Messie Jésus, le principal arbitre et compositeur de tous les différens des Nazaréens, seigneur magnanime en tout honneur, et digne de toute éminence et estat, des administrateurs de la justice le chef, mon puissant frère François*, which, diplomatic hyperbole aside, could not have helped but to assuage Francis' ego; see Charrière, *Négociations de la France*, vol. 1, pp. 129, 408, 417.

powers had agreed to divide the non-European world along a line that sliced through South America, awarding Africa, the routes to Asia, and Brazil to the Portugese, and everything west of Brazil, including all of the New World, to the Spanish. Most of the earliest French ships sailing in the wake of the Portuguese and Spanish resulted from the initiative of private French merchants based in Normandy, especially Dieppe, Honfleur, and Rouen, and Brittany, primarily Saint-Malo. Their foremost interest was fishing the Grand Banks off the coast of Newfoundland. Dieppe merchant Jean Ango was the most famous of these merchant entrepreneurs. Although Francis ennobled Ango and appointed him Governor of Dieppe in 1535, the two had an uneven relationship, largely because Ango persisted in sending ships to Asia and the New World and preying on Iberian shipping with or without royal approval. Ango's fleet served Francis well during times of war with Spain or Portugal, but during times of peace, which usually also meant when Francis was militarily vulnerable and attempting to marshal the support of the Portuguese against Charles V, Ango complicated Francis' diplomatic overtures to John III of Portugal.[28]

Especially alarming to the Portuguese was the 1524 voyage of Giovanni da Verrazano, who explored and mapped the coast of North America from Florida to Cape Breton. The financing and organisation of Verrazano's voyage illustrates the partnership with private capital upon which most early modern French overseas exploration depended. A coterie of Florentine silk merchants based in Lyon, and headed by Ango's relative and banker Bonacorso Rucellai, initiated the voyage, primarily in the hope that Verrazano would succeed in finding an alternative route to the silks of China. Ango and Philippe de Chabot, Admiral of France, also contributed money to the enterprise, which Francis I sanctioned; Francis received Verrazano's official report, and the maps Verrazano produced of his discoveries as well.[29]

[28] Ango and Philippe de Chabot, Admiral de France, eventually had a falling out that undermined Ango's relationship with Francis. After Chabot's fall from grace in 1538 Ango's relationship with Francis improved, and in 1544 he agreed to finance Francis' fleet against the English. The debts which he incurred as a result eventually bankrupted him. See Brunelle, *The New World Merchants*, pp. 30ff; Guénin, *Ango et ses pilotes*, pp. 38-39, 145ff, 163ff; Knecht, *Renaissance Warrior and Patron*, pp. 371, 392-393; Mollat, *Le commerce normand à la fin de Moyen-Age* , pp. 499-507; Wroth, *The Voyages of Giovanni Verrazano*, p. 71ff.

[29] Guénin, *Ango et ses pilotes*, p. 75ff; Julien, *Les voyages de découverte*, p. 79ff; Knecht, *Renaissance Warrior and Patron*, pp. 372-374; Morison, *The European Discovery of America*, pp. 277-319; Wroth, *The Voyages of Giovanni Verrazano*, analyses Verrazzano's maps.

Francis I also sponsored Jacques Cartier's three voyages to the New World. In 1534, he granted Cartier six thousand *livres tournois* toward Cartier's first voyage. With the support of his patron, Admiral Chabot, Cartier undertook a second voyage in 1535, although this time with a contribution of only three thousand *livres* from the royal treasury toward his expenses; private investors paid the rest. Cartier's third voyage, begun in April of 1538, is especially interesting in terms of the theme of this paper, both because of Francis' greater involvement in organising it and because its avowed goal was the search for Saguenay. During his previous voyages to Canada, the Indians had told Cartier tales of a great kingdom called Saguenay where, they assured the French, fabulous riches could be found. Clearly the French explorers themselves elicited such stories through their persistent questions to the Indians about gold, which no doubt suggested to the Indians that the fastest way to get their annoying visitors to move on was to tempt them with stories of greater wealth to be had further inland. It was Saguenay that piqued Francis' interest in Cartier's explorations, because Francis detected an opportunity finally to obtain an empire equal in wealth to that which Cortes had won for Charles V in Mexico. In a conversation with Portuguese navigator João Lagarto, Francis produced two maps of the New World from the royal collection and explained his determination to find Saguenay, which Francis firmly believed had stores of precious spices and gold mines. So important was the search for Saguenay to Francis that he dared not entrust command of the expedition to Cartier, a mere commoner, alone. Instead, Francis put a noble, Jean-François de la Roque, Sieur de Roberval, in charge of the enterprise, with Cartier under Roberval's command. Although Francis' decision is understandable in light of Renaissance cultural attitudes, Roberval was a poor choice, a Protestant with no seafaring experience who quickly alienated Cartier and made a series of bad decisions in Canada. By 1543 the northern climate, Roberval's strategic errors, and Spanish opposition had doomed the initiative and the stragglers who had survived the harsh Canadian winter returned to France without having discovered a trace of Saguenay. By the time Francis died in 1547, dreams of finding a Canadian El Dorado, like so many other versions of the imperial chimeras that had blossomed at the outset of his reign, had vanished.[30] France's claim to Canada remained more symbolic than material until the seventeenth century.

[30] Cf. *Copie de la commission de «capitaine général» donnée par François Ier à Jacques Cartier, enregistrée au Parlement de Rouen', 17 Octobre, 1540* in: Mauduech, *Normandie et la Nouvelle France*, pp. 24-27; *Lettres patentes accordez à François de la Roque, Seigneur de Roberval', 1540*, in: *Collection de manuscrits* [...] *relatifs à la Nouvelle-France*, vol. 1, pp. 30-36. For a list of documents de-

Maps, knowledge, and possession

Fortunately for the French, Europeans in the Renaissance by no means agreed on what it meant to take possession of new territories, especially when they lay thousands of miles across the sea. Although all the European powers seeking to stake their claims in the New World developed their own ceremonies of possession out of their own cultural traditions, it is interesting to note that only the English based their claims of territorial sovereignty on actual effective settlement of the land. In a way, this is not surprising, for the English were latecomers, even more than the French, and sought legal arguments against the sweeping pretensions of their rivals in order to assert their own right to carve out English colonies in areas others had already claimed. Moreover, not even the Spanish could demonstrate effective settlement of more than a small percentage of the territory they claimed on maps, and with few European observers actually in the New World in the sixteenth century, and frequent confusion and disagreement about how much new land lay to the west, and where boundaries between explored and unexplored, claimed and unclaimed, land lay, the best policy was to make the most exaggerated claims possible. Rulers tended therefore to mould their laws and ceremonies validating the creation of territorial sovereignty to best suit their methods of exploration and ability to defend their new lands.[31]

Just as Europeans used language and texts to appropriate the New World, to interpret its meaning in a form they could digest, so too did they invariably enshrine their assertions to new sovereign possessions in maps of which the lines and images also became a way to establish ownership of the newly discovered lands. The maps tended to take on a life of their own, to become arbiters of reality rather than mere reflections of it. Lines on parchment or paper denoted boundaries which only those who could read and interpret the map could comprehend, but which became sufficiently 'real' for men to sacrifice their lives to defend them. Moreover, the images with which map makers filled the as yet unexplored interiors of their maps were not merely decorative. Rather, they interpreted the meaning and significance of the New World to those who saw them. Cartographers put into maps what interested Europeans, economically, militarily, and culturally,

monstrating Francis' interest in Cartier's voyages, see Biggar, *The Early Trading Companies of New France*, pp. 177-181; Julien, *Les voyages de découverte*, p. 118ff; Knecht, *Renaissance Warrior and Patron*, pp. 375-384; Morison, *The European Discovery of America*, pp. 339ff, 395f, 434ff.

[31] Juricek, 'English Territorial Claims in North Ameerica'; Seed, *Ceremonies of Possession*, pp. 2ff.

and what ancient writers had conditioned Europeans to expect to find beyond the borders of what had been the Greco-Roman world. Moreover, Europeans tended to be highly selective in what they observed when they went abroad, and how they interpreted it.[32] As Harley puts it, 'In atlases and wall maps decoration serves to symbolise the acquisition of overseas territory. European navigators – portrayed with their cartographic trade symbol of compasses or dividers in hand – pore earnestly over *terrae incognitae* as if already grasping them before their acts of 'discovery', conquest, exploration, and exploitation have begun'.[33]

Thus it is no accident that early maps tended to be crammed with depictions either of exotic and valuable commodities, such as parrots and brazilwood (from a tree which produced a dyestuff much appreciated in cloth making), or with nearly naked Indians engaged in activities that either promised profit to Europeans (most notably, docile harvest of brazilwood) or justified European conquest and imposition of Christian values (nudity and cannibalism were favourites). Whether noble savages drawn according to classical models, or just plain naked savages, images of Indians in Renaissance maps invariably reflected pre-existing European mental categories of human beings. By the same token, the further a territory was from Europe, the freer map makers were to impose European hopes and fears on their creations. The New World, almost invariably on the edges of maps with Europe at the centre, was the most malleable of all. Early explorers, once they realised that the new lands to the west were not Asia but rather stood as an obstacle between Europe and the riches of China and the Spice Islands, clung as long as possible to the hope that the New World would turn out to be, at best an archipelago, at worst one or two separate continents with navigable passages through or around them. Mirroring this, map makers drew narrow continents and a Pacific Ocean that was little more

[32] This culturally conditioned selectivity is apparent in medieval and Renaissance travel writing about the Middle East, East Asia, and Africa as well as the New World. See Campbell, *The Witness and the Other World*. Campbell's chapters on Columbus and Raleigh are especially interesting in relation to the theme of this essay. See also Brotton, 'Terrestrial Globalism' and *Trading Territories*, pp. 119ff, where he discusses the ways in which the Spanish and Portuguese tried to dupe each other about the correct placement of the eastern part of the line dividing their hemispheres which was designated in the Treaty of Tordesillas. The exact placement of the line mattered because the claims of each to the Moluccas hinged upon it. Since no one knew exactly where it ought to lie, how one drew it depended on how wide each map maker imagined Asia and the Pacific to be, and on which map won acceptance as the 'valid' one. See also Greenblatt, *Marvelous Possessions*, pp. 79-85, and plates 1-10.

[33] Harley, 'Maps, Knowledge, and Power', pp. 298-299.

than a strait, and optimistically put Japan just off the coast of California.[34] Thus Francis' determination to 'see' Saguenay on the two maps he showed Lagarto was no aberration but rather the typical behaviour of a Renaissance gentleman reading a map.

A key, therefore, to establishing effective possession of territory on maps was to attract the services of skilled cartographers, and in this respect Francis I was well served. A set of maps clearly intended to embody the humanist interpretation of the new Valois king are the cordiform maps of Oronce Fine (1494-1555).[35] Like many humanists in the early decades of Francis' reign, Fine was an enthusiastic believer in Francis' glorious destiny, and duly put his considerable talents to work in the service of his royal patron. In 1518, around the time that he became one of the four rectors of the University of Paris, Fine began work on his single cordiform map. His purpose in choosing the heart-shaped projection for his map was twofold. First, he sought to grapple with the technical problem, so familiar to Renaissance cartographers, of depicting a globe on a two dimensional page. Although Mercator's famous projection ultimately won the competition to resolve this dilemma first – and despite the fact that it is not without its own geographical distortions with ideological consequences – there was in the sixteenth century no agreed upon system of projection, which meant that many were tried, including cordiform and conic. Thus like much of his work, Fine's map is not particularly original, and in many aspects conforms to the traditions of late medieval map making more than it presages the cartographic advances of the decades to come.[36]

[34] See for example the 1502 'World Map of Cantino', anonymous, reproduced in Wolff, *America*, pp. 46 and 47; Pierre Desceliers 'World Map' (1550) on pp. 58-59; Sebastian Münster's map of the New World from *Cosmographia* (1546), in which Japan is almost as close to California as Cuba is to Florida on pp. 90-91. Abraham Ortelius grossly exaggerates the width of North America to bring China very close in a map of the Pacific Ocean and America in his 1598 atlas: Wolff, *America* (p. 93). We see the same error in Jodocus Hondius' 1606 map of America from the *Gerardi Mercatoris Atlas*: Wolff, *America*, p. 101. Thus the desire to close the Pacific endured well after the sixteenth century circumnavigations of the world. For examples and discussions of iconography in maps, see Brunelle, 'France and Brazil in the First century of Contact'; Mollat du Jourdin and De la Roncière, *Sea Charts of the Early Explorers*, especially plates 33 and 34 from the 1519 Miller Atlas, plate 40 from Jean Rotz, *Boke of Idrography* (1542) and the 1550 world map of Pierre Desceliers, plate 47.

[35] For illustrations of these maps, see Wolff, *America*. The single cordiform map, a 1556 copy of a map Fine began in 1518 and first printed in the mid-1530s, is reproduced on p. 73, and the 1531 bicordiform map is reproduced on p. 150. Another excellent reproduction of the single cordiform map can also be found in Woodward, *History of Cartography Project*. For my discussion of this map I am also indebted to

The cordiform projection served a second purpose, however, because it permitted Fine to make his map a visual representation of the mystical heart iconography popular in the first decades of Francis I's reign, and especially strongly associated with the 1517 triumphal entries of Francis in Rouen and of Queen Claude in Paris. Identified with the Trinity and the mingling of divine and human love found in the Song of Songs, the heart also was used to symbolise metaphoric union and possession; hence its usefulness in the symbolism of royal entries into cities.[37] The city became the willing bride, of which the lover/king took possession. The king, like a lover, could be expected to rule with justice and the best interests of his subjects in mind, because they were now joined to him legally and metaphysically, like husband and wife. His subjects, like a bride, would in turn submit to Francis governance. Because humanists had already associated the heart in this way with Francis' reign, Fine was able to convey with his cordiform map that Francis was the rightful possessor and protector of the world, for in the map the world is literally within Francis' heart. Thus Francis is the lover/king not only of France, but of all the world.

When the single cordiform map was finally printed in 1534, it incorporated the latest cartographical data available from the courts of Europe, and depicted for the first time the entire coastlines of North and South America with a fair degree of accuracy. Perhaps more significant for Francis I, the map specifically demarcates a sizeable chunk of territory, which Fine calls *Terra Francesca*, designating the region which Verrazano had explored for Francis. Further, Terra Francesca is depicted as part of Asia, unlike the Spanish possessions to the south, and as much closer to Europe as well. Thus, although the French may have held less territory than their rivals, their foothold promised them easier access to the riches of Asia than did the

Conley, *The Self-Made Map*, pp. 88-134, and Pelletier, 'Le monde dans un cœur'.

[36] In fact, Mercator's projection probably succeeded in part *because* it distorted the image of the world, grossly exaggerating the size of the continents of the northern hemisphere, among other things, although his projection did prove a boon to sailors because it allowed them to plot an accurate course, which also played a role in its acceptance. Broc, *La géographie de la Renaissance*, pp. 173ff, 194; Brotton, *Trading Territories*, pp. 161-171; Lewis and Wigen, *The Myth of Continents*, p. 18.

[37] Cities often used royal entries to convey to rulers what they desired from them. By the reign of Henry II, for example, trade between Normandy and the New World was such a significant part of Rouen's economy that the Rouennais city fathers, during Henry's 1550 entry into Rouen staged a performance in which they recreated, with the help of captured Brazilian Indians, a tableau illustrating their determination to overcome Portuguese resistance and establish a French colony in Brazil. Cf. Brunelle, 'Sixteenth-Century Perceptions'; Bryant, *The King and the City*, for a discussion of the significance of royal entry ceremonies; Conley, *The Self-Made Map*, pp. 119-120 and Lecoq, *François Ier imaginaire*, pp. 377ff.

much larger Spanish domains. Further, Fine leaves open the possibility for expansion of the French region, eastward into Asia, and to the north and south, for on either side of *Terra Francesca* lie *Baccalear* (seeming to signify the Labrador coast) and *Terra Florida*, neither of which are demarcated as belonging to other European powers. Despite the fact that, unlike Spain, France had neither conquered nor colonised any territory in the New World in 1534, Fine through his single cordiform map made a compelling argument that Francis was a player in the European race to possess the world.

In part because cartographical knowledge evolved through accretion, once a realm got its territorial claims inscribed on maps that were widely disseminated and respected throughout Europe, features such as islands or imaginary possessions became extraordinarily hard to erase from the maps. Unlike claims to the mythical islands, tenuous claims to New World possessions sometimes materialised into actual settlements and militarily defended frontiers rather than simply fade away over time, perhaps because the maps themselves confirmed for rulers their right to possess the territory marked on the maps as theirs. This seems to have been case for France, whose rulers throughout the sixteenth century struggled against extraordinary odds, including the Wars of Religion, to finance expeditions to explore and settle *Terra Francesca*. In the seventeenth century, with peace restored in France, Henry IV and Louis XIII found the funds and in Samuel de Champlain a leader who finally made that colonial dream a reality. In the sixeenth century, aside from ubiquitous fishing vessels in Newfoundland and interlopers on the coast of Brazil, the French presence in the New World remained primarily in the form of iconography on maps. Fortunately for the French, their royal symbols remained stubbornly planted on the coast of North American maps despite the best efforts of the Spanish and Portuguese to dislodge them.

For this Francis and his sixteenth-century successors had especially the Dieppe cartographers to thank. Established in the city of Jean Ango, and heirs to the strong Norman seafaring tradition, the map makers of the Dieppe school were excellent propagandists for French cartographic knowledge of and interest in the New World. Place-names in their maps were usually at least partly inscribed in French, and the Dieppe map makers tended to assert French territorial possession of the North American coasts which Verrazano and Cartier had explored, sometimes called simply *Terre de France*, but more often entitled *Canada*, and marked with a banner bearing the fleur-de-lys or other symbols of French sovereignty. In a 1550 map Pierre Desceliers went so far as to designate the ocean adjacent to Canada the *Mer de France*. Guillaume Brouscon's 1543 map claimed the entire coast of North America as far south as Florida for the French, although the disastrous French efforts to colonise Florida in the mid-sixteenth century demonstrated that they lacked the ability to wrest the peninsula from the Spanish.[38]

The maps of the Dieppe cartographers borrowed heavily from those of the Portuguese, which is not surprising given the strong commercial ties linking Normandy and Portugal in the sixteenth century. John III needed French support against Spain, despite his discomfiture with the determination of Norman merchants to carve out an enclave for themselves on the coast of Brazil, to facilitate the purchase of brazilwood from the Tupinambá for the Norman cloth trade. Further, French, Basque, and Portuguese fishermen had been plying the waters of the Grand Banks side-by-side since at least 1500. The Norman capital city, Rouen, attracted a significant population of Spanish, Italian, and Portuguese merchants and seamen in the sixteenth century. Thus there existed manifold opportunities for French merchants and sailors to exchange with their Iberian counterparts cartographic information that ended up in the Dieppe maps. Moreover, it is clear that although the appearance of these cartographers in Dieppe owed much to the initiative of Jean Ango and his fellow *armateurs*, Francis was also a significant source of patronage for them. Dieppe cartographer Jean de Clamorgan, for example, produced a *Carte Universelle* which he dedicated to Francis, and a copy of which Francis kept in his library. Furthermore, despite the competition from other European potentates great and small, and especially from Charles V and John III of Portugal, Francis succeeded in luring Portuguese pilots and cartographers into his employ, among them Jean Fontaneau, also known as Alfonse de Saintonge and João Pacheco, whom he appointed royal cartographer. The Portuguese and Spanish authorities of course tried to maintain strict control over the cartographic information that their explorers gathered, but the lure of better rewards elsewhere led not a few Iberian cartographers either to 'leak' information from the official maps in Seville and Lisbon, or to 'defect' themselves. This meant that Portuguese-style maps in particular became the basis for the work of other cartographers produced for courts throughout Europe, so much so that at times Italian, French, German, or Flemish map makers did not even bother to translate the Portuguese inscriptions they had 'borrowed' from Portuguese maps. The Dieppe cartographers' most significant, if

[38] World map, Guillaume Brouscon (1543) reproduced in Mollat du Jourdin and De la Roncière, *Sea Charts of the Early Explorers*, plate 42; world map, Pierre Desceliers (1550) as plate 47; map of the coast of North America by Guillaume Le Testu as plate 49. The most complete study of the Dieppe School of cartography remains Anthiaume's *Cartes marines*. The history of the Laudonnière expedition has been told many times, most recently in McGrath, *The French in Early Forida*.

controversial, innovation, was their insistence on following Marco Polo and placing the island of *La Grande Jave* (Greater Java) on their maps. The significance here is that some historians have detected in its depiction on the maps the outlines of Australia's Northern Peninsula, which is possible because off-course Portuguese sailors seem to have at least sighted the continent from the Moluccas by the early sixteenth century. The debate over whether the Dieppe maps truly represent the first European images of Australia has not been settled.[39]

Perhaps the best example of the way in which cartographic knowledge circulated among Renaissance courts is Jean Rotz's 1542 *Boke of Idrography*, probably the highest-quality atlas created in sixteenth-century France.[40] Rotz originally produced this magnificent atlas for his patron Francis I, primarily to showcase the sophistication of French geographical knowledge and Francis' determination to stake his claim in the New World. In 1542, however, Rotz took his family and his maps to England, where he entered the service of Henry VIII, to whom he finally dedicated his atlas. Rotz was the son of a Scotsman named David Ross who settled with his wife and children in Dieppe, where Jean grew up to sail on the ships of Jean Ango. Jean Rotz became a skilled and experienced sailor and navigator, and in his *Boke of Idrography* he displayed his wide knowledge of mariners' tools such as the compass and the astrolabe, as well as his cartographic abilities. He left Dieppe in 1540, probably to further his formal training in nautical studies in Paris. It has been suggested that his decision to leave France in 1542 resulted in part from disappointment that Francis I had hired Portuguese geographer and map maker João Pacheco rather than Rotz, as royal cartographer, although no one knows for sure the reason for Rotz' decision to relocate to England. Rotz soon became disillusioned with Henry VIII's patronage, however, and after several years of diplomatic manœuvring and

[39] *Catalogue des Actes de François Ier*, vol. 8, p. 189: *'janvier, 1539', A Jean Pechet, portugais, expert en la marine, don de 450 livres pour aller en Portugal chercher sa femme, ses enfants et ses cartes, et s'établir en France pour servir dans la marine. Ibidem*, p. 657: *'juin, 1538', 'A Jean Pachet, portugais, don de 90 livres en récompense de ses services dans la marine et pour l'aider à supporter sa dépense à la suite de la cour*; Anthiaume, *Cartes marines*, I, pp.152-155; Broc, *La géographie de la Renaissance*, pp. 50-69, 169-171; Denuce, *Les origines de la cartographie portugaise*, pp. 33-41, 47ff; Mollat du Jourdin and De la Roncière, *Sea charts of the early Explorers*, p. 30, Teixeira Da Mota, 'Influence de la cartographie portugaise'. See for example Münster's 1546 map of the world, in Wolff *America*, p. 91, as well as Hondius' maps in the *1606 Gerardi Mercatoris Atlas* reproduced on pp. 101-102).

[40] For much of what follows I am indebted to Helen Wallis' beautiful edition of Rotz's *Boke of Idrography*, the original of which is housed in the British Library, and her erudite introduction to it.

negotiations on his behalf on the part of the French ambassador, he was back in France by 1547, where he proceeded to serve the French crown by building and equipping ships for the French navy while also pursuing a career as a merchant. When he returned to France he turned over to the French court all the cartographic intelligence he had gathered during his sojourn in England.[41]

Following the Portuguese example, which in turn was a result of Arab influence, Rotz's maps are oriented with the south at the top of the page. His atlas contains maps of Asia, Africa, Europe, and the New World, all replete with iconography depicting European conceptions of the inhabitants of each of the regions of the world, and what Europeans found curious or valuable there. In what was quite likely a concession to his new patron, Henry VIII, Rotz follows the English conception of possession defined as effective occupation of territory. He does not, therefore, recognise Spanish and Iberian claims to all, or even most, of the New World. Rather, he limits their territorial rights to regions where they had unquestionably conquered the inhabitants and erected institutions of colonial governance. Thus, in his map of the Caribbean, for example, he explicitly demarcates the areas of Spanish settlement in Cuba and the Yucatàn, and calls them *The Indis of occident occupyit be Spain.* Similarly, he denotes the Spice Islands as *The Indis of orient quhayr* (where) *the Portugays doeth occuppye.* Many areas in the New World lacking European settlements are identified – *The londe of florida* and *The new fonde londe quhayr men goeth a fishing* for example – but unlike many contemporary maps, his do not use symbols such as shields and banners to illustrate the claims of European rulers to vast swaths of territory where little more than a handful of Europeans could be found. Nor does he recognise the French claim to all of North America north of the Chesapeake. This style is not surprising since the English, as latecomers to the appropriation of the New World, would have been less likely to approve of an atlas in which every inch of the New World was claimed to their exclusion.

Thus Rotz, like Fine and so many other Renaissance map makers producing for European courts, knew how to tailor his map to the needs, desires, and tastes of his patron. When it was expedient to assert a patron's claim to possess the world or large portions of it, cartographers produced maps that at once imagined a new world for their patrons, and simultaneously confirmed and validated their patrons' sense of their place in that world – at the helm, of course. Early modern cartographers and geographers, whether ensconced in the world of academia like Fine and Guillaume Budé, or sailors, merchants, and explorers like Verrazano, Ango, and Rotz,

[41] Wallis, *The Maps and Text of the Boke of Idrography*, pp. 3-23.

had to be effective courtiers as well, because princes were their most significant, and lucrative, patrons. They of course attempted to elicit and include in their maps the most recent and accurate geographical information to be had, and were by no means above bribery, gossip, and plagarism to get it. But they operated in the cultural milieu of their time, and their maps were not intended to be 'objective' 'scientific' reflections of the world, as we understand those terms today. Putting aside the contemporary debate regarding the extent of cultural bias in contemporary science, we may say that early modern maps were produced for a courtly culture in which political and dynastic rivalries and European cultural superiority were imperatives at least as important as 'science' in determining what went into the maps, and what was left out.[42]

Conclusion

Another significance of cartography to Renaissance courtly culture, which space does not permit me to pursue here, is that maps of course were not one-way conversations, but rather were parts of a dialogue. Courtly patrons exercised a powerful influence on the cartographers whom they attracted to their service, but maps also communicated with the princes and courtiers, and helped to shape their understanding of their power and role in the world. Without a doubt maps contributed to what Stephen Greenblatt has termed 'Renaissance self-fashioning', the process through which princes and their noble followers developed a sense of individual self and destiny, if for no other reason than that maps and globes were a ubiquitous part of élite education in the early modern period.[43] As Europe's knowledge of the world increased, maps surely contributed to the European conviction that it was Europe's duty and destiny to bring Christianity and European civilisation to everywhere that appeared on the maps. By the same token, the very act of seeing regions of the world marked on maps with symbols of European sovereignty doubtless fostered in those viewing a map the sense that the places on the map they possessed were in a manner already theirs, regardless of whether or not they had done more than reconnoitre but a small portion of them.

Francis I was the first French king to be immersed in a map-oriented

[42] Brotton, *Trading Territories*, pp. 178-179; Lestringant, *Mapping the Renaissance World*, p. 104ff.

[43] Conley, *The Self-Made Map*, offers an excellent discussion of the relationship between mapping and Renaissance identity formation. See also Greenblatt, *Renaissance Self-Fashioning*. For noble education in early modern France, see Dewald, *Aristocratic Experience and the Origins of Modern Culture*; Schalk, *From Valor to Pedigree*.

sense of France's imperial destiny, in terms both of European maps commissioned for military purposes and of maps of the non-European world useful for planning expeditions and for locating France's place in the world. The Valois king used maps to plot his route through the Alpine passes into Italy, and to devise battle strategy.[44] He objected vigorously to the Treaty of Tordesillas and the consequent attempt to use maps and lines to exclude him from his share of Europe's imperial conquests. He was not particularly successful militarily and diplomatically in challenging his rival Charles V for pre-eminence in Europe; nor did Francis succeed in establishing an empire in either Asia or the New World. 'Beyond the line', the Portuguese and Spanish still dominated at the end of his reign as they had at its beginning, and the French presence was mostly insecure, in the form of yearly fishing voyages to Newfoundland, attacks on Iberian shipping, and furtive expeditions to secure dyewood from the coast of Brazil. But thanks to the voyages of exploration that Francis sponsored, and to the geographers and cartographers he patronised, by the end of his reign France possessed an empire on the maps that she lacked on the ground. That symbolic possession survived the chaos of the religious wars until the seventeenth century, when France was finally able to claim the cartographic empire that Francis I had already won for her.

[44] Buisseret, 'Monarchs, Ministers, and Maps', pp. 102-103.

PRINCELY CULTURE AND CATHERINE DE MÉDICIS[1]

Margriet Hoogvliet

The name of Catherine de Médicis (1519-1589)[2] evokes almost immediately the Massacre of St. Bartholomew (23-24 August 1572), which began with the assassination of the Protestant leader de Coligny and culminated in the murder of thousands of Huguenots in Paris and elsewhere in France. In sixteenth-century Protestant propaganda and in modern historiography, Catherine is considered to be one of the cruel instigators who planned this massacre immediately after the marriage of her daughter Marguerite to the Protestant Henry de Navarre.[3] The attention paid to the negative aspects of Catherine's political role tends to overshadow her art patronage,[4] and even less attention

[1] The research for this article has greatly benefited from the facilities granted by Prof. Volker Honemann of the Westfälische Wilhelms-Universität (Münster, Germany) and by the Centre d'Études Supérieures de la Renaissance (Tours, France). A research trip to the CERS in Tours was subsidised by the Netherlands Organisation for Scientific Research (NWO).

[2] In France, Catherine's Italian family name 'de' Medici' was rendered as 'de Médicis'. The number of publications on the life and politics of Catherine de Médicis is enormous, but consists largely of romanticised biographies. For scholarly studies, see Cloulas, *Catherine de Médicis*; Knecht, *Catherine de' Medici*; Franke and Welzel, 'Katharina von Medici'. Older, but still useful are: Mariéjol, *Catherine de Médicis*, and Héritier, *Catherine de Médicis*. The study by Bertière, *Les Reines de France au temps des Valois*, vol. 1, pp. 293-377 and vol. 2, pp. 7-409 is interesting, but lacks references. Also interesting but somewhat popular is: Laffont, *Le règne de Catherine de Médicis*.

[3] Knecht, *Catherine de' Medici*, and especially Bourgeon, *Charles IX*, argue that this Black Legend needs reconsidering. For the influence of Catherine's image as the 'wicked Italian queen' in modern historiographical research, see Sutherland, 'Catherine de Medici'. The sinister image of Catherine is also present in recent dramatisations of sixteenth-century France, as, for example, the film *La Reine Margot* (1994) by Patrice Chéreau (based on the novel by Alexandre Dumas *fils* from 1834), and the theatre play *La reine mère ou Catherine de Médicis* by Marie-Thérèse Roy, performed at the Avignon festival in 1998.

[4] The best documented study of Catherine's art patronage is still: Cloulas, *Catherine de Médicis*, pp. 319-369. See also: Mariéjol, *Catherine de Médicis*, pp. 205-245; Knecht, *Catherine de'Medici*, pp. 220-245; Knecht, 'Royal Patronage of the Arts'; Baudouin-Matuszek, ed, *Paris et Catherine de Médicis*, pp. 78-127; ffolliott, 'The Ideal Queenly Patron'.

has been given to the creation of a princely culture by and for Catherine de Médicis.[5]

The life of Catherine de Médicis is the story of the ascent of *la marchande florentine* from the de' Medici family in Florence to the position of Queen of France. She was the only daughter of Lorenzo de' Medici and Madeleine de la Tour d'Auvergne, a duchess from the high nobility of France. In 1533, at the age of fourteen, the orphaned Catherine was given in marriage to Henry d'Orléans (1519-1559), the second son of Francis I (1494-1547), king of France. Like all royal marriages of that time, this marriage served a political goal: the alliance between the de' Medici pope Clement VII and the French king. After the premature death of the Dauphin Francis in 1536, Henry unexpectedly found himself first in line for succession to the French Crown. In 1547, Catherine's husband succeeded to the French throne as Henry II, and she was crowned queen of France. The life of the king ended on 10 July 1559, when he succumbed to the wounds incurred at a jousting party which formed part of the festivities celebrating two royal marriages.[6] Catherine was left behind with young children and a country on the verge of a civil war between Catholics and Huguenots.

I shall concentrate on the period following the death of Henry II in 1559, because before the latter event Catherine's role as queen of France was completely overshadowed by Diane de Poitiers,[7] *maîtresse en titre* of the king. Only after Henry's death and the subsequent exclusion of Diane de Poitiers from court and politics, could Catherine personally shape the cultural and political life at court. From 1559 onwards she would be ever present in the politics of Renaissance France as a powerful queen mother, during the reigns of her sons Francis II (1559-1560), Charles IX (1560-1574), and Henry III (1574-1589). She was officially entrusted with the regency of France during the minority of Charles IX and again in the period prior to the return of Henry III from Poland.

Being a women and thus lacking the uncontestable status of a crowned king, Catherine had to shape her public image carefully. Her first problem was the legitisimation of female power in France, where Salic law could be used to prevent the passage of royal power to the hands of a woman. In Renaissance Europe, female regents could not use the same arguments to

[5] It is only very recently that modern research has started to pay attention to this subject, see: ffolliott, 'Catherine de'Medici', as well as Franke and Welzel, 'Katharina von Medici'.

[6] Knecht, *Catherine de' Medici*, pp. 54-58.

[7] As with Catherine de Médicis, most of the publications on Diane de Poitiers are highly romanticised. For scholarly publications, see: Bardon, *Diane de Poitiers*; Bertière, *Les Reines de France au temps des Valois*, I, pp. 283-292; Cloulas, *Diane de Poitiers*, Ruby, 'Diane de Poitiers'.

legitimise their political power as did emperors, kings and princes. The strategies used by Catherine stand out because of their originality and their effectiveness. Among the latter architectural patronage was of great importance: Catherine spent enormous fortunes on the construction and embellishment of castles and funeral monuments. Another was the cultivation of splendid court festivals, which are probably the most striking element of princely culture during the lifetime of Catherine de Médicis. She used this courtly tradition as a political tool, expressing both the greatness of the Valois kings and her own ideas concerning religious tolerance in a France that risked falling apart as a result of the wars of religion.

The widow as a king

After the death of her husband, Catherine dominated French politics, mostly as a queen mother helping her young sons, but on two occasions she was herself officially in power. During the minority of her second son (1560-1563), Catherine was appointed *gouvernante de France*, which implied that she held almost absolute power.[8] Later, after Charles's death and before the return of Henry III, she was again entrusted with the regency of France (31 May - 6 September 1574).[9] This was remarkable, since in France the regency was traditionally reserved for male relatives from the royal family (the *princes du sang*).[10] Moreover, an exaggerated interpretation of the Salic law was often used as an argument against the possibility that women, although they might be crowned and anointed queen of France, could be invested with political power.[11] Nevertheless, France had in the past had powerful queens who possessed great fiefs, as, for example, Aliénor d'Aquitaine (ca. 1122-1204) and Anne de Bretagne (1477-1514).[12] Important precedents for the regency being handed over to a women were Blanche de Castille (1188-1252) who was regent during the minority of her son (and future saint) Louis (and later during

[8] Cloulas, *Catherine de Médicis*, pp. 154-155; Bertière, *Les reines de France au temps des Valois*, II, pp. 61-65. In 1548 and 1552, during the campaigns of Henry II in Italy, the regency had already been handed over briefly to Catherine, but on these occasions her power was limited. See also Knecht, *Catherine de' Medici*, pp. 42-44.

[9] Cloulas, *Catherine de Medicis*, p. 373; Knecht, *Catherine de' Medici*, p. 172.

[10] Gaehtgens, 'Machtwechsel oder die Übergabe der Regenschaft', pp. 65-66; ffolliott, 'Catherine de' Medici', p. 228; ffolliott 'Casting a Rival into a Shade', p. 138; Bertière, 'Régence et pouvoir féminin'.

[11] A detailed and critical study of the Salic law can be found in: Hanley, 'La loi salique'. See also: Gaehtgens, 'Machtwechsel oder die Übergabe der Regenschaft', pp. 64-67; Zemon Davis, 'Women in Politics', p. 171; Bertière, *Les Reines de France au temps des Valois*, I, pp. 19-31; ffolliott, 'Catherine de' Medici, p. 371, note 4.

[12] Bertière, *Les Reines de France au temps des Valois*, I, pp. 373-374.

his crusade), Anne de Beaujeu (1462-1522) during the minority of her younger brother Charles VIII, and Louise de Savoie (1476-1531) during the Italian captivity of her son Francis I.[13]

A powerful argument in favour of Catherine was that she, as mother of the young kings, had a natural authority.[14] Thus she stressed her motherhood in the text of her royal seal: *Catherine par la grâce de Dieu, Royne de France, Mère du Roy*.[15] The authority of the queen mother was once more confirmed during the proclamation of majority of Charles IX in 1563. The young king declared that from now on he wished to be obeyed by everyone, except by his mother, for whom he reserved the power to command. After the proclamation, Charles descended from his throne to receive homage from his mother and declared that she would govern and command as much, or even more, as she had done in the past.[16] Allusions to Catherine as a mother of both the king and the country also occur, for example during the royal entry of Charles IX into Troyes in March 1564, where the queen mother was hailed as *mere du Roi et mere du païs*.[17] As late as 1588, Henry III, while opening the *états généraux* in Blois, reminded the audience that Catherine was the mother of France.[18]

An even more important key to power was Catherine's widowhood, because it assured her of an unmistakable reference to the fact that she, as a widow, was replacing the deceased King of France.[19] Thus Catherine's lifelong mourning was not only a manner to express grief: it was also the legitimisation of her political role. In her public image, the reminders of her widowhood are countless.[20] On her royal seal, mentioned above, Catherine appears as a standing figure wearing the widow's veil and a crown. Another example stems from the entry of Francis II and Mary Stuart into Catherine's castle

[13] Mariéjol, *Catherine de Médicis*, p. 86; Bertière, *Les Reines de France au temps des Valois*, I, p. 29. Nicolas Houel also refers to Blanche (and other female regents from the history of France) in his *Histoire de la royne Arthemise* (Paris, BnF, ms. fr. 306, ff. 38^r-39^v, transcribed by Von Haumeder, *Antoine Caron*, pp. 227-231).

[14] Zemon Davis, 'Women in Politics', p. 172.

[15] Cloulas, *Catherine de Médicis*, p. 155, plate 11.

[16] "*Et luy faisant ladite dame* (Catherine), *une grande reverence et le baisant, ledit seigneur* (Charles IX) *luy a dit qu'elle gouvernera et commandera autant ou plus que jamais*", Mariéjol, *Catherine de Médicis*, p. 128. See also Cloulas, *Catherine de Médicis*, p. 179; Knecht, *Catherine de' Medici*, p. 97.

[17] Jean Passerat, *Chant d'alegresse*, p. 177.

[18] Boucher, *Société et mentalités autour de Henri III*, p. 127. The source is: *La harangue faite par le roy Henry troisième ... le seizième jour d'oct. 1588* (Blois, 1588), fols. 2^v-3^r.

[19] An in-depth study of this tactics can be found in: Gaehtgens, 'Machtwechsel oder die Übergabe der Regentschaft', pp. 67-72; ffolliot, 'Catherine de' Medici'.

[20] See, for example, the *Hôtel de la Reine*, which counted among its appartments an *appartement de deuil*: Bonnaffé, *Inventaire des meubles de Catherine de Médicis*, p. 18.

Chenonceaux, in March 1560, where an altar in classical style was dedicated to Catherine's grieving over her deceased husband. The accompanying sonnet expressed her wish to withdraw from public functions in order to dedicate herself to her mourning:

> *... Passant, demeure et voy le saint rivage*
> *Où Catherine, en dédaignant l'orgeuil*
> *Des hommes vains, pour témoigner son deuil,*
> *Veult achever les jours de son veuvage.*[21]

> [Passer-by, stop and look at the sacred river bank (of the river Cher)
> where Catherine, who rejects the pride
> of the vain, wants to end the days of her widowhood
> in order to give expression to her mourning].

These eloquent words served solely to underline her widowhood, because in reality Catherine did anything but withdraw from political activities.

After the tragic death of Henry II she appeared in public wearing without exception the black widow's dress instead of the usual white. Sheila ffolliott[22] gives an interesting analysis of this choice: apart from being an important reminder of her widowhood, the colour black was also worn by European rulers such as Charles V, Philip II, and, even more important, by the late Henry II. In this manner Catherine could present herself as a stand-in for her deceased husband and as one who could measure up to her male counterparts.

The widow theme also reoccurs in the references to the *nouvelle Artémise*,[23] modelled on queen Artemisia († 351 B.C.), widow of king Mausolos of Halicarnassus. This *exemplum virtutis* from classical history was a perfect legitimisation for Catherine's political role: Artemisia acted as regent for her son Lygdamis after the death of the king in 353 B.C. She also took charge of educating her son to be a good king. In memory of her beloved husband she

[21] Galitzin, ed, *Le Plessis, Les Triomphes*, p. 10.
[22] ffolliott, 'Catherine de' Medici', pp. 228-229.
[23] An interesting analysis of the Artemisia theme can be found in: Gaehtgens, 'Machtwechsel oder die Übergabe der Regentschaft', pp. 68-70; ffolliott, 'Catherine de' Medici', pp. 229-241; ffolliott, 'A Queen's Garden of Power'. The example of Artemisia had already been used by another female Renaissance regent, Margaret of Austria (1480-1530); see Carpino, 'Margaret of Austria's Funerary Complex'. In the dedication of the *livret* of the entry to Valence, Catherine was compared to another famous female regent and widow from classical antiquity, Queen Zenobia. See La Maisonneuve de Berry, *Description des devises*, p. 213. For other female examples from mythology and history symbolising Catherine, see my study 'The Symbolism of a Queen'.

erected a grandiose tomb, the Mausoleum of Halicarnassus, which was one of the Seven Wonders of the Classical world. According to the legends, queen Artemisia was so afflicted by the death of Mausolos that she drank his ashes mixed with wine and tears. Very shortly after the death of Henry II, Louis Le Roy hailed Catherine as the new Artemisia in a Latin text entitled *Ad illustrissimam reginam D. Catharinam Medicem* (Paris, 1560).[24]

The *nouvelle Artémise* theme served as a base for several works of art dedicated to Catherine. In 1562 Nicolas Houel presented her with the manuscript of his *Histoire de la Royne Arthemise*[25] together with a series of carpet designs, most of which can be attributed to the artist Antoine Caron.[26] These *cartons*, of which sixty-eight survive, visualise important episodes from the story of Artemisia: the funeral ceremonies, the erection of the mausoleum, the regency of Artemisia, the crowning and education of the young king, and the war against Rhodes. The scenes from the life of Artemisia are accompanied by sonnets which were probably also composed by Nicolas Houel.[27] None of the surviving Artemisia tapestries date from Catherine's lifetime: they were all woven in the seventeenth century for the queen regents Marie de Médicis and Anne d'Autriche.[28]

One of the drawings, *La remise du livre et de l'épée,* visualising the education of Lygdamis under the supervision of Artemisia, served as the example for a painting (dated 1575), also attributed to Antoine Caron.[29] It is an allegory of the education and good government of Charles IX. The education of the young king is an important parallel with the story of Artemisia which was exploited by Catherine de Médicis. She herself composed a letter of advice to

[24] Lersch, *Die Grabkapelle der Valois*, p. 106, note 16.

[25] Paris, BnF, ms. fr. 306, partially transcribed by Von Haumeder, *Antoine Caron*, pp. 197-269. See also: Beguin, 'La suite d'Arthémise'; ffolliott, 'Catherine de' Medici', pp. 230-231; ffolliott, 'Exemplarity and Gender', pp. 322-330.

[26] Most of the designs are contained in a separate *recueil* with an introduction by Nicolas Houel (Paris, BnF, Est. Ad. 105. Res). The Cabinet des dessins of the Musée du Louvre in Paris holds another set of the Artemisia drawings. The *cartons* are described in detail by Von Haumeder, *Antoine Caron*, pp. 137-196 and Ehrmann, *Antoine Caron*, pp. 53-78. See also: Ehrmann, 'Antoine Caron. Tapisserie et tableau inédits'; ffolliott, 'Catherine de' Medici', pp. 231-241, fig. 1-6; ffolliott 'Casting a Rival into a Shade'.

[27] The sonnets are inscribed on the verso side of each preceding drawing. For transcriptions, see Von Haumeder, *Antoine Caron*, pp. 270-299.

[28] Von Haumeder, *Antoine Caron*, pp. 11-12; Ehrmann, *Antoine Caron*, pp 55-56; ffolliott, 'Catherine de' Medici, p. 231. The inventory of the Hôtel de la reine, made after Catherine's death, lists a great number of tapestries. Unfortunately it is not possible to establish with certainty whether the Artemisia tapestries were among them. See Bonnaffé, *Inventaire des meubles de Catherine de Médicis*, pp. 12, 56-57, note 2.

[29] Beauvais, Musée Départemental de l'Oise. Von Haumeder, *Antoine Caron*, p. 103; Ehrmann, *Antoine Caron*, pp. 79-81.

Charles IX which still survives in several sixteenth-century manuscript copies.[30] During the reign of Catherine, a great number of educational texts for the young kings were composed by other authors. In 1560 Michel de l'Hôpital dedicated a Latin treatise to Francis II, translated into French by Joachim Du Bellay.[31] Ronsard and Etienne Pasquier, for their part, wrote instructions for Charles IX.[32] In 1575 Antoine de Baïf published a letter in which Catherine gives lessons about good government to her son.[33] Catherine seems to have attached great importance to the humanist ideal of the learned prince, whose power reposes on both *arma et litterae*, and earlier, around 1553-1554, she commissioned a French translation of Erasmus's *Institutio Principis Christiani.*[34]

Following the example of the historical Artemisia, Catherine intended to erect a grandiose mausoleum in memory of her husband.[35] The abbey church of Saint-Denis, just north of Paris, had been the traditional burial place for the Christian French kings since Merovingian times. In Catherine's days, the Saint-Denis abbey church was mainly an early gothic building, approximately as it is nowadays. The Italian artist and architect Francesco Primaticcio designed a spacious twelve-sided Renaissance chapel, known as the *rotonde des Valois*, which was attached to the north transept of the church. The chapel had three levels with six chapels each, and it was to be crowned by a dome with a lantern. Primaticcio's design also envisaged columns, pilasters and epitaphs, in

[30] La Ferrière and Baguenault, eds, *Catherine de Médicis, Lettres*, II, pp. 90-95. The letter is dated 8 September 1563. She also wrote a now lost letter with instructions for her daughter Elisabeth who was to become queen of Spain. For the instructions for princes published during the reign of Catherine de Médicis, see: Von Haumeder, *Antoine Caron*, pp. 107-108.

[31] Michel de l'Hôpital, *De sacra Francisci II, Galliarum regis initiatione, regnique ipsius administrandi providentia* (Paris, 1560). Joachim Du Bellay, *Discours sur le Sacre du tres chrestien Roy François II. Avec la forme de bien regner accomodée aux moeurs de ce royaume* (Paris, 1560). An expanded version of the latter text was published by Du Bellay as: *Discours au Roy contentant une brefve et salutaire instruction pour bien et heureusement regner, accomodée à ce qui est plus necessoire aux moeurs de nostre temps* (Paris, 1566).

[32] Pierre de Ronsard, *Institution pour l'adolescence du Roy treschrestien Charles IX de ce nom* (Paris, 1562); Etienne Pasquier, *Pourparler du Prince* (Paris, 1560).

[33] Antoine de Baïf, *Epistre au Roy, sous le nom de la Royne sa mere, pour l'instruction d'un bon Roy* (Paris, 1575).

[34] Fricke, *Die französischen Fassungen der* Institutio Principis Christiani *des Erasmus*, pp. 59-76.

[35] During Catherine's lifetime, her son Charles IX was also buried in this monument. The best documented studies of the *rotonde des Valois* are: Lersch, *Die Grabkapelle der Valois*; Lersch, 'Remarques sur quelques sculptures'; Martens, *La rotonde des Valois*. See also Blunt, *Art and Architecture in France*, pp. 61, 98-101; ffolliott, 'Catherine de' Medici, pp. 235-236; Pérouse de Montclos, *Philibert De l'Orme*, pp. 328-331.

marble of different colours, on both the inside and the outside of the chapel. For the interior of the chapel, Primaticcio and the French sculptor Germain Pilon designed a grandiose tomb. Pilon and his workshop also executed four freestanding sculptures in marble: a monument representing the *gisants* of Henry and Catherine, a *mater dolorosa*, a Resurrection group and Saint Francis in ectasy. The project for the *rotonde des Valois*, for which work began in 1563, was so ambitious that it could not be finished during Catherine's lifetime.[36]

The tomb by Primaticcio and Germain Pilon[37] is based on the design of the tombs of Louis XII and Francis I, but it is intended to be more impressive than its predecessors. It shows the 'transi' figures of Henry and Catherine in marble, beneath a marble canopy supported by twelve marble columns. Four bronze sculptures representing the cardinal virtues decorate the corners of the monument. On top, Catherine and Henry are represented a second time, now as two kneeling figures in bronze absorbed in eternal prayer. As Thomas Lersch has pointed out, the iconographical programme of the chapel, the tomb and the other sculptures aims to represent the Valois kings as God-sent defenders of the true faith against its enemies.[38] In sixteenth-century France these were beyond any doubt the Protestants.

Catherine's interest in commemorative monuments for Henry II was not limited to the mausoleum in Saint-Denis. In 1560 she commissioned from Germain Pilon and Domenico del Barbiere a marble sculpture for the heart of Henry II; they designed a very refined mannerist work, representing three dancing graces holding a bronze vase. The monument was placed in the convent of the Celestins, which sheltered the hearts of France's deceased kings.[39] A sonnet by Ronsard, engraved on the foot of this sculpture, told the reader not

[36] The building fell into decay and was destroyed in 1719. Parts of the colonnade were transferred to the Parc Monceau in Paris, where they can still be seen.

[37] The tomb displayed nowadays in the north transept of Saint-Denis was reconstructed there in the early nineteenth century, and does not entirely reflect the original design (the pulpits of the *priants* have disappeared). For the tomb see: Lersch, *Die Grabkapelle der Valois*, pp. 19-22, 33-35, 46-53, 162-189. On the sculptures by Pilon, see: Lersch 'Remarques sur quelques sculptures'.

[38] Lersch, *Die Grabkapelle der Valois*, pp. 110-122. See also Cohen, *Metamorphosis of a Death Symbol*, pp. 133-181. The statue by Germain Pilon representing Saint Francis as a Capuchin monk suggests the influence of Henry III; see Lersch, 'Remarques sur quelques sculptures', pp. 104-107.

[39] The sculpture is now in the Musée du Louvre. See Bresc-Bautier, ed, *Germain Pilon*, pp. 16-21, 284-287; Lersch, *Die Grabkapelle der Valois*, p. 354. Catherine also commissioned a commemorative equestrian monument of Henry II from Michelangelo, who, however, declined in favour of Daniele da Volterra; see: Graham and McAllister Johnson, *Estienne Jodelle*, p. 152, plate 41.

to marvel that the heart of such a great king could be contained by a small vase, because Catherine carried his real heart in her breast.[40]

The Artemisia theme reoccurs in the iconography of the 1571 Parisian entry, where Artemisia can be found at the feet of Gallia/Catherine.[41] The *livret* and the accompanying poems refer to Artemisia as a model for Catherine's enterprise at Saint-Denis. The French sonnet gives a hint to Artemisia who literally incorporated the ashes of Mausolus, by suggesting that Henry II continued to live in the person of Catherine: *(...) Henri son espoux qui vit tousiours en elle*. In analogy to the historical Artemisia, Catherine had incorporated the royal power of the dead king,[42] a suggestion similar to the one made by Ronsard's poem on the monument for the heart of Henry II. The continuity of Henry's life through his widow, was one of the important aspects of the legitimisation of Catherine's political functions. Catherine's permanent emphasis on her widowhood was thus a means of suggesting that there had been no break after the premature death of Henry II, and that she was in fact continuing his reign.

The importance of continuity might also be an explanation for the strange phenomenon that after the death of Henry II and the expulsion of Diane de Poitiers, Catherine still used the H(enry)-C(atherine)/D(iane) monogram, consisting of an H with intertwined Cs, which can also be read as Ds. Before 1559, Henry and his mistress Diane shamelessly exploited the ambiguity of the H-C/D monogram.[43] For example, the famous marble sculpture of the goddess Diane, which ornamented Diane de Poitiers' castle, the *château d'Anet*, proudly bears the H-C/D monogram.[44] The *Salle de bal* in Fontainebleau, decorated during the lifetime of Henry II, is literally covered with the H-C/D monogram, crowned Hs and intertwined crescent moons, which could refer to the letter C, but more probably to the crescent moon worn by the goddess Diana, and thus to Diane de Poitiers. The same elements reoccur on the façade of the Henry II wing of the Louvre, whilst hunting scenes, deer crowned with the crescent moon, and, even more obviously, the goddess Diana herself decorate the interior.[45] The crescent moon in Henry II's *impresa*, with the motto

[40] Céard, Ménager and Simonin, eds, *Pierre de Ronsard*, II, p. 897. The engraving has disappeared.
[41] Graham and McAllister Johnson, *The Paris Entries of Charles IX*, plate 11; Yates, *Astrea*, p. 134, plate 20c, Von Haumeder, *Antoine Caron*, pp. 127-129.
[42] Gaehtgens, 'Machtwechsel oder die Übergabe Regentschaft', p. 69.
[43] Rondorf, *Der Ballsaal im Schloß Fontainebleau*, pp. 27-28; Bertière, *Les Reines de France au temps des Valois*, I, p. 345.
[44] For references on the *Diane d'Anet*, see Ruby, 'Diane de Poitiers', p. 256, note 16.
[45] Jenkins, 'The imagery of the Henri II Wing of the Louvre', p. 295; Thomson, *Renaissance Paris*, pp. 90-93; Prinz and Kecks, *Das französische Schloß der Renaissance*, pp. 466-478.

Donec totum impleat orbem, can also be read as a reference to Diane de Poitiers.[46]

After the death of Henry II, Catherine continued to use the H-C/D monogram,[47] in spite of its ambiguous nature. The monogram and crescent moons still decorate the castles of Fontainebleau and the Louvre: it must have been a deliberate strategy not to have them removed. More remarkably, the marble monument in Saint-Denis, mentioned earlier, representing the *gisants* of Henry and Catherine, bears the H-C/D monogram on Catherine's dress and on the bronze cushions. The same goes for the *colonne de l'Horoscope* which formerly belonged to Catherine's Hôtel de la Reine in Paris (it is now attached to the Bourse du Commerce), where the H-C/D monogram also reappears. Besides its function as an astronomical observatory, the column was also a memorial to the dead king and to Catherine's grief over her loss: it was covered with *fleurs de lys*, torn love knots and broken mirrors.[48] At first sight it is astonishing that Catherine should choose to use a device which unmistakably referred to her former rival.[49] Nevertheless, the legitimisation of her political power being based on the authority of the deceased king, a clear break in public imagery and symbolism would have been a great mistake. The use of the H-C/D monogram by Catherine may thus be seen as a conscious policy designed to underline the continuity of the reign of the king in the person of his widow. Moreover, the presentation of Catherine as the *nouvelle Artémise* is yet another sign of continuity, since 'Artémise' is also the name of the goddess Diane.[50]

Unlike other Renaissance rulers, Catherine did not use her *impresa* as an expression of her political power.[51] Just as with all her public imagery, it was

[46] Strong, *Art and Power*, p. 26; ffolliott, 'Casting a Rival into a Shade', p. 139. It can, however, also be read as a symbol of a catholic king fighting heresy. See McGowan, *Ideal Forms in the Age of Ronsard*, pp. 24-27; Lersch, *Die Grabkapelle der Valois*, p. 114. For political interpretations see also Rondorf, *Der Ballsaal im Schloß Fontainebleau*, pp. 25-27; Hoffmann, 'Donec totum impleat orbem'.

[47] See also: Bertière, *Les reines de France au temps des Valois*, I, p. 366. For the continuity of Diane de Poitiers's imagery in Catherine's public image, see ffolliott, 'Casting a Rival into a Shade'.

[48] Cloulas, *Catherine de Médicis*, p. 325; Madoni, 'L'hôtel de la Reine', pp. 121-123.

[49] On the *cartons* by Antoine Caron Catherine's monogram consists of back-to-back Ks, referring to Catherine and to Charles IX, see ffolliott, 'Catherine de' Medici', p. 234.

[50] Béguin, 'La suite d'Arthémise', p. 33; Ehrmann, *Antoine Caron*, p. 53; ffolliot 'Ca-therine de' Medici, pp. 232, 239, ffolliott, 'Casting a Rival into a Shade', p. 141.

[51] Catherine's *imprese* can be found in: Jacobus Typotius, *Symbola divina et humana pontificum imperialum regum* (Prague, 1601), nos XXVI and XXXVII. See also: Cloulas, *Catherine de Médicis*, pp. 66, 121-122; Strong, *Art and Power*, pp. 99-100; Bertière, *Les reines de France au temps de Valois*, I, p. 324; Von Haumeder, *Antoine*

first of all a remembrance of the deceased king. The image of a heap of chalk with drops of rain (or tears) falling on it, occurs most frequently. The accompanying text reads as follows: *Ardorem testantur/ Extincta vivere flamma*, which means that just as living chalk keeps burning once sprinkled with water, her love for Henry still burns after his death. Another *impresa* shows a broken lance with the text *Lacrymae hinc, hinc dolor*. Prior to 1559, Catherine's *impresa* had a completely different character: it showed the rainbow, or the sash of the goddess Iris, with in Greek the motto 'May light henceforth bring calm' (*ΦΩΣ ΦΕΡΟΙ ΗΔΕ ΓΑΛΗΝΗΝ*).[52] Later, during the court festivals, the Valois family and Catherine were again depicted as peacemakers for a France which was torn apart by the conflicts between Catholics and Huguenots.

Architecture and the grandeur of the queen

In her public image as the inconsolable widow, Catherine de Médicis carefully avoided presenting herself as a great and powerful ruler. Her modesty contrasts sharply with the enormous fortunes she spent on architecture and works of art. In particular, the architectural projects she initiated were primarily an expression of her greatness and that of the Valois kings, as with the burial chapel at Saint-Denis, discussed above.[53] Several of Catherine's ambitious building projects for royal residences were published by Jacques Androuet du Cerceau in his *Second volume des plus excellents bastiments de France* (Paris 1579), which was also dedicated to her.[54] The poet Ronsard, however, expressed his disapproval of the vast sums of money which were required for the Queen's residences in a poem to the treasurer of the French Crown:

> *... Il ne faut plus que la Royne batisse*
> *Ny que sa chaux nos trésors appetisse*
> *Molins suffit sans en bastir ailleurs.*
> *Peintres, Maçons, Engraveurs, Entailleurs*
> *Succent l'espargne avec leurs piperies.*
> *Mais que nous sert son lieu des Thuilleries?*

Caron, pp. 10-11. A whole series of *imprese*, all referring to Catherine's grief over her lost husband, were proposed to her by H. de Taffin, seigneur de Torsay (Paris, BnF, ms. fr. 10.451).

[52] See: Graham and McAllister Johnson, *Estienne Jodelle*, pp. 83-85, note 46, ill. 21 who translate: 'let it bring light and calm'.

[53] On Catherine's interest in architecture, see Cloulas, *Catherine de Médicis*, pp. 319-331; Knecht, *Catherine de' Medici*, pp. 288-233; Baudouin-Matuszek, ed, *Paris et Catherine de Médicis*.

[54] Another treatise on architecture was dedicated to Catherine by Philibert de L'Orme, *Architecture* (Paris, 1567).

De rien, Moreau: ce n'est que vanité;
Devant cent ans sera deshabité ....[55]

[The Queen must cease building,
her lime must stop swallowing our wealth.
Moulins will suffice without building elsewhere.
Painters, masons, engravers, stone carvers
drain the treasury with their deceits.
Of what use is the Tuileries to us?
None, Moreau; it is but vanity.
It will be deserted within a hundred years].

In the first half of the sixteenth century, Francis I and Henry II had already begun expanding the medieval Louvre into an impressive Renaissance building,[56] and naturally Catherine's architectural activities focused primarily on the traditional residence of French monarchy in the heart of Paris. After 1559 she had the architect Pierre Lescot, until his death in 1578, continue the work begun under her male predecessors on the west and the south wings of the Louvre.[57] Catherine's architectural zeal did not end here: in 1563 the queen commissioned a new residence for herself to the west of the Louvre on a piece of land called *Terra tegulariorum,* after the tile factories located here. At this place the château des Tuileries[58] was to be built, and the expanding costs of this ambitious project were those to which Ronsard referred in his poem. The square building around a courtyard was designed by Philibert de L'Orme,[59]

[55] *Au tresorier de l'espargne* (ca. 1573). Cf. Céard, Ménager and Simonin, eds, *Pierre de Ronsard*, II, p. 864. English translation by Knecht, *Catherine de' Medici*, p. 233.

[56] The literature covering the architectural history of the Louvre is too extensive to quote here. On the building activities of Francis I and Henry II in the Louvre, see most recently Thomson, *Renaissance Paris*, pp. 84-97; Prinz and Kecks, *Das französische Schloß der Renaissance*, pp. 365-479; Quoniam and Guinamard, *Le palais du Louvre*.

[57] For the works on the Louvre commissioned by Catherine de Médicis, see Thomson, *Renaissance Paris*, p. 165, Quoniam and Guinamard, *Le palais du Louvre*, pp. 54-61; Babelon, *Châteaux de France*, pp. 530-531.

[58] See Blunt, *Philibert de L'Orme*, pp. 91-107; Thomson, *Renaissance Paris*, pp. 165-171; Saintre fare Garnot and Jacquin, *Le château des Tuileries*, pp. 16-24; Jacquin, 'Les Tuileries'; Babelon, *Châteaux de France*, pp. 525-530; Pérouse de Montclos, *Philibert de L'Orme*, pp. 233-237.

[59] Blunt, *Philibert de L'Orme*, pp. 91-107, argues that the drawings in du Cerceau's *Second volume des plus excellents bastiments de la France* (1579) do not reflect the original design by de L'Orme. This seems to be confirmed by recent excavations; see Van Ossel, ed, *Les jardins du Caroussel*, pp. 314-331; yet, according to Pérouse de Montclos, *Philibert de l'Orme*, pp. 233-237, the double foundations indicate that the drawings by du Cerceau nevertheless reflect de L'Orme's original project for a building

who was succeeded by Jean Bullant after de L'Orme's death in 1570. Supervision of the building process was in the hands of one of Catherine's ladies-in-waiting, Marie-Catherine de Pierrevive.[60] Nevertheless, Ronsard was right in predicting the fate of the building: it was left unfinished and construction was halted in 1572. The Louvre was to be converted into an even more prestigious building by the addition of a gallery connecting it to the Tuileries. During Catherine's lifetime only the ground floor of the *Petite galerie* was completed, which could be reached from the *Pavillon du Roi* in the Louvre.[61] Around the palace of the Tuileries an extensive geometric garden[62] was laid out. The garden design included terraces, canals, fountains, and a *grotto*[63] decorated with glazed pottery representing shells and reptiles, designed by Bernard Palissy. Renaissance gardens had several connotations. Geometrical gardens could be read as a reflection of cosmic harmony. Gardens were also collections of botanical and zoological rarities, meant to impress visitors with the immense possessions and power of the owner, and, at the same time, gardens functioned also as a stage for courtly ceremonies.[64] In this spirit, the festival of 1573 for the Polish ambassadors took place in the Tuileries gardens.[65]

In 1572, the project for the château des Tuileries was abandoned, possibly due to a prediction that Catherine would die near Saint-Germain. The Tuileries were located there, and it is likely that the superstitious queen concluded that she should live elsewhere, although there could also have been other reasons for her decision. In 1570, she had already acquired a *hôtel* within the city walls, near the Louvre and the church of Saint-Eustache. On this site the Hôtel

with two oval courtyards.

[60] Cloulas, *Catherine de Médicis*, p. 219; Jacquin, 'Les Tuileries', pp. 89-90; Pérouse de Montclos, *Philibert de l'Orme*, p. 78.

[61] Thomson, *Renaissance Paris*, pp. 171-174; Pérouse de Montclos, *Philibert de l'Orme*, pp. 223-224.

[62] Jacquin, 'Les Tuileries', pp. 95-97.

[63] For symbolic and literary connotations of Renaissance *grotti*, see Liebenwein, *Studiolo*, p. 126.

[64] Boucher, *Société et mentalités autour de Henri III*, vol. 2, pp. 808-810. For Renaissance gardens, their symbolism and their functions, see Comito, *The Idea of the Garden in the Renaissance*; Prinz and Kecks, *Das französische Schloß der Renaissance*, pp. 331-349; Strong, *The Renaissance Garden*, pp. 9-22; Woodbridge, *Princely Gardens*; Cunningham, 'The Culture of Gardens'; Guillaume, ed, *Architecture, jardin, paysage*. Catherine's gardens can be seen as royal collections of *naturalia*. I intend to publish elsewhere a study on Catherine's interest in collections: the maps and *naturalia* in the Hôtel de la Reine (see below) are also a scientific collection in the tradition of the *studiolo* or *Kunst- und Wunderkammer*.

[65] For Catherine's gardens as location of the *magnificences* see Woodbridge, *Princely Gardens*, pp. 77-83.

de la Reine was to be built.[66] In order to be able to erect a residence worthy of a queen, she moved the women of the convent of the *Filles repenties* to another location and annexed other surrounding housings, all of which were demolished. The first design by Jean Bullant could not be executed because it exceeded her financial possibilities, but the final building nevertheless comprised three huge central pavilions joining two *corps de logis*. The colonne de l'Horoscope, mentioned earlier, a tall doric column without precedent in French architecture, was located in the interior courtyard and could be entered from the Hôtel. The pavilions looked out over a spacious garden with terraces, a large water basin and a fountain, orange trees, and an aviary. The central pavilion had an arched passage which led to a second, smaller garden. Here the visitor could admire a marble water basin adorned with a statue of Venus, possibly sculpted by Jean Goujon.[67] Inside the Hôtel Catherine amassed an enormous collection of tapestries, paintings, enamels, maps, and *naturalia*. She even had a *cabinet des miroirs,* covered with 120 mirrors from Venice – an early version of Louis XIV's famous *galerie des glaces* in Versailles.[68]

Catherine's architectural activities were not limited to the city of Paris; the residences of the French kings in Blois and Fontainebleau were also embellished during her reign. In Blois she had an arched gallery added to the wing built by Francis I,[69] and in Fontainebleau, the focal point of French Renaissance art and architecture under Francis I, she ordered several new constructions.[70] In 1559, the architect Philibert de L'Orme was replaced by Primaticcio. Under the direction of the latter, the *Pavillion des Poêles* was transformed into the *Aile des reines mères* (1564-1566). It is highly significant that Catherine chose this wing as her personal residence, because the apartments of the late Henry II had been there. It is yet another sign that the queen-mother wished to stress that she was continuing the reign of the deceased king. For the young king Charles IX, the north wing of the *Cour du Donjon* was doubled (1565-1571) and a completely new wing was added between the *Cour de la Fontaine* and the *Chaussée de l'étang* (1568(?)-1571). Catherine also commissioned for Charles IX a new iconographical programme for the

[66] On the Hôtel de la Reine, see Cloulas, *Catherine de Médicis*, pp. 323-332; Thomson, *Renaissance Paris*, pp. 174-178; Madoni, 'L'hôtel de la Reine'; Boudon, *et al.* eds, *Système de l'architecture urbaine*, pp. 21, 181, 184-191, 195, 217, 224-232, 240, 261, plate 27.

[67] Bonnaffé, *Inventaire des meubles de Catherine de Médicis*, p. 153, note 3.

[68] Bonnaffé, *Inventaire des meubles de Catherine de Médicis*, p. 156.

[69] Prinz and Kecks, *Das französische Schloß*, p. 366; Babelon, *Châteaux de France*, p. 116.

[70] For Fontainebleau during Catherine's lifetime, see Verle-Samoyault, 'Fontainebleau'; Samoyault, 'Le château de Fontainebleau'; Boudon, *Le château de Fontainebleau*, pp. 65-73, 192-194.

Chambre du Roi, painted by the Italian artist Nicolò dell'Abbate.[71] Another work designed by Primaticcio for Catherine was a wooden gallery, which was placed in the garden just in front of the *Galerie François Ier*. The structure was decorated with wooden statues representing the Olympic gods, made by Germain Pilon and Domenico Fiorentino. Furthermore, Catherine possessed a decorated pavilion in the forest of Fontainebleau, designed by Primaticcio, known as *La vacherie* or *Mi-Voye*, which was used during the *magnificences* at Fontainebleau in 1564.[72]

Outside Paris Catherine personally possessed residences in Saint-Maur-les-Fossés[73] and in Montceaux,[74] but she preferred the charming castle of Chenonceaux built over the river Cher.[75] It was given by her husband to Diane de Poitiers, but in 1560, shortly after the king's death, Catherine forced Diane to cede Chenonceaux to her in exchange for the castle of Chaumont. Philibert de L'Orme invented a grandiose scheme in order to change Chenonceaux into an immense residence:[76] it included a vast forefront with colonnades and sculptures on the north side, and a gallery which was to be built over the bridge over the Cher, built earlier for Diane de Poitiers. The plans, once again, exceeded Catherine's financial resources and only parts of the new façade and the gallery were actually built. Nevertheless, here again a richly adorned Renaissance garden was laid out, including waterfalls, fountains, a *grotto*, an aviary, a *bergerie*, and mulberry trees for the production of silk. This garden, too, was to become the decor of several court festivals, in 1560, 1563 and 1577.

[71] Béguin, 'Remarques sur la chambre du Roi', pp. 216-225.

[72] Boucher, *Société et mentalités autour de Henri III*, vol. 2, p. 817; Graham and McAllister Johnson, eds, *The Royal Tour of France*, p. 75; Boudon, *Le château de Fontainebleau*, p. 262; Pérouse de Montclos, *Philibert de l'Orme*, pp. 299-300.

[73] Designed by the architect Philibert de L'Orme; see Blunt, *Philibert de l'Orme*, pp. 89-91; Joudiau, 'De Meudon à Saint-Maur'; Babelon, *Châteaux de France*, pp. 522-525; Pérouse de Montclos, *Philibert de l'Orme*, pp. 338-341.

[74] Babelon, *Châteaux de France*, p. 691-695; Pérouse de Montclos, *Philibert de l'Orme*, pp. 316-318.

[75] For Chenonceaux and Catherine de Médicis, see Blunt, *Art and Architecture in France 1500-1700*, p. 94; Cloulas, *Les châteaux de la Loire*, pp. 134-148, 197-228, 251-258. For the architectural history of Chenonceaux, see Blunt, *Philibert de l'Orme*, pp. 61-64; Prinz and Kecks, *Das französische Schloß der Renaissance*, pp. 525-532; Babelon, *Châteaux de France*, pp. 598-602; Pérouse de Montclos, *Philibert de l'Orme*, pp. 287-290.

[76] The drawings in du Cerceau's *Excellents bastiments* do not reflect the original designs according to Blunt, *Philibert de l'Orme*, pp. 89-91.

Court festivals and politics

Since medieval times, European courts entertained themselves during special occasions with music, dance, banquets, tournaments, and jousting parties. These festive events gradually became more sumptuous and spectacular at the Burgundian court of the fifteenth century. Later, at the court of Francis I, Italian Renaissance *triomfi*, *apparati* and *intermezzi* merged with the existing French-Burgundian tradition.[77] The new fashion of so-called 'musique mesurée', another influence from Italy, enabled the artists to create theatrical performances with sung lyrics, because the audience could now understand the texts without problem.[78] The apogee of sixteenth-century French court festivals was without any doubt reached by Catherine de Médicis: she organised stunning *magnificences* and used them as a part of her internal and external politics.

Because of the tragic death of Henry II at a jousting party, Catherine tried as much as possible to suppress violent chivalric confrontations. Under Catherine's direction, the theatrical side of the court festivals was especially elaborated: these included dramatised tournaments (*tournoi à thème*), theatrical spectacles with sometimes ingenious stage machinery and fireworks, and *ballets de cour* drawing on cosmological symbolism. These *magnificences* were multimedia events where famous artists from different disciplines collaborated closely: poets, painters, sculptors, composers and choreographers. The artists drew primarily on classicising themes and motives, but traditional medieval elements continued to occur.

Catherine used the court festivals as a political instrument.[79] They were intended to impress, to assure loyalty to the French crown, and to reconcile competing political factions. The audience, and frequently also the actors of

[77] The historical forerunners of court festivals are discussed in: Yates, *The Valois Tapestries*, pp. 51-52, Strong, *Art and Power*, pp. 3-62; Rüegger, *Le spectacle total à la Renaissance*, pp. 19-126. For the court festivals of the sixteenth century, see Prunières, *Le ballet de cour en France*; Prunières, 'Ronsard et les Fêtes de cour'; Yates, *French Academies in the 16th Century*, pp. 236-274, and *The Valois Tapestries*, pp. 51-129; McGowan, *L'Art du ballet de cour en France* and *Ideal Forms in the Age of Ronsard*, pp. 209-241; Strong, *Splendour at Court*, pp. 11-78, and *Art and Power*, pp. 98-125; Graham and McAllister Johnson, eds, *The Royal Tour*, pp. 23-70; Rüegger, *Le spectacle total à la Renaissance*.

[78] See for example the *livret* of the festivities in Bayonne: ... *le ton et chant [...] estoit si bien accomodé aux paroles, qu'on entendoit tout ce qu'il recitoit, comme s'il eust parlé, et n'en perdoit on une seule syllabe, tant il prononçoit nettement et distinctement, accordant sa voix à la lyre parfaictement* (Anon., *Recueil des choses*, p. 357).

[79] Mariéjol, *Catherine de Médicis*, p. 144; Yates, *French Academies in the 16th Century* p. 251, and *The Valois Tapestries*, p. 52; Strong, *Splendour at Court*, pp. 121-167; Solnon, *La cour de France*, pp. 127-133.

the *magnificences* consisted of court members. In this way the message was communicated to the high nobility and to the leaders of competing factions, and at the same time the hierarchy of the court could be made explicit. The king was unmistakably the central focus point of attention, but the court festivals were mostly an expression of Catherine's political intentions. Influenced by Italian Neo-Platonism, the classicising and historical themes of the *magnificences* represented the French king symbolically and allegorically as bringer of peace and harmony, the Valois dynasty assuring the unity of France.[80] At the same time the French king was represented as a ruler over the entire world and as the centre of the universe. This royal propaganda was not intended solely for French internal politics: on several occasions, the *magnificences* were intended to impress foreign forces.

A visual impression of the *magnificences* can still be obtained through a series of eight tapestries now in the Uffizi in Florence,[81] and six drawings attributed to Antoine Caron.[82] The drawings probably served as models for some of the tapestries. The tapestries and drawings cannot, however, be considered as eye-witness accounts of the *magnificences*: they were based upon secondary sources and represent different events in one single frame as if they were happening simultaneously.[83] Not all the events represented visually can be identified with the help of textual sources, such as, for example, the painting by Antoine Caron of a nocturnal festival with an elephant, for which no other documentation has yet come to light.[84]

The festival at Chenonceaux, in April 1563 was the first of the political *magnificences*.[85] It was intended to celebrate the recently restored peace with

[80] See especially: Crouzet, *La nuit de la Saint-Barthélemy*, pp. 183-263, who also argues that the violence of St. Bartholomew's night ended the utopian political idea of 'la divine monarchie d'Amour' (546). Nevertheless, an examination of the later festivals reveals that the theme of the French king as the restorer of peace remained a leading idea.

[81] On these tapestries see the study by Yates, *The Valois Tapestries*, although her interpretations have given rise to much debate.

[82] Yates, *The Valois Tapestries*, pp. 3-5, plates IX-XII; Strong, *Art and Power*, pp. 100-101; Graham and McAllister Johnson, eds, *The Royal Tour*, pp. 59-67, plates 2, 7, 24, 25, 26.

[83] For this critique, see: Strong, *Art and Power*, pp. 100-102.

[84] The painting is now in Paris, private collection. For a reproduction, see Yates, *The Valois Tapestries*, plate XII.

[85] The Chenonceaux *magnificences* are not very well documented. A sixteenth-century description can be found on f. 329 of manuscript Paris, BnF, fr. 15.881. For a reproduction of the text, see Boulay de la Meurthe, 'Entrée de Charles IX', pp. 184-189. See also Cloulas, *Les châteaux de la Loire au temps de la Renaissance*, pp. 209-215; Strong, *Splendour at Court*, p. 131, and *Art and Power*, p. 103; Woodbridge, *Princely Gardens*, p. 82.

the edict of Amboise and to welcome the new king Charles IX. Catherine's *filles d'honneur* appeared on several occasions, disguised as singing sirens and nymphs who were saved from attacking satyrs by knights of the court. Other festive events included fireworks, a masked ball, a musical pastorale, a naval combat on the river Cher, and finally a mascarade including six knights in women's clothes. The Chenonceaux festival seems to have been a seminal one, because several of its themes were used again during later *magnificences*.

Another three court festivals with political intentions took place during the royal tour of France (1564-1566), which Catherine undertook in order to present the kingdom to Charles IX.[86] The first festival took place at Fontainebleau and lasted from 6 to 15 February 1564.[87] The festivities at Fontainebleau aimed to represent the young king as a great ruler of France and as the world monarch. The *festin* offered on Monday 14 February by the duc d'Orléans, Charles's brother Édouard-Alexandre, is the most complex and best documented of the *magnificences* at Fontainebleau. Upon entering his brother's residence, Charles was received by singing sirens in one of the canals, who hailed him as the new king of France. Later Jupiter appeared in another canal and offered him his chariot, his trident and the dominion over the seas. The theme of the French king as future world ruler reappeared after dinner, when one of three classical goddesses, Juno, brought him a golden globe, symbolising world dominion. After this there was a combat between two groups of six knights from the court dressed as Greeks and Trojans. They brought with them a letter asking the king to liberate Greece from the enemies of the true faith, so that his brother Édouard-Alexandre, could become king of Greece, and Charles could rule over the entire world. The *festin* was closed by a dramatised siege: three ladies were imprisoned in a tower and could only be liberated by two knights chosen for their descent and courage: Charles and Edouard-Alexandre. Another dramatised siege took place the following day

[86] The main contemporary source is: Abel Jouan, *Recueil et discours du voyage du roy Charles IX* (Paris, 1566). The best study, documented with editions of all surviving primary sources, is Graham and McAllister Johnson, eds, *The Royal Tour*. See also Champion, *Catherine de Médicis*; Boutier, Dewerpe and Nordman, *Un tour de France royal*; see also Vaucheret, 'Les fêtes de cour'. The tour might have been inspired by the systematic visits of Francis I to the provinces of France in the years 1516-1521 and 1531-1534. Cf. Knecht, *Renaissance Warrior and Patron*, p. 129.

[87] The most important sources for this festival are Abel Jouan, *Recueil et discours du voyage du roy Charles IX* and the anonymous *Le Recueil des triumphes et magnificences* [...] *à Fontainebleau*. Description and references to other sixteenth-century sources in: Yates, *French Academies*, pp. 251-253, and *The Valois Tapestries*, pp. 53-54; Strong, *Splendour at Court*, pp. 131-132, and *Art and Power*, pp. 103-105; Graham and McAllister Johnson, eds, *The Royal Tour*, pp. 24-29; Rüegger, *Le spectacle total à la Renaissance*, pp. 109-110, 147-153.

when the king himself offered his *festin*. Here an enchanted castle was attacked and defended by different groups of knights from the court. It is highly significant that the knights defending the castle were grouped around the leader of the Protestants, the prince de Condé, while two of the attacking groups were led by the most fanatic Catholics: the duc de Guise and the duc de Nevers. It is obvious that the Valois family tried to use the *magnificences* as a symbolic though harmless battleground between opposing factions.

During the first days of May 1564 the court made a stop at Bar-le-Duc, where a festival took place to celebrate the baptism of the new-born son of the duc de Lorraine and Charles's sister Claude. No *livret* was published for these festivities, but they are nevertheless interesting because of a masquerade written by Ronsard, which represented the four elements and their planets disputing over the question of which one of them was most appropriate to pay tribute to Charles IX. The discussion was ended by Jupiter, who offered to share the universe with the French king, reserving for himself the skies and leaving the earth to Charles.[88]

The third and most magnificent festival of the royal tour took place in Bayonne from 19 to 25 June 1565 on the occasion of the negotiations between France and Spain over the Council of Trent.[89] With these *magnificences* Catherine intended to impress the Spaniards with the wealth and power of the French crown, and to dissuade Philip II from attacking France, as he had threatened to do because of the French Crown's tolerance of the Protestant heretics. The negotiations were not a great success, for Philip did not deign to come to France. Only his wife, Catherine's daughter Élisabeth (Isabeau), and the duke of Alva travelled to Bayonne. Nevertheless, the festivities did take place, with great pomp and circumstance. Apart from the entries, dances and jousting parties, the meeting at Bayonne included four major *fêtes*. On 19 June, the tournament of nations took place in honour of the two queens, Catherine and her daughter Élisabeth. The knights of the French court appeared disguised

[88] Céard, Ménager and Simonin, eds, *Pierre de Ronsard*, II, pp. 239-242. See also Prunières, 'Ronsard et les fêtes de cour', p. 33; Cloulas, *Catherine de Médicis*, p. 196; Graham and McAllister Johnson, eds, *The Royal Tour*, pp. 23-24, 83; Rüegger, *Le spectacle total à la Renaissance*, p. 110; Simonin, 'Ronsard à Bar-le-duc'. The festivities also included a *Bergerie* by Rémy Belleau.

[89] The most important contemporary sources the anonymous pieces *Le Recueil des choses notables qui ont esté faites à Bayonne* and *Li grandissimi apparati e reali Trionfi* [...] *nella Citta di Baiona*. Description and references to other primary sources in: Yates, *French Academies*, pp. 253-254, and *The Valois Tapestries*, pp. 55-60; McGowan, *L'Art du ballet de cour en France*, pp. 40-41; Strong, *Splendour at Court*, pp. 133-238, and *Art and Power*, pp. 105-109; Graham and McAllister Johnson, eds, *The Royal Tour*, pp. 29-57; Rüegger, *Le spectacle total à la Renaissance*, pp. 111-112, 153-159.

as warriors and ladies from different nations, thus suggesting that the whole world had come to pay tribute to Charles IX. The Gauls were all in women's clothes, because, as the *cartel* explained, the women of Gaul being too proud, the men decided to live as women. The real message emphasised the power of Catherine and Élisabeth: the two Queens from France had the heart and the courage of a man, or, in the words of the *cartel*:

> *Dames, quant est au corps, et, quant au courage, hommes,*
> *Hommes, quant à la force, et quant au reste, Dames*
> *Dames quant aux façons, et hommes, quant aux armes.*[90]
>
> [Ladies in body, men in courage,
> men in strength, and for the rest, ladies.
> Ladies in manners, and men in fighting].

During the festivities on the evening of 21 June the theme of the enchanted castle was used again: Peace, imprisoned by Merlin's magic, could only be rescued by the most perfect prince, who could also restore peace to the Christian world and render the Christian faith more prosperous than ever. This prince was of course Charles IX, and the underlying message in this time of religious conflicts is clear. Another message of this complicated *fête* was addressed to Élisabeth by a fay: six nymphs who refused to love had by way of punishment been changed into trees. They could only be revived through peace and love between France and Spain. This message was emphasised even more during the *fête* on an island in the river Adour on 23 June, offered by Catherine. The guests first saw a nautical spectacle with a whale, a sea turtle with musicians disguised as tritons on its back, Neptune, Arion, and singing sirens. Neptune had come from the seas to greet the great king Charles IX. The central message of this *festin*, however, was the fraternal love between Charles and Élisabeth, which assured peace between France and Spain. This was underlined another time during the pastoral amusements which followed at the island:

> *Tant que vivra Philippe et Isabeau*
> *Tant que vivra Charles et Catherine*
> *Ny l'Espagnol ny le François troupeau*
> *Craindra le Nord ny sa fraiche bruïne*
> *Tant que seront ces quatre d'un accord*
> *Entre bergiers il n'y aura discord.*[91]

[90] *Recueil des choses notables*, p. 341.
[91] *Recueil des choses notables*, p. 377.

[As long as Philip and Elisabeth live,
and as long as Charles and Catherine live,
neither the Spanish and French flocks
will have to fear the northern wind, nor its cool rain,
as long as those four will agree with one another,
there will be no discord among shepherds].

The theme of the closing tournament on 25 June, between the knights of 'Bretagne la Grande' and Ireland, was a dispute over Virtue and Love. Charles led the knights of 'Bretagne la Grande' who pleaded in favour of Virtue, while his brother, the duc d'Orléans, chose for the Irish knights who stood for Love. The knights from both groups offered their ladies golden medals with emblematic inscriptions. These medals are fully described and depicted in the *livret*, a clear sign that the French royal family wished to show off its wealth and learning. The two groups of knights were preceded by two chariots, one with the Five Virtues, the other with the three Graces, Venus and Celestial Love. The latter declared in a song that he was the source of all virtue. The tournament culminated in a ballet of the mounted knights with fireworks, possibly referring to the Neo-Platonic concept of harmony between divine and earthly love. This tournament might have been meant as a reminder for Élisabeth that the love for her family ought to weigh more heavily than opposing political viewpoints.

Nearly seven years later, another set of political *magnificences* took place. These were in honour of the marriage of Catherine's daughter Marguerite de Valois and the Protestant Henry de Navarre.[92] The festivities began on 17 August 1572 and were interrupted on 23 August due to the assassination of the Protestant leader de Coligny and the massacres of Protestants which followed. This was most likely also the reason that no *livret* was published. Other records describe that on Monday, the day after the marriage, the king, the Protestant bridegroom and the leader of the Catholics, the duc de Guise, took part in an indoor marine spectacle and ballet where Charles IX played the role of Neptune. More is known about the *Paradis d'Amour*, a theatrically staged combat which took place on Wednesday 20 August. Charles and his two brothers defended the gate of Paradise against the attacks of the bridegroom

[92] There is no *livret* for this festival. For a description and references to primary sources, voir: Yates, *French Academies*, pp. 254-256, and *The Valois Tapestries*, pp. 61-67; McGowan, *L'Art du ballet de cour en France*, p. 41; Cloulas, *Catherine de Médicis*, pp. 284-285; Strong, *Splendour at Court*, pp. 149-150, and *Art and Power*, pp. 111-115; Rüegger, *Le spectacle total à la Renaissance* , pp. 112-113, 159-160, Crouzet, *La nuit de la Saint-Barthélemy*, pp. 355-371.

and the other Protestants. The latter were defeated by the king and enclosed in an infernal place, called *le Tartare*. While the Protestants were suffering there, a singing Mercury and Cupid descended from the heavens and reminded the Valois brothers of the virtues of Love. The king, his brothers and a group of twelve nymphs from the Elysian fields danced a geometrically choreographed ballet, after which they freed the Protestants. The political message of this spectacle is unequivocal: the French Crown wished to subdue the Protestants, and at the same time the performance expressed the pacifying power of love.

In September 1573 Catherine organised another festival for representatives of foreign countries.[93] These *magnificences* were in honour of the Polish ambassadors who had come to Paris to offer the Polish Crown to Catherine's third son, Henry (formerly Édouard-Alexandre). The festivities included a royal entry of the new Polish king into Paris and several tournaments. The most impressive event was the spectacle offered by Catherine in the gardens of the Tuileries. The recurring themes are Catherine as mother of three crowned sons and the religious peace that the Valois dynasty brought to France. The audience was dazed by the entrance of eighteen nymphs representing Gallia and the provinces of France seated on a huge silver rock decorated with precious stones and shells. The rock was an ingenious piece of machinery: it could move and it was also possible to rotate the different levels. The nymphs offered to the audience medals with emblems based on the region they represented. The symbolism of the emblems emphasised the religous peace brought to France by the Valois family. For example, the emblem of the first nymph (Provence) represented an apple tree and a lemon tree growing from one stem with the Latin motto *Quocumque volent concordia ducet* (Concord will guide them, wherever they may want to go), symbolising the religious tolerance established in France by Valois reign. This message was undoubtedly destined for the Polish ambassadors, a large number of whom were of the Protestant faith. After this scene, the nymphs danced a complicated choreography designed by the Italian Balthasar de Beaujoyeulx (Baltazare di Belgioioso). The descriptions and woodcut in the *livret* indicate that the dancing nymphs formed geometrical patterns according to the new Italian style. According to sixteenth-century dance theories, these geometrical patterns both reflected the harmony of the moving heavens and brought harmony to the terrestrial sphere.[94]

[93] *Livret*: Jean Dorat, *Magnificentissimi spectaculi a Regina Regum matre in hortis suburbanis editi* (Paris, 1573), repr. in: Rüegger, *Le spectacle total à la Renaissance*. Description and references to other primary sources: Yates, *The Valois Tapestries*, pp. 67-72; McGowan, *L'Art du ballet de cour en France* , pp. 41-42; Strong, *Splendour at Court*, pp. 151-153 and *Art and Power*, pp. 114-115; Rüegger, *Le spectacle total*, pp. 114, 160-163.

[94] McGowan, *L'Art du ballet de cour en France*, pp. 17-22, and *Ideal Forms in the*

After the premature death of Charles IX in 1574, his brother returned from Poland to become king of France as Henry III. At first glance, the court festivals organised by Catherine's third son would seem to have been less oriented towards political goals, and more towards entertainment and extravagance. On 15 May 1577, the king organised a transvestite banquet in the gardens of Plessis-les-Tours,[95] and on June, 9 of the same year Catherine organised a banquet at Chenonceaux, where her ladies-in-waiting appeared half nude and with loose hair.[96] One must, however, be reluctant to qualify these festivals as sexual excesses. Travesty was an accepted part of the sixteenth-century court festivals and could even have virtuous connotations, as for example during the *magnificences* of Bayonne, discussed earlier, where one of the *cartels* stated: *Et que changeant de corps le cuer ne change point* (The heart stays the same when the body changes).[97] The same can be said of the topless ladies: the numerous portraits of half nude ladies by the School of Fontainebleau do not have sexual connotations, but refer rather to virtuous concepts, such as marriage and fertility.[98] Catherine's group of beautiful and seductive *filles d'honneur* has also been associated too easily with sexuality by modern scholarship.[99] No doubt love and seduction played an important role in the life of Catherine's court: she used her ladies to appease male opponents and some of her ladies did have love affairs, but one should not forget that

Age of Ronsard, pp. 234-241; Strong, *Art and Power*, pp. 59-61; Rüegger, *Le spectacle total à la Renaissance*, pp. 142-143, 166.

95 The often repeated suggestion that the *Isle des hermaphrodites* (published in 1605), attributed to Artus Thomas, is a condemnation of the cross-gender dressing of this banquet is not correct and is based on an unfounded assumption by Pierre Bayle; it is much more likely that the author wanted to criticise the attitudes of the Libertins in this first French anti-Utopian text. See the introduction to the edition by Dubois (pp. 17-25). It would be too restrictive to characterise Henry III's reign solely by its extravagances. Henry also gave evidence of an enormous religious zeal by organising and participating in elaborate processions and penitences. See: Yates, *Astrea*, pp. 173-207.

96 For these two banquets, see Cloulas, *Catherine de Médicis*, pp. 405-406, and *Les Châteaux de la Loire au temps de la Renaissance*, pp. 249-251; Bertière, *Les Reines de France*, vol. 2, pp. 280, 315; Boucher, *Société et mentalités autour de Henri III*, vol. III, p. 1182.

97 *Recueil des choses notables*, p. 341. For the same point, see Boucher, *La cour de Henri III*, pp. 25-26, 119, 122. The colour green of the Plessis-les-Tours banquet does not stand for folly, as suggested earlier, but refers to Catherine's colours before the death of Henry II (green and white) and to hope. Cf. Graham and McAllister Johnson, *Estienne Jodelle*, p. 121, note 122.

98 An example is the portrait of Gabrielle d'Estrée and her sister (1594), now in the Louvre.

99 On Catherine's ladies-in-waiting, see Mariéjol, *Catherine de Médicis*, pp. 142-144; Cloulas, *Catherine de Médicis*, pp. 189, 353-354, 357, 389, 546; Knecht, *Catherine de' Medici*, pp. 235-236; Bertière, *Les Reines de France*, vol. 2, pp. 99-102.

according to sixteenth-century perception, strongly influenced by Neo-Platonic philosophy, earthly love was virtuous because it helped the elevation of the soul to divine love. Besides, Catherine's ladies-in-waiting were not the just beautiful decorations of an exuberant court life, but they fulfilled official political functions. For example, Claude de Beaune was *trésorière*,[100] and Marie-Catherine de Pierrevive, already mentioned above, was charged with the supervision of the building process of the Tuileries. In fact, Catherine had a female version of the royal household typical of a sixteenth-century king. This is illustrated by an eighteenth-century manuscript copy of a sixteenth-century original, listing the royal households of Henry II, Catherine de Médicis, Francis II, Charles IX, and Henry III,[101] which reveals that Catherine's ladies-in-waiting had the same functions as the male government officials of her husband and sons.

A festival expressing political propaganda for Henry III's reign took place in September and October 1581 on the occasion of the marriage of his favourite, Anne de Joyeuse to Marguerite de Lorraine, half-sister of queen Louise.[102] Unlike his brother Charles, Henry was initially much more oriented towards the fanatically anti-Huguenot family de Guise, from which he had chosen his queen. Nevertheless, an important theme of these *magnificences* was the pacifying power of love, expressing Catherine's policy of pacification. She participated personally in the preparations, and even planned to offer a fête herself; however, because of delays in the preparations, it was postponed to a later date.[103] The festivities lasted for over a fortnight and included the usual chivalric exercises, a horse ballet, a mock combat against and in defence of Love, and a marine combat between the king and the dukes De Guise and Mercœur. The Joyeuse wedding also seems to have been a celebration of the French king as the centre of the universe: one of the festivities was an evening combat between the knights of the sun and the moon, decorated by an ingenious machinery representing the turning planets and heavens. Here Henry III entered the hall on a chariot *comme un grand soleil estival*.[104]

[100] Cloulas, *Catherine de Médicis*, p. 191. It was Anne de Bretagne who introduced female courtiers to the French court. See: Solnon, *La cour de France*, pp. 22-27.

[101] Paris, BnF, ms fr. 7854.

[102] A program for the Joyeuse magnificences is preserved in Paris, BnF, ms. fr. 15.831, f. 90, reprinted in: Yates, 'Poésie et musique dans les magnificences'. For a description and references to primary sources, see: Yates, *French Academies*, pp. 236-251, *Astrea*, pp. 149-172 and *The Valois Tapestries*, pp. 82-88; McGowan, *L'Art du ballet de cour en France*, pp. 42-47, and *Balthazar Beaujoyeulx*: 'introduction'; Strong, *Splendour at Court*, pp. 153-163, and *Art and Power*, pp. 116-122; Rüegger, *Le spectacle total à la Renaissance*, pp. 12-14.

[103] Yates, *Astrœe*, p. 172; Strong, *Art and Power*, p. 119.

[104] The poem by Dorat is cited in Yates, *Astrœa*, p. 164. The sun symbolism had also

The best documented fête of the Joyeuse wedding is the *Ballet comique de la Royne* of 15 October,[105] officially offered by queen Louise, but in fact a continuation of the festival culture created by Catherine de Médicis. One side of the rectangular *grande salle de Bourbon* in the Louvre was occupied by an artificial garden with a view in mathematical perspective. The king and queen mother sat on the opposite side of the hall. The plot of the fête was centred around the enchantress Circe, who stood for change, disorder, mixed elements, and moral corruption.[106] A man came out of the artificial garden, explained in a *harangue* to the king that he was held prisoner by Circe and implored the king to rescue him. Tritons and sirens sang lyrics and a dialogue in the new *musique mesurée*, but most spectacular was the entrance of a huge fountain in gold and silver, crowned by dolphins holding water basins with their tails. In the construction, queen Louise, the bride, and other ladies of the court were seated, dressed as naiads. They started to dance a ballet, forming geometrical patterns. Just when they had formed a crescent moon,[107] Circe came out of her garden, enraged, and immobilised the dancers. The next episode started with loud thunder from the ceiling, accompanying the descent of Mercury from the skies. He succeeded in reviving the ballet, but Circe petrified the ballet a second time, and captured Mercury. The following *intermède* was performed by land creatures – satyrs, driads and Pan – who sang lyrics in *musique mesurée*. During the third *intermède,* the four cardinal virtues invoked the assistance of Minerva, who finally succeeded in vanquishing Circe with the help of the four virtues and Jupiter, who came down from the ceiling accompanied by loud thunder. Jupiter handed over the golden magic wand of Circe to Henry III, and the gods kneeled before the king and the queen mother. Finally, queen Louise and the naiads danced the *grand ballet*, after which they offered golden medals with emblematic inscriptions to the audience.

This complicated *Ballet comique* has several levels of meaning. The defeat of Circe by the combined forces of the four virtues, Minerva and Jupiter stands for the victory of virtue over vice and voluptuousness. The geometrical ballet of the naiads gives expression to the struggle between order and disorder, a battle won by the harmony of virtue. At a political level, the *Ballet*

been used for Charles IX during the entries into Toulouse and especially into La Rochelle. See Graham and McAllister Johnson, eds, *The Royal Tour*, pp. 16, 126, 274. For even earlier examples (Louis XII and Henry II), see: McGowan, *Ideal Forms in the Age of Ronsard*, pp. 19-20.

[105] McGowan, *Balthazar Beaujoyeulx*.

[106] The allegorical meaning of Circe is given in the *livret*; cf. McGowan, *Balthazar Beaujoyeulx*, ff. 74^r-75^v.

[107] The crescent moon fits well in the cosmological symbolism of the Joyeuse *magnificences*, but it might also be a reference to the *impresa* of Henry II.

comique identifies Henry as *Iupiter de France.*[108] Thus it is Henry who vanquishes vice and disorder, not only in the mythological world of the ballet, but also in France, where he restores the golden age of peace. This is also expressed by the lyrics:

> *... O bien heureux encor sous ces princes la terre*
> *O bien heureux aussy le nauire Francoys*
> *Esclairé de ses feux, bien heureuses leurs loix*
> *Qui banniront d'icy les vices & la guerre.*[109]
>
> [Blessed is the earth under their princes,
> blessed is the ship of France
> by the light of its torches, blessed are their laws
> which will banish vice and war from here].

In spite of Henry III's increasing political and financial problems during the last decade of his reign, and consequently, his growing unpopularity, he and the royal family continued to spend great fortunes on marriage festivities and court festivals.[110] Unfortunately, these occasions are less well documented than the *Ballet comique de la Royne.* Catherine organised for the *mardi gras* of 1580 probably her last banquet and ballet with political intentions in the Hôtel de la Reine, attended by Henry III and a large number of foreign ambassadors. The ballet represented Portuguese and Spaniards involved in a game of love and war, implying that the Iberian peoples should be united in harmony and not by the arms of Philip II.[111] Here the French king danced a ballet which spelled out his name and that of Elisabeth I, in order to express the entente between England and France.

[108] McGowan, *Balthazar Beaujoyeulx*, f. 55^r. Minerva is more ambiguous. She could be the queen mother, who is Pallas according to the dedication to the king. However, another poem states that queen Louise is Minerva (f. aiij, f. ej).

[109] McGowan, *Balthazar Beaujoyeulx*, f. 49^v-51^r.

[110] For court festivals organised during the reign of Henry III see: Boucher, *Société et mentalités autour de Henri III*, vol. I, pp. 385-394, vol. II, pp. 789, vol. III, pp. 1049-1115.

[111] Boucher, *La cour de Henri III*, p. 116, and *Société et mentalités autour de Henri III*, vol. 2, p. 787; vol. 3, pp. 1072-1073. Among the last political festivals of the Valois were the feasts in February and March 1585, organised in honour of the Protestant English knights who had come to Paris to offer Henry III the Order of the Garter. This festival is only documented in English and Dutch eye-witness accounts. See: Strong, 'Festivals for the Garter Embassy'; Yates, *The Valois Tapestries*, pp. 116-119; Boucher, *Société et mentalités autour de Henri III*, vol. 1, p. 388.

After her death on 5 January 1589, Catherine left her heirs over 800,000 *écus* of debts.[112] In this respect she lived up to the ideal of magnanimity nourished by all Renaissance rulers.[113] The queen mother seems to have spent the largest sums on the construction and embellishment of her palaces and on the mausoleum for Henry II in Saint-Denis. Renaissance poets and historians encouraged their kings to imitate the example of Roman emperors, who erected grandiose palaces and monuments as eternal signs of their greatness.[114] It is striking that it is especially female regents from this period, as for example Margaret of Austria and Catherine de Médicis, who showed an enormous zeal in the construction of palaces and commemorative monuments.[115] This may be due to the fact that such immense architectural projects were one of the few instruments female rulers could use to express their royal dignity.

For other aspects, female regents could not simply copy the princely culture of their male counterparts. During her lifetime, Catherine very actively led political affairs, but she could only legitimise her governing role by presenting herself either as a mother to her sons and to France, or as a modest widow without any political aspirations. These two arguments, motherhood and widowhood, proved to be highly effective. Because of her motherhood, she had a natural authority over her sons, who were kings of France. As the mother of the nation, she presented herself as a caring mother who had saved the country from civil war and disintegration. In sixteenth-century France, queens could not personally incarnate royal power as did the kings, but by insisting on the fact that she was the widow of Henry II, Catherine could claim that she was continuing his reign. The argument that she had incorporated the royal power of her late husband was an unprecedented and very intelligent move, which, in fact, gave her direct access to a governing role.

Catherine de Médicis did not and could not present herself publically as a great and powerful ruler, and she never explicitly expressed her personal aspirations for political power. This was reserved for the kings of France, her sons, who during court festivals or *magnificences* were represented as great monarchs destined to rule over the entire world. Nevertheless, behind the scenes, it was Catherine who shaped these festivals and used them as a

[112]Cloulas, *Catherine de Médicis*, p. 606.

[113]Some interesting remarks concerning the development of (Neo-Platonic) philosophical theories concerning *liberalitas, magnanimitas* and *magnificentia* in fifteenth-century Florence, can be found in Liebenwein, *Studiolo*, pp. 80-81.

[114]For the importance of architecture, see McGowan, *Ideal Forms in the Age of Ronsard*, pp. 121-128.

[115]Tolley, 'States of Independence'.

political tool, expressing her own ideas concerning the uniting and pacifying role of the French crown.

HENRY IV AND THE DISEASED BODY POLITIC

Annette Finley-Croswhite

The regicide of Henry III, the last Valois king of France, on August 2, 1589 brought the first member of the Bourbon family to the throne, in the person of Henry of Navarre, the new Henry IV. But Henry IV's position in 1589 could not have been more precarious. His legitimacy as France's new king rested on French custom and belief in the fundamental Salic Law. In this instance, twenty-two degrees of cousinage separated Henry IV from the king assassinated by Jacques Clément. Such a distant familial link would, however, have been unquestionable, except for the fact that Henry IV claimed the throne as a Protestant and in the process placed the legitimacy of his reign in jeopardy. In 1589 he thus faced a kingdom in which the majority of cities and towns refused to recognise him as king, and most were united behind a Holy League determined to prevent him from ever wielding real authority. Even many royalist Catholics and noblemen objected to his faith and opted not to follow the Protestant claiming to be king.

The ominous state in which Henry began his kingship can be seen in a Declaration made from Saint Cloud two days after his accession to power. The Declaration was made to Catholic royalists assembled around him who had served Henry III. These included Catholic noblemen in the royal army and important individuals in the deceased king's council and entourage. It was designed to raise their hopes that the new Protestant king might convert to Catholicism in a timely fashion. Henry IV thus promised orally to maintain the Catholic Church, fill vacant offices with Catholics, and seek Catholic religious instruction within six months. The Declaration functioned much like a coronation oath as Henry swore to his subjects that he would uphold the Catholic character of his realm. At the same time it underscored that this was an unanointed king who would not partake in an actual coronation until February 27, 1594 and only then in the recently captured town of Chartres, since the traditional home of the French *sacre*, Reims, was still in Catholic League hands.[1]

[1] Finley-Croswhite, *Henry IV and the Towns*, p. 2; Babelon, *Henri IV*, pp. 317-21; Greengrass, *France in the Age of Henri IV*, p. 78; Wolfe, *The Conversion of Henri IV*, pp. 56-57; Love, 'Winning the Catholics', pp. 372-373, and *Blood and Religion*, pp. 163-164.

Henry also became king at a very inauspicious time since his country had been physically and psychologically devastated by over thirty years of religious warfare that created a moral malaise and divided the country between warring factions. The calamities produced by the wars were also accompanied by the end of a demographic upswing that had brought general prosperity to western Europe in the first half of the sixteenth century, and the downturn was particularly pronounced in France.[2] In Languedoc, for example, grain prices between 1585 and 1600 sextupled, wages did not keep up with price rises, textile production fell off, and the standard of living declined.[3] In the 1580s price curves attained their highest levels of the century throughout the country and taxes continued to rise as well.[4] 1586-87, was a particularly bad year when nearly all of France suffered a crisis of subsistence and wheat prices rose in the north by nearly 700%. This disaster was followed in 1590 by a horrible year of famine in northern France. Between 1589 and 1592, moreover, military engagements became most intense in the north of France between the Loire and the lower Seine rivers and particularly around Paris. The fighting moved south and west after 1595 into Brittany and Burgundy and culminated along the border with the Spanish Netherlands in 1598. Troop movements spread disease, disrupted food production, exacerbated food shortages and high prices, and spread insecurity and disorder. The ravaging of the countryside combined with bad weather meant that the 1580s and the 1590s were marked by the lowest agricultural yields of the century. Peasants were particularly hard hit and succumbed to malnutrition, indebtedness, and a general degradation of their living conditions.[5] Plague epidemics also increased in intensity so that most major French cities experienced recurring plague outbreaks during the last two decades of the sixteenth century.[6] Human suffering during the period additionally included the increased prevalence of influenza, whooping cough, and tuberculosis and the appearance of the new diseases scurvy, rickets, typhus, and scarlet fever.[7] Henry thus became king of a diseased realm in which his own legitimacy was weak. Nonetheless, the metaphor of

[2] Hauser, *Recherches et Documents*; Baulant and Meuvret, *Prix des céreales*; Goubert, *Beauvais et le Beauvaisis*; Appleby, 'Grain Prices and Subsistence Crises in England and France'; Deyon, *Amiens*; Le Roy Ladurie, *The Peasants of Languedoc*, pp. 53-84; Jacquart *La Crise Rurale en Ile-de-France*. This paragraph is also based on a section of a chapter in my book, *Henry IV and the Towns*, p. 14.

[3] Le Roy Ladurie, *The Peasants of Languedoc*, p. 108.

[4] Wolfe, *The Fiscal System of Renaissance France*, pp. 137-184.

[5] Jacquart, 'Économie rurale et démographie sous Henri IV'; Bottin, *Seigneurs et paysans*.

[6] Biraben, *Les hommes et la peste*, vol. 1, pp. 213, 385.

[7] Carmichael, 'Diseases of the Renaissance and Early Modern Europe'.

the diseased body used in association with the diseased state had powerful cultural meaning, and this essay will explore how Henry IV offered himself to his subjects as the remedy for societal ills in ways that strengthened his much needed legitimacy. Indeed, the power to heal and legitimacy were interdependent ideas that had a long history by 1589 and were associated with the French king's divine power to cure scrofula. Henry IV seems to have touched for scrofula more often than any king who ruled before him, attempting to cure up to 1500 people at any given ceremony with the imposition of his royal hands. This emphasis, whereby the king healed a sick individual, moreover, mirrored on a small scale the king's ability to heal his war-torn society.[8] What Henry promised went beyond the ability to cure scrofula and included the return of stable communities and cities that had long been divided and shattered by civil war. Defeating the League involved reincorporating individuals and cities into the larger body politic, reattaching limbs in an effort to make the French state whole. Henry IV effectively used the image of the king as healer to help him win the public opinion campaign for his reign and prove his legitimacy. In the end, French men and women came to believe that only Henry IV could restore order and revive and reinvigorate the French state.

The diseased state

The overwhelming presence of corpses, killed by either war, famine or disease, must have had a tremendous impact on the minds of those living through the French religious wars. As one deputy from Languedoc complained to the king in a letter presented to him in 1589: 'We have suffered from continual warfare for thirty years, mortal famine for twenty, and the plague twice in twelve years, so that in one part or the other, there is almost nothing living'.[9] Death was all pervasive and after thirty years of war, people were powerless to do anything about it. A climate of anxiety thus existed by the late 1580s as the League took hold first in Paris and then elsewhere and that anxiety was brought on not only by the political situation of having a Protestant heir to the French Catholic throne but also by the human environment which infected all groups and created a kind of social pathology in which the language of death and disease permeated the religious and political discourse. Associating heresy with disease was certainly nothing new in the 1580s. The analogy was quite common in European history, perhaps even cliché. The point here is that the League arose on a ter-

[8] Sturdy, 'The Royal Touch in England'; Bloch, *Les Rois Thaumaturges*, pp. 32, 138, 175, 205, 228, 281, 327, 341-344, 356-357, 365, 381, 492.
[9] Roucaute, *Le Pays de Gévaudan*, p. 81.

rible epidemiological landscape that bred disorder and imprinted the minds of men and women with disturbing and consuming images of death.[10]

The most obvious place to find disease-related discourse is in the fiery sermons, which zealous preachers delivered to their congregations during the height of the League's power. The individual clergy who were part of the Sixteen or closely associated with the powerful League leaders took every opportunity to whip up their audiences with frightening invectives and apo-calyptic prophecies. They interpreted the war, famine, and disease that was all around them, not surprisingly, as God's wrath for the sins of the world and proclaimed that deliverance would only come with the eradication of the Protestant heresy. Major themes in their sermons included the right of popular resistance to a tyrannical monarch, the laudable action of Jacques Clément in his assassination of Henry III, and the wrongfulness of Henry IV's succession. These preachers also found places in their sermons, letters, and meditations for reference to sickness and disease. Jean Boucher, for example, was a Parisian doctor of theology and *curé* of Saint-Benoît-le-Bétouné and also a founding member of the Paris League noted for his vehement belief in the righteousness of tyrannicide. Renowned for his eloquence and ferocity, he was said to have inflamed his audiences with fanatical diatribes that inspired his listeners to sedition. His use of language, moreover, also included equating heresy with disease.[11] In referring to the idea of two religions co-existing in one state, he argued in 1587: 'If we have to put up with this contagion [heresy] that stinks everywhere, this canker that invades everything, this gangrene that devours all, this leprosy that infects everything, at least it will be useful and profitable to us [the Catholics] ... since so many [Protestants] will be sent to the lakes of eternal damnation'.[12]

Preachers were not alone in invoking the language of disease. Political leaders also relied on this terminology to hammer home their beliefs. In a

[10] For more on the physiological environment that engulfed the period of the Catholic League, see Delumeau, *Sin and Fear*; Crouzet, *Les guerriers de Dieu*.

[11] Baumgartner, *Radical Reactionaries*, pp. 123-160; Pallier, *Recherches sur l'Imprimerie*, pp. 74, 79; Constant, *La Ligue*, pp. 223-219; Ascoli, *The Sixteen and the Paris League, 1585-1591*, pp. 322-326; De l'Estoile, *The Paris of Henry of Navarre*, pp. 172, 177, 190; Labitte, *De la démocratie chez les prédicateurs de la Ligue*; Cromé, ed. *Dialogue d'entre le maheustre et le manant*.

[12] Quoted in Valois, *Histoire de la Ligue*, 1, p. 165. This is an extremely difficult quote to translate literally because of rambling pronouns. It reads: *Si cette contagion qui empeste tout, ce chancre qui gagne partout, cette gangrène qui dévore tout, cette lèpre qui infecte tout, est utile et profitable, accordons qu'il soit utile de nous voir ainsi bigarrés et que recevions parmi nous cette pierre de scandale qui fera trébûcher tant de gens aux lacs de perdition éternelle.*

speech attributed to Etienne Bernard, deputy to the Estates General of Blois in 1588 and mayor of Dijon in 1592, the League author advised the Estates of Burgundy to 'resist strongly the enemies of our faith, purge France of the venom that has slipped in, and clean the air of the contagion that has been infected by the plague of heretics'.[13] If not, he warned, 'if you follow the party of the King of Navarre and his adherents, the wars will continue, plague, famine, and dearth will destroy you. You will plant the vine and cultivate it and have nothing to drink, all afflictions will seize you and all maledictions, calamities and illnesses written in the book of the Law [of Moses] will follow you'.[14] Such imagery was pervasive in the pamphlet literature as well and permeated the arguments produced by both Leaguers and royalists alike. For example, in a royalist pamphlet produced in 1590 during the siege of Paris, the anonymous author called the League a 'maladie', which he warned his audience, was 'so great and mortal' that it would bring about their destruction.[15] 'Your city is ruined,' he continued, 'your finances are wasted, your forces broken... and famine is upon you'.[16] Similarly in another royalist pamphlet lamenting the death of Henry III, the author notified his League readers that in accepting Sixtus V's papal condemnation of the late king, they had in fact 'vomited the bile of [their] own putrid lungs'.[17] He went on to call Sixtus the doctor who had poisoned them.

If League writers were quick to make comparisons between their physical and political environments, royalist pamphleteers were even more assiduous in employing these analogies once the League began to fail and Henry IV stood on the cusp of victory. Indeed, if the League had popularised the language of disease in condemning Henry IV, royalists writers now turned the imagery around and associated the League with sickness and

[13] Bernard, *Advis des Estats de Bourgongne aux François*, p. 9. Bernard wrote: *Pour en ce temps resister à l'effort violent des ennemis de nostre Foy, purger la France du venin qui s'y glisse, et la nettoyer de l'air contagieux qui l'infecte par la peste des heretiques.*

[14] Bernard, *Advis des Estats de Bourgongne aux François*, p. 37: *Sinon, ou vous ferez le contraire, ou vous suivrez le party du Roy de Navarre et de ses adherans, vous guerres continueront, la peste, famine et disette vous destruiront, vous planterez la vigne et la cultiverez et n'enboirez point, toutes afflictions vous saisiront, toutes maledictions, playes, et maladies escrites au livre du la Loy vous suivront ...*

[15] *Le Manifeste de la France*, reel 4, pp. 3-4: *Il n'est plus temps de faire les idiots ny les insensibles au jugement de ceste maladie, elle est grande, elle est mortelle, & qui porte visiblement vos jours à leur derniere ruine.*

[16] *Le Manifeste de la France*, p. 23: *Votre ville est ruinee, vos finances sont espuisees, vos forces rompues, vos partisans consternez, & tous vos moyens particuliers si à l'estroict, que desia la famine vous press.*

[17] *La Fulminante Pour Feu Tres Grand et Tres-Chrestien Prince Henry III*, reel 5, p. 10: *Tu as vomy la bile de ton pourry poulmon.*

death. The League was viewed as a poison for which the royalist pamphleteers argued that Henry IV was the only sure antidote.[18] Alexandre de Pont-Aimery's pamphlet *Discours d'Estat sur la Blessure du Roy* is filled with the language of disease. He calls the League 'a maladie which is attached to the souls of the French like a fever that is attached to a purulent and unhealthy body'.[19] He interpreted the diseased environment of his natural surroundings and used that environment to project a social pathology of a diseased state. Like many royalist writers, Pont-Aimery prescribed Henry IV as the remedy for the sick realm. Henry is the only good medicine, and if the French fail to submit to this remedy, Pont-Aimery warns, '[t]he gangrene will continue to ulcerate'.[20]

'Henry as the remedy' was a major theme of royalist literature published after 1590 that revealed France in a desperate situation. Because of the war, one author writes, France faces 'the horror, the fear, the threats, the fire, the hell and certain death'.[21] He grieves over 'the poverty, the famine, the plague, the injustice, the atheism, and all the wickness' he sees throughout the realm.[22] But he offers Henry as the solution, remedy, and medicine to France's illness and portrays him as 'full of sweetness and clemency with open arms ready to receive all of us under his protection and guard and lift the yoke of the barbarian foreigners who have almost enslaved us'.[23] Restoring health to the diseased state thus involved throwing off foreign domination. The implication is that under Henry's command, the Spanish will be defeated and the country returned to French control. The pamphlet

[18] *Le Manifeste de la France*, p. 5.

[19] De Pont-Aimery, *Discours d'Estat sur la Blessure du Roy*, p. ii: *La Ligue est une maladie laquelle est attachee aux ames Françoises, comme la fievre aux humerus des corps purulent & mal-sains.C'est pourquoy j'ay dressé ce discours où le remede est plus apparent que le mal mesme ...*

[20] De Pont-Aimery, *Discours d'Estat sur la Blessure du Roy*, p. ii: *La gangrene se met en l'ulcere, & au lieu de cauthere ardent l'on y applique des estoupes oinctes d'huiles & de vinaigre.*

[21] *La Retraitte de la Ligue par P.I.D.G.C*, p. 13: *Devant elle [la guerre] & ses costez marchent l'horreur, la crainte, les menaces, le feu, la gehenne, & les menaces, le feu, la gehenne, & la mort: apres elle retentissent les voix & gemissemens lamentables des pauvres vefues, orphelins, captifs, & mouras: La pauvereté, la famine, la peste, l'iniustice, l'atheisme, & tous les maux, qu'on sçauroit penser ou dire la talonente de pres.*

[22] *La Retraitte de la Ligue par P.I.D.G.C*, p. 13.

[23] *La Retraitte de la Ligue par P.I.D.G.C*, p. 10: *Le voila donc François, le voila tel que ie le vous chaste, que se represente à nous d'un visage Royallement ioyeux, plein de douceur, & clemence, les bras ouverts pour nous recevoir tous soubs sa protection & garde, en secoüant le ioug du Barbare estranger, qui nous a presque villainement asserui.*

ends with a long poem comparing Henry to an expert medical doctor able to repair the broken political body and restore it to good health: 'Just as a doctor procuring the health of someone grievously wounded, cannot return him to good health with a harsh medicine: This strong concoction for the sick [of France] cannot be received, if it is not made palpable with the addition of a mixture of sweet liquor that the expert doctor [Henry] puts in his potion'.[24] As in other political treatises and letters, Henry is portrayed here as the clement conqueror who will use goodness and mercy to strengthen his subjects and reunite all divided and broken parts of the body politic. Only Henry had the healing power associated with sacral monarchy that could revive the state.

Henry IV's political agenda of showing mercy to his enemies and forgiving them for their treasonous association with the Catholic League held out the promise of healing the moral malaise within the country as well. Henry had portrayed himself as a clement conquer almost from the beginning of his reign. On November 28, 1589, for example, he issued letters patent offering his grace to all towns and individuals willing to leave the League immediately.[25] Henry's propagandists also took up this message and portrayed his clemency as 'open and certain: it surpasses all our faults and is immense'.[26] Once Henry finally reconverted to Catholicism in 1593, he began to stress the importance of forgiveness and reconciliation even more. 'After all', Michael Wolfe notes, 'it was highly impolitic to treat the Leaguers in ways which contradicted the very spirit of his reconciliation with the Church'.[27] Thereafter Henry's personal contract with his subjects was based on clemency.[28] Henry wanted to pacify his realm, not destroy it with harsh vengence. When he entered Paris in March, 1594, for example, his soldiers passed out leaflets promising pardons to all but the most notorious Leaguers. In the end he banished no more than one hundred and twenty ringleaders from his capital city, and this pattern of charitable *douceur* was replicated over and over as the other Catholic League strongholds

[24] *La Retraitte de la Ligue par P.I.D.G.C*, p. 43: *Ainsi qu un medecin procurant la santé, de celuy qui d'un mal griefvement agité, Ne peut poiont revenir en sa santé pristine, Sinon par le moyen d'une aspre medecine: Ce brevage facheux du malade debile, Ne peut estre receu, s'il n'est rendu facile, Par une mixtion du quelque ligueur douce, Que l'expert medecin dans ce brevage pousse.*

[25] De Waele, 'Clémence royale et fidélités françaises', p. 232.

[26] Arnauld, *Coppie de l'Anti-Espagnols*, p. 53.

[27] Wolfe, *The Conversion of Henri IV*, pp. 163-164.

[28] De Waele, 'Image de force', p. 58: For an excellent article on Henry's clemency, see his 'Clémence royale'.

capitulated to him.[29] Former Leaguers were often restored to their positions of power or were even promoted or rewarded with gifts, subsidies, and offices. The treaties negotiated with the towns included clauses that encouraged subjects to put the past behind them and consign it to oblivion (*oubliance*).[30] In this way French men and women could emulate their king and forgive each other. This forgiving attitude would restore mental health to the country and help the French people reunite in one political body led by the example of their merciful king. Henry was the Gallic Hercules who could persuade by his words and example and would thus bring France into a golden age.[31] Finally, royal propagandists also linked good health with a strong body politic by reminding the public that Henry possessed the robust body of a warrior that was the personification of a new and healthy state. In countless pamphlets, placards, printed images, and engraved portraits, French people were bombarded with images of the *Vert Galant*, a virile, heterosexual, almost indestructible, man with a huge appetite for life. Cynthia Burlingham argues that the increased production of Henry's image in the graphic medium after 1594 suggest that more of the king's subjects were interested in acquiring pictures of him, and many were inculcating the message that he was a strong and legitimate king.[32] Just as Henry III's sterility served the League as a metaphor for a barren realm, so Henry IV's potency came to be associated with prosperity for the state. The birth of a *dauphin* in 1601, just nine months after his marriage to Marie de Médicis, confirmed Henry's generative power and heralded the return to orderly succession in France. The increased production of portraits and prints of the king with his wife and growing family also emphasised his role as the progenitor of a new dynasty.[33] Wolfe argues that these positive images of Henry IV's royal body 'personified a strong, expansionist France confident of its future'.[34] The French found this image seductive as it reinforced their longings to end years of suffering by giving them hope that Henry could return stability to the kingdom. It thus marked an acceptance of Henry's legitimacy and a return to confidence in the crown.[35] Furthermore, this promise of restoring the body politic was reiterated throughout Henry's

[29] Wolfe, *The Conversion of Henri IV*, p. 179; Finley-Croswhite, *Henry IV and the Towns*, pp. 18-22, 23-62, 122-38.
[30] Wolfe, *The Conversion of Henri IV*, p. 184.
[31] Vivanti, 'Henry IV, The Gallic Hercules'.
[32] Burlingham, 'Portraiture as Propaganda, p. 143.
[33] Burlingham, 'Portraiture as Propaganda p. 146.
[34] Wolfe, 'The strange afterlife of Henry III', p. 478.
[35] This paragraph is based on Wolfe, 'The strange afterlife of Henry III', pp. 474-489, especially 476-479.

reign, in particular after 1594 in association with the king's ability to cure scrofula.

The royal touch

The practice of healing for scrofula by the king's royal touch was a particular religio-political belief with a long history in France and was used for centuries to bolster belief in the authority of monarchy.[36] Consequently, a king such as Henry IV, who employed all possible measures to legitimise his reign, was especially interested in the power of the thaumaturgic rite. The healing ritual not only promoted the power of the French monarchy, but it also allowed the royalists to continue and advance the message of the early 1590s that Henry was the healer of his realm. While the connection between kingship and magical powers existed in the earliest monarchical states in the ancient world, the specific royal touch for scrofula was a medieval creation associated only with the monarchies of France and England. Medieval people considered the royal touch a divine gift (*divinitus)* from God and a mark of divine favour. During the reign of Henry IV, the king's senior physician, André du Laurens, publicised the belief that Clovis (481-511) was the first French king to touch for scrofula.[37] The French medievalist Marc Bloch, however, argued that Philip I (1060-1108) was actually the first to practise the rite, while most contemporary historians, such as Frank Barlow, believe that it was in fact, Louis IX (1226-1270), a king noted for his saintly nature, who first touched for the disease.[38] By the later Middle Ages, touching for scrofula had become a ritual at the French court associated with the king's anointing at his coronation. Traditionally the French coronation ceremony took place at the cathedral of Reims, after which kings journeyed to a nearby shrine at Corbeny, a place associated with the healing power of a sixth-century monk named Marcoul known as the patron saint of those afflicted with scrofula. The journey was necessary before the French kings attempted to use their sacred power and touch for scrofula, also known as *le mal du roy* and *écrouelles*.[39]

Scrofula was a precursor of pulmonary tuberculosis which manifested itself as inflamation of the cervical lymph nodes in the neck and caused by the tubercle bacilli. Sufferers contracted the disease either by drinking the

[36] Turrell, 'The Ritual of Royal Healing', p. 35.
[37] Bloch, *The Royal Touch*, p. 15.
[38] Bloch, *The Royal Touch*, pp. 6-7; Sturdy, 'The Royal Touch in England', p. 171; Barlow, 'The King's Evil', p. 11; Bloch, *Les Rois Thaumaturges*, pp. 30-32, 35, 37-38, 40, 42, 59; Hays, *The Burdens of Disease*, pp. 30-31.
[39] Rice, *Saint Marcoul and the Pilgrimages of the Kings of France*, p. 2; Landouzy, *Le Toucher des Écrouelles*.

tainted milk of tubercular cows or by breathing in the airborne droplets released by scrofula victims.[40] Primary tuberculosis was rarely fatal and frequently went into remission, giving the belief or impression that a cure had occurred. In the early modern period, before the development of bacteriology, moreover, there probably was a great deal of confusion concerning the diseases that attacked the glands, neck, and face. Thus scrofula may have been confused with goitre, thyroid disease, mumps, opthalmic disorders, and even leprosy, anthrax, or lupus.[41] Towards the end of the sixteenth century there was an increased interest in scrofula, stimulated by the worsening disease environment of the time. Just as bubonic plague outbreaks were on the rise, many such as Henry IV's physician, Du Laurens, believed that scrofula was occurring with more frequency as well. In 1578, the *Collège des Médecins* issued a statement warning that the breath of scrofula victims could infect bread, making it dangerous to eat.[42] The Catholic League also circulated propaganda stating that Henry III's wickedness had rendered him incapable of exercising his supernatural power and warning that if France accepted a Protestant king, God would take back his divine gift, and the victims of scrofula would never be healed again.[43]

Henry IV was keenly interested in all aspects of monarchical myth-making and used the healing ceremony to communicate to his subjects the legitimacy of his new dynasty. Undoubtedly Henry's conversion to Catholicism undermined the Catholic League and won him the kingdom, but it was not enough to convince all of his subjects of his sincerity as a Catholic or remove the recriminations of the past. Henry thus used the healing ceremony to his advantage. Even so, he was in a peculiar situation since he was not crowned at Reims and never made the pilgrimage to Corbeny. Yet Henry needed to exploit the healing ceremony and send the message that his power to heal was real and not conferred by coronation but rather by heredity and the infusion of God's grace. Since it had been rumoured that Henry III failed to cure for scrofula and that God would never favour a Protestant, Henry's decision to touch for scrofula visually proved to his subjects his divine favour, especially since the royal doctors and others attending these events publicised the belief that at least half of all those touched by Henry IV were cured within a few days.[44]

[40] Kiple, 'Scrofula', p. 44.

[41] Turrell, 'The Ritual of Royal Healing', p. 4; Bloch, *The Royal Touch*, p. 11; Barlow, 'The King's Evil;, pp. 3, 7, 11; Frzybowski and Allen, 'History and the Importance of Scrofula'.

[42] Landouzy, *Le Toucher des Écrouelles*, p. 12.

[43] Bloch, *Les Rois Thaumaturges*, p. 390, note 88; Blondel, *Genealogiae francicae plenior assertio*, vol. 1, fol. lxx.

[44] Du Laurens, *De mirabili strumas sanandi*; Cayet, *Chronologie Novenarie*, p. 571.

There is no record of Henry IV touching for scrofula after his coronation at Chartres in February 1594. Instead, he waited to display his divinely bestowed power in his capital city after the capitulation of Paris on March 22, 1594. The decision to wait and touch for scrofula in Paris rather than Chartres was probably deliberately planned by the king with an eye to the customary royal processions to Paris that traditionally followed royal coronations.[45] It also increased the drama associated with the arrival of Henry IV in his capital and added to the mystique of kingship. Henry touched for scrofula on Easter Sunday, roughly two weeks after his initial entry into Paris. The fact that he chose the highest holy day of the Christian calendar to demonstrate his healing power was symbolically significant. Henry had been using the period immediately following the capitulation to stress the sincerity of his recent religious conversion. He attended Mass in Notre Dame, participated in religious processions, worshipped in every parish church in Paris, and offered thanks to the Virgin Mary for the capitulation of the capital. Then during Holy Week Henry began acting in ways that clearly emphasised his Christian generosity. Beginning on Maundy Thursday he washed the feet of the poor at a ceremony held at the Louvre and then gave out alms at the Hôtel-Dieu. On Good Friday he visited several prisons in the city, where he freed one man condemned to die and others imprisoned for debt. Next he released members of the Catholic League who were being held in the Châtelet. All of these acts emphasised his benevolence and mercy and underscored his Christ-like nature and willingness to care for his subjects and forgive his former enemies. The association of Henry and Christ was reiterated on Easter Sunday, when the king revealed his divine favour and great compassion as he touched hundreds of his subjects for scrofula.[46] Since there had been no healing rituals held in Paris since Henry III fled his capital after the Day of the Barricades in 1588, public interest in the event was overwhelming. Renewed hope was offered to those afflicted with the disease since the king had returned and reinvigorated the royal rite. Many undoubtedly attended the ceremony, moreover, out of curiosity to see if Henry IV truly possessed divine healing power.

Henry also used the healing rite to set a distinction between himself and his former Protestant self. After the Reformation, many Protestants began to

[45] Wolfe, '"Paris is Worth a Mass" Reconsidered', p. 7. I thank Dr. Wolfe for sharing this paper with me.

[46] *BnF*, mss. fr. 20153, *Recueil de pièces sur l'histoire de France provenant des frères de Sainte-Marte*, fol. 693; Cayet, *Chronologie Novenarie*, p. 571; De l'Estoile, *Journal*, p. 410; Lemoine, Sallois and Deschamps, eds, *1594 Le Sacré d'Henri IV à Chartres*, p. 265; Wolfe, '"Paris is Worth a Mass" Reconsidered', pp. 7-9.

reject the healing ceremony by calling it a pagan ritual. Henry's contemporary, Elizabeth I, seemed reluctant to lay her hands on the sick early in her reign and may have doubted the efficacy of the ritual. She only revived the rite in 1570 after she had been excommunicated from the Catholic church and the papists had accused her of having lost her power to heal.[47] Thereafter, Elizabeth continued to downplay her part in any miraculous cure, even when she did touch for scrofula.[48] Henry needed to show, however, that he possessed none of this Protestant scepticism. By touching for scrofula Henry could inspire belief that his conversion to Catholicism had been real.

The public never really tired of the thaumaturgic rite during Henry's reign, and it was reported that thousands came to attend the royal healing ceremonies that took place, at the very least, four times a year on Easter, Pentecost, All Saints Day, and Christmas. Henry wrote to his mistress, the Marquise de Verneuil, that he touched over 1250 persons inflicted with scrofula on Easter Sunday, 1608.[49] The king was also known to touch for scrofula at other times of the year as well and in other cities besides Paris. He performed the ritual twice in Orléans and once in Reims, for example.[50] He complained of how the ceremony fatigued him, as he often stood for hours to administer the touch, but he continued to lay his hands on the sick throughout his reign and gave the impression that it was out of sheer concern for his subjects and a sincere belief in his power to assuage their miseries.[51] The fact that scrofula often manifested itself as putrid sores on the neck that disappeared in a matter of weeks added to the mystique that the king's hands could miraculously cure.

The thaumaturgic rite functioned as an important means of emphasising the legitimacy of Henry's reign by visually representing the king exercising the power and prerogatives of his kingship and by connecting him with the line of French kings that began with Clovis. Henry's ability to cure, as his propagandists articulated, testified to his proof of belonging to this true line of devout kings and established the divine favour of the new Bourbon dynasty. The entire ritual was intended to reveal Henry's sincere religious devotion in very public ways. The night before he intended to touch for scrofula, he attended vespers. The next morning he went to confession and then heard mass. Then he ventured to a designated open space, such as the courtyard at the Louvre or in front of the cathedral at Reims, where,

[47] Turrell, 'The Ritual of Royal Healing', p. 9; Kiple, 'Scrofula', p. 45.

[48] Turrell, 'The Ritual of Royal Healing', p. 10.

[49] Berger de Xivrey, ed, *Henry IV, Recueil des lettres missives*, p. 510.

[50] Berger de Xivrey, ed, *Henry IV, Recueil des lettres missives*, p. 510; Hennequin, *Henri IV dans ses Oraisons Funèbres*, pp. 181-182.

[51] Bercé, 'Henri IV et la maîtrise des opinions populaires', pp. 121-122; Bloch, *The Royal Touch*, p. 390, note 90.

attended by his body-guards, physicians, almoners, and princes of the blood, Henry laid his hands on the sick. The afflicted were presented to him by a royal physician. The king then made the sign of the cross on each victim's cheeks, perhaps touched visible sores, and uttered the words: *Le Roy te touche et Dieu te guerit*.[52] The king gave credit to God for his miraculous power, but the very essence of the ritual underscored sacral monarchy and sent the message that Henry held special esteem in God's sight. Henry now acted as God's earthly agent and in the process revealed himself as king by virtue of his supernatural deeds.[53] Each person Henry touched, moreover, received a coin or two from the king's almoners. The entire rite thus emphasised the charitable nature of the king and his concern for his subjects. The healing ceremony also mobilised the populace for Henry's reign in a number of ways.

In the first instance, since only the kings of France and England were believed to possess the power to cure by touch, the sick of various nations often attended the rituals. They were ranked in a specific order, in which the Spanish came first and the French last.[54] Given the Spanish involvement with the Catholic League, Henry's willingness to touch and attempt to cure them underscored his forgiving Christ-like nature for all to see. Here was Henry showing sympathy for the greatest enemies of the realm. Secondly, a large percentage of those stricken with scrofula were children, who had low resistence to tuberculosis.[55] It was certainly good publicity for the king to show concern for the smallest sufferers in his realm and his actions reinforced the paternal nature of kingship. Thirdly, the thaumaturgic rite connected the king and his people in a way that brought together the highest and the lowest members of the society.[56] The king appeared more human, even in the moment that revealed his superhuman nature, as he walked bare headed through the crowds. This was an intimate moment when the king became approachable, and although he made himself more vulnerable to disease and bodily threats to his person as he moved from victim to victim in the course of attempting to cure, he probably won the hearts of many victims and by-standers by his selfless actions. Since it was a known fact that would-be assassins stalked the crowds during Henry's reign, the king's

[52] Du Laurens, *De mirabili strumas sanandi*; Landouzy, *Le Toucher des Écrouelles*, p. 11; Crawfurd, *The King's Evil*, pp. 78-81.
[53] Crawfurd, *The King's Evil*, p. 82.
[54] Landouzy, *Le Toucher des Écrouelles*, p. 10.
[55] Kiple, 'Scrofula', p. 44. Adults would have been more likely to have already undergone a bout of primary tubuculosis and recovered from it.
[56] Sturdy, 'The Royal touch in England', p. 169.

survival during these very public events also led credence to the belief that he was divinely protected.[57]

The ritual itself brought together ruler and ruled in a way that offered healing to individuals as well as healing to a factionalised realm.[58] In the process hundreds of individuals were able to look into the king's eyes and imagine his earnestness while thousands more gazed on as spectators and envisaged his grace. All experienced the healing power of sacral monarchy. Finally, the king's propagandists used the opportunity of the healing services to spread the news of Henry's ability to cure. Indeed the king's physician, Du Laurens, published a book during Henry's reign, testifying to the king's healing power. The work went through numerous editions in rapid succession during the seventeenth century.[59] For those who doubted the once-Protestant king and his ability to rule, the healing ceremony for scrofula thus offered striking proof of Bourbon legitimacy and garnered popular support for the new dynasty. It visually revealed a king restoring the health of his subjects, and on a larger scale, rejuvenating the political body of his realm.

Conclusion

Early modern people lived in a world where disease was imperfectly understood and fear accompanied each famine and epidemic. Given this context, the metaphor of the diseased body, used in association with the diseased state, had powerful cultural meaning. For one, it reveals how the experience of ordinary people and their suffering was incorporated into a political language that proposed a variety of methods to combat disease. Thus, while the poor and the sick may have had very little opportunity in their lives to alter their personal situations, their incorporation into the larger rhetorical dynamic of the diseased state not only gave meaning to their particular plights but also created narrative possibilities in which preachers, pamphleteers, political leaders, and Henry IV could offer solutions for the return of peace to the realm and thereby the end of much physical suffering. In a certain sense the preachers and propagandists placed themselves and the poor and the sick in a kind of liminal state that created a community of suffering which was intelligible to everyone, especially the king. All sides in the religious wars adopted the language of pain and suffering and infused their narratives and diatribes with images of the body and its decay. The shared experience

[57] Wolfe, *The Conversion of Henri IV*, p. 169.
[58] Sturdy, 'The Royal touch in England', pp. 171, 180.
[59] Sturdy, 'The Royal touch in England', p. 174; Du Laurens, *De mirabili strumas sanandi*; Bloch, *The Royal Touch*, p. 194.

of disease and death was thus something all readers and listeners could readily identify with and so the projection of the diseased body onto the diseased state, although a common metaphor, had potent rhetorical force.[60]

Since the elimination of disease and the return to good health were goals that all people understood in the early modern world, the use of the lan-guage of disease and death also acted as a rallying cry for the return of peace. Even League incorporation of the diseased state into political propaganda was important – in this instance since it familiarised readers with fantasies of death and provided narrative openings for royalists to promote the healing power of Henry IV. Narratives of horror may have even laid the groundwork for narratives of peace. Peace was associated with the return of a healthy body, and Henry IV was portrayed as the remedy for societal ills. What he offered was not just the promise of food for the poor and weary, the chicken in every pot, but also the return of a peaceful world. His solution fixed a multitude of ills in restoring peace to his realm. The rhetorical language revealed Henry to be the brilliant doctor who held the only antidote that would bring the state back to life and create a new stability. His own good health became the personification of the healthy state which he promised to build. The medical and nosographical emphasis in the pamphlets and illustrations offers one more example of the way in which Henry appealed to his subjects to accept his kingship. By the end of the League, the collective understanding of misery was real. Henry IV became the doctor who promised to take away the pain. He used the public image of the king as healer to posit a miraculous cure for the decayed state. The king and his propagandists articulated, that, by laying his hands on the state, Henry would bring it back to life. This image promoted the king's legitimacy and helped to win him the consent of the French populace. It also connected him strongly with the prerogatives of sacral monarchy and the French king's power to cure scrofula. The king as healer thus became an image that Henry continued to exploit until the end of his reign.[61]

In 1606 Henry IV spent Easter week in the Champagne capital of Reims. For the king it was a most important event, since he was appearing in the sacred coronation site of the French monarchy, but as the one king who had not been crowned there. During Holy Week, therefore, Henry made a point of touching for scrofula and he attempted to cure some 575 persons. The event was captured on an engraving made by Pierre Firens,

[60] Theibault, 'The Rhetoric of Death and Destruction in the Thirty Years War'; Calvi, 'The Florentine Plague of 1630-33'.

[61] This and the preceding paragraph rely heavily on Theibault, 'The Rhetoric of Death and Destruction'.

that was published in 1609 in Du Laurens's medical text on scrofula.[62] Thus in the site most associated with the healing power of kings, Henry popularised his image as a divinely empowered ruler. The inscription beneath the engraving stated that God had given Henry IV the power to cure 'many sicknesses and awful diseases and particularly scrofula'.[63] Undoubtedly the engraving was a wonderful piece of political propaganda. The fact that the inscription credited him with the ability to cure many illnesses, and not just scrofula, deserves notice. It boldly indicated that the Bourbon king could cure his realm as well. By 1606, Henry's throne was secure and his legitimacy well established. Still, however, he continued to disseminate the image of himself as the great healer. The engraving itself shows a bare-headed Henry placing his right hand on the forehead of a victim. The king's eyes are prominent, and one can see and even feel his benevolent gaze. It reveals that in promoting the thaumaturgical rite, Henry never tired of reiterating that he had the power to cure. The healing ceremony itself shows on a small scale how Henry conquered France. Just as the king had always linked fidelity to his person and made separate pacification agreements with key individuals and towns, here Henry was shown curing scrofula and winning his kingdom, one person at a time.[64] In doing so he could also cure disbelief in his legitimacy and promise a bright future for France. By winning the hearts of his people, Henry reunited his realm, and thus the 'king as healer' image validated his ability to restore the diseased state to a healthy body politic.

[62] Thomas, *Henri IV*, pp. 224-226.
[63] Thomas, *Henri IV*, p. 225.
[64] De Waele, 'Clémence royale', p. 250.

PRINCELY CULTURE IN SCOTLAND UNDER JAMES III AND JAMES IV

Alasdair A. MacDonald

Problems and perceptions

In 1424 James I returned to his own kingdom, after a detention of eighteen years in England. There he had been held prisoner by Henry IV and Henry V – sometimes in the Tower of London, sometimes in other castles, and sometimes forced to accompany English armies in their campaigns in France. For a while James overlapped with another illustrious prisoner, Charles of Orleans (1391-1465), who had been captured at Agincourt. The long period spent by the Scottish king in England meant that he was inevitably saturated in the Anglo-French culture of the Lancastrian court. Shortly before he returned home, James married Joanne Beaufort, cousin of Henry V. In such circumstances, it is only natural that the poem which purports to record the inception and progress of the Scottish king's infatuation – the *Kingis Quair* – should follow the literary conventions of the allegorical dream-vision mode favoured by the prestigious English poets Geoffrey Chaucer and John Lydgate; nor is it surprising that this poem is written in a distinctive combination of Scottish and English language forms.[1] Few Scottish kings before James had been so exposed to such strong foreign cultural influences; the effective personal reign of James I (1424-37) may therefore be said to inaugurate a new kind of princely culture in Scotland.

It is of the highest significance that every one of the subsequent Stewart monarchs likewise elected to marry abroad. Such alliances had the effect of enriching Scottish culture, since they exposed the court to international patterns and standards of behaviour.[2] The awareness of Scotland within the

[1] The poem has often been edited (e.g., by Simon, ed, *Le Livre du Roi*, and by Norton-Smith, ed, *The Kingis Quair*). On the language of the poem see Jeffery, 'Anglo-Scots Poetry and the Kingis Quair', pp. 207-221.

[2] On the Stewart kings see the following standard biographies: Brown, *James I*; McGladdery, *James II*; Macdougall, *James III*; *James IV*; Cameron, *James V*. An earlier king of Scotland who had married a foreign princess and also introduced notable cultural innovations to his country was Malcolm III Canmore, successor of

perspective of European politics may be said effectively to begin with James I, who was the first sovereign of his country simultaneously to emulate English, French and Burgundian practice. This king, moreover, used the marriage prospects of his six daughters as a convenient opportunity for forging alliances with other European princes.[3] James II continued the example set by his father through his marriage in 1449 to Mary of Gelderland (Gueldres), grandniece of Philip the Good. This union gave Scottish foreign policy a still stronger focus upon Burgundy, and for the next three decades this concern complemented the traditional preoccupation with the old neighbour England, and the old ally France.[4] It also led directly to the importation into Scotland of Observant Franciscanism, under the leadership of Cornelis of Zierikzee. This order, much favoured by Mary of Gelderland, was especially patronised by later Scottish sovereigns, and, as we shall see, was of especial importance under James IV.[5] The marriages of James III to Margaret of Denmark (1469), and of James IV to Margaret Tudor (1503) followed the by then established trend. During these two reigns – 1460-88, and 1488-1513 respectively – a remarkable development took place. This period of the late Middle Ages has often, and with justice, been singled out as one of the the high-points of Scottish cultural achievement; the roots of this period in the reigns of the first two Jameses should, however, not be forgotten. Likewise, many of the manifestations of culture encountered in the reign of James V (1513-42) may be seen as a continuation (or revival) of patterns laid down under the latter's father and grandfather.

Since in Scotland juvenile succession was a recurring liability, princely culture was as much a matter of fits and starts as of incremental development. Thus, in between the personal reigns of most of the first five Jameses there were periods when political direction slackened. For James I (born 1394, succeeded 1406), there was his imprisonment in England since 1407; James II was six years old at the moment of his father's assassination, and only took personal control in 1448; for his part, James III (born 1452) only began to rule for himself in 1469. In the sixteenth century the problem presented itself anew: on the death of James IV his son was but one year old; more remarkable still, James V's only surviving legitimate child, Mary Stewart, was a mere one week old upon her accession in 1542. The

Macbeth, who in 1069 married Margaret (St Margaret), daughter of Edgar the Ætheling, of the Anglo-Saxon royal house.

[3] Bawcutt and Henisch, 'Scots Abroad', pp. 45-55; Downie, 'La voie quelle menace tenir', pp. 170-191.

[4] On Scoto-Burgundian links see MacDonald, 'Chivalry as a Catalyst of Cultural Change' and 'The Chapel of Restalrig'.

[5] Bryce, *The Scottish Grey Friars*; Durkan, 'The Observant Franciscan Province', pp. 51-57.

exception in this series of interrupted successions was the transition from James III to James IV, where the new king, at the age of almost sixteen, was able to function in office straight away. This fact is in itself a reason for treating the princely culture under these two kings within a single conspectus.

While the cultural blossoming of Scotland at the end of the Middle Ages has long been recognised, it is primarily the reign of James IV which has become fixed in the collective modern memory as the Golden Age of early Scottish culture.[6] The decision adopted here to treat the reigns of father and son together may therefore require further explanation. The *communis opinio* has been preconditioned by awareness of the manner in which James IV came to the throne. In 1488, James III and his supporters were defeated at the battle of Sauchieburn (close to the royal residence of Stirling) by a band of disaffected nobles who had, or claimed to have, the support of the young prince. The king fled the field of battle, only to be murdered, according to legend, by a person disguised as a priest.[7] Whether or not James III deserved to be deposed for political mismanagement, this sorry tale of violence meant that James IV had to confront the issue of his own problematic authority. Not only did the *coup d'État* set a potentially dangerous precedent, it was also sacrilegious for a prince to rebel against his crowned and anointed father. In somewhat parallel circumstances James IV's granduncle, Duke Adolf of Gelderland, had overthrown and imprisoned his own father, and this was used by Charles the Bold as an excuse for annexing that duchy in 1473.[8] Moreover, there was the matter of the character of the Scottish king: James III was by report distinguished by unusually strong piety, especially in his devotion to the Passion of Christ, and only two years before the battle of Sauchieburn had received the Golden Rose from Innocent VIII, as an sign of papal approval.[9] In addition,

[6] This is the basic assumption animating many discussions of the period, e.g.: Mackie, *King James IV*; Wittig, *The Scottish Tradition*; Lindsay, *History of Scottish Literature*. This 'Golden Age' theory has had a negative effect upon the appraisal of the cultural achievements of the reign of James III. However, for a reassessment of the reign of James III see Macfarlane, *William Elphinstone and the Kingdom of Scotland*.

[7] Mackay, ed, *Robert Lindesay*, vol. 1, pp. 208-209.

[8] Nijsten, *Het Hof van Gelre*, p. 152. In a recent essay, Norman Macdougall asks, rhetorically, which other king rebelled against, and murdered, his father; see his 'Henryson's Scotland', p. 54. To this one can say that it is not clear to what extent the young James IV is to be identified with the rebellion; nor is there any evidence that the son willed his father's death.

[9] Burns, 'Papal Gifts to Scottish Monarchs'. On James's piety see Moir, ed, *Hector Boece*, p. 52.

after the death of Margaret of Denmark (1486), James initiated steps which were designed to lead to her canonisation.[10] Rebellion against such a father may have given the son pause for thought.

The disculpation of the new ruler involved a programme of penitential activity, in an attempt to expunge the imputation of regicide.[11] Robert Lindesay of Pitscottie tells a story of how the king, prompted by hearing mass and evensong in the Chapel Royal at Stirling, disburdened his soul to the dean thereof.[12] Some years later, the king's confessor, Patrick Ranwick (or Ranny), Provincial and warden of the Stirling house of Observant Franciscans, advised James to wear, as an act of penance, an iron chain round his waist, the weight of which was increased each year.[13] Furthermore, James often went on very public pilgrimages (on occasion barefoot) which took him throughout the kingdom – whether north, to the shrine of St Duthac, at Tain, or south, to the shrine of St Ninian, at Whithorn.[14] Moreover, every year during Holy Week the king made a retreat to the convent of the Observant Franciscans at Stirling.[15]

From the ostentatious penitence of James IV there emerges an impression of a person at least capable of strong religious engagement. That, however, is not to claim that the young king was egregiously diligent in devotion: he was no saint, even if he regularly regretted being a sinner. It would seem that only on receiving the right stimulus could he attain to something approaching the level of spirituality characteristic of his father. In any event, James IV soon gained the full approbation of the Church: in 1491 Pope Innocent VIII sent him, too, the Golden Rose; later, either Innocent or his successor Alexander VI gave him a silver-gilt Sceptre; and on Easter Sunday 1507 Julius II sent the Scottish king the Sword of State

[10] Macdougall, *James III*, p. 218.
[11] Macdougall, *James III*, pp. 52-53.
[12] Mackay, ed, *Robert Lindesay*, vol. 1, pp. 208-209.
[13] Mackay, ed, *Robert Lindesay*, vol. 1, pp. 217-218. Macdougall, *James IV*, p. 53, gives the impression that James's chain goes back to 1488. This is, however, impossible, since the Stirling Observant house was not founded until 1494. For a representation of the chain, see the Seton Armorial of 1591 (Edinburgh, NLS MS Acc. 9309); photograph in Macdougall, *James IV* (1989) figure 6; (1997) figure 5.
[14] Macdougall, *James IV*, pp. 196-198. It was James III who founded the collegiate church of St Duthac. Cf. Durkan, 'The Sanctuary and College of Tain', pp. 147-156. James III was much interested in pilgrimages, and obtained permission to travel to foreign shrines. Though these projected journeys were never realised, he may have made a vicarious pilgrimage to Sinai and Jerusalem via the peregrination of his Flemish friend, Anselm Adorne: see MacDonald, 'Chapel of Restalrig', pp. 39-44.
[15] MacDonald, 'Catholic Devotion into Protestant Lyric', pp. 71-74.

and the Blessed Hat.[16] These latter gifts were, however, not unconnected with James's desire to lead a crusade against the Turk.

The efforts taken by James IV himself to fortify his reputation have proved compatible with the agenda of not a few later historians, who, in their accounts of the reign of James III, have been systematically deprecatory; in this version of events, the father, in contrast to his brilliant son, is described as weak, ineffectual, indecisive, capricious, out of touch with his nobles, and addicted to base-born minions. These allegations have proved durable, and they have been reiterated in a chain of historiography extending from the early sixteenth to the late twentieth centuries. Only recently has the smear been adequately analysed and refuted.[17] As a result, it has at last become possible to make a more balanced assessment of the respective merits of these two kings, in which justice can be done not only to the mutual differences but also to the similarities. In this adjusted view the symbolic significance of the date of 1488 must necessarily be given greater nuance for, while the political change was dramatic, the cultural continuity was real.

Princes and patronage

It was during the reign of James IV that princely culture in Scotland was first explicitly problematised. This occurred in a poem by William Dunbar (c.1460-1513?): 'Schir, ye haue mony seruitouris'.[18] In the first part of this work, Dunbar lists the many sorts of men busily engaged in working for the king: churchmen, courtiers, craftsmen, doctors of law, doctors of medicine, prognosticators, rhetoricians, philosophers, astrologers, artists, orators, men of arms, knights, musicians, minstrels, singers, mounted soldiers, minters of coin, carvers, carpenters, shipwrights, masons, glaziers, goldsmiths, jewellers, printers, painters and apothecaries.[19] Among all such, Dunbar stakes out a claim for a decent place for himself as poet, and he points out that his art will last at least as long as that of any of these other practitioners. In the second half of the poem Dunbar denounces an equivalent list of parasites and dependents, who are merely exploiting the gracious indulgence of the king. This poem ushers in a novel topic in Scottish poetry, and it may be taken as an adumbration of the general sense of enterprise and bustle in and around the court. At the same time, it is possible that Dunbar's

[16] Burns, 'Papal Gifts to Scottish Monarchs'.
[17] Macdougall, *James III*, pp. 163-64, 269-98, and '"It is I, the Earle of Mar"'.
[18] Bawcutt, ed, *The Poems of William Dunbar*, vol 1, pp. 222-224.
[19] This list as given here is slightly shorter than in the poem, where certain terms are almost doublets, and a few words are obscure.

list of artists and artisans is somewhat protracted for rhetorical effect, and one might observe that the poet's modest plea for the recognition of his art seems to imply no great confidence in the king's appreciation of literature.[20]

As the thrust of this poem suggests, this princely culture may have been more concerned with material than with intellectual matters. There are no records explicitly testifying to the artistic taste of either James III or James IV, or to direct contacts between these kings and contemporary artists: sporadic notes of payment are all that we have to go on. This does not mean, however, that it is impossible to sketch the princely culture of this period. There is a small amount of evidence which may be interpreted as revealing the inclination of the royal will. Moreover, from the material evidence that has survived one can infer the motivations of the princes who caused these works to be made. One can also scrutinise works of literary culture offered to the prince, in the assumption that there is likely to have been a nexus involving the taste of the prince and the works offered to him.[21] Finally, one can point to cultural developments which, though perhaps occurring at some remove from the court, may be assumed to have enjoyed royal approval. In such ways, an account of the princely culture in Scotland during this period does become feasible; unfortunately, however, there is no equivalent of the wealth of evidence available to students of the courts of Italy, France and several other countries.

Literary culture

Readers attaching high value to innovation will have noticed that printers make an appearance near the end of Dunbar's list. In 1507 James IV granted Walter Chepman and Andro Myllar permission to set up the first printing press in Edinburgh; before that date, books by Scottish writers had to be printed abroad.[22] According to the royal patent, the intention was that the works printed should consist of the following: books of the laws of

[20] Bawcutt, *Dunbar the Makar*, pp. 79-80.

[21] On this see Green, *Poets and Princepleasers*, *passim*.

[22] The first work by a Scotsman to be printed was James Liddell's *Tractatus conceptuum et signorum* (Paris, 1498): Broadie, 'James Liddell on Concepts and Signs'. In the sixteenth century many Latin books by Scottish authors continued to be printed at Paris – e.g. John Mair, *Historia Majoris Britanniae tam Angliae quam Scotiae*, published by J. Badius Ascensius in 1521. Scottish vernacular texts of *The Art of Good Living and Good Dying* and of *The kalendayr of the shyppars* were printed at Paris by Vérard in 1503: Duff, 'The two first books printed in the Scottish language'. The first poem in Scots to be printed was the *Contemplacioun of Synnaris*, by William of Touris, which was printed by Wynkyn de Worde (Westminster, 1499); see Mapstone, *The Scots and their Books*.

Scotland; acts of parliament; chronicles; mass books and breviaries after the use of Scotland, with the addition of legends of the Scottish saints.[23] From this list, short as it is, we see some of the specific concerns of the Scottish kings and their advisors. James declares that the patent is granted 'at our instance and request, for our plesour, the honour and proffit of our Realme and Liegis'. This tripartite formulation suggests something of the princely attitude to the new medium; by implication, it encourages one to take a broad view of princely culture, and certainly one which occupies itself with more than merely imaginative literature.

This caveat notwithstanding, Chepman and Myllar are actually best remembered in connection with ten printed booklets containing vernacular poetry. These booklets contain works by the the English poet John Lydgate and by the Scottish poets Robert Henryson and William Dunbar, Andrew Cadiou's Scottish translation of *Le bréviaire des nobles* of Alain Chartier, together with a number of anonymous poems. The genres represented include: romances (*Golagros and Gawain*; *Eglamour*); sundry religious and moral lyrics; moral fable (Henryson, *Orpheus and Eurydice*); treatises on nobility (Chartier) and princely behaviour (*De regimine principum*); allegory (Dunbar, *The Goldyn Targe*); love complaint (Lydgate, *The Complaint of the Black Knight* – known in Scottish texts as *The Maying and Disport of Chaucer*); comic verse (Dunbar, *The Tretis of the tua mariit wemen and the wedo*); flyting (*The Flyting of Dunbar and Kennedy*).[24] The courtly character of this corpus of verse is striking, and it may reflect the taste of the circle of the king and his intimates. However, since one may legitimately assume that these prints were produced as a commercial venture, they may also have been intended to appeal to a somewhat wider circle, one perhaps extending to minor nobility and lairds, churchmen, legal professionals and officials, and members of the *bourgeoisie*.[25] One of these

[23] For the complete text of the letter patent see Dickson and Edmond, *Annals of Scottish Printing*, pp. 7-8.

[24] It may be noted that Dunbar's *Tretis* is not a product of the Chepman and Myllar partnership. It was printed using different letters, possibly when Myllar was still in France. The eleventh and last work in the uniquely surviving convolute containing all these works is the *Gest of Robin Hood*; as a work printed in the types of Jan van Doesborch, it has in reality nothing to do with the Scottish volumes; see Beattie, ed, *The Chepman and Myllar Prints*; *idem*, 'Some early Scottish books'; on Van Doesborch see Franssen, *Tussen Tekst en Publiek*.

[25] It is known, for example, that one Florentine (or Florimund) Martin, a minor landowner in Fife, possessed the now unique copy of the *Goldyn Targe:* Bawcutt, *Dunbar the Makar*, p. 15. Several of these items, for example, were also transcribed by the notary, John Asloan, in his manuscript: Cunningham, 'The Asloan Manuscript'; Van Buuren, 'John Asloan and his Manuscript'.

printed works, however, seems particularly designed to please the king. This is Dunbar's *Ballade of Barnard Stewart*, a poem welcoming the renowned commander on his visit to Edinburgh in 1508.[26] Stuart was a relation of the king's, and was a man with a truly European reputation, having led French armies with distinction in the Italian wars of Charles VIII and Louis XII. As it happened, Stuart died within two months of his arrival, when he was *en route* to the shrine of St Ninian, a melancholy event that led Dunbar to commemorate the general in another poem, known only from manuscript. Stuart himself has been credited with being the author of a treatise on warfare, although it would be more accurate to say that he was the revisor of the earlier work of Robert de Balsac, published at Lyon in 1502 as *La nef des princes et des batailles de noblesse*.[27] As has recently been noted, Stuart was the first Scotsman to bear an *impresa*.[28] From association with Bernard Stuart nothing but reflected glory could accrue to James IV; it therefore seems plausible that Dunbar's welcome poem was either written to commission, or at the least that it was astutely designed to ingratiate royal (and public) taste.[29]

The appearance of three poems by Robert Henryson in the productions of Chepman and Myllar is notable, since it shows the persistent appeal of poetry from the reign of James III.[30] Still other books printed in the types used by Chepman and Myllar, but known today only from fragmentary remains, bear this out: these include the bird-fable of Richard Holland († c.1482), *The Buke of the Howlat* (c.1450), and Hary's fiercely patriotic and quasi-historical romance, *The Wallace* (c.1477-79).[31] In the chief surviving work of Chepman – the *Aberdeen Breviary*, of 1509-10 – we also see continuity. As was noted, James IV was keen to have mass books and

[26] For a discussion of these prints see Fox, 'Middle Scots Poets and Patrons'. Fox (p. 120) points out that the clear overlap between the prints and the contemporary Asloan MS does not extend to Dunbar's welcome for Bernard Stuart. This may support the supposition that it was an 'official' publication, and thus essentially different from the others.

[27] De Comminges, *Bérault Stuart*; Gray, 'A Scottish "Flower of Chivalry"'; Contamine, 'Entre France et Écosse'.

[28] For a reproduction of the *impresa* – with the motto, *Distantia iungit* – see MacDonald, 'Chivalry as a Catalyst of Cultural Change', p. 172.

[29] Bawcutt, *Dunbar the Makar*, p. 4, says that the poem is 'likely to have been commissioned' – presumably by the king.

[30] The standard edition is Fox, ed, *The Poems of Robert Henryson*. The cultural continuity linking the first four kings James – and especially Jameses III and IV – has earlier been stressed in Mapstone, 'Was there a Court Literature in Fifteenth-Century Scotland?'

[31] On Holland see Bawcutt and Riddy, eds, *Longer Scottish Poems*, pp. 43-84; McDiarmid, ed, *Hary's 'Wallace'*.

breviaries for the use of Scotland. Indeed, the king's patent goes on to say that 'na maner of sic bukis of Salusbery use be brocht to be sauld within our Realme in tym cuming', and that any discovered were to be confiscated. The task of compiling the new Scottish national breviary was entrusted to William Elphinstone, bishop of Aberdeen.[32] The latter made great use of legends of the Scottish local saints which had been gathered during the preceding decades, and from these came the lessons for the feast-days of such saints in the Aberdeen Breviary. In this way, Elphinstone's ambition of a reformed breviary dovetailed with James IV's desire for a national (i.e. non-English) use within the Scottish church, and the new medium of print was deliberately imported to effectuate the change.

In many ways, however, the significance of the introduction of printing can be overrated. The great majority of Dunbar's poems, for example, are known only from manuscripts, and of these the most important date from half a century after the efforts of Chepman and Myllar. On the other hand, though there are several surviving Scottish manuscript versions, the earliest known text of the *Contemplacioun of Synnaris* (c.1497) of the Observant Franciscan, William of Touris, is a Westminster print of 1499 by Wynkyn de Worde. The works of Walter Kennedy, for his part, are known exclusively from manuscript.[33] At this date poems written for presentation to the king would most likely be manuscript, and multiple copies would naturally never be required.

An interesting case is that of the prose *Meroure of Wysdome* of John Ireland (Johannes de Irlandia).[34] This large work, which consists in its final version of seven books, carries the date of 1490 on its final page (Edinburgh, NLS Adv MS 18.2.8). In reality, however, it was written for James III and after Sauchieburn was dedicated to the new king.[35] One could hardly find a neater example of cultural continuity from the one reign to the other. In his conclusion, Ireland lays great and explicit stress on his years of service under James III. This may be held to imply that the author is using respectful recollection of the late king as a lever with which to move the conscience of James IV. Were there an ideological chasm between the two

[32] Macfarlane, *William Elphinstone*, pp. 231-46.

[33] On Touris and Kennedy see MacDonald, 'Catholic Devotion into Protestant Lyric'; *Idem*, 'Passion Devotion in Late-Medieval Scotland.

[34] Macpherson, ed, *The Meroure of Wysdome* (vol. 1); Quinn, ed, (vol. 2) and McDonald, ed, (vol. 3).

[35] Burns, 'John Ireland' and *The True Law of Kingship*, pp. 20-39. Curiously, in the Introduction (I, 14-15) Ireland speaks of five books, which, from his summary, would seem to correspond to books i-iii and vi-vii in the final version. Ireland may have added two extra books, though it is possible that he merely expanded his original book iii.

princes Ireland's remarks would have been wholly inappropriate; in fact, he was able for several more years to remain in the service and proximity of the new king. Ireland was a distinguished theologian and preacher, who rose to become rector of the Sorbonne. With his Parisian background, Ireland was used several times by Louis XI and James III as ambassador in diplomatic contacts between the two countries. The *Meroure* is a specimen of the genre of *speculum principis*, and the topics of its seven books are as follows: an exposition of the Lord's Prayer; man's loss of innocence, and its recovery by means of the Incarnation; an exposition of the Creed; the virtues of faith; free will and determination; the sacraments; kingship and its responsibilities. Neither the theology, nor the political and moral advice, in this book is distinguished by great originality of thought[36]: for the present purposes the interest inheres in the fact that such instruction was thought appropriate to two late-medieval Scottish kings.

Early in his work (I, 74), Ireland says that while he will speak of is the 'science and prescience of God'; in this context he pays lukewarm praise to Chaucer, who, though not a trained theologian, also wrote about such matters. Again, in his final address to the king, Ireland apologises for the fact that his thirty years residence in France has prevented him from becoming acquainted with 'the gret eloquens of Chauceir na [nor] colouris that men usis in this Inglis metir' (III, 164). From such passages it would seem that Ireland was aware that Chaucer was regarded as the master poet at the Scottish court, and that he, the theologian, had taken the trouble to acquaint himself with such vernacular literature. This is valuable evidence, since the poems usually listed as demonstrating Scottish acquaintance with Chaucer (Henryson's *Testament of Cresseid*, Dunbar's *The Goldyn Targe* and *Tretis*) have no *explicit* connection with the court. Moreover, there are no features directly connecting the largest contemporary Scottish anthology of Chaucerian material – the so-called '*Kingis Quair* manuscript' (Oxford, Bodl. MS Arch. Selden B. 24) – to royal circles; rather, this important manuscript was owned by the noble family of Sinclair of Roslin and Ravenscraig.[37] Ireland's words, however, let us see that at least with regard to Chaucer the king and his most enlightened nobles *did* share a similar taste. By extension, therefore, this allows one (in lieu of harder evidence) to risk the inference that James IV may well have known the *Kingis Quair*,

[36] Ireland's seventh book has been shown to be a skilfully assembled mosaic of ideas and quotations drawn from Jean Gerson, while in one chapter he makes extensive quotation from Chaucer's *Tale of Melibee*, and in another he carefully refutes a passage on royal election by Marsilius of Padua: McDonald, ed, *Meroure of Wysdome*, p. xxv quoting Lyall, Mason and Mapstone.

[37] Boffey, Edwards and Barker-Benfield, eds, *The Works of Geoffrey Chaucer*, pp. 21-23. See also note 93, below.

which, after all, supposedly narrates the youthful love experience of his great-grandfather.

It has been argued that the *Contemplacioun of Synnaris* of William of Touris and the *Passioun of Crist* of Walter Kennedy are, in their different ways, also mirrors of princes.[38] The former resembles Ireland's *Meroure* in being in seven sections; here, however, they are designed for reading and meditation during the days of one week, and deal with the following topics: the state of the world; man's original innocence; death; judgement; the Passion; hell; heaven. As mentioned earlier, the poem may well have been intended for James's regular Holy Week retreat at the convent of the Observant Franciscans at Stirling. For its part, Kennedy's *Passioun of Crist* contains a striking number of allusions to the Christian knight and the winning of a heavenly crown (also a prominent theme in Touris's poem). Such works seem particularly apt for the spiritual and moral edification of this specific king, and are thus at least a part-reflection of the princely taste.

With Dunbar we are on firmer ground. Many of his poems are directly addressed to the king and make mention of events at the court. While it is true that there is no record of James IV ever rewarding Dunbar for his poetry, he did receive a present from the king on the occasion of celebrating his first mass, and he was the beneficiary of a generous royal pension. It is not impossible that the poet acted as chaplain to either king or queen.[39] At the same time, Dunbar would scarcely have persisted in addressing poems to the king, had he not known that his efforts would elicit a favourable response. Dunbar's *œuvre* displays the typical gamut of the courtly versifier[40]: *commemoration of royal pageantry* ('Blythe Aberdean, thow beriall of all tounis' B8; 'Gladethe, thoue queyne of Scottis regioun' B15; 'Illuster Lodouick, of France most cristin king' B23; 'Quhen Merche wes with variand windis past' B52; 'Renownit, ryall, right reuerend and serene' B56); *comic reminiscence of princely escapades* ('As yung Awrora with cristall haile' B4; 'Lang heff I maed of ladyes quhytt B28; 'Sir Ihon Sinclair begowthe to dance' B70; 'This hindir nycht in Dumfermeling' B76); *poetry on and of love* ('My hartis tresure and swete assured fo' B34; 'Ryght as the stern of day begouth to schyne' B59; 'Sen that I am a presoneir' B69; 'Sweit rose of vertew and of gentilnes' B71); *humour at the expense of royal servitors* ('I maister Andro Kennedy' B19; 'I thocht lang quhill sum lord come hame' B22; 'Schir, I complane off iniuris' B64; 'The wardraip-

[38] This paragraph is based on MacDonald, 'Passion Devotion in Late-Medieval Scotland'.

[39] On Dunbar and court poetry generally see Bawcutt, *Dunbar the Makar*, chapter 3; specifically on the poet's pension: pp. 107-108.

[40] The poems mentioned here are numbered as in the edition by Bawcutt (1998).

per of Wenus boure' B72; 'O gracious princes guid and fair' B73); *aristocratic disdain for the* bourgeoisie *and amusement at the* mores *of craftsmen and rustics* ('In secreit place this hyndir nycht' B25; 'Betuix twell houris and ellevin' B48; 'Quhy will ye, merchantis of renoun' B55; 'Richt arely one Ask Wedinsday' B57); *ingratiating appeals for reward* ('My lordis of chalker, pleis yow to heir' B36; 'My prince in God, gif the guid grace' B37; 'Sanct saluatour, send siluer sorrow!' B61; 'Schir, lat it neuer in toune be tald' B66).[41] By extension, one cannot err greatly in interpreting still other poems by Dunbar in the light of a putative context of performance at court. For example, the exhilarating and vituperative rhetorical exchange with Kennedy in the *Flyting* (B65) seems verily designed to function as general entertainment, and the *Tretis* (B3), with its exposure of the sexual motivations of three *bourgeoises* dressed as ladies of romance, would readily find favour with members of the nobility used to the conventions of courtly and erotic verse. In addition, Dunbar's religious lyrics, which include some of the most accomplished specimens of his poetic art, may well have been intended to give direction to the devotions of the king or queen: it is in any event clear that such poems do not arise from motives of self revelation on the part of the poet.[42] Responsible and sensitive contextualisation, therefore, proceeding from poems where particular features are unambiguously present to others which readily accommodate a similar interpretative 'fit', allows one to use Dunbar's poems to map the taste of the poet's princely master. On this basis, the overall picture of James IV which emerges is one of a restless, energetic, self-conscious, passionate, cultured, intellectually curious and intermittently devout prince.

The literary production of the age of James III confronts us with the same difficulty of how to determine which literary works were actually, probably, or possibly known at court.[43] Many, and perhaps a majority, of the poems known to have been composed during this reign – for example, Henryson's *Fables*; Hary's *Wallace*; the anonymous romance *Lancelot of the Laik*, and *The Talis of the Fyve Bestis* – seem to contain more political advice than spiritual instruction; perhaps naturally, this has been seen as an indication of the inadequacy of James III as a ruler.[44] The problem with this

[41] Despite the tedious length of this list, it yet leaves out of account many excellent poems of a religious and/or moral sort, which are not necessarily courtly.
[42] MacDonald, 'Religious Poetry in Middle Scots, pp. 93-96.
[43] On this difficulty see Mapstone, 'Was there a Court Literature in Fifteenth-Century Scotland?'
[44] McDiarmid, 'The Metrical Chronicles' pp. 27-38; MacQueen, 'Poetry – James I to Henryson'. MacQueen declares (p. 60) that *Lancelot of the Laik* was 'composed for the queen, or another lady of the court'. This literature is surveyed and discussed in Mapstone, *The Advice to Princes*.

deduction is that advice to princes literature is equally prominent under James IV, for whom the same conclusion has not been drawn. One example of cultural continuity in this area is that during the selfsame year which saw the replacement of James III by James IV the scribe, John Ramsay, prior of the Perth Charterhouse, copied out one text of John Barbour's royalistic historical romance, the *Bruce* (written 1375), another copy of that poem, and the only surviving text of the *Wallace*.[45] Again, the romance, the *Buik of King Alexander the Conquerour*, which has been ascribed to Sir Gilbert Hay and is thought to have been composed c.1460, was copied, very possibly with reworking, in 1499 to give the present text.[46] Such *remaniement* in the late century of earlier literary works suggests that conservatism may have been a strong characteristic of Scottish princely culture.

The most imposing single literary composition of medieval Scotland, however, was not any vernacular text but rather *Scotichronicon*, the compilation by Walter Bower (1385-1449), abbot of Inchcolm.[47] This vast history of Scotland, which itself is based on the chronicle of John of Fordun († 1385), begins with the Creation, and continues to the murder of James I. The latter is given a copious eulogy; indeed, this king is presented as an ideal for subsequent princes.[48] An impressive number of copies of *Scotichronicon* survive, some of them dating from the period under discussion.[49] While some of these texts can be connected with the households of particular magnates, it is unthinkable that the book could have escaped kingly attention. Bower gives a comprehensive account of James I's virtues: performance in music; personal intelligence; literary composition; drawing and painting; horticulture; physical games; mechanical and gentlemanly arts; knowledge of the Scriptures; love of country; moral philosophy and the liberal arts; supervision and love of the clergy; peacemaking; upholding

[45] Cunningham, '*Bruce* and *Wallace*', p. 247. McDiarmid and Stevenson, eds, *Barbour's Bruce*; McDiarmid, ed, *Hary's Wallace* (*Wallace*, I, ix) states categorically that: 'Nothing is known of Ramsay's identity'. He also notes (*ibid.*) that the Edinburgh MS of the *Bruce* was made for no-one more exalted than Symon Lochmalony, vicar of Auchtermoonzie, in Fife.

[46] Cartwright, ed, *Gilbert Hay*. The first volume (Introduction) has yet to appear. See also Bunt, *Alexander the Great*, pp. 62-68; McDiarmid, 'Concerning Sir Gilbert Hay'.

[47] Watt *et al.* eds, *Scotichronicon*. See especially Mapstone, 'Bower on kingship'; *Eadem*, 'The *Scotichronicon*'s First Readers'.

[48] Possession of a satisfactory history of the kingdom was a high priority for contemporary princes. For a discussion of how a comparable (Burgundian) chronicle was based on earlier compilations (associated with the abbey of St Denis) see Small, *George Chastelain*.

[49] Watt, ed, *Scotichronicon*, IX, pp. 148-199.

justice; maintenance of decorous music in the chapel royal. Like most eulogies, this one may owe as much to rhetoric as to reality. On the other hand, it may be read as articulating Bower's recommendation to the young James II, and as such it probably set out a pattern of princely culture which could continue to be functional for the latter's descendants.[50]

Church culture

There are a few art objects which, since they contain portraits of the Scottish kings and were doubtless commissioned by the latter, may be taken as being expressive of princely taste. The pair of wings painted by Hugo van der Goes (c.1478-79) as part of the altarpiece for Trinity Church (the central panel is lost) contains a representation of James III and his son, clad in ermine robes, and kneeling in prayer before an altar.[51] Behind them stands Scotland's patron saint, St Andrew, who is shown laying the crown on the king's head, and presenting the king [to Christ].[52] A shield bearing a crowned lion rampant[53] is prominently displayed on the wall behind, topped by a crowned helmet, with another rampant lion as crest. Among the possible subtexts of this panel may be proposed: the spiritual dimension of royalty and its symbols; an interest in making manifest the future succession; a wish to associate the son with the religious devotion of the father. The scene is not realistic, but is rather a portrayal of idealised royal piety.[54] This would have been eminently appropriate to the Trinity Church, since it was founded by Mary of Gelderland as a memorial to her late husband, James II. Mary herself died in 1463; the choir and transepts were completed by James III, though the nave was never built.[55] The piety displayed by

[50] Watt, ed, *Scotichronicon*, VIII, pp. 302-337. In his notes to this passage Watt points out how Bower's account was eked out in later manuscripts with verses commemorating James I.

[51] On these panels see Thompson and Campbell, *Hugo van der Goes*; Ridderbos, *De melancholie van de kunstenaar*; Tolley, 'Hugo van der Goes's Altarpiece', plates xxxiii-xxxiv.

[52] Clearly, one cannot be certain of the subject of the lost central panel: but a representation of the Virgin and Child would be programatically very appropriate. The Holy Trinity is in various ways the subject of the outer panels, as was appropriate to a church with such a dedication.

[53] Another such crowned lion rampant on the royal shield, from the time of James III, appears on the first folio of a manuscript of Virgil (Edinburgh, University Library MS 195). For a colour reproduction see Hall, ed, *Manuscript Treasures*, plate 1.

[54] This panel has often been reproduced, for example: (in colour) Macmillan, *Scottish Art*, p. 20; (black and white) Macfarlane, *William Elphinstone*, opposite p. 182.

[55] Fawcett, *Scottish Architecture*, pp. 174-177.

James III in this masterpiece of Flemish painting may well have been instilled in him by his Burgundian mother, and it may have been his hope that his own son would inherit this spirituality.

A miniature of James IV included in the Book of Hours of James IV and Margaret Tudor (c.1503) shows the new king in a very similar praying pose. This time it is the king's personal patron, St James (the Greater), who is presenting him to Christ, and once again the saint's right hand rests upon the crown. St Andrew appears on the one visible wing of the depicted altarpiece, and also in the chivalric collar which encircles the rampant lion coat of arms on the antependium of the altar.[56] The order of St Andrew was founded by the king's father in 1470, and this miniature may therefore be taken as evoking the bond between father and son, at least in as much as chivalry and spirituality are concerned. One notes that James IV is shown here as wearing a closed, imperial crown; this important signifier of Scottish *imperium* had been introduced by his father, who first used it as a motif on the silver groat coin of 1485.[57] The use of this detail was an unambiguous assertion of Scottish independence from England, France and the Holy Roman Empire, and it may also have been intended to emphasise the perhaps only point of advantage that the kings of Scotland had enjoyed over the mighty dukes of Burgundy.[58] This Book of Hours is one of the most accomplished productions of the Ghent-Bruges school, and the illuminations have been attributed to Simon Bening and Gerard Horenbout.[59] Most recently, however, the miniaturist has been designated, simply, as 'The Master of James IV of Scotland'.[60] The Scottish details included in this illustration made in Flanders must have been inserted at the specifica-

[56] Colour reproduction in Macmillan, *Scottish Art*, p. 14. The manuscript is now Vienna, Österreichische Nationalbibliothek codex 1897, of which there is a facsimile: Unterkircher, ed, *Das Gebetbuch Jakobs IV*. See also Macfarlane, 'The Book of Hours of James IV'.

[57] On the symbolism of the imperial crown see Mason, 'This Realm of Scotland is an Empire?'. Mason notes (p. 77) that the political issue of imperial status evolved in Italy, and was articulated in the writings of Bartolus de Saxoferrato (1314-57). As early as 1469 the Scottish parliament had decreed that James III possessed 'ful jurisdictione and free impire within his realme': Burns, *Lordship, Kingship and Empire*, pp. 14 and 99. Scottish claims to such imperial status would seem to antedate any such made in England.

[58] See MacDonald, 'Chivalry as a Catalyst of Culural Change', p. 152. One might note, in this context, the contemporary motif of the 'five anointed kings' (i.e. of the Empire, France, England, Sicily and Scotland): Van Anrooij, *Helden van Weleer*, p. 113.

[59] Macmillan, *Scottish Art*, pp. 24-27.

[60] Smeyers, *Flemish Miniatures*, pp. 466-467.

tion of the commissioner (one assumes James IV); they may thus be seen as indicating some of his cultural and religious attitudes.[61]

The Stewart kings' ecclesiastical building works confirm the impression of piety sketched above. In a sense, James I set the pattern by founding the Charterhouse at Perth – the only one in Scotland. Fifteenth-century princes were very much in favour of this strict order, and charterhouses often doubled as royal mausolea. James might have known those at London (1371), Sheen (1414) and Mount Grace (1398),[62] but he would also know of French equivalents, not to mention the celebrated charterhouse founded by Philip the Bold (1388) at Champmol, near Dijon. James II seems to have been the person who had the original idea for Trinity College, although it was actually established by Mary of Gelderland. James III, for his part, was responsible for the extraordinary chapel incorporated into the collegiate church of Restalrig (close to the royal palace at Holyrood, just outside Edinburgh). It has been suggested that this edifice may have been intended to function as a relic chapel, or as a place for the perpetual exposition of the consecrated host; it is also possible that it may have accommodated the chapters of the order of St Andrew.[63] In the north of his kingdom, James III founded (1487) the collegiate church of St Duthac at Tain, as mentioned above. James IV's contribution was the Kirk of Steill (Ladykirk), at Upsettlington (Berwickshire), into which he poured a surprising amount of money. This church was on a geographically prominent location, just across

[61] Scottish details in this manuscript should not be taken as portraying any historically realistic scenes. Macdougall (*James IV*, 1989, figure 4) says that the scene of the Office of the Dead 'may represent the funeral obsequies of James III', and Macmillan (*Scottish Art*, p. 24) endorses this supposition, adding that it 'lends a note to the book that is very personal to the king'. Impressed, he reproduces the scene in full-page enlargement. In the 1997 reissue of Macdougall's book (at figure 4) the opinion is maintained, but now mention is also made of the strikingly similar scene in the Grimani Breviary [Venice, Bib. N. Marciana MS lat. I. 99]. For a colour reproduction of the latter see Salmi and Mellini, eds, *The Grimani Breviary*, plate 58. As it happens, a third version of this same scene of the Office of the Dead (c. 1480) is in the Hastings Hours (London, BL Addit. MS 54782), conveniently reproduced in Backhouse, ed, *The Hastings Hours*, p. 56. In truth, these three miniatures are (very close) variations on the same model, and the only significant changes are those affecting the heraldic identification of the arms and pennants of the commissioner. Apart from such specific details and a general thematic relevance, any supposed Scottishness in the Hours of James and Margaret should be treated *cum grano salis*.

[62] On the Carthusian houses in England see Knowles and Hadcock, *Medieval Religious Houses*, pp. 133-136.

[63] MacDonald, 'Chapel of Restalrig'. Work began on the chapel around 1477, but it was clearly finished by 1486, when James, Bishop Elphinstone, and the bishop of Imola, Giacomo Passarella, made a formal Easter visit there.

the Tweed from the castle of the bishop of Durham, at Norham. The site was politically significant, since it was the traditionally neutral meeting-place for boundary negotiations between the two neighbouring kingdoms. Interestingly, this church belonged to the king's favourite order, the Observant Franciscans. At Stirling nothing now remains of the church and convent of this order, but this building, close to the castle, may well have been impressive, since it was considered suitable for James's Easter retreats. This survey does not exhaust the list of churches founded, expanded or reconstructed in Scotland during the late Middle Ages, but it does indicate the Stewart kings' direct interest in promoting the exercise of piety through prestige building projects.

Much of the impetus to construction was linked to particular institutions. Of the latter, one of the most significant was the Chapel Royal. Until the time of James III, the Chapel had had its permanent base at the church of St Mary on the Rock, beside St Andrews cathedral.[64] It has been plausibly suggested, however, that the erection of Restalrig to collegiate status may have been connected with a wish on James's part to transfer the Chapel to a place closer to his normal residence.[65] In 1501 James IV was to refound the Chapel Royal, with a larger permanent choir, and a new building within Stirling Castle.[66] In this chapel, modern polyphony would have been heard alongside traditional Gregorian melody. The newest repertoire would have included works by Robert Carver, the outstanding composer of late-medieval Scotland, whose remarkable, nineteen-part motet, *O bone Iesu*, was written before 1513.[67] At the Scottish Chapel Royal leading Burgundian musical fashions were combined with the influences of the stately *Eton Choirbook* style, knowledge of which arrived with Margaret Tudor, in 1503. The high musical standards at Restalrig and at Stirling meant that the Chapel Royal in Scotland was able to impart to the piety of the royal family an aesthetically fitting musical dimension, one which could

[64] In another sense, however, the Chapel Royal was the choir which travelled around with the king, mentioned by Bower in his praise of James I. This was also true in England, on which see Baldwin, *The Chapel Royal*.

[65] Macdougall, *James III*, pp. 231-232. James III differed from earlier kings, in making Edinburgh his permanent capital.

[66] Rogers, *History of the Chapel Royal*; MacQueen, ed, *Ballattis of Luve*; Van Heijnsbergen, 'The Chapel Royal'. It may be noted that, even after the king's new foundation at Stirling, musical standards at Restalrig remained high. James IV's chapel was a casualty of the Reformation, and the present building at Stirling was erected by James VI. Cf. Fawcett, *Stirling Castle*.

[67] Ross, *Musick Fyne*; Preece, *Music in the Scottish Church*. For the music of Carver's motet see Elliott, ed, *The Complete Works of Robert Carver*, vol. 1, pp. 219-239.

withstand comparison with equivalent institutions at other European courts.[68]

Princely display

Rulers who value culture tend to want princes abroad and subjects at home to register the fact. It is noticeable that, during the period of James III and IV there comes to be a change in the Latinity of the royal correspondence, as the new humanism begins to gain sway. Scotland had had a foretaste of humanist culture through the visit of Æneas Silvius Piccolomini (later Pope Pius II) to the court of James I, in 1435.[69] James III's friend, Anselm Adorne of Bruges,[70] was someone who appreciated the new style of writing, and also notable in this context is Archibald Whitelaw († 1498), the humanist secretary of James III.[71] From 1505 James IV's secretary was Patrick Paniter, friend of Erasmus, and correspondence between the Scottish king and his equals could be conducted with fitting eloquence.[72] Self-fashioning is always easier with professional help.[73]

Another way in which the prince presented himself to the world was through the circulation of his likeness. If James III had been the first Scottish king to have his portrait painted (on the Van der Goes altarpiece), his son went further: in addition to the miniature already mentioned, there are two panel portraits and one drawing, all of which are firmly rooted in the secular world.[74] One painting, now at Abbotsford, is dated 1507, and is

[68] On such institutions see, for example, Reese, *Music in the Renaissance*; Perkins, *Music in the Age of the Renaissance*, pp. 89-98. It may be noted that high quality church music was available at other churches in late-medieval Scotland (e.g. the cathedrals of Glasgow and Aberdeen).

[69] There is a fanciful painting (c. 1507-8) of this embassy, by Pinturicchio, in the Piccolomini Library at Siena. Reproduced (black and white) in Jusserand, *The Romance of a King's Life*, frontispiece.

[70] Heers and de Groër, ed, *Itinéraire d'Anselme Adorno*; Macquarrie, 'Anselm Adornes of Bruges'.

[71] On Whitelaw see Durkan, 'The Cultural Background in Sixteenth-Century Scotland', p. 290; MacQueen, 'The Literature of Fifteenth-Century Scotland', p. 194, and 'Aspects of Humanism', p. 19; Durkan, 'Education', pp. 130-131.

[72] On Paniter see Macdougall, *James IV*, pp. 209-211 and *passim*; Durkan, 'The Be-ginnings of Humanism in Scotland'.

[73] If we may go by the evidence of Don Pedro de Ayala, the Spanish ambassador who visited the Edinburgh court in 1498, James himself had a real gift for languages, speaking – in addition to Scots/English – Latin (very well), French, German, Flemish, Italian, Spanish and Gaelic: Dickinson, Donaldson and Milne, eds, *A Source Book*, p. 3.

[74] I leave out of consideration here kings' heads in manuscript initials, on coins,

said to be 'rather in the French rather than the Flemish manner'.[75] One of the points of interest here is that the king is shown wearing a collar with a pendant of St George. Since James IV was never admitted to the English order of the Garter (of which St George was the patron), the pendant shown in the portrait may be that of the order of St George of Carinthia, founded by Frederick III in 1468, and which was in the personal gift of the Habsburg emperor.[76] The second portrait is a seventeenth-century copy by Daniel Mytens of a now lost original of c.1500; in it James appears, below the royal motto, 'In my defens', as a magnificent young prince with hawk on hand. The *significatio* may be that he is being shown as ripe for marriage. Thirdly, in Arras, Bibliothèque Municipale MS 266, once in the possession of Jacques le Boucq († 1573), 'roi d'armes du Hainault', there is a drawing of James IV. This shows some lively detail about the face, but it is difficult to know to what extent, if any, it may correspond with reality.[77]

In Edinburgh, several painters received money from James IV. One was David Prat († 1503), who is recorded in the account books from 1496. Prat, together with an anonymous 'Almayn' (presumably a Fleming), received payments in 1502-03 in connection with work on a marble tomb for James III at Cambuskenneth Abbey (adjacent to Stirling).[78] Prat also painted an altar for a church in that town. In 1505 a triptych of Our Lady and Son with angels carrying musical instruments was given to the Chapel Royal, and it is possible that this is the work by Prat.[79] Other painters visited the Scottish court, for example, the Frenchman 'Piers', from 1505 until 1508, and the Englishman 'Mynours' (i.e. John Maynard, or de Mayne), in 1502. Portraits of non-aristocratic dignitaries also begin to appear at this time. There is a panel (c.1488-1505) showing Bishop Elphinstone, and there is a miniature (1498) of James Brown, dean of Aberdeen; both of these works were executed in Flanders and imported.[80] Two Scottish

and in drawings in armorials, since these are to a large degree schematic.

[75] The information in this paragraph depends largely on Macmillan, *Scottish Art*, pp. 30-31 (with reproductions, pp. 28-29).

[76] On this order see Boulton, *Knights of the Crown*, p. 399.

[77] See Beard, 'Early Stewart Portraits'. Beard reproduces several drawings from the 'Recueil d'Arras'; the one of King James IV is also in Mackie, *James IV of Scotland*, opposite p. 53. See also Campbell, 'The Authorship of the "Recueil d'Arras"', plates 23-26.

[78] Margaret of Denmark had been buried at Cambuskenneth in 1486, and, after the battle of Sauchieburn, the corpse of James III was also brought there.

[79] Macmillan, *Scottish Art*, pp. 30-31.

[80] For the Elphinstone portrait see Macfarlane, *William Elphinstone*, frontispiece. For the Brown miniature see Macmillan, *Scottish Art*, p. 26; Smeyers, *Flemish Miniatures*, p. 467. On the manuscript (Edinburgh, NLS MS 10270) see McRoberts, 'Dean Brown's Book of Hours', pp. 144-167.

painters, Alexander Chalmers and Sir Thomas Galbraith (a clerk of the Chapel Royal at Stirling) painted various heraldic and decorative works for the king. Although little of this applied art has survived, William Dunbar was clearly justified in including painters in the list of skilled people pullulating at the court of James IV.

Of the artists and artisans mentioned by Dunbar, a large number would doubtless be involved with the construction and equipping of royal residences. It was in fact a contemporary cultural imperative that there be a correspondence between the prince and the quality of the buildings which housed him. Although the Scottish court was still to a certain extent peripatetic, there was from the fifteenth century a definite trend towards more stable residence at a small number of places. Of these, Edinburgh (Holyrood), Linlithgow and Stirling were easily the most important, and throughout the fifteenth and sixteenth centuries a great deal of construction and reconstruction went on there. Linlithgow, over which Anselm Adorne was appointed lieutenant, was never a place designed for serious defence; in fact, it has been aptly designated as a 'palatium ad modum castri'.[81] At Edinburgh the kings largely abandoned the castle on its impregnable crag, and (first under James III) opted rather for the palace of Holyrood, beside the abbey and next to the park. Stirling, however, was different, and was a combination of palace and castle. James IV had his Great Hall constructed there, and later erected the new Chapel Royal between the hall and the so-called 'King's Old Building'.[82] On account of the obvious security which Stirling, by virtue of its position, could offer, it was regularly the residence of the queen (especially Margaret of Denmark) and of the royal children. New kings habitually, when need arose, made improvements to the work of their predecessors – as when James IV had Holyrood made fit for the reception of Margaret Tudor in 1503, and when he expanded his hunting-lodge at Falkland, in Fife. This building activity continued through the sixteenth century, during which time Holyrood, Linlithgow and Stirling continued to receive the lion's share of royal munificence.

When once the Scottish princes had provided themselves with fitting backdrops, they could begin to cultivate the contemporary enthusiasm for pageantry. In this area, the contribution of James III was the foundation, noted above, of the chivalric order of St Andrew. This was an attempt to emulate the order of the Garter of Edward III (1349) and the Golden Fleece of Philip the Good (1430), though the most immediate parallels were with the Louis XI's order of St Michael (1469) and Christian I's order of St

[81] Campbell, 'Linlithgow's "Princely Palace"'.

[82] On Holyrood and Stirling see Fawcett, *Scottish Architecture*, pp. 301-330, and *Stirling Castle*; Dunbar, *Scottish Royal Palaces*.

Mary – or the Elephant – (1457?).[83] In establishing the chapel of Restalrig, James III may have been thinking of the chapel of St George at Windsor, the location of the chapters of the Garter. However, it was James IV who was really to exploit chivalry and pageantry for political effect. In doing this, the Scottish king may usefully be compared with such illustrious contemporaries as Henry VIII and, especially, Maximilian of Habsburg; all these princes, in fact, evince their Renaissance magnificence through the cultivation of neo-medieval display. In the case of James IV this emerges from the account made by John Younge, the Somerset Herald, of the reception of Margaret Tudor to Scotland, and in particular to Edinburgh.[84] In circumstances of make-believe romance, James could play before his bride, for example, the role of knight on a white horse rescuing damsels in distress.[85] The comparison with Maximilian's fashioning of himself in the pseudo-autobiographical romance works *Freydal*, *Theuerdank* and *Weisskünig* is what immediately springs to mind.[86] But James did not stop here. In 1507, and again in 1508, he convened tournaments in Edinburgh, in which he himself starred as the Black Knight.[87] As has also been noted above, this was also the period in which James gave most consideration to the plan of leading a crusade against the Turk.[88] Such an enterprise, which proved beyond the power of Pius II in 1465, was altogether unrealistic fifty years on; James, however, does not seem easily to have been dissuaded from his chivalric ambitions. If he had acquired such ideas from his reading of courtly romances, that would make him something of a Don Quixote *avant la lettre*.

Princely culture in national perspective

It has sometimes been taken for granted that culture in medieval Scotland was coterminous with princely culture. Such a view, however, demands qualification. For a start, there is the problematic issue of the position of culture in relation to the geographical constraints on royal power. Orkney

[83] See Boulton, *Knights of the Crown*, pp. 103, 360, 501.
[84] For the text see Leland, ed, *De Rebus Britannicis Collectanea*, vol. 3, pp. 258-300.
[85] The symbolism of this episode has been ably analysed by Fradenburg, *City, Marriage, Tournament*, pp. 91-149.
[86] Müller, *Gedechtnus*, pp. 104-146.
[87] Bawcutt, *Dunbar the Makar*, pp. 54-55.
[88] Mackie, *King James IV*, pp. 201-206; Macdougall, *James IV*, pp. 199-207; Macquarrie, *Scotland and the Crusades*, pp. 107-112; Housley, *The Later Crusades*, pp. 124-125. Housley, p. 426, characterises James as suffering from 'spontaneous if naive enthusiasm'.

and Shetland fell under Scottish domination only in 1469, when they were part of the dowry pledge (never redeemed) made by Christian I, father of Margaret of Denmark, on the occasion of his daughter's marriage to James III. Before that event, and for some time thereafter, the inhabitants of those islands lived mainly within a Scandinavian world. Then again, the Highland part of Scotland (half of the superficies), had its own Celtic culture and language, connected with that of Ireland. This area was for practical purposes outside royal control during the period, although James III began to make inroads, with the forfeiture (1475) of, and attack (1476) on, John Macdonald, earl of Ross. Under James IV, the quasi-independent Macdonald Lordship of the Isles was forfeited in 1493. Even in those regions of the Lowlands remote from Edinburgh, the authority of the king was often of lesser importance than that of the local magnates, though once again we see changes to this during the period.[89] While it is true that James III left Edinburgh only rarely, the expeditions, travels and pilgrimages of James IV were, among other things, an assertion of royal authority throughout the kingdom.

James IV, however, did not possess a monopoly on culture, and many manifestations thereof were of non-princely nature.[90] Bishops could be powerful patrons, though not every bishop was as closely involved with the affairs of the royal court as were William Elphinstone and Gavin Douglas. Monastic culture was governed by the demands of the relevant rule, and decisions of the general chapter. Robert Henryson, as (presumably) a teacher at the school at Dunfermline, is without question one of the greatest poets of medieval Scotland, but his credentials as a courtly writer are not strong. The friars were organised in their own provinces, exempted from episcopal control. To take the Observant Franciscans as an example, whereas the works of certain members of that order, especially at the Stirling house, may have impinged upon the conscience of the king, that is not necessarily the case with all such. For their part, the universities (St Andrews 1411; Glasgow 1451; Aberdeen 1495) were from the beginning controlled and staffed by churchmen, but the contacts of the latter were not so much with the royal court but more with intellectuals and theologians at other universities (e.g. Paris, Oxford, Leuven, Cologne, Padua, Bologna) in the rest of learned Europe. The burghs, with their own merchant and craft guilds and their growing interest in fraternities, with their own altars and chaplains, were also capable of autonomous cultural initiatives. For

[89] Brown, 'Scotland Tamed?'.

[90] For this paragraph see Ross, 'Some Notes on the Religious Orders', pp. 185-240; Durkan, 'The Cultural Background in Sixteenth-Century Scotland'; Dilworth, *Scottish Monasteries*; Lynch, Spearman and Stell, eds, *The Scottish Medieval Town*.

example, the Bruges cult of the Holy Blood was welcomed in Edinburgh and Aberdeen, the two principal Scottish ports trading with the Flemish staple. More important still, however, was the nobility, some members of which took an active interest in culture. Several collegiate churches were founded by such families: Crichton (William, Lord Crichton, 1449); Roslin (William Sinclair, earl of Caithness and Orkney, c.1450); Guthrie (Sir David Guthrie, c.1479); Seton (George, Lord Seton, 1492).[91] Men like these may, within the limits of their own power and inclination, be said to have promoted a courtly, if non-royal, culture within their own territories. To the extent that these minor centres followed the trend set by the king's court one might, however, claim such local initiatives as an indicator (albeit at second hand) of the percolation of (at least aspects of) princely culture.

The area of literature is especially interesting from this point of view, and even before the reign of James III it is known that several families of the gentry were encouraging the production of literature, or, at the least, commissioning for their own use copies of existing texts.[92] In this context, the family of the Sinclairs of Roslin, and of Ravenscraig deserves particular mention. It was at Roslin for William Sinclair, earl of Orkney and Caithness and chancellor of Scotland, that the prose works of Sir Gilbert Hay (translations, from the French, of Honoré Bouvet, *L'Arbre des Batailles*; Ramon Lull, *Livre de l'ordre de Chevalerie*; and pseudo-Aristotle, *Secreta Secretorum*) were written, and it was doubtless at Roslin, later, that the only surviving manuscript copy was made. Also at Roslin (or Ravenscraig) was the manuscript of the *Kingis Quair*, noted above, and in the last year of the reign of James IV Gavin Douglas dedicated his translation of the *Aeneid* not to the king but to Henry, Lord Sinclair.[93] In subsequent times the trend towards pockets of local culture would develop further, especially among the gentry. A Lowland example is that of the poet, family-historian and judge, Sir Richard Maitland (1496-1586), who spent his formative years under James IV, and later commented on court and national affairs from the

[91] For details of these and other foundations see Cowan and Easson, *Medieval Religious Houses Scotland*.

[92] For example, Richard Holland's poem, the *Buke of the Howlat*, was written at Darnaway Castle (Morayshire) for Elizabeth Dunbar, wife of Archibald Douglas, earl of Moray: Riddy, 'The Alliterative Revival'.

[93] Bawcutt, *Gavin Douglas*, p. 93. For other MSS owned by Sinclair see Stevenson, ed, *Gilbert of the Haye's Prose Manuscript*, vol. 1, pp. xxxiv-xxxv. Sally Mapstone believes that Ravenscraig is the more likely place for the *Kingis Quair*: see her review of Boffey *et al.*, *The Works*.

position of his own residence, at Lethington.[94] A (near) Highland example is provided by the family of the Campbells of Glenorchy.[95]

There is a considerable corpus of literature in Middle Scots for which we know little concerning author or provenance. Among the texts which could be mentioned here are: alliterative romances, *Golagros and Gawain* and *Rauf Coilyear*; non-alliterative romances, *Lancelot of the Laik*, *The Buik of Alexander*, *Clariodus*, the Scottish *Troy Book* fragments; burlesque romances, *Christis Kirk on the Green*, *Peblis to the Play*; moral tales, *The Thre Prestis of Peblis*, *The Book of the Chess*; love poetry, *The Quair of Jelusy*; prose treatises, *The Spektakle of Luf*, *The Cart of the Warld*, *The Sex Werkdayis and Agis*.[96] Some of these works – especially, perhaps, the romances – might well have appealed to princely taste. However, as has been discussed above, it is difficult to delimit what might, potentially, belong to courtly literature. One cannot be certain that such works were indeed known at the court, and it is entirely possible that they got no further than the more literate members of the nobility, gentry, professionals, merchants and more prosperous tradespeople.

On the other hand, there are many literary works which long have been interpreted as alluding to the political and social situation in contemporary Scotland. To the extent that such interpretations are warranted, it might be necessary to classify these works as culture that is *potentially* princely, by virtue of its message and likely destination. But if such works might have been intended to send a signal to the king, they were also designed to make a more popular appeal. Even though the king might be unlikely to derive unalloyed pleasure from the political animadversions made in such literature, it is probable that these works would reach a large and enthusiastic readership. There is a fine dividing line sometimes between the literature criticising, and that adhorting, princes.

State of the art, or art of the state?

In the matter of culture, late-medieval Scotland was making considerable progress, in many areas, in both the religious and secular domains. This is already perceptible during the reigns of James I and James II, but it comes to real fruition under James III and James IV. Scotland at this period was

[94] See MacDonald, 'Sir Richard Maitland and William Dunbar'.

[95] Gillies, 'The Gaelic Poems of Sir Duncan Campbell', part i (1978), pp. 18-45; part ii (1981), pp. 263-288; 14, part i (1983), pp. 59-82; Meek, 'The Scots-Gaelic Scribes'.

[96] On these (and other) works see MacQueen, 'The literature of fifteenth-century Scotland'; Edwards, 'Contextualising Middle Scots Romance'.

open and receptive to foreign influences – especially from England, France, Burgundy, the Empire, and Denmark. Such contacts had a fertilising and invigorating effect on Scottish culture, and the latter, on a respectable scale not unbefitting a small and geographically peripheral country, followed as closely as possible the trends and fashions set in the most advanced parts of Europe. In this development, the role of the prince was of the greatest significance, since most international contacts went via the ruler and his court; alternatively, as in the case of the church, they involved ecclesiastics who themselves were working with (if not necessarily for) the king.

It would seem that the Scottish monarchs well understood the political *kudos* which would accrue to them from pursuing an active policy of cultural innovation and expansion: the position of the Scottish king in the eyes of contemporary European rulers was thereby considerably raised, and the nobility at home were more and more outclassed. A visible testimony to the ultimate success of this policy is the inclusion of the bust of the king of Scotland on the *Ehrenpforte* which Albrecht Dürer designed for Emperor Maximilian.[97] Indeed, one might even claim that the seeds of Stewart absolutism – often thought of as characteristic of James VI and his son in the seventeenth century – were beginning to be sown even as early as the fifteenth.[98] In this context, the new emphasis on royal piety exhibited by Jameses III and IV might for its part be said curiously to anticipate the self-awareness of such a king as Charles I.

In the *rayonnement* of princely culture, James IV was clearly more successful than his father, but the two kings, as has been seen, have much in common and the significance of the sudden change of rulers in 1488 can be seen to have been exaggerated. However, when in 1515 the regent, Governor Albany, acting on behalf of the infant James V, decreed that James III's chapel of Restalrig should be given over to a memorial where masses be said in perpetuity for the repose of the souls of the founder and his son, both of whom had died sudden and violent deaths, we are confronted with a clear and fitting marker of closure for the two reigns.[99]

The battle of Flodden, unlike that of Sauchieburn, was a disaster on a truly national scale, and not surprisingly caused a clear hiatus. Nothing more is heard of William Dunbar after 1513, and Gavin Douglas forsook literature for political and ecclesiastical intrigue. Only in 1528, when James V finally escaped from the dominance of the Douglas family and began to

[97] See Lüken, 'Kaiser Maximilian I', (with reproduction of the whole). For the detail of the Scottish king see MacDonald, 'Chivalry as a Catalyst of Cultural Change', p. 173.
[98] Goodare, *State and Society*, p. 71.
[99] MacDonald, 'Chapel of Restalrig', pp. 55-56.

rule for himself, can one again speak of a full princely culture in Scotland.[100] To some extent there then occurs an attempt to revert to patterns of culture typical of the former age: for example, William Stewart writes as an epigone of Dunbar, and Robert Carver resumes composing music for the Chapel Royal.[101] But there was also a real change of national mood, and the political circumstances were quite different. Nonetheless, the pursuit of chivalric honours, the passion for architecture, the importation of art works to decorate royal palaces and chapels were all aspects of princely culture that re-established themselves strongly. That this was possible is due in no small measure to the real progress made during the reigns of James III and James IV.[102]

[100] See the article by Janet Hadley Williams in the present volume.

[101] Various aspects of Scottish culture in the reign of James V are discussed in the following: Hadley Williams, *Stewart Style*; Ross, *Musick Fyne*; Macmillan, *Scottish Art*; McRoberts, *Essays on the Scottish Reformation*; MacDonald *et al.*, eds, *The Renaissance in Scotland*; Houwen *et al.*, eds, *A Palace in the Wild*; Edington, *Court and Culture in Renaissance Scotland*; Hadley Williams, ed, *Sir David Lyndsay. Selected Poems*; Thomas, *'Princelie Majestie'*.

[102] For their helpful reactions to an earlier draft of this essay I am greatly obliged to Dr J. Hadley Williams and Dr S.L. Mapstone.

JAMES V OF SCOTS AS LITERARY PATRON

Janet Hadley Williams

At the command of the richt hie, richt excellent, and noble prince James ... : thus, in confident conventional terms, does the cleric and court servant, John Bellenden, allude to the royal sponsorship of his vernacular translation of Hector Boece's *Scotorum Historia* (see fig. 1).[1] The words selected for the patron are perforce linked also to the context in which the commission was fulfilled. His *Hystory and Croniklis of Scotland* (see fig. 2), Bellenden implies, was written in a stable and conservative era, when patronage of contemporary writers was a well-established expression of the king's power.[2] The content of the commissioned work itself (of which more detail later) further supports these inferences. Yet Bellenden was writing during the reign of James V, more specifically its middle years of the 1530s. His brief image – of a mature monarch to whom literary patronage is important – encourages further investigation: it is strikingly at odds with the opening indicators for James and his reign. Unlike his own father, James IV, who was fifteen years old at his accession, or his future father-in-law, Francis I, who was twenty-one when he succeeded to the French throne in 1515, James V had not yet reached two when he was crowned King of Scots in

[1] This is on fol. 6^{v} of the printed version of Bellenden's work; see the facsimile of *STC* 3203, confusingly titled (by the modern publisher), Chambers, R.W., Batho, R.C. and Husbands, H.W., eds, *Hector Boethius, Chronicle of Scotland, Edinburgh, (1540?)*. Bellenden's earlier manuscript version (New York, Pierpont Morgan Library, M 527) differs only slightly: *at the desyre of the richt hye, richt excellent, nobill and michty Prince* ...; see Bellenden, *Chronicles*,1, p. 13.

[2] Literary patronage is understood to refer to that relationship between a patron (here, specifically, a princely patron) and a writer to whom he offers favour, protection, or support (by commissions or influence), and from whom he accepts dedications, presentation copies, and, in some cases, also commentary (of support, apology, flattery, explanation, propaganda, advice) concerning his [the patron's] own position in contemporary affairs; see further Lucas, 'The Growth', pp. 219-248; Asch, 'Court and Household', pp. 1-38; Carlson, *English Humanist Books*, pp. 1-19. Green, *Poets and Princepleasers*, although not specifically about princes and literary patronage, covers many aspects of the topic throughout; see also Mason, '*Regnum et Imperium*', pp. 104-138.

1513,[3] soon after the unexpected death of his father at the battle of Flodden.[4] It was to take the following fifteen troubled years before he was truly in a position (and that for only fourteen years) to offer personal patronage of any kind.

It could be argued, all the same, that even such a lengthy minority as this one would not have obliterated all the remains of literary patronage at the previous court: although James IV had favoured diverse live entertainments rather than written artefacts,[5] what had existed of the latter would not have perished, since, at least initially, the widowed Queen Margaret was Regent. Nor, it could be suggested, need the minority leaders have prevented the king from receiving an education that would equip him with the intellectual and moral discipline necessary for enlightened rule. It might even be added that the long period of regents, lieutenants, protectors and guardians would have enabled the young king to observe and learn from a variety of examples about the operation of patronage, and to begin to understand the roles that literary patronage, in particular, might play in the wise governing of his kingdom and in the nurturing of his own interests. There is some surviving evidence to support these propositions. Working against them, however, are the facts that those who held power in the king's name did not retain it for long (as one political faction overcame another); that the king's education (though it began well when James was five years old, with the appointment of a learned *maister* and a co-ordinated recreational programme)[6] was brought prematurely to an end; and that faction leaders, as far as can be known, infrequently resorted to literary patronage, whether in James V's name or not.

Those part-time writers (otherwise clerks, chaplains, ushers, or grooms) at court during the minority provided confirmation of the latter point. Altogether, they found *Better hap to court nor gude serviss* [Luck is more important at court than good service].[7] One poet, surely without hope of obtaining the patronage of the addressees, sharply admonished those Lords

[3] James V was born on 10 April 1512 and was crowned at Stirling on 21 September 1513.

[4] The decisive battle in the intermittent border war between England and Scotland occurred on 9 September 1513; see Phillips, *The Anglo-Scots Wars*, pp. 117-133.

[5] Bawcutt, *Dunbar the Makar*, pp. 47-62, 79; Ross, *Music Fyne*, pp. 6-7, 25-39.

[6] See, for example, *TA*, V. pp. 146, 147, 195-196, 252, 254, 258, 259, 265, 275, 277, 381; VI. 261, VII. 118, 271, 414; Lyndsay, *Works*, I, pp. 31-46; *Testament ... of the Papyngo*, pp. 283-286; *SP Henry VIII*, IV, p. 243; *James V Letters*, pp. 163, 169, 170; Wode, *Cantus Part-book*, pp. 483, 176.

[7] *Rolling in my remembrance*, *Bann. MS*, II, pp. 249-251. In this and following quotations, letter conventions of Middle Scots have been normalised, and words written in abbreviated forms have been expanded and romanised.

who had James *in steir* [in governance] (26), to *do rycht and perseveir* [do right and persevere] (33).[8] Another, speaking as a powerless smallholder, wrote a prayer that gradually modulated into a series of allegations – against the Lords who *will nocht* [not] *our complaint heir* [hear] (14), the Council that *makis* [makes] *no correctioun* (26), the Regents *ane or ma and sindre divers* [one or more different individuals] (34) who allow thieves to prosper, and the Chancellor and the Chamberlain who, for the licence they permit informers, *The mekill deill be of thame fane* [The great devil be glad of them] (51).[9] Notwithstanding its comments on the abuse of power by those temporarily possessing it in the king's name, the central issue in this poem and contemporary pieces is the urgent need for an adult monarch as dispenser of justice, as *man to plenye* [complain] *to* (17). The need for the royal literary patron is closely related.

If the impression left by a brief survey of writing at court during the early minority is of the sparseness of literary patronage, the data gathered from extant administrative records caution against generalising assumptions about the several regents. Their experience and perspectives were varied, and their influence, if any, on James V's attitudes to literary patronage was unlikely to be straightforward. It must be remembered, for instance, that the first of the regents (and probably the most important from James V's perspective), the king's mother, Margaret Tudor,[10] had left the household of her father, Henry VII, before she could observe the full impact that the king's desires for the royal library had made on literary patronage at the English court.[11] On her Scottish marriage in 1503, however, Margaret had been the recipient of a key instance of patronage. For that occasion she had been given a splendidly illuminated Book of Hours, produced for her in Flanders by commission, probably that of her new husband, James IV.[12] It is uncertain, all the same, if her son in turn saw this important example of kingly sponsorship. Annotations reveal that Margaret gave the volume to her sister. If this was Mary, the gift was perhaps made at her marriage to

[8] *Suppoiss I war in court most he* [If I were highest in court], *Bann. MS*, II, pp. 233-234.

[9] *Jesu chryst that deit on tre* [Jesus Christ who died on the tree], *Bann. MS*, II, pp. 245-257. Cf. also, in the voice of Jock Upland, the poem *Now is our king in tendir aige* [Now our king is in childhood], *Bann. MS*, II, pp. 247-249.

[10] Margaret was Regent from 9 September 1513 to 21 September 1514. She regained and held power from June 1524 to 23 February 1525.

[11] Kipling, 'Henry VII', pp. 123-134.

[12] Vienna, Öst. Nationalbibl., Codex Vindobonensis 1897; in facsimile, Unterkircher, ed, *Das Gebetbuch Jakobs IV*. On the specific points see Macfarlane, 'The Book of Hours', pp. 6-8 and Fradenburg, 'Sovereign Love', p. 84. Margaret also received a Book of Hours from her father; see Whitworth Art Gallery, *Medieval and Early Renaissance Treasure*, p. 31 (no. 56).

Louis XII in 1514;[13] if to her sister-in-law, Catherine, then perhaps during Margaret's visit of 1516. Both would preclude her son's exposure to the volume and its significance. Margaret was not responsible, however, for the probable loss of the *Meroure of Wyssdome*, a work dedicated in 1490 to her husband, James IV, by the author John Ireland. It is likely that this volume had passed out of royal hands even before Margaret's widowhood.[14] If so, her son had no chance to know an advisory text notable for both its author's understanding of continental kingship theory and awareness of its relevance to the Scottish monarchy.[15] But it could be said that Queen Margaret continued the patronage of Gavin Douglas into the minority, although it did not take the form of literary commissions or, on his part, dedications. Her favour, politically motivated, was concerned with Douglas as a noble churchman (and, soon, as relative of her second husband, Archibald Douglas, Earl of Angus). Yet when, very early in her regency, Margaret put forward his name for high promotion, her praise included the point that Douglas was 'second to none [of this kingdom] in letters'.[16] Did she also, in time, say this to her son? She must have kept the manuscript of Douglas's *Palice of Honour*,[17] another work dedicated to James IV, for, to anticipate, it was first published during James V's personal reign.

James probably also saw the vernacular literary works that have been viewed as the unofficial offshoots of his father's policy to sponsor the Southgait printing press of Walter Chepman and Andro Myllar (This licence was for the more overtly political purposes of publishing laws, parliamentary acts, chronicles, mass books, portable breviaries, and legends of the Scottish saints, but the words, *al utheris bukis that salbe necessar*, leave some room for conjecture.)[18] Despite their possible status as pieces outside the 1507 patent, several of these printed literary texts were linked closely to the court of James IV and Queen Margaret[19] – among them the *Flyting* of Dunbar and Kennedy, Dunbar's public eulogy, *The Ballade of ... Barnard Stewart* and his dream vision, *The Goldyn Targe.* It therefore is possible (if,

[13] Macfarlane, 'The Book of Hours', pp. 5-6.
[14] Ireland, *Meroure*, pp. xi-xiii.
[15] See Mapstone, 'A Mirror', pp. 308-323. The same seems likely of a *Gestorum de Gower* owned by James IV (*ER* XI. p. 123), of which not a trace is found in the following reign; see Bawcutt, *Dunbar the Makar*, p. 79 and Boffey, Edwards and Barker-Benfield, *The Works of Geoffrey Chaucer*, p. 18, n. 53.
[16] See Douglas, *Eneados*, I, p. 9 and note 32. See also *James V Letters*, p. 14.
[17] Bawcutt, *The Shorter Poems of Gavin Douglas*, pp. xvi and 1-133; Douglas, *Eneados*, I, p. 8.
[18] See Beattie, *The Chepman and Millar Prints;* Macfarlane, *William Elphinstone*, pp. 236-237; *RSS*, I, no. 1546.
[19] Parkinson, 'Scottish Prints', pp. 304-310.

as seems likely, they were kept at court or with Margaret during her widowhood) that the prints influenced the young king in ways worth noting in the present context. It is plausible that they kindled an interest in the idea of sponsored publications, in the value to the monarchy of particular writing styles and genres, or in the variety of ways a king and his poet-servitors might respond to each other and to Scotland at large.

The further claim has been made that the Queen Mother commissioned her servant, William Stewart, to translate Boece's *Scotorum Historia* for James.[20] Boece's work was published in 1527, but probably was in existence in 1526 (the date of its dedicatory epistles). At that time Margaret had returned briefly to court (20 November 1526-26 March 1527). It seems reasonable that she might then have commissioned the translation of a work by the Scottish colleague of Erasmus (in line with her brother Henry VIII's literary patronage, which she had witnessed during her lengthy visit in 1516-17).[21] Even if the difficulties arising from Stewart's extremely common name are set aside, however, no evidence survives of a direct relationship between the queen, a poet-servitor called William Stewart, and the metrical *Croniclis*.[22] The work's start and completion dates, in any case, are established from internal evidence as 1531-35 (thus during the king's personal reign).[23] This does not necessarily eliminate Margaret, acting on her son's behalf, as Stewart's early patron. Lines in a carol attributed to Stewart allude to an earlier time when Margaret was a generous sponsor (to at least one writer), and to more recent obstacles preventing her from continuing.[24] Yet without certainty of date for the carol, it is difficult to be sure whether Stewart's diplomatic allusion is to Margaret's days as Queen before her widowhood, to those before she lost the Regency, or simply to any time before her death (1541), when the poet laments, *for an scho war as scho hes*

[20] See Stewart, *Croniclis*, I, pp. vii-xiv, and Sanderson, 'Two Stewarts', pp. 25-46.

[21] Emond, 'The Minority', p. 166.

[22] These difficulties are discussed by MacDonald, 'William Stewart', pp. 182-183.

[23] Margaret and a *Maister* William Steward are linked directly only once; but this man almost certainly was the Bishop of Aberdeen of that name; see *Hamilton Papers*, I, pp. 9-10. The earliest record of a *Maister* William Stewart at court is December 1526 (*TA*, V, p. 309), which falls after the date of Margaret's temporary return, when her estranged second husband, Angus, had control of the government. The idea that this Stewart was connected to Margaret possibly is strengthened by the fact that on 27 August 1527 (after Margaret had left the court again) the auditors of exchequer (as part of their attempts to correct the imbalance between royal income and expenditure) refused to accept Master William Stewart's letters of pension and livery; see Emond, 'The Minority', p. 537, who cites the unpublished Acts of the Lords of Council 37, fol. 221, 27 August.

[24] *Ffirst lerges the king my cheife*, *Bann.MS*, II, pp. 254-255.

bene / scho wald be lerger of lufray / Than all the laif ... [if she were as she was once, she would be more generous than all the rest].[25]

A different style of literary patronage might have been expected from the heir apparent, French-born John Stuart, Duke of Albany, who at the request of the Lords had replaced Margaret in 1515.[26] He was welcomed to Scotland in high rhetorical mode, as *noble prudent seigneur* (4), by one hopeful poet.[27] As his later actions in the Franco-imperialist wars were to confirm,[28] however, Albany's strengths, during his three periods of residential rule in Scotland,[29] were those of the able military commander: Scottish administrative records show him greatly pre-occupied with establishing internal order and pacifying the Anglo-Scots border.[30] He also took care to protect his power-base. John Bellenden, the clerk in royal service who was to shine as a writer during James's personal rule, was one dismissed for his Douglas sympathies during Albany's second visit to Scotland.[31] Nonetheless it is from this time (1521-22), when the king was between nine and ten, that there survives some further evidence of official thought being given to James V's curriculum: he was to be instructed in *all gude vertuis, to reid and write, and to speke Latin and Fransh.*[32] The impression that Albany's governorship was not detrimental to the young king, seems corroborated by later praise of him as 'the prudent Duke'.[33] This was expressed, in a poem written in 1530, by David Lyndsay, a servant who had been closely associated with James V for most of his childhood. Too much should not be made of it: in illustrating his mutability argument, Lyndsay had treated all

[25] This stanza is omitted in the Maitland Folio version (*Maitland Folio Manuscript*, ed. Craigie, I, pp. 248-249, where the poem is not attributed to Stewart. On date see MacDonald, 'William Stewart', pp. 195-196; Hadley Williams, 'Dunbar and His Immediate Heirs', p. 97.

[26] She had lost her rights as the king's *tutrix testamentar* on her marriage to the Earl of Angus; Cf. *APS*, II, p. 282.

[27] Only the French translation of this work, *Ballade faicte pour la venue du duc d'Albanie en Escosse* (1515), is preserved; see Shire, *The Thrissil*, pp. 10-11 (from Paris, Bibliothèque nationale, MS fr 20055, fol 73^{v}), and commentary, p. 26.

[28] Knecht, *Renaissance Warrior*, pp. 216-218, 227, 229, 244.

[29] Albany was governor in residence first, from 26 May 1515 to 24 September 1517 (partly by deputy, Seigneur De La Bastie), secondly, from 18 November 1521 to 27 October 1522 and, thirdly, from 23 September 1523 to 31 May 1524.

[30] See, for example, *ADCP*, 54 (22 August 1515); and *APS*, II, p. 126 (concerning the action against the Humes).

[31] See Sheppard, 'John Bellenden', pp. 424-427.

[32] HMC, *Report*, pp. 111-12.

[33] Lyndsay, *Works, I: Papyngo*, p. 534.

minority leaders with similarly careful words.[34] But another estimate altogether of the Duke can be read in an earlier anonymous poem, *We lordis hes chosin a chiftane mervellus* [We, lords, have chosen a marvellous leader],[35] probably composed towards the end of the period between 1517 (Albany's first departure to France) and 1521 (his return to Scotland). The author presents himself as one of the Lords of Council,[36] ostensibly offering Albany an urgent appeal to end his 'tardation' in France and return to Scotland, where his continuing absence, it is claimed, has caused slaughter, war, and controversy (21, 33, 35). The poet addresses the French-speaking Albany in Scots, which could suggest that it is not Albany's literary patronage, but another audience – fellow Lords, perhaps –that is his real target. Though the opening complimentary stance is later reinforced, it is also undercut. This *chiftane mervellus* has *wylis cautelus* [cunning wiles] (3), and although his *prudent wit* (17) is noted, so is the detail that, by remaining absent from Scotland, he has *abusit* his good sense (17). Also suspect is the fact that the poet's own voice is never distinct from those he is either representing (the suffering population of Scotland?) or else surreptitiously addressing (the Lords?): throughout he uses 'we' and 'us' as he offers Albany a considered opinion of his behaviour and its effect on Scotland. The tone, similarly, becomes increasingly ambiguous. What could be lament is just as possibly criticism. The overwhelming emphasis on the lack of trust, the great dissension, the pleasure that Scotland's present demise in Albany's absence is causing *our auld Innamy* (England), and the pain suffered by *Thy leigis leill* [Your loyal vassals] may be read two ways. If he knew of it, this poem gave the young king an opportunity to observe how patronal literature could sustain political strategies.

In the intervals of Albany's absence, initially because the French deputy, Anthony De La Bastie, was murdered, James Hamilton, Earl of Arran (who was next in line to the throne after Albany), was elected Regent and Lieutenant of the Merse.[37] It is a simplification to say that he clashed to an increasing degree with the Queen's (by then estranged) second husband, Archibald, Earl of Angus.[38] To answer him, Arran's patronage was of the kind likely to bolster his position – 'gifts of lucrative wardships and marriages, given either as rewards for past service or inducements to future ser-

[34] Lyndsay, *Works, I: Papyngo*, pp. 528-562; 589-597 (Albany, *Lufetentis*, Margaret, James Beaton; Angus).
[35] *Bann. MS*, II, pp.197-199.
[36] Among them, Gavin Douglas and Adam Otterburn are known to have been poets. Both were supporters of Scotland's closer ties with England; for the list of Lords see Emond, *The Minority of James V*, Appendix E, pp. 647-664.
[37] Emond, *The Minority of James V*, pp.167-190.
[38] A helpful account is Bawcutt, *Gavin Douglas*, pp. 18-19.

vice.'[39] There is no sign in these prosaic records (and few further sources are available) that literary patronage was found equally useful. This was so also for Angus, whose early primary concern was to strengthen the position he had created for himself as stepfather to the king. Indeed, when Albany returned to Scotland in November 1521, Angus sought the legal, rather than the literary, skills of his uncle, Gavin Douglas, to present in London the formal list of complaints against the Duke.[40]

Yet the hope of royal literary patronage, expressed in substantial published form, was not altogether wanting: 1521 was also the year in which John Mair, the eminent scholastic theologian, chose to address the then nine-year-old James V directly.[41] In the dedicatory preface to his *Historia Majoris Britanniae tam Angliae quam Scotiae* [A History of Greater Britain, both England and Scotland],[42] Mair spoke to the king in the traditional didactic manner of the *glorious deeds of your ancestors*.[43] Its concluding hope, that James may *read to good purpose*, however, although seemingly in the same vein, alluded to the king's acquaintance with material that did not always offer continuing or unqualified support for traditional attitudes – to the origin myths of James's ancestors, for instance, which Mair questioned.[44] Mair also examined anew (and most pertinently given the currently complex political conditions in Scotland) the issue of what powers (and what limitations of these powers) were appropriate for the king, community, and magnates.[45] He also advocated the union, on an equal footing, of England and Scotland.[46] Like the direct address to James, child of a Scottish prince and an English princess, Mair's union proposal may be seen as that of the cosmopolitan scholar, able to view the destabilising factional politics of the time from the more detached vantage point acquired by his studies in England and France, even more, perhaps, than it could be considered partisan-supportive of the Douglas cause.[47]

Mair's volume was prefaced (Ai^{V}) by a large engraving of the royal arms of Scotland,[48] seemingly especially prepared. This was not necessarily

[39] See, for example, *RSS*, I, nos. 2977, 3041, 3043, 3061.
[40] See *LL & P Henry VIII*, 3, ii (no. 1886); Small, ed, *Poetical Works of Gavin Douglas*, I, pp. xcii-xcvi; Emond, 'The Minority', pp. 293-296.
[41] See Major, *Historia*, pp. 183-222.
[42] See Constable, ed, *A History of Greater Britain ... by John Major*.
[43] Constable, ed, *A History of Greater Britain ... by John Major*, p. cxxxiii.
[44] Constable, ed, *A History of Greater Britain ... by John Major*, p. cxxxv. On this as a widespread change in attitude, see also Duncan, 'Hector Boece', p. 6.
[45] See Burns, *The True Law*, pp. 67-75.
[46] Burns, *The True Law*, pp. 63-67.
[47] See Mason, 'Kingship', pp. 182-183.
[48] For an accessible illustration, see Mapstone, *Scots and their Books*, p. 21.

with Mair's involvement: beneath it was a Latin dedication to James V by Jodocus Badius Ascensius, the Flemish humanist-printer whose Paris press was known for its series of annotated editions of the Latin classics, and for its significant number of works by Scots, including those of Galbraith and Vaus.[49] The dedication spoke to James as 'a boy of hope and outstanding talents', calling attention in highly traditional terms to James's duty to 'Examine the deeds of your ancestors / And defend the rights of your freedom'.[50] Several components of the engraving above, however, were more distinctive. An open crown is placed above the crest helmet (a tilting helm now designating the knight or baron, but in 1521 probably a less precise reference to chivalric ideals).[51] Another open crown is worn by the demi-lion above, who holds in his paws the two other elements of the Honours of Scotland, the sceptre and sword. Helm style and open crown may also allude to Scotland's minority, and, perhaps, to the regency of Albany. His presence in France at this time must have helped to put forward a view of Scotland's affairs that was Franco-centric.[52]

When Albany left Scotland for the last time in 1524, Angus, although supported by Henry VIII, was at first forestalled from seizing power by Margaret, who rapidly had the king declared of age to govern.[53] By 1526 the Earl had gained the upper hand, by refusing to relinquish his charge after the expiry of the period legally allotted to him as a keeper of the king.[54] James, then fourteen, was again declared of age to rule (again in name only for the next few years),[55] but on this basis his formal studies were ended.[56] (Later, James's personal servant, David Lyndsay, was to refer scathingly to the *wytles fullis* who had prevented the king from continuing his educa-

[49] See Renouard, *Bibliographie*.

[50] I am greatly indebted to Dr Nicola Royan for her helpful discussion of the translation, especially of the non-classical and less common senses of Badius Ascensius's words.

[51] See Innes of Learney, *Scots Heraldry*, p. 17; Burnett and Dennis, *Scotland's Heraldic Heritage*, p. 28.

[52] If so, it had its equal in Scotland, where the Parliament of October 1515 had received Albany in his ducal coronet, the sword and sceptre being borne before him as signs of his right to govern; *L & P Henry VIII*, II, pt i, no. 779. It should be added that the arms are not Albany's own; for those see the contemporary armorial manuscript of Lyndsay, Edinburgh, NLS Adv. MS 31.4.3., more accessible as Laing, *Facsimile of an Ancient Heraldic Manuscript*, no. 50.

[53] Thomson, *A Diurnal*, p. 9 and *APS*, II, p. 286.

[54] Emond, 'The Minority', p. 493; Thomson, *A Diurnal*, p. 10.

[55] *APS*, II, p. 301.

[56] Allusions to the king's *maister*, Gavin Dunbar, do not appear in record after June 1526; see *SP Henry VIII*, iv, p. 401.

tion.)[57] Angus gave household offices or offices of state, also grants of land, wardships and pensions, chiefly to family members or closest supporters.[58] The literary lacuna in his patronage must have been more noticeable, the opportunity (and duty) it presented to continue the king's education (and thereby to secure his future favour) more urgent, as he grew older. A growing number of writers began to address the young king directly.

Many poems written to James V in these latter years, just before he began to govern in his own right, speak to him after a well-tried pattern. With few exceptions,[59] what is explicit in these pieces, as, for example, the references to Flodden Field, concerns the contemporary situation as a whole (and what it means for the writers) as much as it does the particular king. As their young monarch, James is the proper object of their counsel, but as yet he is neither a distinctive leader nor fully able to be their patron in return.

Poems such as the dream vision *This hindir nycht neir by the hour of nyne* [The other night near nine o'clock],[60] and Alexander Kyd's *The rich fontane* [fountain],[61] focus on the quality of the king's advisers. *This hindir nycht* perhaps is distinguished by the attractions of its dream guide, Lady 'varite' [verity] (16). Her naked and translucent body is calculated to appeal to the king, already something of a libertine, but it also allows the dreamer to see the moralising mottoes on the wall behind her. Verity's answer to the dreamer's question, 'when will Scotland be favoured with the peace, rest and plenty of other lands?' (30-31), has a crisp directness that might have been designed to create a momentary frisson of fear among James's present counsellors. Her *solutioun sufficient* (34) involves the declaration of the names and the subsequent exiling of those men involved in council, session and parliament who have corrupted the king. Those she mentions, however, although carefully chosen, are allegorical figures, including *wilful wrang* [obstinate wrong] (41), *hid hatreit* [secret hatred] (42) and *yung counsale* [inexperienced advisers] (43). She demands that they be replaced by those despised since Flodden Field (60-61), and provides a balancing list of names, these chiefly of the virtues – cardinal, moral and theological – that are the familiar foundations of good government.

[57] See *Complaynt*, pp. 131-132, 161-166.

[58] See Emond, 'The Minority', pp. 494-500, 529-57, 547-549.

[59] See Hadley Williams, 'Dunbar'; on Stewart's *Schir, sen of men ar divers sortis* [Sir, since men are of all kinds], *Bann. MS*, II, pp. 256-257.

[60] *Bann. MS*, II, pp. 228-231. It is attributed to William Stewart in *Maitl. Folio MS*, no. cxxviii.

[61] *Bann. MS*, II, pp. 242-245.

Other contemporary pieces, among them William Stewart's *Precelland prince* [Excellent prince][62] and the intricate, now anonymous, *Be gratious ground and gate to sapience* [Be gracious foundation and gate to wisdom],[63] also address James on the commonplaces of statecraft.[64] Two stanzas in *Be gratious ground* expound the scripturally-based meanings of the king's symbols of office: the sword of honour for power, sceptre for sapience, crown for *bonyte* [excellence] (37-40), the robe royal of blue purple for justice with godly intent (41), the white lining for innocence and clear conscience, the chair of state for the heavenly throne of the Trinity, and the richly-clad lords for heaven's ministers on earth (45-56). The extended poetic reference is uncommon, and provides a small link to James V's later interest as patron in royal heraldic imagery.[65]

Lyndsay's *Dreme* probably was presented in about 1526, when, for the second time, James was declared of age to rule, but when, because of the associated 'general revocation' of offices, Lyndsay's own position had become less secure.[66] In this long poem there is a marked change of tone from that of earlier minority pieces. Like them, *The Dreme*'s main concerns are advisory, with the underlying stress that of earthly mutability.[67] Yet that discussion is combined with the provision of a systematic compendium of useful facts and figures on the cosmos, the earth, and present-day Scotland. Moreover, although the content of the poem's opening epistle to the king affectionately relates the extent of Lyndsay's past personal service (to demonstrate without a heavy hand the justice of his present claims for recompense), it also emphasises James V's new-found ability to offer real patronage in return. Lyndsay, who had once held the royal infant in his arms 'full tenderlie' (9), here recasts himself a *wratcheit worme* before such a prince (27-28). In the formal closing *Exhortatioun* traditional counsel remains prominent, but there is also a new firmness of purpose: although he has yet to use it, Lyndsay suggests, James now has the power to act:

Thov may weill wyt...
Quhat sorrow and quhat trubulatioun

[62] *Bann. MS*, II, pp. 231-251.
[63] *Bann. MS*, II, pp. 221-224.
[64] See Kantorowicz, *The King's Two Bodies*; Born, 'The Perfect Prince', pp. 470-504. For Scotland's advisory literature in this period, see Mapstone, *The Advice*.
[65] John Ireland, in Bk 7 of his prose *Meroure of Wyssdome*, provides a similar yet less extended passage on the symbols of royal office (III, p. 159).
[66] *APS*, II, p. 300; Emond, 'The Minority', pp. 498-501, and, on the poem's date, Edington, *Court and Culture*, pp. 24-25.
[67] See, for example, lines 127-133, 1118-1126.

Haith bene in this pure realme infortunate.
Now conforte thame that hes bene desolate (1058-61)

[You well know what sorrow and what trials have been in this unfortunate realm; now comfort those who have been afflicted].

This period near the June 1526 declaration also was chosen by Hector Boece,[68] a fellow Scot and scholar-contemporary of John Mair, as appropriate for the presentation of his epistles to James V (April 1526) and Archbishop James Beaton (May 1526). These letters dedicated to them his *Scotorum Historiæ a prima gentis origine* [A History of the Scottish People from their First Origins], the volume itself published in Paris in 1527.[69] In 1526 the king might have been officially of age, but he was still in Angus's custody; Boece's timing therefore gave added meaning to his moralising stress, significantly placed within his epistle to James V, on the unfailing fate (disgraceful death) of those kings and, *much more so*, those nobles 'puffed up with unbridled power'.[70] Within the text itself such deserved ends for the overmighty are a recurring feature.[71] Boece's patriotic emphases therein are also evident; for example (unlike the more critically rigorous Mair), in his return to the myths of Scotland's origins,[72] which made James V the last of the kings of Scots in a line unbroken since Fergus; or in his prefacing account of a *Scotorum regni descriptio*, which detailed the regions of the Scottish realm.[73] In a variety of ways, such as his care to establish Scotland's antiquity as the equal of Rome, and admit a Gaelic component to Scotland's past,[74] or his restrained rhetorical-humanist style, modelled on Livy and Sallust, Boece shows his desire for an audience beyond Scotland,[75] but also his concern to 'place Scotland in the right position in European political geography'.[76] That Hector Boece's version of the Scottish

[68] From 1505-36 he was principal of the University of Aberdeen.
[69] A continuation by Giovanni Ferrerio was published in Paris in 1574, but there is no modern edition.
[70] See Burns, *The True Law*, p. 79, quoting in translation *Scotorum Historia*, sig. a iiii^{v}. The present discussion of Boece is heavily dependent on Burns and on Royan, 'The Relationship'.
[71] Burns, *The True Law*, pp. 80-81.
[72] They were based on John of Fordun's works. See, however, Bower, *Scotichronicon*, pp. 8, 235.
[73] III^{r}-XVII^{r}; I wish to thank Dr Nicola Royan for her expert help, patiently given, on this and several other aspects of Boece's *Scotorum Historia*. Dr Mason considers this the earliest example of such a description; see his 'This Realm of Scotland', p. 83.
[74] Royan, 'The Relationship', p. 138.
[75] Royan, 'The Relationship', p. 138; Farrow, 'The Substance', p. 6.
[76] Royan, 'The Relationship', p. 144.

past found favour with James V is attested by the speed at which he commissioned a translation of the *Scotorum Historiæ* after the personal rule began.[77]

Boece's history, published by Jodocus Badius Ascensius, shares several physical features with Mair's volume issued six years earlier. One is the prefacing engraving of the royal arms, already described, but, in 1527, less appropriate. In Boece's work, however, the engraving shares the page (aii) with a liminary Latin verse, *De insignibus Scotorum Regum Carmen* [Song about the standard of the kings of Scots], by the humanist, Pierre Rosset.[78] The verse stresses the colourful symbolism of the lion,[79] rather than that of the crowns, but later evidence suggests that their open form was noticed in Scotland. Another shared feature is the clear Roman typeface, evidence of the scholarly pretensions of both printer and authors. (Despite the fact that one was writing in the older dialectic mode, the other in the humanist rhetorical, both had been influenced by the new learning.)[80] The elegant type had further implications for the image of the dedicatees, the royal and ecclesiastical patrons of both works: at this time in Scotland nothing had appeared that was not printed in the medieval blackletter or Textura type.

Some confirmation of Scottish sensitivity to this aspect of literary patronage is provided by the format of a gratulatory poem addressed to James V as he at last assumed personal authority (June 1528). This was a Latin *Strena* [New Year's Gift] *Ad Serenissimum Scotorum Regem Iacobum Quintam de suscepto Regni Regimine a diis feliciter ominatio* [To his most serene King of Scots, James V ...],[81] thought to have been written by James Foullis.[82] He, like Mair and Boece, had studied in France, where a volume of his Latin verses had been published, c. 1512, from the press of Gilles de Gourmont. In contrast, the *Strena* was the work of an Edinburgh printer, Thomas Davidson.[83] From this local press, the poem's title-page was arresting. As far, perhaps, as available printing type had allowed,[84] Davidson had used spacious Roman type. He also had added, in the style then fashion-

[77] From 1527, the king authorised an annual payment to him of £50: *ER*, XVI. li-lii, pp. 41-42.
[78] On Rosset (d. 1532), see McFarlane, 'Religious Verse', p. 175.
[79] On this topic see Bawcutt, 'Dunbar's Use of the Symbolic Lion and Thistle', pp. 84-89.
[80] Burns, *The True Law*, p. 76.
[81] *STC* 14425; for a facsimile and a nineteenth-century translation, see *Bann. Misc.*, pp. 2, 1-8. I am grateful for Mrs Kathleen Loncar's help with my translation.
[82] See IJsewijn and Thompson, 'The Latin Poems', pp. 102-160.
[83] See Dickson and Edmond, *Annals of Scottish Printing*, pp. 104-135.
[84] Watry, 'Sixteenth Century Printing Types', pp. 71-72.

able on the continent,[85] a compartment with heavily decorated pillars at each side, symmetrically opposed cornucopiae held by part-human part-beast figures (not cockatrices) at the top, and a group of cherubic boys at the foot.[86] This gave the first page a look of a humanist text, although the work following was printed in the usual blackletter.

The eulogistic opening of the *Strena* also is deft in its implications. The king's fruitfulness, asserts the author, is foretold in the stars, and James V must bring the poem to life (7-8): as Fradenburg notes, it seems that the *Strena* is 'really the king's gift to the poet', becoming 'the effect, rather than the cause of royal patronage'.[87] Like a humanist historian, the poet speaks of Scotland in terms of imperial Rome. The country lately has been taken over, he claims, by those unworthy to govern, latter-day Catilines rather than Catos (43-46). Now, in James, Scotland rejoices more than Troy of Hector, or Greece of Pelides (Achilles) (61-63). Because of the abilities and character of the new king, who is aided by the ancient gods – for Jupiter looks on James V as his offspring (27) and Phoebus assists him (74-76) – the country will see the return of justice, peace and plenty.

Although Davidson's publication of the *Strena* provides some early evidence that James V was aware of his printing press, it is not known when an association between them was formalised,[88] but surviving records of the middle 1530s show that the printer was by then in receipt of royal grants and an annual pension.[89] For James V as king and literary patron, this was an important move. First, it went some way towards fulfilling what his own father had achieved only in part by his 1507 patent to the press of Chepman and Myllar. By the late 1540s, Davidson had published under James's auspices in a further two of the categories James IV had listed, those of chronicle and acts of Parliament, in both instances for the first time in Scotland. James's formal recognition of Davidson, secondly, established in yet another way his realm's claim to equal status within a larger European context. In surviving colophons Davidson styles himself *prenter to the kyngis nobyll grace CVM PRIVILEGIO* and *regii impressoris CVM privilegio*, his manner reminiscent of (or presaging) printers Pynson, Berthelet and others in England, or Estienne in France.[90]

[85] Kerrow and Ferguson, *Title-page Borders*, p. xxi.
[86] Kerrow and Ferguson, *Title-page Borders*, p. 12, no. 14.
[87] Fradenburg, *City, Marriage, Tournament*, p. 58.
[88] It was perhaps in 1529, when Foullis, who later was involved in choosing the printer for the *New Actis*, was secretary to the king; see further, Dickson and Edmund, *Annals of Scottish Printing*, pp. 105, 109-110.
[89] *ER*, XVI, 398, 480K.
[90] Dickson and Edmund, *Annals of Scottish Printing*, pp. 114-115; Thomas Berthelet was King's printer, in succession to Pynson, from February 1529-30 to

Lyndsay's *Complaynt* to the king was written during the early years of the personal reign, c. 1530, and probably printed by Davidson not long afterwards.[91] Its four-stress couplets establish conversational informality, but mask its careful design. Once again, although this time chiefly for a local Scottish audience, the poem signals a change in James's position as patron. Throughout, he is addressed flatteringly as an able monarch, in control of his political powers *in his aistait* [estate] *Royall, / Havand power Imperyall*, 115-116. Direct (if carefully expressed) criticism of the one aspect of government still needing his attention adds to the impression that his position is secure.[92] Although the interim governments, the corrupt dealings, and the deliberate seduction of the youthful king during the minority years are all recalled (the several levels of diction giving to the account the liveliness of dramatic narrative) they are put firmly in the past. The potent present tense dominates the latter part of the poem, first in the sober traditional affirmation (*The foure gret verteous Cardinalis / I see thame with the principalis*, 379-80) that all is well with James's rule, and then in the striking reassertion of the petitionary tone, now playfully exaggerated, with which Lyndsay began (*Schir ... / Heir my complaynt ...*).[93] James is described as a king whose great riches have advanced his honour 'In Scotland, Ingland, and in France' (456). Assuming therefore that his generosity as a patron is unequalled (461-62), Lyndsay asks the king for a loan, promising to repay it when a series of 'impossibilities' have come to pass: when local geographical landmarks, for instance, have been removed to unlikely alternative sites – Mt Sinai, or across the border into Northumberland – or when churchmen no longer desire high status.[94] Lyndsay's audacity is in part a therapeutic lightening of tone before the stern final reminder to the king that he *is bot ane Instrument / To that gret kyng* ... (499-500). Yet it also makes the point that literary patronage is now so established at James V's court that it can, with safety, be presented in terms of a lighthearted transaction between patron and poet.

1547; Robert Estienne was made King's printer in Hebrew and Latin in 1539, and in Greek in 1540. On the latter, see Knecht, *Renaissance Warrior*, p. 477.

[91] The argument has a plausible bibliographic basis; see Hamer, 'The Bibliography', p. 21.

[92] This was ecclesiastical corruption; see *Complaynt*, pp. 409-412.

[93] The passage was compared to Clément Marot's *Au Roy, pour avoir esté desrobé* by Borland, *The Influence of Marot*, pp. 34-36, but Marot's epistle (beginning *On dit bien vray, la malvaise Fortune*), composed 1531 and presented 1532, postdates Lyndsay's piece; see Mayer, ed, *Clément Marot. Les Epîtres*, pp. 171-176.

[94] These 'lying' poems were especially popular in (although not exclusive to) late medieval Scotland; see Utley, *The Crooked Rib*, pp. 133-134.

By the end of 1530 Lyndsay had composed (and Davidson printed soon after) a more ambitious poem, *The Testament and Complaynt of our Soverane Lordis Papyngo*, in which the speaking role and the near-death state of a pretty, plump, but proud royal parrot are used to draw together the poem's several major themes.[95] These are focused, in sequence, on James V (his proper government of self and realm), his court (the papyngo in her literal and metaphorical fall representing all over-ambitious and proud *princis*), and his realm (its corrupt clerical aspects in particular). James V's role as literary patron is thus a significant thread in earlier sections of the *Papyngo*.

Lyndsay's prefacing stanzas list James's courtier-writers in formal detail, associating them, in a chronological order that nevertheless emphasises some writers at the cost of others, with the 'greats' from antiquity to the recent past.[96] Among the latter is William Dunbar, to whose *Goldyn Targe* reference is made confidently, as if further elaboration to the court of James IV's son is unnecessary (thus providing a small piece of circumstantial evidence that this Chepman and Myllar print remained at court after James IV's death). Gavin Douglas is singled out, his learning and eloquence praised. Five of his works are mentioned, but only his *Eneados*, the vernacular translation of Virgil, named. Later sections of Lyndsay's poem, nonetheless, show that he knew (and, less certainly, that he expected his courtly audience to know) Douglas's *Palice of Honour*, printed, as previously noted, during the reign.[97] Reference is also made to the enthusiastic composition and daily presentation to James V of ballats and lays (37-39). (Later, the papyngo herself also alludes to this, with self-deprecating irony, as she presents him with yet another, 236.) Lyndsay mentions the generic variety of these offerings (38, 41), as well as their stylistic range (44, 45, 48, 52). There is a hint, too, that these lively writers compete for pre-eminence (52-54). From among them, possibly assisted by information not disclosed in the poem, Lyndsay draws attention to one called *Ballentyne* [Bellenden] (51), predicting a bright future if circumstances at court favour him.[98]

Lyndsay's own poem is a demonstration of the contemporary court talent vying for the king's notice. A medley of genres (including *chanson*

[95] See Lyndsay, *Works*, IV, pp. 15-16.

[96] For greater detail, see Hadley Williams, 'Dunbar'.

[97] It is not known when Davidson published the *Palice* and whether James V was directly involved. A date of c. 1530-40 has been postulated by Bawcutt, *The Shorter Poems of Gavin Douglas*, p. xvi. For possible Douglas echoes, see *Papyngo*, p. 2, *Palice*, p. 250; *Papyngo*, pp. 113-114, 126, *Palice*, pp. 49-50, 52, and note also the use of internal rhyming in the concluding traditional disclaimers, *Papyngo*, pp. 1179-1185, *Palice*, pp. 2161-2169.

[98] Few of Bellenden's poetic works survive; of those four pieces now known, three are attached to his translations of Boece (2) and Livy (1).

d'aventure, bird assembly, complaynt to Fortune, and literary testament) is used entertainingly (for both comic and serious purposes).[99] Two formal stanza forms, internally ornamented, allude with skill to outstanding examples in earlier writing, especially those of Chaucer, Douglas, and *The Kingis Quair*. A dextrous interplay of voices (narrator, parrot, three clerical birds of prey) provides this long work with the semi-dramatic aspect it needs. The role of James V's parrot also recalls more generally, but with intent, other bird speakers in literature within and beyond Scotland (Holland's *Howlat*, Skelton's *Phyllyp Sparowe* (387-587), Lemaire's *Epîtres de l'Amant vert*).

Similarly, the parrot's pleasing portrait of the Scottish king in his courtly activities in the first epistle (227-345), helps to put James V forward as a monarch of *vertew* (262). Cleverly, the dying bird, offering him traditional counsel, also presages James's early acts as literary patron. With a comic despair the parrot appeals to the king to study *bot half one hour / The Regiment of princelie governyng* (306-307). Her metaphoric description of what he will learn of the principles of good rule (*Quhow thou suld use thy sceptour, swerd and croun*, 310) hints at the enhanced role that James was so soon to give to these symbols of office in re-fashioning his image as king. Likewise, the parrot exhorts him to know *the Cronecklis* for the *gude and evyll report / Off everilk Prince* contained therein (313-314), setting out James's rightful place in that royal line according to Boece: *Sen first kyng Fergus bure ane Dyadame / Thou art the last kyng, of fyve score and fyve* (323-324).

Lyndsay's poem is well aware, it would appear, of the royal commission to John Bellenden: to prepare a vernacular translation of Boece's *Scotorum Historia*. By April 1531 Bellenden had received £30 *for translating of the cronykill* and by October a further £30 for the same task.[100] These payments probably are related to the 1533 presentation manuscript for James V, with decorated capitals, fine borders, and an illuminated title-page of the royal arms.[101] In its present overpainted configuration, the latter shows modifications appropriate to early 1537: the arms of James's first wife, Madeleine de Valois, have been impaled with his.[102] Enough of the original

[99] Another ambitious poem was the elegantly-shaped *chanson d'aventure* by Stewart (possibly one of those courtier-writers Lyndsay listed), *Furth over the mold at morrow* [Forth over the land in the morning], *Bann. MS*, IV, pp. 40-42, which alludes in a variety of ways to Chaucer's *Troilus and Criseyde*. Like Lyndsay's *Complaynt*, it makes use of a distinctively Scottish list of 'impossibilities'.

[100] *TA*, V, p 434; VI, p 37 (where two separate payments appear, amounting to £36, but only the first explicitly *for his translatyng of the croniculis*).

[101] See Sheppard, 'John Bellenden', p. 437.

[102] See Burnett, 'Outward Signs', pp. 292-293. This is a possible indication that in its original form this page was in existence even before 1530.

design is visible, however, to show that it had resembled the arms as depicted in the histories of Mair and Boece.

Recent studies have looked in some detail at the complex textual differences between Boece's Latin work and Bellenden's vernacular translation(s) in manuscript and printed forms.[103] Of special interest here are the observable responses of Bellenden and, later, Boece (as corrector and reviser),[104] to the perceived or imposed requirements of James as literary patron. Dr Royan has noted many of them, including Bellenden's 'glorification of the monarch' by way of his title change from Boece's *retain of the Scottish people* to '*of Scotland*' (its emphasis on Scotland as an entity reinforced in the text by the use of 'realm').[105] She has shown how the volume as a whole was made more accessible to the less learned reader (as James V and some of his lay courtiers might have been described) by structural divisions and headings in a text hitherto without breaks; by occasional facilitating insertions (some demonstrating Bellenden's independent use of sources); reiteration of dates; omissions (such as those discussing the ancient classical authorities), and stylistic changes (towards greater narrative dramatisation).[106]

The printed version (c.1536-40), with its many textual changes,[107] is perhaps most revealing of James V's own desires to re-shape his image as both literary patron and ruler. This is evident, for instance, in the fine binding of the royal copy (one of those Davidson printed on vellum),[108] which features two medallions, of Dido and Plato, and an Italianate arabesque frame, similar to those deriving form the work of Etienne Roffet, French royal bookbinder, 1539-48.[109] There are notable preliminaries and insertions not found in either Boece or in Bellenden manuscript versions, including Davidson's poetic *Excusation* on the title-verso, desiring that he *Mycht first pleis god, and syne our noble kyng*, and Bellenden's following *Proheme of the Cosmographe*, a tour de force of forty elaborate nine-line stanzas (those used by Dunbar, in tribute to Chaucer's skill in *Anelida and Arcite*, in *The*

[103]Burns, *The True Law*, pp. 86-89; Royan, 'The Relationship'; Mapstone, 'Shakespeare and Scottish Kingship', pp. 161-177. The date of the printed version is unknown, conjecturally c. 1536-42.

[104]See the full title of Thomas Davidson's printed edition, with its reference to a *newly correckit* text by Boece, fol. 6^{v}.

[105]Royan, 'The Relationship, pp. 138-139.

[106]Royan, 'The Relationship, pp. 139-53.

[107]One was the inclusion of the *Cosmographe and discription of Albion* (a translation of Boece's *Scotorum regni descriptio*) omitted from the early MS version.

[108]Dickson and Edmond, *Annals of Scottish Printing*, pp. 131-132.

[109]Doughty, 'Renaissance books', p. 119 and Appendix no. 7; Hobson, *Humanists and Bookbinders*, pp. 135-136.

Goldyn Targe), signal that this is a volume of some pretensions.[110] A revised form of Bellenden's poetic address to his book, or *proheme of the history*, inserted at folios F4^{V}-F6^{V}, drew attention to James's *Hie nobilite* and natural gifts, and to the fact that the stories of James's progenitors *neuir was sene in to his toung afore*. Bellenden's *Epistil ... to the kyngis grace* had been placed as 'preface' to the manuscript version. It was added, rewritten, to the end of the printed text. Its opening allusion, not simply to Erasmus, but to his *institutioun of cristin kingis* [*Institutio Principis Christiani*, 1517], flatteringly inferred a link between James V and the Emperor Charles V,[111] for whom Erasmus had written the *Institutio*. This reaffirmed the position of James V as set out on the first page of the *Hystory and Croniklis*, in a woodcut, newly designed, of the royal arms.[112] Badius Ascensius's armorial woodcut, which had been copied in Bellenden's presentation manuscript, was at once acknowledged and corrected: its depiction of the sceptre in the lion's left paw was retained, but the earlier open crowns were replaced with imperial crowns (as sign of James's independent and absolute authority over the peoples of his kingdom), and the helm now used was unmistakeably that of the sovereign.[113] Since the *Hystory* was a royal commission, James V's approval of the changes to the royal arms is guaranteed; the re-use of the unchanged cut in 1540, on the title-page of *The New Actis and Constitutionis of Parliament Maid Be The Rycht Excellent Prince Iames the Fift Kyng of Scottis*, confirms it.[114] David Lyndsay's involvement in the re-design is plausible – by this time he was senior herald. Yet in his own armorial manuscript of c. 1536-42 the depiction of the royal arms was more conservative. The closed crown was featured, but the seated lion held a sword in the right paw and the saltire flag, not the sceptre, in the other.[115] As a whole, Lyndsay's manuscript is highly relevant to the present

[110]Note also the link this stanza form makes with two works in Oxford, Bodleian Library, MS Arch. Selden B. 24, *The Lay of Sorrow*, fols. 217-19 and *The Lufaris Complaynt*, fols. 219-221^{v}.

[111]On Charles V and the revival of the idea of empire, Yates, *Astraea*, pp. 1-28 and Ullmann, '"This Realm"', pp. 175-203. On the contemporary debate see, for example, Koebner, '"The Imperial Crown', pp. 29-52; Hoak, 'The Iconography', pp. 54-103.

[112]It differed from the two second-hand woodcuts within the text (fols. H3^{r} and Nn4^{r}) used previously by the Antwerp printer Jan van Doesborch; see Beattie, 'Fragments', pp. 34-35; Watry, 'Sixteenth Century Printing Types', p. 72.

[113]The new engraving was by no means the earliest use of the closed crown in a Scottish setting; see, for example, the Beaton panel of the royal arms illustrated in Caldwell, 'The Beaton Panels', pp. 174-184 and plate XXIXA.

[114]See further, Dickson and Edmond, *Annals of Scottish Printing*, pp. 109-118.

[115]Laing, *Facsimile of an Ancient Heraldic Manuscript*, no. 18.

discussion. Its unique heraldic representation of James V's Scotland is a supportive visual commentary on this king's majesty.

James V's literary patronage played its part in the creation of several works related to the religious debates of the 1530s. The Piedmontese humanist, Giovanni Ferrerio, who was much later to write a continuation of Boece, was a visitor to the Scottish court at the time of a royal visit to Perth in 1531, when the appearance of a comet (generating the fear that James V's death had been foretold) prompted him to write *De vera cometae significatione contra astrologorum omnium vanitatem libellus* [On the true significance of comets ...].[116] Anti-astrological excerpts from Boece were one means used to support his argument.[117] James's response, disappointingly, is unknown. In the form in which *De vera significatione* was eventually published in Paris by Vascosan, in 1540, Ferrerio had extended earlier associations with the Scottish king by adding lines to mourn the death of Queen Madeleine and, at the front, lines to rejoice in the subsequent wedding of James V to Marie de Guise.[118]

Ferrerio was addressing a king who took some heed of long-held, if increasingly challenged beliefs about unusual natural phenomena. Two other scholars saw James V otherwise, as alert to the current reformist debate. They sought his support, from opposing positions, on a controversial issue – whether the New Testament should be translated into the vernacular.[119] During 1533 and 1534, the exiled Scottish reformer, Alexander Alesius (Alane) published two short tracts in the form of letters to James V, in which he advocated biblical translation.[120] With better tactics, the German Catholic theologian, Johannes Cochlaeus, who had gained the backing of both Erasmus and Ferdinand, king of the Romans, formally invited the Scottish king to accept the dedication that would preface his response to Alesius.[121] With his agreement, James V's involvement became that of the literary patron, albeit one with politico-religious objectives. His responses to the participants also showed his interest. To Erasmus, James re-empha-

[116]See Durkan, 'Giovanni Ferrerio, Humanist' pp. 181-94 esp. 193 as well as his 'Giovanni Ferrerio, Gesner', pp. 350-53, esp. 356.

[117]Durkan, 'Giovanni Ferrerio, Humanist', p. 190.

[118]Durkan, 'Giovanni Ferrerio, Humanist', pp. 183, 185, 189-90; Johnston and Robertson, *Bibliographia*, p. 40.

[119]On this brief period of moderation, see Baker-Smith, 'Florens Wilson', pp. 1-14.

[120]*Alexandri Alesii Epistola* and *Alexandri Alesii responsio*; see also *James V Letters*, pp. 241, 260-261, and Baxter, 'Alesius', pp. 93-102. As a canon of St Andrews during the 1520s Alesius's attacks on heresy had drawn favour, but his growing interest in Lutheran theology had forced him to flee to the Continent in 1532; see McGoldrick, *Luther's Scottish Connection*, pp. 58-60.

[121]See *James V Letters*, pp. 241, 252, 271; the response was *An expediat laicis*.

sized the 'old connection' (his role as tutor to Alexander Stewart, James V's half-brother) that had been raised in the letter recommending Cochlaeus, and agreed cordially that Erasmus 'did not write to a prince with whom he had no acquaintance'.[122] To Cochlaeus, the king sent written thanks for his dedication and, more revealing of his own opinion on the biblical translation issue, a gift of £50.[123] Alesius, who had been associated (by Cochlaeus) with the reformers Melanchthon and Luther,[124] was less fortunate, as far as is known receiving only silence.

Both the writer-patron relationship and the religious position disclosed are less certain in James V's connections with George Buchanan, at court from 1536-38 as tutor to Lord James Stewart.[125] Buchanan possibly wrote his four Latin *justa*, on James IV and Queen Madeleine, at this time, but, if so, although the subject matter is suggestive of the king's special interest, it is not documented.[126] Equivocal evidence, however, links Buchanan's satires on the Franciscan order, or at least the last of them, the *Franciscanus*, to James V's sponsorship. It has been suggested that James's supposed involvement in the work was kindled by Buchanan's first satire, the *Somnium* (c. 1535), which drew upon the self-mocking anti-Franciscan poem, *This nycht befoir the dawing cleir* by William Dunbar.[127] Yet the *Somnium* is selective in its use of elements from Dunbar's poem and also alludes to the classical writers (Martial, Lucan, and Cicero).[128] The following *Palinodiæ* and *Franciscanus*, moreover, look beyond Scottish writers altogether, to Juvenal and others. Nonetheless, Buchanan himself made several subsequent claims, the first some fifteen years later, that James V had commissioned the *Franciscanus*. In his address to the Lisbon Inquisition, during a trial that he initially believed had been prompted by the controversial contents of the *Franciscanus*,[129] Buchanan maintained that James V had requested him to write it, and, further, that he had presented the king with the

[122]*James V Letters*, p. 271.

[123]*James V Letters*, p. 271; *TA*, VI, p. 236.

[124]*James V Letters*, pp. 273-274.

[125]*TA*, VI, pp. 289, 353, 430; *RSS*, II, p. 383. Stewart was James's eldest illegitimate son by Elizabeth Shaw of Sauchie.

[126]See Burmann, *Georgii Buchanani Opera Omnia*, II, pp. 377-378.

[127]See Ford, *George Buchanan*, pp. 48-54; Bawcutt, *Dunbar the Makar*, pp. 273-274. Dunbar's poem had not then been printed, as far as is known; Buchanan and the king must have seen a manuscript copy. For hint of James's attitudes to the Franciscans see *James V Letters*, pp. 275-276 (16 September 1534).

[128]Ford, *George Buchanan*, pp. 52-53.

[129]See Aitken, *The Trial*, pp. xxii-xxiii; McFarlane, 'George Buchanan's *Franciscanus*', pp. 133-134.

only copy of the finished composition.[130] By that time James V had suffered the defeat of Solway Moss, and his own fatal illness; he could not confirm or contradict Buchanan's assertions of royal literary patronage.

The longstanding French influence on Scottish literary works and literary interests continued in James V's personal reign, especially in its last seven years, when the court was augmented and changed in character as a result of the king's marriages to Madeleine de Valois (1537) and, after her early death, to Marie de Guise Lorraine (1538).[131] As seen earlier, genres such as the *chanson d'aventure* and the dream vision (which looked back to *Le Roman de la Rose*), endured in high regard. James's 1533 commission to Bellenden, the translation of Livy's *History of Rome*, was perhaps as much a gesture in emulation of Francis I, whose interest in Roman history was well known (and was gathering to the subject considerable prestige),[132] as it was a response to a widespread trend that gave the classics an important place in the education of rulers.[133] The courtly lyric, newly fashionable at the French court, was enjoying concurrently a period of renewed vigour at the Scottish.

One such Scots courtly lyric was *Lanterne of lufe and lady fair of hew*,[134] attributed to James V's favoured servitor, George Steill.[135] He was not among the courtier-writers listed in Lyndsay's *Papyngo* (1530), but Steill was very much a personality of James V's reign and not after – named, for instance, in Lyndsay's *Complaint and Publict Confessioun of the Kingis Auld Hound, callit Bagsche*, as the dog handler who had introduced to court the hound Bawte, the supplanter of Bagsche in the king's affections (17-18).[136] Many details of Lyndsay's poem suggest that it was

[130]See Aitken, *The Trial*, pp. xvi-xix, xxii-xxiii; McFarlane, 'George Buchanan's *Franciscanus*, pp. 127-128.

[131]References in the accounts include those to the *Frenche tailȝeour*, the *Frenche maister houshald* and the queen's fool, *Jane the Frenche droche* [dwarf] (*TA*, VII, pp. 149, 167, 151). Among court visitors are the French king's envoy, Monsieur de Lassigny, a pursevant called *De la Plume*, and the Duke of Guise's master of household (*TA*, VII, pp.149-150). *Peris, gunnar* is sent to France (*TA*, VII, pp. 150), masons from France bring with them jousting spears (*TA*, VII, p. 184), and *Andro Mentioun, wrycht, Frencheman, and his collegis* construct the royal chambers aboard the *littill new bark* (*TA*, VII, p. 189. James himself orders *ane cote of ane new fassoun cum out of France* (*TA*, VII, p. 173).

[132]Knecht, *Renaissance Warrior*, p. 473.

[133]MacQueen, 'Aspects', p. 19.

[134]*Bann. MS*, III, pp. 312-313.

[135]*James V Letters*, p. 166; *TA*, VII, pp. 17, 151, 254, 464; Knox, *Works*, I, p. 68.

[136]A veiled meaning seems implied, but Steill had real links with the royal kennels; see *TA*, VI, p. 203.

composed in the late 1530s,[137] but Steill's lyric, with its traditional terms of love service, alliteration, and a refrain that smoothly gathers the lover's elaborated complaint, is comparable with *Support your servand peirles paramour*,[138] or even the older *O Lady, I schall me dress with besy cure.*[139] Other Scots lyrics were translated from the French, not always word-for-word: the anonymous *Support your servand*[140] just mentioned, for example, is a Scots version of Clément Marot's *Secourey moy, ma Dame, par amours*, a chanson composed before 1527, and published for the first time with the musical setting of Claudin de Sermisy in 1528.[141] The style of the Scots poem, conservative in its heavy alliteration (unlike Marot's chanson) and in its courtly-love terms, suggests that it could belong as easily to the earlier as the later years of James's reign and literary interests. Another, sung in parts, *Richt soir opprest,*[142] seems later, its anonymous musical accompaniment said to reflect the newer chanson forms associated with the later work of Claudin.[143] This later period is also reflected in the works of the cleric and song-school teacher, John Fethy, who by 1532 had returned from musical studies abroad, and by 1542 had well-established connections at the Scottish court.[144] Fethy's *Pansing in hairt* [Pensive in heart],[145] with its traditional terms but slow-developing change of mood, via both the increasingly cynical refrain *Cauld, cauld, culis the lufe that kendillis our hett* [Cold, cold, cools the love that kindles too hot] and a skilfully colloquial secondary repetition *lat dolour be and gang ane vther gett* [let sadness be, and go another way], seems an elder sister to poems such as *Returne the, hairt* by Alexander Scott, whose compositions were to be pre-eminent in Mary's reign.[146] So, too, with its similar tonal uncertainties and mix of the

[137] A dog named *Begsche* was in the royal kennels in 1538 (*TA*, VII, p. 96), and one called *Bawte* is mentioned 1539-40 (Murray, ed, 'Accounts of the King's Pursemaster', p. 40), but both names could be recalling Lyndsay's earlier poem.

[138] Elliott and Shire, eds, *Musica Britannica* XV, no. 39; Shire, *Song, Dance and Poetry*, p. 64.

[139] MS Arch Selden B.24, fol. 231^r, 230^r. It is printed in Robbins, ed, *Secular Lyrics*, no. 196.

[140] *Bann. MS*, III, p. 295.

[141] Mayer, ed, *Clément Marot. Œuvres Lyriques*, pp. 174-175 and 12-13. For the French and Scots texts in parallel see Shire, *The Thrissill*, pp. 12-13, 27-28. For Claudin, see Ross, *Musick Fyne*, p. 124.

[142] Elliot and Shire, *Musica Britannica*, XV, no. 40.

[143] Shire, *Song, Dance and Poetry*, p. 38; Elliot, '*Trip and Go*', p.153.

[144] He is first mentioned in royal record in 1540: *RSS*, II, p. 524; see *TA*, VIII, p. 54 (payment for liveries for Fethy's *childer that plays on the viols*); Shire, *Song, Dance and Poetry*, pp. 37-39; van Heijnsbergen, 'The Scottish Chapel', p. 303.

[145] *Bann. MS*, III, pp. 343-344.

[146] *Bann. MS*, IV, pp. 8-9.

colloquial with the courtly address to the King of Love, does *Thir Lenterne dayis* [These Lenten days], by Stewart.[147]

A hint of early royal interest in poetic making in an ornate style is suggested in Bellenden's prologue to the Livy of 1533, *Armipotent Lady Bellona serene*.[148] In an appeal to James to be *muse and ledare of my pen*, Bellenden portrays the king himself as a participant in literary activities, referring to him as one who *writis in ornate stile poeticall / Qwik flowand vers of rethorik cullouris* [Lively flowing verse of figures of speech] (17-18). The idea of the king as literary participant as well as patron possibly was not an extreme distortion of flattery. A few years on, when the negotiations for the first French marriage were well under way, Lyndsay referred similarly to James V's 'ornate meter' in his *Answer to the Kingis Flyting* (c. 1535-36), but the context of his remarks is worth note. This is an exchange with the king (whose poem has not survived), not of the expected courtesies (which expression had in these years achieved a high point in the lighter epistles of Marot to the French court circle).[149] James's poem is said to have been *vennemous* (16); Lyndsay's *Answer*, although highly patterned with puns, similes and dense alliteration, is written as a mock-reluctant reflection of it, as much insulting as flattering, although nonetheless skilled. Like Marot's use of the revealing personal anecdote, James V, it is implied, has told a scurrilous story against Lyndsay's virility, and by this means has caused his ejection from *Venus' court*. Lyndsay deploys one in turn, using it to expose (and resolve) the multi-faceted portrait he has drawn of the king – on the one hand a writer of *flowand Rethorik* (70) and a chivalric lover, and on the other, a poet with a *prunyeand pen* (6) and the irresponsible amorous behaviour of *a restless Ram* (36). Lyndsay remembers (complicitly) an unseemly, furtive, but hilarious encounter between the king and a female servant in a brewery, which ended with each of them *Drowkit* [drenched] *with dreggis* (60). With the punning line, *But yit be war with lawbouring of your lance* (67), the poet predicts another. This one, he implies, will supplant the first, since it will be a public, nationally-approved encounter with a *bukler furth of France* (literally, a small round shield, 68), who will be the king's fitting partner in all senses. Here, the advice is threaded artfully through a poem in which the relationships of poet to patron, and of both men to poetic composition, are presented in a mature and easy form.

The king as *potent Prince ... and knicht* (64) is uppermost a short time later, in Lyndsay's poem of national mourning, *The Deploratioun of the Deith of Quene Magdalene* (1537). Its bilingual title, alluding to a common

[147] *Bann. MS*, IV, pp. 6-8.
[148] Bellenden, *Livy*, I, p. 1.
[149] See Smith, *Clément Marot*, pp. 91-124.

French elegiac form,[150] diplomatically acknowledges present Franco-Scots grief and an ongoing alliance. This is maintained within the poem. The traditional apostrophes to, and conventional imagery of, Death – as *creuell* (1) or *Gredie* (26), as *dreidfull Dragoun, with ... dulefull dart* (15) – owe as much to earlier English and Scots examples as to French. But the careful symmetries – of France and Scotland, Paris and Edinburgh, Madeleine and James (both of *blude Imperiall* (41)), the *laud and glorie* (72) of colourful French celebrations, and the *dulefull Dirigeis* (133) of Scotland's mourning, for example – in emphasising the strength and logic of the alliance, both suggest that Scotland's welcome to Madeleine would have equalled France's to James, and help to prepare the political ground for a second French marriage. In this light the poem may also be read as a conscious literary response not only to earlier French *complaintes* and *déplorations* in general but to the more recent poems celebrating this wedding, including Clément Marot's *Chant nuptial du Roy d'Escosse et de Madame Magdalene Premiere Fille de France*.[151]

Madeleine's *hame cumming* at St Andrews, organised and spoken by Lyndsay, had included a *trieumphant frais* [farce, play], during which the new queen, in accord with tradition, had been given the *keys of haill Scotland* and instructed on her duties to God and to her husband.[152] The language of the address is not specified, but in his later *Deploratioun* Lyndsay refers to the (French) cries of *Vive la Royne*! (157) that were to have greeted Madeleine in Edinburgh, and to the planned presence of *ornate oratouris* (162) (also a feature of James's Paris reception).[153] The acceptance of a French presence, by the city as at the Scottish court, is evident a year later, in the brief details, noted in the burgh records, of Marie de Guise's Edinburgh entry: a welcome speech *in Fransche* was prepared by the best of James V's orators – James Foullis and Adam Otterburn (neo-Latin poets, lawyers and royal servitors) and David Lyndsay (royal servant, senior herald and vernacular poet), and delivered by Henry Lauder (king's advocate).[154]

Much direct evidence of literary patronage at that Franco-Scots court of James and Marie seems lost or fragmentary, perhaps prey to the changing political and religious attitudes of the mid sixteenth century. Beside the

[150] See Bawcutt, 'A Medieval Scottish Elegy', pp. 5-13.

[151] Mayer, ed, *Clément Marot. Œuvres Lyriques*, pp. 314-318. The poem, distinctive for its use of the Psalms, was first published in 1538, but Lyndsay, in Paris for the ceremonies, possibly heard it then; see Hadley Williams, ed, *Sir David Lyndsay*.

[152] Pitscottie, *Historie*, I, p. 379.

[153] Teulet, ed, *Papiers d'État*, I, p. 124.

[154] *Edin. Recs.*, II, pp. 90-91. On Otterburn and Lauder, see further Finlay, 'James Henryson', pp. 25-26.

vogue for the musically-accompanied and inventively developed love lyric, noted briefly above, Lyndsay's mock-chivalric *Justing of Watsoun and Barbour* is possibly indicative of another kind of in-group entertainment in royal favour (as it had been at the previous court).[155] *The Justing* may have been performed as part of one of the court's tournaments, held at St Andrews in 1538, 1539 and 1540.[156] It is purportedly a record of a joust before the king and queen, between two actual, but ludicrously inappropriate, royal servitors, who are comically unskilled for their tasks as knights.[157] Yet a further and more important aspect of James V's literary patronage at this time can be glimpsed in the report, compiled by the director of the royal chancery, the Protestant sympathiser, Thomas Bellenden (who sent it to the English ambassador Sir William Eure, who sent it in turn to Thomas Cromwell), of a dramatic performance acted before the king and queen at Linlithgow.[158] The unresolved questions about the interlude's author, and the relationship of the interlude itself to Lyndsay's *Ane Satyre of the Thrie Estaitis* (1552, 1554)[159] are of less interest here than James V's reported involvement. Reminded during the performance of his obligations as God's earthly representative, and likewise flattered as the king 'who had pacified the country / and *stanched thifte*, James was said to have also spoken out – in a sense to have continued the play – after it had ended. According to the reported *nootes*, the king had threatened the bishops (whose corruption had been a topic of the play) that unless they reformed he would *sende sex of the proudest of thaym vnto his vncle in england.*[160] This seems a stage-managed act, designed for circulation (as indeed it most efficiently was), rather than a certain sign of James's reformist stand. Whether it can be considered further, as a deliberate use of literary patronage for political ends, is debateable, but, if so, it shows just how much James V had learned of his role as literary sponsor since his coronation twenty-seven years earlier.

[155]Cf. Dunbar's *Off Februar* (B47), stanzas 12-20.
[156]*TA*, VI, pp. 412-413; VII, pp. 164-166, 317.
[157]See further Hadley Williams, ed, *Sir David Lyndsay,* pp. 267-70.
[158]Lindsay, *Works*, II, pp. 1-6; *TA*, VII, pp. 276-277 (references to the costume for one of the players, and to *play cotis*).
[159]See Graf, 'Audience Involvement', pp. 423-435; Lyall, 'The Linlithgow Interlude', pp. 409-421.
[160]Lindsay, *Works*, II, p. 2.

THE REASSERTION OF PRINCELY POWER IN SCOTLAND THE REIGNS OF MARY, QUEEN OF SCOTS AND KING JAMES VI

Michael Lynch

In June 1552, *Ane Satyre of the Thrie Estatis*, by the poet and royal herald, Sir David Lindsay (*c.*1486-1555), was performed for the first time at Cupar, a royal burgh situated between the royal hunting lodge at Falkland and the university town of St Andrews.[1] This sophisticated court drama in the medieval genre of a mirror for princes was also a powerful but orthodox exercise in pointed anticlericalism, directed against the ecclesiastical hierarchy.[2] One version of the play survived the Reformation of 1560, preserved as a series of extracated comic 'interludes' in the Bannatyne Manuscript, a large and heterogeneous collection of late medieval poetical works compiled by an Edinburgh merchant and scribe, George Bannatyne.[3] The play at Cupar was performed only fifteen kilometres from St Andrews, centre of the archdiocese of St Andrews and seat of Scotland's metropolitan. By 1552, after a long flirtation with early Protestantism which had begun in the late 1520s and had climaxed in 1546 with the assassination of Cardinal David Beaton and a twelve-month occupation of his castle, St Andrews had become an acknowledged centre of Catholic reform, focused in the new College of St Mary. Early in 1552, a provincial council of the Scottish church, called by its primate Archbishop John Hamilton, had met. Believing that the 'many frightful heresies' which had afflicted Scotland 'within the last few years ... seem almost extinguished' and also heavily influenced by the orthodox reforms which had been masterminded by Archbishop Hermann von Wied at Cologne in the later 1540s, this council commissioned a vernacular catechism. The *Hamilton Catechism*, as it came to be known, professed itself as 'a plain and easy statement and explanation of the rudiments of the faith'. The book, which was an orthodox assault on clerical illiteracy and incom-

[1] The most convenient modern edition is Lyall, ed, *Ane Satyre of the Thrie Estatis*. The authoritative text, however, remains Hamer, ed, *The Works of Sir David Lindsay*.

[2] Edington, *Court and Culture in Renaissance Scotland*, pp. 168-192.

[3] Ritchie, ed, *The Bannatyne Manuscript*; Van Heijnsbergen, 'The Interaction between Literature and History in Queen Mary's Edinburgh'.

petence, probably appeared within two months of the first performance of Lindsay's *Satyre*.[4]

Although both play and catechism have, on occasion, been seen by some historians as forerunners of the Reformation or even as tainted with heretical thought,[5] each, in context, should rather be seen as a defence of the established order against the alarming pressures which had threatened the realm since the death of James V in 1542 and the accession of an infant, Mary, as queen of Scots. A parliament which met in February 1552 re-enacted legislation against disruption of the Mass and reinforced penalties for other religious and moral offences.[6] In the *Satyre*, a comic highlight, and one which tends to feature prominently in modern productions, comes when the anarchic figure of John the Commounweill occupies the throne vacated by King Humanitie, who has hitherto spent much of the play in a drunken slumber. To much of the play's audience in 1552, caught up in a royal minority which had seen the murder of Scotland's primate by an assorted group of minor Protestant figures and political dissidents,[7] the message of this episode in the *Satyre* surely represented the dangers of letting loose the 'many-headed monster' of the common people. The motive for staging the next recorded performance of the play, in August 1554, at the playfield of the Greenside just outside Edinburgh 'in presence of the Quene Regent [Mary of Guise-Lorraine] and ane greit part of the nobilitie',[8] is unclear. It is possible that this was a conciliatory gesture towards those of a reforming mind for this was only four months after the ratification of the regent's appointment by parliament. But it is more likely that the set-piece event was part of the process of establishing her court and administration in the capital.

The dangers foreseen by Lindsay and others in the royal court and the church hierarchy were dramatically realised during the year-long revolt in 1559-60 of the 'Lords of the Congregation', who were the vehicle for a Protestant Reformation in Scotland. The revolt began with an inflammatory sermon preached in the royal burgh of Perth by John Knox, a radical Calvinist recently returned from exile in Geneva. This provoked a 'rascal mul-

[4] Sanderson, *Cardinal of Scotland*, pp. 148-176; Winning, 'Church Councils in Sixteenth-Century Scotland'; Cameron, 'Catholic reform in Germany and in the pre-1560 Church of Scotland'. For the provincial council of 1552, see Patrick, ed, *Statutes of the Scottish Church*, pp. 135-136, 143-144. For the catechism, see Law, ed, *The Catechism of John Hamilton*.

[5] Donaldson, *The Scottish Reformation*, p. 35; Donaldson, *The Faith of the Scots*, p. 52.

[6] *APS*, II, pp. 486-487.

[7] Sanderson, *Cardinal of Scotland*, pp. 223-230.

[8] Cited in Hamer, ed, *The Works of Sir David Lindsay*, vol. 1, p. 398.

titude' to sack the town's two friaries and the great Charterhouse, founded by James I (1406-37). The iconoclasm and destruction in Perth was the spontaneous action of an urban mob, but the concerted campaign of 'cleansing' towns and their churches of 'idolatry' which followed in the next two months across east-central Scotland is likely to have been orchestrated by a small band of Protestant notables. It was thus not unlike the *Beeldenstorm* which seemed to spread like wildfire across parts of Flanders in 1566.[9] St Andrews experienced a reformation virtually overnight on 10\11 June 1559, with the parish church transformed from one of the most richly decorated Catholic churches in the realm into a Protestant preaching house in the space of a few hours.[10] The destruction of the Perth Charterhouse, which contained the tombs of James I and his queen, had been an act of desecration of a royal mausoleum which, though probably inadvertent, had been a propaganda gift to the royal administration of Mary of Guise.[11] Yet, the single most dramatic act of deliberate iconoclasm of the Reformation of 1559-60 was to be found elsewhere. The royal chapel at Restalrig, a little more than a kilometre from the palace of Holyroodhouse beside Edinburgh, had very possibly been founded by King James III (1460-88) *c.*1470 as the base for the new chivalric order of St Andrew, which was closely linked to the Burgundian Order of the Golden Fleece. The chapel was singled out for demolition by the first meeting of the General Assembly of the new Protestant church (Scotland's equivalent of the Huguenot national synod in France) in December 1560. Its protector, a local minor noble or laird called Robert Logan of Restalrig, was carted through the town of Edinburgh in an act of ritual humiliation on the orders of a new, aggressively Protestant town council brought to power in a *coup* during the Reformation crisis.[12] No other church or chapel in Scotland was officially targeted in the same way. The interconnecting trinity of chivalry, sainthood and the conspicuous iconography of a pious, orthodox monarchy was directly challenged by the new Protestant regime shortly after it seized power.

Continuities and discontinuities

It is difficult to think of two examples more dramatic than the respective fates of the *Satyre* and the chapel at Restalrig to demonstrate the different cultural and religious patterns of continuity and discontinuity which marked the Scottish experience of the Reformation. As at Restalrig, many of the

[9] Parker, *The Dutch Revolt*, pp. 74-80, 288 (note).
[10] Dawson, "'The face of ane perfyt reformed kyrk'".
[11] Henry II to Pope Paul IV, 29 June 1559, *CSP Rome*, vol. 1, pp. 12-13.
[12] MacDonald (A.A.), 'The Chapel of Restalrig'; *Edin. Recs.*, III, pp. 79-82.

cultural relics of the past were calculatedly destroyed; the capital of Edinburgh even cut the image of its 400-year old patron saint, St Giles, out of its town flag. Many royal burghs – towns which owed their chartered status to the crown – auctioned off the vestments, plate and valuables of the Catholic cult and its clergy. Scotland experienced a 'stripping of the altars'[13] in and after its Reformation of 1560 more ruthless than in most Protestant countries. The results were stark. Only a small handful of pre-Reformation altarpieces survive for the whole of Scotland, along with only one craft banner, the so-called Fetternear Banner of the prestigious Edinburgh merchant guild which had figured King James IV (1488-1513) amongst its honorary members.

Yet other cultural artefacts and works did survive the Reformation. *The Contemplacioun of Synnaris*, a penitential poem grounded in the cult of the Passion, and composed by the Observant Franciscan William of Touris in the last years of the fifteenth century was reprinted, in England, as an Anglican work, shorn of most of its references to Mary, the saints, good works and other Catholic observances. Part of the poem, as a lyric of the Passion, appears in the Bannatyne Manuscript, which contained a significant amount of religious poetry.[14] Bannatyne came from an intellectual circle in the capital, made up of merchants, lawyers and other professional men, some with connections to the royal court and administration, who were infused with a mixture of Erasmian humanism and a conservative patriotism. Their 'concern for continuity'[15] was evident in cultural and intellectual terms as well as social or political; a desire to preserve the social order matched an ingrained allegiance to the crown. The preservation of the cultural treasury of the late Middle Ages was another reflection of this political conservatism; it provided a significant underpinning of existing patterns of culture in an age when religious upheaval, royal minority and rapid socio-economic change threatened to overwhelm the way that the upper reaches of society behaved and thought.

The fate of the *Satyre* was less clear-cut than it has sometimes been made out to be. Despite its anti-clerical comic highlights, it did not quickly achieve the status of a celebrated Protestant obituary for the corrupt church jettisoned by the Reformation. The only surviving sixteenth-century copy of the text is that in the Bannatyne Manuscript. After the Reformation, Lindsay's collected poetical works, of which the first surviving printed edition dates to 1568 but were then minus the *Satyre*, became a regular production

[13] Cf. the English example in Duffy, *The Stripping of the Altars*.
[14] MacDonald (A.A.), 'Catholic devotion into Protestant lyric'.
[15] Van Heijnsbergen, 'The Interaction between Literature and History in Queen Mary's Edinburgh', p. 209.

of the Scottish printing press.[16] Yet the conjunction of a royal herald who escaped sanction in his own lifetime and his post-Reformation reputation as an early Protestant was uneasy. In a 'preface to the reader' composed by his first post-Reformation publisher Henry Charteris, he was hailed as the victim of attempts by Catholic clergy 'to rage and raill aganis him as ane Heretike' but was also described, somewhat oddly, as 'Schir David Lyndesay of the Mount, *alias* Lyoun King of Armes'.[17] By 1568, with Queen Mary deposed and a programme of black propaganda in print directed against her reputation under way, holders of royal office under that queen had to be beyond all reproach. Lindsay's collected poems, still without the *Satyre*, figured prominently in booksellers' inventories in the 1580s and 1590s. But the first copy of a printed text of the *Satyre* dates only from 1602. It may well be that it was only after that this date that this court drama became a 'popular' Protestant printed work, enjoyed by a much wider audience. The 1602 edition of the play was probably the result of royal patronage: by 1604, when the 1602 edition was reissued with an English title page bearing the royal arms of James VI as king of England, Robert Charteris had become 'Printer to the Kinges most Excellent Maiestie'.[18]

The example of the *Satyre* suggests three cautionary points. The first is that audience matters. Lindsay's lyric poetry was readily reconfigured in print for a new reading public after the Reformation. So were wholesome religious works by other pre-Reformation poets, such as Robert Henryson's *Testament of Cresseid* (a coda to, and part reworking of, Chaucer's *Troilus and Criseyde*) and even some examples of devotional pieces, such as the *Contemplacioun of Synnaris*. But court drama, with its private in-jokes or butts of satire, did not always translate easily into a public arena. Secondly, anticlericalism was a double-edged weapon. By the 1590s, a generation af-

[16] Allan, *The Scottish Book Trade*, pp. 110, 212. Lindsay's poems had, of course, been printed before 1560, in editions variously published at Edinburgh, London and Paris.

[17] The office of Lord Lyon became an issue of controversy in 1568: the existing holder, a Marian (and therefore in the eyes of the new regime highly suspect), was dismissed and an investigation was subsequently ordered into the operation of the office. His replacement was Lindsay's half brother, David Lindsay of Rathulit: *RPC*, I, 638, 660; *RSS*, VI, no. 489; Burnett, 'The Officers of Arms', pp. 14-15.

[18] Axton, '*"Ane Satyre of the Thrie Estaites"*', pp. 21-23. Lindsay's *Works* were printed in 1580 and 1582, both by or for Charteris: Aldis, *A List of Books printed in Scotland*, nos. 172, 186. See Laing, ed, *The Bannatyne Miscellany*, II, pp. 197, 224 for inventories: Thomas Bassenden had 5 bound and 595 unbound copies of Lindsay's poems in 1580 and Henry Charteris had 788 bound copies in 1599; the bound copies cost 8s. In contrast, Robert Bryson had 1,150 copies of the collected works, which now included the *Satyre*, priced at £2 each, in 1646 (Laing, ed, *The Bannatyne Miscellany*, II, p. 264).

ter the Reformation, the anticlerical elements in the *Satyre* could have found a new target: there was some loud criticism of the new Protestant clergy, who 'live like lairds'. In 1592, two anonymous sonnets attacking ministers' restraints on trade were tossed into the pulpit of St Giles', Edinburgh's parish church, during a sermon.[19] And thirdly, there can be little doubt that a fear of the urban mob affected both the court and the reformed church. Each, for good reason, would have been wary of performances open to the populace at large, such as those at Cupar in 1552 and Edinburgh in 1554. Monarchical ceremony was now largely confined to set-piece royal entries or new versions of chivalric display; and religious spectacle was largely restricted to the public humiliation of sinners.[20]

There were other reasons for the diversification of court culture and the seeming diminution of princely power. The most obvious was the series of royal minorities which afflicted every reign from the death of James I onwards. Half of the period between 1437 and the departure in 1603 of James VI to London to claim the English throne following the death of Elizabeth Tudor saw rule by minors and regents. The effect of this series of royal minorities, both on the authority of the crown and on court patronage of the arts, is the subject of much debate and disagreement. It is unlikely that matters were as bleak in either the minority of Mary or that of James VI as one poet rhetorically complained, saying that, with the death of James V in 1542, the fire went out leaving poets to shiver in a cold climate. Patrick Hume of Polwarth was sitting in the chimney 'neuk' [corner] at Holyrood before the re-establishment of the court there in 1579.[21] A certain amount of *ad hominem* continuity between reigns, across long minorities, can be demonstrated: Robert Carver (*c*.1485-*c*.1568), Augustinian canon of Scone,[22] in music, and Sir Richard Maitland (1496-1586)[23] in poetry, are the best exam-

[19] Calderwood, ed, *History of the Kirk*, V, pp. 177-178.

[20] There were only occasional exceptions. The most striking was the triumphal procession staged in 1582 to mark the return of John Durie, one of Edinburgh's radical presbyterian ministers. Cast into internal exile for criticism of the immorality of the court under Esmé Stuart, his return took the form of an inversion of the standard route of royal entries through the streets of the capital, accompanied by a large crowd singing the Calvinist battle hymn, Psalm 124, 'Now Israel may say'. Calderwood, *History of the Kirk*, VIII, p. 226.

[21] His poem, *The Promine*, addressed to the young king is dated as June 1579, at least three months before James left Stirling for Edinburgh and his royal entry. It was published in 1580. See Lawson, ed, *Poems of Alexander Hume*, pp. 204-210, for a convenient edition of the text.

[22] In Carver's case, the linkage extends back to the reign of James IV: Ross, *Musick Fyne*.

[23] MacDonald (A.A.), 'Early modern Scottish literature', pp. 82-86; MacDonald (A.A.), 'The Poetry of Sir Richard Maitland', pp. 7-19.

ples of a bridge between the reigns of James V and Mary. Rather more such linkages can be traced between the reigns of Mary and that of James VI after 1579: they include Maitland (again), Alexander Scott (*c.*1520-83), John Stewart of Baldynneis (*c.*1539-1606) and perhaps Alexander Montgomerie (c.1545-98) amongst practitioners of poetry, and a significant number of musicians, prominent among them the four English Hudson brothers and James Lauder (*c.*1535-*c.*1595).[24]

What also seems self-evident is that Protestantism, though rumoured to have infiltrated the court of James V in the later 1530s – the king was alleged to have drawn up a 'black list' of heretics – did not flourish long at court after his death. After the brief 'godly fit' in mid-1543 of the regent and prince of the blood, James Hamilton, first earl of Arran (later duke of Châtelherault), who promoted Protestant preachers and encouraged the import of English heretical works, heresy was left to fend for itself in regional pockets.[25] The greenhouse effect of the court, which was seen in France where, it has been estimated, almost two-thirds of noblewomen had flirted with Protestantism by the late 1550s,[26] was not experienced in Scotland in the same period. The quasi-court which existed during the minority of Mary, queen of Scots (without its child queen after 1548, when she was taken to France for safe-keeping) did not act, so far as can be judged, as a hothouse for political intrigue or religious controversy. Seigneurial Protestantism, nurtured in the country house, acted as a substitute. Courtly Protestantism, as a result, took time to develop, even after 1560.

These two reigns were preceded by long minorities: both Mary and James VI succeeded (as had James V before them) as infants. Yet there was a significant difference in the character of these two later reigns. James V's minority had seen something of a tug of war amongst rival factions at court but the end of the minority was signalled by the king's escape, aged sixteen, from the most formidable of these factions, the Douglases, who were subsequently forced into exile. A fairly familiar pattern then took charge: the reassertion of royal power and patronage. Mary's minority saw war and inva-

[24] Shire, *Song, Dance and Poetry of the Court of Scotland,* pp. 44-116; Ross, *Musick Fyne*, pp. 130-133. The Hudsons first appeared in the retinue of Darnley in 1565. Scott's whereabouts are difficult to establish c.1568-80. He had, however, enjoyed a pension as canon of Inchmahome Priory as well as being a prebend of the Chapel Royal. Both sinecures link him to the family of the Erskines of Mar, hereditary keepers of the royal castle at Stirling and administrators of the priory as well as guardians of the young James VI from 1568-79. A possibility is that he continued to be based at Stirling. It is thought that some of Montgomerie's work may be included in the Bannatyne Manuscript but there is no other trace of him in Mary's reign.

[25] Merriman, *The Rough Wooings*, p. 89-100.

[26] Roelker, 'The role of noblewomen in the French Reformation'.

sion by English armies (it was Sir Walter Scott who first dubbed this the 'Rough Wooing'), followed by her escape to France for safe-keeping, and then by a Reformation, led by rebel nobles in 1559-60. Mary returned in 1561, already at nineteen a dowager queen of France, to a realm which had seen, at best, only a shadow of a court during the long minority. An assessment of court culture in her period is made difficult by the shortness of her personal reign (1561-7), the crisis in which it ended and the campaign of iconoclasm which followed. This took two forms, one radical and the other conservative in motivation: a systematic destruction by Protestant enthusiasts of books and manuscripts which had a whiff of papistry about them or the camouflage of works with questionable subjects by poets and collators of poetry.[27]

In the case of James VI, the boy king was shut up in a place of safety, the formidable fortress at Stirling, with a skeleton household for the first thirteen years of his life, which saw a six-year-long civil war (1568-73) between the 'King's men' and 'Queen's men' (the latter supporting his deposed mother), four successive regents and the assassination of two of them. Here, there can be little doubt that the court culture normally associated with the king's household was largely in abeyance, though it seems likely that there was an alternative court, based in Regent Morton's 'palace' at Dalkeith, near Edinburgh, which was criticised by the General Assembly in 1575 for its luxury and excess.[28] In contrast, there were a few musicians in the boy king's household at Stirling (including the Hudsons) but little else to suggest the arts until immediately before his departure to Edinburgh in 1579. The length of James's minority is an almost metaphysical question. Technically, he assumed the reins of power in 1578, when just twelve; his formal entry into his capital and the establishment of a court there took place in 1579, when he had not long entered his fourteenth year. But he is usually thought not to have taken command of politics until 1585, by which time he was nineteen. And he deferred the search for a wife, despite recurrent pressures, until 1589.

The golden years of the 'Castalian Band', a group of vernacular poets who surrounded the young 'Apollo', were a period when the king had as yet, despite his age, not fully grounded himself in either politics or the art of

[27] Shire, *Song, Dance and Poetry*, pp. 21-23, gives examples of the Janus-like character of the 'ballatis of luve' in the Bannatyne Manuscript, where 'one can feel the blue pencil [of the self-censor] on the page' (p.21); see also MacDonald, 'Politics, Poetry and Reformation', p. 417.

[28] Morton's demonstrable interests focused on music, architecture and ornamental gardens, to be seen at Dalkeith and at Drochil and Aberdour castles. McQuaid, 'Scottish Musicians of the Reformation', pp. 49-52, 61. Ross, *Musick Fyne*, pp. 89-94; Howard, *Scottish Architecture*, pp. 81, 83-84.

kingship. The period between 1579 and 1585 saw four *coups* at court, all of them successful. This is a cautionary tale: instability and political factionalism are not necessarily inimical to the well-being of a court culture.[29] There is an analogy to be made here between these years and those between 1526-8, when James V, though formally declared of age to rule, was a king in name only.[30] Despite calculated attempts, in both public propaganda and in the private performance art of the court, to hail a return to the golden years of James IV and James V, who both had assumed control of government by the age of sixteen, James spent an extraordinary length of time for his political novitiate. In the perorations of the Castalian poets, James might be a philosopher king; but in politics, he was a probationer.

The reclaiming of power: the role of the court in Mary's personal reign (1561-67)

If the effects of royal minorities are debatable, what is less in doubt is the recurrent pattern, when monarchs came of age, of an immediate assertion of princely power. Kingship was still intensely personal. Scottish monarchs ruled through the force of their collective personality, in the court. Sir Richard Maitland, a veteran of three reigns, wrote a poem to instruct his son in statecraft; its repeated refrain would have been acknowledged in every Stewart reign: 'He reulls weill that weill in court can guyde'.[31] The beginning of a personal reign usually saw fresh investment in the household, a burst of propaganda insisting on the venerable lineage of the royal house, a renewed emphasis on court ceremony, and the re-invention of iconographic images and themes underlining the continuity of kingship. It happened in 1528, when the sixteen-year-old James V escaped from the clutches of his mentors and gaolers. It accompanied the return of the nineteen-year-old Queen Mary from France to reclaim her kingdom in 1561, despite the stark challenge to royal authority posed by the Reformation. And it was carefully devised for the young, godly prince James VI, who at the age of thirteen

[29] The *coup* which brought to power the Ruthven regime between 1582 and 1583 is usually thought to have interrupted the heyday of the Castalian Band; the court was reported to be 'very quiet and small' (*CSP Scot*, VI, pp. 322, 474). But the household continued to grow in size during that period: Juhala, 'The Household and Court of King James VI', p. 43 (also Appendix 1, pp. 310-339).

[30] Again, James V, aged 16, had been formally declared of age to rule in 1526. See Wiliams, ed, *Stewart Style*.

[31] 'The laird of Lethingtounis Counsale to his sone beand in the court', in: Craigie, *Maitland Quarto Manuscript*, pp. 32-36; Bawcutt, *Dunbar the Makar*; MacDonald (A.A.), 'Sir Richard Maitland and William Dunbar'.

was on the brink of passing from the second to the third 'Age of Man', when he was taken from his schoolroom in Stirling Castle to an elaborately staged royal entry into his capital in 1579.

In the late medieval period, the mainspring of much culture had been the royal court. The sudden, premature end of the reign of James V seems to have accelerated the trickle-down impact of court culture into a society which was by then already enmeshed in a process of complex and accelerating social and economic change. The spread of literacy, together with an active property market, encouraged the emergence of new professions; lay lawyers became more prominent, both in government and outside of it; the wholesale selling-off of church lands, in the form of feuing, helped produce new landed classes; and increasingly presence at court was marked by the ennoblement of many minor families.[32] There was a search, by each of these groups of *arrivistes*, for emblems of their new-found status. Conspicuous consumption and a renewed fascination with chivalry, reflected in all the arts but most notably in heraldry,[33] architecture[34] and decorative work of various kinds, ranging from painted ceilings or plasterwork to bookbinding,[35] were the result. Except for family histories and armorials which proliferated in the period, literary patronage, in the form of dedications or commissions, is more difficult to detect.[36] Yet closer analysis of some of the court literature of the reign of James VI, in particular, is likely to yield results. The barrier to understanding is most often the intricacy of court factionalism, which makes allusions difficult to trace.

The effect of the long minority of Mary, between her birth in 1542 and her return from France in 1561, was a truncated or muted court culture. The repeat performance in 1554 of Lindsay's *Satyre,* four months after the formal induction of Mary of Guise-Lorraine as regent, suggests an attempt to

[32] Lynch, *Scotland*, pp. 171-185.

[33] See Burnett, 'The Officers of Arms and Heraldic Art'; Burnett, 'Outward signs of majesty', pp. 289-302.

[34] See Howard, *Scottish Architecture*, esp. chapters 2 and 3; Glendinning, MacInnes and MacKechnie, *A History of Scottish Architecture*, chapts 1 and 2; MacKechnie, 'James VI's Architects', pp. 154-169.

[35] Such as John Gibson, appointed King's bookbinder in 1581 until his death in 1600, when he was succeeded by his son: Mitchell, *A History of Scottish Bookbinding*, pp. 57, 121; Allan, *Scottish Book Trade*, p. 119. Burnett lists 12 painters, two embroiderers, two decorative masons, a geneaologist, a calligrapher and a bookbinder in royal service in the period up to 1603: 'The Officers of Arms' (Appendix 3), pp. 260-261, 263-279. Only two of the painters were foreigners, both from the Low Countries. Although most of these craftsmen were based in Edinburgh, a significant number were either based in other towns or did commissioned work on noble houses.

[36] Brown, *Noble Society in Scotland*, p. 221.

re-establish a court based in Edinburgh rather than on a peripatetic circuit. In 1556, the Queen Regent founded two royal lectureships, based on the Collège de France in Paris, in the capital, hinting at a pro-active patronage of learning and the law outside of the universities which were largely still clerical preserves; a third lectureship may have followed in 1559. The Queen Regent's role in prompting a third and final meeting of the provincial council of the Scottish church, again in Edinburgh, on the very eve of the Reformation, suggests a return to the interventionist kingship of James V.[37] All these initiatives reflect the familiar investment of male Stewart kings in the court as a literary centre, and also their growing interests in both educational and religious reform.

In such circumstances, it is not surprising that the re-emergence of a royal court, once Queen Mary returned to her kingdom, offered a series of opportunities for a sovereign anxious to re-establish royal authority after a long minority and a religious revolt. The climate was also full of promise for ambitious suitors and claimants, ranging from nobles to poets, eager to enjoy their rightful place on the gravy train of royal favour. The process of restoring royal power proved troublesome. The formidable problems facing the young Catholic queen can be illustrated by the juxtaposition of two remarkable set-piece events: her official entry into her capital of Edinburgh a week days after her return and the three-day Renaissance 'triumph' organised in December 1566 at Stirling Castle to mark the baptism of her son and heir.

In European perspective, Scotland experienced one of the last national reformations of the sixteenth century. As well as being late, the reformation 'settlement' contained within itself an unresolved mixture of radical and conservative ingredients. Mary returned to a capital city which had experienced a *coup* by a radical minority. This was the town council which organised her official entry into her capital a week after her arrival. Yet, despite the appointment of the firebrand preacher John Knox as burgh minister, only one in six of the town's population attended the new Protestant communion at the Easter before the queen's return.[38] The entry was a mixture of conventional ceremony and explicit Protestant propaganda.[39] The first greeting for the queen came in the form not only of the keys to the burgh but also a Protestant (and probably English) bible and psalm book.

[37] Durkan, 'The Royal Lectureships under Mary of Lorraine, pp. 73-78; *Statutes of the Scottish Church*, pp. 156-162.

[38] Lynch, *Edinburgh and the Reformation*, pp. 75-91, 97, 190.

[39] MacDonald'(A.A.), 'Mary Stewart's Entry', pp. 101-110, and 'The Triumph of Protestantism'; Davidson, 'The Entry of Mary Stewart'; Gray, 'The Royal Entry in Sixteenth-Century Scotland', pp. 26-28.

Worse was to follow, including a pageant recounting the burning of the three Israelites, Corah, Dathan and Abiron, who had defied the authority of Moses. Less a civic entry than a 'triumphal entry into hell',[40] the ritual humiliation of the queen set the scene, two days later, for the first of her interviews with Knox. It is hardly surprising that the Catholic queen demanded of the Protestant minister of her capital why it was that she perceived her 'subjects shall obey you and not me and shall do what they list'.[41] Yet Knox's unrelenting hostility towards the queen exposed him to criticism from a significant section of Protestant nobles, and this came to a head in the General Assembly in 1564. He was particularly disparaging of his fellow rebels in the Congregation of 1559-60 who had gone 'courting' after the queen's return.

The second set-piece event of Mary's reign provided a dramatic contrast. Elaborate plans were laid after the birth of a son to the queen in June 1566 for an extravagant Renaissance festival, copying some of the features of the 'triumph' at Bayonne in June 1565, which had been organised to mark the final stage of the royal progress through France of the young Charles IX after the end of the first war of religion.[42] For some Protestant observers, the triumphs at both Bayonne and Stirling were of a piece with the march of the duke of Alva up the 'Spanish road' to establish a Council of Blood in the Netherlands, marking the onset of a Catholic international conspiracy against Protestantism.[43] The Stirling baptism, which was important enough for Mary to levy the only tax of her personal reign to help pay for it, demonstrated its borrowings from the ceremony, iconography and literature of the Valois court, but it was also a restatement of the extravagant ambitions made by the Scottish royal house in the three previous reigns. As in France in the year before, reconciliation rubbed shoulders with triumphalism. Although the baptism itself was conducted by Catholic rite, in what is likely to have been the most 'high' Mass conducted in Scotland since Mary's return, it was immediately followed by a formal banquet in which elaborate lengths were taken to show to the two guests of honour, ambassadors from Catholic France and Protestant England, a nobility divided by religion but united in purpose; it was in every sense a 'meal of domestic reconciliation'.[44] On the final day, late in the evening, came a sensational *feu d'artifice*. A mock fort, assaulted by the enemies of the state including Moors, *Landesknechten* and 'wild Highland men', survived intact, as a visi-

[40] Kipling, *Enter the King*, pp. 352-356, esp. 356.
[41] Dickinson, ed, *John Knox's History of the Reformation in Scotland*, II, p. 17.
[42] See Lynch, 'Queen Mary's Triumph', and the references therein.
[43] *CSP Foreign, 1566-8*, nos. 836, 842.
[44] Cf. Boutier, Dewerpe and Nordman, *Un tour de France royal*, p. 316.

ble demonstration of the claim that the Stewart monarchy had not only survived the vicissitudes of Reformation and noble *coups* but was the only guarantor of 'peace in our time'. The three-dimensional message was rammed home by poetic eulogy: 'The importance of kingship is eternal; it will be in the power of the Stewart family. The crown of Mary awaits her grandsons'.[45] The Stirling triumph is one of the best examples in Renaissance Scotland of how new kinds of iconography and novel devices, including the first fireworks show which the country had seen, could reinforce a familiar message about royal power.

The re-establishment of a cult of honour is one of the less well recognised themes of the personal reign of Mary. Yet there is ample, other evidence to sustain it, below the surface of the complex and often tangled events of the brief, six-year personal reign. Mary enjoyed the income of a dowager queen of France and it was this, amounting in the early years to some £30,000 Scots (almost matching the ordinary income of the Scottish crown), which seems to have paid for the royal household.[46] There is little direct evidence to reveal the atmosphere of the re-established court, other than indirectly through the work of some poets, principally Alexander Scott, a canon of the Chapel Royal at Stirling, which had acted as a focal point for certain strands of court culture since its foundation by James IV.[47]

Tracing the revived cult of chivalry becomes easier from 1565 onwards, when the queen married her cousin, Henry Stewart, Lord Darnley. He was the product of a mixed marriage in terms of religion and an English upbringing, since his father (the earl of Lennox) had spent twenty-two years in exile. Darnley's establishment at court as a royal consort took the form of a remarkable inflation of honours, amounting to five earldoms and fourteen knighthoods. A court party was created for him: by late 1565, it was claimed that 'every man does what he likes if he has either credit or friend at court'.[48] Its impact was swift. His chief rival at court, the former regent, Arran, now duke of Châtelherault, who was still first in line of succession to the throne, declared his 'house quite overthrown' and the Protestant party at court eclipsed. By early 1566, this cult of honour, which underpinned the Lennox Stewart axis, took on an explicitly Catholic face when Darnley was given the French order of St Michael in an elaborate ceremony at Can-

[45] Adamson, *Serenissimi ac Nobilissimi Scotiae Angliae Hyberniae Henrici Stuardi at Mariae Reginae Epithalamium*. Further extracts are given in Lynch, 'Queen Mary's Triumph', p. 13.

[46] Greengrass, 'Mary, dowager queen of France'.

[47] Van Heijnsbergen, 'The love lyrics of Alexander Scott'. See the contribution of MacDonald in this volume (note 65).

[48] Quoted in Goodare, 'Queen Mary's Catholic interlude', p. 14; *CSP Scot*, II, no. 247.

dlemas. Mary used the occasion to try to attract conservative nobles at court back to the Mass. Although Darnley turned from Catholic worshipper to Protestant conspirator in a matter of a few weeks, when he became involved in the murder of the queen's Savoyard servant, David Rizzio, the challenge to Protestantism which emanated from the court continued, though in a different guise. The birth of a son and heir in June 1566 gave the queen a fresh opportunity to re-establish courtly Catholicism. Despite a near-fatal illness suffered by Mary which delayed the celebrations, the baptism was made the centrepiece of the elaborate triumph, which used to its full potential the dramatic theatre of Stirling Castle, which was (uniquely in Scotland) both royal palace and a formidable fortress.

A simple recital of events in the period from mid-1565 until the baptism in December 1566 suggests that it was one in which court culture was increasingly exploited for explicitly political motives: the Queen married, helped create a new court party for her consort, tried to promote the Mass at court, survived two attempted *coups*, gave birth to a son, staged the Stirling triumph, commissioned the first full edition of the acts of parliament of Scotland,[49] and rehabilitated both the earl of Huntly (son of the Catholic magnate whom she had quashed in 1562), and the Catholic primate, Archbishop Hamilton. The triumph was immediately followed by the marriage, across the religious divide, between William Maitland of Lethington, chief adviser to the queen, and one of her ladies-in-waiting, Mary Fleming. One of Maitland's closest co-religionists reacted in amazement, claiming that he was as fit to be pope as this Catholic lady was to marry the Protestant intellectual.[50] The recent redating of the verse play *Philotus*, in which the central theme is the marriage of an elderly man to an attractive, young woman, to the mid-1560s is plausible. It is, however, difficult to be certain which love match it celebrates for there were many opportunities between the marriage of the queen herself in 1565 and the Maitland match, which took place on the last of the twelve days of Christmas spent by the court at Stirling immediately after the baptism.[51] Birth, love and marriage crowded this period.[52]

[49] Aldis, *A List of Books printed in Scotland before 1700*, nos. 50, 51.

[50] *CSP Scot.*, II, no 93; Loughlin, *The Career of William Maitland*, p. 238.

[51] Reid Baxter, 'The authorship of Philotus'. I am grateful to Dr Reid Baxter for discussion of this point. Both authorship and date of composition are disputed, not least because it was first printed in 1603. If it can be attributed to the young Alexander Montgo-merie, and linked to the Lennox Stewart connection at Mary's court, it is a further example of continuity between that reign and the next.

[52] Amongst other possible butts of the satire was the English ambassador Thomas Randolph, who had fruitlessly pursued another of the queen's ladies-in-waiting, Mary Beaton. He had been exiled from the Scottish court in February 1566 because of his involvement in Protestant conspiracies and the scandal caused by a satire

This was the time – appropriately enough – when the large section of love poems in the Bannatyne Manuscript was assembled: the scribe later altered the relevant date from 1565 to 1568, by which time there was not only an outbreak of plague but also a new mechanism of censorship imposed by the Protestant reformers.[53]

The ingredients of the cult of honour promoted at Mary's court in 1565-1566 need to be pieced together for little was printed at the time and much was destroyed after Mary's fall. The honeymoon period was described as a 'triumphal time' even by contemporaries and the theme of Venus, which recurs frequently in the poems of Alexander Scott, is a predictable preoccupation.[54] Yet there was an additional point to it in 1565. In France, after the end of the first war of religion in 1564, an extensive royal tour had been staged to bring messages of peace and harmony to a divided kingdom. One of the pageant masters was Mary's favourite French poet, Pierre de Ronsard, who in June 1564 orchestrated a royal entry into Lyon, where Catholic and Protestant children walked hand in hand, strewing the streets with flower petals, the muses singing of a new age of gold that would banish the folly of civil war. In this propaganda campaign, Venus and Astraea became key metaphors: political union would be achieved only through love; Astraea was the restorer of harmony to a world in chaos.[55] Such messages were just as appropriate to Scotland in 1565-1566, when two Protestant-inspired *coups* had, so it was feared, brought the country to the brink of a war of religion. In the work of George Buchanan, virtual Latin court poet in Mary's household, can be found mention of a 'golden age and the end of warfare' brought on by the birth of an heir in 1566.[56] The theme of Mary and Darnley as bringers of peace and harmony must have percolated the court from the time of their marriage onwards. In Buchanan's *Pompae Deorum Rusticorum*, a masque performed at both the marriage of 1565 and the baptismal celebrations of 1566, a series of images intertwined: Mary was not only Astraea but a female version of the shepherd prince played by Charles IX of France during his tour of his kingdom. She was

highly critical of the court: see 'Maister Randolphes Phantasey', in: Cranstoun, ed, *Satirical Poems*, I, pp. 1-29. Another possibility is John Knox, arch-critic of both the queen and her court, who had married the seventeen-year-old daughter of a noble in 1564, when aged about fifty: see MacDonald (A.A.), 'The Poetry of Sir Richard Maitland'.

[53] MacDonald, (A.A.), 'The Bannatyne Manuscript'.

[54] *Pepys MSS* (London, 1911), 77; Shire, *Song, Dance and Poetry*, pp. 60-61.

[55] Strong, *Art and Power*, pp. 103-106; Strong, *Splendour at Court*, p. 133; Armstrong, *Ronsard and the Age of Gold*, p. 37; Yates, *Astraea*, pp. 39, 133.

[56] 'Genethliacon', in: McGinnis and Williamson, eds, *George Buchanan*, pp. 154-162.

also another Arthur, bringer of the age of gold and fulfiller of the prophecy of Merlin.[57] The same elaborate claims were made in the Latin panegyric, *Serenissimi ac Nobilissimi Scotiae ... Epithalamium,* composed by Patrick Adamson to mark the baptism: 'Our leader [Mary] has transposed Mars ablaze with civil war into peace in our time ... Perhaps now the hardness of iron is softening into gold and the golden age of Saturn is returning.'

Although the staging was novel – a pointed Renaissance triumph explicitly copied from the festival at Bayonne in June 1565 – the political messages were intended to stress the continuity of monarchical power. These heady claims had a real precedent in previous reigns. The device of Arthur had been used by both James IV and James V to underline the claims of the Stewart dynasty to the English succession, which was weak from the point in 1502 at which Henry VII's first son, Arthur, died. Both of these Stewart kings named second sons (who did not survive infancy) after Arthur. A round table, like that of Arthur, was regularly used during the reign of James IV in formal court banquets to embarrass English diplomats,[58] as it was again in December 1566. And the image of the goddess Astraea was conventionally linked with imperial monarchy as well as the return of peace and the age of Saturn.[59] The claims of the Scottish monarchy from the reign of James III onwards,[60] seen in the adoption of a closed imperial crown on their coinage, were being revived in a new form.

The baptismal triumph was not an isolated set-piece event. It was the culmination of a year and a half of the increasing use of the court as political theatre. Harmony could also be reflected in the new *ballet de cour*. The conjunction of song, dance and poetry in court drama, which was borrowed from France and was new to Scotland, belongs to this period.[61] But such performance art needs a visual setting, as the next reign would amply demonstrate.[62] The ambitious building or reconstruction of royal palaces, at Holyrood, Stirling and Linlithgow, belonged to the reigns of James III, IV and V.[63] But it was in the next two reigns, of Mary and James VI, that greatest use was made of their dramatic possibilities as the setting for court entertainment, both indoors and outside.

[57] Buchanan, *Opera omnia*, II, pp. 404-405; Macfarlane, *Buchanan*, pp. 233-234.
[58] Macdougall, *James IV*, p. 295.
[59] Yates, *Astraea*, pp. 30-34.
[60] See MacDonald (A.A.), 'Princely culture', in this volume.
[61] Strong, *Splendour at Court*, pp. 129, 138; Carpenter, 'Early Scottish Drama', p. 203.
[62] Howard, *Scottish Architecture*, p. 23, where the point is made in relation to the reign of James VI rather than that of Mary.
[63] Dunbar, *Scottish Royal Palaces*, pp. 39-55.

At least two of the poets who later emerged as prominent members of the so-called Castalian Band around the young James VI in the early 1580s, Alexander Montgomerie and John Stewart of Baldynneis, can be traced, through family connections, to Mary's court twenty years before.[64] What is much more difficult to establish is which among their works may have linkages to the court of Mary rather than that of her son. Mary was an amateur poet of sorts[65] but, unlike her son, had no ambitions to be a poetic arbitrator. Apart from Alexander Scott, the most prominent poet of the 1560s (to judge from the number of his works in the Bannatyne Manuscript), there was no single outstanding literary exponent of vernacular literature at the court. In Latin scholarship, Buchanan was an outstanding figure, but his court laureate poetry has been described as run-of-the-mill.[66] Yet as in France, where she had inspired Ronsard, Brantôme, Maisonfleur and others, Mary's importance was as a patron or inspirer rather than a practitioner. As in previous reigns, the monarch's cultural patronage was widely cast: it extended to musicians, portrait painters, lawyers and historians as well as poets.

Various other authors who were not court poets can also be shown to have dedicated works to the royal couple: Thomas Craig, prominent lawyer and judge and a Catholic, penned Latin verses as a wedding hymn.[67] Another lawyer, Edward Henryson, who held one of Mary of Guise's royal lectureships in Edinburgh in the late 1550s, dedicated his French translation of Plutarch's attack on Stoicism to Mary and Darnley.[68] David Chalmers of Ormond, like Henryson a clerical lawyer, dedicated a manuscript dictionary of Scots law to the Queen in 1566.[69] And John Lesley, promoted bishop of Ross in 1565, had already devised briefing notes for an emissary to Rome to give a history lesson to Pope Pius V in April 1566; this was presumably part of the first draft of Lesley's *Historie of Scotland*, first published in 1570.[70]

Who were these legal figures? Lawyers, mostly clerics, had been prominent in the administration of Stewart kings from at least James III onwards. Yet there was also a difference here from these earlier reigns. The

[64] Lynch, ed, *Mary Stewart*, p. 15, 27 (note).
[65] Arbuthnot, ed, *Queen Mary's Book*.
[66] MacQueen, 'Scottish Latin poetry', p. 217.
[67] Craig, *Henrici et Mariae epithalamium*; Aldis, *A List of Books printed in Scotland*, no. 46.
[68] Durkan, 'Henry Scrimgeour', p. 20; Durkan, 'The Library of Mary Queen of Scots', pp. 77, 93; Kirk, *Patterns of Reform*, pp. 30-31.
[69] Durkan, 'The Library of Mary Queen of Scots', pp. 77-78.
[70] Pollen, ed, *Papal Negotiations*, p. 235. Lesley, in his introduction to the 1570 edition (conveniently published by the Bannatyne Club, 1830), claimed that he brought 'some notes' compiled on Scottish kings before he went to England in 1568-70. See Lynch, 'Queen Mary's Triumph', p. 16 (note).

reign of Mary came at a transitional point for the operation of kingship. No Stewart monarch except for James IV went on progress as much as Mary; the display of royal authority reverted to some of its medieval, peripatetic habits. On the other hand, despite its difficulties and recurrent crises, this reign was also the first to see a decisive growth of the machinery of the state. The *Register of the Privy Council* first emerged as a separate record of monarchical government in 1545. Mary's policy after her return in 1561, and especially that on religion, was conducted through her privy council, which mostly sat in Edinburgh. It has been argued that there was a 'certain coolness'[71] and tension between the queen's 'two bodies' – her household and privy council. This was undoubtedly so in the early part of the reign, when the privy council was dominated by former Lords of the Congregation, who had steered a Protestant settlement through parliament in 1560; a Jesuit visitor in 1562 complained that Mary was surrounded by heretics. Yet the composition of the privy council changed significantly as a result of the two failed *coups* of 1565 and early 1566 – the so-called 'Chaseabout Raid' and the Rizzio murder. Prominent amongst the newcomers was a circle of lawyers, both clerics (or former clerics) and laymen, who were responsible for the two editions of the acts of parliament produced late in 1566.[72] These were the legal men with literary ambitions – such as Chalmers, Craig, Henryson and Lesley - who surfaced in 1565-6. It is significant that none belonged to the Bannatyne circle, which was urban rather than courtly in nature.[73] They were definitely within her administration.

Rival court cultures in the reign of Mary

Queen Mary's return and the tensions which it provoked resulted in rival cultures, both located for the most part within the court. There was some spillage of one or other of these into country-house culture or urban literary circles. The tower house at Seton, which was rebuilt as a 'palace' in the 1580s, was testimony to the rise to prominence of a Catholic family which provided Queen Mary's master of the household in the 1560s. It was almost certainly at Seton that the poet Alexander Scott, a prebendary of the Chapel Royal, delivered his *New Year's Gift* to the queen in January 1562. As mentioned above, it is possible that a rival 'palace' at Dalkeith, also some ten kilometres from the capital and the house of one of the leading Protestant nobles of the 1560s and 1570s, the earl of Morton, acted as an alterna-

[71] Donaldson, *All the Queen's Men*, pp. 76-77.
[72] For others, see Lynch, ed, *Mary Stewart*, pp. 16, 77-8, 160 (and notes).
[73] Cf. the list of the Bannatyne circle in Van Heijnsbergen, 'The Interaction between Literature and History in Queen Mary's Edinburgh', pp. 224-225.

tive, Protestant cultural centre, as it did in the 1570s. But the focus of both culture and cultural patronage remained the court.

The tension after 1560 was partly to do with rival religious patronage of the arts. The queen's household was heavily French in both numbers and its cultural leanings, largely Catholic in its sympathies, and on the whole made up of lesser nobles. Her privy council was committed to the new 'amity' with England, a term which had overtly Protestant overtones, and was composed of most of the greater nobles of the realm.[74] In the early and mid-1560s, there was a 'battle of the books' and of rival printing presses in the capital.[75] The royal household had close links with the press of John Scot, which produced anti-Protestant tracts by both Ninian Winzet and the queen's confessor, René Benoist, before being shut down by the town authorities in 1562, forcing both polemicists into exile. Yet the same press, or at least the same printing irons, re-opened in 1564, under the control of Thomas Bassendyne, who had family links with Scot.[76] The rival printing press of Lekpreuik, who was official printer to the General Assembly, had a different connection with the royal court. Its sponsor was James Stewart, bastard half-brother of the queen, prior of the Augustinian house at St Andrews, who had emerged as one of the leaders of the Protestant Lords of the Congregation during the Reformation crisis of 1559-60. Lord James, created earl of Moray in 1562, remained the effective leader of the Protestant party at court and in the country throughout his half-sister's personal reign and was made regent after she was deposed in 1567. He also acted out a role which is less generally acknowledged, as the chief court patron of Protestant culture. He financed, via one of his clients, an Edinburgh merchant called Alexander Clerk, the printing by Lekpreuik in 1564 of the *Book of Common Order*, the product of radical English exiles in Geneva, as the primer of the new Protestant church. It seems likely that he was also the

[74] Donaldson, *All the Queen's Men*, pp. 66-67, 76-78.
[75] Lynch, ed, *Mary Stewart*, pp. 16-17.
[76] Watry, 'Sixteenth Century Printing Types and Ornaments of Scotland', pp. 23-25, 36, 40. The drawing of too ready a connection between the nature of the output and the political or religious allegiances of the printer is criticised by Mann, *The Scottish Book Trade*, pp. 150-151. It is true that all three main printers operating in the 1560s – Scot, Bassendyne and Lekpreuik – had a mixed output. Bassendyne was probably a Protestant; he held office as an elder in the Edinburgh kirk session during the civil war. But he also twice fell foul of the Protestant regime after 1567: for producing the Erastian work, *The fall of the Roman kirk* (1568) and for printing sixteen pro-Marian pamphlets during the civil war. Similarly Lekpreuik printed Thomas Craig's *Henrici et Mariae Epithalamium* (1565) celebrating Mary's wedding, but his output after 1568 was so overwhelmingly pro-King's party that he had to follow Knox into exile in St Andrews in 1571.

hidden hand which financed Lekpreuik's printing in 1565 of two works by reformist Italian authors which would surely otherwise have been unfamiliar to Scottish readers and were presumably intended to counter the Italian and Catholic influence at court. It was almost certainly his intellectual interests in demonology which produced the first act of the Scottish parliament against witchcraft, in 1563. And it was his pro-active patronage of Thomas Wode, an ex-monk of Lindores Abbey who gained office in the reformed church after 1560, which did much to produce an alternative musical liturgy for the new church.[77]

The most important figure in Moray's circle was Buchanan. He played a double role at the court during the personal reign, before he took on the part of leading character assassin of the queen after she was deposed. After 1568, he became a leading propagandist of the King's Men in the civil war. In his role as Latin court poet of the queen, both his poems and his dramatic works echoed themes that were familiar elsewhere: he, like Lesley, wrote of her as the descendant of the legendary hundred Scottish kings. This was not entirely sycophantic. Buchanan had at least three political masters – Mary, Moray and the earl of Lennox[78] – and it had been the latter's return to Scotland in 1564, followed by his son Darnley in the following year, which had transformed court politics. Buchanan, like the vernacular poets, indulged in comparisons with Diana and Astraea and hailed the shepherd princess who, like Charles IX of France, watched over her kingdom; he, too, revelled in descriptions of a 'golden age', seen in his *Genethliacon*, written to mark the birth of her son.[79] Buchanan's changing fortunes and changing masters leave considerable doubt as to whether he was anything more than a conventional, fawning court poet until Mary was deposed.[80]

[77] Durkan, 'Contract between Clerk and Lekpreuik'; Durkan, 'Native influences on George Buchanan'. The Italian works, by Celio Secondo Curione and Lelio Capilupi, are listed in Aldis, *A List of Books printed in Scotland*, nos. 49, 46; Doughty, 'The library of James Stewart'; Ross, *Musick Fyne*, pp. 65-66, 88.

[78] Buchanan described himself as a 'man of Lennox', the Highland area to the north and west of Glasgow.

[79] McGinnis and Williamson, eds, *George Buchanan. Political Poetry*, p. 154. See also the poem, 'For Lord Walter Haddon' (150-53), probably written in late 1564 or early 1565, before the Darnley marriage, for more testimony to a golden age. It has been argued that an undercurrent of pointed criticism can be detected in Buchanan's work: the golden age in *Genethliacon* was more like a commonwealth than an imperial monarchy; this 'mirror for princes' had a strong whiff of morally righteous sentiment: McGinnis and Williamson, eds, *George Buchanan. Political Poetry*, pp. 29-30.Yet it cannot be proved that the copy which survives was not retouched after Mary's fall. The first printed edition, by Robert Estienne, Paris, dates to 1567: McFarlane, *Buchanan*, pp. 298, 507, no. 166.

[80] See McGinnis and Williamson, ed, *George Buchanan. Political Poetry*, nos. B7

If explicit criticism of the queen is difficult to detect – or at least to prove – from within the court, a series of attempts have been made to trace a populist polemic both before and after her fall. In some respects there is a disjunction of interpretation between most historians of the reign and students of its literature. The origins of a *querelle des femmes* have been traced to the episode early in 1563 when an otherwise obscure French member of her household, Pierre de Boscosel, seigneur de Chastelard, infiltrated the queen's bedchamber.[81] His execution a few days later did, in this view, little to mend the damage done to the queen's honour, although the chief witnesses for this particular persecution are Knox and Thomas Randolph, the English ambassador, both of whom had good reason to play up the incident. Yet everything is relative and this episode pales into insignificance when compared with the scandal provoked at the court of Elizabeth Tudor in 1560 by the mysterious death by a fall down a flight of stairs of Amy Robsart, wife of her master of horse, Robert Dudley. There can be little doubt that the openness which poets and courtiers urged on kings – as William Stewart had done with James V[82] – could be interpreted in the case of queens or queen regents (such as Mary of Guise or Catherine de Medici) as over-familiarity. A polemical paper trail, beginning with the Chastelard incident, can be pursued. It becomes much thicker in 1567, following the murder of Darnley. By 1568, a steady stream of vitriolic works, dubbed 'ballattis of despyit' by one commentator,[83] was coming off the Lekpreuik press. Yet there are three sets of objections to this interpretation. The first is that women rulers made for easy targets and this interpretation does not allow for the political backlash which misogyny caused if it called sovereignty into question. Secondly, the authors of these libels were mostly marginal figures, although in April 1567 parliament did, it is true, take action to ban the 'slander, reproche and infamye' caused by such works. Petitions on behalf of the self-termed 'professors of the Evangel of Jesus Christ' were a regular feature of the personal reign.[84] They represented the politics of a radical but largely powerless faction, held at arm's length by the real Protestant power-brokers amongst the nobility. And lastly, despite the amount

and B8 (pp. 274-275), a psalm paraphrase addressed to Mary, 'You surpass your lot in life by your merits, your years by your virtues, /Your sex by your powers of mind, and your nobility of birth by your character'; and a Strena of New Year 1566, addressed to King Henry (Darnley). 'since with things going well for you, /All things go well for your kingdom too'.

[81] Parkinson, '"A Lamentable Storie"', pp. 146-147, 155-159.

[82] See Ritchie, ed, *The Bannatyne Manuscript*, II, p. 256, ll. 16-25; MacDonald (A.A.), 'William Stewart'.

[83] Kratzmann, 'Sixteenth-century secular poetry', p. 115.

[84] *CSP Scot.*, II, pp. 178, 323.

of vituperative works which Lekpreuik printed against the queen after she was deposed, it remains a fact that most leading figures in politics expected her to return from her detention in England. The real debate was about whether she should rule in her own right or as part of some kind of joint monarchy with her son, under the control of Moray. That position changed only when events in England took an unexpected turn in 1569, with the Norfolk plot and the simultaneous rising of Catholic nobles in the north.

The assertion of princely power in the reign of James VI

As in other courts of north-western Europe, royalist propaganda in Scotland became steadily more pointed and more overtly political as the century progressed. We have seen that Queen Mary used the baptism of her son to stage a multi-dimensional Renaissance triumph full of symbolic significance. An elaborate panegyric in Latin, composed to mark the occasion, hailed the new-born product of the Stewart line, the successor of a hundred kings before him, as a fulfilment of the prophecy of Merlin and guarantor of the 'age of gold' to come; he was lauded as the new 'Arthur', king of the Britons, who would succeed to the English throne.

The next great set-piece ceremony, which came in 1579, also had a very specific political agenda. In simple terms, it marked the formal entry into his capital of Edinburgh of that same son, James VI, now in his fourteenth year and a Protestant prince.[85] Its centrepiece was a group portrait of the five previous Stewart kings, all with the same name, who had ruled from 1406 until 1542. His mother was conspicuous by her absence. If female rule had brought discontinuity, the official memory of it was expunged. The message was clear: the confusing years of James's mother's reign, which had seen a religious reformation, successive revolts against royal authority culminating in her deposition in 1567, followed by civil war, were over. A new Stewart age, redolent of the golden years of the past, had begun.

The 'joyous entry' was also designed to ensure the success of one of the largest political *coups* of the sixteenth century – namely, the maximising of attendance at a parliament called to forfeit the 'race of Hamiltons', the premier noble family in Scotland for the past two generations. It coincided with the arrival from France of the king's cousin, Esmé Stuart, and the beginnings of the restoration of an extended family of Stewarts around the king (the first such grouping since the reign of James III). It marked the further diminution of the influence of the earl of Morton, who had been re-

[85] Gray, 'The Royal Entry in Sixteenth-Century Scotland', pp. 28-29; Lynch, 'Court ceremony and ritual', Mill, *Mediaeval Plays in Scotland*, pp. 80, 89-90, 192-194.

gent between 1572 and 1578, and the setting-up, after a hiatus of more than a dozen years, of a royal court now largely based at Holyrood.[86]

The icons of previous Stewart kings were redeployed. The sword and sceptre, ironically gifts of successive Medici popes to King James IV,[87] were made, along with the closed imperial crown manufactured for James V in 1540, the symbols of a new Protestant monarchy which asserted its unbroken continuity with the past. These, which together came to be known as the 'Honours of Scotland', were made the focal point of an elaborate new ceremonial procession, the 'riding of parliament', devised to mark the opening of each meeting of the Estates.[88] Kingly power was finding new means of self-expression in the age of what is sometimes called 'state formation'. Even the role of pious king and religious reformer, which had featured in the reign of James V, was reworked. The teenage James VI, hailed in his royal entry of 1579 as successor of the biblical King David and as a Solomon belying his youth, was made the focal point of a new Protestant iconography. A week-long set of festivities following a marriage at court in January 1581 was climaxed by the adoption by the 'whole council and court', on their knees, of the 'King's Covenant', a national bond between Protestant king and his subjects, composed by the royal chaplain John Craig, which was ordered to be read out in every pulpit in the realm. A wave of religious legislation, initiated by the crown, followed in the next parliament.[89] A Protestant king, court (both chamber and council) and nation were yoked together.

Apart from conventional messages from the genre of advice to princes, there had been two main themes of the entry of 1579: the celebration of a philosopher king, and the claim of a now restored continuity with a past golden age. The future was guaranteed by the restoration of the Stewart line, the personal accomplishments of the young king (who was addressed in Latin, Greek and Hebrew),[90] and by fate itself. As a result, the entry re-

[86] By the 1590s, the court spent more time at Holyroodhouse than at all the other royal palaces put together: Juhala, 'The Household and Court of King James VI', p. 125.

[87] See MacDonald, 'Princely power', in this volume, at note 16.

[88] Innes of Learney, 'The Scottish Parliament'.

[89] Russel and Napier, eds, *History of the Church of Scotland*, II, p. 268; Calderwood, ed, *History of the Kirk of Scotland*, III, p. 501; Lynch, 'Court ceremony and ritual', pp. 70-72. *APS*, III, pp. 210-213 (Oct. 1581).

[90] He was acclaimed by Montgomerie as 'in eviry language eloquent'. Cf. Cranstoun and Stevenson, eds, *The Poems of Alexander Montgomerie*, II, no. XLVIII, l.80. The address in Hebrew was made, on the steps of the church of St Giles', by 'Dame Religion', who invited him to hear a sermon of the duty of kings by the burgh's chief minister, John Craig, who was also appointed king's chaplain in 1579.

sembled an astrological pageant: the Wheel of Fortune was burned outside the burgh church and Ptolemy explained the happy conjunction of planets at the time of the king's birth; the four moral virtues of Temperance, Prudence, Fortitude and Justice who flanked Ptolemy celebrated the accomplishments of the four ages yet to come for a king who had just entered, at fourteen, the third age of man.[91] The authorship of the various ingredients of the 1579 entry is unknown, and no pageant book survives.[92] Yet it established much of the iconography of the rest of the personal reign: the Scottish David was already on the way to becoming the British Solomon.

After 1585, when James at last began to take charge of his administration, the image of a just king and lawgiver was fortified in various ways. The most striking example, which also illustrates how much his rule was determined by what might now be called government by photo opportunity, was the 'love feast' of May 1587. On the last day of an acrimonious meeting of the Estates, held in Holyroodhouse,[93] the king processed feuding nobles, hand in hand as a symbol of their reconciliation, the kilometre from the palace to the market cross, the centre of his capital (and also, in a sense, of his kingdom), where a banquet was laid out in the street. Debtors were released from prison, the gibbets at the cross were ritually destroyed, and musicians, trumpeters, fireworks and cannon fired from the nearby Castle combined to proclaim a new peace in King James's time. The 'love feast',

Dame Religion is reminiscent of the central, moral figure in Lindsay's *Satyre*, Lady Veritie, who, in the play, was a 'representation of the living Word of God which sustains the king's new found commitment to divine precept'. See Edington, *Court and Culture in Renaissance Scotland*, p. 138.

[91] This theme had both traditional and novel aspects. It had been common in European entry spectacle and in Scots poetry, as in Lindsay's *Squire Meldrum*. But there were also intellectual novelty in a Protestant 'reconstituted astrology': see Williamson, 'Numbers and national consciousness'.

[92] Alexander Montgomerie, 'maister poete' of the Castalian Band, cannot have been involved unless he returned to Scotland at an earlier date than has been hitherto established. It is likely that more than one hand was involved, particularly because of the range of languages employed. But it is possible that the main conceiver of the pageant was the one poet who can be proved to have been resident at Holyrood before October 1579 – Patrick Hume of Polwarth; see Juhala, 'The Household and Court of King James VI', p. 177. If this is the case, it may help explain the dynamics of the later 'flyting' between Hume and Montgomerie and the latter's efforts, in *The Navigatioun*, to outdo some of the rhetoric of the entry: in it, James is hailed as a 'Solomon', who was 'the chosen vessel of the Lord': Cranstoun, and Stevenson, eds, *The Poems of Alexander Montgomerie*, I, no. XLVIII, ll. 78-79, 82.

[93] The holding of meetings of parliament or conventions of Estates in royal palaces was both unusual and controversial. Normally, they met in the Edinburgh tolbooth, at least notionally in public.

transforming court politics into theatre, was a Renaissance triumph in miniature.[94]

The marriage to a queen gave a further opportunity for monarchical display. The medals struck to commemorate the occasion depicted James as a Roman emperor, wearing a laurel wreath: clearly, the imperial monarchy first claimed on James III's coinage a century before was taking on added meaning.[95] Scotland had not had a combined coronation and royal entry of a queen since that of Margaret Tudor in 1503. It was usual in Renaissance Europe – and was the case both in 1503 and 1590 – that the entry of a queen was more elaborate and more pointed in its political messages than the previous entry of the king himself. Predictably, the entry of Anna of Denmark in 1590 was dominated by images of love and fecundity, peace and plenty, together with the lineage of the Stewart family and the succession, which the marriage would guarantee.[96] But there were more elements of a popular festival than in 1579, because the entry also signified a marriage between the new queen and her capital city. The houses along the route, according to a celebratory poem by John Burel, were decorated with paintings and tapestries; many of these had been borrowed for the purpose from the royal household.[97] Some of the stage effects were novel, at least in Scotland. On two occasions, actors spoke on behalf of the king: one, 'in the garb of an astronomer ... pretending to be a mathematician' repeated the theme of astrological learning, which had been omnipresent in 1579. Such allegorical personification of majesty was fairly new to entry spectacle; in France it had first been used in 1571 at the entry into Paris of Charles IX. The ultimate purpose was clear enough: Anna was proclaimed as Sheba, a fitting queen for a king already hailed as Solomon.[98]

The only set-piece court ceremony of the personal reign to have a pageant book is the baptism of Prince Henry, at Stirling Castle, in August 1594.

[94] Goodare and Lynch, eds, *The Reign of James VI*, pp. 4, 83. Cf. Mason, *Scots and Britons*, ed, pp. 112-137, 183-184.

[95] Goldberg, *James I*, p. 45.

[96] Gray, 'The Royal Entry', pp. 29-31; Lynch, 'Court ceremony and ritual', pp. 83-87; McManus, 'Marriage and the performance of the romance quest'. A Danish account of the coronation and entry is reprinted and translated in Stevenson, *Scotland's Last Royal Wedding*.

[97] John Burel, 'The Discription of the Quennis Maiesties Maist Honorable Entry into the Toun of Edinburg, Upon the 19 Day of Mai 1590', pp. i-vii. Cf. Manuscript Town Treasurer's Accounts (1581-96), fol. 581; I owe this reference to Dr Juhala, 'The Household and Court of King James VI', p. 264.

[98] Bryant, *The King and City*, pp. 157-158; the 'Danish account', pp. 109-119, is the only one to mention Solomon and Sheba.

The deviser of the three-day festival was the poet William Fowler.[99] As a result, the highlight of the elaborate banquet arranged in the Great Hall on the final day of the celebrations is well known. Described in a brilliant essay by Sir James Fergusson called 'A Ship of State',[100] the climax came with an enormous set-piece engine which brought in the third course of the banquet. It was a ship in full sail measuring almost six metres in length and over twelve metres from its bottom to its topmost pinnacle, with a crew of more than forty, including the classical gods Arion, Triton and Neptune and six assorted goddesses (Ceres, Fecundity, Faith, Concord, Liberality and Perseverance), and surrounded by an undisclosed number of 'syrenes' or mermaids. Less attention has been given to what else happened over the course of the three days' festivities and the reason for the huge expenditure, which eclipsed even the spending on the king's own baptism. In 1566, Mary had raised a tax of £10,000. In 1594, James demanded a tax of £100,000. Even given price inflation, the difference was phenomenal.

As before, the baptism was the signal for an extravagant three-day festival.[101] It began with a tilting tournament, with four sets of knights, each with their own shields bearing an *impresa* - Amazons, Turks, Moors (who failed to appear), and Knights of Malta (who included the king himself). A second day's tournament, which would have added exotic, fake animals to the proceedings, including a camel, elephant, dragon and unicorn, had to be abandoned because the workmen required to stage it were needed in the Great Hall. There, in the presence of ambassadors from England, Brunswick, Mecklenburgh, Denmark, Holland and Zeeland, a series of engines conveyed the different courses along the length of the Hall. First, to a fanfare of trumpets and hautboys, came a triumphal chariot, seemingly hauled along by a blackamoor with six goddesses riding in it (the same six who later appeared on the Ship of State). Here was a standard symbol of imperial monarchy, a message which would have been reinforced if the original plan, to have it pulled in by a lion, the emblem of Scottish kings for over 400 years, had been put into action. At the last moment the pageant master had a failure of nerve and, thinking the lion might frighten the ladies of the court, substituted it. Next came the Ship of State, resplendent in the colours of the Scottish royal house, red and yellow, and complete with the armorials of the crowns of Scotland and Denmark, representing the heroic voyage which James had undertaken, 'like a newe Jason',[102] to claim his

[99] *A True Reportaire of the Baptisme of the Prince of Scotland* (Edinburgh, n.d. [*c*.1594-5]) in: Meikle, ed, *The Works of Thomas Fowler*, vol. 2, pp. 169-195.

[100] 'Ship of State' in Fergusson, *The White Hind*, pp. 84-96.

[101] Lynch, 'Court ceremony and ritual', pp. 88-89.

[102] Meikle, ed, *The Works of Thomas Fowler*, vol. 2, p. 193.

bride four years before. Its entry into the Hall, according to one account, was by 'hiddin and unperceaved convoy' and its exit was no less dramatic: amidst the sound of a round of cannonfire from the ship and a pall of smoke, suddenly the ship was gone. The proceedings ended with a rendition of Psalm cxxviii, sung in a seven-part harmony: *Blest are thou that fearest God/And walkest in his way.*

The dramatic, hugely expensive appearance of the Ship of State, rich in classical iconography, has to a great extent drawn attention away from the purpose and the overall context of the baptismal celebrations. In the sixteenth century, a ship had become a powerful metaphor, for both church and imperial monarchy. Charles V and his son Philip had been borne into the city of Lille in 1548 on such a ship, and the Emperor was carried in funeral procession through the street of Brussels in another great ship of state in 1558.[103] There are numerous pictorial images of the 'Ship of the Kirk' which survive, especially from the Netherlands, which was well represented amongst the ambassadors at the baptism. This was portrayed as a stately, safe and stable vessel, in full sail, with dissenters, Anabaptists and other heretics consigned to the murky waters around it. William Fowler's 'Ship of State' was an outrageous plagiarism, accreting to the monarch rather than the church metaphors of power and divinity. It was no longer church bells which rang out to celebrate monarchy: it was literal cannonfire from the guns mounted on the Ship of State.

This theme of divine kingship, however, had already been established before the celebrations in the Great Hall. In the Chapel Royal, specially rebuilt for the baptism as a Protestant place of worship 'more large, long and glorious',[104] the king sat on his throne on a raised dais. The font and pulpit were placed in the centre. The text of the sermon, from Genesis xxi and Psalm xxi, on the duty of kings, both emphasised the divinity of kingship. Yet the claims were far more extravagant than that. The new chapel, dubbed the 'great temple of Solomon' by a keen observer of the court, was built to the same dimensions as Solomon's Temple, and the king sat in the section called the holy of holies.[105] Clearly, an imaginative linkage was being sug-

[103]Strong, *Splendour at Court*, pp. 103, 113. A 'Ship of France' had been displayed atop one of the triumphal arches in Charles IX's entry into Paris in 1571, but by 1581 the symbol had taken on three dimensions: Henry III's entry in the celebrations of the marriage of the Duc de Joyeuse at Paris in 1581 took the form of a 'marine triumph, being in a great ship' (Yates, *Astraea*, pp. 135-136, 157, 166, 171).

[104]Meikle, ed, *The Works of Thomas Fowler*, vol. 2, pp. 169-170.

[105]Laing, ed, *Original Letters of Mr John Colville*, pp. 106-108; *CSP Scot*, XI, p. 377; Mackechnie, 'James VI's architects', pp. 163-165. Only the second ecclesiastical building in Scotland constructed since the Reformation, it demonstrated a royal prestige building project akin to those of James III and IV: see the contribution of

gested between the Chapel Royal, atop the hill in the citadel of Stirling, and the Jewish Temple on its Mount in Jerusalem. Five years before James VI laid claim in print in his *Trew Law of Free Monarchies* to being a king by divine right, the claim was being made for him in three dimensions, in stone. James, as God's lieutenant on earth – it was in effect claimed – was now simultaneously King Solomon (the fount of wisdom), the biblical King David (whose Psalms the king had translated)[106] and the Christian Emperor Constantine (responsible for the official adoption of a new religion).

The baptism of 1594 was unusual in having relatively few political messages directed at James's own nobility. That was because the real audience for the baptism of a child named Henry Frederick, after Henry VIII of England and Frederik IV of Denmark, was the English ambassador and his entourage. On the tourney field, the king had dressed up as a Knight of Malta, a living recreation of the theme of his poem *Lepanto*. The image was not understood by ministers of the Scottish kirk, who thought it papist. Yet Knights of Malta, as surrogate Protestant crusaders, a new St George to fight off the Turks, had been, since the 1580s, a commonplace of English tourneys on the anniversary (17 November) of Elizabeth's accession to the throne. It was, in effect, an English tournament that James was staging. At the banquet in the Great Hall, the seating plan was different from the usual arrangements, according to which the king sat with his hard-drinking gentlemen of the chamber at separate tables from the queen and her household. Instead, 'betweixt everie noble man and gentil man stranger was placed a ladie of honour or gentil woman'. This was the court in the English style developed during the reign of a female ruler in England. In Scotland, the celebrations of 1594 as a whole were, in effect, a triumph of the Elizabethan succession, copying English chivalric festivals.[107] Even the pageant book by William Fowler, describing the events, was written in English rather than Scots.[108]

Ironically, the most ambitious set-piece ceremony in terms of the claims made for princely power in both reigns – the baptisms of 1566 and

MacDonald in this volume, at note 63.

[106]Printed in Craigie, ed, *The Poems of James VI*, vol. 2, pp. xi-xxii, xxix-xxxviii, 1-63.

[107]Meikle, ed, *The Works of Thomas Fowler*, vol. 2, p. 186; Lynch, 'Court ceremony and ritual', p. 89. Cf. Young, *Tudor and Jacobean Tournaments*, pp. 35-36, 157; Strong and Van Dorsten, *Leicester's Triumph*, pp. 69-70; Guy, *Tudor England* (Oxford, 1988), pp. 427, 431.

[108]Two editions were printed, one in Edinburgh, the other in London. Fowler was familiar with English. He had been in England 1582-3 and recruited by Elizabeth I's secretary of state, Francis Walsingham. Cf. Meikle, ed, *The Works of Thomas Fowler*, vol. 3, pp. xxvii-xxviii.

1594 – each had a foreign provenance. 1566 was a French triumph in miniature, while 1594 was an ambitious imitation of the revels of the Tudor court. Yet this was in itself not novel. From at least the time of a spectacular tournament staged at Stirling in 1449, the Burgundian court had acted as a template for the court of James II (1437-60), who married a princess of Gelderland, and that of their son, James III.[109]

The king's 'two bodies': politics and patronage in chamber and council

One result of the complicated events of 1579-80 was a highly fluid and complex state of court politics. There were three sets of 'loyalists' close to the king for much of the next twenty years. The first of these networks emerged from the events of the king's minority. The Erskine family, hereditary keepers of Stirling Castle, had had charge of the boy during his formative years, between 1568 and 1579 and two nobles who had long careers during the reign – the second earl of Mar and the Master of Mar – were fellow classmates in the hard school run by George Buchanan, who had also been tutor to the young Lord James, bastard son of James V, in 1536-8.[110] A second group came from the household formed in 1579-80, when the court was established at Holyrood.[111] Long service in the chamber became a virtual guarantee of further preferment, either in the household or in the king's administration. The final group, which is the most difficult to categorise since it sprawled so extensively, was the extended family of greater and minor Stewarts who thronged the court in the 1580s and 1590s.

Neither Erskines nor Stewarts could be described as a well-organised or tight-knit faction. The two wings of the Erskine family had fallen out in a murderous quarrel played out in the presence of the terrified boy king in the Great Hall of Stirling Castle in 1578, when his guardian had been severely wounded and a classmate killed.[112] John Erskine, second earl of Mar, was involved in two attempted political *coups* against the king, both staged in Stirling, in 1582 and 1584. For much of the 1580s, he and other dissident Protestant nobles belonged to the so-called 'party of Stirling'. The revived Stewart network was also fissiparous. Initially clustered around the figure of Esmé Stuart, who reorganised the household on his arrival in Scotland in 1579, it split in 1582 with the successful but short-lived *coup* orchestrated

[109]See MacDonald (A.A.), 'Princely culture', in this volume; also his 'Chivalry as a Catalyst'.
[110]See Williams, 'James V', in this volume.
[111]The household is exhaustively listed in Juhala, 'The Household and Court of James VI', Appendix 1, pp. 310-339.
[112]Lynch, 'The Great Hall of Stirling Castle'.

by the Ruthven regime, and formed again after its fall, this time around the controversial figure of James Stewart of Bothwellmuir, earl of Arran. The competition for place amongst the extended Stewart family intensified in the early 1590s with the coming of age of Esmé Stuart's son, Ludovick, duke of Lennox,[113] the new prominence as a royal favourite of George, sixth earl of Huntly after his marriage to Esmé's daughter Henrietta in 1588,[114] and the increasing demands made by another Stewart with an ingrained conviction of his right to a place in the sun of the king's favour, Francis Stewart, Earl Bothwell.[115]

James VI was a polymath – an arbiter of poetry as well as a practitioner and translator of it, a theologian, demonologist and political theorist. He was wide-ranging, obsessive yet fickle in his intellectual interests. After 1588, when he wrote a masque for the marriage of Henrietta and Huntly, James, the Apollo figure, 'prince among poets', increasingly turned philosopher king.[116] His literary career moved away from poetry to prose and from performance arts to introspective pursuits of the intellect. Its formidable range and voluminous production were reflected in the size and eclecticism of his *Complete Works*, published in London in 1616; the title page, reminiscent of the triumphal arches devised for his entry into London in 1604, with the figures of Religion and Mercy acting as supporters of a closed imperial crown, was a monument to both the philosopher king and to divine right monarchy.[117]

The transition was predictable. Until 1585, the king was an apprentice in the arts of government, the creature of a series of masters – Esmé Stuart, duke of Lennox (1579-82); the Ruthven regime (1582-3); and Captain James Stewart, earl of Arran (1583-5).[118] After 1585, although James had

[113]Ludovick was born in France in 1574, was sent to Scotland in 1583 after his father's death, married Sophia Ruthven without the king's permission in 1589, but was left in nominal charge of the kingdom during the King's absence in Denmark in 1589-90. As high chamberlain (an office his father had held), he had full control over lodgings within all royal palaces. In 1600, he combined this office with the title of first gentleman of the chamber: Juhala, 'The Household and Court of James VI', pp. 102-103.

[114]From 1588 until Ludovick came of age, Huntly exercised control over access and accommodation: Brown, *Bloodfeud in Scotland*, p. 145.

[115]McPherson, 'Francis Stewart'; Melville, *Diary*, pp. 328-329.

[116]Although his earlier poetry was printed in his collection, *Poeticall Exercises at Vacant Houres* (1591). Goodare and Lynch, eds, *The Reign of James VI*, pp. 17, 69-70, 248-251.

[117]James's *Basilikon Doron* and his poem *Lepanto* were alluded to in one of the triumphal arches erected for his entry into London in 1604: Bergeron, *Royal Family, Royal Lovers*, p. 76.

[118]Arran's wife, the formidable Elizabeth Stewart, who had been granted a divorce

become the single predominant figure in politics, there is little evidence that he had firmly gasped the helm of the ship of state. His attendance at meetings of his privy council tells its own story: between 1585 and 1592, he was present at an average of ten meetings a year; but in the years 1592-1603, his attendance increased threefold.[119] In those intervening years, between 1585 and 1592, a new kind of figure emerged: James's leading adviser was his chancellor, John Maitland of Thirlestane (second son of Sir Richard Maitland), whose power base lay in the exchequer. The result was a persistent tension between council and chamber which lasted until Maitland's death, in 1595. On occasion, it exploded into violence, but usually on the streets of the capital rather than within the royal palace.[120] In effect, the king, like his mother during her personal reign, was caught between the mutual dislike felt by his 'two bodies' – chamber and council – towards each other. After 1595, new suspicion of the exchequer fell on the so-called Octavians, a group of eight of its officials, originally formed to monitor the queen's income and expenditure, who took control of royal finances as a whole in the brief period 1596-1598.

Two patterns formed, dissipated and re-formed in the years between *c*.1585 and 1598. Courtiers were frustrated by repeated attempts to restrict their access to the king; there were frequent, sometimes violent disputes over the size of noble retinues allowed at court, precedence and protocol. Administrators were repeatedly exasperated by the reckless spending of the household and the profligacy of the king's patronage of the gentlemen of his chamber. Factions, usually based on place and personality rather than on principle or ideology, also proliferated within both the household and privy council. If the battle was a head-on one between the king's two bodies, it was the courtiers who usually won, although the struggle could be bitter and

from the Earl of March in 1581 on the grounds of his impotency and was pregnant when she married Arran, was described in official records of 1582-5 as the 'king's consignis', nearest in blood to him. As such, she probably fulfilled the central female role at the court during Arran's period in power, and perhaps also for part of the Esmé Stuart period. It has been argued that she provided Shakespeare with some of the material for Lady Macbeth. Calderwood, *History of the Kirk of Scotland*, IV, pp. 27-31; Moysie, *Memoirs of the Affairs of Scotland*, p. 34; Fergusson, *The Man behind Macbeth*, p. 34; Juhala, 'The Household and Court of James VI', pp. 106-107; *Scots Peerage*, I, p. 397.

[119]Goodare and Lynch, eds, *The Reign of James VI*, p. 4.

[120]The 'Diary of Robert Birrell' in: Dalyell, ed, *Fragments of Scottish History*, records with relish a series of violent episodes in the 1590s. See Brown, 'Burghs, lords and feuds', pp. 112-113. It is likely that Robert, a schoolmaster, was the brother of the poet John Burel, who also had a low opinion of a lawless aristocracy, whom he stigmatised as 'cannibals': see Baxter, 'Politics, passion and poetry in the circle of James VI', p. 207.

prolonged. The decisive moment came in 1598, when the Octavians were dismissed.[121] The chamber then took over the king's government, with those who had served longest in it given office in the exchequer and treasury. Restraints on patronage and spending were eased. An inflation of honours followed, which was much greater than that in Mary's reign; it took place against a background of a near-bankrupt crown and spiralling taxation. In total James created two dukes, two marquises and six viscounts (both novel titles in Scotland), twenty-seven earls and twenty-nine lords during his reign; most came after 1598. It is hardly surprising that the scramble for status among the nobility, both new and old, became frenetic in the 1590s. It was reflected in a new stress on ceremony (seen in the increasingly elaborate regulation of the riding of parliament) and a revived cult of honour (demonstrated in set-piece events such as the English-style tournament which preceded Prince Henry's baptism; a heightened enthusiasm for family histories and heraldry;[122] and a fashion for architectural totems such as internal picture galleries and outdoor viewing platforms, which increasingly became standard features of tower houses of the nobility, now built for decoration rather than defence). The ultimate architectural icon was crenellation, which required a royal licence; it was reserved for the king's favourites.[123]

Court patronage and its audiences

A paradoxical set of cultural patterns operated during James VI's reign. Most of the distinguished poets of the 1580s and 1590s were clients of the royal court. The Castalian Band had as its honorary leader the young Apollo whose first printed work, in 1584, was a set of laws regulating vernacular poetry.[124] Yet the golden years of the Castalian poets, when Alexander

[121]Goodare, 'Scottish Politics in the reign of James VI', pp. 41-43.

[122]Two of the more elaborate armorials were the *Seton Armorial* (1591) and the *Lindsay Secundus* (c. 1598): cf. Burnett, 'The *Officers of Arms* and Heraldic Art', pp. 24, 28.

[123]McKean, 'The Scottish château'; MacKechnie, 'James VI's Architects', pp. 160, 167. The Earl of Gowrie had a long gallery installed in his house at Perth in 1584; the Seton family, the most prolific patrons of the visual arts and architecture amongst the nobility on the rise, had two galleries in their 'palace' at Seton. The most ostentatious example of crenallation was at Huntly Castle. The names of the sixth earl and his wife, Henrietta, daughter of Esmé Stuart and cousin of the king, were lettered in stone across elaborate battlements.

[124]*Essayes of a Prentise in the Diuine Art of Poesie* (1584), which included the treatise, 'Reulis and Cautelis' for the writing of verse in Scots; see Craigie, ed, *The Poems of James VI*, vol. 1, pp. xxviii-xliii.

Montgomerie was 'at the zenith of Fortune's wheel',[125] belonged to a prelude to a personal reign which, in political terms, had scarcely yet begun. Within a very few years of the king's assumption of power in 1585, his own poetical career had come to an end and the close-knit circle of court poets had begun to break up. Before the end of the 1580s the single, intimate circle had given way to rival factions, each with its own stake in literary patronage. Yet, to be set against the increasing dependency of poets on one or other of the court factions, were the increasing, general effects of a trickle-down court culture, which can be seen more sharply in the fields of architecture, heraldry and interior decoration, especially in a vogue for elaborately painted ceilings,[126] where iconography conveyed messages of status more directly. Literary patronage at court became an instrument of faction, whereas 'court' culture in its more general and visible forms became an increasingly necessary badge of status for the landed classes.

It had taken time for an alternative Protestant court to devise new, acceptable forms of performance entertainment after the deposition of the Catholic Mary. Although insufficient is known of the court set up by Mary's half-brother, the earl of Moray in 1567, the uneasy relationship between a godly church and a Protestant royal court was immediately apparent. The coronation of the infant king at Stirling avoided the traditional rite of anointing and took place in the town's parish church, with a sermon on the Book of Kings by Knox, arch-critic of Queen Mary. The Chapel Royal, where James had been baptised by Catholic rites just a year before, was avoided but, after the service, 'great feasts were made in the castle to the nobility and gentlemen'.[127] The first recorded examples of a new-style Protestant court all belong to the period 1579-82. The work of the Castalian poets, who grouped (or regrouped) around the young king after the re-establishment of a court, now at Holyrood, in 1579 was essentially performance literature, confined to royal palaces. Little of it was published in print in these poets' lifetimes – except for the work of the poet king himself. Very little of it can be dated with precision. The self-conscious device of a 'flyting' between rival poets (reminiscent of that between the poets William Dunbar and Walter Kennedy in James IV's reign) to claim the status of 'master poet', which supposedly marked the inception of the Castalian Band, may have been part of a running battle rather than a single, set-piece event. The cacophony of elaborate praise which greeted the young king during his formal entry into Edinburgh, in effect, set the gold standard, and poets over the next three years (until the Ruthven *coup*) vied to outdo it.

[125] Jack, *Alexander Montgomerie*, p. 8.
[126] Apted, *The Painted Ceilings of Scotland*; Bath, 'Painted ceilings, 1550-1650'.
[127] *CSP Scot.*, II, p. 370.

Montgomerie, usually acknowledged as the most gifted of the Castalian poets, hailed in *The Navigatioun* 'so sapient a ying and godly king' as a new Solomon; and his *A Cartell of the Three Ventrous Knichts* glorified the traditional role of the king as knight and crusader. Both pieces – one with an invitation to the ball and the other with a call to the tourney field – contain hints that they were for performance as a play or masque.

When the court did resort to public spectacle, it took a different form – the re-enactment in January 1581 on the Water of Leith, the port of Edinburgh, of a water tournament, involving an assault upon the pope's palace of Castel S. Angelo in Rome, first staged for Henry VIII of England on the Thames at Westminster in 1539.[128] English muscular Protestantism and a new kind of knockabout farce took the place of Lindsay's anti-clerical drama.[129] Otherwise, the tournament reasserted itself as the most visible face of chivalry. One of the first changes made to make the palace of Holyroodhouse fit for a royal court after a hiatus of over a decade was the laying out of a practice tourney field in the close of the former Augustinian abbey next door. That and the hunt provided alternative means of access to the king for the throng of suitors who crowded the rooms of Holyroodhouse.[130]

Added to the general scramble for place and preferment, the period from 1588 onwards saw an increasing sharpness in the divisions between different constituents of the court. It was not confined to the tension between the chamber dominated by Stewarts and the council largely controlled by Maitland of Thirlestane. It also affected the relationship between the queen's household and Maitland, who controlled the administration of her dower lands, and it spread among the Stewart network itself, which dissolved into acrimonious infighting. At various points between 1589 and 1594, both Huntly and Bothwell withdrew from court, at least technically in rebellion against the crown. Maitland was forced out of the court for much of 1592 by threats of violence made against him by Lennox and, although the chancellor did not attend the baptism of Prince Henry in 1594, he was given custody of the child as part of an effort to balance court factions.[131] While little effort was spared to glorify the personality of princely power, the court in this period was dominated by acrimony, recrimination and violence and poets became the instrument of court factionalism.

[128]Calderwood, *History of the Kirk of Scotland*, III, pp. 486-487; Loades, *The Tudor Court*, p. 31.

[129]It may not be coincidence that two editions of Lindsay's collected works were printed during this period and that they both excluded the *Satyre*.

[130]Goodare and Lynch, ed, *The Reign of James VI*, p. 82.

[131]Lee, *John Maitland of Thirlestane*, pp. 246, 258, 261.

The careers in the 1590s of three poets – Fowler, Montgomerie and Burel – show the difference between the enclosed circle of the Castalian Band in the first half of the 1580s and the fragmented cultural atmosphere of the next decade. To first appearances, Fowler seems to have been the new master poet. The fact that he contributed commendatory sonnets to the king's *Essays of a Prentise* and to Thomas Hudson's translation (made at James' request) of Du Bartas's *Historie of Judith*, both of 1584, suggests that Fowler had already by then joined the Castalian circle. The fact that he accompanied James, as a representative of the burgh of Edinburgh, during his five-month stay in Denmark in 1589-90, his contribution of a sonnet in the preface to the king's *Poeticall Exercises at Vacant Houres* (1591), and his pre-eminent role in devising the elaborate ceremonial for the baptism of 1594, equally suggest a close and continuing bond between king and poet. Yet Fowler owed his first sinecure, granted in 1585, to Bothwell, and his continuing links with the increasingly wayward earl, together with his own appointment to the queen's household in 1590, may reflect a client in search of a reliable patron and a poet who was willing to write to order – as he did (in English) for the baptism of 1594.[132]

The career of Montgomerie, former favourite poet of the king, who briefly found a new patron (and pension) in the rising star of the duke of Lennox, starkly illustrated the vicissitudes of fortune at the Jacobean court. In 1587, he had written a sonnet linking the virtues of the king's chancellor (who was himself a Latin poet) to Mars, Minerva, Mercury and the Muses. By 1591, in *Rob Stene's Dream* (sometimes attributed to Montgomerie), Maitland is the victim of a biting allegory, depicting him as greedy, insatiable and intent on subverting Stewart sovereignty. Yet the poetic offensive did not bring either job security or a pension. By 1595, Montgomerie was living in self-imposed exile in a rural backwater and flirting with Catholic plotters. The result was that he died an outlaw, although he was buried, on the orders of James himself, within the parish church of the Canongate, next door to the palace of Holyroodhouse.[133]

The output of John Burel was modest in comparison to that of either Fowler or Montgomerie. A merchant burgess of Edinburgh and stepson of Thomas Acheson, master of the royal mint, Burel was not a courtier, though he did become involved in the war of words at the court, which reached new heights of acrimony after 1590. It has been shown that his translation of the

[132]Meikle, ed, *The Works of Thomas Fowler*, vol. 3, pp. xxi-xxvii; Lee, *John Maitland of Thirlestane*, p. 245.

[133]Cranstoun and Stevenson, eds, *The Poems of Alexander Montgomerie*, vol. 1, p. 93; Fleming, Motherwell and Smith, eds *Rob Stene's Dream*; Shire, *Song, Dance and Poetry*, pp. 110-113; Lee, *John Maitland of Thirlestane*, p. 225.

twelfth-century dramatic poem *Pamphilus de amore* was made at the request of 'ane Scollar', who was almost certainly Maitland himself. This was a new kind of 'mirror for princes', with a twist to the Venus tradition: it was an explicit warning to Lennox (still at that point heir to the throne), to whom the drama is addressed, about the unsuitability of his forthcoming marriage to the daughter of a noble executed in 1584 for rebellion against the crown. *Pamphilus* and *Rob Stene's Dream* gave expression in verse to the conflict at the heart of James VI's court in the early 1590s.[134] Burel, a stern critic of the feuding and violence of the nobility who thronged the streets of his native town, became with his *Pamphilus* both an instrument of the Maitland faction and the spokesman for a new force at court – the king's capital. After all, the royal burgh of Edinburgh had a significant investment in the court: it not only underwrote set-piece royal events, such as the entry of 1590, but it also provided a series of loans to both James and Anna and even supplied a guard for the king, both in Edinburgh and, on occasion, as far away as Stirling.[135]

Elite and non-elite culture and their audiences

The culture of late sixteenth-century Scotland revolved around three sets of groups: one was the strictly court culture of an ennobled elite, mainly (but not wholly) in the medium of the vernacular – mostly Scots, French or Italian; a second was a 'clerical and academic culture', learned in the law or theology, and mostly (though not exclusively) operating in Latin; the third was a pot-pourri of more 'popular' – or populist – strains of vernacular culture, in Scots, much of it connected with the educational or evangelisation programmes of the Protestant church.[136] Paradoxically, in the age of Mary and James VI, the influence of all three groups, and the media which they employed, was expanding.

To take each group in turn: the household of James VI is difficult to quantify with precision. It was undoubtedly larger than that of James V and at least as numerous as that of James IV. As measured strictly by named officials and servants, the households of king and queen after 1590 were about 450 strong. But the combined complement is more likely to have been nearer to 800.[137] One of the most striking features of the court of James VI

[134]See Reid Baxter, 'Politics, passion and poetry', *passim*, which, more than any other single piece, captures the adversarial atmosphere of court poetry in the 1590s.
[135]Juhala, 'The Household and Court of James VI', pp. 235-293.
[136]MacDonald (A.A.), 'Early modern Scottish Literature', p. 95.
[137]Juhala, 'The Household and Court of James VI', pp. 59, 302. Both figures are significantly higher than the 180 estimated for the king's and queen's households in Cuddy, 'The revival of the entourage', p. 179.

was the stability of the household and especially that of the chamber,[138] despite the maelstrom of factions and faction-fighting in and around the court. Gentlemen of the chamber enjoyed a far greater job security than did the poets of the Castalian Band. The complaint made by the poet William Dunbar to James IV, 'Schir ye haue mony seruitoris',[139] echoed loudly in the court of James VI, where the scramble for place and preferment often became a search for payment by a king whose conspicuous consumption was matched by his persistent impecuniousness. One result was the increasing dependence of poets on patronage and their persistent complaints of poverty, allied to a high risk of redundancy. Another, hardly surprising, consequence was that rival factions within the court or at its margins gave temporary employment to hired propagandists. By 1594-6, a series of reports of anonymous pasquils and satirical verses directed against the court, which provoked condemnation by the privy council, suggests that criticism of the court was no longer confined to insiders.[140]

Despite the factionalism which swamped it, the influence of the court was increasing. By the 1590s, with peripatetic kingship having virtually disappeared, both the royal court and the organs of government, which included centralised law courts and exchequer as well as privy council, insisted that prominent subjects came regularly to the seat of what was now called the 'incuntrey': Edinburgh. The wider impact of a culture which had previously largely been confined to the court or to court nobles in their own households must have increased as a result, although this tends to be more easily detected in architecture and interior decoration rather than in the arts.

The rise of Edinburgh as a capital, which can first be dated to the reign of James III, reached a new dimension in the 1580s and 1590s. It was central to a new, more diffuse dissemination of court culture. Because Holyrood[141] did not have the capacity to house the whole court, many nobles took lodgings in Edinburgh or, more often, in an urban court precinct adjacent to the Palace.[142] They were joined there by significant numbers of Ed-

[138]Juhala, 'The Household and Court of James VI', p. 180; Brown, *Bloodfeud in Scotland*, p. 117.

[139]See MacDonald, 'Princely culture', in this volume.

[140]Chambers, *Domestic Annals of Scotland*, p. 274; Meikle, ed, *The Works of Thomas Fowler*, vol. 3, p. xxviii; Brown, *Bloodfeud in Scotland*, p. 195.

[141]The same applied to all the royal palaces. This may have been why, in the early 1620s, the accommodation in the north range of Linlithgow Place was substantially increased.

[142]This court precinct, which can be seen in meticulous detail in Gordon of Rothiemay's map of Edinburgh (1647), is part of the site of the new Scottish parliament; see Dennison, *An Archaeological and Historical assessment*; Juhala, 'The Household and Court of James VI', p. 141.

inburgh's mercantile elite, who acquired houses near to the palace, which was a kilometre from the centre of the town itself. This was a novel kind of *milieu* for Scotland and it must have promoted even closer relationships between court and town, at different levels. For the first time, some of the leading poets of the period – such as Fowler and Burel – had burgess rather than aristocratic backgrounds. The town houses of the nobles or of their burgess clients and bankers, it is likely, became alternative centres of patronage, literary discourse and political intrigue. The lavishly furnished house of the money-lender, Janet Fockart, was one example: she had provided accommodation for Esmé Stuart on both his first arrival in 1579 and his departure in 1582. In the intervening years, this house became a base for the mixed group of former Queen's Men, opponents of ex-Regent Morton, francophiles and Stewarts who held sway at court. As such, although the point cannot be proved, it is likely to have been an alternative venue for the Castalian Band. Both Janet's house and that of her son, William Fowler, seem frequently to have been used by the earl of Huntly as a place to play the host, both before and after Fowler became secretary to Queen Anna in 1590.[143]

Both the ministry of the church and other professions were increasing in numbers. By 1600, the church in Lowland Scotland had a virtually all-graduate ministry: the universities were producing some fifty or sixty graduates a year; and most parish schools were staffed, though grammar schools were to be found only in larger towns. Even so, the constituency of the second grouping was one of the key phenomena of the later sixteenth and early seventeenth centuries. The expansion of a wider cultural base is more debatable since the question turns to a significant extent on the unproveable – the rates of literacy amongst the population as a whole.

At times, the borders between these three groupings were thin. Until a breakdown in communications in 1596, prominent Protestant clergymen were accustomed to direct access to the king in his chamber. It was only after the breakdown that they regretted their years of 'courting'.[144] Andrew Melville, who has a reputation as *doyen* of the 'awkward squad' amongst presbyterian ministers in the generation after Knox, was also a Latin court poet, who composed some two hundred verses for the reception given to James's Danish bride; these he insisted in delivering in person, although he

[143]Calderwood, ed, *History of the Kirk of Scotland*, V, p. 37; Moysie, *Memoirs of the Affairs of Scotland*, p. 73; Sanderson, *Mary Stewart's People*, pp. 98-99. For Fowler, who was appointed in 1589, see Juhala, 'The Household and Court of James VI', p. 58, and Appendix 1. The link between Queen Anna's household and the exchequer may help explain why it met there in Fockart's house in 1593: Stuart *et al.*, eds, *The Exchequer Rolls*, pp. xxii, 309.

[144]Melville, *Diary*, pp. 328-329; MacDonald (A.R.), *The Jacobean Kirk*, p. 177.

boycotted her coronation because of the 'popish' ceremony of anointing. One of the most celebrated of the poets of the Castalian Band, Patrick Hume of Polwarth, had a younger brother, Alexander Hume (c.1557-1609), from 1597 minister of Logie near Stirling whose work (such as his poem *The Day Estivall*, in his *Hymnes or Sacred Songs* (1599)) marks him out as one of the most talented of the poet-clergymen. Yet he seems to have had an earlier career as an advocate and as a secular poet with connections to the royal court; he repudiated both roles *c.*1587. No radical, he was as critical of Edinburgh's troublesome ministers as he was of the pleasures of the court which had seduced him for so long.[145]

Hume's spiritual pilgrimage paralleled that of James himself, away from being the Apollo of the adoring Castalian poets to philosopher king. Hume was unusual only because he deserted the court early. The group of ministers around the king, including Robert Pont, James Melville (nephew of Andrew), and Robert Bruce, became a new coterie, set apart from the factionalism of the nobles at court, and they survived as a group until shortly before the crisis of 1596.[146] They offered theological rather than poetic discourse. They were, in effect, the replacements for the Castalian Band, as the king's agenda moved from poetics to matters of state and his own divinity. The Apollo of the Muses became the 'nursing father' (James's own phrase) of the church.

The prolonged crisis of the civil war which dominated the first years of James VI's reign is often taken to mark a new streak of populist, polemical literature, in both verse and prose. Almost all of the collection, *Satirical Poems of the Reformation*, belongs to the civil war of 1568-73 rather than to the Reformation crisis of 1559-60. Yet the audience for the 'ballattis of despyit' is uncertain. Too few copies survive to give meaningful clues. The content of some of these poetic works, however, suggests a sophisticated audience, despite the adoption of a populist persona. The anonymous 'Dialogue of the Twa Wyfeis' (1570), which attacked the leading Marian, William Maitland of Lethington, as a 'Machiavel', was an intellectual *tour de*

[145]See 'His Recantation'. Only one sonnet from his earlier period survives. The uncle of the Hume brothers was Alexander Hume of North Berwick, a member of the king's household since 1580, who was imposed by James VI on the capital as its provost for successive terms between 1593-7. As such, he was more than a 'minor favourite': Hume, *Works*, pp. xxiii, xxvi-xxix, 9, 11-16; Juhala, 'The Household and Court of James VI', pp. 246-247.

[146]In the summer of 1592, at the time of the 'Golden Act' which exerted an Erastian settlement with a number of concession to the church, there were even rumours that three ministers in this circle were to be put on the privy council. MacDonald (A.R.), 'Ecclesiastical representation in post-Reformation Scotland', pp. 48-49.

force in disguise.[147] At most, such works reflected a dialogue between courtiers and an urban-based intelligentsia.

The strains which an urban court brought in the years after its establishment at Holyrood in 1579 had two, paradoxical, effects. Greater familiarity with the extravagance and violent behaviour of the court gave rise to an ever-growing criticism of it from outside. The work of John Burel is symptomatic of a new partnership between king and capital and of a new, more critical relationship. On the other hand, the very proximity of the court guaranteed a wider reception for what hitherto could properly be classed as court literature. Again, one example must suffice. The 1590s saw the publication in a new and more accessible form of one of the key icons of the reign of James V: this was the official history of the kingdom remained the chronicle of Hector Boece,[148] translated into Scots by royal commission in the 1530s. Already translated into Italian and published in Antwerp in 1588 for an international audience,[149] this work reached a wider audience within Scotland itself in the 1590s, with the appearance of two abridged editions. This was the point at which a newly visualised version of a national community, based on a recycled mythology of the past, began to reach a larger reading public.[150] Its essence was a glorification of princely power, which reached new heights in both the private and the public propaganda which surrounded James VI in the mid- and later 1590s.Yet its nemesis, a critique of the new claims of kingship, which would climax in revolt against the crown in Scotland in 1638, was already taking shape.[151]

[147] Loughlin, '"The Dialogue of the twa Wyfeis"'.

[148] Williams, 'James V', in this volume.

[149] *Descrittione del regno di Scotia di Petruccio Ubaldini* (reprinted Edinburgh, 1829).

[150] Aldis, *A List of Books printed in Scotland*, nos. 247 (?1594), 303 (1597). Both editions were compiled by John Monipenny. A comparison with the Danish experience suggests itself: an official nine-volume history was written in 1600 by the courtier Arild Huitfeld; it was printed in 1645 in an abridged form of 138 pages, and reprinted in the same year. Lynch, 'A nation born again?', p. 89.

[151] Mason, ed, *Scots and Britons*, pp. 8-13.

A CULTURAL CENTRE IN THE SOUTHERN NETHERLANDS THE COURT OF ARCHDUCHESS MARGARET OF AUSTRIA (1480-1530) IN MECHELEN

Dagmar Eichberger

In the course of the fifteenth century, the Burgundian dukes Philip the Good and Charles the Bold set new standards for court culture in Europe by their extravagant lifestyle, their elaborate court rituals and their concern for administrative structures.[1] As Thérèse de Hemptinne and others have pointed out, the term 'court' indicates a number of things and it encompassed many different facets of everyday life. It could refer to the residence in which the ducal family stayed during their sojourn, the social hierarchies between the various members of the ducal household or the organisational structures which had been built up to govern the country.[2] Life at the ducal court was dominated by a strictly regulated court ritual and was carefully defined by several court ordinances.[3] Werner Paravicini has shown that these Burgundian traditions remained alive in the Low Countries well after the death of the last Burgundian duke, Charles the Bold († 1477). Charles's daughter, Mary of Burgundy, adopted the same structures for her court, and her son, Philip the Handsome (1478-1506), equally followed the Burgundian model until he became king of Spain in 1504.[4]

On the premature death of Mary of Burgundy in 1482 and the early death of her only son, Philip the Handsome, the predominance of the Burgundian dynasty was in danger of disappearing from the political scene.[5] The Habsburgian element, which had come into play for the first time in 1477 with the marriage between Mary of Burgundy and Maximilian I, increasingly gained ground in the southern Low Countries and the two dynasties began to merge. Soon after the death of Philip the Handsome, his sister,

[1] Paravicini, 'The Court of the Burgundian Dukes', pp. 71-90; Prevenier, ed, *Le Prince et le peuple*, pp. 14-111, 154-161.
[2] De Hemptinne, 'Princes et courtisans', pp. 14-33.
[3] Kruse and Paravicini, eds, *Höfe und Hofordnungen*, pp. 141-174.
[4] Paravicini, 'The Court of the Burgundian Dukes', pp. 97-98.
[5] Kren, ed, *Margaret of York*, pp. 13-18.

Margaret of Austria (1480-1530), was made governor-general (1506) and regent (1509) of the Burgundian-Habsburgian Netherlands. She established a princely court in the city of Mechelen, which was to become one of the most influential cultural centres of the region.

Archduke Charles (1500-1558) spent his childhood years in the Burgundian-Habsburgian Netherlands, mostly in Mechelen and Brussels, where he was brought up under the tutelage of his aunt, Margaret of Austria, and was educated by Guillaume de Croy and Adriaan of Utrecht, the future Pope Adrian VI. Charles's court did not leave a particularly strong mark on the cultural life of this region, because he left the Low Countries for Spain soon after reaching maturity.[6] This meant that for more than twenty years Margaret's court was effectively the centre of political power in this economically important part of the empire (1507-1515 and 1517-1530). As Prevenier and Blockmans have pointed out, Margaret's reign can be regarded as a phase of relative peace and concord. Charles and Margaret were both accepted by the various provinces as natural heirs to the collective territories which were soon called the 'Low Countries by the Sea'. Margaret's aspiration to represent the interests of the imperial family in a dignified manner was as significant for her regency as her strong interest in art and culture. She also played a crucial role in shaping the younger generation, in particular Charles V and two of his sisters, Mary of Hungary and Eleanor of Austria.[7] As proxy to Emperor Maximilian I and Emperor Charles V, Margaret ruled her court in Mechelen with strength and decisiveness. The first female regent in the Low Countries, she also had to explore new ways of negotiating between her powerful role as head of a politically significant territory and her gender role as a single woman, widowed and without children of her own.[8]

[6] In 1516, shortly after the death of Ferdinand of Aragon, Charles was appointed king of Castile and he left for Spain in 1517. One of the few studies which examines closely the early years of Archduke Charles is Saintenoy's investigation of the court of Brussels; see Saintenoy, *Les arts et les artistes à la cour de Bruxelles*, pp. 175-189; more recently: De Jonge, 'Le palais de Charles-Quint', pp. 107-125 and 'The Architectural Enterprises of the Emperor', pp. 35-53.

[7] Soly and Van de Welde, *Carolus*, p. 43; Blockmans and Prevenier, *The Promised Lands*, p. 230.

[8] Eichberger, 'A Renaissance Princess named Margaret', pp. 10-24, and 'A noble Residence for a Female Regent', *passim*; Triest, *Macht, vrouwen en politiek, 1477-1558*, pp. 115-122.

Margaret of Austria's European upbringing

As a young girl, Margaret of Austria had been a popular princess on the European marriage market and consequently she spent most of her childhood and teenage years away from the Low Countries at distinguished courts in France and Spain (fig. 3).[9] At the young age of three, she was sent to the Loire valley to be brought up as the future wife of the French dauphin, Charles VIII. When this marriage arrangement failed, Margaret was married off to Charles of Castile, the young heir to the Spanish throne, and spent a few years in the orbit of her highly cultured mother-in-law, Queen Isabella of Spain. Her second husband, Philibert of Savoy, who had also been educated at the French royal court in Amboise, shared Margaret's passion for the literature, music and art, as well as the court festivities and hunting, of court culture.

When Margaret returned to the Low Countries, she garnered experience in a wide range of different cultural contexts. Over the years, she had been exposed to high-quality works of art by Italian, Spanish, Flemish and French artists and she knew what was considered fashionable elsewhere. She had developed a fairly clear idea as to what she expected from her own courtiers and the artists attached to her court. The following analysis will look at the structure of her court, at the role played by her court artists and at examples of Margaret's art patronage. Special attention will be given to her important collection of art and artefacts, which conveys her notion of artistic quality.

The courts of Margaret's male relatives, Philip the Good, Charles the Bold, Philip the Handsome and Maximilian I, had all been itinerant and highly mobile. Moving from one palace or castle to the next was considered a political and diplomatic necessity. Margaret of Austria's itinerary shows, that she, too, made an effort to visit the important cities within her Netherlandish realm.[10] However, despite a certain amount of travelling, she chose Mechelen as her constant base. She regarded her residence in Mechelen – the so-called 'court of Savoy' – as her permanent home and made a strong effort to turn it into a centre of European court culture.

On a large block of land, situated between Keizerstraat, Korte Madgenstraat and Voochtstraat, the city of Mechelen commissioned and paid for the erection of a noble residence for the young archduchess, which was to be-

[9] Bruchet, *Marguerite d'Autriche*, pp. 7-26; Tamussino, *Margarete von Österreich*, pp. 25-123; De Boom, *Marguerite d'Autriche-Savoie*, pp. 1-63. See figs. 3 and 4 in the plates-section following upon the list of plates (p. xi).

[10] Bruchet and Lancien, *Itinéraire de Marguerite d'Autriche*, *passim*. Every year Margaret spent a few weeks at the Coudenberg palace in Brussels.

come the stage on which she performed her role as regent.[11] The spacious architectural complex was structured according to the traditions of Burgundian court architecture and comprised all that was needed for the comfortable life of a princely household.[12] In addition to the official living quarters and the reception rooms, there was a court chapel, a library, a garden cabinet, a treasury, two baths, living quarters for a small number of courtiers, a kitchen, storage rooms, stables, etc. (fig. 4).[13] Margaret paid particular attention to the furnishing of her library and her personal suite (*Cabinetz*). The *Cabinetz* comprised a dining room, a small reception room, a bedroom, a study and a garden cabinet. The decoration of Margaret's official residence played a major part in her effort to create a positive public image of herself and her dynasty.

The structure of the 'Court of Savoy' in Mechelen

The overall structure of her court followed the pattern established by the Burgundian dukes in the course of the fifteenth century. It comprised the principal services: the pantlers (*pannetiers*), the cup-bearers (*échansons*), carvers (*écuyers tranchants*) and the equerries (*écuyers d'écurie*).[14] In keeping with tradition, a basic distinction was made between the positions taken up by gentlemen of the chamber, mostly men from the high nobility, and the posts filled by valets, usually men of lower social standing.[15] In 1525, there were around 150 people in Margaret's permanent service. Compared to the exceptionally large households of Philip the Good and Charles the Bold, the size of her court seems small. However, if one takes into account, that Margaret was not the head of the empire, but was acting on behalf of Maximilian I, her court was quite substantial in size.[16]

In 1525, Margaret's household was headed by Antoine de Lalaing, the count of Hochstraten. Her *chevalier d'honneur* was a longstanding friend of

[11] The architects in charge were Anthonis I († 1512) and Rombaut II Keldermans (c. 1460-1531), both official city architects of the city of Mechelen, see: Eichberger, 'A noble Residence for a Female Regent'.

[12] De Jonge, 'Der herzogliche und kaiserliche Palast zu Brüssel', pp. 256-260, and 'Het paleis op de Coudenberg te Brussel', pp. 28-34.

[13] Eichberger, *Leben mit Kunst*, chap. 2.

[14] Paravicini, 'The Court of the Burgundian Dukes', p. 72; Müller, *Der Fürstenhof*, p. 18. In 1525 there were 27 gentlemen of the chamber serving in these four categories, see: court ordinance of 3 April 1525, as quoted by De Quinsonas, *Matériaux pour servir à l'histoire de Marguerite d'Autriche*, vol. 3, p. 283.

[15] Paravicini, 'The Court of the Burgundian Dukes', p. 72.

[16] Paravicini, 'The Court of the Burgundian Dukes', p. 76.

the imperial family, a man whom Margaret trusted completely.[17] His wife, the countess of Hochstraten, was Margaret's most senior lady-of-honour. She was in charge of all the other women at the court, including the nine girls of honour who lived there at the time.[18] There were four masters of the household and twenty-seven gentlemen of the chamber, who served in one of the four principal offices mentioned above. As was customary during the fifteenth century, these officers served in turns, so that more nobility had access to the court without having to be on duty at the same time. The *chapelle* comprised eight members, among them a confessor, an almoner and three chaplains. Six men were listed under the heading *conseil*, three of whom were Margaret's personal advisers, the rest were her secretaries.[19] In addition, Margaret employed a marshal for lodging and eight guards to serve in her private bedroom (*seconde chambre à chemynée*) and her dining hall (*première chambre à chemynée*). Twenty-four officers were employed in the various offices providing food and drink. Sixteen men were in charge of the horses, litter and chariots.

Margaret of Austria and her court artists

Of particular interest for assessing the cultural significance of Margaret of Austria's court are all those members of the household who were not concerned with the daily needs of the regent and her court, but who contributed to a positive public image and helped to give her residence a more stately appearance. Keeping several artists of international standing in permanent employment was considered essential for a sixteenth-century ruler since that projected an image of grandeur and refinement to the outside world. Already Margaret's forebear, duke Philip the Good, had enhanced the reputation of his court by binding Jan van Eyck, one of the most famous painters of his time, to his household.

Margaret's contacts with several leading courts in France and Spain may explain why she was remarkably ambitious in her choice of artists. More than once she attempted to commission work from men internationally renowned. After the death of her second husband, Philibert of Savoy, Margaret initiated and paid for the construction of the monastic church of

[17] Debae, *La bibliothèque de Marguerite d'Autriche*, p. 488; Eichberger, *Leben mit Kunst*, chap. 4; Triest, *Macht, vrouwen en politiek*, pp. 122-124.

[18] In all there were 20 women, ladies-of-honour and servants, who were given close access to the regent.

[19] As advisors are listed: Claude de Boisset, Nicolas Perrenot and Jehan de Marnix. Marnix is described both as adviser and as secretary. Cf. De Quinsonas, *Matériaux pour servir à l'histoire de Marguerite d'Autriche*, vol. 3, p. 284.

St. Nicholas de Tolentin in Brou, close to Bourg-en-Bresse.[20] In the second decade of the sixteenth century, she sought a suitable design for the complex funerary monument which she intended to put up in the choir of her church. She invited Jean Perréal and Michel Colombe, two well-known artists in the service of the French king, to furnish designs for the tombs in Brou. Cahn and Tolley have convincingly argued that in this instance Margaret was competing with her French rival, Anne de Bretagne, for the best French artists available at the time.[21] When Pietro Torrigiani, the Italian court sculptor of Henry VII of England, passed through Brussels in 1510, he was also approached by Margaret of Austria for advice regarding the monument in Brou.[22] Even if she did not always succeed in these endeavours, she was obviously interested in gaining respect from her peers by employing significant artists for her projects.

Margaret took great pains to attract artists who promised to raise the public profile of her court. In 1525, for instance, five artists were listed as being permanently on her payroll: the painter Bernard van Orley, the sculptor Conrat Meit, an embroiderer, Pieter Nieuwland, a goldsmith, Martin des Abliaux, and a tapestry maker with his two assistants.[23] While the daily pay of these artists was not very high compared to the remuneration given to the nobility, they did receive an annual pension and enjoyed a number of privileges, which set them apart from the ordinary guild artists.[24] Once an artist had entered the court system, he often preferred to stay in the service of the patron's family or to move on in the wider patronage network. For instance, after Margaret's death in 1530, Van Orley was appointed court painter by her niece and successor as regent, Mary of Hungary. Jan Vermeyen stayed in the service of the Habsburg family by continuing to work for Margaret's nephew, Charles V.

In the course of her regency, Margaret employed five different painters as court artists: the South Netherlandish painter-designer Jan van Roome,[25]

[20] Hörsch, 'Architektur unter Margarethe von Österreich', pp. 24-148.

[21] Cahn, 'Towards the enduring monument', pp. 56-63; Tolley, 'States of independence', pp. 249-251.

[22] Duverger, 'Margareta van Oostenrijk', p. 133.

[23] Pieter de Pannemaker was employed by patent of 20 July 1527. While he had already been commissioned to execute work for Margaret in 1523, he only became a member of the household a few years later. See De Quinsonas, *Matériaux pour servir à l'histoire de Marguerite d'Autriche*, vol. 3, p. 290.

[24] Duverger, 'Het statuut van de zestiende-eeuwse hofkunstenaar', pp. 81-91; Warnke, *Hofkünstler*, pp. 16-78. Artists such as Jan Mostaert tried to attract Margaret's interest by giving her paintings in the hope of being eventually elevated into court service, see Duverger, 'Jan Mostaert', p. 113.

[25] Dhanens, 'Jan van Roome', pp. 41-146.

the little known painter Jan Marlart,[26] the widely-travelled Venetian painter-engraver Jacopo de' Barbari († 1516),[27] the Brussels painter-designer Bernard van Orley[28] and the painter-designer Jan Vermeyen.[29] As far as we know, these five court painters were never employed at the same time, but entered Margaret's service one after the other. Painters were in high demand for a number of reasons. They could be commissioned to produce large quantities of portraits for the court.[30] Portraits were traditionally employed to negotiate marriages for the younger members of a dynasty. This well-established tradition was continued by Margaret, who was involved in the negotiations for her nieces and nephews. In addition, painters were often asked by their patrons to prepare designs for those tapestry weavers and glass painters, who were involved in courtly commissions.[31] More noteworthy was, however, the exhibition of numerous likenesses in Margaret's Mechelen portrait gallery. This portrait gallery had been installed in the *première chambre à chemynée* to serve dynastic and diplomatic purposes, and it also highlighted the noble status of the head of the household.[32]

Jacopo de' Barbari, court painter

Not long after her first encounters with Torrigiani, Perréal and Colombe, Margaret succeeded in appointing a well-known Italian to her household. The Venetian painter-engraver Jacopo de' Barbari stayed in her service for a few years, before he died of old age in or before 1516.[33] Francis I had a similar experience with the even more famous Leonardo da Vinci. Leonardo chose to spend the last two years of his life in the Loire valley, before he died close to Amboise in 1519. While Margaret had never travelled to Italy apart from a brief visit to Turin, she was well aware of the fact that many contemporary artists and patrons looked to Italy for inspiration and innovation. Before de' Barbari entered Margaret's court, he had already worked at

[26] Duverger, 'Het statuut van de zestiende-eeuwse hofkunstenaar', pp. 94 (doc. 1).
[27] Levenson, *Jacopo de Barbari, passim*.
[28] Van Orley is the one who is listed in the ordinance of 1525 as *Bernard Dorleck*. See De Quinsonas, *Matériaux pour servir à l'histoire de Marguerite d'Autriche*, vol. 3, p. 290.
[29] Horn, *Jan Cornelisz Vermeyen*, pp. 7-9.
[30] Eichberger and Beaven, 'Family Members and Political Allies', pp. 227-228.
[31] Delmarcel, 'De passietapijten van Margareta van Oostenrijk'; Van den Boogert, 'Hapsburgs Imperialisme', p. 63. Occasionally, court painters would restore objects or estimate the value of a work of art.
[32] Eichberger and Beaven, 'Family Members and Political Allies', pp. 229-238, 247.
[33] Duverger, 'Jacopo de' Barbari en Jan Gossart', pp. 8-9.

several European courts north of the Alps. He had been in the service of Margaret's father, Emperor Maximilian I, of Duke Frederick the Wise of Saxony and temporarily he had worked for another relative, namely bishop Philip of Burgundy (1465-1524). Margaret of Austria owned several paintings by de' Barbari and she kept his valuable sketchbook in her personal collection.[34] De' Barbari supported Margaret's artistic interests in more than one way. In 1510, he presented his patroness with a painting set which had the shape of a book. Margaret's fake book was covered in violet-coloured velvet and had gilded silver clasps with her coat of arms, so that it imitated the bound manuscripts in her rich library.[35] It contained several paintbrushes as well as three silver shells, designed as receptacles for the oil paint.[36] The regent kept these precious utensils in her stately bedroom. According to her inventory of 1523, she would occasionally '*paint to pass the time*'.[37] It has been suggested by Jozef Duverger that at some stage de' Barbari may have given Margaret painting lessons.[38] The whimsical nature of this personalised paintbox calls to mind the relaxed relationship between Duke Jean de Berry and his equally famous court illuminators. The Limbourg brothers had given a fake book to their bibliophile patron as a New Year's gift.

[34] She owned an image of Saint Anthony on canvas, a panel painting with a crucifixion, a large painting of Actaeon, a small grisaille portrait of a Portuguese man and a portrait of herself.

[35] Most of her books were bound in green, red or violet velvet, some in satin or gold brocade; see the various catalogue entries in Debae, *La bibliothèque de Marguerite d'Autriche*, for instance cat. no. 81, p. 120.

[36] Ms Lille, AdN, B 19167, Nr. 4057 [1510]: *Au dict follio LXXIII et LXXV à maistre Jacques Barbaris pour une layette de bois à maniere d'ung livre, servant à mettre roles de painctures, couvert de velours violet et doublé de satin. Pour VII onces II estrelins d'argent employés ès deux fermailles de la dicte layette dorées. Pour VII estrelins demy et I frelind'or employé en petits escussons d'or aux armes de ma dicte dame, fay en icelles dessus dicts fermailles. Pour 1 marc, 2 onces, 3 estrelins demie d'argent pour pottekins à mettre huylles et 3 estrelins à mettre rollets de paincture*s. See Duverger, 'Margareta van Oostenrijk', p. 140.

[37] Ms Paris, BnF., Cinq Cents de Colbert 128, fol.87^{r} [1523-4]: *Item, ung fainct livre, couvert de velours violets à deux fermiletz d'argent dorez aux armes de Madame, a trois escailles, une petite boîte d'argent et 5 pinceaux garniz d'argent dedans le dit livre, le tout servant pour le passe-temps de Madame à paindre*. See also Michelant, 'Inventaire des vaisselles, ... de Marguerite d'Autriche, pp. 77-78.

[38] Duverger, 'Margareta van Oostenrijk', p. 141.

Conrat Meit, court sculptor

Margaret's most successful court appointment was perhaps the German master sculptor Conrat Meit from Worms. In contrast to many of her Flemish court artists, Meit lived and worked for an extended period of time in the immediate neighbourhood of her residence. He stayed in Margaret's service for more than fifteen years.[39] He worked in a range of different techniques using wood, clay, alabaster, marble and various types of metal. Meit produced a number of remarkably modern small-scale sculptures for Margaret and her courtiers, such as several representations of the classical hero Hercules and of Adam and Eve. The surviving Adam and Eve images by Meit in Vienna and Gotha (fig. 5) give us some idea as to how Margaret's deluxe version, made from gilded brass, may have looked.[40] These free-standing cabinet pieces combine the awakening interest in the nude with a more general interest in gender relations. As a result, there is little left of the broader religious framework in which the first human couple was generally placed during the fifteenth century. Margaret kept these Renaissance statuettes in a room close to the garden of her Mechelen residence (*cabinet emprès le jardin ou sont les coraulx*). I have argued elsewhere that this room had no other function than to house and display part of her valuable collection of artefacts, naturalia and curiosities. This room, which was located in the vicinity of the garden, is described as one of the earliest documented collection cabinets north of the Alps.[41]

Meit also specialised in three-dimensional portraits as can be seen on the marble portrait busts of Philibert of Savoy and Margaret of Austria. These images of the regent and her late husband were displayed in her well-furnished library.[42] In addition, Meit produced several smaller wooden portrait busts of Margaret and Philibert and sculpted a fine portrait medallion in

[39] Lowenthal, *Conrad Meit*, pp. 5-24. A new monograph on Conrat Meit is currently in preparation by Jens Burk (München).
[40] Margaret bought these sculptures from Meit in 1519: Ms Lille, AdN, B 19032, Nr. 40170 [1519]: *comptant à Conrat Meyt nostre tailleur dymaiges 25 lb ...et ce pour Adam et Esve de letum, qu'il nous a vendu, chargeant les dictes de quitances seullement dudict Conrat. Fait à Malines, le 4 d'aoust, l'an 1519.* Cf. Lowenthal, *Conrat Meit*, p. 152. They appear in her inventory of 1523-4: Ms. Paris, BnF, Cinq Cents de Colbert 128, fol. 105^r [1523-4]: *Item, deux personnaiges de Adam et Eve, nuz, de leton dorez, bien faiz.* Cf. Michelant, 'Inventaire des vaisselles, ... de Marguerite d'Autriche, p. 110.
[41] Eichberger, *Leben mit Kunst*, pp. 342-350, and 'A noble Residence for a Female Regent'.
[42] Eichberger and Beaven,'Family Members and Political Allies', pp. 238-241; Eichberger, 'A Renaissance Princess named Margaret', pp. 14-17.

clay of his patroness in 1528. His most important task, however, was to create several life-size portrait sculptures for the already mentioned funerary church in Brou.[43]

Margaret's appreciation for Conrat Meit's artistic achievement and his fine craftsmanship was expressed in several ways, not least by the fact that she had a small wooden portrait head of the artist in her library.[44] By exhibiting a likeness of one of her best court artists in this part of her residence, Margaret was making a public statement about the status of her *familiaris* within the hierarchy of her court. Meit was not a man of noble birth and therefore belonged to the lower echelons of her household. Nevertheless, his likeness was admitted to her prestigious library, a space which housed a colourful mixture of portraits.[45] Meit's carved self-portrait shared the same room with painted images of Neutken, Margaret's female court jester, the dwarfs of the King of Denmark, Sultan Süleyman I, the King and Queen of France. There were also several portraits of members of Margaret's own family, such as Maximilian I and Joanna of Castile.[46]

Margaret of Austria and her collection

The arts generally played a prominent role at the court of Margaret of Austria. Her most ambitious and most costly act of patronage was the construction and furnishing of her funerary church in Brou. Like many other European rulers, Margaret wished to express her concern for *Memoria* and remembrance by financing a lavish tomb for herself, her late husband Philibert and her mother-in-law.[47] Still, her most notable contribution to European court culture was to establish an unusually large collection of artefacts and collectable items. The household inventories of her residence in Mechelen reveal that Margaret owned approximately 385 paintings, sculptures, embroidered images and tapestries, which she kept in her residential suite and in her spacious library. Under the same roof, she also brought together 132

[43] Bruchet, *Marguerite d'Autriche*, pp. 171-175; Poiret, *Le monastère royale de Brou*, pp. 90-112.

[44] Ms Lille, AdN, B 3513, Nr. 123962 [1516]: *ung visaige de bois, taillé par Conrad à sa semblance*. See Finot, 'Inventaire', p. 237; the same object is described in 1523-4 in ms Paris, BnF, Cinq Cents de Colbert, fol. 46^v: *Item, ung petit manequin, taillé aussi de mesme bois, à la semblance de Maitre Conrat*. See also Michelant, 'Inventaire des vaisselles, ... de Marguerite d'Autriche', p. 58.

[45] Eichberger and Beaven, 'Family Members and Political Allies', p. 241.

[46] Ms Paris, BnF, Cinq Cents de Colbert 128, fol. 46^v. See also Michelant, 'Inventaire des vaisselles, ... de Marguerite d'Autriche', pp. 58-59.

[47] Poiret, *Le monastère royale de Brou*, pp. 90-93; Hörsch, 'Architektur unter Margarethe von Österreich', pp. 48-53.

items which can be grouped under the terms *Naturalia* and *Exotica*. This section included a large number of carved and uncarved corals, exotic shells, minerals, stones and a spectacular display of Indian objects from the recently conquered middle-Americas. In addition, there were forty-seven decorative art objects, such as clocks, games and *Curiosa*, often made from precious materials. Her library was stocked with about 380 illuminated manuscripts, printed books and genealogies.[48]

Collecting art and artefacts has always been an integral part of human behaviour, which is not specific to the Renaissance.[49] Yet, such activities played a particularly important role as works of art become increasingly important in the secular realm of the private household or palace. From the late fifteenth century onwards, sovereigns and local rulers used their private collections more and more to make a visual statement about their position in society, their knowledge of the world and their appreciation of art and artefacts. The history of the *Studiolo* and its uses is a case in point.[50] Renaissance collections frequently reflect the owner's vision of the world and thus give us insight into how he or she wished to be seen by others.

Most accounts of the early history of Renaissance collecting start with the developments in Italy during the second half of the fifteenth century.[51] In the past, northern Europe collections were closely associated with the rise of the so-called 'art- and curiosity cabinet' (*Kunst- und Wunderkammer*) during the second half of the sixteenth century.[52] Recent research has shown, however, that north of the Alps collecting activities had already begun much earlier and gained momentum in the first half of the sixteenth century. Several French, Spanish, German and Netherlandish sovereigns looked upon their possession of artefacts as an important sign of their public status as cultured and well-educated rulers. Margaret's important collection of artefacts in Mechelen is one of the earliest, richest and best documented collections in the Low Countries, if not in the Habsburgian empire.[53] The structure and the display of her collection parallel some of the developments taking place in contemporary Italy.

Renaissance collections have little in common with our modern conception of an art collection or a museum. First of all, there existed no division in principle between 'art objects' and *Naturalia*, that is objects manu-

[48] Eichberger, *Die Sammlung der Margarete von Österreich*, p. 352.
[49] Von Schlosser, *Kunstl- und Wunderkammern*.
[50] Liebenwein, *Studiolo*, pp. 56-127.
[51] Bergvelt, Meijers and Rijnders, eds, *Verzamelen*, pp. 93-116; Grote, ed, *Macrocosm in Microcosm*, pp. 107-242.
[52] The only exception to the rule is Jean de Berry, who pursued his collecting activities in relative isolation.
[53] Eichberger, *Die Sammlung der Margarete von Österreich*, pp. 351-370.

factured by man or produced by nature. Neither was there a clear distinction between 'high art' and 'low art': the medium of painting had not yet established itself as the queen of arts. In most cases, a painting or a sculpture offered more than one level of meaning to the beholder. Religious works of art were often cherished as much for their content as for their artistic value. Many of Margaret's artefacts were displayed in order to convey dynastic or political messages to courtiers and high-ranking visitors. Other objects were installed to underline Margaret's exemplary moral qualities, her piety and her female *decorum*. A third reason for displaying a work of art could be its high artistic quality. The number of art objects which were collected purely for art's sake was probably small. In my view, this has partly to do with the fact that art was predominantly exhibited in multi-functional spaces, a dining room, a stately bedroom, a library, a festive hall, etc. Only very rarely were works of art displayed in rooms which did not serve at least one other function.

Margaret's love of art was well known to her courtiers and peers and artefacts were used widely as tokens of esteem in the diplomatic exchange of gifts at her court. Philip of Burgundy, bishop of Utrecht, and Christian I, king of Denmark, each gave Margaret a painting by Jan Gossaert. This may also explain why the *Arnolfini wedding* by Jan van Eyck was passed on to Margaret and not to Charles V or another collector (fig. 6). The famous panel had belonged to the Spanish nobleman Don Diego de Guevara, who was a well-known collector and had been in the service of Margaret's family for several decades.[54] To be able to acquire a painting of such artistic value is clearly an indication of Margaret's privileged status in society. The portrait of Arnolfini and his wife is only one of numerous objects which give testimony of Margaret's discerning taste and her appreciation of art.

Most of Margaret's artefacts were distributed throughout her living quarters, her library, her small audience room, her dining hall, her stately bedroom and her small study. All her paintings, sculptures and ethnographic objects had been integrated into the domestic household. Only Margaret's precious plate and her valuable collection of tapestries were stored in separate rooms, probably for reasons of safety.

Between 1516 and 1523 Margaret changed the display in her residence in several ways. The most significant transformation was the addition of a second collection cabinet on the ground floor. The so-called 'garden' or 'coral cabinet' (*cabinet emprès le jardin ou sont les coraulx*) was designed as an extension to the small study, which was situated next to her bedroom (*petit cabinet*). Her study upstairs may have become too small for her collection over the years. The new cabinet housed many precious objects,

[54] Campbell, *National Gallery Catalogues*, pp. 174-211.

paintings and sculptures, which had previously been displayed upstairs. In 1523, the garden cabinet contained 248 objects, compared to only sixty-eight pieces in the study upstairs. In addition, access to the garden cabinet was probably easier than to the *petit cabinet*. While the garden cabinet was still part of Margaret's personal suite of rooms, it was conceived as an exhibition space from the start.[55] This cabinet can be regarded as one of the first quasi-autonomous collection rooms used by their owners to show off a specific part of the collection.

In the context of early collections, it is of particular interest that Margaret of Austria employed a full-time treasurer (*garde joyaulx*), Richard Contault, who was responsible for the management and display of her art objects and collectable items. He was supported in his task by a personal assistant and by Etienne Lullier, one of Margaret's *valets de chambre*. Contault and Lullier were responsible for the whole of the valuable collection of moveable items comprising gold and silver plate, art objects, and precious furniture.[56] It was one of their duties to monitor the movement of objects and to keep the household inventories in good order.[57] There are only a few documented instances in this early period where a full-time treasurer is known to have been employed for the safe-keeping of the collection.

Patterns of collecting

In the past, Margaret has often been characterised as a woman who was only interested in religious imagery and dynastic portraiture. Denhaene is one of the authors who tried to create a marked contrast between the Renaissance-minded bishop Philip of Burgundy and the 'old-fashioned' and somewhat conservative archduchess from Mechelen.[58] In the light of her entire collection of sculptures and paintings, this dated image of Margaret of Austria calls for readjustment. There is no question that Margaret had a strong predilection for devotional objects and cherished portraits of family members and friends. However, she also owned a considerable number of

[55] There is no indication of tables and chairs, beds and cupboards which might suggest that the regent actually lived in this room.

[56] The only group of objects missing from the inventory of 1523-4 are Margaret's jewels. It may well be that there existed a separate inventory for these which is now lost.

[57] A distant relative of Margaret, the famous collector Jean de Berry, had also employed a treasurer. Cf. Minges, *Das Sammlungswesen der frühen Neuzeit*, p. 21.

[58] Denhaene, 'Les collections de Philippe de Clèves', pp. 320-322. This polarity was developed by Hans van Miegrot in a paper presented at the University of Louvain in November 2000: 'Eenheid en Tweespalt. Architectonische relaties tussen de Zuidelijke en Noordelijke Nederlanden 1530-1700'.

artefacts which do not fit into either of these two categories because of their secular nature and content. She owned several artefacts with mythological subject matter or objects referring back to the Roman period. The Regent even displayed a small number of nude figures in different sections of her palace, preferably in her library and her garden cabinet.[59]

In the library, Margaret kept a wooden image of the honourable Lucretia and a marble copy of youthful Spinario, a popular classical sculpture from Rome.[60] On the wall of the same chamber hung a large painting by Gossaert with the nude dwarfs of Christian II, king of Denmark.[61] It appears that Gossaert depicted the male and female dwarfs as Adam and Eve, standing on a green lawn and holding an apple in their hands. Margaret's library was a comparatively public and accessible area within the court of Savoy.

Sometime after 1524 Margaret purchased a white marble sculpture of a female nude from her tapissier De Pannemaker.[62] In the garden cabinet, the regent kept one of her most stunning pieces, a small painting by Jan Gossaert of the unhappy encounter between Hermaphroditus and the nymph Salsmacis (fig. 7). Gossaert's interpretation of this classical story, based on Ovid's *Metamorphoses* and later commentaries highlights the struggle be-

[59] Eichberger, 'Hoofse hobby's', pp. 32-37.

[60] Ms Paris, BnF, Cinq Cents de Colbert 128, fol. 46^{r} [1523-4]: Item, *ung petit manequin tirant une espine hors de son pied, fait aussi de marbre blanc, bien exquis*, and fol. 46r [1523-4]: *Item, une petite Lucresse, aussi taillé en bois*. See also Michelant, Inventaire des vaisselles, ... de Marguerite d'Autriche, 'Inventaire des vaisselles, joyaux, peintures, manuscrits etc.', p. 58.

[61] *Ibidem*, fol. 46^{v} [after 1524]: *Item, delivré audit Garde-joyault depuis cest inventaire fait, la portraicture des nayn et nayn du roy de Dannemarcque, faicte par Jehanin de Maubeuge, fort bien fait*. See Michelant, Inventaire des vaisselles, ... de Marguerite d'Autriche, 'Inventaire des vaisselles, joyaux, peintures, manuscrits, etc.', p. 58. The entry in the Vienna copy of the 1523-24 inventory provides additional information: Vienna, Österreichisches Staatsarchiv, Haus-, Hof- und Staatsarchiv, Habsburgisch-Lothringisches Familienarchiv, no. 1176, fol. 97^{r} [after 1524]: *Ung grant tableau de paincture d'ung nain et une nayne nuz, tenant une pomme, le champ du dit tableau bleu et vert, donné par le roy de Dannemarque à Madame*. See also Zimerman,'Inventoire des parties de meubles', cxix, nr. 878.

[62] Ms Paris, BnF, Cinq Cents de Colbert, fol. 88^{v} [after 1527]: *Plus une femme nue en marbre blanc, fort bien faicte, achetée de Pennemacre*. See also Michelant, 'Inventaire des vaisselles, ... de Marguerite d'Autriche', p. 97. In the Vienna copy of the inventory the statuette is described in more detail. Cf. Österreichisches Staatsarchiv, HLF 1176, [after 1524]: *Une ymaige de marbre blanc d'une femme nue, ayant les cheveux noir et le pied sus ung estoq d'ung arbre, et une serpent tortillée a l'entour, que la mort au pied; la dite ymaige joincte a une table de mesme marbre, asiz en bois painct noir, achetée de Pannemake*. See Zimerman,'Inventoire des parties de meubles', p. xcix, nr. 155.

tween the love-striken nymph and her human victim. Both figures are depicted in the nude, standing in the treacherous water.[63] The fact that Christian of Denmark and Philip of Burgundy presented Margaret with such examples of contemporary art seems to suggest that both tried to satisfy her demand for high-quality art. It is difficult to image that either of these men would have intended to annoy, embarrass or provoke the regent of the Netherlands by confronting her with such paintings. This reading is supported by the fact that Gossaert's paintings are highly praised in her inventory (*beau tableau* and *fort bien fait*) and that they were both displayed in important parts of her residence.

A detailed analysis of her collection and the frequently used value judgements attached to individual works of art has brought to light that art appreciation played a significant role at the court of Margaret of Austria. It appears that the regent did not have a clear preference for either early-Netherlandish painting, contemporary Northern or Italian art, but that she chose the best of each period and each cultural region.[64]

Margaret of Austria's artistic talents

In the sixteenth century, the status and the recognition of a patron like Margaret could increase, if he or she not only appreciated works of art produced by others but also practised painting or music herself. According to her contemporaries, Margaret not only painted, but also wrote poems, played an instrument and was a skilled singer. Both her court poets, Jean Lemaire de Belges and Agrippa of Nettesheim, commented explicitly on her serious commitment to the arts.[65] In his *Le Premier epistre de l'Amant Vert* (1505) Lemaire uses the voice of Margaret's pet parrot, her so-called 'green lover', to comment in a fashion more intimate than would otherwise be acceptable on the personality, the outer appearance and the multiple talents of his honourable lady. He says:

> *Bien me plaisoit te voire chanter et rire*
> *Dancer, jouer, tant lire et escrire,*
> *Peindre et pourtraire, accorder monocordes*
> *Dont bien tu scais faire bruire les cordes.*[66]

[63] Ms Paris, BnF, Cinq Cents de Colbert 128, fol. 105^r [1523-4]: *Item, ung beau tableau auquel est painct ung homme et une femme nuz, estant les pieds en l'eaue; le premier bort de marbre, le second doré et en bas ung escripteau, donné par Monsr. d'Utrecht.*

[64] Eichberger, *Leben mit Kunst*, chap. 6.

[65] See the funerary speech by Agrippa von Nettesheim, 1531, pp. 1121-1149.

[66] Stecher, ed, *Œuvres de Jean Lemaire de Belges*, vol. 3, pp. 7-8.

Lemaire makes far-reaching comments in a contemporary piece of court writing, his panegyric treatise *La Couronne Margaritique* (1504-5).[67] He stresses the fact, that Margaret had the command of more than traditional female skills, such as needlework and embroidery. He writes:

> *Oultre la notice de tous ouvrages feminins en esguille et broderie, elle s'excerya louablement en musique vocale et instrumentaire, en peinture et rhétorique, tant en langue Françoise comme Castillane.*[68]

Musicologists have suggested that Margaret wrote the texts of several secular songs in her famous *chansonnier*.[69] Margaret's favourite contemporary musician was the singer and composer, Pierre de la Rue, who served at the court of Archduke Charles between 1508 and 1512. The Nuremberg patrician Petrus Imhoff, also known by the name of Pierre Alamire, was a well-known singer, composer and copyist of musical manuscripts. He was employed by Charles as his *escripvain et garde de livres* and produced several musical manuscripts for Margaret and her relatives. Illuminated choir books were frequently used as diplomatic gifts and often carried meaning that went well beyond the religious content of any musical piece.[70] Her strong interest in secular and religious music is reflected both in her large collection of manuscripts of this sort and in the active musical life at her court.[71] While the archduchess occasionally employed an organist and a tambourine player, she profited considerably from the presence of the *grande chapelle* of her under-age nephew Charles. Until 1517, Charles lived in a mansion just opposite her own residence on the Keizerstraat.[72]

[67] *La Corone Margarétique qui se nomme Plume Infélice* (= Jean Lemaire, *La Couronne margaritique*), Vienna, Österreichische Nationalbibliothek, Cod. 3441, Savoy, 1504-5. See also Stecher, ed, *Œuvres de Jean Lemaire de Belges*, vol. 4, pp. 15-167; Debae, *La bibliothèque de Marguerite d'Autriche*, cat. no. 374, pp. 504-7.

[68] Stecher, ed, *Œuvres de Jean Lemaire de Belges*, vol. 4, pp. 110-111. Margaret's excellent knowledge of Spanish is also confirmed by Antonio de Beatis, who accompanied Cardinal Louis d'Aragon on his journey through the Low Countries, quoted in Bruchet and Lancien, eds, *Itinéraire de Marguerite d'Autriche*, p. 182.

[69] Ms Brussels, Bibl. Roy. d'Albert, Ms. 228. See Debae, *La bibliothèque de Marguerite d'Autriche*, p. 12; Schreurs, *De schatkamer van Alamaire*, pp. 65-67.

[70] Kapp, 'Musikhandschriften am Hof der Margarethe', pp. 16-17; Schreurs, *De schatkamer van Alamaire*, pp. 67-71.

[71] Debae, *La bibliothèque de Marguerite d'Autriche*, cat. no. 2, pp. 11-12, cat. no. 39, pp. 61-62 and cat. no. 66, pp. 94-96; Kapp, 'Musikhandschriften am Hof der Margarethe von Österreich', p. 15.

[72] De *De Quinsonas, Matériaux pour servir à l'histoire de Marguerite d'Autriche*, vol. 3, pp. 285, 290; Duverger, 'Floris Nepotis', pp. 3-5. Much new light has been

Margaret occasionally borrowed Charles's singers for the sung mass in her own court chapel and also paid the choirboys from the church of St. Rombaut for entertaining her during dinner. Musical performances were particularly important on special occasions such as New Year's festivities and diplomatic banquets.[73]

Culture in the context of the court

Why was so much attention given to the arts by early sixteenth-century rulers? Why did patrons spend so much time, money and effort to get from their artists what they desired? Was it only a general convention to use art for the purpose of self-representation or was art employed for sending out subtle messages to one's subjects or enemies? Were there any Renaissance patrons who were exclusively motivated by their love of the art and by their appreciation of good craftsmanship? Such questions can only be answered on an individual basis, as there was no generally accepted theory of collecting and no common code of patronage, which was followed by everybody.[74] In the case of Margaret of Austria it was probably a mixture of all such considerations.

Commissioning, purchasing and collecting religious works of art was high up on Margaret's agenda, first because she was a devout ruler and second, because she wanted to appear as such in the public eye. This is apparent in her donations of altarpieces and sculptures – for instance to the Sainte Chapelle of Chambéry and to the Anonciade monastery of Bruges.[75] Her religiosity is equally expressed by the large number of devotional objects which she kept in her bedroom and in other parts of her residence (fig. 8).[76]

Margaret also used works of art and artefacts for conveying political messages to her subjects. Her heraldic tapestries (fig. 9) and her portrait gal-

shed on musical practice at Margaret's and Charles's court in the recent exhibition catalogue edited by Schreurs (*De schatkamer*). Klaartje Proemans has shown that a tambourine player was normally a multi-skilled musician, who was also expected to entertain his audience by dancing and clowning: 'Margaretha's hof en de muziek', pp. 60-61. The regent's annual accounts of the city of Mechelen reveal that Margaret's chapel was equipped with a pulpit for singers. As to the choirboys from St. Rombaut, see Bruchet and Lancien, eds, *Itinéraire de Marguerite d'Autriche*, p. 291.

[73] The regent paid regularly for musicians and dancers who performed for her as she passed through the cities of her realm; see: Bruchet and Lancien, eds, *Itinéraire de Marguerite d'Autriche*, pp. 237, 242, 296, 299, etc.

[74] Bergvelt, Meijers and Rijnders, eds, *Verzamelen*, pp. 11-13.

[75] Bruchet, *Marguerite d'Autriche*, p. 371; Lowenthal, *Conrat Meit*, p. 152, nr. 16.

[76] Eichberger, *Leben mit Kunst*, chap. 4.

lery in the *première chambre* stressed her own position within a large dynastic network of rulers and dignitaries reaching as far as Spain, Portugal, Poland and Hungary. The exotic collection of Indian artefacts prominently displayed in the library, was tangible evidence of the new territories which Cortèz and others had conquered on behalf of Charles V.

There are many indications, that Margaret cherished works of art for their artistic value and that she was a most discerning patron. One of the most remarkable aspects of the Mechelen inventory of 1523-4 is the close attention which is paid to quality judgements. The following terms are used to define the relative value of a work of art:[77] *bon,*[78] *fort bonne,*[79] *beau,*[80] *beau et grant,*[81], *fort belle facon,*[82] *bien faict, bien fete et paincte, fort bien faict,*[83] *exquis,*[84] *bien exquis, fort exquis* and *riche et fort exquis.*

[77] Further expressions are used to describe good craftsmenship in decorative art pieces.

[78] Ms Paris, BnF, Cinq Cents de Colbert 128, fol. 73^{v} [1523-4]: *Item, ung aultre bon tableau de la pourtraiture d'ung Espaignol, habille d'ung manteau noir, joince de velours noir, ayant une petite chayne a son col, ayant aussi une fauce parruqe*. See Michelant, 'Inventaire des vaisselles, ... de Marguerite d'Autriche', p. 86.

[79] Ms Paris, BnF, Cinq Cents de Colbert 128 fol. 113^{r} [1523-4]: *Premier la pourtraicture de l'empereur moderne, Charles V(me), de ce nom, tiree apres le vif et faict par compas sur toille, fort bonne*. See Michelant, 'Inventaire des vaisselles, ... de Marguerite d'Autriche', p. 116.

[80] See note 61, above.

[81] Ms Paris, BnF, Cinq Cents de Colbert 128, fol. 51^{v} [1523-4]: *Item, ung riche manteau, beau et grant*. See also Michelant, 'Inventaire des vaisselles, ... de Marguerite d'Autriche', p. 63. This is one of the Indian artefacts.

[82] Respectively ms Paris, BnF, Cinq Cents de Colbert 128, fol. 127^{r}: [1523-4]: *quatre pièces de belle et exquise tappisserie faictes de soye et de sayette par grans feullaiges, et a fort belle façon, armoyées des armes de la genealogie et descente de Madite Dame*; fol. 94^{r}: *Item, ung petit sainct George, son habit esmaillé de gris et son cheval esmaillé de blanc ossez, a ung dragon d'argent esmaillé, bien fait*; *ibid.*, fol. 105^{r}: *Item, une fiole de verre, dedans laquelle il y une naviere, bien fete*; fol. 62^{v}: *Item, une naviere, fete de bois, bien fete et paincte, pendant au milieu de ceste chambre*. See Michelant, 'Inventaire des vaisselles, ... de Marguerite d'Autriche', respectively pp. 125, 102, 110.

[83] See note 60.

[84] Ms Paris, BnF, Cinq Cents de Colbert 128, fol. 64^{v} [after 1527]: *Item, Madame a fait fere ung tableau de XX petites painctures exquises, des XXII cy apres escriptes, à la garniture duquel tableau y a entre seize marcs d'argent de net* (These are the panels by Juan de Flandes); 46^{r}: *Item, ung petit manequin tirant une espine hors de son pied, fait aussi de marbre blanc, bien exquis* (This is the marble copy of the Spinario); 73^{r} [1523-4]: *Item, ung aultre tableau fort exquis, qui se clot à deux fulletz, ou il y a painctz ung homme, et une femme estantz desboutz, touchantz la main l'ung de l'aultre, fait de la main de Johannes, les armes et divise de deu Don Dieghe esdits deux feulletz, nommé le personnaige Arnoult Fin* (This is the des-

Another indication of Margaret's appreciation of artefacts for their artistic value can be found in the section describing the content of the garden cabinet. Margaret obviously instructed her *garde-joyaux* to provide detailed descriptions of each item, but to omit the weight of objects which were made from precious metal. Richard Contault was not happy with this order, which in his view called into question his professional integrity. He added a long statement stressing that he deviated from common practice at the express wish of his patroness. Margaret regarded the garden cabinet as a collector's cabinet and not a treasury, which is why she insisted on new ways of cataloguing the collection.

As mentioned earlier, high-quality works of art often combined a number of different aspects, so that it is not always possible to decide for what reason a painting or a sculpture might have been acquired in the first place. The group of objects which belonged neither to the category of religious works nor to that of dynastic portraiture is quite substantial. Margaret's collection of mythological and classical objects is small but choice. They are a clear sign of her familiarity with the latest trends in Renaissance culture.

Conclusion

During her extended reign as regent of the Low Countries, Margaret of Austria established and administered a considerable court in the city of Mechelen. Her international experience in court culture, her familiarity with contemporary art patronage in its various forms and her call for excellence were only a few reasons for her success as a political and a cultural leader in her region. Margaret paid particular attention to the construction and the furnishing of her court in Mechelen, which she regarded as her permanent base. She gathered a considerable collection of art objects and artefacts which she displayed throughout her residence. She employed works of art to express her political ideas, her dynastic interests, her religious concerns

cription of Van Eyck's Arnolfini wedding); 75^{v} [1523-4]: *Item, ung riche et fort exquis double tableau de Notre Dame, doublé par dehors de satin brochier, et Monseingeur le duc Charles de Bourgogne painct en l'ung desdits fulletz*; 97^{r} [1523-4]: *Toutes lesquelles pieces et menutez, d'or et d'argent cy dessus escriptes, estans et gisans ausdits cabinetz, ensemble les aultres pieces garnies dargent doré et d'argent simplement, Madite Dame n'a voulu icelles estre pesées, ains a dit et declere se contente et contentera cy apres, en luy rendant les pieces et selon qu'elles sont escriptes et speciffiées en cest présent inventoire.* See Michelant, 'Inventaire des vaisselles, ... de Marguerite d'Autriche', respectively pp. 58, 86, 88.

and her appreciation of the arts. Margaret of Austria respected the cultural traditions which had been introduced by her Burgundian ancestors. At the same time, the archduchess explored new ground and went beyond the established modes of cultural practice. Margaret of Austria was an eminent collector and patron of the arts who made a significant contribution to the shaping of the European landscape of court culture.

COURTS AND CULTURE IN RENAISSANCE SCANDINAVIA

Alan Swanson

From the perspective of Florence, say, or Flanders, fifteenth- and sixteenth-century Scandinavia had but little to offer by way of princely culture. Seen from within the North, however, the growth of that culture after a slow start was rapid and its presence manifold. To understand the general development in this period of high culture in Scandinavia, and a court culture in particular, it is necessary to understand the growth and success of two important and intertwined political/intellectual developments, nationalism and reformation. The context of these developments can best be understood as taking place within an historic interaction between Periphery and Centre which, with respect to Scandinavia and Europe, seems to act in alternating directions. For example, the Viking incursions into the heart of Europe which brought peripheral Scandinavia so dramatically to the centre's attention were succeeded by the intellectual advance of Christianity into Scandinavia from the South and, to some extent, the West. These were, in turn, followed by a period of isolation or, rather, indifference, save for the essentially mercantile attention of the Hanseatic League. The flow of humanist ideas into sixteenth-century Scandinavia, in a large degree as a result of a Reformation largely steered by the courts, was followed, in the seventeenth, by the direct intervention of Scandinavia in the political and theological affairs outside itself. On the larger scale, this effect is, thus, less one of an intermingling of culture than of an alternation of interest.

In the fifteenth and sixteenth centuries, Scandinavia consisted of territory extending from Finland and the eastern shores of the Baltic to Greenland. As a result of the agreement known as the Union of Kalmar (1397), Scandinavia was, formally, one political unit of three kingdoms: Denmark (of which Iceland, the Faroes, Greenland, the western and southern coasts of modern Sweden, and certain islands in the Baltic were part), Norway (which at various times included parts of northern Sweden), and Sweden (of which Finland was a part), united under one monarch. The first three of those monarchs were Margaret [I] of Denmark and Norway (r. 1387-97), her great-nephew, Erik of Pomerania (r. 1397-1438),[1] and, after the latter's deposition, Chris-

[1] Erik was a minor when he succeeded and the general impression of historians is

topher of Bavaria (r. 1440-48). Christopher left no heir at his death, and the councils chose Christian [I] of Oldenburg (r. 1448-81) as their monarch. His long reign, during which Swedish dissatisfaction with the Union entered its serious final stage, was followed by the equally long reign of his son, Hans (r. 1481-1513). By the end of the fifteenth century, Norway had fallen completely under Danish suzerainty (becoming formally a part of Denmark in 1537), while Sweden, just powerful enough to assert a degree of independence, maintained its Council of State with an elected regent (and occasional king). The most important of these were Sten Sture (regent several times from 1470-1503), Svante Nilsson (regent 1503-12), and Sten Svantesson – called Sten Sture, the younger – (regent 1512-20). Despite a reign of considerable material and administrative improvement, a series of grave political misjudgements on the part of Hans's successor, Christian II (r. 1513-23), together with the persistent pressure of the Swedes, led to a final sundering of the Union in 1521 and the re-establishment of an independent Swedish kingdom, under Gustaf Eriksson Wasa (r. 1523-60). The tension in the relationship between Denmark and Sweden came into balance in the sixteenth century, as each side sought to stabilise its internal political situation.

Thus, at the beginning of the sixteenth century, we see the historic rivalry between eastern and western Scandinavia developing into the creation of two power blocs, with the far-flung, if waning, presence of the Hanseatic League always to be taken into account. Formally a trading organisation, the wealthy and aggressive League, based in Lübeck, had long followed a political course essentially aimed at securing safe and toll-free passage for its cargo ships within the Baltic and through the Øresund (the sound separating Sweden from Denmark). Its economic weight was such that it had permanent seats on the councils of most important cities within its sphere of influence, such as Stockholm, Bergen and Visby. The growing rivalry between Denmark and Sweden, therefore, constituted a clear danger to the economic pre-eminence of the League. Indeed, by the 1520s its long dominance of Northern trade was clearly coming to an end; this allowed other powers, especially England and, after 1580, the United Provinces, to enter the Baltic market. These new political and economic impulses left their effects upon the culture of the courts of Scandinavia.

Compared with the splendours of Florence or Flanders, Scandinavia in much of this period appeared to offer little by way of genteel culture and even less in the tradition of knightly culture. Though there was much contact between Scandinavia and the rest of Europe, advanced forms of feudalism made little headway in the North. On the other hand, though the earliest re-

that, even after Erik's majority in 1401, Margaret effectively ruled the Union until her death in 1412. See Derry, *A History of Scandinavia*, pp. 69-78.

corded appearance in Scandinavia of Baldassare Castiglione's *Cortegiano* (1528) seems to be a copy of a French translation given to Erik XIV by the English ambassador, John Dymock, in 1561, it is clear from the structure and language of Erik's speeches, for example, that he had already benefited from a humanist rhetorical education.[2] Apart from coronations, however, there appear to have been few grand public ceremonies and state occasions intended to impress natives and visitors. The Swedish ruler did not marry the sea, as did his Venetian counterpart, nor could the Danish king bestow so prestigious an honour as the Burgundian Golden Fleece, though he could (after 1457) award the Order of the Elephant to other sovereigns.[3] The reason is certainly that after the exhaustion caused by frequent internal wars in the late fifteenth century, culminating in the decisive conflict in Sweden (1519-21), there simply were insufficient resources to elaborate such celebratory moments as there were. Further, the political chaos of the first two decades of the sixteenth century was such as to create other political priorities and limit severely opportunities for exploring new cultural ideas: after all, culture other than military requires peace, as well as pence and population.

This is not to say that there was no ostentation nor that the courts did not play a role in furthering the arts and learning. On the contrary, the achievement in 1521 of something resembling peace gave both Denmark and Sweden the chance to reach out to a Europe whose renaissance of culture was at its apogee.

In both Scandinavian countries, national and religious reform, originating in the courts, led most noticeably to a modest invigoration of the school system, largely influenced by the humanist ideals of the German reformers, particularly as formulated by Philip Melanchthon.[4] In both countries, the curriculum was similar. Students were taken through Cicero, Vergil, Ovid, Plautus, Erasmus, Melanchthon, and parts of the Bible, all in Latin, though the reformers had a clear interest in furthering the study of vernacular languages as well. More advanced study took students into classical rhetoric and eloquence, through the work of Quintilian and others.[5] The direction of this

[2] Roberts, *The Early Vasas*, pp. 199-201, and Burke, *The Fortunes of the Courtier*, p. 64.

[3] This order was founded by Christian I, who perhaps used it to confirm his own sovereignty. It was disbanded at the Reformation and re-instituted in 1580, by Frederik II. Cf. Boulton, *The Knights of the Crown*, pp. 399-402.

[4] Skafte Jensen, ed, *A History of Nordic Neo-Latin Literature*, pp. 20-21; Garstein, *Rome and the Counter-Reformation*, pp. xvi-xxxi, xxxix-xlvi, 7-39; Roberts, *The Early Vasas*, pp. 273-296. Of the early decades of Gustaf Wasa's reign, however, Roberts takes a more acerbic view, 'In no country in Europe, perhaps, was the Reformation more immediately disastrous for education than in Sweden' (p. 115).

[5] Garstein, *Rome and the Counter-Reformation*, pp. 7-9. For a more nuanced view

education was toward preparing students not only to be clerics but to be well-formed citizens. Such a curriculum was clearly also intended to produce students whose formal competence would place them on an equal footing with their counterparts in the rest of Europe. At the university level, however, the situation differed considerably.

The first Swedish university had been founded in 1477 at Uppsala, the seat of the archbishop, and was intended initially to foster the development of the Swedish clergy. Political unrest and the consequent economic devastation in late fifteenth-century Sweden had an especially hard effect upon Uppsala, however, and by the first decades of the new century, teaching there had virtually ceased. Though Gustaf Wasa had good intentions toward the place, he did little to improve its economic and scholarly position. The university was re-financed in 1566 by Gustaf's son and successor, Erik XIV (r. 1560-68), who also appointed an historian, Laurentius Petri Gothus, as professor of Greek. Erik's successor, Johan III (r. 1568-92), appointed four more professors, but by 1576, teaching seems to have ceased again, for in that year, Johan had also established a rival (Jesuit-oriented) college in Stockholm, the *Collegium Regium Stockholmense*. This notably zealous institution gave the Counter-Reformation a brief (1576-80) place in Stockholm life.[6] This is not the place to discuss the entire movement of the Reformation in Sweden; suffice it to say that, unlike its counterpart in Denmark, the Lutheran reform in Sweden took most of the century to arrive at complete official status, gaining such recognition only with the declarations of the Uppsala Meeting of 1593.[7]

One practical result of this slow development was that many of the statutory acts needed to regulate the Church and the university which provided for it, took decades to set in motion, and the development of the school curriculum in Sweden was, like the development of the university, conservative in nature, and remained within the reformed tradition. Despite modest improvement – given the generally moribund character of Uppsala university through most of the sixteenth century – the brightest students from

than Garstein's, see Brask, *et al.*, eds, *Dansk litteraturhistorie,* vol. 2, pp. 84-85, 309-321. For the German background of Reformation educational theory and practice, see Strauss, *Luther's House of Learning*, esp. pp. 31-70, 108-131.

[6] Garstein, *Rome and the Counter-Reformation*, pp. xxii-xxviii; Roberts, *The Early Vasas*, pp. 283-287; Derry, *A History of Scandinavia*, pp. 99-100.

[7] A brief survey in English of the Reformation in Scandinavia can be found in Österlin, *Churches of Northern Europe*, pp. 49-87. Garstein's own hardly dispassionate view of the whole Reformation in Sweden is summarised as 'the forcible introduction of Protestantism into the far North through the avarice of their sovereign lords and masters, who had cast their greedy eyes on the wealth of the cathedrals, parish churches, and monasteries ...': *Rome and the Counter-Reformation*, p. xvi.

the schools were usually sent abroad, often to Wittenberg, though there were Swedes at other institutions as well. This built upon the practice of earlier times; there were, for example, three Swedish student houses in Paris as early as the end of the thirteenth century, and by the middle of the fourteenth there were Scandinavian students in Prague.[8] In the sixteenth century, students from both kingdoms studied in Germany, if they were Lutheran, especially at Wittenberg, Rostock, and Greifswald, and, if they were Roman Catholic, at Paris, Louvain, and some Italian universities. Later still, the Northern Netherlands were to become a popular stop on the study tour, especially for those intended for political or military careers.

The first Danish university, on the other hand, founded in 1478 at Copenhagen, was intended initially to train administrators. 'Within weeks of the religious change-over, in 1536, King Christian III had decided to overhaul the ecclesiastical and educational legislation of the country', including the introduction into schools of arithmetic and geometry, based on a textbook by the Dutchman Gemma Frisius.[9] From the start, the stability of the Reformation in Denmark meant that educational reform could be, with a few brief interruptions, consistently and coherently directed. Consequently, the university in Copenhagen continued to operate more or less fully throughout the century with a reformed, heavily Classical, curriculum.[10]

The humanist impulse in Scandinavia was fostered by a deep, even if largely political, interest in the history of each kingdom, especially from the point of view of demonstrating its antiquity, the legitimacy of its sovereign, and its peculiar Danishness or Swedishness.[11] The first sign of this new historical interest was the publication, by Gotfred af Ghemen, in 1495, of the first printed book in Danish, *Den danske Rimkrønike* ('The Danish Rhyming Chronicle').[12] This was followed by the humanist Christiern Pedersen's edi-

[8] Aili, Ferm and Gustavson, *Röster från svensk medeltid*, pp. 180-207.

[9] Garstein, *Rome and the Counter-Reformation*, pp. 17, 21.

[10] Brask, *Dansk litteraturhistorie*, vol. 2, pp. 357-367.

[11] For the development of the idea of *patria* in Denmark, see Ilsøe, 'Danskerne og deres fædreland', pp. 27-88, esp. 32-44, 57-78.

[12] Skautrup, *Den danske Sprogs Historie* vol. 2, pp. 124-125. See also Klemming and Nordin, *Svensk boktryckeri-historia*, pp. 117-124, where, however, the presses in the 'Swedish' part of Denmark, especially in Malmö, are not discussed until those parts become formally Swedish. The first book printed in Denmark was the *De obsidione et bello rhodiano* (Odense, 1482). This was the work of a Dutchman from Lübeck, Johan Snell, who moved to Stockholm the following year and printed the first, or possibly second, book in Sweden, the *Dialogus creaturarum*. Klemming and Nordin are of the opinion (pp. 143-145) that Snell was beaten into second place, in Sweden, by a Lübeck colleague, Bartholomeus Ghotan (or Gothan), whose (much shorter) *Vita Katharine* – about the daughter of St. Birgitta, founder (c. 1345) of a double order of nuns and monks at Vadstena, in central Sweden – seems to have come out slightly earlier in

tion of Saxo's late-twelfth/early-thirteenth century *Gesta Danorum* (Paris, 1514). This singular medieval document became for long the cornerstone of Danish national history and pride. '[T]he very existence of this remarkable work written in elegant Latin became one of the most important testimonies in the sixteenth century that Denmark was no barbarian country'.[13]

Sweden had nothing to rival the great Saxo, and one of Gustaf Wasa's initiatives was the stimulation of the writing of a history of Sweden. The first result, *En swensk cröneka* (1541-42 ['A Swedish chronicle']), by his onetime secretary, Olaus Petri, so displeased him that, in 1554, he ordered all copies destroyed.[14] The offence seems to have been that it neither sufficiently acknowledged the king's God-granted supreme authority nor Sweden's role as the home of the Goths. This latter was an old claim, prominent in the fifteenth century, and one attractive to a usurping monarch.[15] Ironically enough, this Gothic assumption was the central thesis of the monumental *Historia de omnibus Gothorum Sveonumque regibus* (written before 1540, publ. Rome, 1554) by Johannes Magnus, the Roman Catholic titular archbishop of Uppsala, in exile in Rome, who argued the Gothic glory of Sweden. This was much more to Gustaf Wasa's taste and his eldest son, Erik, certainly knew the work well.[16]

Of more international consequence was Olaus Magnus's publication in Venice in 1539 of his great map of the North, the *Carta marina*, said to have been the largest single-sheet map of its day[17] and the first to give a reasonably accurate view of the geography of Scandinavia. The map seems to have had some influence on Sebastian Münster's *Cosmographei* (1544) and, in any event, Münster's book was dedicated to Gustaf Wasa.[18] Olaus Magnus's map

1483. What *is* important to note is that the courts soon moved to control the printing industry through centralisation in Copenhagen and Stockholm. After establishing his own press in Stockholm, Gustaf Wasa quickly put that of his rival, Bishop Hans Brask in Linköping, out of business. See Klemming and Nordin, *Svensk boktryckeri-historia*, pp. 149-150.

[13] Skafte Jensen, ed, *A History of Nordic Neo-Latin Literature*, p. 19.

[14] Sahlgren, ed, *Olavus Petri*, p. v.

[15] This assertion was first publicly made by the bishop Nils Ragvaldsson on November 12, 1434, at the Council of Basel. The entire speech, together with a Swedish translation by Eva Odelman, can be found in Aili, Ferm and Gustavson, *Röster från svensk medeltid*, pp. 286-299. The theme was recycled later in the century in the chronicle of Ericus Olai, written in the 1460s and 1470s.

[16] The best study of the Gothic revival in sixteenth century Sweden is Johannesson, *Gotisk renässans*, chapter 6, pp. 270-285, esp. illustration, p. 283, which shows Erik's own marginal annotations.

[17] The image measures 107 x 78.5 cm.

[18] Sebastian Münster, *Cosmographei* (Bazel, 1544), of which the second edition of 1550 has been reprinted in facsimile, gathering A II, r-v.

was followed in 1555 by a promised commentary on it, the *Historia de gentibus septentrionalibus*, a massive, generously illustrated, well-indexed, 'book of knowledge' about Scandinavia in general and Sweden in particular. Based in part on a journey to the north of Sweden in 1518-19, it sought to be a comprehensive guide to the fauna, resources, social customs, and governance of the country. The book, aimed essentially at a non-Swedish audience, was much reprinted, translated, and exploited in the hundred years following its publication, in Rome.[19]

The impulse toward national definition brought about by the rupture in 1520-21 of the Union of Kalmar into two states had, in the end, two different linguistic effects. On the one hand, it stimulated in Scandinavia the use of Latin as an international language of diplomacy, and on the other, it encouraged writing in Danish and Swedish (as well as in Icelandic and Finnish). This latter effect came about as much as an expression of nationality as an attempt to reach a literate but not necessarily Latinate public.

In encouraging the development of national languages, the reformers in Scandinavia, as elsewhere, found translation of the Bible to be a potent force. A Danish New Testament, translated by Christiern Pedersen from Luther's German and Erasmus's Greek texts appeared in Antwerp in 1529, followed there two years later by Pedersen's psalter, while the whole Bible appeared in Danish in 1550. This translation, using part of Pedersen's Old Testament material, based on Luther's German version, was the work of a committee of five, among whom were the bishop Peder Palladius, and a Scottish Lutheran, John MacAlpine (also known as Johannes Macchabaeus), a professor at Copenhagen University.[20] These translations, with their subsequent improvements were used in Norway as well, since Christian III (r. 1534-59) insisted upon Danish as the administrative and therefore ecclesiastical language of the country; this policy was to retard the development of a strong tradition of written Norwegian. In Sweden, on the other hand, Gustaf Wasa's active interest in a Swedish Bible promoted Olaus Petri's and Laurentius Andreae's Swedish New Testament, made from Luther's translation and Erasmus's Greek and Latin editions of the text; this was published in Stockholm in 1526 by Richloff, the royal printer.[21] The complete Swedish Bible, by an anonymous committee probably headed by the archbishop, Laurentius Petri, Olaus's brother, appeared in 1541.

[19] Swanson, 'The Idea of Map', pp. 65-76, and further references there.

[20] Brask *et al.*, eds, *Dansk litteraturhistorie*, vol. 2, p. 161.

[21] Klemming and Nordin, *Svensk Boktryckeri-historia*, p. 151. An interesting survey of the complicated construction of this translation can be found in Bergendoff, *Olavus Petri*, pp. 86-111.

This renewed interest in the local language echoed quite differently in Iceland, where there had always been a strong tradition of written Icelandic through the Middle Ages. This tradition ran, of course, in parallel with the Latin used in the church. Indeed, even in the fourteenth century there had been translation into Icelandic of parts of the Bible.[22] There was a printing press in the 1530s in Hólar, the seat of the last Roman Catholic bishop of the country, and from this press came a stream of vigorous anti-Reformation tracts until the bishop's execution in 1550. A complete Icelandic Bible was not available until 1584, when one – based on that of Luther – was printed at Hólar.[23] On the eastern extremity of Scandinavia, in Finland, the situation was just the opposite. Finnish was not a written language before the middle of the sixteenth century. The return from Wittenberg of, among others, Michael Agricola, whose translation of the New Testament was printed in Stockholm in 1548, brought the first scholarly interest in developing written Finnish.[24] A complete Finnish Bible was not available, however, until one was printed in Stockholm in 1642.

This interest in the vernacular languages was fostered by the compelling needs of religious reformation and nationalistic renewal. Out of this interest stemmed, likewise, the awareness that education itself was also important for convincing people – and helping them convince themselves – of the truths of the Reform; hence the active support by the Church as well as the state. Indeed, the showing forth of the 'pure Word' became something of a Swedish slogan for the aims of the Church, the success of which ideally required an educated and sophisticated populace. Yet, at the same time as the educational needs of Denmark and Sweden increased and stabilised written Danish and Swedish, the larger educational project, originally developed in Wittenberg,[25] aimed at creating Latin schools in every large city, where pupils could be brought into direct contact with the international world of learning, based on Classical authors, Biblical commentary, and rhetorical training. This orientation itself is probably due to the fact that the German and French beginnings of the sixteenth-century Reformation had their roots within the university tra-

[22] Österlin, *Churches of Northern Europe*, p. 51, picture on p. 52.

[23] For more on the inverted situation in Iceland, see Péttursson, 'Iceland', pp. 96-104.

[24] Agricola produced some Lutheran manuals after his return to Finland (1539), and an ABC-book around 1543, which, though published in Stockholm, seems to have been the first example of printed Finnish. Cf. Derry, *A History of Scandinavia*, p. 92; Schoolfield, *A History of Finland's Literature*, pp. 35-36; Laitinen, *Suomen kirjallisuuden historia*, p. 109, who suggests that the ABC-book might have been printed any time between 1537 and 1543.

[25] See Bolger's discussion of Melanchthon's organisation of and contribution to the educational programme of the German reformers: *The Classical Heritage*, pp. 344-349.

dition. The importation of this educational project was, however, a deliberate initiative of the monarchy.

In Scandinavia in general, but perhaps in Denmark in particular, it is useful to see the Latin renaissance as a 'modernising' movement, bringing a whole new view of, attitude toward, and stimulation of (a mostly poetic) literature. One reason for this, Kurt Johannesson suggests, is pedagogical: 'Poetry was thought to awaken the interest of young people in the art and beauty of language'. The Swedish school rules of 1571 expressed the belief that if the teacher included songs and sayings in his teaching, the pupils would maintain a keen interest in their lessons. Poetry was seen as a demonstration of all the aspects of rhetoric in a compact form.[26] Those educated in this manner often wrote poetry because it was fashionable and was considered a social accomplishment. Such poetry is most charmingly represented, perhaps, by Martin Børup's *Carmen vernale*, from the end of the fifteenth century. As the courts stimulated learning, through their importation of foreign scholars and the training of native students at home and abroad in the new educational reforms, elegaic literary hybrids, in all the Classical forms and genres, often combining or applying Classical references to local matters,[27] were encouraged, probably even expected, by monarchs as an appropriate reflection of their station. Christian III (r. 1534-59), Frederik II (r. 1559-88), and Christian IV (r. 1588-1648) of Denmark, and Erik XIV (r. 1560-69) and Johan III (r. 1569-92) of Sweden had all certainly been raised to expect the highest in Renaissance standards of flattery. Among the finest of these encomiastic elegies in Denmark are the *Bucolica* (Wittenberg, 1560) by Erasmus Laetus, an ambitious pastoral praising the life of Christian III and the coronation of Christian's son, Frederik II, and the *De regibus Daniæ epigrammaton* (1569) by Hans Jørgensen Sadolin, a poetic demonstration of the antiquity of the Danish throne.[28] In Sweden, Gustaf Wasa had a court Latinist, Henricus Mollerus, whose function seems to have been that of poetic apologist for the king, a role similarly performed by the Uppsala professor of Greek, Laurentius Petri Gothus, for Gustaf's sons.[29] Such patriotic composition, how-

[26] Johannesson, 'Latinsk skolpoesi', p. 160 [my translation].

[27] We can see this function expressed later in the *Buch von der Deutschen Poëterey* of Martin Opitz, which describes and illustrates standard Classical prosodic forms, metaphors and motifs. More to the point, Opitz understands that the secular instruction which he offers also has an underlying religious basis; he opens chapter 2 as follows, *'Die Poeterey ist anfanges nichts anders gewesen als eine verborgene Theologie, und unterricht von Göttlichen sachen'* [From its inception, poetry has been nothing other than hidden theology, and teaches of godly matters].

[28] Skafte Jensen, ed, *A History of Nordic Neo-Latin Literature*, pp. 25-28.

[29] Skafte Jensen, ed, *A History of Nordic Neo-Latin Literature*, p. 137. An interesting, and fairly large, Latin genre that runs parallel to this consists of valedictory poems; see

ever, especially in Sweden, seems to have been a continuation of a fairly strong vernacular tradition of chronicle writing, mostly directed against the Union of Kalmar as represented by its first head, Erik of Pomerania. The popular 'Song of Freedom', written no later than 1439, for instance, by Bishop Tomas Simonsson of Strängnäs, is openly in this vein.

Beyond its literary uses, there was a broad acceptance of Latin as a scholarly language. There were several large-scale history projects in Denmark, for instance, which aimed not only to fill in the gaps in the knowledge of Danish history from Saxo to the recent past but also to attempt a world history. The task begun by Hans Svaning, a polemicist as well as an historian (all of whose historical work was unfortunately lost in the great Copenhagen fire of 1728), was brilliantly continued by his son-in-law, Anders Sørensen Vedel (1542-1616). Indeed, Vedel's contribution to Danish cultural history is enormous: not only did he write scholarly and poetic work in Latin, he extended his scholarship into the vernacular through his translations into Danish (notably of Saxo, 1575). His historical curiosity led to what we would today call cultural anthropology, for, in 1591, he published the first of the great collections of old Danish folk ballads which constitute Denmark's greatest Renaissance vernacular literary treasure.[30] Vedel is a key figure at the meeting point of Latin humanist and Danish vernacular culture. Lars Boje Mortensen argues that he 'had never been a typical classicizing humanist in the style of the nationalist poets'. All along his main interests were Danish medieval history and the Danish language.[31]

It is hard to say whether or not this scholarly use of Latin in the end really accomplished its international purpose. There is no sure way of knowing who read these books and little even to tell us how widely they were distributed. It is certain, however, that much of contemporary European culture came into Denmark, and Scandinavia, through Latin, either through books purchased and (presumably) read, or through visiting scholars, who brought new ideas in the international language.

It may perhaps almost go without saying that many of these ideas and books were on theological matters. Since Reformation preceded Renaissance in Scandinavia, this was probably inevitable. Since this theology was exclusively Lutheran, in the sense that it was aimed at creating an understanding and clarification of what the Lutheran reform meant and intended for Denmark and Sweden, little of it was exported outside Scandinavia; indeed, much of it was initially heavily dependent upon Wittenberg and Rostock models.

Harsting, 'Latin valedictory poems', pp. 203-218.

[30] Vedel, *Et Hundrede udvalgte danske Viser*, later taken into Grundtvig *et al.*, eds, *Danmarks gamle Folkeviser*.

[31] Mortensen, 'Anders Sørensen Vedel', p. 269.

Though in both Scandinavian countries the reform took place from the top down, there seems to have been relatively little lay opposition to it. This was certainly because the most obvious practical change, the liturgical switch to the vernacular, was an idea whose time had come.[32] In this entire period, then, there is a parallel movement of Latin, used largely as a language conduit to the outside world, and the vernaculars, used largely for the internal communication of political and theological ideas. This is hardly unexpected. It was, indeed, the re-infusion of Latin into Scandinavia as a secular language that gave Scandinavians a contemporary voice in a larger world which had recently ignored them. Far from suppressing indigenous intellectual life, the Reformation opened Scandinavians to the most recent scientific, æsthetic, theological and philosophical ideas and discoveries available in a Europe teeming with intellectual ferment.

Thus, Erik XIV's letter (1560) of proposal of marriage to Elizabeth of England was written in Latin to the strict requirements of Classical rhetoric, and his brother Johan's use of Latin in delivering it was favourably commented upon.[33] Indeed, though his speeches were spoken in Swedish, Erik apparently wrote drafts for them in Latin. He is thought, moreover, to be the anonymous author of a Latin reply to an attack by the Danish historian, Hans Svaning, on the merits of Johannes Magnus's *Historia.*

The adoption by sixteenth-century intellectuals of the New Latinity for literature, history, theology, and administration is well-known; it was, however, in the natural sciences and medicine, where it perhaps had the most long-lasting effect, and where it formed the standard of communication well into the eighteenth century. An example of the first effects of this development comes in the appearance of a Latin-Danish glossary by Christiern Pedersen, printed in Paris in 1510, and its reverse counterpart, the Danish-Latin *Hortulus synonymorum*, published by Henrik Smith [=Henricus Faber/ Fabricius] in Copenhagen in 1520,[34] the sort of necessary reference material that younger scholars might well need for a modern education. The *Hortulus* is, in fact, a particularly interesting book, since its glossary (really a kind of thesaurus), while not neglecting, for example, the Latin words for 'love', is clearly directed toward scientific discourse. While a student in Rostock, a city

[32] See the discussion of the introduction in Stockholm of Swedish in the Mass, in Bergendoff, *Olavus Petri*, pp. 148-159. It is useful to emphasise that the change was only linguistic: the structure and most of the formulæ of the Mass remained much the same. Theological interpretation, however, might show new emphases. There was also substantial renovation in the daily offices.

[33] Aili, 'Sweden', p. 134. On Erik's broad humanistic background and abilities, see Roberts, *The Early Vasas*, pp. 199-200.

[34] The latter is available in a facsimile edited by Inger Bom, as number II in the series, *Det 16. århundredes danske vocabularier.*

which had quickly adopted the reformed theological position and had thereby become an important transmitter of new ideas to Scandinavia, especially to Denmark, Smith took a great interest in medical questions and later even wrote a book on the subject, of which the last edition appeared in the middle of the nineteenth century.[35]

The history of early medicine in the North has not been much studied. In 1526, Frederik I tried, without success, to import two doctors into Denmark to work in Odense and Århus. As late as 1600 there were apparently only ten or twelve physicians and two pharmacists in the whole country. Medicine in Denmark was, however, internationalised by the influence later in the sixteenth century of Peter Sørensen [=Severinus], whose *Idea medicinæ philosophiæ* (Basel, 1571) brought into Denmark the Paracelsian idea of diagnosis based on observation rather than theory. On his return to Denmark in 1571 or 1572, Sørensen became court physician to Frederik II, and later to Christian IV, and he remained in this influential position for thirty years. Through his book, 'in civilised Latin', in which he reorganised and rethought Paracelsus' notions, he transformed the diagnostic ideas of, among others, Thomas Muffet, who was greatly to influence the subsequent development of Paracelsian medicine in England.[36]

Without question, the most internationally known Scandinavian natural scientist of the sixteenth century was the older contemporary of Galileo, Tycho Brahe (1546-1601). Brahe achieved international prominence through his discovery of a supernova, about which he wrote and published a long elegaic poem, *De nova stella* (1573), thereby combining science with art. Though Brahe has been recently credited with writing a long Ovidian heroid, *Urania Titani* (1594),[37] much of his other work was more prosaically devoted to locating and accurately describing the positions and movements of stars. In discussing the Copernican 'revolution', Elizabeth Eisenstein points out the importance for Tycho Brahe of the availability of the printed tables and measurements of other astronomers and mathematicians, and Brahe's own ability, in turn, to communicate with many other scientists through print.[38] The importance of Brahe's astronomical work persuaded Frederik II to grant him a fief of the island of Hven, in the Øresund. Here Brahe built his famous observatory, Uraniborg, which was visited by many well-known contemporaries. Among them was James VI of Scotland, who visited Uraniborg

[35] Brask, *Dansk litteraturhistorie*, vol. 2, pp. 480-482.
[36] Trevor-Roper, *Renaissance Essays*, pp. 149-199, esp. 160-163, 178-180.
[37] Zeeberg, *Tycho Brahes* Urania Titani.
[38] Eisenstein, *The Printing Press as an Agent of Change*, pp. 480, 575-635, esp. 580-584, 623-626.

on March 20, 1590, while he was in the area at the time of formalising his marriage to Anne of Denmark.[39]

It is important to understand that the Scandinavian courts used the relative peace after the first two decades of the sixteenth century to consolidate their historical, intellectual, and patronal positions. Denmark was incomparably the more powerful and wealthier of the two kingdoms but by the last decades of the century, the Swedes had also asserted their place in the European mainstream. A simple, outward, sign of this new status can be seen in the different kinds of clothing worn by Gustaf Wasa and his sons in contemporary portraits (even allowing for changes of fashion and some discreet touching-up by the artists). A portrait of Gustaf Wasa by Jacob Binck (1542) shows us a thickly-clothed, somewhat stolid, powerful man of wealth, while an anonymous Dutch portrait of his eldest son, Erik, reveals a slender, alert young man, dressed in the recent looser fashion of central Europe, a style also to be seen in J.B. van Uther's portrait of Erik's brother, Johan. It is, I think, fair to see the cultural activity at the courts of the Scandinavian kings as being acquisitively directed outside their borders, not solely in an attempt to catch up with more fashionable courts elsewhere, but also as policies aimed deliberately at bringing modern ideas into their realms to aid the great social renewal then under weigh.

In our present age of great diffusion of cultural impulse, we must not underestimate the energy expended on cultural projects by the Scandinavian courts in a time when the strengthening of their political position was a central administrative task in both countries. Just as the relationship between Europe and Scandinavia can be seen within the context of Centre and Periphery, so within Scandinavia there was a parallel tension, most obvious in the sundering of Sweden from Denmark. That tension gave rise subsequently to internal tensions of a similar kind in either country.

In Denmark, the nobility, the great landlords, had always been relatively powerful and a source of much unrest and rebellion against a nonetheless established and acknowledged central administration in the court, whose responsibilities and attention were often occupied with people and events outside Denmark itself. Hence, the monarch's chief home interest was to exert his centrality; appropriately, the display of high culture played a central role in presenting the king to his country. We are vouchsafed a glimpse of this in the

[39] A close study of Tycho Brahe's time on Hven is by Christianson, *On Tycho's Island*. See further Zeeberg, 'The inscriptions at Tycho Brahe's Uraniborg', pp. 263-264, 266. The marriage itself is presumably the subject of a now-lost Latin poem by Anders Sørensen Vedel, *Carmen gratulatorium ad serenissimum Jacobum Scotiae regem*, printed in Copenhagen in 1590. See Mortensen, 'Anders Sørensen Vedel', pp. 276, 280. The wedding is discussed extensively in Stevenson, *Scotland's Last Royal Wedding*.

engraving by Caspar von Ens representing *Herredagen*, a grand meeting in Odense in 1580 of all the nobles subject to Frederik II. The city square is clearly a scene of great pomp and festivity. Similarly, the coronation of Christian IV in 1598 took place in an elaborate public manner. Such spectacles were naturally focused on the monarch. It is at this time, too, that the whole notion of *patria* began to take on a more specific complexion, splitting into *fædernelandet* and *fæderne rige* (loosely, Denmark, and places subject to the Danish crown).[40]

In Sweden, on the other hand, the magnates were historically and constitutionally much more powerful and prominent in the running of the country than was any regent. Their power was exercised through their permanent presence in the Council of State, where they elected one of their own as regent or governor. On the whole, this caused little problem as long as their actions and animus were directed at the central authority in Copenhagen. Thus, once so elected, Gustaf Wasa's foremost political task was to transform his regency into a kingship, thereby formally separating Sweden from the Union.[41] His great administrative task, however, as he himself well understood, was to create a court essentially *ex nihilo*, to create a new Centre and to push the nobility to the thereby newly-created Periphery. In a sense, then, this required nothing less than the creation and cultivation of the idea of court and the culture associated therewith.

For Gustaf Wasa, one powerful expression of this idea, in a place and period when the notion of 'capital city' scarcely existed, came through the building and re-building of castles. His first large-scale project was the re-building, between 1537 and 1544, of the fourteenth-century fortress of Gripsholm, on Lake Mälar, which allowed him to strengthen his hold on this important trade route through central Sweden.[42] One of the effects of this project was, in the end, to transform a fortress into a Renaissance castle. Most of the designers and artisans who effected this transformation came from abroad: its master builder was the German, Heinrich von Köllen. In this castle, refurbished yet again from 1567 onwards, Duke Carl's Room was given decorations derived from Netherlandish designs by Cornelis Floris and Vredeman de Vries. Far more completely Renaissance in feeling and detail, however, was the new Vadstena Castle, also situated on an important waterway in West Central Sweden. This small castle – built next to the fourteenth-

[40] Ilsøe, 'Danskerne og deres fædreland', pp. 32-36.

[41] From the time of his proclamation as king, in 1523, it took him another twenty-one years to make his kingship formally hereditary by male primogeniture, in the Succession Pact agreed with the nobility at the meeting of the Estates in Västerås, 1544. Roberts, *The Early Vasas*, pp. 141-143.

[42] For Gustaf Wasa's claim to this castle, see Roberts, *The Early Vasas*, p. 67.

century mother abbey of the Birgittine nuns and monks, which was itself built next to the main buildings of the early-medieval Folkung kings of central Sweden – was worked on from 1555 under the direction of Pierre de la Roche. A third reconstruction was Kalmar Castle, on the southeast coast, close to the border with Denmark. This castle was, indeed, the bulwark of Sweden's southern defence, and was re-fortified in the 1570s for Johan III by members of the Milanese family of architects, Pahr. Its splendid interior well was built by the Fleming, Roland Mackle, to a design by Domenicus Pahr. In the same period, much of the decoration of the old castle in Stockholm, Tre Kronor (devastated by fire in 1697), was carried out under the direction of the Netherlander, Wilhelm Boy, a sculptor, who designed the church of St. James in central Stockholm, as well as making (1558-60) a fine, full-length, oak relief of the king himself.[43]

Gustaf Wasa and his sons were not alone in their interest in castles, however. In 1574, across the sound at Helsingør, Frederik II began the building of Kronborg, the foremost Renaissance castle of Denmark. Like Gustaf Wasa, Frederik also imported foreign artists and artisans, mostly Netherlanders. The whole work was under the direction of Hans van Paeschen and the principal sculptor was Gert van Groningen, whose grand Royal Portal was executed in 1573-76, and who was succeeded in the royal project by his son, Harmen. The main courtyard of the castle was decorated in 1583 with an especially elaborate fountain by the Nürnberg founder, Georg Labenwolff. Thomas Frandsen, thought to have come originally from Utrecht, carved the magnificent altar in the chapel. As with Gustaf Wasa, Frederik II also had his Netherlandish relief portrait, this one by Gert van Egen.[44]

This passion for bricks and mortar reached new heights under the long reign of Christian IV. Where the father had been content to create Kronborg and to refurbish a few castles, the son created, or recreated, whole towns, of which the jewel was the new chief city of Norway, which he renamed Christiania (since 1925, once again Oslo). Indeed, Christian had a special interest in Norway, visiting the country often in his reign and leaving his name on much of the landscape.

It was inevitable that, once begun, the Scandinavian Renaissance cultural project should in the sixteenth century have imported much of its direct impetus from abroad, largely from Northern Europe, and from Western and Southern Europe in succeeding centuries. This continued, after all, an old pattern. Though there was a long (probably) native tradition of church painting throughout the Middle Ages, much of the fine Gothic sculpture and altar-carving in Scandinavia was done by foreign, largely German, artisans,

[43] Sandström, '1520-1728', pp. 131-134, 142-147.
[44] Bøggild Johannsen and Johannsen, *Ny dansk Kunsthistorie* vol. 2, pp. 50-69.

such as the Lübecker, Bernt Notke, whose high altar in Roskilde Cathedral was finished in 1479, and whose 'St George and the Dragon' in Stockholm Cathedral was consecrated on New Year's Day, 1489.

The Scandinavian courts and their associated institutions became an attractive new market for art, artists, and artisans from outside Scandinavia. One of the reasons for this was the shift in patronage from the Church to the court. This was not so much attributable to the Reformation itself, which exhibited almost no iconoclastic tendencies in Scandinavia, as to the fact that the churches were largely complete before the Reformation and did not need much in the way of new art. At the same time, the courts had a use for artists and artisans. Hence, for instance, the many portrait painters who travelled to the Northern courts. Jacob Binck's portrait of Gustaf Wasa has its parallel in one from his hand, at about the same time, of Christian III's chancellor, Johan Friis, while the Fleming, Jost Verheiden, painted Christian III himself. Indeed, so many Netherlanders worked in the building of Kronborg that Helsingør was referred to by contemporaries as 'Little Amsterdam'.[45] A further contributing cause was the availability of so many artists. This can be attributed to the political and social unrest of the times, not least in the Low Countries, where the struggle against the Spanish left limited time, money, and opportunity for artists and artisans; this created a sort-of artistic 'push-pull' effect in the direction of Scandinavia in general, and Denmark in particular.

The opportunities for cultural work in Scandinavia were markedly increased by the creation and expansion of the function of the courts, whose cultural interests were not limited to visual artists and architects, scientists, and historians, but were also given expression in the performing arts.

Compared with courts elsewhere, the Scandinavian courts were rather late in the creation of musical establishments, and though there is some record of musicians more or less permanently attached to court and church in the sixteenth century, their development into large, musically broad ensembles really belongs to the seventeenth. This does not at all suggest that there was no music or theatre. Indeed, there is ample Swedish evidence, for instance, of a widespread musical culture within and without the Church, which throughout the fifteenth century was the principal patron of musicians. Many fifteenth-century wall paintings in Swedish churches, such as those at Estuna, about 1463, and at Härkeberga, painted in the 1480's by Albertus Pictor (both

[45] Bøggild Johannsen and Johannsen, *Ny dansk Kunsthistorie* vol. 2, pp. 45-49. It would, indeed, be hard to guess how many foreign artists and artisans worked in Scandinavia in the sixteenth century, but the Low Countries certainly furnished a disproportionately high number.

places in Uppland), attest to secular as well as to sacred use of instruments and song.[46]

The first instrumentalists known to have been attached to the Scandinavian courts were brass players, and almost certainly included drummers, as well. The trumpet and trombone were princely instruments, essential for calling public attention to the king and his family. Indeed, as early as 1527-28, Gustaf Wasa hired such musicians to enhance his prestige.[47] Traditionally, these (usually brass) wind instruments were considered outdoor instruments – as with the English *waits* and the German *Stadtpfeiffer* – small bands in the service of the town, and are so depicted in Olaus Magnus's *Historia*.[48] In Scandinavia, as often elsewhere, they were mostly used at public moments in the life of the sovereign; as in Italy, for instance, they were also lent to the Church for festive occasions.

There were also string players and lutenists at the courts. Tradition has it that Gustaf Wasa himself took lute lessons and that both Prince Erik and Prince Johan played that instrument. It is a fact that, in addition to some Italian string players who seem to have arrived in 1556, Gustaf Wasa hired a series of court lutenists, one of whom, Hieronymus Hofman, probably wrote a lute piece dedicated to Prince Erik.[49] Erik himself seems to have composed at least two motets while incarcerated after his deposition, and his library contained music scores for what we would today refer to as chamber music.[50] The first known Swedish polyphonic composition, a parody mass by Bertil Kellner, probably from the 1570s, is based on Orlando di Lasso's motet, *Lauda Jerusalem*. Clearly, the Swedish court and its institutions had a direct contact with some of the finest continental music. The Wasas took a close interest in the music of the German Church in Stockholm, which seems to have functioned as something of a branch of the royal chapel. Its musicians also worked together with those of the court and the cathedral in the 1580s, during the reign of Johan III. The earlier music in its large collection, both in manuscript and printed form, consists of a great quantity of then-recent music from central Europe, and was acquired through donations from the royal family.[51]

This high musical culture had its parallel in Denmark. During the reign of Frederik II (r. 1559-88), the first large royal ensemble, *Det kongelige Kapel*,

[46] Öberg, 'Kyrkans bild', pp. 153-168 and 138.
[47] Kjellberg, 'Vasadynastins renässanskultur', p. 200; Norlind and Troback, *Kungl. Hovkapellets historia*, pp. 7-32.
[48] *Historia de gentibus septentrionalibus*, XV: 30, 523.
[49] Kjellberg, 'Vasadynastins renässanskultur', pp. 204-205.
[50] Kjellberg, 'Vasadynastins renässanskultur', pp. 208-212.
[51] A broad study of this important collection is to be found in Norlind, *Från Tyska kyrkans glansdagar*, esp. vol. 1.

was formed, largely with musicians from England, Germany, and the Low Countries. However, the incomparably great patron of the arts in late sixteenth- and early seventeenth-century Scandinavia was Christian IV, who made himself the complete Renaissance prince. The early years of his long reign saw an immense upsurge of visible cultural activity: in addition to his architectural and town-planning interests, music played a prominent part in the cultural expression of his court. He continued the tradition of inviting foreign musicians to his court, of whom his most distinguished early guest was the English composer and lutenist, John Dowland, who stayed for eight years and was paid even more than the court architect. At the same time, Christian sought out and encouraged Danish musicians, for example, Mogens Pedersøn, whom in 1599 he sent to study with Giovanni Gabrieli in Venice; another was Thomas Schattenberg, who studied in Northern Germany about the same time. Their work bore fruit early in the following century.[52]

Music was also associated with theatrical performance. Indeed, one might not improperly consider most royal appearances as a kind of theatre, as Christian IV's coronation in 1596 certainly was.[53] Theatre itself, however, took a long time to arrive in something like permanent fashion in Scandinavia. Church plays were the most common form of theatre through the Middle Ages in Scandinavia as elsewhere; likewise, there were travelling troupes of entertainers, some of whom performed plays. King Christopher (r. 1440-48) had certainly hired a court jester by 1447 and probably also had some kind of players, as well. In any event, the *Ludus de Sancto Kanuto Duce* (circa 1500), though formally a play about a saint, Knut Lavard (c. 1096-1131), included a great deal of Danish history derived from Saxo, and required many players, a fair amount of scenic apparatus, and was surely played out of doors.[54] On the whole, however, formal theatre was kept within the church and the school in Denmark and Sweden, where it was seen as providing good models of action and rhetoric for impressionable minds.

Sixteenth-century Denmark did produce one playwright with a royal connection: this was Hieronymus Justesen Ranch, whose play, *Kong Salomos Hylding* ('Homage to King Solomon', 1584), was written in honour of Frederik II and the newly-proclaimed crown prince, the seven-year old Christian, who responded with a *skål*. The play required a great many players and musicians, and contained elements of *ballet de cour* and other southern

[52] See the articles on 'Denmark', 'Christian IV', and 'Mogens Pedersøn' in: Sadie, ed, *The New Grove Dictionary*. For Mogen Pedersøn, see also Glahn, ed, *Musik*, vol. 4, p. iii.; for Thomas Schattenberg, see vol. 7, pp. iii-iv.

[53] See the description of this elaborate event in Kvam, Risum and Wingaard, *Dansk teaterhistorie*, vol. 1, pp. 48-49, and Marker and Marker, *A History of Scandinavian Theatre*, pp. 30-31.

[54] Risum, 'De tidligste teaterformer', pp. 9-49.

theatrical novelties. Ranch's finest play is *Karrig Niding* ('Niding the Miser'), from about 1598, conceived as a counterpart to Plautus's *Aulularia*.[55] One assumes, moreover, the occasional presence of visiting foreign troupes during Frederik's and Christian's reigns – not least the visit in 1586-87 of members of the Earl of Leicester's troupe, who later formed the Lord Chamberlain's Men, of which Shakespeare was to be an important member.[56] Christian may also have had the services of the great stage architect, Inigo Jones, who was in Copenhagen in 1603.[57] There appears, however, to have been no permanent professional troupe in Scandinavia in the period under consideration.

The great age of court theatre in both countries, but especially in Sweden, lay in the seventeenth century. Nonetheless, interest in spectacle, if not expressly the theatrical elements therein, is clear at least from the time of Erik XIV, whose Court Order decrees that great public occasions in his court shall be celebrated 'as is the custom in the courts of other kings and princes'.[58] A troupe with English players in it visited the Nyköping court of Gustaf Wasa's youngest son, Duke Carl, in 1591-92, though it is not absolutely certain that they performed plays in the traditional sense.[59] A 'comedy' was certainly performed in Uppsala Castle on February 12, 1594, during the coronation of Sigismund (r. 1592-99), but what it consisted of is difficult to say.[60] About a year later, on 3 March 1595, a 'comedy' was performed in Stockholm Castle for Duke Carl. Yet, it seems clear from the paucity of references that, outside of festive occasions, the Wasas did not particularly favour theatre. On the whole, an interest in locally-generated theatre did not take hold in Sweden before the beginning of the seventeenth century, when Johannes Messenius planned and began his series of history plays on Swedish themes. Though not sponsored by the court, the historical direction of this series did not contradict the court's interests.[61]

The political instability of the fifteenth century inherent in the structure of the Union of Kalmar and the latter's subsequent dissolution into two states, the

[55] Risum, 'Die tidligste teaterformer', pp. 41-45, and Marker and Marker, *A History of Scandinavain Theatre*, pp. 41-42.

[56] Marker and Marker, *A History of Scandinavain Theatre*, pp. 40-41, and Risum, 'De tidligste teaterformer'', pp. 47-48.

[57] See the article on 'Jones' in Sadie, ed, *The New Grove Dictionary*.

[58] Dahlberg, *Komediantteatern*, p. 73.

[59] Dahlberg, *Komediantteatern*, pp. 86-88.

[60] For theatre at the courts of Carl and Sigismund: Dahlberg, *Komediantteatern*, pp. 86-95.

[61] Sauter, ed, *Messenius*, pp. 7-60. Messenius planned fifty plays on Swedish history, but only managed to write six. A still-useful longer study of Messenius' plays is by Lidell, *Studier*.

relative poverty and weakness of central government with respect to its periphery, and a small and dispersed population, hindered the formation of a courtly culture on a level with that to be seen elsewhere on the continent. There was nothing in Scandinavia faintly approaching, even at a distance, the brilliance of the Italian *Quattrocento*. The increasing centralisation of authority in the sixteenth century, however, and the increasing prosperity brought about by peace and expansion of royal income, allowed the general direction of courtly culture in Scandinavia in the period to be one of acceleration toward a European norm, associated with and manifest at the court, as we see in Erik XIV's regulation. This motion continued through the seventeenth century, rising to spectacular heights during the reigns of Christian IV (r. 1588-1648) in Denmark and Christina (r. 1632-54) in Sweden.

The development of a courtly culture in Scandinavia, perhaps most dramatically to be observed in Sweden-Finland but in no way absent from Denmark-Norway, is closely connected with nation-building and the establishment of a strong, royal Centre to counteract an often recalcitrant Periphery. Indeed, in Sweden, the acquisition of an internationalised culture can be seen as part of a process of identifying, even of defining, the central court. By comparison with the far wealthier courts to the south and west, the courtly culture of Scandinavia in the fifteenth and sixteenth centuries is modest. It is of no little interest, however, that this came about in part as the result of actions taken as a consequence of the Reformation in Scandinavia, which imported many of the humanist aspects of the Italian Renaissance, particularly the revival of the learning of antiquity. Far from sounding the death knell of 'the classical tradition', there is a clear sense in which the Reformation in Scandinavia was, in fact, the agent which brought about a renewal of courtly and civil life.[62] During the course of the sixteenth century, that culture, through the discourse rapidly diffused by printing, New Latin and improved education, became modern and international at the same time as, in so doing, it furthered the nationalistic political and social development of the region.

[62] A contrary and rather shrill view is taken by Highet, *The Classical Tradition*, pp. 367-368, where he asserts that Luther and, by extension, Lutheranism crushed any spark of the Renaissance in Germany, delaying its benefits there and denying the potential development of a German Shakespeare.

POWER AND CREATIVITY AT THE COURT OF HEIDELBERG

Rita Schlusemann

> Especially after Frederick's successor, Philip the Upright (1476-1508), Heidelberg became a nursery garden of aristocratic intellectuality. Philip himself was a real humanist who had translated antique classical literature and who preferred to stay in the library rather than to go hunting. A quiet and sensitive personality, who was celebrated like a second Numa, he was convinced of the inner value of humanism, collected new writings and stimulated the production thereof.[1]

These words by Wolfgang Stammler, in one of the leading histories of German literature, are representative of the *communis opinio* concerning Philip the Upright, Elector Palatine from 1476 to 1508. The dominant picture of the Elector is that of a sensitive sovereign who had received a classical education, who had predominantly aesthetic interests in humanist literature, and who dedicated his court to the muses.[2]

In the present paper I shall argue against this traditional view, in two different ways. The first section gives an overview of the function of 'lay' humanist literature produced and collected under Philip's predecessor, Frederick the Victorious, and this literature is examined as to what it tells us about the relationship of power and creativity.[3] Two texts, it is proposed, are typical of the literary works produced during Frederick's reign: Peter Luder's speech when he entered the university of Heidelberg, and Matthias von Kemnat's

[1] Stammler, *Von der Mystik zum Barock*, p. 64.

[2] In her dissertation Backes (*Das literarische Leben*) argues for a change in this picture of Elector Philip.

[3] For the late Middle Ages the term 'lay' should not be opposed to *clericus* in the sense of priest, 'clerical' or a learned man. Nor is the modern opposition of 'lay' to 'expert' relevant here. The humanist ideal created the learned layman who is not only an expert in one discipline but who is able to participate and communicate in others and enjoys therefore a higher prestige than by virtue of his ability. On the other hand, this ideal is directly linked with a command of some learned language. For a fuller description of these considerations see Müller, *Wissen für den Hof*, and especially the introduction to the volume. See for a broad discussion also Kock and Schlusemann, *Laienlektüre und Buchmarkt*.

prose chronicle. Together with these, Michel Beheim's verse chronicle deserves to be mentioned, since both Matthias von Kemnat and Michel Beheim incorporated Luder's speech into their texts. The second section begins with a short survey of the literature traditionally associated with the court of Heidelberg during Philip's reign, before proceeding to focus on literature which does not fit into the traditional view. The interpretation given here of one text produced at court under Philip's patronage, the verse romance *Die Kinder von Limburg* (1480), is a first step towards a more detailed future investigation which will be centrally concerned with elucidating the complexities of literary production at the court of Heidelberg during the second half of the fifteenth century. Creativity is to be understood as a synonym for court literature (in German *Hofliteratur*), a term reintroduced by Jan-Dirk Müller for literature of all kinds intended for the laity at court.[4] Court literature should not be equated with courtly literature, however, and it should not be regarded as standing in opposition to bourgeois literature. Works of court literature in this definition were not intended exclusively for use at court: they could also be of interest for religious groups, people in towns, or learned people in general outside the court.

Several factors are responsible for the development of the small residence at Heidelberg during the second half of the fifteenth century into one of the earliest centres of German humanism. Although several authoritative, modern literary histories point to the Emperor Maximilian as the person mainly responsible for the development of humanism in Germany,[5] it should not be forgotten that as early as 1386 the university of Heidelberg was founded, and that this institution was to become a centre for wide-ranging exchanges of knowledge. In the fifteenth century the Elector Palatine chose university teachers for diplomatic, advisory and judicial tasks. Heidelberg, it may be noted, was the most important territorial centre in the German southwest, with a well-organised chancellery and an ever more influential group of learned advisors. The Elector Palatine held a leading position among the seven Electors of the Holy Roman Empire, by virtue of his caretaker role when the emperor was absent. The politics of the Palatinate, therefore, were of importance beyond the frontiers of that relatively small territory. Under the reign of Frederick the Victorious (1449-1476), a prince who was succesful with regard to both territorial expansion and military actions, the Elector Palatine became the most important counterweight to the Habsburg emperor in the third quarter of the fifteenth century.[6]

[4] Müller, ed, *Wissen für den Hof*, 22.

[5] See Wehrli, *Geschichte der deutschen Literatur*, p. 907; Rupprich, *Die deutsche Literatur*, p. 469.

[6] Rolf, *Kurpfalz*, pp. 36, 64, 67; Schaab, *Geschichte der Kurpfalz*, vol. 1: *Mittelalter*,

Frederick was a controversial sovereign for two main reasons: the questionable legitimacy of his rule, and his violent politics. After the early death of his brother Louis IV (1438-1449), Frederick on 16 September 1451 adopted the latter's one-year-old son Philip,[7] and, contrary to the provisions for primogeniture laid down in the Golden Bull,[8] made himself Elector of the Palatinate through the so-called *arrogatio* of 13 January 1452.[9] Frederick, however, promised never to marry, in order not to have legal descendants and heirs.[10] Although he succeeded in securing both papal approval and the agreement of the six other Electors for this *arrogatio*, the emperor Frederick III at first contested the arrangement.[11] Opponents of the Elector took the opportunity to impugn the legitimacy of his claim to the position. Frederick responded to these attacks not only with warfare but also by promoting at his court the production of songs, pamphlets, and literary and historical works. He used literature written both in Latin and in the vernacular as a means of legitimising both his position and his politics.[12] The practice – also shared by humanists – of glorifying the sovereign in speech and making him the ideal of every virtue suited Frederick's political goals. It would be too simple, however, to regard humanist rhetoric as a compensation for an absent political legitimacy, since there was an element of reciprocity between the two, and, insofar as it concerned the legal basis for Frederick's reign, the relationship did have to be reformulated in response to the arguments of his opponents.[13]

Peter Luder, who was appointed to a position at the university of Heidelberg in 1456 and is considered to be that university's first humanist, delivered a panegyric on Frederick on 11 February 1458.[14] Luder himself des-

pp. 174-183.

[7] Rolf, *Kurpfalz*, p. 32.

[8] The conditions for *arrogatio*, as defined in the Golden Bull, did not apply in this case, since *arrogatio*, as a matter of principle, was simply not possible between the prince and his adopted child.

[9] Rolf, *Kurpfalz*, p. 33ff. See also Berg and Bodemann, 'Wie ludwigen von Beyern', p. 3.

[10] Frederick did, however, have a relationship with Clara Dettin, whom he had met at the court of Munich in 1458. It is likely that she came to Heidelberg sometime before 1461. After the birth of their two sons, Frederick (born 1 May 1461) and Louis (born 29 September 1463), Frederick not only sought material security for his family but also endeavoured to assimilate the status of his illegitimate sons to that of legal descendants. For a full account of these efforts see Berg and Bodemann, 'Wie ludwigen von Beyern', pp. 4-7.

[11] In the document arranging the *arrogatio*, imperial agreement is not mentioned, but it must have been given. See Schaab, *Geschichte der Kurpfalz*, p. 176.

[12] Müller, 'Der siegreiche Fürst', pp. 17-50.

[13] Müller, 'Der siegreiche Fürst', p. 23.

[14] For more information on Luder see, for example, Baron, *The Life and Work of the*

cribed the Latin speech, given at the university, in a letter that he sent to Frederick along with a written copy of the text, which was to function as a *memoria* (an act of encomiastic remembrance) for the sovereign, his ancestors and his models.[15] Not only a stylistic model of the new rhetoric – one of Luder's sources was Cicero's *Pro archia poeta* – the speech was directly linked to the political circumstances of the Palatinate in the late 1450s. Frederick's power both as Elector and ruler of Heidelberg was viewed positively, and the reign was declared to be based on *virtus* rather than on hereditary succession.[16] A defence of the questionable *arrogatio* then followed, and Frederick was presented as the intellectual father of Philip, a view that was supported by many quotations and comparisons from Virgil, especially references alluding to Aeneas's relationship to his son Ascanius.[17] Luder states that Frederick's *pietas* and *clemencia* even exceed that ancient model: Aeneas loved his son, but Frederick went so far as to renounce marriage and father-hood on behalf of his adopted son Philip.[18] Aeneas, out of *pietas* for his father and his son, risked everything but had to abandon his native country; Frederick, who similarly acted out of love for his brother's son, saved his country and thus surpassed the classical exemplar.[19] *En passant* it may be noted that one of the gifts that Philip received on his wedding day in February 1474 was a manuscript of Virgil, containing the *Bucolics*, the *Georgics* and the *Aeneid*.[20] Frederick is not only presented as the new and even better Aeneas, but he appears as a *princeps litteratus* who had learnt the *artes liberales* and some of the *artes mechanicae*.[21] In the above-mentioned letter to Frederick, Luder emphasises the superiority of written records and literature.[22] He refers to Alexander the Great, who is said to have appreciated the

Wandering Humanist Peter Luder.

[15] See Müller, 'Peters Luders Panegyrikus', pp. 289-322, especially 289.

[16] Müller, 'Peters Luders Panegyrikus', p. 290.

[17] Müller, 'Der siegreiche Fürst', pp. 36-38.

[18] *Ut omnem amorem, pietatem, affectum denique paternum, in fratris sui filium, et ut verius dicam suum, conferre posset* quoted in Müller (Müller, 'Der siegreiche Fürst', p. 37).

[19] Müller, 'Der siegreiche Fürst', p. 38.

[20] Ms. Rome, Bibl. Vat., Cod. pal. lat. 1632. It is possible that it was given by Frederick. See Frommberger-Weber, 'Spätgotische Buchmalerei', pp. 114-118; see also Mittler, ed, *Bibliotheca Palatina*, pp. 195-196; Müller, 'Der siegreiche Fürst', p. 38, and Backes, *Das literarische Leben*.

[21] In their article on Frederick's testament ('"Wie ludwigen von Beyern etliche bucher verschriben sin"') Berg and Bodemann emphasise the importance which the chronicles of Matthias von Kemnat and Michel Beheim assign to Frederick's education. This applies especially to the *artes liberales*, the *artes mechanicae*, and courtly behaviour.

[22] See for an elaborate discussion of this aspect Müller, 'Peter Luders Panegyrikus', p. 294.

writings of Callisthenes.[23] The latter is called by Luder a writer and not a historiographer or a poet, and it is emphasised that the written character of the *memoria* of Alexander is the precondition of its durability.

Luder's speech was copied and translated into German by Matthias von Kemnat. Probably born in 1429, Matthias began his study at Heidelberg university in 1447. He left Heidelberg in 1449, but returned again in the same year together with Peter Luder. By 1460 at the latest he was made the Elector's chaplain. Matthias's prose chronicle was begun in the 1460s and was finished by 1475. The first part is a history of the Wittelsbach-Bavarian house within the framework of universal history. Matthias von Kemnat placed Luder's speech at the beginning of the second part of his chronicle; this part, which deals with Frederick I, covers the reign of Matthias's patron.[24] Not only was the prose chronicle copied quite frequently at the Heidelberg court in the fifteenth and sixteenth centuries,[25] its function as *memoria* was especially em-phasised; this was of course relevant for those who could not understand Latin. Recently, Studt has shown that on the whole the chonicle had a prag-matic function in respect to the confirmation, legitimation and stabilisation of the Elector's lordly authority.[26] For his part, Müller speaks about a change of function, from form to content.[27] It should also be mentioned that a translation (with amplifications) of Luder's letter to Frederick accompanied the speech in Von Kemnat's chronicle. The vernacular version of the speech has been preserved in an even older manuscript, once belonging to Matthias himself.[28]

The speech was incorporated into yet another text produced at the court, namely, Michel Beheim's *Pfälzer Reimchronik*, for which one of the major sources was Matthias's prose chronicle. Born in Sülzbach (northern

[23] According to the tradition Alexander had himself painted by Apelles, had himself carved in stone by Pyrgoteles, and had an image of himself cast in bronze by Lysippus: *Calistenem scriptorem semper secum duxit, ut res suas tam gestas quamque gerendas scripturis posteritatis memorie commendaret*, quoted by Müller ('Peter Luders Panegyrikus', p. 294).

[24] In recent years the prose chronicle has been the object of detailed research. Studt's *Fürstenhof und Geschichte* concentrates on the making and the tradition of the chronicle as well as on its sources and pragmatic functions. See also Müller, *Wissen für den Hof*; Studt, '*Exeat aula qui vult esse pius*', pp. 113-136.

[25] Studt (*Fürstenhof und Geschichte*) mentions seven manuscripts containing the chronicle.

[26] Studt, *Fürstenhof und Geschichte*.

[27] Müller, 'Peter Luders Panegyricus'.

[28] Ms. Rome, Bibl. Vat., Cod. pal. lat. 870, probably written between 1458 and 1469 (fols. 158^r - 166^v). The translation in this manuscript seems to be the oldest one and in it there are traces of corrections, especially with regard to choice of words. See Müller, 'Peter Luders Panegyricus', pp. 291, l.8.

Württemberg) in 1420, Beheim first worked as a weaver. In the 1440s he began working as a poet and singer at different courts. In 1468, he came to Heidelberg, but left the court four years later. He was murdered in his birthplace in 1472. Beheim called himself 'the German language-poet and writer of my gracious lord Frederick, Pfalzgraf of the Rhine'.[29] His verse chronicle was written between 1469 and 1471.

Luder's Latin speech was first delivered orally; then a written copy was presented to Frederick accompanied by a letter, also in Latin. Subsequently a vernacular translation was produced by Matthias von Kemnat; this was integrated into a written *memoria* in Matthias' prose chronicle. And finally, a version in rhymed couplets appears in Michel Beheim's chronicle, and was probably intended to be read aloud. These varying forms of the same text in Latin and in the vernacular, were produced for different occasions and for different recipients. They should be seen as interactive forms of literature,[30] and as such typical of the literary production at the Heidelberg court from the late 1450s to the 1470s.

Whether spoken or written, heard or read, in Latin or the vernacular, the text traces Frederick's predecessors back to the time of the birth of Christ.[31] The most important thing is not the continuous chronology of Frederick's predecessors but the genealogical evidence for his right to reign. A second set of arguments in his defence can be summarised as those which grounded his nobility in virtue rather than in dynastic legitimacy. Genealogy, in this perspective, is to be regarded merely as a framework for the idea of nobility of birth.[32] Although the compass of the present contribution precludes a treatment of such men as Matthias Ramung[33] and works like *De dignitate principum* by Petrus Antonius de Clapis,[34] or, for example, the very interesting collection of 118 books which Frederick bequeathed to his son Louis,[35] it is

[29] *Meines genedigen hern her Fridrichs pfalcz graven bei Rein teutscher poet und tichter*. For more detailed information see Müller, U., 'Michel Beheim', pp. 672-680 as well as MacDonald (W.C.), '*Whose Bread I Eat*'.

[30] Müller, 'Peter Luders Panegyricus', p. 293.

[31] Luder goes back to the time of the Frankish kings as the ancestors of the Bavarian House.

[32] *Felix Germanus, dum te domus alta tenebit/ Bavarie, vis te ledere nulla potest* quoted by Müller ('Der siegreiche Fürst', p. 35).

[33] Ramung was Frederick's chancellor from the second half of the 1450s. From 1464 he was bishop of Speyer. In Heidelberg Ramung supported the early humanists Peter Luder, Petrus Antonius de Clapis and the young Jacob Wimpfeling.

[34] In 1465 the lawyer and early humanistic poet Petrus Antonius de Clapis (d. 1512) came to Frederick's court. The year before he had sent the Elector his *laudatio*. For an assessment of the text as a specimen of humanistic thinking on education see Müller, 'Der siegreiche Fürst', pp. 38-39.

[35] These include classical texts such as Horace, *Ars poetica*; Cicero, *De Officiis*;

abundantly clear that at Heidelberg there was a stimulating and profitable combination of literary and public interest in the service of the legitimation of the Elector's rule.

Philip the Upright, Frederick's successor and nephew, has for long been considered the great humanist patron at Heidelberg.[36] While Philip's role is important in itself, the development of humanist and non-humanist literature must be seen against a more complex background, one which takes fully into account tradition and change, new developments and the revalorisation of old texts.

The claim of Heidelberg as the earliest humanist centre in the German-speaking world is, of course, based on the presence at the court of celebrated humanists and their works. Philip is traditionally held to be responsible for this development, since during his reign most of the humanists came to his court to become teachers of the Elector's sons. People like Conrad Celtis (1459-1508),[37] Johannes Reuchlin (1455-1522) and Adam Werner von Themar (1462-1537) gravitated there, as also Johann von Dalberg (1482-1503), whose merit it was, among other things, to be a great spreader of humanist ideas. It was at the latter's intitiative that Rudolf Agricola (1444-1485) came to Heidelberg in 1484.[38]

Celtis had fled to the university of Cologne in order not to have to become a wine-grower, and he was in 1477 the first German poet to become a *poeta laureatus*. He founded the literary circle *sodalitas litteraria rhenania* in Heidelberg, probably in 1495, after the example of comparable academic literary circles in Florence and Rome. In 1492 Celtis dedicated his *Panegyris ad duces bavariae* to Elector Philip in order to thank him for his help in gaining a professorship at Ingolstadt. Johannes Reuchlin was for a long time in the service of Eberhard of Württemberg, at Stuttgart. He came to the court of Heidelberg in 1497, where it was his duty to supervise the teachers of Philip's sons. In 1499 he went back to Stuttgart. It is not known whether he produced any texts. Adam Werner came to the court in 1484, left it in 1485, but returned in 1488 in order to teach the Elector's sons. After his study of the law, Werner became a member of Philip's law-court in 1498. He wrote more than

Boethius, commentary on Cicero, *Topica*, juridical texts (nos. 42, 44, 46) as well as songs and recipes in German (nos. 48, 49). For further information and the text of Frederick's testament see Berg and Bodemann, 'Wie ludwigen von Beyern'.

[36] Müller, ed, *Wissen für den Hof*, p. 13.

[37] For more information, see Backes, *Das literarische Leben*, pp. 151-152.

[38] Rudolf Agricola, the most famous representative of humanistic teaching north of the Alps, came to Heidelberg for an earlier visit in 1482. Although he died on 27 October 1485 he had been in Heidelberg only little more than a year. Nevertheless, Agricola's influence on the humanists can hardly be overestimated. See for recent information, Akkerman and Vanderjagt, eds, *Rodolphus Agricola Phrisius*.

150 Latin poems, most of them dedicated to humanist friends and acquaintances, and he also made translations of classical authors. He was the first to translate Virgil and Horace into German: two eclogues from the former's *Bucolics* and one of the latter's satires. He also translated the Alda-story by the Italian humanist Guarino Veronese. Johann von Dalberg, born in Oppenheim in 1455, studied in Erfurt, Pavia and Padua. He became the chancellor of the Electorate, and in 1482, bishop of Worms. He had connections with many humanists among whom, as has been mentioned, was Rudolf Agricola.

It is quite impossible here to give an adequate account of the importance of all these men for the development of humanist literature in the late fifteenth century. Despite this caveat, at least Jacob Wimpfeling deserves special mention. Wimpfeling (1450-1528) may be used to exemplify some of the problems which arise when it is claimed that all the writings of such men are strictly humanist.[39] He studied at Heidelberg from 1469 to 1483.[40] He returned there in 1498, when Philip promised him a professorship in the *Lectio humanitatis* in the new college of law. After three years, however, he left Heidelberg again, perhaps because the promise of an academic position had been an empty one.[41] Wimpfeling wrote educational and moralising treatises. These included the *Philippica*, dedicated to Philip's second son, Philip (1480-1541),[42] as well as his major work, *Agatharchia*.[43] A mirror for princes, this latter work is dedicated to Philip's eldest son Louis, Elector Palatine from 1508 till 1544. Not surprisingly, several more humanist and fatherly virtues are praised in this work, such as Philip's *affabilitas* and his *placabilitas*, as well as his interest in and promotion of the sciences. But although Wimpfeling is normally characterised as a humanist of the first rank, the text is on the whole more a product of the scholastic tradition than of humanism.[44] Singer wonders, in fact, whether Wimpfeling ought not better to be described as a 'scholastic under a cloak of humanism'.

[39] For more information see, for example, Backes, *Das literarische Leben*, pp. 138-142.

[40] In order to escape the plague he left in 1483 for Speyer, where he became a preacher at the cathedral.

[41] After his second stay in Heidelberg Wimpfeling worked as a teacher and writer in Basel, Freiburg and Strasbourg.

[42] This was written in August 1498 and recited in Heidelberg on 9 October 1498. See Singer, *Die Fürstenspiegel in Deutschland*, p. 176.

[43] Finished 18 October 1498.

[44] 'Der Fürst ist nicht im Sinn der Renaissance das große Individuum, das mit Taten für den Nachruhm sorgt, der Philosophenherrscher, der *Princeps optimus*, sondern der *Princeps bonus*, der mittelalterlich-christliche Herr' (Singer, *Die Fürstenspiegel in Deutschland*, pp. 196-199).

Although Conrad Celtis, for his part, has often been called the German 'Erzhumanist', his ideal of harmony is to be seen rather as a reconciliation of antiquity and christianity. According to Wuttke, Celtis is not concerned with the individual but, interested in making visible 'superindividual truth and/or the natural law'.[45] It might also be asked whether Philip himself was actually as influential in the cause of humanism as has been claimed. Philip himself attracted the attention of famous humanists to the court at Heidelberg, but the importance of bishop Johann von Dalberg in this matter should also not be underestimated. Furthermore, quite a few of the so-called humanists left Heidelberg after a relatively short period of time: for example, Wimpfeling left in 1501, Reuchlin in 1499, and Celtis in 1497.

The notion that one should not judge all that is written during Philip's reign from the single viewpoint of humanism is supported by Backes' survey.[46] This production is rather characterised by a variety of texts and genres: *artes*-literature with calendars and astronomical tables, mantic texts; short historical writings, didactic texts, advices for prayer and confession. Among the books on weapons, and especially, the treatises on warfare, Hans Lecküchner's treatise on the technique of fencing has recently been the subject of detailed analysis, with regard to the development of the transmission of such a treatise and the relationship between text and picture.[47] All such texts must be seen as part of the great mass of vernacular *Gebrauchstexte*, or pragmatic texts in the narrower sense of the word, produced at the Heidelberg court under the patronage of Frederick and Philip. In a broader sense, however, the label 'pragmatic' also includes fictional literature or *litterae bonae*. As in the Middle Ages, epic, romance, love lyric and allegory retain important pragmatic functions: they offer norms and orientation for behaviour and conduct, and they provide knowledge and specific – although differing – world views.[48]

With these considerations in mind, we may return to the romance *Die Kinder von Limburg* written by Johann von Soest.[49] This work reveals interesting information about the relationship between Philip the Upright and the author. In addition, however, the reception of this courtly romance seems to indicate that, besides the interest in humanism, there was also a clear in-

[45] Wuttke, 'Conradus Celtis Protucius', pp. 173-199, esp. p. 186. These examples of recent interpretations of texts by traditional humanists working at the Heidelberg court are mentioned in order to indicate the necessity of more detailed studies on various so-called humanist authors.
[46] Backes, *Das literarische Leben*.
[47] Müller, 'Hans Lecküchners Messerfechtlehre'.
[48] Müller, *Wissen für den Hof*, p. 14.
[49] See for a diplomatic edition of the text Klett, ed, *Johannes von Soest*.

terest in chivalric literature during Philip's reign. This interest deserves to be studied more closely.

Johann von Soest (1448-1506), born in Soest/Westphalia, became a singer as a young boy and worked in various places: Cleves, Bruges, Aardenburg (near Bruges), Maastricht, Cologne and Kassel. In 1472, under Elector Frederick, he was appointed choirmaster at the court of Heidelberg. In 1476, he started studying medicine at the university, only two weeks before Frederick's death. After more than twenty-three years of service at the Heidelberg court he became a doctor in Worms in 1495, in Oppenheim in 1499 and in Frankfurt a.M. in 1500, where he died in on May 2, 1506.[50]

The German romance *Die Kinder von Limburg*, comprising some 23000 verses, must have been written in the 1470s, since it was dedicated and presented to Philip in 1480. The only extant manuscript, indeed, is that very presentation text. Philip is addressed directly several times, for example in the prologues to book 6, 8 and 9: 'This take to your heart, my prince and lord, and do not despise my lesson' (9, 19-20). The romance may be interpreted as a typical example of literature within the context of the 'help for life' (in German: 'Lebenshilfe'), a term used by Hugo Kuhn to label the function of most literature in the fifteenth century. Right from the beginning, the author of the *Limburg* romance leaves no doubt that he wants the poem to be understood as a text with an abundance of good teaching in it (*hubschen leren*, 1, 29-32). The manuscript includes many visual aids, including hands with the index-fingers drawing attention to important parts of the text, *nota bene* signs, or red lines drawn next to the text, especially at those parts containing strong moralising or advice.[51]

The German romance *Die Kinder von Limburg* is in fact an adaptation of the Dutch verse romance, *Roman van Heinric ende Margriete van Limborch*, completed at the beginning of the fourteenth century. The original version has been preserved in two manuscripts. The first is a manuscript in Brabantish (A) from the first half of the fourteenth century.[52] A second complete manuscript

[50] For more information about Johann von Soest see his own autobiography in Von Fichard, 'Gedichte Johanns von Soest', pp. 75-153; Bonath, 'Johann von Soest', pp. 744-755; Heimann, 'Stadtbürgerliches Selbstverständnis', pp. 239-262; Pietzsch, *Quellen und Forschungen zur Geschichte der Musik*; Pietzsch, 'Soest, Johann', pp. 824-825; Schläder, 'Johann von Soest', pp. 25-43; Von Bahder, ed,'Johann von Soest', pp. 129-158. See also the recent study by Von Santen, *Die Person Johanns von Soest*, and Schlusemann, 'Selbstbekenntnis bei Johann von Soest'.

[51] See for example, Klett, ed, *Johannes von Soest*, book 10, pp. 692-693; book 10, pp. 1082-1083. On prologues in general, see Sonnemans, *Functionele aspecten van Middelnederlandse versprologen*.

[52] Edited in a diplomatic edition by Van den Bergh, *Roman van Heinric ende Margriete*. For more information about the manuscript tradition of the Dutch version

(B) is a word by word translation into Ripuarian dialect.[53] This manuscript preserves the text of the Dutch original even better than manuscript A, and can therefore be called the best representative of the Dutch version.[54] In the following, the Dutch version will be quoted according to the Ripuarian manuscript.

A comparison of two of the eleven books of the Dutch and the German versions shows that the German text makes the didactic moralisation most explicit: in book ten, a mirror for princes, Jonas, the servant, arrives at the castle of Adventure, where an allegory of virtues is presented to him. He is taught the good characteristics of a king and the right manner of reigning. After this introduction the four different kinds of king are described (706-735), and a summary of the most important qualities of a king is given, with truth as ultimately the most important of these. Up to this part, the Dutch and German texts are very similar. From then on, however, in the German adaptation more than 250 verses are added (799-1067), which most explicitly describe daily life at court. These are combined with advice to the prince, especially as to how to handle his employees: the poor faithful servants (804-815), the civil servants (816-867), the priests (868-869), the singers (870-963) and the valets (964-1005). The narrator not only describes correct courtly behaviour and the right way to reign, but he also gives concrete advice to the Elector about daily practice at the court. All in all, the patron's shortcomings are emphasised and the Elector, who is addressed directly several times, is warned to take strong measures should the people abuse their positions.[55]

A second major didactic tendency evident in the German adaptation could be called the condemnation of different kinds of love, or the defence of chastity. Book seven deals with the adulterous relationship between Evax, one of the main figures, and Sibille, queen of Aragon. In the prologue to this book, Johann tells the reader that he should understand book seven as a negative example:

> You should learn by this how you can resist someone who lusts after you – that you are not dishonoured, just as Sibilla the queen was honoured by

see Kienhorst, *De handschriften van de Middelnederlandse ridderepiek* and De Wachter and Schlusemann *et al.*, eds, *Fragmenten van de 'Roman van Heinric ende Margriete van Limborch'*.

[53] Edited by Meesters, *Roman van Heinric ende Margriete.*

[54] For more information about this matter see De Haan, 'De Roman van Heinric en Margriete van Limborch', pp. 139-155; Schlusemann, 'Een kopiist als redacteur'. On the problem of whether to characterise the Ripuarian text as German or Dutch see Klein, 'Die Rezeption mittelniederländischer Verdichtung im Rheinland'.

[55] See also Bonath and Brunner, 'Die Kinder von Limburg', pp. 129-152.

> Venus's love. This should be an example to you; do not let your temple be destroyed, lest your body and soul be ruined altogether. (7, 18-26).

A little later, Johann adds in his adaptation:

> I ask you, lords and ladies all, if you intend to be pure, do not let trouble overrun you, but shun those who treat you wrongly and who betray you. For, if you are not full of pity, you are not worth a penny. For my sake, take queen Sibilla as an example! Do not let yourselves be seduced in such a manner by any pleasure. You are too highly born for that. The game would be totally lost. (book 7, 1627-1640).

This second quotation mentions different important ways in which the text should, according to the author, be read by the sovereign and other princes. It is useful as an instruction in the following qualities: pureness, attention to falseness and betrayal, piety and fear of God, condemnation of Sibilla's behaviour, and responsibility for noble descent. With regard to the matter of love, the Dutch and German text show completely different attitudes:

Roman van Heinric ende Margriete van Limborch	*Kinder von Limburg*
Help, what does love do! Her power is not small That she led the chosen knight to such a loss. was so brave in his deeds ... Venus, lady, why do you separate courtly people? (B 6, 1469-1478)	Here you see what the power of Venus is able to do. By the contract the queen became a poor whore, she who was previously so good. (7, 1503-1506)

In the Dutch version, Venus's power is made responsible, but in the German text adulterous lovers are condemned. It seems that the power of love is the most important aspect in the Dutch romance. First of all, it causes men to become real knights. Secondly, it turns foreigners into neighbours: this is the message expressed in book twelve, when some of the Saracens become Christians in order to be able to marry their beloveds. Thirdly, in the Dutch version, love serves as an allegory for the uselessness of war. In the game 'le roi qui ne ment', played in book eleven,[56] those who have not yet succeeded

[56] For a more elaborate discussion of the differences between the Dutch and German versions with regard to the concept of love, see Schlusemann, 'das yr begyr wolt

in conquering their beloveds with weapons should not use violence, but be humble and show their tears and sighs (11, 541-552). Book twelve tells us that trying to win a woman with violence is as useless as using war to pursue one's political aims. Is it not possible that the association of love and war attracted the Elector's interest? With these and other changes, the author of the German version moved from the discussion on courtly love, present in his source, to a judgement and condemnation of several forms of love. In the Dutch source the ambivalence between the theory (book eleven) and the practice of love (book twelve) is discussed thoroughly. The ambivalence between these poles, which forms the core of the Dutch epic, Johann von Soest presents from the point of view of society. For Bonath and Brunner 'courtly ideality and representation' and the duty of giving good and concrete advice are one of the things expected of the sovereign: namely, the representation of nobility. In this kind of literature, they claim, the awareness of the exclusivity of status was propagated.[57]

While this affirmation is of course, on the whole, true, Bonath and Brunner incorrectly identify the author's intention, as expressed in comments and moralising passages, with the patron's intention and with the function that the text was to have at court when the Elector ordered the translation. It is not credible that Philip ordered the adaptation of the Dutch romance, with special instructions to add this strong criticism of himself and with so much overt moralising.[58] Philip might have known about the romance in its Dutch version via his aunt Mathilda, Frederick's sister, who was known for her interest in romance. The Dutch manuscript, owned by Mathilda, may have been the source for the Ripuarian version in manuscript B and even also the source for Johann von Soest's adaptation of the text into Middle High German.[59] It is certain that the Ripuarian manuscript and the German manuscript by Johann von Soest had a common predecessor. According to the *Ehrenbrief* by Püterich von Reichertshausen (1462),[60] the Dutch work was one of the twenty-three manuscripts in Mathilda's library about which Püterich had not previously known.[61] Philip might have known about the text as a consequence

halten reyn'.

[57] Bonath and Brunner, 'Die Kinder von Limburg', p. 152.

[58] Schlusemann, '*das yr begyr wolt halten reyn*'.

[59] Beckers, '*Der püecher haubet*', pp. 17-47; De Haan, '"De Roman van Heinric en Margriete van Limborch"', who supports Beckers' idea. For a discussion of the hypothesis and the role that Wirich VI von Daun zu Oberstein might have played in this matter see Schlusemann, 'Literarische Vernetzung'.

[60] See Berend and Wolkan, eds, *Der Ehrenbrief des Jakob Püterich von Reichertshausen*; Goette, *Der Ehrenbrief des Jakob Püterich*; and Kultur-stiftung, eds, *Jacob Püterich*.

[61] Kulturstiftung, eds, *Jacob Püterich*, Strophen 98 and 99; Duijvestijn, 'Nieder-

of good family relationships between aunt and nephew. There were also at least two occasions in 1474 at which he could have heard the text: at the occasion of his own wedding with Margaret of Bavaria-Landshut in February 1474, and that of Mathilda's son, count Eberhard of Württemberg, to margravine Barbara of Mantua in Urach in July of the same year. It is known that the wedding mass on the latter occasion was sung by Philip's choir. The Dutch *Limborch* romance might have been read or (re)told during one or both of these occasions. This in itself may be enough to explain Philip's interest in the text. Furthermore, there are at least three elements in the romance which could have attracted the latter's attention. First, the main female figure is called Margaret, the name of his wife. Second, many tournaments take place in the romance, and Philip was renowned for his horsemanship and his skills in tournament. He even twice besieged Emperor Maximilian. Third, the romance starts with a hunting-party, which initiates the action of the romance. Philip's addiction to all kinds of hunting was likewise famous, contrary to the picture presented by Stammler.

Philip, who, as it was shown, knew the contents of the romance as it was preserved in Mathilda's manuscript, may have ordered the translation, but it is not likely that he commissioned the adaptation in the form we now know it.[62] Johann himself frequently uses the word *transferyren* to characterise his use of the source. Nevertheless, Johann von Soest obviously could not restrain himself from tampering with the contents, commenting on good and bad behaviour and explicitly criticising his patron. Johann is known for his stubborn and self-willed character. As was said above, two weeks before Frederick's death, in 1476, he began to study medicine at the university of Heidelberg, doubtless in order to have the possibility of leaving the court again later. In 1495, in fact, he settled as a doctor in Worms. After a quarrel with the singers of the Elector's choir Johann was thrown into prison by Philip who, in 1485, took back the estates he had bestowed upon Johann. Thus the relationship between the Elector and his choirmaster was not without its tensions.

Another argument for the hypothesis that Philip may have ordered this translation must be viewed in the context of the literary production at the court of Heidelberg. The *Limburg*-romance, as an adaptation of a Dutch work, is a striking exception within the overall reception of literature at the court during Philip's reign. The other German translations of Dutch originals are faithful translations of their sources,[63] as has been pointed out in detail by

ländische Dichtung', p. 25; De Haan, '"De Roman van Heinric en Margriete van Limborch"', p. 153.

[62] Schlusemann, *'das yr begyr wolt halten reyn'*.

[63] Duijvestijn, 'Middelnederlandse literatuur in Duitse overlevering', pp. 153-168; Beckers, 'Frühneuhochdeutsche Fassungen'. For a more detailed discussion on the

Duijvestijn for the *Malagis*.[64] The same can be said of *Reinolt von Montelban*,[65] *Ogier von Dänemark*[66] and the prose-*Lancelot*.[67] Moreover, certain Middle High German texts were merely copied at the court in the last quarter of the fifteenth century: Heinrich von dem Türlin, *Der aventiure crone*[68]; Hartmann von Aue, *Iwein*[69]; and a huge collection (more than 28000 verses) of fifty-six treatises on love, or *Minnereden*.[70] The latter has been characterised as the most important volume of this genre, but it has never been studied as a whole.[71]

With this in mind, it is necessary to search in the Dutch version, as representated by the Ripuarian manuscript, for the interests of the maecenas in the *Limburg*-romance. Moreover, this is the closest to Johann's source, with which it shares a common predecessor. Of the texts translated from Dutch into German at the Heidelberg court, most can, like the Dutch *Limborch*-text, be characterised as discourses on courtly love. In such works, special attention is paid to the conflict between inward feelings of love and love that is influenced by the outer norms of society.

Should we, then, see the production of the *Limburg*-romance and other romance texts at the Heidelberg court as exemplifying a renaissance of chivalry and a renewal of old ideals? Is it an indicator of aristocratic attitudes, or of the awareness of status on the part of the nobility? In this context, another factor deserves to be taken into consideration. The contemporary transmission and production of 'old' and 'new' texts, of texts going back to antiquity and others from the High Middle Ages, of humanist and non-humanist literature, testifies to a late fifteenth-century consciousness of literary tradition, to which one might attach the label of 'Renaissance'. Philip could be regarded almost as a publisher – someone who would give old books a

translation techniques from Dutch into German in the late Middle Ages see Schlusemann and Wackers, eds, *Die spätmittelalterliche Rezeption niederländischer Literatur*.

[64] Ms. Heidelberg, UB, Cod. pal. germ. 340, c. 1476 and Cod. pal. germ. 315, c. 1480. See Haase, Duijvestijn, *et al.*, eds, *Der deutsche Malagis*; Duijvestijn, *Der deutsche und der niederländische 'Malagis'*; Duijvestijn, '"Uss dem flemischen"', pp. 111-134.

[65] Ms. Heidelberg, UB, Cod. pal. germ. 340, c. 1476 as well as Cod. pal. germ. 399, c. 1480.

[66] Ms. Heidelberg, UB, Cod. pal. germ. 363, 9 February 1479.

[67] Ms. Heidelberg, UB, Cod. pal. germ 147. Schlusemann, 'The Late Medieval Reception of Dutch Arthurian Literature'.

[68] Ms. Heidelberg, UB, Cod. pal. germ. 374, 1479, copied by Ludwig Flugel.

[69] Ms. Heidelberg, UB, Cod. pal. germ. 316.

[70] Ms. Heidelberg, UB, Cod. pal. germ. 313.

[71] Its position with regard to typology and tradition has been compared to that of the Manesse manuscript for the *Minnesang*. See Glier, *Artes amandi*.

new cover or would arrange for the publication of editions and translations of old but still interesting subjects. As it happens, this literature could also be pressed into service for contemporary pragmatic purposes, as was the case with the humanist texts under Frederick and the *Limburg* romance under Philip. If Philip can be viewed somewhat in the role of a publisher, it should no longer be thought surprising that he fostered humanist literature, *artes*-literature or *Gebrauchsliteratur* side by side with fictional literature, such as romances. The latter functioned as self-representation of the nobility, and the life depicted in that literature was imitated in the tournaments which were held at the court of Heidelberg, for example during the great tournament in 1481.[72] On one folio, the German *Limburg* romance produced for Philip has a dedication page, which shows the author Johann von Soest handing over his manuscript to the Elector. This page, drawn by a famous artist, imparts to the manuscript a somewhat exclusive character, in its representation of a new princely ideal.[73] This, admittedly is hypothetical, and one would have to test it through a study of several relevant texts within the context of the production and function of literature at the Heidelberg court in the second half of the fifteenth century. The intertextual relations of such texts, their respective functions, and the interests of the patrons should all be taken into account in research into the actual use of the texts within everyday historical practice.

The examples selected here to illustrate Frederick's patronage seem to suggest that he was a sovereign who had a principal interest in 'static' humanist literature, especially to legitimise his reign and his politics. Nevertheless, one should not forget that his doctor, Heinrich Münsinger, advised him to listen to histories (stories), and that Hermann von Sachsenheim described him as a lover of chivalric romance. The traditional view of his successor Philip as patron of humanist literature is too narrow and too simplistic. Although it is unlikely that the latter promoted the production of literature to legitimate his reign, it is probable that he favoured the production for the representation of the splendour of his court and his power as Elector, and also to promote various kinds of princely behaviour and practice. A close analysis of the several sorts of literature, especially the medieval fictional texts, reproduced, translated or adapted at the court during his reign, should shed more light on the functioning of such texts as well as on Philip's intentions and interests. In the late Middle Ages the court remained both a political and a cultural centre, and in that centre politics impinged on the acceptance of renaissance novelties and the publication of the literary past.

[72] Rüxner, *Anfang* [...] *des Thurniers*, pp. 214-246.

[73] The name of the artist is not known but the consensus is that it was the work of the *Meister des mittelalterlichen Hausbuchs*. See Hess, *Meister um das "mittelalterliche Hausbuch"*. See fol. 6[+].

THE COURT OF EMPEROR MAXIMILIAN I

Jan-Dirk Müller

How should we define the court of Emperor Maximilian I? If we define 'court' as the idea of a permanent residence with a certain life-style or a relatively fixed personnel, then the court of Maximilian did not exist. Like his medieval predecessors, Maximilian ruled by travelling all over the Empire accompanied by his government apparatus and the royal household. Although his father, Frederick III, did not leave his Austrian territories very often, especially towards the end of his reign, the 'actual residence' of Maximilian 'was the saddle'.[1] Maximilian is as it were on the turning-point dividing medieval 'travelling kingship' [*Reisekönigstum*] and early modern government from the princely capital [*Residenz*]. Maximilian's grandson Ferdinand I was the first Emperor to draw his power from his ancestral estates [*Erblande*], and from that time onwards Vienna (and for a time Prague) became the centre of Empire politics as well as the residence of the Habsburgs.

Maximilian's 'court' was an open system to and from which princes from the various territories of the Empire, their officials, nobleman knights [*Ritter*], representatives of the free cities and the envoys of foreign powers came and went. Even the central parts of Maximilian's own government apparatus fluctuated strongly, in composition as well as total number. He did not desire to attract as many people as possible to his court – as absolutist princes in later times tended to do – nor did he have the ambition to regulate them, for that would have been costly. The size of his household never exceeded that of a powerful territorial prince [*Landesfürst*] – for example, that of his uncle and predecessor Siegmund of the Tyrol – and it was noticeably smaller than that of Duke Charles of Burgundy, whose heiress he had married. Only under Ferdinand I would the imperial court reach the size

[1] Wiesflecker, *Kaiser Maximilian I.*, vol. 5, p. 380; in general for this: *Maximilian I. 1459-1959*; Müller, *Gedechtnus*; Maximilian was never crowned Emperor by the pope, but allowed himself to be proclaimed Emperor at Trent in 1508. Until that moment, his correct title would be 'king'. A number of statements below refer to him both before *and* after 1508; hence the title 'Emperor' will be used throughout this article.

of the former Burgundian household.[2] The Emperor even met his death while travelling in the Upper-Austrian Wels.

There were quite a number of centres, such as the free imperial cities [*Reichsstädte*], from which Maximilian reigned for longer periods (e.g. Augsburg, Strasburg, Cologne), or the larger cities of his territories, which served him for a time as residences (especially Innsbruck). But often the centre of imperial politics and the court were separated; as a result, the territorial bureaucracies of the *Erblande*, were often burdened with affairs of imperial government, depending on where the Emperor happened to be staying. The *Erblande* disintegrated into a group of Upper-Austrian territories with Innsbruck as their centre, and a Lower-Austrian group centred on Vienna. In addition, there were the centres of the Burgundian territories, where Maximilian ruled not by his own authority but by that of his son or grandson. The imperial city of Augsburg was an important focal point of Empire politics. Its town clerk [*Stadtschreiber*] Konrad Peutinger was keeper of Maximilian's imperial and personal seals while the Emperor was absent; he coordinated Maximilian's policies, public relations and intelligence-gathering, and directed his scientific and artistic projects. As imperial councillor [*Rat*] he belonged to the king's most important advisors. Thus the 'court' was scattered over many places and associated with different groups of people.

The image of the court and courtly society, however, had changed significantly over the past decades. We no longer assume that during the later Middle Ages and the beginnings of the early modern era courts were definitive, institutionalised structures which were fixed spatially and architecturally, which cultivated certain ways of life, and which were closed, fully rationalised and fully functionalised systems.[3] Such were the views of the sociologists of courtly society during the age of absolutism. We rather expect courts to be more or less open, fluctuating associations of people in close proximity to the sovereign, which were more or less governed by ceremony, where there existed different restrictions on access to the sovereign, which were to greater or lesser degree organised hierarchically, and which were only in the long run clearly distinguished from the administrative and judicial institutions of the princely territorial state. If the absolutist courts were already complex and manifold constructs, this was even more true for the constitutive phase around 1500, when the institutionalisation

[2] Wiesflecker, *Kaiser Maximilian I.*, vol. 5, pp. 381ff.; Niderkorn, *Der Hof*; Moraw, *The Court*.

[3] Crucial studies are: Elias, *Die höfische Gesellschaft*, and Von Kruedener, *Die Rolle des Hofes*; see also the critical discussion by Bauer, *Die höfische Gesellschaft*, pp. 9-53.

and differentiation of the personnel around the sovereign according to rank and function was beginning to be established in patterns that would come to be characteristic of the seventeenth and eighteenth centuries. Maximilian's court belonged in this constitutive phase, and it was thus marked by a lack of differentiation between personnel, between imperial and territorial tasks, and between bureaucracy and representation.

The centre of the court was not the band of feudal followers of the sovereign, but his government agencies. Throughout his reign Maximilian was busy reorganising the latter; despite this, his reforms consistently failed, partly because of a failure of persistence, partly because of a lack of money.[4] It is rather revealing that Wiesflecker's monumental biography does not include a section on court and court society under Maximilian; it does, however, include one with the title 'Der Kaiserhof. Hof- und Reichsregierung' [The Imperial Court. The Government of Court and Empire], the greatest part of which deals with the officials in the Empire and the territories.[5] Only later (pp. 380-409) are we informed about daily life at court with its festivities [Das Hofleben. Alltag und Festkultur], in a chapter containing a mass of historico-cultural details. Maximilian's court was untypical of either feudal society or absolutist aristocracy.

As Roman King under his father, Emperor Frederick III, Maximilian managed with only one chancery. As ruler of the Tyrol (from 1490) and later also of Lower-Austria, he used the institutions already existing there, though one should not attach too much importance to their special status and institutional consolidation.[6] The Tyrol supplied a large number of some of the most important men around Maximilian. The relations between the sovereign and the estates, despite the controversies that occasionally arose, did not affect the functionality of the territorial government but the antagonism between the imperial estates [*Reichsstände*] and the Executive [*Reichs[spitze]regiment*] led to considerable tensions. The imperial chancery [*Reichskanzlei*] or Roman chancery, which was dominated by the estates under the archbishop of Mainz as imperial chancellor [*Erzkanzler*], was opposed by Maximilian's own Privy Council [*Hofrat*], which operated in Maximilian's vicinity, and which had the Upper House [*Hofkammer*] and court chancery [*Hofkanzlei*] subordinate to it. The tensions would increase

[4] On this, see Noflatscher, *Räte*; Kögl, *Studien über das niederösterreichische Regiment unter Maximilian I.*, pp. 48-74 as well as numerous monographs from the school of Wiesflecker (mostly in the form of typed dissertations).

[5] Wiesflecker, *Kaiser Maximilian I.*, vol. 5, pp. 220-305; especially pp. 220-279 (officials); only towards the end briefly dealing with mail, archive, library and Treasury; pp. 279-293 (Council, Upper House, and Chancery), pp. 293-296 (Mails); pp. 296-305 (Archives, Portraits and Treasury).

[6] Kögl, *Studien*, p. 50.

in the years after the Diet of Worms (1495), with the conflict lasting from about 1495 to 1502; in these years the estates temporarily gained the upper hand, though eventually the royal ministries asserted themselves. Maximilian's Privy Council usually followed the court, but sometimes it was separated from it and would remain in one place for a longer period of time; for example, in the late 1490s it remainded in Innsbruck.[7] The court chancery, which was subordinate to the Privy Council, and which originally dealt with matters concerning Maximilian as territorial prince, came to deal also with affairs of the Empire, just like the imperial chancery. The division between government institutions run by the prince and those run by the estates was not always effective. There were disputes over respective areas of responsibility, and various attempts were made to define clear borderlines, but finally the estates had to abandon their plan of a council and a government which could have functioned largely independently of Maximilian – although they never accepted Maximilian's Privy Council as an independent authority. Several unsuccessful attempts at reform were made before 1518, but from 1502 onwards Maximilian's court chancery had been the decisive government institution for the Empire.

After the chancery, the financial administration [*Schatzkammer*, *Raitkammer*, *Hofkammer* and others] was most in significance. Everything that needed financial expenditure fell under its responsibilities: law courts, public finances, the military, care of royal property, maintenance of royal castles, implementation of royal instructions. Especially influential was the Innsbruck Chamber under Paul von Liechtenstein, which was frequently entrusted with affairs that did not concern the territory, but Maximilian as German king. Here, too, the area of the competence between the different offices and their officials overlapped; members of the chancery were often concerned with questions of finance, as were other servants [*Diener*] in Maximilian's vicinity. Yet, the many efforts to reform the different institutions of administration proved a need for better defined duties.

In the multifarious and rapidly changing institutions members of the old nobility worked next to social climbers who had qualified themselves through their specialised knowledge. Maximilian's retinue included princes of the Empire [*Reichsfürsten*], prelates, members of princely houses, counts, knights of the Empire, envoys of the imperial cities and foreign envoys who happened to be present. All these people could likewise be entrusted with tasks by the Emperor. Initially there were princes of the Empire and other high-ranking dignitaries among the twelve members of Maximilian's Privy

[7] Moser, *Die Kanzlei Kaiser Maximilians I*; for the organisation in general, see Heinig, 'Theorie und Praxis'; Moraw, 'Organisation'; Noflatscher, *Räte*.

Council. Elector Duke Frederick the Wise of Saxony was occasionally at its head, although he left court in 1499 after a dispute with the Emperor. From then on the number and influence of the aristocratic members gradually diminished in favour of advisers of non-aristocratic origin, who were responsible to Maximilian. Gradually the princes of the Empire and the members of their houses were displaced from the inner circle of government. Over the years Maximilian relied increasingly on the aristocracy of his own territories [*Erblande*], and on councillors and secretaries who were schooled in law, humanist rhetoric or chancery activities, and who stemmed especially from the Habsburg territories, and the neighbouring southern-German area; for foreign languages he relied on secretaries from Burgundy or Italy. For the offices of his own territories he chose especially the nobility, clergy and other natives of these lands. But distinctions between the different groups are artificial; the different governmental institutions always remained interpenetrable as to personnel. Very often an official who proved himself in territorial politics would be given an appointment close to the Emperor; when this in turn led to social advancement and the conferment of aristocratic titles or benefices in the Empire, that did not in any way rule out subsequent activity in the service of the Emperor's own lands.

Around the core of government were councillors from the different territories or cities of the Empire who were only intermittently called to court.[8] An appointment as imperial councillor [*Rat*] was supposed to bind influential politicians of the Empire to the ruler. Often nothing more than the title of councillor or one-off service was all that would be involved, but in other cases the nomination would be the beginning of a longer collaboration. It seems, however, that the sovereign took it for granted that he could call these people whenever he needed them, especially from the free imperial cities, whose nominal head the Emperor was. Altogether the subjects of his own territories, who came from the Habsburg territorial authorities, were more influential. Although they would often continue to work in the service of the latter regions, Maximilian regularly employed them to deal with imperial affairs. This was especially true for that group of officials whom Maximilian found as an 'Austrian party' at the court at Innsbruck, when he took over the Tyrol following the abdication of his uncle Siegmund.

In this respect, too, the 'court' was an open system, not an exclusive formation. And if it is already difficult clearly to distinguish between the staff of the different authorities, it is almost impossible to determine which group of people could actually be counted as belonging to the court. In ad-

[8] Gatt, *Der Innsbrucker Hof*, p. 113. At the end of his government Maximilian ordered a list of all men appointed as councillors, but this aim proved to be almost unattainable (cf. Heinig,' Theorie und Praxis').

dition to those already mentioned one must also consider the hangers-on, the domestic staff who belonged to the royal household, and the servants and amanuenses of the noble courtiers or the non-aristocratic office bearers. It is therefore difficult to talk about a court society in respect to this heterogeneous group of people. Crucial was the proximity to the ruler, and the persons surrounding him tend to be recognised as belonging to the court.[9] Maximilian's government represented in type the 'personal rule' which was predominant in the sixteenth century.[10] It is also true that the Emperor, to the distress of those close to him, preferred to do everything himself. In this respect the court is perhaps best described as the 'surroundings of the ruler'

Thus Maximilian's court was by no means dominated by the aristocracy. Even his interest in chivalric orders was inspired by military and financial aims. The order of St George, which he especially promoted, had no influence at court and was not exclusive to the nobility. It was more an instrument designed for the financing of and recruitment for, the planned war against the Turks. Later the order was given the task of maintaining the cult at Maximilian's grave. If we exclude the princes of the Empire and their entourage then we find that the nobility of the Habsburg lands and other territories, who were all trying to catch Maximilian's attention, found themselves in almost the same situation as the non-aristocratic advisers of the prince; for all of these, service at court offered a chance to rise out of small, urban or half-rural conditions, and their career at court could begin with very subordinate tasks.[11] Both would be similarly rewarded with estates, castles, income from feudal rights, trusteeships, ecclesiastical benefices, shares in salt, silver or copper mines, aristocratic titles, advantageous marriage alliances, etc. While commoners were often elevated to aristocratic status, with their families in the next generation blending in with the landed nobility, noblemen would be rewarded for their services – not the least of which consisted of military commands – with an improvement in their position in the hierarchy of the landed estates, and a commensurate increase in property. Some of these nobles, like Siegmund von Dietrichstein, were so successful that they surpassed the most powerful aristocratic houses in their homelands. Service to the Emperor (who was the most powerful prince in the southeast and southwest of the Empire) often opened up access to lucrative ecclesiastical benefices: bishoprics, prebends, canonries, etc.

Society in the first half of the sixteenth century was changing; class distinctions were losing a part of their former meaning, and the lifestyles of the respective groups who had influence with Maximilian – nobles, clergy,

[9] Lotz, *Am Hof Kaiser Maximilians I*, p. 1.

[10] Oestreich, 'Das persönliche Regiment der deutschen Fürsten', pp. 201-234.

[11] Hyden, *Zyprian von Serntein*, p. 2.

rich burghers, secretaries – were blending in many respects. This can be demonstrated through a study of the biographies of individuals. There were marriage alliances between families of noble and of common origins, which ignored class distinctions. The court chancellor, Dr Konrad Stürzel, who came from Kitzingen, attained a respected position among the Breisgau knights, while his son, though a doctor of canon law, already behaved like a member of the landed gentry.[12] A politician such as Siegmund von Dietrichstein, who came from small nobility in Carinthia, was advanced to the status of baron, and became the head [*Landeshauptmann*] of the provincial government of the Steiermark; he also busied himself as supplier of weapons and cattle dealer and regarded feudal holdings and rights from the point of view of their profitability.[13] In general, bishoprics and abbeys were taxed according to their annual income and distributed among loyal servants. Important financiers, such as the Fuggers, became Counts of Kirchberg; bishop Thurzo was a mining entrepreneur, as was the imperial treasurer, Jakob Villinger. Other prelates, such as Melchior of Meckau were more likely to be involved in financial affairs, as shareholders of the Fuggers. The trade in silver, cattle, cloth and soap together with the mining of coal and iron, etc. were all sources of supplementary income for the powerful people at court. Some of them would invest their personal fortune in advantageous loans to the Emperor, and – albeit at a significant risk – would attempt to make a profit from the dismal financial situation of the sovereign.

A special group was formed by scholars like Konrad Stürtzel, Sebastian Sprentz, Jakob de Banissis, Petrus and Franciscus Bonomus, Johannes Cuspinianus, Jakob Spiegel and others. The majority of the latter, though by no means all of them, chose a clerical career and were rewarded with ecclesiastical benefices; it was particularly the group of lawyers that was becoming increasingly more important. It is difficult to define clearly the tasks of the scholars in general, since they were specialists in 'communication', who could be used for all sorts of affairs. The most influential of them were imperial councillors and were concerned with diplomatic affairs or legal transactions; however, they would also have been consulted for other tasks, such as researching the genealogy of the Habsburgs, developing dynastic plans or offering advice on artistic projects. Scholars would be involved in anything to do with knowledge. On various occasions the estates protested against their influence. The most important of the scholars might even be ennobled – sometimes, as in the case of Matthäus Lang, along with his entire family – so that they would be able to compete with the old ruling estates at court.

[12] Bücking, 'Das Geschlecht der Stürtzel', p. 250ff.
[13] Von Moltke, *Siegmund von Dietrichstein*.

Besides these officials, who wielded significant political influence, there was a host of *literati* who sought alimentation and advancement at Maximilian's court and whose skills were in demand for his literary propaganda: the abbot Johannes Trithemius, the 'arch poet' Konrad Celtis, the astronomer and historian Johannes Stabius or the many orators and poets at imperial assemblies or other representative occasions.[14] Sometimes they actually found employment in the chancery, but sometimes they would only claim to be *a secretis*, i.e. serving Maximilian as secretary. Especially when they had not yet gained a foothold at court they would use pompous titles such as *Kayserlicher Maiestat cappelan, historicus* and *astronomus* [chaplain, historian and astronomer of his Imperial Majesty] (Joseph Grünpeck) to draw attention to themselves.[15] Most of the scholars saw themselves as followers of the Roman rhetoricians; they aligned themselves with the new humanism and defined their high social status through their erudition. *Arma et litterae*, a 'chivalrous' and 'literary' qualification, was propagated equally as occupations of the prince and his surroundings. With many of the court *literati* this remained mere pretence, since their self-esteem did not reflect either their actual status or their influence. Yet, *studia humanitatis* was believed to be an equivalent counterweight to noble origin. Humanist education frequently served as decoration for non-aristocratic social climbers. Thus a book of panegyrical humanist poetry dedicated to the secretary and financier Blasius Hölzl was celebrated by the *docti* as a *specimen* of humanist culture at the imperial court and the addressee himself was accepted as a member of humanist élite, although Hölzl could hardly be counted as a humanist poet. Rather, he had already attained a social position of which the poets could only dream.[16] Cardinal Lang, from an Augsburg burgher family, surrounded himself with secretaries who had literary ambitions, such as Ricardo Bartolini or Caspar Ursinus Velius, and allowed himself to be praised in panegyrics by a member of the University of Vienna. Furthermore, men like Laurenz Saurer[17] from a middle-class background, or Florian Waldauf from a rural background, emerged as patrons of humanist literati.

A rigid distinction of professions, however, was still missing among the different occupations at court:[18] the cook was also occasionally employed as a courier (or vice versa), the musician or merchant or prince of the Empire

[14] Mertens, 'Reichstag'.
[15] Schack, *Der Kreis um Maximilian I.*, p. 21.
[16] *Complurium eruditorum uatum carmina.*
[17] He was first factor of the court dressmakers (Wiesflecker, *Kaiser Maximilian I.*, vol. 5, p. 266).
[18] Gollwitzer, 'Zur Geschichte der Diplomatie', p. 189.

as diplomat, the senior territorial official [*Landeshauptmann*] as poet, the town clerk as historian, the court painter as commissioner of buildings, and so forth.[19] But on the whole, the experts in government affairs, especially in the chancery, were advancing. There was competition, moreover, between the different groups. The dispute between Maximilian and the influential elector Duke Frederick the Wise, which led to the latter's retreat from court, was welcome news to the less distinguished advisors in the circle around Maximilian – such as the bourgeois Matthäus Lang, the later bishop of Gurk (Carinthia) and cardinal archbishop of Salzburg, or the court chancellor Cyprian of Northeim, called Sernteiner, who came from the Sarntal north of Bolzano – since it boosted their influence.[20] The traditional hierarchies of the estates were turned upside-down by new differentiations determined by function, in which proximity to the Emperor was more important than inherited rank. Many a secretary of humble origins had more influence than the offspring of the old territorial nobility. Thus there were frequent disputes about status, and some of these can still be documented.[21] Some of Maximilian's most important advisers seemed to be *parvenus* to the old noble elite, and like *parvenus* they were busy to enrich themselves and unscrupulously pursue benefices. Lang and Serntein belonged to this group, and nothing worked without them at Maximilian's court. Their advancement resulted in snobbery of a new sort: when Lang became prince of the Empire after many failed attempts as bishop of Gurk, he instructed that in correspondence addressed to him the title '*Fürst*' [prince] should not be forgotten.[22]

It was not easy to command attention in the intrigues around the Emperor; people talked of a 'hedge' of favourites, which even the highest dignitaries of the Empire and foreign envoys had to struggle through, should they wish to be admitted to Maximilian.[23] In principle, however, access was not exclusive and – unlike the customs of absolutist courts – it was not controlled by complicated ceremonial. Maximilian set great store on being accessible to all. When Weisskunig was reproached for his excessive passion for hunting, he replied that

> *du bist wider dich selbs, dann wann ich nit an der valkenpaiß rit, darann jederman zu mir kumen mag, so rittest du jetzo nit neben mir, du hettest auch auf*

[19] Lotz, *Am Hof Kaiser Maximilians I*, p. 7.
[20] Hyden, *Zyprian von Serntein*, p. 65.
[21] Schubert, 'Blasius Hölzl'.
[22] Legers, 'Kardinal Matthäus Lang', p. 483. For a similar the concern about prestige see the case of Zyprian von Serntein, who attempted to have his wife accommodated in the royal women's quarters; cf. Hyden, *Zyprian von Sernteim*.
[23] Wiesflecker, *Kaiser Maximilian I.*, vol. 5, p. 232.

> *dasmal nut mit mir geredt und wurdest gar selten mit mir redn und ain anderer, der jetzt mynder ist dann du, dem wurdest du mit grosser begerung nachlaufen.*[24]

The court was where the ruler dwelt, and that could be in one of the centres of the Habsburg lands, any other place within them, one of the princely castles which Maximilian had renovated for his use and which would accommodate him for a time, or any other place in the Empire. A permanent court establishment existed only temporarily, for example in Innsbruck for the Empress Bianca Maria (1494-1511). Maximilian, too, would often stay in Innsbruck, and sometimes for a longer period of time.[25] Yet these periods were of no consequence to the development of an aristocratic, courtly way of life.[26] While it was reported that at the queen's court at Innsbruck virgins were strictly supervised,[27] only a part of the personnel that belonged to the court in the wider sense ever actually lived in Innsbruck castle.

Maximilian stayed in the free imperial cities just as often as he did in his territories. Occasionally he described himself as a burgher of Augsburg, the place where messages from all over Europe came together and which was the financial centre of the Empire. The Augsburg burgher Georg Gossembrot was for a time his top financier and to him the revenues of the Austrian countries were to be leased for a time. The merchants of Augsburg, moreover, financed Maximilian's wars. In the vicinity of the Emperor the lifestyle of the burghers, of scholars and financiers prevailed. Maximilian himself wanted to be portrayed in the habit of a burgher. His noble passion for hunting and his fondness for tournaments were part of an aristocratic chivalric tradition, but for him it was mainly an exercise and sport; thus it is not surprising that he participated in a joust of young Nuremberg citizens [*Gesellenstechen*]. When he opened up the former knightly order of St George to people of both sexes from any social class, he did this primarily to create a means of financing his military plans. Thus the 'last knight' would again and again take up chivalrous models of the High Middle Ages, but he would often imbue them with new meaning and direct them to his own ends. While in late-medieval Burgundy chivalry was staged in imitation of courtly romances,[28] Maximilian hardly ever bothered, even in his literary works, to invent a plot for what to his mind was chivalric behaviour.

[24] *Weisskunig* in: Musper *et al.*, eds, *Kaiser Maximilians Theuerdank*, p. 233.

[25] Benecke, *Maximilian I.*, p. 94.

[26] For the personnel of the court at Innsbruck, meals, daily routine, consumption of light, clothes, wages, etc, see Benecke, *Maximilian I.*, pp. 105-111; for Maximilian's meals, p. 128.

[27] Gatt, *Der Innsbrucker Hof*, p. 41.

[28] Cf. Melville: 'Der Held in Szene gesetzt'.

In his *Theuerdank* the knight's quest becomes a series of dangerous situations [*Gferlicheiten*], sometimes senseless tests of courage.

Although Maximilian was impressed by the extravagant and highly formalised Burgundian court culture he did not copy it. He held court as unpretentiously as the Habsburg rulers had done before him. The royal household – court offices, domestic staff, hangers-on, etc. – swallowed a lot of money, and money was often lacking. The ordinary imperial household (including councillors, secretaries, servants, entertainers) was, as mentioned above, no bigger than that of a territorial prince. Nevertheless clothing, catering, accommodation, upkeep of horses, etc., were huge cost factors. The Empress Bianca Maria was considered to be particularly extravagant; she often had financial problems and occasionally had to pawn her jewels; when she travelled with the imperial court, she was sometimes detained as security for accumulated debts and the court had to go on without her.[29] Maximilian attempted in vain to control and curb the expenses of the household.[30] The paymaster of the court occasionally followed the court, in order to redeem securities which had been left behind. Strictly speaking, there is little evidence of a courtly form of life. The traditional court offices remained honorary positions, exercised only on the few ceremonial occasions when the Empire assembled; normally they would be filled by servants in the imperial household. The division between the administration of the imperial household and the imperial government was not yet fully developed, so that clashes were unavoidable (as with major-domo or steward).

On his travels Maximilian lived rather modestly: a few simple, often only sparsely furnished rooms would suffice him, though the rooms of the Emperor would be decorated with tapestries, like those of the Dukes of Burgundy.[31] Necessities would be transported along on wagons, and the furnishings sometimes appeared shabby to foreign envoys.[32] On occasion not even the provisioning of the many people around the Emperor was safeguarded, and in such a case silverware or jewellery had to be pawned. What precious objects Maximilian owned were mostly locked in treasure vaults and only taken out and shown at ceremonial occasions. At larger festivities there could be exceptional problems – as for instance, during the celebrations of the royal marital consummation in Burg Hasegg near Hall in the Tyrol, the wives of the burghers of Hall had to help out with linen.[33]

[29] Benecke, *Maximilian I.*, pp. 96; 102; Hyden, *Zyprian von Serntein*, p. 9.

[30] Wiesflecker, *Kaiser Maximilian I.*, vol. 5, pp. 252, 258; Heinig, 'Theorie und Praxis'. Cf. Benecke, *Maximilian I.*, p. 101ff. for the expenses of holding court.

[31] Wiesflecker, *Kaiser Maximilian I.*, vol. 5, p. 303.

[32] Wiesflecker, *Kaiser Maximilian I.*, vol. 5, p. 384.

[33] Gatt, *Der Innsbrucker Hof*, p. 167.

Life in Maximilian's vicinity, at the actual 'court', was as turbulent, unsettled and confused as anything described in the court-critical literature written at any time since the twelfth century. For example, the same had been reported of the court of Maximilan's father, Frederick III's, by Enea Silvio Piccolomini: no ceremonial etiquette, bad manners, usually bad meals, frictions and petty jealousies of the courtiers. Maximilian himself was not a man of formalities. Envoys like Machiavelli reported that he was always on the move, extremely volatile, never focused for long on the same thing, constantly changing his intentions, and, what is more, always in financial difficulties. In *Weisskunig*, Maximilian boasts of his ability to dictate to half a dozen secretaries at the same time, and thus outdo Caesar. If this really were government practice, he would probably have driven his employees insane.

The typical modesty of Maximilian stood in contrast to the enormous courtly splendour he displayed at grand occasions, attended by the Empire and its outstanding representatives assembled: these included coronations, imperial Diets [*Reichstage*], signing ceremonies in connection with peace treaties, and royal weddings. The concept of 'court', in an emphatic sense, therefore refers to something quintessentially ephemeral, and the sometimes impoverished everyday life at court was in stark contrast to the tremendous pomp displayed at those splendid moments.[34] But a regular shortage of money often imposed tight restrictions, and meetings did not take place, because Maximilian was afraid that he might not be attired magnificently enough. Throughout the period, there are reports of the poor appearance of the Emperor; that began with the meeting of Emperor Frederick III and Charles the Bold in Trier, and it continued to Maximilian's meeting with Henry VIII (1513). Yet, there were also repeated demonstrations of royal *splendors*, such as at Hagenau (1505) or at the Congress of Vienna (1515). The latter was estimated to have cost 120,000 fl.; the mounted guard wore dress uniforms and treasures were exhibited. For all this, Maximilian obtained money from the Fuggers, with which he borrowed jewels in order to display imperial magnificence. Throughout his life he commissioned magnificent robes, in particular, splendid suits of armour. Marriages of his servants with rich heiresses, arranged by Maximilian, provided occasions for splendid banquets, dances, masques and tournaments.

On these occasions – ceremonial entries, which mirrored the hierarchical order of the estates, assemblies, solemn masses, tournaments, banquets or masques – Maximilian's court would represent the Empire to a greater public, and numerous reports of such festivities have been preserved. The

[34] Legers, 'Kardinal Matthäus Lang', p. 489. This was true of Maximilian as well as of his most important adviser, cardinal Lang.

scholars, too, played their part at these events. Feudal rituals were complemented by recitations of praise poetry, solemn speeches and the ritual of the poet's coronation, which Maximilian awarded to deserving eulogists and historiographers. Maximilian also maintained a famous court orchestra and had Paul Hofhaymer, one of the best organists of the times in his employ. But holding court in this emphatic sense was always a temporary business, and the riches and resources which came together on these occasions would normally soon be dispersed again far and wide.

What kept these different groups of people together and drew them in towards a common centre was not the force exerted by any institution but rather the person of the ruler himself. His charisma had to be significantly greater than that of all the other princes. His monstrous *Gedechtnus* [memory] project was aiming at this by consciously modelling his image for both contemporaries and posterity.[35] In the knights Freydal and Theuerdank and the young *Weisskunig* he created literary figures, who, hardly disguised, were meant to portray him and his astonishing exploits. It is said about Theuerdank that 'he is but a human being' [*Er ist ein mensch vnd doch nit mer*], but this is said in utmost admiration of Maximilian's supernatural deeds: no one should attempt to copy them, for such an ambition would be bound to end in disaster.[36] Such imaginations raised the hero (and his idol) above the level of any ordinary man. This is the tenor of all Maximilian's self-portrayals: his distinction from all others. With this he anticipated absolutism, in which the ruler is the embodiment of sacral authority. In this style the court *literati*, too, speak of the *adoratio* of the *divus Maximilianus*. Majesty is a quasi-religious *arcanum*, and it is not only the person of the ruler that is made sacral, but his entire dynasty, the house of Austria, the noblest lineage in Christendom.[37] By means of genealogical research, reaching back to the biblical forefathers, Maximilian's court historiographers tried to prove that the house of Austria united all noble blood since the creation of the world.[38] The ultimate focal point of Maximilian's 'court' and his government was the idea of the superiority of the House of Austria as represented by himself; however, this claim only became reality after his death, thanks to the marriage alliances entered into during his reign.

Maximilian tried to compensate for his factual powerlessness and the lack of centralisation of his court by displaying his image and the symbols

[35] Müller, *Gedechtnus*; see also Schauerte, *Die Ehrenpforte für Kaiser Maximilian I.*

[36] Musper, *et al.*, eds, *Kaiser Maximilians Theuerdank*, p. P_7^v; vgl. Bl. A_2^v; N_6^r; O_4^r; cf. Unger, ed, *Kaiser Maximilian I., Teuerdank*, pp. 6, 285, 292; see also Müller, *Gedechtnus*, pp. 228-238.

[37] Müller, *Gedechtnus*, pp. 157-159, 188, 265.

[38] Benecke, *Maximilian I.*, pp. 174-181.

and claims of his rule as often and in as many places as possible. He made use of the print medium, by which he could be present within the Empire in diverse ways and in many places, in mandates and memoranda, war reports and proclamations, portraits, arms and insignia of royalty. In his territories he added durable forms of representation, such as monuments, pictures and sculptures. His coat of arms could be found everywhere, on churches, castles, secular buildings, on furniture and other items of everyday use. This demonstrated the power that he actually exercised as well as the power that he claimed.[39] Moreover, Maximilian's image represented the many roles which he wished to assume: sometimes it depicted the ruler in his majesty, sometimes also the private man, the commander, the knight, the father of the family, etc.; he was thus often stylised as Hercules, as St George, or in the guise of another saint. In this way Maximilian, even when physically absent, sought to be present in as many places as possible, and in this fashion he tried to maximise his imperial aura.

Maximilian was less concerned with the actual appearance of his court than with the way that its image would appear to the contemporary public and in future memory [*Gedechtnus*]. His court literally existed on paper: to a large extent it was a virtual quantity. For Maximilian the public echo of grand events was just as important as reality itself. It is not certain that he understood the speeches, travel reports and panegyrics which the humanist scholars dedicated to him. But he did cause them to be printed in order to be circulated. An event like the Congress of Vienna in 1515, which laid the foundations of the Habsburgs' world power through marriage alliances with the kings of Hungary and Poland, were intended not only to be witnessed by those who were present: reports by participants, a collection of speeches in Latin, pictures, a woodcut for the *Weisskunig* or one depicting a carriage in his triumphal procession, turned the entire Empire into potential witnesses. The symbolic character of political actions was always more important than their actual execution. In 1508, Maximilian's plan of leading a campaign to Rome failed, where he wanted to have himself crowned Emperor. Instead he assumed the title of Emperor in the Cathedral of Trent, where he was acclaimed by only a relatively small and not very prominent retinue. However, by means of the public echo generated by the media, the acclamation was elevated to a political event with a significance for the entire Empire. For this reason, the text of the proclamation was printed; Maximilian from then on acted as Emperor, and as a ruler far elevated above all other monarchs.

[39] Compare the survey by Hye, 'Die heraldischen Denkmale', pp. 56-77; concerning their sacral background, see Egg, 'Der Wappenturm' (with further reading).

Even if we set aside the agendas of everyday politics, Maximilian's court can be described in terms of the images and texts which were meant to secure his lasting fame. The most complete of them are not portrayals of a real court, but of a substitute, intended to stand in its stead. Especially his printed triumphal procession [*gedechtnus Triumpf*] shows how Maximilian imagined his court, and in it a fifty-seven metres long succession of woodcuts depict an imaginary triumph. Its participants were – as in the triumphs of the Roman generals – soldiers, prisoners, representatives of subjugated peoples, standard-bearers and heralds, as well as weapons (especially artillery) and spoils; there are displayed portraits of ancestors and relatives. Representations of outstanding events in Maximilian's reign were pulled along on ceremonial carriages. Finally, the royal household appears on foot or on horse, sometimes on triumphal carriages: the holders of court offices (cook, cupbearer, barber, cobbler, tailor), huntsmen, pipers and drummers, lutenists, wind players, the court organist, the 'masters' of different martial games, 'natural' jesters (i.e. the mentally disturbed) and professional fools, most of them mentioned by name.[40] What in reality would never have come together is here united within one single picture.

The autobiographical works in the vernacular – *Freydal*, *Theuerdank* and *Weisskunig* – are also depictions of an imaginary court. The *Freydal* was supposed to display Maximilian's knightly games (jousting on horseback, as well as foot combat) and masques [*Mummereyen*], strictly ordered by category and narrated as stations in the young Freydal's quest in the service of his noble lady. The joustings and festivities, which had taken place in reality on this or that occasion, events more or less lavish which had been held in front of few witnesses, received the appropriate courtly setting only in this work, through literary stylisation and the provision of fitting images. Scholars were astonished that the court tailor had been consulted for the miniatures of the masques and that Maximilian himself took care of every detail of the weapons and armour; but this was necessary if the pictures were to represent the ideal court Maximilian was dreaming of.[41]

Among the woodcuts of the *Weisskunig* (more than in the text itself) we can also find such idealised designs of an imaginary court-life – funerals, marriages, coronations, assemblies of princes and the like. Sometimes

[40] See also *Der Triumphzug Kaiser Maximilians I. 1516-1518*, and Schestag, 'Kaiser Maximilian I. Triumph'; Winzinger, *Die Miniaturen zum Triumphzug Kaiser Maximilians I.*

[41] See also Gottlieb, *Büchersammlung Kaiser Maximilians I.*, p. 57. Not much was completed of *Freydal*: there is a prose introduction of the narrative frame, a list of the celebrations and a list of participants, added to which are 255 drafts of miniatures for woodcuts for 64 tournament courtyards (of which only five were implemented by Dürer).

events – such as sober administrative acts or the signing of treaties by authorised representative – are translated into ceremonial acts which never happened in the way shown. Courtly accomplishments and the practice of knightly skills appear here mainly as models pertaining to the education of the young Weisskunig, who like every ideal prince masters them brillantly. Also the quest of a knight, *Theuerdank* concludes at an imaginary court, the court of Dame Ehrenreich, with a series of courtly jousts and celebrations. Maximilian's court thus appears as a figment of the imagination of his artists and poets.

Overall the literature which Maximilian patronised was not courtly in the sense that it was meant for a courtly society, whose rituals, manners and norms of communication created ideals and served as their illustration. Maximilian had stylised his life after the example of romances and prose novels, because he believed it was thus given the appropriate traditional setting. The literary format was subordinate to the aim of putting his real life as a ruler into public memory; the addressees were not the group of people surrounding him, but a wider, albeit more exclusive public, whom he wanted to present with evidence of his deeds. Triumphal processions and arches,[42] too, drew contemporaries and future generations into the contemplation of an imaginary court, before which the ruler's fame was displayed.

These works of memory-shaping show how access to this virtual court was an almost exclusive prerogative, and the claim throughout is that they reveal an *arcanum* which was not meant for everyone. In *Theuerdank* Maximilian's deeds as a knight are related symbolically, while a key (*Clavis*) reveals the historical models for the happy few. The *Weisskunig* encodes military actions (all of which, it is suggested, were successful) with anagrams and heraldic symbols; like *Freydal*, it was to be read only by initiates. Furthermore, the hero of *Weisskunig* excels at profound riddles [*scharpf Red*], which – so the instruction says – cannot be understood by the common people, but only by those familiar with the ruler's secrets. The imposing carriage on which the Emperor was enthroned and which formed the climax of this triumphal procession, tells us in allegorical figures and symbols about the *arcanum* of imperial power, and the triumphal arch, a woodcut arch, contains at its heart a *mysterium hieroglyphicum*: an image of Maximilian in company with animal figures which are to be interpreted 'hieroglyphically', each representing a virtue that a good ruler should possess. The message is always the same: wisdom and knowledge are the keys opening the door to the Emperor, and only a small group of initiated people may enter the inner *sanctum* of the imaginary court. The access to the *arca-*

[42] Chmelarz, 'Die Ehrenpforte'; Schauerte, *Die Ehrenpforte*.

num of power, which in later times would be regulated by ceremonial, was here effectuated by literature.

Maximilian's court was a hybrid. We find precursors of the bureaucracy of the absolutist territorial state, as well as the descendants of the medieval feudal nobility. The latter were not the people with influence; they were rather the 'experts', who were often of the most humble origins. At the same time, this sober government routine was complemented by magnificent appearances at imperial Diets and assemblies of princes, at which the head of the Empire, as the tradition was, represented the unity of Christianity. Strictly speaking, the court existed only on paper, in woodcuts, romances, and panegyrics. Here, aspects of early modern court culture were anticipated, and the *adoratio* of the ruler which was inspired by classical concepts was blended with medieval traditions. Yet the old and the new often coexisted only in an imperfect amalgam. The Latin court literature remained mostly the concern of scholars, but it also served as a decorative accomplishment for social climbers from middle-class backgrounds. The subject matter, however, was always the praise of the prince.[43] It is notable, however, that the vernacular court culture distanced itself more and more from its late medieval roots, as a result of the influence of the new ruling elite at court, and of the new tasks which the ruler imposed upon the court.[44] Court culture and court society drifted apart, therefore; on the one hand we see the heirs of a medieval feudal tradition, on the other hand the representatives of an aristocracy of the mind. Both aspects came to be integrated into the early modern state, albeit that such an integration, which would lead to a new type of courtly society, was under Maximilian only something that was coming into being.

[43] Müller, *Gedechtnus*, pp. 159-179.
[44] Müller, *Gedechtnus*, pp. 212-228.

BIBLIOGRAPHY

Abelard, J., *Les Illustrations de Gaule et Singularitez de Troye de Jean Lemaire de Belges. Etude des éditions – Genèse de l'œuvre* (Geneva, 1976).

Actes des journées internationales Claus Sluter (Septembre 1990) (Dijon, 1992).

Adamson, J., ed, *The Princely Courts of Europe. Ritual, Politics and Culture under the* Ancien Régime *1500-1750* (London, 2000).

Adamson, P., *Serenissimi ac Nobilissimi Scotiae Angliae Hyberniae Henrici Stuardi at Mariae Reginae Epithalamium* (Paris, 1566).

ADCP: Hannay, R.K., ed, *Acts of the Lords of Council.*

Agrippa ab Nettesheim, H.C., *Henrici Cornelii Agrippae oratio, habita in divae Margaritae Austriacorum et Burgundionum principis aeterna memoriae dignissimae*, *Opera*, vol. 2 (Leiden, 1600), pp. 1129-1149.

Aili, H., 'Sweden', in: Skafte Jensen, M., ed, *A History of Nordic Neo-Latin Literature*, pp. 129-158.

———, Ferm, O. and Gustavson, H., *Röster från svensk medeltid* (Stockholm, 1990).

Aitken, J.M., *The Trial of George Buchanan before the Lisbon Inquisition* (Edinburgh/London, 1939).

Akkerman, F. and Vanderjagt, A.J., eds, *Rodolphus Agricola Phrisius 1444-1485* (Groningen, 1994).

Aldis, H.G., *A List of Books printed in Scotland before 1700* (Edinburgh, [2]1970).

Alesius, Alexander, *Alexandri Alesii Epistola contra decretum quoddam Episcoparum in Scotia* (Wittenberg, 1533).

Alesius, Alexander, *Alexandri Alesii responsio as Cochlei calumnias* (*s.l.*, 1533-1534).

Allan, D., *The Scottish Book Trade, 1500-1720: Print Commerce and Print Control in Early Modern Scotland* (East Linton, 2000).

Almquist, J.A., 'Tornérspelet vid kröningen 1617. Ett bidrag till 1600-talets bibliografie', in: *Donum Grapeanum*. Festschrift Anders Grape (Uppsala, 1945), pp. 1-7.

Althoff, G., 'Ungeschriebene Gesetze. Wie funktioniert Herrschaft ohne schriftlich fixierte Normen', in: Althoff, G., *Spielregeln der Politik im Mittelalter. Kommunikation in Frieden und Fehde* (Darmstadt, 1997), pp. 282-304.

Anglo, S. 'Humanism and the Court Arts', in: Goodman, A and MacKay, A., eds, *The Impact of Humanism on Western Europe* (London/New York, 1990).

Anthiaume, l'abbé A., *Cartes marines, constructions navales, voyages de découverte chez les normands, 1500-1650*, 2 vols. (Paris, 1916).

Appleby, A.B., 'Grain Prices and Subsistence Crises in England and France, 1590-1740', *The Journal of Economic History* 39 (1979), pp. 865-887.

APS: Thomson and Innes, eds, *Acts of the Parliaments of Scotland.*

Apted, M.R., *The Painted Ceilings of Scotland* (Edinburgh, 1966).

Arbuthnot, P. Stewart-Mackenzie, ed, *Queen Mary's Book: a Collection of Poems and Essays by Mary Queen of Scots* (London, 1907).

Ariani, M., ed, *Il teatro italiano II. La tragedia del Cinquecento, tomo secondo* (Turin, 1977).

Armstrong, C.A.J., 'Had the Burgundian Government a Policy for the Nobility?' in:

Armstrong, C.A.J., *England, France and Burgundy in the Fifteenth Century* (London, 1983), pp. 213-236.

———, 'Les ducs de Bourgogne, interprètes de la pensée politique du 15e siècle', in: Jongkees, A.G. and Vanderjagt, A.J., eds, *Annales de Bourgogne* 67 (1995), pp. 5-34.

Armstrong, E., *Ronsard and the Age of Gold* (Cambridge, 1961).

Arnade, P., *Realms of Ritual. Burgundian Ceremony and Civic Life in Late Medieval Ghent* (Ithaca, 1996).

Arnauld, A., *Coppie de l'Anti-Espagnol fait à Paris* (s.l., 1590).

Asch, R.G., 'Court and Household from the Fifteenth to the Seventeenth Centuries', in: Asch and Birke, eds, *Princes, Patronage, and the Nobility*, pp. 1-38.

Asch, R.G. and Birke, A.M., eds, *Princes, Patronage and the Nobility. The Court at the Beginning of the Modern Age c. 1450-1650* (Oxford, 1991).

Asch, R. and Durchhardt, H., eds, *Der Absolutismus – ein Mythos? Strukturwandel monarchischer Herrschaft* (Cologne/Weimar/Vienna, 1996).

Ascoli, P., *The Sixteen and the Paris League, 1585-1591* (Ph.D. diss. University of California, Berkeley, 1972).

Atkinson, G., *Les nouveaux horizons de la renaissance française* (Geneva, 21969).

Axton, M., '*Ane Satyre of the Thrie Estaitis*: The First Edition and its Reception', in: Gardner-Medwin, A. and Williams, J. Hadley, eds, *A Day Estivall: Essays on the Music, Poetry and History of Scotland and England* (Aberdeen, 1990), pp. 21-34.

Babelon, J.P., *Henri IV* (Paris, 1982).

———, *Châteaux de France au siècle de la Renaissance* (Paris, 1989).

Baccou, R., transl., *Platon. La République* (Paris, 1966).

Backes, M., *Das literarische Leben am kurpfälzischen Hof zu Heidelberg im 15. Jahrhundert. Ein Beitrag zur Gönnerforschung des Spätmittelalters* (Tübingen, 1992).

Backhouse, J., ed, *The Hastings Hours* (London, 1996).

Baelde, M., ed, *Les Chevaliers de l'Ordre de la Toison d'or au XVe siècle. Notices bio-bibliographiques* (Frankfurt am Main, 1994).

Bain, J. *et al.*, eds, *Calendar of the State Papers relating to Scotland and Mary, Queen of Scots*, 13 vols. (Edinburgh, 1862-1954).

———, ed, *Hamilton Papers*, 2 vols. (Edinburgh, 1890-1892).

Bak, J.M., 'Symbolik und Kommunikation im Mittelalter. Ein Rohbericht', in: *Kommunikation und Alltag im Mittelalter* (Vienna, 1992), pp. 39-46.

Baker-Smith, D., 'Florens Wilson: A Distant Prospect', in: Hadley Williams, ed, *Stewart Style*, pp. 1-14.

Baldwin, D., *The Chapel Royal ancient and modern* (London, 1990).

Balfour Paul, Sir J., ed, *The Scots Peerage* (Edinburgh, 1904-1914).

Bann. Misc.: Laing, D., ed, *The Bannatye Miscellany*.

Bann. MS: Tod Ritchie, W., ed, *The Bannatyne MS.*

Barbiche, J., *Les institutions de la monarchie française à l'époque moderne* (Paris, 1999).

Bardon, F., *Diane de Poitiers et le mythe de Diane* (Paris, 1963).

Barker, E., Webb, N and Woods, K., eds, *The Changing Status of the Artist* (New Haven/London, 1999).

Barlow, F., 'The King's Evil', *English Historical Review* 95 (1980), pp. 3-27.

Baron, F.A., *The Life and Work of the Wandering Humanist Peter Luder* (Michigan, 1966).

Baron, H., *The Crisis of the Early Italian Renaissance* (Princeton, 1955).

Barrault, J.-M., *Le Sacre et la Pensée: 1529, de Dieppe à Sumatra. Les capitaines-poètes de Jean Ango ouvrent la route des Indes fabuleuses* (Paris, 1989).

Barudio, G., *Gustav Adolf – der Große. Eine politische Biographie* (Frankfurt-am-Main, 1982).

Barzman, K.-E., *The Florentine Academy and the Early Modern State.The Discipline of Disegno* Cambridge, 2000).

Bath, M., 'Painted ceilings, 1550-1650: applied emblematics in Scotland', *Emblematica* 7 (1993), pp. 259-305.

Baudouin-Matuszek, M.-N., ed, *Paris et Catherine de Médicis* (Paris 1989).

Bauer, V., *Die höfische Gesellschaft in Deutschland von der Mitte des 17. bis zum Ausgang des 18. Jahrhunderts* (Tübingen, 1993).

———, *Hofökonomie. Der Diskurs über den Fürstenhof in Zeremonial-wissenschaft, Hausväterliteratur und Kameralismus* (Vienna/Cologne/Weimar, 1997).

Baulant. M. and Meuvret, J., *Prix des céreales extraits de la mercuriale de Paris (1520-1698)*, 2 vols. (Paris, 1960).

Baumgärtel, B. and Neysters, S., eds, *Die Galerie der starken Frauen. Die Heldin in der französischen und italienischen Kunst des 17. Jahrhunderts* (Düsseldorf/ Darmstadt, 1995).

Baumgartner, F.J., *Radical Reactionaries. The Political Thought of the French Catholic League* (Geneva, 1976).

———, *Louis XII* (New York, 1994).

Bawcutt, P., ed, *The Shorter Poems of Gavin Douglas* (Edinburgh/London, 1967).

———, *Gavin Douglas: A Critical Study* (Edinburgh, 1976).

———, 'A Medieval Scottish Elegy and its French Original', *Scottish Literary Journal* 15.1 (1988), pp. 5-13.

———, 'Dunbar's Use of the Symbolic Lion and Thistle', *Cosmos* 2 (1986), pp. 83-97.

———, *Dunbar the Makar* (Oxford, 1992).

———, ed, *The Poems of William Dunbar*, 2 vols. (Glasgow, 1998).

Bawcutt, P. and Henisch, B., 'Scots Abroad in the Fifteenth Century: The Princesses Margaret, Isabella and Eleanor', in: Ewan, E. and Meikle, M.M., eds, *Women in Scotland c.1000-c.1750* (East Linton, 1999), pp. 45-53.

Bawcutt, P. and Riddy, F., eds, *Longer Scottish Poems: Volume One, 1375-1650* (Edinburgh, 1987).

Baxandall, M., *Painting and Experience in Fifteenth-Century Italy: a Primer in the Social History of Pictorial Style* (Oxford, ²1988).

Baxter, J. Reid, 'Politics, Passion and Poetry in the Circle of James VI: John Burel and his Surviving Works', in: Houwen, MacDonald and Mapstone, *Palace in the Wild*, pp. 199-248.

Baxter, J. Reid, 'The authorship of Philotus'. Forthcoming.

Baxter, J.H., 'Alesius and Other Reformed Refugees in Germany', *Records of the Scottish Church History Society* 5 (1935), pp. 93-102.

Beard, C.R., 'Early Stewart Portraits: A Discovery', *The Connoisseur* 71 (1925), pp. 5-15.

Beattie, W., *The Chepman and Myllar Prints* (Oxford, 1950).
———, ed, *The Chepman and Myllar Prints* (Edinburgh, 1950).
———, 'Fragments of The Palyce of Honour', *Edinburgh Bibliographical Society Transactions* 3.1 (1951), pp. 33-46.
———, 'Some early Scottish books', in: Barrow, G.W.S., ed, *The Scottish Tradition: Essays in Honour of Ronald Gordon Cant* (Edinburgh, 1974), pp. 107-120.
Beaune, C., *The Birth of an Ideology: Myths and Symbols of Nation in Late-Medieval France*, transl. by Susan Ross Huston (Berkeley, 1991).
Beckers, H., '*Der püecher haubet, die von der tafelrunde wunder sagen.* Wirich von Stein und die Verbreitung des "Prosa-Lancelot" im 15. Jahrhundert', *Wolfram-Studien* 9 (1986), pp. 17-47.
———, 'Frühneuhochdeutsche Fassungen mittelniederländischer Erzählliteratur im Umkreis des pfalzgräflichen Hofes zu Heidelberg um 1450-80', in: Cockx-Indestege and Hendrickx, *Miscellanea Neerlandica*, pp. 230-242.
Béguin, S., 'La suite d'Arthémise', *L'Œil* 38 (1958), pp. 32-39, 74.
———, 'Remarques sur la chambre du Roi', in: Chastel, A., ed, *Actes du colloque international sur l'art de Fontainebleau* (Paris, 1975), pp. 199-230.
Bellenden, *Chronicles*: Chambers, Batho and Husbands, eds, *Bellenden.*
Bellenden, *Livy*: Craigie, W.A., ed, *Livy's History of Rome.*
Belyea, B., 'Images of Power: Derrida/Foucault/Harley', *Cartographica* 29,2 (1992), pp. 1-9.
Benecke, G., *Maximilian I. An analytical biography* (London, etc., 1982).
Bercé, Y.M., 'Henri IV et la maîtrise des opinions populaires', in: Tucoo-Chala, P., ed, *Henri IV, le Roi et la Reconstruction du Royaume* (Pau, 1990), pp. 111-123.
Berend, F. and Wolkan, U., eds, *Der Ehrenbrief des Jakob Püterich von Reichertshausen an die Erzherzogin Mechthild (*Weimar, 1920).
Berg, Th. and Bodemann, U., '"Wie ludwigen von Beyern etlich bucher verschriben sin". Buchbesitz und Bildungsfunktion am Heidelberger Hof zur Zeit Friedrichs des Siegreichen', *Bibliothek und Wissenschaft* 24 (1990), pp. 1-35.
Bergendoff, C., *Olavus Petri and the Ecclesiastical Transformation in Sweden 1521-1552* (New York, 1928).
Berger de Xivrey, J., ed, *Henry IV, Recueil des lettres missives*, vol. VII (Paris, 1858).
Bergeron, D.M., *Royal Family, Royal Lovers: King James of England and Scotland* (Columbia, 1991).
Bergvelt, E., Meijers, D.J. and Rijnders, M., eds, *Verzamelen. Van Rariteitenkabinet tot Kunstmuseum* (Heerlen, 1993).
Bernard, E., *Advis des Estats de Bourgongne aux François touchant la resolution prise aux estates de Blois, l'An 1588. Fait à Dijon le premier jour de Janvier, 1590* (Troyes, 1590); repr. in: Chevreul, H., ed, *Pièces sur la Ligue en Bourgogne* (Paris, 1883).
Berns, J.J., 'Luthers Papstkritik als Zeremoniellkritik. Zur Bedeutung des päpstlichen Zeremoniells für das fürstliche Hofzeremoniell in der Frühen Neuzeit', in: Berns, J.J. and Rahn, Th., eds, *Zeremoniell als höfische Ästhetik in Spätmittelalter und Früher Neuzeit* (Tübingen, 1995), pp. 157-173.

Bertière, S., *Les Reines de France au temps des Valois*, vol. 1: *Le beau XVIe siècle*; vol. 2: *Les années sanglantes* (Paris, 1994).

———, 'Régence et pouvoir féminin', in: Wilson-Chevalier, K. and Viennot, E., eds, *Royaume de fémynie. Pouvoirs, contraintes, espaces de liberté des femmes de la Renaissance à la Fronde* (Paris, 1999), pp. 63-70.

Besnier, G., 'Quelques notes sur Arras et Jeanne d'Arc', *Revue du Nord* 40 (1958), pp. 183-194.

Bideaux, M., 'Le discours expansionniste dans L'*Histoire de la Nouvelle-France* de Marc Lescarbot', in: Lestringant, F., ed, *La France-Amérique (XVIe-XVIII siècles). Actes du XXXVe colloque international d'études humanistes* (Paris, 1998), pp. 167-191.

Biggar, H.P., *The Early Trading Companies of New France: A Contribution to the History of Commerce and Discovery in North America* (Toronto, 1901).

Biraben, J.N., *Les hommes et la peste en France et dans les pays européens et méditerranéens*, vol. 1: *La peste dans l'histoire* (Paris, 1975).

Black, J., *Maps and History: Constructing Images of the Past* (New Haven/London, 1997).

Blake, N.F., *Selections from William Caxton* (Oxford, 1973).

———, ed, *The Canterbury Tales by Geoffrey Chaucer. Edited from the Hengwrt Manuscript* (London, 1980).

Blanchard, J., *Commynes L'Européen. L'invention du politique* (Geneva, 1996).

Blanchet, J. et al., ed, *Collection de manuscrits contentant lettres, mémoires, et autres documents historiques relatifs à la Nouvelle-France*, vol. 1, 1492-1712, (Quebec City, 1883).

Blickle, P., *Unruhen in der ständischen Gesellschaft (1300-1800)* (Munich, 1988).

Bloch, M., *Les Rois Thaumaturges. Étude sur le caractère surnaturel attribué à la puissance royale particulièrement en France et en Angleterre* (Paris/ Strasbourg, 1924; repr. 1961).

———, *The Royal Touch, Sacred Monarchy and Scrofula in England and France*, transl. by J.E. Andersen (London, 1973).

Blockmans, W.P., ed, *Le privilège général et les privilèges régionaux de Marie de Bourgogne pour les Pays-Bas:1477/Het algemene en de gewestelijke privilegien van Maria van Bourgondië voor de Nederlanden* (Kortrijk/ Heule, 1985).

Blockmans, W. and Donckers, W., 'Self-Representation of Court and City in Flanders and Brabant in the Fifteenth and Sixteenth Centuries', in: Blockmans, W. and Janse, A. eds, *Showing Status. Representation of Social Positions in the Late Middle Ages* (Turnhout, 1999), pp. 81-112.

Blockmans, W. and Prevenier. W., 'The second Flowering 1492-1530', in: Blockmans and Prevenier, eds, *The Promised Lands*, pp. 206-234.

Blockmans, W.P. and Prevenier, W., *The Promised Lands. The Low Countries under Burgundian Rule, 1369-1530* (Fackelman, E. and Peters, E., transl.) (Philadelphia, 1999).

Blondel, David, *Genealogiae francicae plenior assertio* (Amsterdam, 1654).

Blume, F., *Die Musik in Geschichte und Gegenwart. Allgemeine Enzyklöpadie der Musik* (Kassel/etc., 1949-1989).

Blumenthal, A.R., *Theater Art of the Medici* (Hanover, 1980).

Blunt, A., *Art and Architecture in France 1500-1700* (Harmondsworth, 1953).

———, *Philibert de L'Orme* (London, 1958).

Boece, Hector, *Scotorum Historiae a prima gentis origine cum aliarum et rerum et gentium illustrione non vulgari* (Paris, 1527).

Boffey, J., Edwards, A.S.G. and Barker-Benfield, B.C., eds, *The Works of Geoffrey Chaucer and 'The Kingis Quair'* (Cambridge, 1997).

Bøggild Johannesen, B. and Johannesen, H., *Ny dansk Kunsthistorie* vol. 2 (Copenhagen, 1993).

Bojcov, M.A., 'Qualitäten des Raumes in zeremoniellen Situationen: Das Heilige Römische Reich, 14.-15. Jahrhundert', in: Paravicini, ed, *Zeremoniell und Raum*, pp. 129-153.

Bolger, R.R., *The Classical Heritage* (Cambridge, 1954, New York).

Bom, I., *Det 16. århundredes danske vocabularier* (Copenhagen, 1974).

Bonath, G. and Brunner, H., 'Die Kinder von Limburg (1480)', in Harms, W. and Johnson, L.P., eds, *Deutsche Literatur des späten Mittelalters. Hamburger Colloquium 1973* (Berlin, 1975), pp. 129-152.

Bonath, G., 'Heinric en Margriete van Limborch' in: Ruh, K. (from vol. 9 onwards Wachinger, B.), ed, *Die deutsche Literatur des Mittelalters. Verfasserlexikon* (Berlin/New York,) 1978ff. (^{2}*VL*), 1981), cols. 657-659.

———, 'Johann von Soest', in: ^{2}*VL* 4, cols. 744-755.

Bonino, G.D., ed, *Ludovico Ariosto. Satire* (Milan, 1990).

Bonnaffé, E., *Inventaire des meubles de Catherine de Médicis en 1589. Mobilier, tableaux, objets d'art, manuscrits* (Paris, 1874; repr. Geneva, 1973).

Borland, L., *The Influence of Marot on English Poetry of the Sixteenth Century* (Chicago, 1913).

Born, L.K., 'The Perfect Prince: A Study in Thirteenth and Fourteenth-Century Ideals', *Speculum* 3 (1928), pp. 470-504.

Bottin, J., *Seigneurs et paysans dans l'ouest du pays de Caux* (Paris, 1983).

Boucher, J., *Société et mentalités autour de Henri III*, 4 vols. (Lille/Paris, 1981).

———, *La cour de Henri III* (Rennes, 1986).

Boudon, F., *Le château de Fontainebleau de François Ier à Henri IV: les bâtiments et leurs fonctions* (Paris, 1998).

Boudon, F., Chastel, A., Couzy, H. and Haman, F., eds, *Système de l'architecture urbaine. Le quartier des Halles à Paris*, 2 vols. (Paris, 1977).

Boudou, R, *L'idéologie ou l'origine des idées reçues* (Paris, 1986).

Boulay de la Meurthe, comte, 'Entrée de Charles IX à Chenonceaux', *Mémoires de la société archéologique de Touraine* 61 (1900), pp. 151-189.

Boulton, D'A.J.D., *The Knights of the Crown. The Monarchical Orders of Knighthood in Later Medieval Europe 1325-1520* (New York, 1987).

Bourdieu, P., 'Espace social et genèse de "classe"', *Actes de la recherche en sciences sociales* 52/53 (1984), pp. 3-15.

Bourgeon, J.L., *Charles IX devant la Saint-Barthélemy* (Geneva, 1995).

Bousmanne, B. and Van Hoorebeeck, V., eds, *La librairie des ducs de Bourgogne. Manuscrits conservés à la Bibliothèque royale de Belgique*, vol. I: *Textes liturgiques, ascétiques, théologiques, philosophiques et moraux* (Turnhout, 2000).

Boutier, J., Dewerpe, A. and Nordman, D., *Un tour de France royal: le voyage de Charles IX, 1564-1566* (Paris, 1984).

Bower, *Scotichronicon*: Watt, D.E.R., ed, *Scotichronicon by Walter Bower*.

Brask, P. *et al.*, ed, *Dansk litteraturhistorie*, 9 vols. (Copenhagen, 1984-1985).
Bresc-Bautier, G. ed, *Germain Pilon et les sculpteurs français de la Renaissance. Actes du colloque du Musée du Louvre organisé par le service culturel les 26 et 27 octobre 1990* (Paris, 1993).
Brewer, J.S. *et al.*, eds, *Calendar of Letters and Papers, Foreign and Domestic, Henry VIII*, 21 vols. (London, 1864-1932).
Britnell, J., ed, *Jean Lemaire de Belges. Traicté de la différence des schismes et des conciles de l'Eglise avec l'Histoire du prince Sophy et autres œuvres* (Geneva, 1997).
Broadie, A., 'James Liddell on Concepts and Signs', in: MacDonald, Lynch and Cowan, eds, *The Renaissance in Scotland*, pp. 82-94.
Broc, N., *La géographie de la Renaissance (1420-1620)* (Paris, 1980).
Brotton, J., *Trading Territories: Mapping the Early Modern World* (Ithaca/New York, 1997).
———, 'Terrestrial Globalism: Mapping the Globe in Early Modern Europe', in: Cosgrove, D., ed, *Mappings* (London, 1999), pp. 71-89.
Brown, J.H. and Elliott, J.H., *A Palace for a King: The Buen Retiro and the Court of Philip IV* (New Haven, 1980).
Brown, K., *Bloodfeud in Scotland, 1573-1625* (Edinburgh, 1986).
Brown, K., *Noble Society in Scotland: Wealth, Family and Culture from Reformation to Revolution* (Edinburgh, 2000).
Brown, K.M., 'Burghs, lords and feuds in Jacobean Scotland', in: Lynch, M., ed, *The Early Modern Town in Scotland* (London, 1987), pp. 102-124.
Brown, M., *James I* (Edinburgh, 1994).
Brown, M.H., 'Scotland Tamed? Kings and Magnates in Late Medieval Scotland a review of recent work', *Innes Review* 45 (1994), pp. 120-146.
Bruchet, M., *Marguerite d'Autriche, Duchesse de Savoie* (Lille, 1927).
Bruchet, M. and Lancien, E., *Itinéraire de Marguerite d'Autriche, gouvernante des Pays-Bas* (Lille, 1934).Brunelle, G.K., *'France and Brazil in the First Century of Contact: The Lure of Brazilwood'* (Chicago, 1989).
Brunelle, G.K., 'Sixteenth-Century Perceptions of the New World: Rouennais Commerce and a Renaissance Tableau', *Proceedings of the Annual Meeting of the Western Society for French History* 17 (1990), pp. 71-81.
———, The New World Merchants of Rouen, 1559-1630 (Kirksville, Mo., 1991).
———, 'The World Economy and Colonial Expansion', in: Stearns, P.N. *et al.*, ed, *Encyclopedia of European Social History from 1350 to 2000*, 6 vols. (Detroit, 2001), vol. 1, pp. 461-474.
Bryant, L.M., *The King and the City in the Parisian Royal Entry Ceremony: Politics, Ritual, and Art in the Renaissance* (Geneva, 1986).
Bryce, W.M., *The Scottish Grey Friars*, 2 vols. (Edinburgh/London, 1909).
Buchanan, George, *Opera omnia* (Leiden, 1725).
Bücking, J., 'Das Geschlecht der Stürtzel von Buchheim (1491-1790). Ein Versuch zur Sozial- und Wirtschaftsgeschichte des Breisgauer Adels in der frühen Neuzeit', *Zeitschrift für Geschichte des Oberrheins* 118 (1970), pp. 218-279.
Budé, Guillaume, *De l'institution du prince* (first published 1518-1519) (Paris, 1547; repr. Farnborough, 1966).
Buisseret, D., ed, *Monarchs, Ministers, and Maps: The Emergence of Cartography as a Tool of Government in Early Modern Europe* (Chicago, 1992).

Bunt, G.H.V., *Alexander the Great in the Literature of Medieval Britain* (Groningen, 1994).
Burel, J., 'The Discription of the Quennis Maiesties Maist Honorable Entry into the Toun of Edinburg, Upon the 19 Day of Maii 1590', in: Craig, J.T.G., ed, *Papers relative to the Marriage of King James the Sixth of Scotland* (Edinburgh, 1828), pp. i-vii.
Burke, P., *The Italian Renaissance* (Oxford, 1987).
———, *The Fabrication of Louis XIV* (New Haven/London, 1992).
———, *The Fortunes of the Courtier* (Oxford, 1995).
Burkhardt, J., 'Die entgipfelte Pyramide. Kriegsziel und Friedenskompromiß der europäischen Universalmächte', in: Bußmann and Schilling, vol. 1: *1648 – Krieg und Frieden in Europa*, pp. 51-60.
Burkolter, V., *The Patronage System. Theoretical Remarks. Some Analytical Approaches to the Study of Patronage* (Basel, 1976).
Burlingham, C., 'Portraiture as Propaganda, Printmaking during the reign of Henry IV', in: Jacobson, K, ed, *The French Renaissance in Prints from the Bibliothèque nationale de France* (Los Angeles, 1994), pp. 139-151.
Burmann, P., ed, *Georgii Buchanani ... Opera Omnia*, 2 vols. (Leiden, 1725)
Burnett, C.J. 'The Officers of Arms and Heraldic Art under King James VI & I, 1567-1625' (unpublished Edinburgh University M.Litt., 1991).
———, 'Outward Signs of Majesty, 1535-1540', in: Hadley Williams, ed, *Stewart Style*, pp. 289-302.
Burnett, C.J. and Dennis, M.D., *Scotland's Heraldic Heritage* (Edinburgh, 1997).
Burns, C., 'Papal Gifts to Scottish Monarchs: the Golden Rose and the Blessed Sword', *Innes Review* 20 (1969), pp. 150-194.
Burns, J.H., 'John Ireland: Theology and Public Affairs in the Late Fifteenth Century', *Innes Review* 41 (1990), pp. 21-42.
———, *Lordship, Kingship and Empire: the Idea of Monarchy, 1400-1525* (Oxford, 1992).
———, *The True Law of Kingship: Concepts of Monarchy in Early-Modern Scotland* (Oxford, 1996).
Burton, J.H. *et al.*, eds, *The Register of the Privy Council of Scotland*, 14 vols. (Edinburgh, 1877-1898).
Bußmann, K. and Schilling, H., eds, *1648 – Krieg und Frieden in Europa*, 3 vols. (Münster, 1998).
Byles, A.T.P., ed, *The book of the ordre of chyvalry translated and printed by William Caxton from a French version of Ramón Lull's "Le libre del orde de cavayleria", together with Adam Loutfut's Scottish transcript (Harleian MS. 6149)* (London, 1926).
Cahn, W., 'Towards the enduring monument: Nantes, Brou, Margaret of Austria', *Masterpieces. Chapters on the History of an Idea* (Princeton, 1979), pp. 43-64.
Calderon, T., *Étude biographique sur Ango et son époque* (Paris, 1891).
Calderwood, D., ed, *History of the Kirk of Scotland*, 8 vols. (Edinburgh, 1842-1849).
Caldwell, D., 'The Beaton Panels – Scottish Carvings of the 1520s or 1530s', in: Higgit, J., ed, *Medieval Art and Architecture in the Diocese of St Andrews* (Leeds, 1994), pp. 174-184.

Calmette, J., *Les grands ducs de Bourgogne* (Paris, 1949).

Calvi, G., 'The Florentine Plague of 1630-33: Social Behaviour and Symbolic Action', in: Bulst, N. and Delort, R., eds, *Maladies et Société (XIIe-XVIIIe siècles). Actes du colloque de Bielefeld, novembre 1986)* (Paris, 1989), pp. 327-336.

Cameron, J., *James V: The Personal Rule, 1528-1542* edited by Macdougall, N. (East Linton, 1998).

Cameron, J.K., 'Catholic reform in Germany and in the pre-1560 Church of Scotland', *Records of the Scottish Church History Society* 22 (1984), pp. 105-17.

Camesasca, E., ed, *Benvenuto Cellini. Vita* (Milan, 1985).

Campbell, I., 'Linlithgow's "Princely Palace" and its influence in Europe', *Architectural Heritage* 5 (1995), pp. 1-20.

Campbell, L., 'The Authorship of the "Recueil d'Arras"', *Journal of the Warburg and Courtauld Institutes* 40 (1977), pp. 301-313; plates 23-26.

Campbell, L., *National Gallery Catalogues. The Fifteenth Century Netherlandish Schools* (London, 1998).

Campbell, M.B., *The Witness and the Other World: Exotic European Travel Writing, 400-1600* (Ithaca, 1988).

Campbell, St., *Cosmè Tura of Ferrara. Style, Politics and the Renaissance City 1450-1495* (New Haven/London, 1997).

Canuti, F., *Il Perugino*, 2 vols. (Siena, 1931).

Carlson, D.R., *English Humanist Books: Writers and Patrons, Manuscript and Print 1475-1525* (Toronto, 1993).

Carmichael, A., 'Diseases of the Renaissance and Early Modern Europe', in: Kiple, K., ed, *The Cambridge World History of Human Disease* (Cambridge, 1993), pp. 279-286.

Carnazzi, G. and Battaglia, S., eds, *Baldassar Castiglione. Il Libro del Cortegiano* (Milan, 1987).

Caron, M.-T., *Le Banquet du voeu du faisan. Fête de cour et prise de conscience européenne* (Lille, 1995).

Caron, M.-T. and Clauzel, D., eds, *Le Banquet du Faisan 1454: l'Occident face au défi de l'Empire ottoman* (Arras, 1997).

Carpenter, S., 'Early Scottish Drama', in: Jack, R.D.S, ed, *The History of Scottish Literature*, vol. 1: *Origins to 1660: Mediaeval and Renaissance* (Aberdeen, 1988), pp. 191-212.

Carpino, A., 'Margaret of Austria's Funerary Complex at Brou', in: Lawrence, C., ed, *Women and Art in Early Modern Europe: Patrons Collectors and Connoisseurs* (University Park, PA, 1997), pp. 37-52.

Cartwright, J., ed, *Gilbert Hay, The Buik of King Alexander the Conquerour*, 2 vols. (Edinburgh, 1986-1990).

Cassagnes, S., *D'art et d'argent. Les artistes et leurs clients dans l'Europe du Nord (xive-xve siècle)* (Rennes, 2001).

Cast, D., 'Aurispa, Petrarch, and Lucian. An Aspect of Renaissance Translation', *Renaissance Quarterly* 27 (1974), pp. 157-173.

Cauchies, M., 'Antoine de Bourgogne, dit le Grand Bâtard' in: Baelde, ed, *Les Chevaliers*, pp. 118-120.

Cayet, P.V., *Chronologie Novenarie contenant l'histoire de la guerre sous le règne du très-Chrestien roy de France et de Navarre, Henry IV*, in: Michaud, J. and Poujalat, B., eds, *Nouvelle Collection des Mémoires pour servir à l'Histoire de France depuis le XIIIe siècle jusqu'à la fin du XVIIIe*, vol. 12 (Paris, 1838).

Céard, J., Ménager, D. and Simonin, M., eds, *Pierre de Ronsard, Œuvres complètes*, 2 vols. (Paris, 1993-1994).

Cervantes, F., *The Devil in the New World: The Impact of Diabolism in New Spain* (New Haven, 1994).

Chamard, H. and Bellinger, Y., eds, *Joachim du Bellay. Œuvres complètes*, vol. 1: *L'Olive. L'Antérotique. XXX Sonnetz de l'Honneste Amours* (Paris, 1989).

Chambers, D.S., 'The Earlier 'Academies' in Italy', in: Chambers and Quiviger, *Italian Academies*, pp. 1-14.

Chambers, D.S. and Martineau, J. eds, *Splendours of the Gonzaga (Catalogue of the Exhibition 4 november 1981-31 January 1982) Victoria and Albert Museum, London* (Milan, 1981).

Chambers, D.S. and Quiviger, F., ed, *Italian Academies of the Sixteenth Century* (London, 1995).

Chambers, R., *Domestic Annals of Scotland* (2nd edn., Edinburgh, s.d.).

Chambers, R.W., Batho, R.C. and Husband, H.W., eds, *Bellenden, John. Hector Boethius, Chronicle of Scotland, Edinburgh (1540?),* English Experience 851, facsimile edition of Bellenden's Hystory and Chronicles (Amsterdam/ Norwood, 1977).

Chambers, R.W., Batho, R.C. and Husbands, H.W., eds, *The Chronicles of Scotland compiled by Hector Boece, Translated into Scots by John Bellenden*, 2 vols. (Edinburgh/London, 1938-1941).

Champion, P., *Catherine de Médicis présente à Charles IX son royaume (1564-1566)* (Paris, 1937).

Champollion, A., ed, *Poésies du roi François Ier, de Louise de Savoie, duchesse d'Angoulême, de Marguerite, reine de Navarre. Correspondance intime du roi avec Diane de Poitiers et plusieurs autres dames de la cour* (Geneva, 1970/Paris 1847).

Charrière, E., *Négociations de la France dans le Levant*, vol. 1 (New York, 1966).

Chastelain, G., *Chronique* in: Kervyn de Lettenhove, *Œuvres*, vols. 1-5.

———, *Advertissement au duc Charles soubs fiction de son propre enten-dement parlant à luy-mesme, autre personnage de luy, lequel l'instruit en sa cause* in: Kervyn de Lettenhove, ed, *Œuvres*, vol. 7, pp. 285-333.

Chaunu, P., *Conquête et exploitation des nouveaux mondes, XVIe siècle* (Paris, 1995).

Chmelarz, E., 'Die Ehrenpforte des Kaisers Maximilian I.', *Jahrbuch der Kunsthistorischen Sammlungen des Allerhöchsten Kaiserhauses* 4 (1886), pp. 289-319.

Christianson, J.R., *On Tycho's Island. Tycho Brahe and His Assistants, 1570-1601* (Cambridge, 2000).

Chroscicki, J., 'Ceremonial Space', in: Ellenius, A., ed, *Iconography, Propaganda, and Legitimation* (Oxford, 1998), pp. 193-216.

Clendinnen, I., *Ambivalent Conquests: Maya and Spaniard in Yucatan, 1517-1570* (Cambridge, 1987).

Cloulas, Y., *Catherine de Médicis* (Paris, 1979).
———, *Les châteaux de la Loire au temps de la Renaissance* (Paris, 1983).
———, *Diane de Poitiers* (Paris, 1997).
Cochleus, Johannes, *An expediat laicis Novi Testamenti libros lingua vernacula* (Basel or Augsburg, 1533).
Cockshaw, P. *et al.*, eds, *Karel de Stoute 1433-1477* (Brussels, 1977).
———, 'La présence de l'ordre de la Toison d'or ou de ses symboles dans les monnaies', in: Van den Bergen-Pantens, ed, *L'ordre de la Toison d'or*, pp. 163-165.
Cockx-Indestege, E. and Hendrickx, F.P.M., eds, *Miscellanea Neerlandica. Opstellen voor Dr. Jan Deschamps ter gelegenheid van zijn zeventigste verjaardag* (Louvain, 1987).
Cohen, K., *Metamorphosis of a Death Symbol. The Transi Tomb in the Late Middle Ages and the Renaissance* (Berkeley, 1973).
Coldwell, D.F.C., ed, *Virgil's 'Aeneid' translated into Scottish Verse by Gavin Douglas*, 4 vols. (Edinburgh/London, 1957-1964).
Coleman, J., 'The science of politics and late medieval academic debate', in: Copeland, R., ed, *Criticism and Dissent* (Cambridge, 1996), pp. 181-214.
*Collection des ordonnances des rois de France. Catalogue des Actes de François Ier*, 8 vols. (Paris, 1905-1908).
Comito, T. *The Idea of the Garden in the Renaissance* (New Brunswick, 1978).
Complurium eruditorum uatum carmina ad magnificum uirum D. Blasium Holcelium (Augsburg, 1518).
Conley, T., *The Self-Made Map: Cartographic Writing in Early Modern France* (Minneapolis, 1996).
Constable, A., ed and transl, *A History of Greater Britain as well England as Scotland, by John Major* (Edinburgh, 1892).
Constant, J.M., *La Ligue* (Paris, 1996).
Contamine, P., 'Entre France et Écosse: Bérault Stuart, seigneur d'Aubigny (vers 1452-1508), chef de guerre, diplomate, écrivain militaire', in: Laidlaw, J., ed, *The Auld Alliance: France and Scotland over 700 Years* (Edinburgh, 1999), pp. 59-76.
Cools, H. *Mannen met macht. Edellieden en de Moderne Staat in de Bourgondisch-Habsburgse landen, ca. 1475-ca.1530* (Amsterdam, 2000).
Cormier, J.-P., *An Edition of the Middle French Prose Romance, Gilles de Chyn based on mss. No. 10237 of the Bibliothèque Royale of Brussels and No. 134 fonds Godefroy of the Bibliothèque Municipale of Lille* (Evanston, 1983).
Cosgrove, D., ed, *Mappings* (London, 1999).
Couton, G., ed, *Corneille. Théâtre complet*, 2 vols. (Paris, 1993).
Cowan, I.B. and Easson, E.D., *Medieval Religious Houses Scotland* (London/New York, 1976).
Craig, Thomas, *Henrici et Mariae epithalamium* (Edinburgh, 1565).
Craigie, W.A., ed, *Livy's History of Rome. The First Five Books Translated into Scots by John Bellenden in 1533*, 2 vols. (Edinburgh/London, 1901-1903).
———, *Maitland Folio Manuscript*, 2 vols. (Edinburgh/London, 1919-1927).
———, ed, *The Poems of James VI of Scotland*, 2 vols. (Edinburgh/London, 1955-1958).

Cranstoun, J., ed, *Satirical Poems of the Time of the Reformation*, 2 vols. (Edinburgh/London, 1891-1893).

Cranstoun, J. and Stevenson, G., eds, *The Poems of Alexander Montgomerie* (Edinburgh/London, 1887-1910).

Crawford, B.E., ed, *Church, Chronicle and Learning in Medieval and Early Renaissance Scotland* (Edinburgh, 1999).

Crawfurd, R., *The King's Evil* (Oxford, 1911).

Cromé, F., ed, *Dialogue d'entre le maheustre et le manant* (Geneva, 1977).

Crosby, A.W., *Ecological Imperialism: The Biological Expansion of Europe, 900-1900* (Cambridge, 1986).

Crouzet, D., *Les guerriers de Dieu. La violence au temps des troubles de religion, vers 1525-vers 1610*, 2 vols. (Seyssel, 1990).

———, *La nuit de la Saint-Barthélemy. Un rêve perdu de la Renaissance* (Paris, 1994).

CSP Foreign: Stevenson *et al.*, eds.

CSP Rome: Rigg, ed.

CSP Scot: Bain *et al.*, eds.

Cuddy, N., 'The revival of the entourage: the bedchamber of James I, 1603-1625', in: Starkey, D., ed, *The English Court: from the Wars of the Roses to the Civil War* (London, 1987), pp. 173-196.

Cunningham, A., 'The Culture of Gardens', in: Jardine, L. *et al.*, eds, *Cultures of Natural History* (Cambridge, 1996), pp. 38-56.

Cunningham, I.C., '*Bruce* and *Wallace* (National Library of Scotland Advocates' Manuscript 19.2.2)', *Edinburgh Bibliographical Society Transactions* 4 (1955-71), pp. 245-252.

———, 'The Asloan Manuscript', in: MacDonald, Lynch and Cowan, eds, *The Renaissance in Scotland*, pp. 107-135.

Cuvelier, J. *et al.*, eds, *Actes des États Généraux des anciens Pays-Bas*, vol. 1 (Brussels, 1948).

DaCosta Kaufmann, *Court, Cloister & City. The Art and Culture of Central Europe 1450-1800* (London, 1995).

Dahlberg, G., *Komediantteatern i 1600-talets Stockholm* (Stockholm, 1992).

Dalyell, J.G., ed, *Fragments of Scottish History* (Edinburgh, 1798).

Damen, M., *De staat van dienst. De gewestelijke ambtenaren van Holland en Zeeland in de Bourgondische periode (1425-1482)* (Hilversum, 2000).

Davidson, P., 'The Entry of Mary Stewart into Edinburgh, 1561, and other Ambiguities', *Renaissance Studies* 9 (1995), pp. 416-429.

Dawson, J., '"The face of ane perfyt reformed kyrk": St Andrews and the early Scottish Reformation', in: Kirk, J., ed, *Humanism and Reform: the Church in Europe, England and Scotland, 1400-1643* (Oxford, 1991), pp. 413-435.

De Boom, G., *Marguerite d'Autriche-Savoie et la Pré-Renaissance* (Brussels, 1935).

De Comminges, É., *Stuart, B., Traité sur l'Art de la Guerre* (The Hague, 1976).

De Haan, C., '"De Roman van Heinric en Margriete van Limborch": Middelhoogduitse receptie van Middelnederlandse literatuur', *Queeste. Tijdschrift over middeleeuwse letterkunde in den Nederlanden* 1 (1994), pp. 139-155.

De Hemptinne, Th., 'Princes et courtisans', in: Prevenier, ed, *Le Prince*, pp. 14-33.

De Jonge, K., 'Der herzogliche und kaiserliche Palast zu Brüssel und die Entwicklung des höfischen Zeremoniells im 16. und 17. Jahrhundert', *Jahrbuch des Zentralinstituts für Kunstgeschichte* 5/6 (1989/90), pp. 253-282.

———, 'Het paleis op de Coudenberg te Brussel in de vijftiende Eeuw. De verdwenen hertogelijke Residenties in de zuidelijke Nederlanden in een nieuw Licht geplaatst', *Revue Belge d'Archéologie et d'Histoire de l'Art* 59 (1990), pp. 5-38.

———, 'Le palais de Charles-Quint à Bruxelles', in: Guillaume, J., ed, *Architecture et Vie Sociale. L'organisation des grandes demeures à la fin du Moyen Age et à la Renaissance*, vol. 1 (Paris, 1994), pp. 107-125.

———, 'The Architectural Enterprises of the Emperor and his Court in the Low Countries. The European Context', in: Soly and Van den Welde, eds, *Carolus*, pp. 35-53.

De L'Estoile, Pierre, *Journal de L'Estoile pour le règne de Henri IV*, vol. 1 *1589-1600*, ed. by R.L. Lefèvre (Paris, 1948).

———, *The Paris of Henry of Navarre as seen by Pierre de l'Estoile, Selections from his Mémoires-Journaux*, transl. by N.L. Roelker (Cambridge, Mass., 1958).

De Nolhac, P., *Ronsard et l'Humanisme avec un portrait de Jean Dorat et un autographe de Ronsard* (Paris, 1921).

De Pont-Aimery, Alexandre, *Discours d'Estat sur la Blessure du Roy* (Paris, 1595).

De Quinsonas, E., *Matériaux pour servir à l'histoire de Marguerite d'Autriche, Duchesse de Savoie, Regente des Pays-Bas*, 3 vols. (Paris, 1860).

De Wachter, L., Schlusemann, R. *et al.*, eds, *Fragmenten van de 'Roman van Heinric ende Margriete van Limborch'.* (Leuven 2001).

De Waele, M., 'Image de force, perception de faiblesse: La clémence d'Henri IV', *Renaissance and Reformation* 17 (New Series, 1993), pp. 51-60.

———, 'Clémence royale et fidélités françaises à la fin des Guerre de Reli-gion', *Historical Reflections/Reflexions Historiques* 24 (1998), pp. 231-252.

Debae, M., *La bibliothèque de Marguerite d'Autriche: essai de reconstruction d'après l'inventaire de 1523-24* (Louvain/Paris, 1995).

Del Hoyo, A., ed, *Baltasar Gracián. Obras completas* (Madrid, 1960).

Delacourcelle, D., ed, *Rémy Belleau, La Bergerie. Texte de l'édition de 1565 publié avec une introduction, des notes et un glossaire* (Geneva, 1954).

Delenda, O, 'Sainte Marie Madeleine et l'application du décret tridentin (1563) sur les Saintes Images', in: Duperray, E., ed, *Marie Madeleine dans la mystique, les arts et les lettres* (Paris, 1989), pp. 191-210.

Delmarcel, G., 'De passietapijten van Margareta van Oostenrijk (ca. 1518-1524). Nieuwe gegevens en documenten', *Revue Belge d'Archéologie et d'Histoire de l'Art* 61 (1992), pp. 127-160.

Delumeau, J., *Sin and Fear. The Emergence of a Western Guilt Culture, 13th-18th Centuries*, transl. by E. Nicholson (New York, 1990).

Demerson, G., *La Mythologie dans l'œuvre de la 'Pléiade'* (Geneva, 1972).

Denhaene, G., 'Les collections de Philippe de Clèves, le goût pour le nu et la Renaissance aux Pays-Bas', *Bulletin de l'Institut Historique Belge de Rome* 45 (1975), pp. 310-342.

Dennison, E.P., *An Archaeological and Historical assessment of the proposed New Parliament of Scotland Site* (Edinburgh, 1998).

Denuce, J., *Les origines de la cartographie portugaise et les cartes des Reinel* (Amsterdam, 1963).

Der Triumphzug Kaiser Maximilians I. 1516-1518 [...] Mit dem von Kaiser Maximilian diktierten Programm und einem Nachwort von Horst Appuhn (Dortmund, 1979).

Derolez, A., 'Vroeg humanisme en middeleeuwse bibliotheken. De bibliotheek van de Adorne's en van de Jeruzalemkapel te Brugge', *Tijdschrift voor Geschiedenis* 85 (1972), pp. 161-170.

———, *The Library of Raphael de Marcatellis, Abbot of St. Bavon's Ghent, 1437-1508* (Ghent, 1979).

Derry, T.K., *A History of Scandinavia* (Minneapolis/London, 1979).

Deschaux, R., *Un poète bourguignon du XVe siècle, Michault Taillevent* (Geneva, 1975).

Descrittione del regno di Scotia di Petruccio Ubaldini (repr. Edinburgh, 1829).

Dewald, J., *Aristocratic Experience and the Origins of Modern Culture: France, 1570-1715* (Berkeley, 1993).

Deyon, P., *Amiens Capitale Provinciale étude sur la société urbaine au 17e siècle* (Paris, 1967).

Dhanens, E., 'Jan van Roome alias van Brussel, schilder', *Gentse Bijdragen tot de Kunstgeschiedenis en Oudheidkunde* 11 (1945-48), pp. 41-146.

Dickinson, J.G., *The Congress of Arras 1435. A Study in Medieval Diplomacy* (Oxford, 1955).

Dickinson, W.C., ed, *John Knox's History of the Reformation in Scot-land*, 2 vols. (Edinburgh, 1949).

Dickinson, W.C., Donaldson, G. and Milne, I.A., eds, *A Source Book of Scottish History* (London, 1958).

Dickson, R. and Edmond, J.P., *Annals of Scottish Printing* (Cambridge, 1890; reissued Amsterdam, 1975).

Dickson, T. and Balfour Paul, J., eds, *Accounts of the Lord High Treasurer of Scotland*, 12 vols. (Edinburgh, 1877-1916).

Dilworth, M., *Scottish Monasteries in the Late Middle Ages* (Edinburgh, 1995).

Dogaer, G. and Debae, M., eds, *La librairie de Philippe le Bon* (Brussels, 1967).

Donaldson, G., *The Scottish Reformation* (Cambridge, 1960).

———, *All the Queen's Men: Power and Politics in Mary Stewart's Scotland* (London, 1983).

———, *The Faith of the Scots* (London, 1990).

Doughty, D.W., 'The library of James Stewart, earl of Moray, 1531-1570', *Innes Review* 21 (1970), pp. 17-29.

———, 'Renaissance books, bindings and owners in St Andrews and elsewhere: the humanists', *Bibliotheck* 7.5 (1975), pp. 117-31.

Douglas, *Eneados*: Coldwell, D.F.C., ed, *Virgil's 'Aeneid'*.

Doutrepont, G., *La littérature française à la cour des ducs de Bourgogne. Philippe le Hardi, Jean Sans Peur, Philippe le Bon, Charles le Téméraire* (Paris, 1909; repr. Geneva, 1970).

Dowell, G.S. and Donnell, V., *Propaganda and Persuasion* (London/New Delhi, 1986).

Downie, F., 'La voie quelle menace tenir: Annabella Stewart, Scotland, and the European Marriage Market, 1444-56', *Scottish Historical Review* 78 (1999), pp. 170-191.

Drijvers, J.W. and MacDonald, A.A., eds, *Centres of Learning* (Leiden, 1995).

Du Laurens, André, *De mirabili strumas sanandi vi solis Galliae regibus Christianissimis divinitus concessa liber unus et de strumarum natura, differentiis, causis, curatione quae fit arte & industria medica liber alter* (Paris, 1609).

Dubois, C.-G., *Celtes et Gaulois au XVIe siècle* (Paris, 1972).

———, *L'Imaginaire de la Renaissance* (Paris, 1985).

———, ed, *Artus Thomas, L'Isle des Hermaphrodites nouvellement descouverte* (Geneva, 1996).

Duff, E.G., 'The two first books printed in the Scottish Language', *Publications of the Edinburgh Bibliographical Society* 1 (1892-1893), No. 3.

Duffy, E., *The Stripping of the Altars: Traditional Religion in England, c.1400-c.1580* (New Haven, 1992).

Duijvestijn, B.W.Th., *Der deutsche und der niederländische 'Malagis'. Eine vergleichende Studie*, 2 vols. (Ghent, 1985).

———, 'Niederländische Dichtung in der Privatbücherei der Pfalzgräfin Mechthild (1418/1419-1482)', in: Cockx-Indestege and Hendrickx, *Miscellanea Neerlandica*, pp. 251-261.

———, 'Middelnederlandse literatuur in Duitse overlevering. Een arbeidsveld voor Neerlandici', in: Van Oostrom, F.P. and Willaert, F., eds, *De studie van de Middelnederlandse letterkunde: stand en toekomst* (Hilversum, 1989), pp. 153-168.

———, '"Uss dem flemischen". Zum Arbeitsverfahren spätmittelhoch-deutscher Übersetzer am Beispiel des *Malagis* und des *Karlle ind Elegast*', in: Sonderegger, S. and Stegeman, J., eds, *Geben und Nehmen. Vorträge über Theorie und Geschichte deutscher Rezeption niederländischer Sprache und Literatur an der Universität Zürich* (Dordrecht, 1993), pp. 111-134.

———, '"Reinolt von Montelban", eine niederländische Dichtung in deutschen Landen', in: Schlusemann and Wackers, *Die spätmittelalterliche Rezeption*, pp. 49-64.

Duindam, J., *Myths of Power. Norbert Elias and the Early Modern European Court* (Amsterdam, 1995).

Dunbar, J.G., *Scottish Royal Palaces: the Architecture of the Royal Residences during the Late Medieval and Early Renaissance Period* (East Linton, 1999).

Duncan, A.A.M., 'Hector Boece and the Medieval Tradition', in: Doig, R.P., ed, *Scots Antiquaries and Historians* (Dundee, 1972), pp. 1-11.

Durkan, J., 'The Beginnings of Humanism in Scotland', *Innes Review* 4 (1953), pp. 5-24.

———, 'The Cultural Background in Sixteenth-Century Scotland', in: McRoberts, D., ed, *Essays on the Scottish Reformation 1513-1625* (Glasgow, 1962), pp. 274-331.

———, 'The Sanctuary and College of Tain', *Innes Review* 13 (1962), pp. 147-156.

———, 'Henry Scrimgeour, Renaissance bookman', *Edinburgh Bibliographical Society Transactions* 5 (1978), pp. 1-31.

———, 'Giovanni Ferrerio, Gesner and French Affairs', *Bibliothèque d'Humanisme et Renaissance* 42.2 (1980), pp. 349-360.

———, 'Giovanni Ferrerio, Humanist: His Influence in Sixteenth-Century Scotland', in Robbins, K., ed, *Religion and Humanism* (Oxford, 1981), pp. 181-194.
———, 'The Royal Lectureships under Mary of Lorraine', *Scottish Historical Review* 62 (1983), pp. 73-78.
———, 'Contract between Clerk and Lekpreuik for printing the Book of Common Order, 1564', *The Bibliotheck* 11 (1983), pp. 129-135.
———, 'The Observant Franciscan Province of Scotland', *Innes Review* 35 (1984), pp. 51-57.
———, 'Native influences on George Buchanan', in: McFarlane, I.D., ed, *Acta Conventus Neo-Latini Sanctandreani* (New York, 1986), pp. 31-42.
———, 'The Library of Mary Queen of Scots', in Lynch, *Mary Stewart*, pp. 71-104.
———, 'Education: The Laying of Fresh Foundations', in: MacQueen, *Humanism*, pp. 123-160.
Duverger, J., 'Jacopo de' Barbari en Jan Gossart bij Filips van Burgondië te Souburg (1515)', *Mélanges Hulin de Loo* (Brussels, 1931), pp. 142-153.
———, 'Floris Nepotis, orgelist van Margareta van Oostenrijk en Karel V (na 1495-1537)', in: *Miscellanea Musicologica Floris van der Meuren*, (Ghent, 1950), pp. 1-15.
———, 'Jan Mostaert, ereschilder van Margareta van Oostenrijk', *Aachener Kunstblätter* 41 (1971), pp. 113-117.
———, 'Margareta van Oostenrijk (1480-1530) en de Italiaanse Renaissance', *Relations artistiques entre les Pays-Bas et l'Italie à la Renaissance: Etudes dédiées à Suzanne Sulzberger* (Brussels/Rome, 1980), pp. 127-142.
———, 'Het statuut van de zestiende-eeuwse hofkunstenaar in de Nederlanden', *Jaarboek van het Koninklijk Museum voor Schone Kunsten-Antwerpen* (1982), pp. 61-95.
Eamon, W., 'Court, Academy, and Printing House', in: Eamon, W., *Age and Institutions. Science, Technology, and Medecine at the European Court 1500-1750* (Woodbridge, 1991), pp. 25-50.
Edin. Recs: Marwick.
Edington, C., *Court and Culture in Renaissance Scotland* (Amherst, Mass., 1994; reissued East Linton, 1995).
Edwards, A.S.G., 'Contextualising Middle Scots Romance', in: Houwen, MacDonald and Mapstone, eds, *A Palace in the Wild*, pp. 61-73.
Egg, E., 'Der Wappenturm – Zur Vorgeschichte einer heraldisch-künstlerischen Idee', *Veröffentlichungen des Tiroler Landesmuseums* 70 (1990), pp.99-109.
Ehrmann, J., 'Antoine Caron. Tapisserie et tableau inédits dans la série de la reine Artémise', *Bulletin de la Société de l'histoire de l'art français* (1964), pp. 25-34
———, *Antoine Caron. Peintre des fêtes et des massacres* (Paris, 1986).
Eichberger, D., 'A Renaissance Princess named Margaret. Fashioning a Public Image in a Courtly Society', *Melbourne Art Journal*, 4 (2001), pp. 4-24.
———, 'A noble Residence for a Female Regent. Margaret of Austria and the Construction of the Court of Savoy in Mechelen', in: Hills, H., ed, *Gender, Architecture and Power in Early Modern Europe* (Aldershot, 2002).
———, 'Hoofse hobby's – over humanisme en mecenaat in de vroee 16de eeuw', *Kunstschrift* 1 (2002), pp. 32-37.
———, *Leben mit Kunst-Wirken durch Kunst. Sammelwesen und Hofkunst unter*

Margarete von Österreich, Regentin der Niederlande (Turnhout/London, 2002).
Eichberger, D. and Beaven, L., 'Family Members and Political Allies: The Portrait Gallery of Margaret of Austria in Mechelen', *Art Bulletin*, 77,2 (1995), pp. 225-248.
Eisenstein, E.L., *The Printing Press as an Agent of Change. Communications and cultural transformations in early-modern Europe*, 2 vols. (Cambridge, 1979; as one vol., 1980).
Elam, C., 'Mantegna at Mantua', in: Chambers and Martineau, eds. *Splendours of the Gonzaga*, pp. 15-25.
Elias, N., *Die höfische Gesellschaft. Untersuchungen zur Soziologie des Königtums und der höfischen Aristokratie* (Darmstadt/Neuwied, [5]1981).
Elliott, J.H., *The Old World and the New, 1492-1650* (Cambridge, 1970).
———, 'A Europe of Composite Monarchies', *Past and Present* 137 (1992), pp. 48-71.
Elliott, K., 'Trip and Go, Hey: "A Truly Scottish Song"', in: Hadley Williams, ed, *Stewart Style*, pp. 53-173.
———, ed, *The Complete Works of Robert Carver* (Glasgow, 1996).
Elliott, K. and Shire, H.M., eds, *Musica Britannica XV: Music of Scotland 1500-1700* (London, 1964).
Emond, W.K., *The Minority of James V, 1513-1528* (Ph.D. diss. St Andrews, 1988).
Enders, J., 'Rhetoric, coercion, and the memory of violence', in: Copeland, R., ed, *Criticism and Dissent in the Middle Ages* (Cambridge 1996), pp. 24-55.
ER: Stuart, J. *et al*, eds, *The Exchequer Rolls of Scotland.*
Falconer, W.A., ed. and transl, *Cicero. De Senectute, De Amicitia, De Divinatione* (London/Cambridge, Mass., 1964).
Färber. H., ed, *Horaz. Sämtliche Werke. Lateinisch und Deutsch* (Munich, 1967).
Farrow, K.D., 'The Substance and Style of Hector Boece's Scotorum Historiae', *Scottish Literary Journal* 25.1 (1998), pp. 5-25.
Fawcett, R., *Scottish Architecture from the Accession of the Stewarts to the Reformation 1371-1560* (Edinburgh, 1994).
———, *Stirling Castle* (London, 1995).
Fergusson, Sir J., *The White Hind and Other Discoveries* (London, 1963).
———, *The Man behind Macbeth, and Other Stories* (London, 1969).
Fernández-Armesto, F., ed, *The European Opportunity* (Brookfield/Vermont, 1995).
Ferrerio, Giovanni, *De vera cometae significatione contra astrologorum omnium vanitatem libellus* (Paris, 1540)
ffolliott, S., 'Catherine de' Medici as Artemisia: Figuring the Powerful Widow', in: Ferguson, M.W., Quilligan, M. and Vickers, N.J., eds, *Rewriting the Renaissance. The Discourses of Sexual Difference in Early Modern Europe* (London/Chicago, 1986), pp. 227-241.
———, 'Casting a Rival into a Shade: Catherine de' Medici and Diane de Poitiers', *Art Journal* 18/2 (1989), pp. 138-143.
———, 'A Queen's Garden of Power: Catherine de'Medici', in: Di Cesare, M.A., ed, *Reconsidering the Renaissance* (Binghamton, NY, 1992), pp. 245-255.
———, 'Exemplarity and Gender: Three Lives of Queen Catherine de'Medici', in: Meyer, T.F and Woolf, D.R., eds, *The Rhetorics of Life-Writing in Early*

Modern Europe. Forms of Biography from Cassandra Fedele to Louis XIV (Ann Arbor, 1995), pp. 321-340.
———, 'The Ideal Queenly Patron of the Renaissance: Catherine de'Medici Defining Herself or Defined by Others?', in: Lawrence, C., ed, *Women and Art in Early Modern Europe: Patrons Collectors and Connoisseurs* (University Park, PA, 1997), pp. 99-110.
Finlay, J., 'James Henryson and the Origins of the Office of King's Advocate in Scotland', *Scottish Historical Review*, 72,1: No. 207 (2000), pp. 17-38.
Finley-Croswhite, S.A., *Henry IV and the Towns: The Pursuit of Legitimacy in French Urban Society, 1589-1610* (Cambridge, UK, 1999).
Finot, J., *Inventaire sommaire des Archives Départementales antérieures à 1790*, vol. VIII (Lille, 1895).
Finscher, L., (re)ed of Blume, F. ed, *Die Musik in Geschichte und Gegenwart. Allgemeine Enzyklöpadie der Musik* (Kassel/etc., 1994–...).
Firth Green, R., *Poets and Princepleasers. Literature and the English Court in the Late Middle Ages* (Toronto/Buffalo/London, 1980).
Fisher, P., 'Introduction III to Olaus Magnus', in: Foote, P., ed, *History of the Northern Peoples*, 3 vols. (London, 1996-1998).
Fleming, W., Motherwell, W. and Smith, J., eds, *Rob Stene's Dream* (Maitland Club, 1836).
Fletcher, J.M., 'Isabella d'Este. Patron and Collector', in: Chambers and Martineau, eds, *Splendours of the Gonzaga*, pp. 51-63.
Ford, P.J., *George Buchanan: Prince of Poets* (Aberdeen, 1982).
Forster, R., ed, *European and Non-European Societies, 1450-1800*, 2 vols. (Brookfield, 1997).
Foucault, M., 'Questions on Geography', in: Gordon, C., ed, *Power/Knowledge: Selected Interviews and Other Writings, 1972-1977, Michel Foucault* (New York, 1980), pp. 63-77.
Foulkes, A.P., *Literature and Propaganda* (London/New York, 1983).
Fox, D., 'Middle Scots Poets and Patrons', in: Scattergood, V.J. and Sherborne, J.W., eds, *English Court Culture in the Later Middle Ages* (London, 1983), pp. 109-127.
Fox, D., ed, *The Poems of Robert Henryson* (Oxford, 1981).
Fradenburg, L.O., *City, Marriage, Tournament: Arts of Rule in Late Medieval Scotland* (Madison, 1991).
———, 'Sovereign Love: The Wedding of Margaret Tudor and James IV of Scotland', *Cosmos* 7 (1992), pp. 78-100.
Franke, B., *Assuerus und Esther am Burgunderhof. Zur Rezeption des Buches Esther in den Niederlanden (1450-1530)* (Berlin, 1998).
Franke, B. and Welzel, B., 'Katharina von Medici (1519-1589)', in: Zimmermann and Böhm, eds, *Französische Frauen der frühen Neuzeit*, pp. 65-80.
Franssen, P.J.A., *Tussen Tekst en Publiek: Jan van Doesborch, drukker-uitgever en literator te Antwerpen en Utrecht in de eerste helft van de zestiende eeuw* (Amsterdam/Atlanta, 1990).
Frappier, J., ed, *Jean Lemaire de Belges. La Concorde des deux Langages* (Paris, 1947).
French Political Pamphlets, 1560 through 1653 from the collection in the Newberry Library, 28 reels (Cleveland, 1968).

Fricke, D., *Die französischen Fassungen der* Institutio Principis Christiani *des Erasmus von Rotterdam* (Geneva, 1967).

Frommberger-Weber, U., 'Spätgotische Buchmalerei in den Städten Speyer, Worms und Heidelberg (1440-1510)', *Zeitschrift für die Geschichte des Oberrheins* 121 NF 82 (1973), pp. 35-145.

Frzybowski, S. and Allen, E., 'History and the Importance of Scrofula', *The Lancet* 346, No. 8988 (December 2, 1995), pp. 1472-74.

Fubini, M. and Maier, B., ed, *Torquato Tasso. Aminta* (Milan, [4]1988).

Funck-Brentano, F., 'Le caractère religieux de la diplomatie du moyen âge', *Revue d'histoire diplomatique* 1 (1887), pp. 113-125.

Gachard, L.P., ed, *Collection des documens inédits concernant l'histoire de la Belgique* (Brussels, 1833).

Gadoffre, G., *Du Bellay et le sacré* (Paris, 1978).

Gaehtgens, B., 'Machtwechsel oder die Übergabe der Regentschaft', in: Baumgärtel and Neysters, *Die Galerie der Starken Frauen*, pp. 64-78.

Galitzin, le Prince A., ed, *Le Plessis, Les Triomphes faictz a l'entree de Françoys II et de Marye Stuart au chasteau de Chenonceau le dymanche dernier iour de mars MDLIX* (Tours, 1559; Paris, 1857).

Gallet-Guerne, D., *Vasque de Lucène et la* Cyropédie *à la cour de Bourgogne 1470. Le traité de Xenophon mis en français d'après la verion latine du Pogge* (Geneva, 1974).

Garstein, O., *Rome and the Counter-Reformation in Scandinavia. Jesuit Educational Strategy 1553-1622* (Leiden, 1992).

Gatt, A., *Der Innsbrucker Hof zur Zeit Kaiser Maximilians 1493-1519* (Innsbruck, 1943.

Gerhard, D., *Old Europe. A Study of Continuity, 1000-1800* (New York, 1981).

Giesey, R.E., 'The "King Imagined"', in: Baker, K.M., ed, *The French Revolution and the Creation of Modern Political Culture*, vol. 1 (Oxford, 1987), pp. 41-59.

Gillies, W., 'The Gaelic Poems of Sir Duncan Campbell of Glenorchy', *Scottish Gaelic Studies* 13, part i (1978), pp. 18-45; 13, part ii (1981), pp. 263-288; 14, part i (1983), pp. 59-82.

Gillot, H. *La Querelle des Anciens et des Modernes en France* (Nancy, 1914).

Gimeno, R., ed, *Juan del Encina. Teatro (Segunda producción dramática)* (Madrid, [3]1987).

Glahn, H., ed, *Musik i Danmark på Christian IV:s tid*, 7 vols. See Jensen and Krabbe.

Glendinning, M, MacInnes, R. and MacKechnie, A., *A History of Scottish Architecture* (Edinburgh, 1996).

Glier, I., *Artes amandi. Untersuchung zu Geschichte, Überlieferung und Typologie der deutschen Minnereden* (München, 1971).

Goette, A., *Der Ehrenbrief des Jakob Püterich von Reichertshausen an die Erzherzogin Mechthild* (Straßburg, 1899).

Goldberg, J., *James I and the Politics of Literature* (Stanford, 1983).

Gollwitzer, H., 'Zur Geschichte der Diplomatie im Zeitalter Maximilians I.', *Historisches Jahrbuch der Görresgesellschaft* 74 (1955), pp. 189-199.

Gombrich, E.H., *Symbolic Images. Studies in the art of the Renaissance II* (Oxford, [3]1985).

Goodare, J., 'Queen Mary's Catholic interlude', in: Lynch, M., ed, *Mary Stewart*,

Queen in Three Kingdoms (Oxford, 1988), pp. 154-170.

———, *State and Society in Early Modern Scotland* (Oxford, 1999).

———, 'Scottish Politics in the reign of James VI', in: Goodare and Lynch, *Reign of James VI*, pp. 32-54.

Goodare, J. and Lynch, M., eds, *The Reign of James VI* (East Linton, 2000).

Gosman, M., 'La matière "classique" dans la littérature française: les métacommentaires auctoriels (12e-16e siècles)', in: Welkenhuysen, A., Braet, H. and Verbeke, W., eds, *Mediaeval Antiquity* (Louvain, 1995), pp. 255-276.

———, *La légende d'Alexandre le Grand dans la littérature française du 12e siècle. Une réécriture permanente* (Amsterdam, 1997).

———, 'The Best Present Ever. The Notion of Time in sixteenth-century French Royal Entries', in: Gosman, M., Vanderjagt, A.J. and Veenstra, J.R., eds, *The Growth of Authority in the Medieval West* (Groningen, 1999), pp. 39-61.

———, 'Ariosto's *Orlando Furioso* and the Restoration of the Este image', in: Suntrup, R. and Veenstra, J.R., eds, *Normatieve Zentrierung in Herrschaftsausübung, Kirchenreform und kultureller Organisation*, forthcoming.

———, 'Le nationalisme' naissant et le sentiment de la *natio*: la tradition épique et la politique de Philippe le Bon', *Actes du XVe Congrès International de la Société Internationale Rencesvals pour l'étude des épopées romanes* (Poitiers, 2000). Forthcoming.

———, 'Les académies du Cinquecento: aventure scientifique ou politique?', in: *Les premiers siècles de la république européenne des Lettres (1368-1683). Actes du colloque international, Paris 3-4-5 décembre 2001*, forthcoming.

Gottlieb, T., *Büchersammlung Kaiser Maximilians I.* (Leipzig, 1900).

Goubert, P., *Beauvais et le Beauvaisis de 1600 à 1730. Contribution à l'histoire sociale de la France du XVIIe siècle* (Paris, 1960).

———, *Louis XIV et vingt millions de Français* (Paris, 1966).

Goyet, F., ed, *Traités de poétique et de rhétorique de la Renaissance* (Paris, 1990).

Graf, C., 'Audience Involvement in Lindsay's Satyre of the Thrie Estaitis', in: Strauss, D. and Drescher, H.W., eds, *Scottish Language and Literature, Medieval and Renaissance*, vol. 4 (Frankfurt am Main, 1986), pp. 423-35

Graham, V.E. and McAllister Johnson, W., *Estienne Jodelle, Le Recueil des Inscriptions, 1558. A Literary and Iconographical Exegesis* (Toronto, 1972).

———, eds, *The Paris Entries of Charles IX and Elisabeth of Austria, 1571. With an Analysis of Simon Bouquet's "Bref et sommaire recueil"* (Toronto, 1974).

———, eds, *The Royal Tour of France by Charles IX and Catherine de'Medici. Festivals and Entries, 1564-6* (Toronto, 1979).

Gray, D., 'A Scottish "Flower of Chivalry" and his Book', *Words* 4 (1974), pp. 22-34.

———, 'The Royal Entry in Sixteenth-Century Scotland', in: Mapstone and Wood, *The Rose and the Thistle*, pp. 10-37.

Green, R.F., *Poets and Princepleasers: Literature and the English Court in the Late Middle Ages* (Toronto, 1980).

Greenblatt, St., *Renaissance Self-Fashioning: From More to Shakespeare* (Chicago, 1980).

———, *Marvelous Possessions: The Wonder of the New World* (Chicago, 1991).

———, ed, *New World Encounters* (Berkeley, 1993).

Greengrass, M., 'Mary, dowager queen of France', in: Lynch, *Mary Stewart*, pp. 171-194.
———, *France in the Age of Henri IV. The Struggle for Stability* (London/ New York, 1984; repr. 1995).
Grote, A. ed, *Macrocosm in Microcosm. Die Welt in der Stube - Zur Geschichte des Sammelns 1450 bis 1800* (Opladen, 1994).
Grundtvig, S. *et al.*, eds, *Danmarks gamle Folkeviser*, 12 vols. (Copenhagen, 1853-1976).
Guenée, B. and Lehoux, F., *Les entrées royales françaises de 1328 à 1515* (Paris, 1968).
Guénin, E., *Ango et ses pilotes* (Paris, 1901).
Guerdan, R., *François Ier: le roi de la Renaissance* (Paris, 1981).
Guillaume, J., ed, *Architecture, jardin, paysage. L'environnement du château et de la villa aux XVe et XVIe siècles. Actes du colloque tenu à Tours du 1er au 4 juin 1992* (Paris, 1999).
Guy, J., *Tudor England* (Oxford, 1988).
Haase, A., Duijvestijn, Bob W. Th. *et al.*, eds, *Der deutsche Malagis: nach den Heidelberger Handschriften unter Benutzung der Vorarbeiten von Gabriele Schieb und Sabine Seelbach* (Berlin, 2000).
Hacke, D., 'Isabella d'Este (1474-1539)', in: Osols-Wehden, I., ed, *Frauen der Italienischen Renaissance. Dichterinnen, Malerinnen, Mäzeninnen* (Darmstadt, 1999), pp. 211-226.
Hadley Williams, J., ed, *Stewart Style 1513-1542: Essays on the Court of James V* (East Linton, 1996)
———, ed, *Sir David Lyndsay: Selected Poems* (Glasgow, 2000).
———, 'Dunbar and His Immediate Heirs', in: Mapstone, S., ed, *William Dunbar: the nobill poet*. Forthcoming.
Haggh, B., 'The Virgin Mary and the Order of the Golden Fleece' in: Caron and Clauzel, eds, *Le Banquet du Faisan*, pp. 273-287.
Hall, J.T.D., ed, *Manuscript Treasures in Edinburgh University Library* (Edinburgh, 1980).
Hamer, D., 'The Bibliography of Sir David Lindsay (1490-1555), *The Library*, 4th ser., 10.1 (1929), pp. 1-42.
———, ed, *The Works of Sir David Lindsay of the Mount*, 4 vols. (Edinburgh/ London, 1931-6).
Hamilton Papers: Bain, J. ed, *The Hamilton Papers*
Hanley, S., 'La loi salique', in: Fauré, Chr., ed, *Encyclopédie politique et historique des femmes* (Paris, 1997), pp. 11-30.
Hannay, R.K., ed, *Acts of the Lords of Council in Public Affairs 1501-1554* (Edinburgh, 1932).
Hannay, R.K. and Hay, D., eds, *The Letters of James V* (Edinburgh, 1954).
Harley, J.B., 'Silences and Secrecy: the Hidden Agenda of Cartography in Early Modern Europe', *Imago Mundi* 40 (1988), pp. 57-76.
———, 'Maps, Knowledge, and Power', in: Cosgrove, D. and Daniels, St., eds, *The Iconography of Landscape: Essays on the Symbolic Representation, Design, and Use of Past Environments* (New York, 1988), pp. 277-312.
———, 'Deconstructing the Map', *Cartographica* 26,2 (1989), pp. 1-20.

———, 'Historical Geography and the Cartographic Illusion', *Journal of Historical Geography* 15,1 (1989), pp. 80-91.
———, 'Rereading the Maps of the Columbian Encounter', *Annals of the Association of American Geographers* 82,3 (1992), pp. 523-542.
Harley, J.B. and Zandvliet, K., 'Art, Science, and Power in Sixteenth-Century Dutch Cartography', *Cartographica* 29,2 (1992), pp. 10-19.
Harsting, P., 'Latin valedictory poems of the 16th century', in: Skafte Jensen, M., ed, *A History of Nordic Neo-Latin Literature*, pp. 203-218.
Hauser, A., *The Social History of Art*, 2 vols. (London, 1951).
Hauser, H., *Recherches et Documents sur l'histoire des Prix en France de 1500-1800* (Paris, 1936).
Hays, J.N., *The Burdens of Disease, Epidemics and Human Response in Western History* (New Brunswick, N.J, 1998).
Heers, J., 'Le rôle des capitaux internationaux dans les voyages de découverte aux XVe et XVIe siècles', in: Fernández-Armesto, *The European Opportunity*, pp. 65-85.
Heers, J. and De Groër, G, ed, *Itinéraire d'Anselme Adorno en Terre Sainte, 1470-1471* (Paris, 1978).
Heijnsbergen, T. van, 'The Scottish Chapel Royal as a Cultural Intermediary between Town and Court', in: Drijvers, J.W. and MacDonald, A.A., eds, *Centres of Learning* (Leiden, 1995), pp. 299-313.
Heimann, H.-D., 'Stadtbürgerliches Selbstverständnis und Reform-mentalität des Heidelberger Hofkapellmeisters und Frankfurter Stadtarztes Johann von Soest genannt Steinwert (1448-1506)', *Westfälische Zeitschrift. Zeitschrift für vaterländische Geschichte und Altertumskunde* 135 (1985), pp. 239-262.
Heinig, P.-J., 'Theorie und Praxis des 'höfischen' Ordnung unter Friedrich III. und Maximilan I', in: Von Kruse, H. and Paravicini. W., eds., *Höfe und Hofordnungen* (Sigmaringen, 1999), pp. 223-242.
Helenius-Öberg, E., 'Kyrkans bild av den profana musiken', in: Jonsson, L., Nilsson, A.-M. and Andersson, G., eds, *Musiken i Sverige*, vol. 1, pp 153-168.
Hennequin, J., *Henri IV dans ses Oraisons Funèbres ou la naissance d'une légende* (Paris, 1977).
Henshall, N., *The Myth of Absolutism: Change and Continuity in Early Modern European Monarchy* (London, 1992).
Héritier, J., *Catherine de Médicis* (Paris, ²1994).
Hermann Schubert, F., 'Blasius Hölzl und die soziale Situation in der Hofkammer Maximilians', *Vierteljahresschrift für Sozial- und Wirtschaftsgeschichte* 47 (1960), pp. 105-115.
Hess, D., *Meister um das "mittelalterliche Hausbuch". Studien zur Hausbuch-meisterfrage* (Mainz, 1994).
Hexter, J.H., transl., *Claude de Seyssel, The Monarchy of France* (New Haven, 1981).
Highet, G., *The Classical Tradition* (New York, 1949, repr. 1957).
Hinrichs, E., *Fürsten und Mächte. Zum Problem des europäischen Absolutismus* (Göttingen, 2000).
HMC Historical Manuscripts Commission, *Report on the Manuscripts of the Earl of Mar and Kelly* (London, 1904).

Hoak, D., 'The Iconography of the Crown Imperial', in: Hoak, D., ed, *Tudor Political Culture* (Cambridge, 1995), pp. 54-103.
Hobson, A., *Humanists and Bookbinders* (Cambridge, 1989).
Hofmann, C. and Lecoq, D., eds, *Tours et contours de la Terre: Itinéraires d'une femme au cœur de la cartographie* (Paris, 1999).
Hofmann, H., 'Der spätmittelalterliche Rechtsbegriff der Repräsentation in Reich und Kirche', in: Ragotzky and Wenzel, *Höfische Repräsentation*, pp. 17-42.
Hoffmann, V., 'Donec totum impleat orbem: symbolisme impérial au temps de Henri II', *Bulletin de la Société de l'histoire de l'art français* (1978), pp. 29-42.
Hollingsworth, M., *Patronage in sixteenth-century Italy* (London, 1996).
Hommel, L., *Marie de Bourgogne ou le grand héritage* (Brussels, [4]1951).
Hoogvliet, M., 'The Symbolism of a Queen: Texts and Images Representing Catherine de Médicis at Royal Entries', forthcoming.
Horn, H.J., *Jan Cornelisz Vermeyen, painter of Charles V and his conquest of Tunis: paintings, etchings, drawings, cartoons and tapestries* (Doornspijk, 1989).
Hörsch, M., 'Architektur unter Margarethe von Österreich, Regentin der Niederlande (1507-1530)', *Verhandelingen van de Koninklijke Academie voor Wetenschappen, Letteren en Schone Kunsten van België. Klasse der Schone Kunsten*, 56 (1994), pp. 1-236.
Housley, N., *The Later Crusades, 1274-1580* (Oxford, 1992).
Houston, R.A., *Literacy in early Modern Europe. Culture & Education 1500-1800*, (London/New York 1988).
Houwen, L.A.J.R., MacDonald, A.A. and Mapstone, S.L., eds, *A Palace in the Wild: Essays on Culture and Humanism in Late-Medieval and Renaissance Scotland* (Louvain, 2000).
Howard Adams, W., *The French Garden* (New York, 1979).
Howard, D., *Scottish Architecture: Reformation to Restoration, 1560-1660* (Edinburgh, 1995).
Howarth, D., *Images of Rule. Art and Politics in the English Renaissance, 1485-1649* (London, 1997).
Huizinga, J., 'De Bourgondische macht en Frankrijk' in: Huizinga, J., *Verzamelde Werken*, 9 vols. (Haarlem, 1948), vol. 2, pp. 110-124.
———, *Herfsttij der middeleeuwen. Studie over levens- en gedachtenvormen der veertiende en vijftiende eeuw in Frankrijk en de Nederlanden* (1919), Van der Lem, A. ed (Amsterdam, 1999)
Hume, *Works*: Lawson, ed.
Huse, N., *Studien zu Giovanni Bellini* (Berlin/New York, 1972).
Hyden, R., *Zyprian von Serntein im Dienste Kaiser Maximilians I. in den Jahren 1490-1508* (Graz, 1973).
Hye, F.H., 'Die heraldischen Denkmale Maximilians I. in Tirol', *Der Schlern* 43 (1969), pp. 56-77.
IJsewijn, J. and Thomson, D.F.S., 'The Latin Poems of Jacobus Follisius or James Foullis of Edinburgh', *Humanistica Lovaniensia* 24 (1975), pp. 103-152.
Ilsøe, H., 'Danskerne og deres fædreland. Holdninger og opfattelser ca. 1550-1700', in: Feldbæk, O., ed, *Dansk identitetshistorie*, 4 vols. (Copenhagen, 1991), vol. 1, pp. 27-88.

Innes of Learney, T., 'The Scottish Parliament: its Symbolism and its Ceremonial', *Juridical Review* 44 (1932), pp. 87-124.

Innes, T. of Learney, *Scots Heraldry*, rev. ed M. Innes of Edingight (London/Edinburgh, 1977).

Ireland, *Meroure*: MacPherson, Quinn and McDonald, eds, *Johannes de Irlandia*.

Isenmann, E., *Die deutsche Stadt im Spätmittelalter (1250-1500). Stadtgestalt, Recht, Stadtregiment, Kirche, Gesellschaft, Wirtschaft* (Stuttgart, 1988).

Israel, J., *The Dutch Republic. Its Rise, Greatness, and Fall 1477-1806* (Oxford, 1995).

Jack, R.D.S., *Alexander Montgomerie* (Edinburgh, 1985).

———, ed, *The History of Scottish Literature: volume I: Origins to 1600* (Aberdeen, 1988).

Jacobus Typotius, *Symbola divina et humana pontificum imperialum regum* (Prague, 1601; repr. Graz, 1972).

Jacquart, J., 'Économie rurale et démographie sous Henri IV', in: Tucoo-Chala, ed, *Henri IV*, pp. 207-219.

Jacquart, J., *La Crise Rurale en Ile-de-France 1550-1670* (Paris, 1974).

———, *François I*[er] (Paris, 1981).

Jacquin, E., 'Les Tuileries', in: Baudouin-Matuszek, *Paris et Catherine*, pp. 87-107.

Jacquot, J. *et al.*, ed, *Fêtes de la Renaissance* (Paris, 1956).

James V, King, *Letters*: Hannay, R.K. and Hay, D., eds, *The Letters of James V*.

James VI, King, *Poeticall Exercises at Vacant Houres* (Edinburgh, 1591).

Jardine, L., *Wordly Goods. A New History of the Renaissance* (London, 1996).

Jeffrey, C.D., 'Anglo-Scots Poetry and the Kingis Quair', in: Blanchot, J.J. and Graf, C., eds, *Actes du 2*[e] *colloque de langue et de littérature écossaises (Moyen Age et Renaissance)* (Strasbourg, 1978), pp. 207-221.

Jenkins, M., 'The Imagery of the Henri II Wing of the Louvre', *Journal of Medieval and Renaissance Studies* 7 (1977), pp. 289-307.

Jensen, N.M. and Krabbe, N., eds, *Musik i Danmark på Christian IV's tid*, 7 vols. (Copenhagen, 1988).

Jex-Blake, K. and Sellers, E., eds, *The Elder Pliny's Chapters on the History of Art* (Chicago, 1968).

Johannesson, K., *Gotisk renässans* (Stockholm, 1982).

———, 'Latinsk skolpoesi', in: Lönnrot, L. and Delblanc, S., eds, *Den svenska litteraturen*, 7 vols. (Stockholm, 1987-1990), vol. I, pp. 159-179.

———, *The Renaissance of the Goths in Sixteenth-Century Sweden. Johannes and Olaus Magnus as Politicians and Historians* (Berkeley/Los Angeles, 1991).

Johnston, J.F.K and Robertson, A.W., *Bibliographia Aberdonensis: 1472-1640* (Aberdeen, 1929).

Jongkees, A.G., 'Het koninkrijk Friesland in de vijftiende eeuw', in: Van der Werff, Linssen and Ebels-Hoving, eds, *Burgundica et Varia*, pp. 27-47

———, 'Vorming van de Bourgondische staat' in: Van der Werff, Linssen and Ebels-Hoving, eds, *Burgundica et Varia*, pp. 232-234.

Jonsson, L., Nilsson, A.-M. and Andersson, G., eds, *Musiken i Sverige*, 4 vols. (Stockholm, 1992-1994).

Jouan, Abel, *Recueil et discours du voyage du roy Charles IX* (Paris, 1566), in: Graham and McAllister Johnson, eds, *The Royal Tour of France*, pp. 71-143.

Jouanna, A., *Ordre social. Mythes et hiérarchies dans la France du XVIe siècle* (Paris, 1977).
Jouanny, R., ed, *Molière. Théâtre complet*, 2 vols. (Paris, 1962).
Joudiau, G., 'De Meudon à Saint-Maur', in: Baudouin-Mauszek, *Paris et Catherine de Médicis*, pp. 160-171.
Juhala, A., 'The Household and Court of King James VI of Scotland, 1567-1603' (unpublished Edinburgh University Ph.D., 2000).
Julien, Ch.A., *Les voyages de découverte et les premiers établissements (XVe-XVIe siècles)* (Paris, 1948).
Jung, R., *Hercule dans la littérature française du XVIe siècle. De l'Hercule gaulois à l'Hercule baroque* (Paris, 1966).
Juricek, J.T., 'English Territorial Claims in North America under Elizabeth and the Early Stuarts', *Terrae Incognitae* 7 (1976), pp. 7-22.
Jusserand, J.J., *The Romance of a King's Life* (London, 1896).
Kamen, H., *Philip of Spain* (New Haven/London, 1997).
Kantorowicz, E.H., *The King's Two Bodies. Studies in Medieval Political Theology* (Princeton, 1957).
Kapp, M., 'Musikhandschriften am Hof der Margarethe von Österreich. Herstellung, Inhalt und Ausstellung', *Jaarboek van het Vlaamse Centrum voor oude muziek* 3 (1987), pp. 15-26.
Keen, M., *Chivalry* (New Haven, 1984).
Kelley, D.R., *The Beginning of Ideology. Consciousness and Society in the French Reformation* (Cambridge, 1983).
Kempers, B., *Painting, Power and Patronage. The Rise of the Professional Artist in Renaissance Italy* (London, 1987).
Kervyn de Lettenhove, J.B.M.C., ed, *Oeuvres de Georges Chastellain*, 8 vols. (Brussels, 1863-1866).
Kettering, S., *Patrons, Brokers and Clients in Seventeenth Century France* (Oxford, 1986).
Kienhorst, H., *De handschriften van de Middelnederlandse ridderepiek. Een codicologische beschrijving* (Deventer, 1988).
Kiple, K.F., 'Scrofula: The King's Evil and Struma Africana', in: Kiple, K.F., ed, *Plague, Pox & Pestilence* (New York, 1997), pp. 44-49.
Kipling, G., *The Triumph of Honour. Burgundian Origins of the Elizabethan Renaissance* (Leiden, 1977).
———, 'Henry VII and the Origins of Tudor Patronage', in: Lytle, G.F. and Orgel, S., eds, *Patronage in the Renaissance* (Princeton, 1981), pp. 117-64
———, *Enter the King: Theatre, Liturgy and Ritual in the Medieval Civic Triumph* (Oxford, 1998).
Kirk, J., *Patterns of Reform: Continuity and Change in the Reformation Kirk* (Edinburgh, 1989).
Kjellberg, E., 'Vasadynastins renässanskultur', in: Jonsson, L., Nilsson, A.-M. and Andersson, G., eds, *Musiken i Sverige*, vol. 1, pp. 199-219.
Klein, Th., 'Die Rezeption mittelniederländischer Versdichtung im Rheinland und Augustijns 'Herzog von Braunschweig', in: Schlusemann and Wackers, *Die spätmittelalterliche Rezeption*, pp. 79-107.
Klemming, G.E. and Nordin, J.G., *Svensk boktryckeri-historia 1483-1883* (Stockholm, 1883; repr. 1983).

Klett, M., ed, *Johannes von Soest. Die Kinder von Limburg (*Vienna, 1975).

Knecht, R.J., 'Royal Patronage of the Arts in France, 1574-1610', in: Cameron, K., ed, *From Valois to Bourbon* (Exeter, 1989), pp. 145-160.

———, *Renaissance Warrior and Patron. The Reign of Francis I* (Cambridge, 1994).

———, *Catherine de' Medici* (London/New York, 1998).

Knowles, D and Hadcock, R.N., *Medieval Religious Houses: England and Wales* (London, 1971).

Knox, *Works*: Laing, D., ed, *The Works of John Knox*..

Kock, T. and Schlusemann, R., eds, *Laienlektüre und Buchmarkt im späten Mittelalter* (Frankfurt am Main, 1997).

Koebner, R., '"The Imperial Crown of this Realm": Henry VIII, Constantine the Great and Polydore Vergil', *Bulletin of the Institute of Historical Research* 26 (1953), pp. 29-52.

Koenigsberger, H.G., 'Dominium Regale or Dominium Politicum et Regale', in: Koenigsberger, H.G., ed, *Politicians and Virtuosi. Essays in Early Modern History* (London, 1986), pp. 1-25.

Kögl, W., 'Studien über das niederösterreichische Regiment unter Maximilian I. Mit besonderer Berücksichtigung der Finanzverwaltung (1490-1506)', *Mitteilungen der IÖG* 83 (1975), pp. 48-74.

Kratzmann, G., 'Sixteenth-century secular poetry', in: Jack, *History of Scottish Literature*, pp. 105-124.

Kren, T., ed, *Margaret of York, Simon Marmion and 'The Visions of Tondal'* (Los Angeles, 1992).

Kruse, H. and Paravicini, W., eds, *Höfe und Hofordnungen, 1200-1600* (Sigmaringen, 1999).

Kulturstiftung der Länder and Bayerische Staatsbibliothek München, eds, *Jakob Püterich von Reichertshausen, Der Ehrenbrief Cgm 9220* (Stuttgart, 1999).

Kunisch, J., 'Formen symbolischen Handelns in der Goldenen Bulle von 1356', in: Stollberg-Rilinger, *Vormoderne politische Verfahren*, pp. 263-280.

Kvam, K., Risum, J. and Wingaard, J., *Dansk teaterhistorie*, 2 vols. (Copenhagen, 1992).

La Ferrière, H. de, and Baguenault de Puchesse, eds, *Catherine de Médicis, Lettres*, 10 vols. (Paris 1880-1909).

La Fulminante Pour Feu Tres Grand et Tres-Chrestien Prince Henry III. Roy de France & de Polonge. Contre Sixte V soy disant Pape de Rome & les Rebelles de la France, in: *French Political Pamphlets*, reel 5.

La Maisonneuve de Berry, Jean de, *Description des devises qui estoient en la ville de Valence à l'entrée du treschrestien Roy Charles IX* (Avignon, 1564), in: Graham and McAllister Johnson, eds, *The Royal Tour of France*, p. 213

La Marche, O. de, *Mémoires*, 4 vols., Beaune, H. and d'Arbaumont, J., eds (Paris, 1883-1888).

La Retraitte de la Ligue par P.I.D.G.C. (Lyons, 1594).

La Taverne, A. de, *Journal de la Paix d'Arras (1435)*, Bossuat, A., ed (Arras, 1936).

Labitte, C., *De la démocratie chez les prédicateurs de la Ligue* (Paris, 1841).

Laffont, R., *Le règne de Catherine de Médicis* (Paris, 1971).

Lafortune-Martel, A., *Fête noble en Bourgogne au XVe siècle. Le* banquet du Faisan *(1454): Aspects politiques, sociaux et culturels* (Montréal/Paris, 1984).

Laing, D., ed, *Facsimile of an Ancient Heraldic Manuscript Emblazoned by Sir David Lyndsay of the Mount* (Edinburgh, 1822).
———, ed, *The Bannatyne Miscellany*, 3 vols. (Edinburgh, 1827- 1855).
———, *The Works of John Knox*, vol. 1 (Edinburgh 1846).
———, ed, *Original Letters of Mr John Colville* (Edinburgh, 1858).
Laitinen, K., *Suomen kirjallisuuden historia* (Helsinki, 1991).
Landouzy, L., *Le Toucher des Écrouelles. L'Hôpital Saint-Marcoul, Le Mal du Roi* (Paris, 1907).
Laumonier, P., ed, *Pierre de Ronsard. Œuvres complètes* (Paris, 1928-1982).
Lavisse, C., *Louis XIV. Histoire d'un grand règne. 1643-1715* (Paris, 1989).
Law, T.G., ed, *The Catechism of John Hamilton* (Oxford, 1884).
Lawson, A., ed, *Poems of Alexander Hume (?1557-1609)* (Edinburgh/London, 1902).
Le Manifeste de la France aux Parisiens & à tout le peuple François, in: *French Political Pamphlets*, reel 4.
Le Recueil des triumphes et magnificences qui ont estez faictes au logis de Monseigneur le Duc d'Orleans [...] estant à Fontainebleau [...], Troyes, 1564, in: Graham and McAllister Johnson, eds, *The Royal Tour of France*, pp. 147-169.
Le Roy Ladurie, E., *The Peasants of Languedoc*, transl. by J. Day (Chicago, 1974).
———, *The Royal French State, 1460-1610*, transl. by Juliet Vale (Oxford, 1994).
Lecoq, A.-M., 'La città festeggiante. Les fêtes publiques aux XVe et XVIe siècles', *Revue de l'Art* 35 (1976), pp. 83-100.
———, *François Ier imaginaire: symbolique et politique à l'aube de la renaissance française* (Paris, 1987).
Lee, M., *John Maitland of Thirlestane and the Foundations of Stewart Despotism in Scotland* (Princeton, 1959).
Lefèvre, L. and Martin, H.J., *L'apparition du livre* (Paris, 1971).
Legers, P., 'Kardinal Matthäus Lang. Ein Staatsmann im Dienste Kaiser Maximilians I.', *Mitteilungen der Gesellschaft für Salzburger Landeskunde* 46 (1906), pp. 437-518.
Leiner, W., 'Mars et Minerve sur le statut des écrivains' in: Mousnier and Mesnard, eds, *L'Age d'or*, pp. 161-169.
Leland, J., ed, *De Rebus Britannicis Collectanea*, vol. 3 (London, 1770).
Lemaire, C. and Henry, M., eds, *Isabelle de Portugal. Duchesse de Bourgogne, 1397-1471* (Brussels, 1991).
Lemoine, G., Sallois, J. and Deschamps, D., eds, *1594 Le Sacre d'Henri IV à Chartres* (Chartres, 1994).
Lersch, T., *Die Grabkapelle der Valois in Saint Denis* (Munich, 1995).
———, 'Remarques sur quelques sculptures de la rotonde des Valois', in: Bresc-Bautier, *Germain Pilon*, pp. 89-111.
Lestringant, F., *Mapping the Renaissance World: the Geographical Imagination in the Age of Discovery*, transl. by David Faussett (Berkeley, 1994).
Levenson, J.A., *Jacopo de Barbari and Northern Art of the Early Sixteenth Century* (unpublished Ph.D. thesis, New York University, 1979).
Levey, M., *High Renaissance* (Harmondsworth, 1987).
Lewis, M.W. and Wigen, K.E., *The Myth of Continents: A Critique of Metageography* (Berkeley, 1997).

Li grandissimi apparati e reali Trionfi fatti per il Re e Regina de Francia nella Citta di Baiona (Padova/Milan, 1565), in: Graham and McAllister Johnson, eds, *The Royal Tour of France*, pp. 321-327.
Lidell, H., *Studier i Johanness Messenius dramer* (Uppsala, 1935).
Liebenwein, W., *Studiolo. Die Entstehung eines Raumtyps und seine Entwicklung bis um 1600* (Berlin, 1977).
Lindgren, M, *et al.*, ed, *Svensk konsthistoria* (Lund, 1986).
Lindsay, *Works*: Hamer, D., ed, *The Works of David Lindsay*.
Lindsay, M, *History of Scottish Literature* (London, 1977).
Livingstone, M., *et al.*, eds, *Registrum Secreti Sigilli Regum Scotorum*, 8 vols. (Edinburgh, 1908-1966).
Loades, D., *The Tudor Court* (Bangor, 1992).
Lönnrot, L. and Delblanc, S., *Den svenska litteraturen*, 7 vols. (Stockholm, 1987-1990)
Lotz, R., *Am Hof Kaiser Maximilians I. Ein Beitrag zur Kulturgeschichte der Wende vom 15. zum 16. Jahrhundert* (Diss. Graz, 1963).
Loughlin, M., '"The Dialogue of the Twa Wyfeis": Maitland, Machiavelli and the propaganda of the Scottish civil war', in: MacDonald, Lynch and Cowan, *The Renaissance*, pp. 226-245.
———, *The Career of William Maitland of Lethington, c. 1526-1573* (unpublished Edinburgh University Ph.D., 1991).
Love, R.S., 'Winning the Catholics: Henri IV and the Religious Dilemma in August 1589', *Canadian Journal of History/Annales canadien-nes d'histoire* 24 (1989), pp. 361-379.
———, *Blood and Religion. The Conscience of Henri IV 1553-1593* (Montreal, 2001).
Lowenthal, C., *Conrat Meit* (unpublished Ph.D thesis, New York University, 1977).
L & P Henry VIII: Brewer, J.S., *et al.*, *Calendar of Letters and Papers*.
Lucas, P.J., 'The Growth and Development of English Literary Patronage in the Later Middle Ages and Early Renaissance', *The Library*, Sixth Ser., 4.3 (1982), pp. 219-248.
Lüken, S., 'Kaiser Maximilian I. und seine Ehrenpforte', *Zeitschrift für Kunstgeschichte* 61 (1998), pp. 449-490.
Lünig, J.Chr., *Theatrum Ceremoniale Historico-politicum Oder Historisch- und Politischer Schau-Platz Aller Ceremonien*, 2 vols. (Leipzig, 1719-1720).
Luzio, A. and Renier, R., 'La coltura e le relazioni lettterarie di Isabella d'Este Gonzaga', *Giornale storico della letteratura Italiana* 34 (1899), pp. 1-162.
Lyall, R., 'The Linlithgow Interlude of 1540', in: Blanchot, J.-J. and Graf. C., eds, *Actes du 2è Colloque de Langue et Littérature Écossaises (Moyen Âge et Renaissance)*, Université de Strasbourg, 5-11 juillet 1978 (Strasbourg, 1978), pp. 409-421.
———, ed, *Ane Satyre of the Thrie Estatis* (Edinburgh, 1989).
Lynch, M., *Edinburgh and the Reformation* (Edinburgh, 1981).
———, ed, *Mary Stewart: Queen in Three Kingdoms* (Oxford, 1988).
———, 'Queen Mary's triumph: the baptismal celebrations at Stirling in December 1566', *Scottish Historical Review* 69 (1990), pp. 1-21.
———, *Scotland: a New History* (London, 1991).

———, 'A nation born again? Scottish Identity in the Sixteenth and Seventeenth Centuries', in: Broun, D., Finlay, D.J. and Lynch, M., eds, *Image and Identity; the Making and Re-making of Scotland through the Ages* (Edinburgh, 1998), pp. 82-104.

———, 'Court ceremony and ritual during the personal reign of James VI', in: Goodare and Lynch, *Reign of James VI*, pp. 74-78.

———, 'The Great Hall of Stirling Castle in the reigns of Mary, Queen of Scots and James VI', in: Fawcett, R., ed, *Stirling Castle: the Restoration of the Great Hall* (Council for British Archaeology, 2001), pp. 15-22.

Lynch, M., Spearman, M. and Stell, G., eds, *The Scottish Medieval Town* (Edinburgh, 1988).

MacClintock, C. and L., *Le Balet comique de la Royne* (New York, 1971).

MacDonald, A.A., 'The Poetry of Sir Richard Maitland of Lethington' *Transactions of the East Lothian Antiquarian and Field Naturalists' Society* 13 (1972), pp. 7-19.

———, 'Politics, Poetry and Reformation: Censorship in sixteenth-century Scotland', *English Studies* 64 (1983), pp. 410-421.

———, 'Catholic devotion into Protestant lyric: the Case of the *Contemplacioun of Synnaris*', *Innes Review* 35 (1984), pp. 58-87.

———, The Bannatyne Manuscript: a Marian anthology', *Innes Review*, 37 (1986), pp. 36-47.

———, 'Religious Poetry in Middle Scots', in: Jack, R.D.S., ed, *The History of Scottish Literature*. vol. 1 (Aberdeen, 1988), pp. 91-104.

———, 'Mary Stewart's entry to Edinburgh: an ambiguous triumph', *Innes Review* 42 (1991), pp. 101-110.

———, 'William Stewart and the Court Poetry of the Reign of James V', in: Hadley Williams, ed, *Stewart Style*, pp. 179-200.

———, 'The triumph of Protestantism: the burgh council of Edinburgh and the entry of Mary, Queen of Scots, 2 September 1561', *Innes Review* 48 (1997), pp 73-82.

———, 'Passion Devotion in Late-Medieval Scotland', in: MacDonald, Ridderbos and Schlusemann, eds, *The Broken Body*, pp. 109-131.

———, 'Early modern Scottish literature and the parameters of culture', in: Mapstone, S. and Wood, J., eds, *The Rose and the Thistle: Essays on the Culture of Late Medieval and Renaissance Scotland* (East Linton, 1998), pp. 77-100.

———, 'The Chapel of Restalrig. Royal Folly or Venerable Shrine' in: Houwen, L.A.J.R., MacDonald, A.A. and Mapstone, S.L., eds, *The Palace in the Wild: Essays on Vernacular Culture and Humanism in Late-Medieval and Renaissance Scotland* (Leuven, 2000), pp. 27-59.

———, 'Chivalry as a Catalyst of Cultural Change in Late-Medieval Scotland', in: Suntrup, R. and Veenstra, J.R., eds, *Tradition and Innovation in an Era of Change/Tradition und Innovation im Übergang zur Frühen Neuzeit* (Frankfurt am Main, 2001), pp. 151-174.

———, 'Sir Richard Maitland and William Dunbar: textual symbiosis and poetic individuality', in: Mapstone, S.L., ed, *William Dunbar, 'The Nobill Poyet'* (East Linton, 2001), pp. 134-149.

MacDonald, A.A., Lynch, M. and Cowan, I.B., eds, *The Renaissance in Scotland: Studies in Literature, History and Culture* (Leiden, 1994).
MacDonald, A.A., Ridderbos, H.N.B. and Schlusemann, R.M., eds, *The Broken Body: Passion Devotion in Late-Medieval Culture* (Groningen, 1998).
MacDonald, A.R., *The Jacobean Kirk: Sovereignty, Polity and Liturgy* (Aldershot, 1998).
———, 'Ecclesiastical representation in post-Reformation Scotland: the two kingdoms theory in practice', *Journal of Ecclesiastical History* 50 (1999), pp. 38-61.
MacDonald, W.C., *'Whose Bread I Eat': The Song-Poetry of Michel Beheim* (Göppingen, 1981).
Macdougall, N., *James III: A Political Study* (Edinburgh, 1982).
———, *James IV* (Edinburgh, 1989).
———, '"It is I, the Earle of Mar": In Search of Thomas Cochrane', in: Mason, R. and Macdougall, N., eds, *People and Power in Scotland: Essays in Honour of T.C. Smout* (Edinburgh, 1992), pp. 28-49.
———, *James IV* (Edinburgh, 1989; reissued East Linton, 1997).
———, 'Henryson's Scotland: Two Renaissance Kings and their Subjects', in: Fleming, M.R., ed, *The Cloak of Poetry* (Dunfermline, 2001), pp. 35-60.
Macfarlane, I.D., *Buchanan* (London, 1981).
———, ed, *The Entry of Henri II into Paris. 16 June 1549* (Binghamton, 1982).
Macfarlane, L.J., 'The Book of Hours of James IV and Margaret Tudor', *Innes Review* 11 (1960), pp. 3-21.
———, *William Elphinstone and the Kingdom of Scotland 1431-1514: The Struggle for Order* (Aberdeen, 1985; reissued, with some extra references, 1995).
Mackay, Æ.J.G., ed, *Robert Lindesay of Pitscottie. The Historie and Cronicles of Scotland*, 3 vols. (Edinburgh/London, 1899-1911).
MacKechnie, A., 'James VI's Architects and their Architecture', in: Goodare, J. and Lynch, M., eds, *The Reign of James VI* (East Linton, 2000), pp. 154-169.
Mackie, R.L., *King James IV of Scotland* (Edinburgh/London, 1958).
Macmillan, D., *Scottish Art 1460-1990* (Edinburgh, 1990).
Macpherson, C. , Quinn, F. and McDonald, C., eds, *Johannes de Irlandia, The Meroure of Wyssdome composed for the use of James IV*, 3 vols. (Edinburgh/London/Aberdeen, 1926-1990).
Macquarrie, A., 'Anselm Adornes of Bruges: Traveller in the East and Friend of James III', *Innes Review* 33 (1982), pp. 15-22.
———, *Scotland and the Crusades* (Edinburgh, 1985; reissued 1997).
MacQueen, J., ed, *Ballattis of Luve* (Edinburgh, 1970).
———, 'The Literature of fifteenth-century Scotland', in: Brown, J.M., ed, *Scottish Society in the Fifteenth Century* (London, 1977), pp. 184-208.
———, 'Scottish Latin Poetry', in: Jack, *History of Scottish Literature*, pp. 213-226.
———, 'Poetry – James I to Henryson', in Jack, R.D.S., ed, *The History of Scottish Literature*, vol 1 (Aberdeen, 1988), pp. 55-71.
———, 'Aspects of Humanism in Sixteenth- and Seventeenth-Century Literature', in: MacQueen, J., ed, *Humanism in Renaissance Scotland* (Edinburgh, 1990), pp. 10-31.
———, ed, *Humanism and Renaissance Scotland* (Edinburgh, 1990), pp. 10-31.

Madoni, C., 'L'hôtel de la Reine', in: Baudouin-Matuszek, *Paris et Catherine*, pp. 108-127.
Mair, *Historia*: Constable, A., ed and transl, *A History of Greater Britain*.
Mair, J., *Historia Maioris Britanniae tam Angliae quam Scotiae* (Paris, 1521).
Maitl. Folio MS: Craigie, W.A., ed, *Livy's History of Rome*.
Mann, A.J., *The Scottish Book Trade, 1500-1720 : Print Commerce and Print Control in Early Modern Scotland: an Historiographical Survey of the Early Modern Book in Scotland* (East Linton, 2000).
Mapstone, S., '*The Advice to Princes Tradition in Scottish Literature, 1450-1500*' (Ph.D. diss. ,Oxford, 1986).
———, 'A Mirror for a Divine Prince: John Ireland and the Four Daughters of God', in: McClure, J.D. and Spiller, M.R.G., eds, *Brycht Lanternis: Essays on the Language and Literature of Medieval and Renaissance Scotland* (Aberdeen, 1989), pp. 308-323.
———, 'Was there a Court Literature in Fifteenth-Century Scotland?', *Studies in Scottish Literature* 26 (1991), pp. 410-422.
———, *Scots and their Books* (Oxford, 1996).
———, 'The *Scotichronicon*'s First Readers', in: Crawford, *Church*, pp. 31-55.
———, 'Shakespeare and Scottish Kingship: A Case History', in: Mapstone, S. and Wood, J., eds, *The Rose and the Thistle* (East Linton, 1998), pp. 158-193
———, 'Bower on Kingship', in: Watt *et al.*, *Scotichronicon*, vol. IX, pp. 321-338.
———, Review of Boffey *et al.*, *The Works*, *Review of English Studies* 200 (1999), pp. 504-505.
———, ed, *William Dunbar, 'The Nobill Poyet'* (East Linton, 2001).
Mapstone, S. and Wood, J., eds, *The Rose and the Thistle* (East Linton, 1998)
Maravall, A., *Teatro y literatura en la sociedad barroca* (Madrid, 1972).
Mariéjol, J.-H., *Catherine de Médicis (1519-1589)* (Paris, 1920).
Marker, F.J. and Marker, L.-L., *A History of Scandinavian Theatre* (Cambridge, 1996).
Martens, M.P.J., ed, *Lodewijk van Gruuthuse. Mecenas en europees diplomaat ca.1427-1492* (Bruges, 1992).
Martens, W.P., *La rotonde des Valois à Saint Denis* (Brussels, 1988).
Martindal, A., 'The Patronage of Isabella d'Este at Mantua', *Apollo* 79 (1964), pp. 183-191.
Märtl, C., *Kardinal Jean Jouffroy († 1473). Leben und Werk* (Sigmaringen, 1996).
Marwick, J.D., ed, *Extracts from the Records of the Burgh of Edinburgh A.D. 1528-1557*, vol. 2 (Edinburgh, 1871).
Mason, R.A., 'Kingship, Nobility and Anglo-Scottish Union: John Mair's History of Greater Britain (1521)', *Innes Review* 41.2 (1990), pp. 183-222.
———, ed, *Scots and Britons: Scottish Political Thought and the Union of 1603*, (Cambridge, 1994).
———, ed, 'Regnum et Imperium: Humanism and the Political Culture of Early Renaissance Scotland', in: *Kingship and the Commonweal* (East Linton, 1998), pp. 104-138.
———, 'This Realm of Scotland is an Empire? Imperial Ideas and Iconography in Early Renaissance Scotland', in: Crawford, *Church*, pp. 73-91.
———, 'This Realm of Scotland is an Empire? Imperial Ideas and Iconography in Early Renaissance Scotland', in: Crawford, B.E., ed, *Church, Chronicle*

and Learning in Medieval and Early Renaissance Scotland (Edinburgh, 1999), pp. 73-91.

Mauduech, G., ed, *Normandie et la Nouvelle France d'Amerique du Nord, 1508-1658* (Rouen, 1978).

Maximilian I. (Katalog Exposition, Innsbruck, 1969).

Maximilian I. 1459-1959. Katalog der Ausstellung der Österreichischen Nationalbibliothek (Vienna, 1959).

Mayer, C.A., ed, *Clément Marot. Œuvres Lyriques* (London, 1964).

McDiarmid, M.P., ed, *Hary's 'Wallace'*, 2 vols. (Edinburgh/London, 1968-69).

———, 'The Metrical Chronicles and Non-alliterative Romances', in: Jack, R.S.D., ed, *The History of Scottish Literature*, vol 1 (Aberdeen, 1988), pp. 27-38.

———, 'Concerning Sir Gilbert Hay, the Authorship of *Alexander the Conquerour* and *The Buik of Alexander*', *Studies in Scottish Literature* 28 (1993), pp. 28-54.

McDiarmid, M.P., and Stevenson, J.C., eds, *Barbour's Bruce*, 3 vols. (Edinburgh, 1980-85).

McDonald, C., ed, *John Ireland. The Meroure of Wysdome* (Aberdeen, 1990).

McFarlane, I.D., 'George Buchanan's Franciscanus – the History of a Poem', *Journal of European Studies* 4 (1974), pp. 126-139.

———, 'Religious Verse in Neo-Latin Poetry until the Death of Francis I and Marguerite de Navarr, in: Kirk, J., ed, *Humanism and Reform: The Church in Europe, England, and Scotland, 1400-1643* (Oxford, 1991), pp. 171-186.

McGinnis, P.J. and Williamson, A.H., eds, *George Buchanan: the Political Poetry* (Edinburgh, 1995).

McGladdery, C., *James II* (Edinburgh, 1990).

McGoldrick, J.E., *Luther's Scottish Connection* (London/Toronto, 1989).

McGowan, Margaret, *L'Art du ballet de cour en France 1581-1643* (Paris, 1963).

———, ed, *Balthazar Beaujoyeulx, Le Balet comique (Paris, 1582)* (Binghamton, 1982).

———, *Ideal Forms in the Age of Ronsard* (Berkeley/Los Angeles/London, 1985).

McGrath, J.T., *The French in Early Florida: In the Eye of the Hurricane* (Gainesville, 2000).

McKean, C., 'The Scottish château', *Review of Scottish Culture* 12 (2000), pp. 3-21.

McKerrow, R.B. and Ferguson, F.S., *Title-page Borders Used in England and Scotland 1485-1640* (London/Oxford, 1932).

McManus, C., 'Marriage and the performance of the romance quest; Anne of Denark and the Stirling baptismal celebrations for Prince Henry', in: Houwen, Maconald and Mapstone, *Palace in the Wild*, pp. 175-198.

McPherson, R., 'Francis Stewart, fifth Earl Bothwell, and James VI: perception politics', in: Brotherstone, T. and Ditchburn, D., eds, *Freedom and Authority: Scotland c.1050-c.1650* (East Linton, 2000), pp. 155-164.

McQuaid, J., 'Scottish Musicians of the Reformation' (unpublished Edinburgh University Ph.D., 1949).

McRoberts, D., 'Dean Brown's Book of Hours', *Innes Review* 19 (1968), pp. 144-167.

———, *Essays on the Scottish Reformation, 1513-1625* (Glasgow, 1962).

Meek, D.E., 'The Scots-Gaelic Scribes of Late Medieval Perthshire: an overview of the orthography and contents of the Book of the Dean of Lismore', in:

McClure, J.D. and Spiller, M.R.G., eds, *Bryght Lanternis: Essays on the Language and Literature of Medieval and Renaissance Scotland* (Aberdeen, 1989), pp. 387-404.

Meesters, J.A., ed, *Roman van Heinric ende Margriete van Limborch. Uitgegeven volgens het Brusselse handschrift* (Amsterdam, 1951).

Meikle, W., ed, *The Works of Thomas Fowler*, 3 vols. (Edinburgh/ London, 1914-1940).

Melville, *Diary*: Pitcairn, ed.

Melville, G., 'Der Held in Szene gesetzt. Einige Bilder und Bilder und Gedanken zu Jacques de Lalaing und seinen *Pas d'armes de la Fontaine des Pleurs*', in: *'Aufführung' und 'Schrift' in Mittelalter und Früher Neuzeit. Germanistische Symposien* 17 (Stuttgart, 1996), pp. 255-286.

Ménager, D., *Introduction à la vie littéraire du XVIe siècle* (Paris, 1984).

Merriman, M.H., *The Rough Wooings: Mary Queen of Scots, 1542-1551* (East Linton, 2000).

Mettam, R., *Power and Faction in Louis XIV's France* (Oxford, 1988).

Michalski, S., *The Reformation and the Visual Arts. The Protestant Image Question in Western and Eastern Europe* (London/New York, 1993).

Michelant, M., 'Inventaire des vaisselles, joyaux, peintures, manuscrits etc., de Marguerite d'Autriche, régente et gouvernante des Pays-Bas, dressé en son palais de Malines, le 9 juillet 1523', *Compte rendu des séances de la Commision royale d'histoire. Académie royale des Sciences, des Lettres et des Beaux-Arts de Belgique (Bruxelles)*, 3e série, 12 (1871), pp. 5-78, 83-136.

Mignet, M., *Rivalité de François Ier et de Charles-Quint* (Paris, 1876).

Mignolo, W.D., *The Darker Side of the Renaissance: Literacy, Territoriality, and Colonization* (Ann Arbor, 1995).

Mill, A.J., *Mediaeval Plays in Scotland* (Edinburgh, 1927).

Minges, K., *Das Sammlungswesen der frühen Neuzeit. Kriterien der Ordnung und Spezialisierung* (Münster, 1998).

Mitchell, W.S., *A History of Scottish Bookbinding, 1432-1650* (Aberdeen, 1955).

Mittler, E., ed, *Bibliotheca Palatina. Katalog zur Ausstellung vom 8. Juli bis 2. November 1986 Heiliggeistkirche Heidelberg*, 2 vols. (Heidelberg, 1986).

Moir, J., ed, *Hector Boece. Murthlacensium et Aberdonensium Episcoporum Vitae* (Aberdeen, 1894).

Mollat, M., *Le commerce normand à la fin du Moyen-Age: étude d'histoire économique et sociale* (Paris, 1952).

Mollat du Jourdin, M. and La Roncière, Ch., *Sea Charts of the Early Explorers, 13th to 17th Century*, transl. by L. le R. Dethan (New York, 1984).

Möller, H., *Fürstenstaat oder Bürgernation. Deutschland 1763-1815* (Berlin, 1989).

Morand, K., *Claus Sluter. Artist at the Court of Burgundy* (Austin, 1991).

Moraw, P., 'Organisation und Funktion von Verwaltung im ausgehenden Mittelalter (ca. 1350-1500)', in: Jeserich, K.G.A., Pohl, H and Unruh, G.Ch., eds, *Deutsche Verwaltungsgeschichte*, vol. I (Stuttgart, 1983), pp. 21-65.

———, *Von offener Verfassung zu gestalteter Verdichtung. Das Reich im späten Mittelalter – 1250 bis 1490* (Berlin, 1985).

———, 'The Court of the German King and of the Emperor at the End of the Middle Ages', in: Asch and Birke, eds, *Princes, Patronage, and the Nobility*, pp. 103-137.

———, 'Fürsten am spätmittelalterlichen Königshof;, in Nolte, C., Speiss, K. and werlich, R.-G., eds, *Principes. Dyanstien und Höfe im späten Mittelalter* (Stuttgart, 2002), pp. 17-32.

Morche, G. (Siegfried Hermelink), 'Heidelberg', in: Finscher, *Die Musik*, Sachteil, vol. 4, pp. 234-243.

Morison, S.E., *The European Discovery of America: The Northern Voyages* (New York, 1971).

Mörke, O., 'Bataver, Eidgenossen und Goten: Gründungs- und Begründungsmythen in den Niederlanden, der Schweiz und Schweden in der Frühen Neuzeit', in: Berding, H., ed, *Mythos und Nation* (Frankfurt am Main, 1996), pp. 104-132.

Morse, R., *The Medieval Medea* (Cambridge, ^{2}1998).

Mortensen, L.B., 'Anders Sørensen Vedel. The Latin writings of a vernacular humanist', in: Skafte Jensen, M., ed, *A History of Nordic Neo-Latin Literature*, pp. 267-279.

Moser, H., *Die Kanzlei Kaiser Maximilians I. Graphematik eines Schreibusus*, 2 vols. (Innsbruck, 1977).

Mousnier, R and Mesnard, J., eds, *L'Age d'or du Mécénat 1598-1661* (Paris, 1985).

Moysie, D., *Memoirs of the Affairs of Scotland, MDLXXVII-MDCIII* ed. J. Dennistoun (Edinburgh, 1830)

Muchembled, R., *Culture populaire et culture des élites dans la France moderne (XVe-XVIIIe siècles)* (Paris, 1978).

Muir, E., *Ritual in Early Modern Europe* (Cambridge, 1997).

Müller, J.D., *Gedechtnus. Literatur und Hofgesellschaft um Maximilian I* (Munich, 1982).

———, 'Der siegreiche Fürst im Entwurf der Gelehrten. Zu den Anfängen eines höfischen Humanismus in Heidelberg', in: Buck, A., ed, *Höfischer Humanismus* (Weinheim, 1989), pp. 17-50.

———, 'Hans Lecküchners Messerfechtlehre und die Tradition. Schriftliche Anweisungen für eine praktische Disziplin', in: Müller, *Wissen*, pp. 355-384.

———, 'Peters Luders Panegyrikus auf Friedrich d. S., die Chronik des Matthias von Kemnat und die Pfälzer Reimchronik des Michel Beheim', in: Müller, *Wissen*, pp. 289-322.

———, ed, *Wissen für den Hof. Der spätmittelalterliche Verschriftlichungsprozeß am Beispiel Heidelberg im 15. Jahrhundert* (Munich, 1994).

Müller, R.A., *Der Fürstenhof in der frühen Neuzeit* (München, 1995).

Müller, U., 'Michel Beheim', ^{2}*VL 1*, cols. 672-680.

Münster, S., *Cosmographei* (Basel, 1544, facsimile of edition 1550/Houten, 1987).

Murray, A.L., ed, 'Accounts of the King's Pursemaster 1539-40', *Miscellany X* (1965), pp. 13-51.

Musper, T. *et al*, eds, *Kaiser Maximilians Theuerdank. Faksimile* (Stuttgart/Plochingen, 1968).

Neuhaus, H., *Das Reich in der frühen Neuzeit* (Munich, 1997).

Nieuwstraten, R., 'Vervaardigers en bezitters van Raoul Lefèvre's *Histoire de Jason*: kanalen voor de verbreiding van een idee', *Millennium* 8 (1994), pp.

134-147.
Nijsten, G., *Het Hof van Gelre: cultuur ten tijde van de hertogen uit het Gulikse en Egmondse huis (1371-1473)* (Kampen, 1992).
Noflatscher, H., *Räte und Herrscher. Politische Eliten an den Habsburgerhöfen der österreichischen Länder* (Mainz, 1999).
Norlind, T., *Från Tyska kyrkans glansdagar*, 2 vols. (Stockholm, 1944-1945).
Norlind, T. and Trobäck, E., *Kungl. Hovkapellets historia 1526-1926* (Stockholm, 1926).
Norton-Smith, J., ed, *James I of Scotland, The Kingis Quair* (Oxford, 1971; reissued Leiden, 1981).
Noufflard, A., transl., *Vie de Michelange racontée par son élève et ami Ascanio Condivi en 1553* (Paris, 1949).
Öberg, 'Kyrkans bild av den profana musiken', in: Jonsson, Nilsson, A.-M. and Anderson, eds, *Musiken i Sverige*, vol. 1, pp. 153-168.
Oestreich, G., 'Das persönliche Regiment der deutschen Fürsten am Beginn der Neuzeit', in: *Geist und Gestalt des frühmodernen Staates*, 2 vols. (Berlin, 1969), pp. 201-234.
Olaus Magnus, *Historia de gentibus septentrionalibus* (Rome, 1555).
Opitz, M., *Buch der Deutschen Poëterey* (Breslau, 1624).
Orvieto, P., ed, *Lorenzo de' Medici. Tutte le Opere*, 2 vols. (Rome/Salerno, 1992).
Österlin, L., *Churches of Northern Europe in Profile* (Norwich, 1995).
Painter, S., *William Caxton. A Quincentenary Biography of England's First Printer* (London, 1976).
Pallier, D., *Recherches sur l'Imprimerie à Paris pendant la Ligue, 1585-1594* (Geneva, 1975).
Paravicini, W., *Karl der Kühne. Das Ende des Hauses Burgunds* (Göttingen, 1976).
———, 'The Court of the Dukes of Burgundy. A Model for Europe?' in: Asch, R.G., and Birke, A.M., eds, *Princes, Patronage, and the Nobility. The Court at the Beginning of the Modern Age c.1450-1650* (Oxford, 1991), pp. 69-102.
———, 'Zeremoniell und Raum', in: Paravicini, *Zeremoniell und Raum*, pp. 11-36.
———, ed, *Zeremoniell und Raum* (Sigmaringen, 1997).
———, '"Ordre et régle". Charles le Téméraire en ses ordonnances de l'hôtel', *Académie des inscriptions & belles-lettres. Comptes rendus 1999 janvier-mars* (Paris, 1999), pp. 311-359.
Paravicini, A. and W., 'L'arsenal intellectuel d'un homme de pouvoir. Les livres de Guillaume Hugonet, chancelier de Bourgogne' in: Boutet, D. and Verger, J., eds, *Penser le pouvoir au moyen âge. VIIIe – XVe siècle. Mélanges offerts à Françoise Autrand* (Paris, 2000), pp. 261-325.
Parker, G., *The Dutch Revolt* (London, 1977).
Parkinson, D., 'Scottish Prints and Entertainments, 1508', *Neophilologus* 75.2 (1991), pp. 304-310.
———, '"A Lamentable Storie": Mary Queen of Scots and the inescapable *querelle des femmes*', in: Houwen, MacDonald and Mapstone, *Palace in the Wild*, pp. 141-160.
Parry, J.H., *The Age of Reconnaissance* (London, 1963).
Passerat, Jean, *Chant d'alegresse pour l'entree de treschrestien, treshault, trespuissant, tresexcellent, tresmagnamine, et tresvictorieux Prince Charles*

IX de ce nom, Roi de France, en sa ville de Troïe (Paris, 1564), in: Graham and McAllister Johnson, eds, *The Royal Tour of France*, p. 177.

Patrick, D, ed, *Statutes of the Scottish Church, 1225-1559* (Edinburgh, 1907).

Paviot, J., 'Ghillebert de Lannoy, seigneur de Santes' in: Baelde, ed, *Les Chevaliers de l'Ordre de la Toison d'or au XVe siècle*, pp. 42-45.

———, *La politique navale des ducs de Bourgogne 1384-1482* (Lille, 1995).

Peck, L.L., *Court Patronage and Corruption in Early Stuart England* (London, 1990).

Pedersøn, M., *Messe og motetter*, in: Glahn, *Musik*, vol. 4.

Pelletier, M., 'La symbolique royale française: des globes et des rois', in: Hofmann and Lecoq, *Tours et contours de la Terre*, pp. 57-79.

———, 'Le monde dans un cœur: les deux mappemondes d'Oronce Fine', in: Hofmann and Lecoq, *Tours et contours de la Terre*, pp. 117-197.

———, 'Les enjeux de la cartographie européenne aux XVIe et XVIIe siècles', in: Hofmann and Lecoq, *Tours et contours de la Terre*, pp. 161-176.

Pepys MSS: Historical Manuscripts Commission, *Calendar of Pepys MSS* (London, 1911).

Perkins, L.L., *Music in the Age of the Renaissance* (New York/London, 1999).

Pernot, J.-F., 'De l'importance des territoires extérieurs et du contrôle des voies maritimes pour un État moderne. Analyse de géostratégie proposée par Claude de Seyssel dans *La Monarchie de France (1515)*', in: Balard, M., ed, *État et colonisation au Moyen Age* (Lyon, 1989), pp. 477-485.

Pernoud, R., 'L'inventeur de la monarchie', in: Seward, D., ed, *Prince of the Renaissance: The Golden Life of François Ier* (New York, 1973), pp. 161-199.

Pérouse de Montclos, J.-M., *Philibert de l'Orme. Architecte du roi (1514-1570)* (Paris, 2000).

Petto, Chr.M., 'Cartography and Power in Early Modern France', *AB Bookman's Weekly* 99,22 (1997), pp. 1761-1766.

Pétursson, S., 'Iceland', in: Skafte Jensen, M., ed, *A History of Nordic Neo-Latin Literature*, pp. 96-104.

Phillips, G., *The Anglo-Scots Wars, 1513-1550* (Woodbridge, 1999).

Picker, M., ed, *The Chanson Albums of Marguerite of Austria: Mss. 228 and 11239 of the Bibliothèque royale de Belgique, Brussels. A Critical Edition and Commentary* (Berkeley/Los Angeles, 1965).

Pietzsch, G., 'Soest, Johann', in Blume, *Die Musik*, vol. 12, pp. 824-825.

———, *Quellen und Forschungen zur Geschichte der Musik am kurpfälzischen Hof zu Heidelberg bis 1622* (Wiesbaden, 1963).

Pitcairn, R., ed, *The Autobiography and Diary of Mr James Melville* (Edinburgh, 1842)

Pitscottie, *Historie*: Mackay, Æ.J.G., ed, *Robert Lindesay*.

Poiret, M.-F., *Le Monastère de Brou. Le chef-d'œuvre d'une fille d'empereur* (Paris, 1994).

———, *Le Monastère royal de Brou, l'église et le musée* (Bourg-en-Bresse, 2000).

Pollen, J.H., ed, *Papal Negotiations with Mary Queen of Scots during her Reign in Scotland, 1561-1567* (Edinburgh, 1901).

Preece, I.W., *Music in the Scottish Church up to 1603* (Glasgow/Aberdeen, 2000).

Prevenier, W., ed, *Le prince et le peuple. Images de la societé du temps des ducs de Bourgogne 1384-1530* (Antwerpen, 1998).

Prevenier, W. and Blockmans, W., *Die burgundischen Niederlande* (Weinheim, 1986).
Prietzel, M., Guillaume Fillastre der Jüngere (400/1407-1473). Kirchenfürst und herzoglich-burgundischer Rat (Stuttgart, 2001).
Prinz, W. and Kecks, R.G., Das französische Schloß der Renaissance (Berlin, 1985).
Proemans, M., 'Margaretha's hof en de muziek. De hoogstaande cultuur van Margaretha', in: Schreurs, *De schatkamer*, pp. 59-61.
Prunières, H., *Le ballet de cour en France* (Paris, 1914).
———, 'Ronsard et les fêtes de cour', *Revue musicale* 5 (1924), pp. 27-44.
Py, A., ed, *Ronsard. Hymnes* (Geneva, 1978).
Quilliet, B., *Louis XII* (Paris, 1986).
Quinn, D.B., 'Maps in the Age of European Exploration', in: Quinn, *European Approaches*, pp. 92-119.
———, 'The Americas in the Rotz Atlas of 1542', in: Quinn, *European Approaches*, pp. 69-92.
———, *European Approaches to North Americia, 1450-1640* (Aldershot, 1998).
Quinn, F., ed, *John Ireland. The Meroure of Wysdome*, vol. 2 (Edinburgh/London, 1965);
Quiviger, F., 'The Presence of Artists in Literary Academies', in: Chambers and Quiviger, eds, *Italian Academies*, pp. 105-112.
Quoniam, P. and Guinamard, L., *Le palais du Louvre* (Paris, 1988).
Rabil, Jr., A., ed, *Knowledge, Goodness, and Power: The Debate over Nobility among Quattrocento Italian Humanists* (Binghamton, 1991).
Ragotzky, H. and Wenzel, H., eds, *Höfische Repräsentation. Das Zeremoniell und die Zeichen* (Tübingen, 1990).
Rau, V., 'Les marchands-banquiers étrangers au Portugal sous le règne de João III (1521-1557)', in: Mollat, M. and Adam, P., eds, *Les aspects internationaux de la découverte océanique aux XVe et XVIe siècles* (Paris, 1966), pp. 295-307.
Raynaud, C., 'Humanism and Good Government: A Burgundian Rendering of the *Romuleon* by Roberto Della Porta', *Fifteenth-Century Studies* 24 (1998), pp. 159-182.
Recueil des choses notables qui ont esté faites à Bayonne à l'entreveuë du Roy Treschrestien Charles neufieme de ce nom avec la Royne Catholicque sa sœur (Paris, 1566), in: Graham and McAllister Johnson, eds, *The Royal Tour of France*, pp. 328-380.
Reese, G., *Music in the Renaissance* (London, 1954).
Reinhard, W., *Geschichte der Staatsgewalt. Eine vergleichende Verfassungsgeschichte Europas von den Anfängen bis zur Gegenwart* (Munich, 1999).
Renouard, P., *Bibliographie des Impressions et Œuvres de Josse Badius Ascensius* (Paris, 1908).
Rèpaci-Courtois, G. 'Blaise de Vigénère et l'expérience des arts visuels', in: *Blaise de Vigénère. Poète et mythographe au temps de Henri III, Cahiers V. L. Saulnier* 11 (1994), pp. 101-110.
Rice, M.M., *Saint Marcoul and the Pilgrimages of the Kings of France to His Shrine at Corbeny* (M.A. thesis, Catholic University of America, 1939).
Richet, D., *La France moderne: l'esprit des institutions* (Paris, 1973).

Ridderbos, H.N.B., *De melancholie van de kunstenaar: Hugo van der Goes en de oudnederlandse schilderkunst* (The Hague, 1991).

Riddy, F., 'The Alliterative Revival', in: Jack, R. D. S., ed, *the History of Scottish Literature*, vol 1 (Aberdeen, 1988), pp. 39-54.

Rigg, J.M., ed, *Calendar of State Papers relating to English Affairs, preserved at Rome...* (London, 1916-1926).

Rinaldi, R., *Storia della civiltà letteraria italiana, II,2* (Turin, 1993).

Ringmar, E., *Identity, interest, and action: a cultural explanation of Sweden's intervention in the Thirty Years War* (Cambridge, 1996).

Risum, 'De tidligste teaterformer', in: Kvam, Risum and Wingaard, *Dansk teaterhistorie*, pp. 9-49.

Ritchie, W. Tod, ed, *The Bannatyne Manuscript writtin in tyme of pest, 1568, by George Bannatyne*, 4 vols. (Edinburgh/London, 1928-1934).

Robbins, R.H., ed, *Secular Lyrics of the XIVth and XVth Centuries* (Oxford 1955).

Roberts, M., *Gustavus Adolphus. A History of Sweden (1611-1632)*, 2 vols. (London, 1953-1958).

———, *The Early Vasas. A History of Sweden 1523-1611* (Cambridge, 1968).

Roelker, N.L., 'The role of noblewomen in the French Reformation', *Archiv für Reformationgeschichte* 63 (1972), pp. 168-195.

Rogers, C., *History of the Chapel Royal of Scotland* (London, 1877).

Rolf, B., *Kurpfalz, Südwestdeutschland und das Reich 1449-1476. Die Politik des Pfalzgrafen und Kurfürsten Friedrich des Siegreichen* (Heidelberg, 1981).

Rondorf, D., *Der Ballsaal im Schloß Fontainebleau. Zur Stilgeschichte Primaticcios in Frankreich* (Bonn, 1967).

Ross, A., 'Some Notes on the Religious Orders in Pre-Reformation Scotland', in: McRoberts, D., ed, *Essays on the Scottish Reformation 1513-1625* (Glasgow, 1962), pp. 185-240.

Ross, D.J., *Musick Fyne: Robert Carver and the Art of Music in Sixteenth Century Scotland* (Edinburgh, 1993).

Rothstein, M., 'Jean Lemaire de Belges' *Illustrations de Gaule et Singularitez de Troyes*: Politics and Unity', *Bibliothèque d'Humanisme et Renaissance* 52 (1990), pp. 593-606.

Roucaute, J., *Le Pays de Gévaudan au temps de la Ligue* (Paris, 1900).

Royan, N., 'The Relationship between the Scotorum Historia of Hector Boece and John Bellenden's Chronicles of Scotland', in: Mapstone, S. and Wood, J., eds, *The Rose and the Thistle* (East Linton, 1998), pp. 136-157.

RPC: *The Register of the Privy Council of Scotland*: Burton *et al.*

RSS: Livingstone, M., *et al.*, eds, *Registrum Secreti Sigilli Regum Scotorum.*

Rubinstein, N., 'Lorenzo de' Medici: his Statecraft', in: Holmes, G., ed, *Art and Politics in Renaissance Italy* (Oxford, 1993), pp. 113-136.

Rublack, H.-Ch., 'Political and Social Norms in Urban Communities in the Holy Roman Empire', in: Von Greyerz, K., ed, *Religion, Politics and Social Protest. Three Studies on Early Modern Germany* (London, 1984), pp. 24-60.

Ruby, S., 'Diane de Poitiers (1500-1566)', in: Zimmermann and Böhm, *Französische Frauen der frühen Neuzeit*, pp. 45-54.

Rudd, N., *Themes in Roman Satire* (London, 1986).

Rüegger, E., *Le spectacle total à la Renaissance: Genèse et premier apogée du ballet de cour* (Zürich, 1995).
Runeby, N., *Monarchia mixta. Maktfördelningsdebat i Sverige under den tidigare stormaktstiden* (Uppsala, 1962).
Rupprich, H., *Die deutsche Literatur vom späten Mittelalter bis zum Barock 1370-1520 Geschichte der deutschen Literatur von den Anfängen bis zur Gegenwart*, vol. 4, part 1 (München, 1970).
Russell, J.G., *The Field of the Cloth of Gold: Men and Manners in 1520* (London, 1969).
Russel, M. and Napier, M., eds, *History of the Church of Scotland ... by the Right Rev. John Spottiswoode*, 3 vols. (Edinburgh, 1847-1851).
Rüxner, G., *Anfang, vrspru[n]g vnd herkom[m]en des Thurniers inn Teutscher nation / Wieuil Thurnier biß vff den letstenn zu Wormbs: Auch wie vnnd an welchen orten die gehalten, vn[d] durch was Fürsten, Grauen, Herrn, Ritter vn[d] vom Adel, sie iederzeit besucht worden sindt* (Siemern, 1532).
Sadie, S., ed, *The New Grove Dictionary of Music and Musicians* (London, 1980).
Sahlgren, J., ed, *Ola[v]us Petri, En swensk crönika* (Uppsala, 1917).
Saintenoy, P., *Les arts et les artistes à la cour de Bruxelles* (Brussels, 1934).
Saintre fare Garnot, P.N. and Jacquin, E., *Le château des Tuileries* (Paris, 1988).
Salet, F. 'Mécénat royal et princier au Moyen Age', Lecture faite dans la séance publique annuelle du 22 novembre 1985, *Académie des Inscriptions et Belles-Lettres* (Paris, 1985).
Salmi, M. and Mellini, G.L., eds, *The Grimani Breviary* (London, 1972).
Salvini, R., *Michel-Ange* (Paris, 1977).
Samoyault, J.-P., 'Le château de Fontainebleau sous Charles IX', *Hommage à Hubert Landais. Art, objets d'art, collections. Etudes sur l'art du Moyen Age et de la Renaissance sur l'histoire du goût et des collections* (Paris 1987), pp. 116-124.
Sanderson, J.M., 'Two Stewarts of the Sixteenth Century: Mr William Stewart, Poet, and William Stewart, Elder Depute Clerk of Edinburgh', *The Stewarts* 17.1 (1984), pp. 25-46.
Sanderson, M.H.B., *Cardinal of Scotland: David Beaton, c.1494-1546* (Edinburgh, 1986).
———, *Mary Stewart's People* (Edinburgh, 1987).
Sandström, B., '1520-1728,' in: Lindgren *et al.*, *Svensk konsthistoria*, pp. 89-134.
Sauter, W., ed, *Messenius. Disa* (Stockholm, 1989).
Sawyer, P., *Medieval Scandinavia. From Conversion to Reformation (circa 800-1500)* (Minneapolis, 1993).
Scailliérez, C., *François Ier et ses artistes dans les collections du Louvre* (Paris, 1992).
Schaab, M., *Geschichte der Kurpfalz. Bd. 1. Mittelalter* (Stuttgart, 1988).
Schack, G., *Der Kreis um Maximilian I.* (Hamburg/Berlin, 1963).
Schalk, E., *From Valor to Pedigree: Ideas of Nobility in France in the Sixteenth and Seventeenth Centuries* (Princeton, 1986).
———, 'The Court as "Civilizer" of the Nobility. Noble Attitudes and the Court in France in the Late Sixteenth and Early Seventeenth Centuries', in: Asch, R.G. and Birke, A.M., eds, *Princes, Patronage, and the Nobility. The Court at the Beginning of the Modern Age (c. 1450-1650)* (Oxford, 1991), pp. 245-263.

Schattenberg, T., *Jubilus S. Bernhardi*, in: Barfod *et al.*, *Musik*, vol. 7.

Schauerte, T.U., *Die Ehrenpforte für Kaiser Maximilian I.* (Munich/Bern, 2001).

Schestag, F., 'Kaiser Maximilian I. Triumph', *Jahrbuch der Kunsthistorischen Sammlungen des Allerhöchsten Kaiserhauses* I (1883), pp. 154-181.

Schläder, J., 'Johann von Soest, Sängermeister und Komponist' in Heimann, H.-D., ed, *Von Soest - aus Westfalen. Wege und Wirkung abgewanderter Westfalen im späten Mittelalter und in der frühen Neuzeit* (Paderborn, 1986), pp. 25-43.

Schlesinger, R., *In the Wake of Columbus: The Impact of the New World on Europe, 1492-1650* (Wheeling, Illinois, 1996).

Schlusemann, R., 'Een kopiist als redacteur. Nederlandse en Duitse *Limborch*-handschriften met elkaar vergeleken', *Amsterdamer Beiträge zur älteren Germanistik* 46 (1996), pp. 171-187.

———, '*das yr begyr wolt halten reyn.* Zur Rezeption des *Limborch*-Romans bei Johann von Soest' in: Schlusemann and Wackers, *Die spätmittelalterliche Rezeption*, pp. 175-196.

———, 'Literarische Vernetzung als Quelle für buchhistorische Fragen. Adelshäuser in den mittel- und rheinfränkischen Rheinlanden in der zweiten Hälfte des 15. Jahrhunderts', in: Schlusemann, R., Hermans, J.M.M. and Hoogvliet, M., eds, *Sources for the History of Medieval Books and Libraries* (Groningen, 1999), pp. 95-110.

———, 'The Late Medieval Reception of Dutch Arthurian Literature in Heidelberg and Blankenheim', in: Claassens, G. and Johnson, D.F., eds, *Arthur in the Medieval Low Countries* (Leuven, 2000), pp. 97-111.

———, 'Selbstbekenntnis bei Johann von Soest', in: Suntrup, R. and Veenstra, J., eds, *Personen(selbst)darstellung in Spätmittelalter und früher Neuzeit.* Forthcoming.

Schlusemann, R. and Wackers, P., eds, *Die spätmittelalterliche Rezeption niederländischer Literatur im deutschen Sprachgebiet* (Amsterdam/Atlanta, 1997).

Schmidt, G., *Geschichte des alten Reiches. Staat und Nation in der Frühen Neuzeit (1495-1806)* (Munich, 1999).

Schmidt, I., *'De clara antiquitate et antiqua claritate Gothorum'. Gotizismus als Identitätsmodell im frühneuzeitlichen Schweden* (Kiel, 2003). Forthcoming.

Schnerb, B., 'Les funérailles de Jean sans Peur', *Annales de Bourgogne* 54 (1982), pp. 122-136.

———, *Les Armagnacs et les Bourguignons. La maudite guerre* (Paris, 1988).

———, *L'État bourguignon 1363-1477* (Paris, 1999).

Schoolfield, G., ed, *A History of Finland's Literature* (Lincoln, NB, 1998).

Schreurs, E. ed, *De schatkamer van Alamire. Muziek en miniaturen uit Keizer Karels Tijd (1500-1535)* (Louvain, 2000).

Schubert, F.H., 'Blasius Hölzl und die soziale Situation in der Hofkammer Maximilians', *Vierteljahrschrift für Sozial- und Wirtschaftsgeschichte* 47 (1960), pp.105-115.

Schück, H., 'Sweden's Early Parliamentary Institutions from the Thirteenth Century to 1611', in: Metcalf, M.F., ed, *The Riksdag: A History of the Swedish Parliament* (Stockholm, 1987), pp. 5-60.

Schwartz, S.B., ed, *Implicit Understandings: Observing, Reporting, and Reflecting on the Encounters between Europeans and Other Peoples in the Early*

Modern Era (Cambridge, 1994).
Schwarz, K., *Aragonische Hofordnungen im 13. und 14. Jahrhundert. Studien zur Geschichte dr Hofämter und Zentralbehörden des Königreichs Aragon* (Berlin, 1914).
Scots Peerage: Balfour.
Seed, P., *Ceremonies of Possession in Europe's Conquest of the New World, 1492-1640* (Cambridge, 1995).
Seward, D., *Prince of the Renaissance. The Life of François I* (London, 1973).
Sheppard, E.A., 'John Bellenden', in: Chambers, Batho and Husbands, eds, *Chronicles of Scotland*, vol. 2, pp. 411-461.
Shire, H.M., ed, *The Thrissil, the Rois and the Flour-de-lys* (Cambridge, 1962).
———, *Song, Dance and Poetry of the Court of Scotland Under King James VI* (Cambridge, 1969).
Simon, J.R., ed, *Le livre du Roi (The Kingis Quair) attribué à Jaques Ier d'Écosse* (Paris, 1967).
Simonin, M., ed, *Du Perron. Oraison funèbre sur la mort de Monsieur de Ronsard (1586)* (Geneva, 1985).
———, 'Ronsard à Bar-le-duc', *Revue d'histoire littéraire de la France* 87/1 (1987), pp. 99-109.
Singer, B., *Die Fürstenspiegel in Deutschland im Zeitalter des Humanismus und der Reformation* (München, 1981).
Skafte Jensen, M., ed, *A History of Nordic Neo-Latin Literature* (Odense, 1995).
Skautrup, P., *Den danske Sprogs Historie*, vol. 2 (Copenhagen, 1947, repr. 1968).
Skelton, R.A., *Maps: A Historical Survey of their Study and Collecting* (Chicago, 1972).
Slerca, A., ed, *André de la Vigne. Le voyage de Naples. Edition critique avec introduction, notes et glossaire* (Milan, 1981).
Small, G., *George Chastelain and the Shaping of Valois Burgundy: Political and Historical Culture at Court in the Fifteenth Century* (London/-Woodbridge, 1997).
Small, J., ed, *Poetical Works of Gavin Douglas*, 4 vols. (Edinburgh, 1874).
Smeyers, M., *Flemish Miniatures* (Louvain, 1999).
Smith, P.M., *The Anti-Courtier Trend in Sixteenth-Century French Literature* (Geneva, 1966)
———, *Clément Marot: Poet of the French Renaissance* (London, 1970).
Solnon, J.-F., *La cour de France* (Paris, 1987).
Soly, H. and Van de Welde, J. *Carolus. Charles Quint 1500-1558* (Ghent, 2000).
Sommé, M., *Isabella de Portugal, duchesse de Bourgogne. Une femme au pouvoir au XVe siècle* (Lille, 1998).
Sonnemans, G., *Functionele aspecten van Middelnederlandse versprologen*, 2 vols. (Boxmeer, 1995).
Spencer, J.R., transl, *Leon Battista Alberti. On Painting* (New Haven/London, 1966).
SP Henry VIII State Papers of Henry the Eighth, 11 vols. (London, 1832-1852).
Spottiswoode, *History*: Russel and Napier.
Spufford, P., *Monetary Problems and Politics in the Burgundian Netherlands 1433-1496* (Leiden, 1970).
Stammler, W., *Von der Mystik zum Barock. 1400-1600* (Stuttgart, 1950).
Stanesco, M., *Jeux d'errance du chevalier médiéval. Aspects ludiques de la fonction*

guerrière dans la littérature du Moyen Age flamboyant (Leiden, 1988).
Starkey, D., ed, *Henry VIII: A European Court in England* (London, 1991).
Statutes of the Scottish Church: Patrick.
Stecher, J., ed, *Œuvres de Jean Lemaire de Belges*, 4. vols (Louvain, 1882-1885).
Steiger, H., 'Konkreter Friede und allgemeine Ordnung – Zur rechtlichen Bedeutung der Verträge vom 24. Oktober 1648', in: Bußmann and Schilling, *1648 – Krieg und Frieden in Europa*, vol. 1, pp. 437-446.
Stein, F., *Geschichte des Musikwesens in Heidelberg bis zum Ende des 18. Jahrhunderts* (Heidelberg, 1921).
Stevenson, D., *Scotland's Last Royal Wedding: the Marriage of James VI and Anne of Denmark* (Edinburgh, 1997).
Stevenson, J.H., ed, *Gilbert of the Haye's Prose Manuscript (A.D. 1436)*, 2 vols. (Edinburgh/London, 1901-1914).
Stevenson, J. *et al.*, ed, *Calendar of State Papers, Foreign Series, of the Reign of Elizabeth* (London, 1863-1950).
Stewart, *Croniclis*: Turnbull, W.B., ed, *The Buik of the Croniclis of Scotland.*
Stollberg-Rilinger, B., 'Zeremoniell als politisches Verfahren. Rangordnung und Rangstreit als Strukturmerkmale des frühneuzeitlichen Reichstags', in: Kunisch, J., ed, *Neue Studien zur frühneuzeitlichen Reichsgeschichte* (Berlin, 1997), pp. 91-132.
———, 'Zeremoniell, Ritual, Symbol. Neue Forschungen zur symbolischen Kommunikation in Spätmittelalter und Früher Neuzeit', *Zeitschrift für Historische Forschung* 27 (2000), pp. 389-405.
———, ed, *Vormoderne politische Verfahren* (Berlin, 2001).
Strauss, G., *Luther's House of Learning. Indoctrination of the Young In the German Reformation* (Baltimore, 1978).
Strong, R., 'Festivals for the Garter Embassy at the Court of Henri III', *Journal of the Warburg and Courtauld Institutes* 22 (1959), pp. 60-70.
———, *Splendour at Court: Renaissance Spectacle and Illusion* (London, 1973).
———, *The Renaissance Garden in England* (London, 1979).
———, *Art and Power: Renaissance Festivals, 1450-1650* (London, [2]1984).
Strong, R.C., and Van Dorsten, J.A., *Leicester's Triumph* (London, 1962)
Stroo, C., *De celebratie van de macht. Presentatieminiaturen en aanverwante voorstellingen in handschriften van Filips de Goede (1419-1467) en Karel de Stoute (1467-1477)* (Brussel, 2002).
Stuart, J. *et al.*, eds, *The Exchequer Rolls of Scotland*, 23 vols. (= *ER*) (Edinburgh 1878-1908).
Studt, B., *Fürstenhof und Geschichte* (Köln, 1992).
———, '*Exeat aula qui vult esse pius* – Der geplagte Alltag eines Hofliteraten', in: Paravicini, W., ed, *Alltag bei Hofe, 3. Symposium der Residenzen-Kommission der Akademie der Wissenschaften in Göttingen, Ansbach, 28. Februar - 1. März 1992* (Sigmaringen, 1995), pp. 113-136.
Sturdy, D., 'The Royal Touch in England', in: Duchhardt, H., Jackson, R. and Sturdy, D., eds, *European Monarchy Its Evolution and Practice from Roman Antiquity to Modern Times* (Stuttgart, 1992), pp. 169-84.
Sutherland, N.M., 'Catherine de' Medici: The Legend of the Wicked Italian Queen', *The Sixteenth Century Journal* 9/2 (000), pp. 45-56.
Svennung, J., *Zur Geschichte des Goticismus* (Stockholm, 1967).

Swanson, A., 'The Idea of Map and the Maps of Olaus Magnus', *Tijdschrift voor Skandinavistiek* 16 (1995), pp. 65-76.
TA: Dickson, T. and Balfour Paul, J., eds, *Accounts of the Lord High Treasurer*.

Tamussino, U., *Margarete von Österreich. Diplomatin der Renaissance* (Graz, 1995).
Teixeira Da Mota, A., 'Influence de la cartographie portugaise sur la cartographie européenne á l'époque des découvertes', in: Mollat and Adam, *Les aspects internationaux*, pp. 223-248.
Teulet, A., ed, *Papiers d'État: pièces et documents inédit ou peu connus relatifs à l'histoire de l'Ecosse au XVIe siècle*, 3 vols. (Paris, 1852-1860)
Theibault, J., 'The Rhetoric of Death and Destruction in the Thirty Years War', *Journal of Social History* 27 (1993), pp. 271-290.
Thibaut, F., *Marguerite d'Autriche and Jehan Lemaire de Belges ou de la littérature et des arts aux Pays-Bas sous Marguerite d'Autriche* (Paris, 1888; repr. Geneva, 1972).
Thomas, A., *'Princelie Majestie': The Court of James V of Scotland, 1528-1542* (East Linton, forthcoming).
Thomas, D., *Henri IV. Images d'un roi entre realité et mythe* (Paris, 1992).
Thomas, M., Zink, M. (commentary) and Guerrand, R.H. (adaptation into modern French), *Girart de Roussillon ou l'épopée de Bourgogne* (Vesoul, 1990).
Thompson, C. and Campbell, L., *Hugo van der Goes and the Trinity Panels in Edinburgh* (Edinburgh, 1974).
Thomson F. and Innes, C., ed, *A Diurnal of Remarkable Occurrents that have passed within the country of Scotland since the death of King James the Fourth till the year MDLXXV* (Edinburgh, 1833).
Thomson, D., *Renaissance Paris. Architecture and Growth, 1475-1600* (London, 1984).
Thomson, T. and Innes, C., eds, *The Acts of the Parliaments of Scotland*, 12 vols. (Edinburgh, 1814-1875).
Thrower, N.J.W., *Maps and Civilization: Cartography in Culture and Society* (Chicago, 1972; repr. 1996).
Tod Ritchie, W., ed, *The Bannatyne MS*, 4 vols. (Edinburgh/London, 1928-1934).
Tolley, T., 'Hugo van der Goes's Altarpiece for Trinity College Church in: Edinburgh and Mary of Gueldres, Queen of Scotland', in Higgit, J., ed, *Medieval Art and Architecture in the Diocese of St Andrews* (Leeds, 1994), pp. 213-231.
———, 'States of independance: women regents as patrons of the visual arts in Renaissance France', *Renaissance Studies* 10 (1996), pp. 237-258.
Tooley, R.V, 'Mapmaking in France from the Sixteenth Century to the Eighteenth Century', *Proceedings of the Huguenot Society of London* 23, 6 (1952), pp. 473-479.
Tooley, R.V. and Bricker, Ch., *Landmarks of Mapmaking* (New York, ^{2}1989).
Toussaint, J., *Les relations diplomatiques de Philippe le Bon avec le concile de Bâle, 1431-1449* (Louvain, 1942).
Trevor-Roper, H., *Renaissance Essays* (London, 1985).
———, *Princes and Artists. Patronage and Ideology at four Habsburg Courts 1517-1633* (London, ^{2}1991).
Triest, M., *Macht, vrouwen en politiek 1477-1558. Maria van Bourgondië, Marga-*

reta van Oostenrijk, Maria van Hongarije (Louvain, 2000).

Trudel, M., *Histoire de la Nouvelle-France*, vol. 1, "Les vaines tentatives", (Montreal, 1963, ^{2}1983).

Turnbull, W.B., ed, *The Buik of the Croniclis of Scotland, or A Metrical Version of the 'History' of Boece by William Stewart*, 3 vols. (London, 1858).

Turrell, J.F., 'The Ritual of Royal Healing in Early Modern England: Scrofula, Liturgy, and Politics', *Anglican and Episcopal History* 68 (1999), pp. 3-36.

Ullman, W., '"This Realm of England is an Empire"', *Journal of Ecclesiastical History* 30.2 (1979), pp. 175-203.

Unger, H., ed, *Kaiser Maximilian I., Teuerdank* (Munich, 1968).

Unterkircher, F., ed, *Das Gebetbuch Jakobs IV. von Schottland und seiner Gemahlin Margaret Tudor* (Graz, 1987).

Ursu, J., *La politique orientale de François Ier (1515-1547)* (Paris, 1908).

Utley, F.L., *The Crooked Rib: An Analytical Index to the Argument about Women in English and Scots Literature to the End of the Year 1568* (Ohio, 1944).

Vale, M., *War and Chivalry* (London, 1981).

———, 'An Anglo-Burgundian Nobleman and Art Patron: Louis de Bruges, Lord of La Gruthuyse and Earl of Winchester' in: Barron, C. and Saul, N., eds, *England and the Low Countries in the Late Middle Ages* (Stroud, 1995), pp. 115-131.

Valois, C., *Histoire de la Ligue. Œuvre inédite d'un contemporain*, vol 1: *1574-1589* (Paris, 1914).

Van Anrooij, W., *Helden van Weleer: de negen besten in de Nederlanden (1300-1700)* (Amsterdam, 1997).

Van Buuren, C., 'John Asloan and his Manuscript', in: Hadley Williams, J., ed, *Stewart Style 1513-1542: Essays on the Court of James V*, pp. 15-51.

Van den Bergen-Pantens, C., ed, *L'ordre de la Toison d'or de Philippe le Bon à Philippe le Beau (1430-1505). Idéal ou reflet d'une société?* (Brussels, 1996).

Van den Bergh, L.Ph.C., ed, *Roman van Heinric ende Margriete van Limborch, gedicht door Heinric,* 3 vols. (Leiden, 1846/47).

Van den Boogert, B., 'Hapsburgs Imperialisme en de Verspreiding van Renaissance – Vormen in de Nederlanden: De Vensters van Michiel Coxcie in de Sint-Goedele te Brussel', *Oud Holland* 106 (1992), pp. 57-80.

Van der Werff, E.O., Linssen, C.A.A. and Ebels-Hoving, B., eds, *Burgundica et Varia. Keuze uit de verspreide opstellen van prof.dr. A.G. Jonkees* (Hilversum, 1990).

Van Heijnsbergen, T., 'The Chapel Royal as Intermediary between Church and Court', in: Drijvers and MacDonald, *Centres of Learning*, pp. 299-313.

———, 'The Interaction between Literature and History in Queen Mary's Edinburgh: the Bannatyne Manuscript and its prosopographical Context', in: MacDonald, Lynch and Cowan, eds, *The Renaissance*, pp. 183-225.

———, 'The love lyrics of Alexander Scott', *Studies in Scottish Literature* 26 (1991), pp. 366-379.

Van Hijum, L.M., *Grenzen aan macht. Aspecten van politieke ideologie aan de hoven van Bourgondische en Bourgondisch-Habsburgse machthebbers tussen 1450 en 1555* (Groningen, 1999).

Van Leeuwen, C.G., *Denkbeelden van een vliesridder. De* Instruction d'un jeune

Prince *van Guillebert de Lannoy* (Amsterdam, 1975).
Van Ossel, P., ed, *Les jardins du Carrousel: de la campagne à la ville: la formation d'un espace urbain* (Paris, 1998).
Van Rompaey, J., *De Grote Raad van de hertogen van Boergondië en het Parlement van Mechelen* (Brussel, 1973).
Van Veen, H.T., *Cosimo de' Medici. Vorst en Republikein* (Amsterdam, 1998).
Vanderjagt, A.J., *"Qui sa vertu anoblist". The Concepts of* noblesse *and* chose publicque *in Burgundian Political Thought. Including Fifteenth Century French Translations of Giovanni Aurispa, Buonaccorso da Montemagno, and Diego de Valera* (Groningen, 1981).
———, 'Three solutions to Buonaccorso's *Disputatio de nobilitate*' in: Gosman, J., and Van Os, J., eds, *Non nova, sed nové. Mélanges de civilisation médiévale dédiés à Willem Noomen* (Groningen, 1984), pp. 247-159.
———, *Laurens Pignon, OP: Confessor of Philip the Good. Ideas on jurisdiction and the estates* (Venlo, 1985).
———, 'Il pubblico dei testi umanistici nell'Italia settentrionale ed in Borgogna: Buonaccorso da Montemagno e Giovanni Aurispa', *Aevum. Rassegna di scienze storiche linguistiche e filologiche* 70 (1996), pp. 477-487.
———, '"En in de zomer doorkruisten zij de hele Zwarte Zee". De Bourgondische vloot in de Oriënt', *Madoc*: theme issue: *Middeleeuwen aan zee* 13:4 (1999), pp. 236-45.
———, 'Terechtgesteld te Rome en te Ghent: Stefano Porcari (†1453) and Guillame Hugonet (†1477) over volk en recht' in: Von Martels, Z.R.W.M., Steenbakkers, P. and Vanderjagt, A., eds, *Limae labor et mora. Opstellen voor Fokke Akkerman ter gelegenheid van zijn zeventigste verjaardag* (Leende, 2000), pp. 32-44.
———, 'Expropriating the past. Tradition and innovation in the use of texts in fifteenth-century Burgundy' in: Suntrup, R. and Veenstra, J., eds, *Tradition and Innovation in an Era of Change/Tradition und Innovation im Übergang zur Frühen Neuzeit* (Frankfurt am Main, 2001), pp. 177-201.
———, 'Practicing nobility in fifteenth-century Burgundian courtly culture: ideology and politics', in: Knechtges, D. and Vance, E., eds, *The Dragon and the Unicorn* (Seattle, 2002), forthcoming.
Vaucheret, E., 'Les fêtes de cour dans le sud-ouest durant le tour de France de Charles IX', in: Hepp, N., ed, *La cour au miroir des mémorialistes, 1530-1682* (Paris, 1991), pp. 13-25.
Vaughan, R., *Philip the Bold. The Formation of the Burgundian State* (London, 1962).
———, *John the Fearless. The Growth of Burgundian Power* (London, 1966).
———, *Philip the Good. The Apogee of Burgundy* (London, 1970).
———, *Charles the Bold. The Last Valois Duke of Burgundy* (London, 1973).
Vec, M., *Zeremonialwissenschaft im Fürstenstaat. Studien zur juristischen und politischen Theorie absolutistischer Herrschaftsrepräsentation* (Frankfurt am Main, 1998).
Vedel, A.S., *Et hundrede udvalgte danske Viser* (Ribe, 1591).
Veenstra, J.R., *Magic and Divination at the Courts of Burgundy and France. Text and Context of Laurens Pignon's* Contre les devineurs *(1411)* (Leiden, 1998).

Verle-Samoyault, C., 'Fontainebleau', in: Baudouin-Matuszek, *Paris et Catherine*, pp. 150-159.

Verlinden, Ch., 'Italian Influences in Iberian Colonization', in: Fernández-Armesto, *The European Opportunity*, pp. 87-99.

Vermeersch, V., ed, *Brügge und Europa* (Antwerp, 1992).

Vivanti, C., 'Henry IV, The Gallic Hercules', *Journal of the Warburg and Courtauld Institutes* 30 (1967), pp. 176-197.

Von Bahder, K., ed, 'Johann von Soest. Dy gemein bicht', *Germania Vierte-jahresschrift für deutsche Alterthumskunde* 43, NF 21 (1888), pp. 129-158.

Von Beyme, K., *Die Kunst der Macht und die Gegenmacht der Kunst. Studien zum Spannungsverhältnis von Kunst und Politik* (Frankfurt am Main, 1998).

Von Fichard, J.C., 'Gedichte Johanns von Soest eines Hofsängers und Arzts. Von 1501-1504', *Frankfurtisches Archiv für ältere deutsche Litteratur und Geschichte* 1 (1811), pp. 75-153.

Von Haumeder, U., *Antoine Caron. Studien zu seiner Histoire d'Arthémise* (Heidelberg, 1976).

Von Kruedener, Freiherr J., *Die Rolle des Hofes im Absolutismus* (Stuttgart, 1983).

Von Moltke, K., *Siegmund von Dietrichstein. Die Anfänge ständischer Institutionen und das Eindringen des Protestantismus in der Steiermark zur Zeit Maximilians I. und Ferdinands I.* (Göttingen, 1970).

Von Santen, C., *Die Person Johanns von Soest in seiner Zeit. Leben und Werk. Der Einfluß der deutschen Frühhumanisten auf einen ihrer Zeitgenossen* (Groningen, 1996).

Von Schlosser, J., *Die Kunstl- und Wunderkammern der Spätrenaissance: ein Beitrag zur Geschichte des Sammelwesens* (Leipzig, ^{2}1923).

Wallis, H., ed, *The Maps and Text of the Boke of Idrography presented by Jean Rotz to Henry VIII now in the British Library* (Oxford, 1981).

Warnke, M., *Hofkünstler. Zur Vorgeschichte des modernen Künstlers* (Cologne, 1996).

Waterschoot, W., 'Hieroglyphica te Gent in 1584', *Verslagen en Mededelingen van de Koninklijke Academie voor Nederlandse Taal- en Letterkunde* 1 (1978), pp. 48-85.

Watry, P.B., *Sixteenth Century Printing Types and Ornaments of Scotland with an Introductory Survey of the Scottish Book Trade* (Ph.D. diss., Oxford University, 1993).

Watt, D.E.R., *et al.*, eds, *Scotichronicon by Walter Bower in Latin and English*, 9 vols. (Aberdeen/Edinburgh, 1987-1998).

Weddige, H., 'Johann von Soest', in: Killy, W., ed, *Killy Literaturlexikon. Autoren und Werke deutscher Sprache* (CD-ROM) (Berlin, 1998), vol. 9, cols. 9994-9996.

Wehrli, M., *Geschichte der deutschen Literatur vom frühen Mittelalter bis zum Ende des 16. Jahrhunderts* (Stuttgart, ^{2}1984).

Welch, E., *Art and Society in Italy 1350-1500* (Oxford, 1997).

Wellens, R., *Les États généraux des Pays-Bas des origines à la fin du règne de Philippe le Beau (1464-1506)* (Heule, 1974).

Wheatcroft, A., *The Habsburgs. Embodying Empire* (Harmondsworth, 1996).

Whitworth Art Gallery, *Medieval and Early Renaissance Treasure in the North West* (Manchester, 1976).
Wiesflecker, H., *Kaiser Maximilian I. Das Reich, Österreich und Europa an der Wende zur Neuzeit*, 5 vols. (Munich, 1971-1986).
Williams, J. Hadley, ed, *Stewart Style, 1513-1542: Essays on the Court of James V* (East Linton, 1996).
Williamson, A.H., 'Numbers and National Consciousness: the Edinburgh Mathematicians and Scottish Political Culture at the Union of the Crowns', in: Mason, R.A., ed, *Scots and Britons: Scottish Political Thought and the Union of the Crowns* (Cambridge, 1994), pp. 187-212.
Winn, M.B., *Anthoine Vérard. Parisian Publisher, 1485-1512: Prologues, Poems, and Presentations* (Geneva, 1997).
Winning, T., 'Church Councils in Sixteenth-Century Scotland', in: McRoberts, D., ed, *Essays in the Scottish Reformation, 1513-1625* (Glasgow, 1962), pp. 332-358.
Wintle, M., 'Renaissance Maps and the Construction of the Idea of Europe', *Journal of Historical Cartography* 25,2 (1999), pp. 137-165.
Winzinger, F., *Die Miniaturen zum Triumphzug Kaiser Maximilians I.* (Graz, 1969).
Wittig, K., *The Scottish Tradition in Literature* (Edinburgh/London, 1958).
Wode, T., *Cantus Part-book*, Edinburgh University Library, MS Laing III.483.
Wolfe, M., *The Fiscal System of Renaissance France* (New Haven, Conn., 1972).
———, *The Conversion of Henri IV. Politics, Power, and Religious Belief in Early Modern France* (Cambridge, Mass., 1993).
———, "'Paris is Worth a Mass' Reconsidered: Henry IV and the Leaguer Capital, March 1594' (Unpublished paper presented at the Society for the French Historical Studies Conference, Wilmington, Delaware, March, 1994; private circulation).
———, 'The strange afterlife of Henry III: dynastic distortions of early Bourbon France', *Renaissance Studies* 10 (1996), pp. 474-191.
Wolff, H., ed, *America: Early Maps of the New World* (Munich, 1992).
Woodbridge, K., *Princely Gardens. The Origins and Development of the French Formal Style* (London, 1986).
Woodward, D., ed, *History of Cartography Project*: *http://feature.geography. wisc. edu/hstcart/v3cap.html.*.
Wroth, L.C., *The Voyages of Giovanni Verrazano* (New Haven, 1970).
Wuttke, W., 'Conradus Celtis Protucius', in: Füssel, St., ed, *Deutsche Dichter der frühen Neuzeit (1450-1600). Ihr Leben und Werk* (Berlin, 1993), pp. 173-199.
Yates, F.A., *The French Academies of the Sixteenth Century* (London, 1947).
———, 'Poésie et musique dans les magnificences au mariage du Duc de Joyeuse, Paris, 1581', in: Lebègue, R. *et al.*, eds, *Musique et Poésie au XVIe siècle* (Paris, 1954), pp. 237-263.
———, *The Valois Tapestries* (London, 1959).
———, *Astraea: the Imperial Theme in the Sixteenth Century* (London, 1975).
Young, A., *Tudor and Jacobean Tournaments* (London, 1987).
Žak, S., 'Die Gründung der Hofkapelle in Heidelberg', *Archiv für Musikwissenschaft* 50 (1993), pp. 145-163.

Zeeberg, P., 'The inscriptions at Tycho Brahe's Uraniborg', in: Skafte Jensen, M., ed, *A History of Nordic Neo-Latin Literature*, pp. 251-266.

———, *Tycho Brahes* Urania Titani. *En digt om Sophie Brahe* (Copenhagen, 1994).

Zeitz, L., *Tizian. Teurer Freund. Tizian und Federico Gonzaga. Kunstpatronage in Mantua in 16. Jahrhundert* (Petersburg, 2000).

Zemon Davis, N., 'Women in Politics', in: Zemon Davis, N. and Farge, A., eds, *A History of Women in the West. III. Renaissance and Enlightenment Paradoxes* (Cambridge, Mass./London, 1993), pp. 167-183.

Zimerman, H., 'Inventoire des parties de meubles estans es cabinetz de Madame en sa ville de Malines, estans a la garde et charge de Estienne Luillier, varlet-de-chambre de ma dite dame, lequel en doit respondre a Richard Contault, garde-joyault de ma dite dame, et le dit Contault en tenir compte a icelle ma dite dame' [20. April 1524], *Jahrbuch der kunsthistorischen Sammlungen des allerhöchsten Kaiserhauses* 3 (1885), pp. xciii-cxxiii.

Zimmermann, M. and Böhm, R., eds, *Französische Frauen der frühen Neuzeit. Dichterinnen - Malerinnen – Mäzeninnen* (Darmstadt, 1999).

INDEX

This index does not list modern authors. Problem names are treated in the following way: for names such as Olivier de La Marche, see under 'De'; for Van Eyck, see under 'Van'.

Adolf, duke of Gelderland, 149

BRILL'S STUDIES IN INTELLECTUAL HISTORY

56. PRANGER, M.B. *Bernard of Clairvaux and the Shape of Monastic Thought.* Broken Dreams. 1994. ISBN 90 04 10055 5
57. VAN DEUSEN, N. *Theology and Music at the Early University.* The Case of Robert Grosseteste and Anonymous IV. 1994. ISBN 90 04 10059 8
58. WARNEKE, S. *Images of the Educational Traveller in Early Modern England.* 1994. ISBN 90 04 10126 8
59. BIETENHOLZ, P.G. *Historia and Fabula.* Myths and Legends in Historical Thought from Antiquity to the Modern Age. 1994. ISBN 90 04 10063 6
60. LAURSEN, J.C. (ed.). *New Essays on the Political Thought of the Huguenots of the* Refuge. 1995. ISBN 90 04 09986 7
61. DRIJVERS, J.W. & A.A. MacDONALD (eds.). *Centres of Learning.* Learning and Location in Pre-Modern Europe and the Near East. 1995. ISBN 90 04 10193 4
62. JAUMANN, H. *Critica.* Untersuchungen zur Geschichte der Literaturkritik zwischen Quintilian und Thomasius. 1995. ISBN 90 04 10276 0
63. HEYD, M. *"Be Sober and Reasonable."* The Critique of Enthusiasm in the Seventeenth and Early Eighteenth Centuries. 1995. ISBN 90 04 10118 7
64. OKENFUSS, M.J. *The Rise and Fall of Latin Humanism in Early-Modern Russia.* Pagan Authors, Ukrainians, and the Resiliency of Muscovy. 1995. ISBN 90 04 10331 7
65. DALES, R.C. *The Problem of the Rational Soul in the Thirteenth Century.* 1995. ISBN 90 04 10296 5
66. VAN RULER, J.A. *The Crisis of Causality.* Voetius and Descartes on God, Nature and Change. 1995. ISBN 90 04 10371 6
67. SHEHADI, F. *Philosophies of Music in Medieval Islam.* 1995. ISBN 90 04 10128 4
68. GROSS-DIAZ, T. *The Psalms Commentary of Gilbert of Poitiers.* From *Lectio Divina* to the Lecture Room. 1996. ISBN 90 04 10211 6
69. VAN BUNGE, W. & W. KLEVER (eds.). *Disguised and Overt Spinozism around 1700.* 1996. ISBN 90 04 10307 4
70. FLORIDI, L. *Scepticism and the Foundation of Epistemology.* A Study in the Meta-logical Fallacies. 1996. ISBN 90 04 10533 6
71. FOUKE, D. *The Enthusiastical Concerns of Dr. Henry More.* Religious Meaning and the Psychology of Delusion. 1997. ISBN 90 04 10600 6
72. RAMELOW, T. *Gott, Freiheit, Weltenwahl.* Der Ursprung des Begriffes der besten aller möglichen Welten in der Metaphysik der Willensfreiheit zwischen Antonio Perez S.J. (1599-1649) und G.W. Leibniz (1646-1716). 1997. ISBN 90 04 10641 3
73. STONE, H.S. *Vico's Cultural History.* The Production and Transmission of Ideas in Naples, 1685-1750. 1997. ISBN 90 04 10650 2
74. STROLL, M. *The Medieval Abbey of Farfa.* Target of Papal and Imperial Ambitions. 1997. ISBN 90 04 10704 5
75. HYATTE, R. *The Prophet of Islam in Old French:* The Romance of Muhammad *(1258) and* The Book of Muhammad's Ladder *(1264).* English Translations, With an Introduction. 1997. ISBN 90 04 10709 2
76. JESTICE, P.G. *Wayward Monks and the Religious Revolution of the Eleventh Century.* 1997. ISBN 90 04 10722 3
77. VAN DER POEL, M. *Cornelius Agrippa, The Humanist Theologian and His Declama-tions.* 1997. ISBN 90 04 10756 8
78. SYLLA, E. & M. McVAUGH (eds.). *Texts and Contexts in Ancient and Medieval Science.* Studies on the Occasion of John E. Murdoch's Seventieth Birthday. 1997. ISBN 90 04 10823 8
79. BINKLEY, P. (ed.). *Pre-Modern Encyclopaedic Texts.* 1997. ISBN 90 04 10830 0
80. KLAVER, J.M.I. *Geology and Religious Sentiment.* The Effect of Geological Discoveries on English Society and Literature between 1829 and 1859. 1997. ISBN 90 04 10882 3
81. INGLIS, J. *Spheres of Philosophical Inquiry and the Historiography of Medieval Philosophy.* 1998. ISBN 90 04 10843 2

82. McCALLA, A. *A Romantic Historiosophy.* The Philosophy of History of Pierre-Simon Ballanche. 1998. ISBN 90 04 10967 6
83. VEENSTRA, J.R. *Magic and Divination at the Courts of Burgundy and France.* Text and Context of Laurens Pignon's *Contre les devineurs* (1411). 1998. ISBN 90 04 10925 0
84. WESTERMAN, P.C. *The Disintegration of Natural Law Theory.* Aquinas to Finnis. 1998. ISBN 90 04 10999 4
85. GOUWENS, K. *Remembering the Renaissance.* Humanist Narratives of the Sack of Rome. 1998. ISBN 90 04 10969 2
86. SCHOTT, H. & J. ZINGUER (Hrsg.). *Paracelsus und seine internationale Rezeption in der frühen Neuzeit.* Beiträge zur Geschichte des Paracelsismus. 1998. ISBN 90 04 10974 9
87. ÅKERMAN, S. *Rose Cross over the Baltic.* The Spread of Rosicrucianism in Northern Europe. 1998. ISBN 90 04 11030 5
88. DICKSON, D.R. *The Tessera of Antilia.* Utopian Brotherhoods & Secret Societies in the Early Seventeenth Century. 1998. ISBN 90 04 11032 1
89. NOUHUYS, T. VAN. *The Two-Faced Janus.* The Comets of 1577 and 1618 and the Decline of the Aristotelian World View in the Netherlands. 1998. ISBN 90 04 11204 9
90. MUESSIG, C. (ed.). *Medieval Monastic Preaching.* 1998. ISBN 90 04 10883 1
91. FORCE, J.E. & D.S. KATZ (eds.). *"Everything Connects": In Conference with Richard H. Popkin.* Essays in His Honor. 1999. ISBN 90 04 110984
92. DEKKER, K. *The Origins of Old Germanic Studies in the Low Countries.* 1999. ISBN 90 04 11031 3
93. ROUHI, L. *Mediation and Love.* A Study of the Medieval Go-Between in Key Romance and Near-Eastern Texts. 1999. ISBN 90 04 11268 5
94. AKKERMAN, F., A. VANDERJAGT & A. VAN DER LAAN (eds.). *Northern Humanism between 1469 and 1625.* 1999. ISBN 90 04 11314 2
95. TRUMAN, R.W. *Spanish Treatises on Government, Society and Religion in the Time of Philip II.* The 'de regimine principum' and Associated Traditions. 1999. ISBN 90 04 11379 7
96. NAUTA, L. & A. VANDERJAGT (eds.) *Demonstration and Imagination.* Essays in the History of Science and Philosophy Presented to John D. North. 1999. ISBN 90 04 11468 8
97. BRYSON, D. *Queen Jeanne and the Promised Land.* Dynasty, Homeland, Religion and Violence in Sixteenth-Century France. 1999. ISBN 90 04 11378 9
98. GOUDRIAAN, A. *Philosophische Gotteserkenntnis bei Suárez und Descartes im Zusammenhang mit der niederländischen reformierten Theologie und Philosophie des 17. Jahrhunderts.* 1999. ISBN 90 04 11627 3
99. HEITSCH, D.B. *Practising Reform in Montaigne's* Essais. 2000. ISBN 90 04 11630 3
100. KARDAUN, M. & J. SPRUYT (eds.). *The Winged Chariot.* Collected Essays on Plato and Platonism in Honour of L.M. de Rijk. 2000. ISBN 90 04 11480 7
101. WHITMAN, J. (ed.), *Interpretation and Allegory:* Antiquity to the Modern Period. 2000. ISBN 90 04 11039 9
102. JACQUETTE, D., *David Hume's Critique of Infinity.* 2000. ISBN 90 04 11649 4
103. BUNGE, W. VAN. *From Stevin to Spinoza.* An Essay on Philosophy in the Seventeenth-Century Dutch Republic. 2001. ISBN 90 04 12217 6
104. GIANOTTI, T., *Al-Ghazālī's Unspeakable Doctrine of the Soul.* Unveiling the Esoteric Psychology and Eschatology of the Iḥyā. 2001. ISBN 90 04 12083 1
105. SAYGIN, S., *Humphrey, Duke of Gloucester (1390-1447) and the Italian Humanists.* 2002. ISBN 90 04 12015 7
106. BEJCZY, I., *Erasmus and the Middle Ages.* The Historical Consciousness of a Christian Humanist. 2001. ISBN 90 04 12218 4
107. BRANN, N.L. *The Debate over the Origin of Genius during the Italian Renaissance.* The Theories of Supernatural Frenzy and Natural Melancholy in Accord and in Conflict on the Threshold of the Scientific Revolution. 2002. ISBN 90 04 12362 8
108. ALLEN, M.J.B. & V. REES with M. DAVIES.(eds.), *Marsilio Ficino: His Theology, His Philosophy, His Legacy.* 2002. ISBN 90 04 11855 1
109. SANDY, G., *The Classical Heritage in France.* 2002. ISBN 90 04 11916 7
110. SCHUCHARD, M.K., *Restoring the Temple of Vision.* Cabalistic Freemasonry and Stuart Culture. 2002. ISBN 90 04 12489 6

111. EIJNATTEN, J. VAN. *Liberty and Concord in the United Provinces.* Religious Toleration and the Public in the Eighteenth-Century Netherlands. 2003. ISBN 90 04 12843 3
112. BOS, A.P. *The Soul and Its Instrumental Body.* A Reinterpretation of Aristotle's Philosophy of Living Nature. 2003. ISBN 90 04 13016 0
113. LAURSEN, J.C. & J. VAN DER ZANDE (eds.). *Early French and German Defenses of Liberty of the Press.* Elie Luzac's *Essay on Freedom of Expression* (1749) and Carl Friedrich Bahrdt's *On Liberty of the Press and its Limits* (1787) *in English Translation.* 2003. ISBN 90 04 13017 9
114. POTT, S., MULSOW, M. & DANNEBERG, L. (eds.). *The Berlin Refuge 1680-1780.* Learning and Science in European Context. 2003. ISBN 90 04 12561 2
115. GERSH, S. & ROEST, B. (eds.). *Medieval and Renaissance Humanism.* Rhetoric, Representation and Reform. 2003. ISBN 90 04 13274 0
116. LENNON, T.M. (ed.). *Cartesian Views.* Papers presented to Richard A. Watson. 2003. ISBN 90 04 13299 6
117. VON MARTELS, Z. & VANDERJAGT, A. (eds.). *Pius II – 'El Più Expeditivo Pontefice'.* Selected Studies on Aeneas Silvius Piccolomini (1405-1464). 2003. ISBN 90 04 13190 6
118. GOSMAN, M., MACDONALD, A. & VANDERJAGT, A. (eds.). *Princes and Princely Culture 1450–1650.* Volume One. 2003. ISBN 90 04 13572 3
119. LEHRICH, C.I. *The Language of Demons and Angels.* Cornelius Agrippa's Occult Philosophy. 2003. ISBN 90 04 13574 X
120. BUNGE, W. VAN (ed.). *The Early Enlightenment in the Dutch Republic, 1650–1750.* Selected Papers of a Conference held at the Herzog August Bibliothek, Wolfenbüttel 22–23 March 2001. 2003. ISBN 90 04 13587 1
121. ROMBURGH, S. VAN, *For My Worthy Freind Mr. Franciscus Junius.* An Edition of the Correspondence of Francis Junius F.F. (1591-1677). 2004. ISBN 90 04 12880 8
122. MULSOW, M. & POPKIN, R.H. (eds.). *Secret Conversions to Judaism in Early Modern Europe.* 2004. ISBN 90 04 12883 2
123. GOUDRIAAN, K., J. VAN MOOLENBROEK & A. TERVOORT (eds.). *Education and Learning in the Netherlands, 1400-1600.* 2004. ISBN 90 04 13644 4
124. PETRINA, A. *Cultural Politics in Fifteenth-Century England: The Case of Humphrey, Duke of Gloucester.* 2004. ISBN 90 04 13713 0
125. SCHUURMAN, P. (ed.). *Ideas, Mental Faculties and Method.* The New Logic of Descartes and Locke and Its Reception in the Dutch Republic. 2004. ISBN 90 04 13716 5